D1611266

BIOETHICS

Readings & Cases

BIOETHICS
Readings & Cases

Baruch A. Brody

Baylor College of Medicine and Rice University

H. Tristram Engelhardt, Jr.

Baylor College of Medicine and Rice University

Prentice-Hall, Inc., Englewood Cliffs, New Jersey 07632

Library of Congress Cataloging-in-Publication Data

Bioethics : readings & cases.

Includes bibliographies.
1. Medical ethics. 2. Bioethics. 3. Medical
ethics—Case studies. 4. Bioethics—Case studies.
I. Brody, Baruch A. II. Engelhardt, H. Tristram
(Hugo Tristram), 1941–
R724.B484 1987 174′.2 86-25302
ISBN 0-13-076522-8

Editorial/production supervision
  and interior design: Virginia L. McCarthy
Cover design: Ben Santora
Manufacturing buyer: Harry P. Baisley

Printed in the United States of America

10 9 8 7 6 5 4

ISBN 0-13-076522-8 01

Prentice-Hall International (UK) Limited, *London*
Prentice-Hall of Australia Pty. Limited, *Sydney*
Prentice-Hall Canada Inc., *Toronto*
Prentice-Hall Hispanoamericana, S.A., *Mexico*
Prentice-Hall of India Private Limited, *New Delhi*
Prentice-Hall of Japan, Inc., *Tokyo*
Prentice-Hall of Southeast Asia Pte. Ltd., *Singapore*
Editora Prentice-Hall do Brasil, Ltda., *Rio de Janeiro*

This book is dedicated to the faculty, house officers,
and medical students
of
Baylor College of Medicine
from whom we have learned so much about these issues.

CONTENTS

PREFACE   xv

ACKNOWLEDGMENTS   xvii

PART I
Moral Theory

SECTION A
Introduction   1

SECTION B
The Major Moral Considerations   3

1. APPEALING TO THE CONSEQUENCES OF OUR ACTIONS   3
2. APPEALING TO RIGHTS   11
3. APPEALING TO THE VIRTUES   22
4. APPEALING TO JUSTICE AND EQUALITY   28

SECTION C
A Brief Introduction to the Major Moral Theories   34

PART II
Readings in Bioethics

SECTION A
Decision Making   43

INTRODUCTION   43

1. CAPACITIES AND COMPETENCIES OF PATIENTS   47

Not All Can Be Free, *John Stuart Mill*   47

The Status of Children, *John Locke*   48

Minors' Assent or Dissent to Medical Treatment, *Sanford L. Leikin*   49

The Logic of Competency, *Bernard Gert and Charles Culver*   55

Who Is Incapacitated and How Is It To Be Determined? *President's
Commission*   57

Compassion, Control, and Decisions About Competency, *Virginia
Abernethy*   60

**2. THE ROLES AND VIRTUES OF DIFFERENT PROFESSIONALS AS
PROVIDERS**   66

Physicians and Nurses: A Historical Perspective, *Andrew Jameton*   66

From Loyalty to Advocacy: A New Metaphor for Nursing, *Gerald
R. Winslow*   74

Why Physicians Need to Maintain Control of Health Care Delivery,
Robert H. Bartlett   84

Licensing, Certification, and the Restraint of Trade: The Creation
of Differences Among the Health Care Professionals, *Susan Costello,
H. Tristram Engelhardt, Jr., and Mary Ann Gardell*   89

The Virtues of a Physician, *Hippocrates*   95

The Enlightenment Picture of the Virtuous Physician, *Dietrich von
Engelhardt*   95

How Virtues Become Vices, *Alasdair MacIntyre*   100

3. THE ROLE OF THE PATIENT AND THE PROVIDER   102

The Patient as Decision-Maker, *President's Commission*   102

Types of Autonomy and Their Significance, *Bruce Miller*   105

Medical Ethics' Assault Upon Medical Values, *Colleen D. Clements
and Roger C. Sider*   109

Beyond Medical Paternalism and Patient Autonomy: A Model of Physician Conscience for the Physician-Patient Relationship, *David C. Thomasma*   113

4. INFORMED CONSENT   **121**

The Information Desired by a Reasonable Patient, *Canterbury v. Spence*   121

The Subjective Standard: Canterbury Can Require Too Little, *Alexander Capron*   125

The Best Interest of the Patient: Canterbury Can Require Too Much, *Jewish Compendium on Medical Ethics*   128

SECTION B

Persons and Their Lives   **132**

INTRODUCTION   **132**

5. THE CONCEPT OF A PERSON   **136**

The Species Principle and the Potentiality Principle, *Philip E. Devine*   136

The Criterion of Sentience, *L. W. Sumner*   141

The Criterion of Brain Functioning, *Baruch A. Brody*   143

The Criterion of Awareness of Self as a Continuing Entity, *Michael Tooley*   146

Multiple Concepts of Personhood, *H. Tristram Engelhardt, Jr.*   152

6. THE SANCTITY OF THE LIVES OF PERSONS   **156**

The Morality of Killing: A Traditional View, *Germain Grisez and Joseph M. Boyle, Jr.*   156

Principle of Double Effect, *H. Tristram Engelhardt, Jr., and John P. Kenny*   160

A Non-Consequentialist Argument for Active Euthanasia, *Baruch A. Brody*   161

A Consequentialist Argument for Active Euthanasia, *Peter Singer*   165

The Traditional Distinctions Are Unhelpful, *President's Commission*   169

Roots of the Belief in the Sanctity of Life, *Law Reform Commission of Canada*   174

A Jewish Statement on the Sanctity of Life, *Jewish Compendium on Medical Ethics*   177

Life Is Sometimes a Modest Benefit, *President's Commission*   179

Some Qualities of Life Are Not Worth Living, *H. Tristram Engelhardt, Jr.* 181

SECTION C

Health Care and Justice   **185**

INTRODUCTION   **185**

7. THE RIGHT TO HEALTH CARE   **188**

The Right to an Adequate Level of Health Care, *President's Commission* 188

When Is the Best Care Too Expensive? *Allan Gibbard* 192

Health Care as Fair Opportunity, *Norman Daniels* 195

Equality in Health Care, *Amy Gutmann* 197

Liberty and the Purchase of Health Care, *Baruch A. Brody* 201

8. FINANCING AND DELIVERY OF HEALTH CARE   **206**

The Money We Spend and Its Sources, *Carol McCarthy* 206

The Consumer Choice Health Plan, *Alain Enthoven* 213

National Health Plan: Why We Need to Follow the British, *Peter Singer* 218

9. INDIVIDUAL PATIENTS AND SOCIAL NEEDS   **221**

The Primacy of the Physician as Trusted Personal Advisor and Not as Social Agent, *Charles Fried* 221

Costs and Clinicians as Agents of Patients, *Baruch A. Brody* ... 226

PART III

Case Areas

SECTION A

Reproductive Issues   **229**

1. DECISIONS TO REPRODUCE   **229**

2. NEW REPRODUCTIVE TECHNOLOGIES   **233**

3. ABORTION   **237**

4. GENETIC AND PRENATAL COUNSELING   **241**

SECTION B

Perinatal Issues 246

5. FETAL TREATMENT 246
6. ALTERNATIVE BIRTH SETTINGS 249
7. CESAREAN SECTIONS 253
8. DEFECTIVE NEWBORNS 256
9. TRIAGE IN THE NEONATAL INTENSIVE CARE UNIT (NNICU) 260

SECTION C

Pediatric Health Care 265

10. ASSENT AND CONSENT TO PEDIATRIC TREATMENT AND EXPERIMENTATION 265
11. PEDIATRIC DONATION OF ORGANS 269
12. CONFIDENTIALITY AND ADOLESCENT SEXUALITY 274
13. RELIGIOUS OBJECTIONS TO TREATMENT OF MINORS 277

SECTION D

Adult Patients: General Issues 282

14. CONSENT OF ADULTS TO TREATMENT 282
15. CONSENT OF ADULTS TO EXPERIMENTATION 286
16. CONFIDENTIALITY 291
17. ACCESS TO HEALTH CARE 294
18. PREVENTIVE MEDICINE 298
19. OCCUPATIONAL SAFETY AND THE SOCIAL RESPONSIBILITY TO PREVENT JOB-RELATED ILLNESS AND DEATH 301
20. ALTERNATIVE FORMS OF CARE 305

SECTION E

Adult Patients: Special Issues 310

21. CHRONIC PAIN AND CHRONIC PROBLEMS 310
22. RELIGIOUS OBJECTIONS TO TREATMENT BY ADULT PATIENTS 313

23. PSYCHIATRIC PATIENTS   318

24. CANCER SURGERY   322

25. PATIENTS WITH SERIOUS BURNS   326

26. ORGAN TRANSPLANTATION   328

27. SEX THERAPY AND COUNSELING   332

SECTION F

Geriatric Health Care   **336**

28. ASSESSMENT OF COMPETENCY   336

29. THE HIGH COSTS OF GERIATRIC HEALTH CARE   339

30. INDEPENDENCE OF THE ELDERLY PATIENT   342

SECTION G

Death and Dying   **347**

31. TRUTH-TELLING   347

32. THE USE OF INTENSIVE CARE UNITS   351

33. ADVANCE DIRECTIVES   354

34. DNR ORDERS   358

35. THE FAMILY'S ROLE IN DECISIONS FOR TERMINAL PATIENTS   364

36. HOSPICE CARE   369

37. SUICIDE AND EUTHANASIA   373

38. DEFINITION OF DEATH   377

39. AUTOPSIES AND ORGAN DONATIONS   381

APPENDIX

Codes of Ethics

Hippocratic Oath   387

A Patient's Bill of Rights, *American Hospital Association 1973*   388

Principles of Medical Ethics, *American Medical Association*—1984   389

Current Opinions of the Judicial Council of the American Medical   390
Association—1984

Code for Nurses: Ethical Concepts Applied to Nursing (1973),
International Council of Nurses   393

Code for Nurses (1976, 1985), *American Nurses' Association*   394

Code of Federal Regulations   396

PREFACE

This volume grew out of the experience of teaching bioethics to medical students, interns, and residents at Baylor College of Medicine, and to undergraduate students at Rice University. Conversations with patients have also contributed their share. This volume is also the result of years of discussion with our colleagues at Baylor and with physicians and nurses at the Baylor-affiliated hospitals concerning the ways in which modern health care involves moral issues that cannot be avoided either by patients or health-care providers. We are indebted to many individuals and are especially grateful to Eugene Boisaubin, M.D., who read through large portions of the manuscript.

The moral and public policy problems that characterize contemporary health care raise fundamental questions regarding the role of physicians, patients, and the government in health-care decisions. Such fundamental questions are philosophical. They are questions about how patients, nurses, and physicians can justify the choices they make or would wish to make. They force us to engage in ethical analysis and a reassessment of the moral and philosophical underpinnings of contemporary health-care policies. Our experience in the Baylor-affiliated hospitals has shown that such philosophical analysis does take place, if only implicitly, in the actual care of patients. This volume attempts to make the content and character of such philosophical analysis and questioning explicit and to look at its foundations.

The selection of readings reflects the current areas of major development in the field of bioethics. Through them we provide the reader with an introduction to the philosophical, moral, and public policy issues underlying contemporary health care. The issues analyzed in the selections are then integrated in a range of case analyses. The cases in this text do not correspond to any case histories or actual patients. Rather, they are composites of numerous encounters with actual case problems at Baylor and other institutions, either on the part of the authors or on that of our colleagues. All identifying material has been removed. Any resemblance to actual patients is at most coincidental. The cases, however, convey the tensions and conflicts that are inherent in making health-care decisions.

Even if one is neither a physician nor currently a patient, we believe that the selection of case analyses will be of interest. All of us will someday die, and most of us will be ill before we die, thus necessitating the need for hospitalization and a confrontation with the moral issues raised in this text. Because we are all either prospective patients or family members of prospective patients, the bio-ethical issues raised by contemporary health care are unavoidable. For physicians and nurses, these issues are a part of everyday life.

Baruch A. Brody
H. Tristram Engelhardt, Jr.
Houston, Texas

ACKNOWLEDGMENTS

John Stuart Mill, "Not All Can Be Free"
from John Stuart Mill, *On Liberty*.

John Locke, "The Status of Children"
from John Locke, *Second Treatiste*.

Sanford L. Leikin, "Minors' Assent or Dissent to Medical Treatment"
from The President's Commission for the Study of Ethical Problems, *Making Health Care Decisions*, vol. 3, pp. 175–183 (Government Printing Office: Washington, D.C.), 1983.

Bernard Gert and Charles Culver, "The Logic of Competency"
excerpted from *Philosophy in Medicine: Conceptual and Ethical Issues in Medicine and Psychiatry* by Charles M. Culver and Bernard Gert. Copyright © 1982 by Oxford University Press, Inc. Reprinted by permission.

President's Commission, "Who Is Incapacitated and How Is It To Be Determined?"
from The President's Commission for the Study of Ethical Problems, *Making Health Care Decisions*, vol. 1, pp. 169–175 (Government Printing Office: Washington, D.C.), 1983.

Virginia Abernethy, "Compassion, Control, and Decisions About Competency"
reprinted by permission of the author and the publisher from *The American Journal of Psychiatry*, 141:1, 53–58. Copyright 1984 by the American Psychiatric Association.

Andrew Jameton, "Physicians and Nurses: A Historical Perspective"
from Andrew Jameton, *Nursing Practice: The Ethical Issues*, © 1984, pp. 36–46. Reprinted by permission of Prentice-Hall, Inc., Englewood Cliffs, N.J.

Gerald R. Winslow, "From Loyalty to Advocacy: A New Metaphor for Nursing"
reprinted by permission of the author and the publisher from *The Hastings Center Report* (June 1984). © Institute of Society, Ethics and the Life Sciences, 360 Broadway, Hastings-on-Hudson, N.Y. 10706

Robert H. Bartlett, "Why Physicians Need to Maintain Control of Health Care Delivery"
from Marc Basson, *Troubling Problems in Medical Ethics* (New York: Alan R. Liss, Inc., 1981). Reprinted by permission of the publisher.

Susan Costello, H. Tristram Engelhardt, Jr., and Mary Ann Gardell, "Licensing, Certification, and the Restraint of Trade: The Creation of Differences Among the Health Care Professions"
original essay prepared for this volume.

Hippocrates, "The Virtues of a Physician"
reprinted with gratitude from "The Physician," in *Hippocrates,* trans. W. H. S. Jones (Cambridge: Harvard University Press) 1962, vol. 2, pp. 311, 313.

Dietrich von Engelhardt, "The Enlightenment Picture of the Virtuous Physician"
from Dietrich von Engelhardt, "Virtue and Medicine During the Enlightenment in Germany," Section: The Physician, pp. 65–71. In Earl Shelp, *Virtue and Medicine,* 1985. Copyright © 1985 by D. Reidel Publishing Co., Dordrecht, The Netherlands.

Alasdair MacIntyre, "How Virtues Become Vices"
from H. T. Engelhardt and S. Spicker, *Evaluation and Explanation in the Biomedical Sciences,* 1975, pp. 107–111. Copyright © 1975 by D. Reidel Publishing Co., Dordrecht, The Netherlands.

President's Commission, "The Patient as Decision-Maker"
from The President's Commission for the Study of Ethical Problems, *Making Health Care Decisions,* (Government Printing Office: Washington, D.C.), 1983.

Bruce Miller, "Types of Autonomy and Their Significance"
reprinted by permission of the author and the publisher from Bruce Miller, "Autonomy and the Refusal of Life-Saving Treatment," *Hastings Center Report* (August 1981). © Institute of Society, Ethics and the Life Sciences, 360 Broadway, Hastings-on-Hudson, N.Y. 10706

Colleen D. Clements, and Roger C. Sider, "Medical Ethics' Assault Upon Medical Values"
reprinted by permission of the authors and the publisher from *The Journal of the American Medical Association,* Vol. 250, No. 15 (Oct. 21, 1983), 2011–2015. Copyright 1983, American Medical Association.

David C. Thomasma, "Beyond Medical Paternalism and Patient Autonomy: A Model of Physician Conscience for the Physician-Patient Relationship"
reprinted by permission of the author and the publisher from the *Annals of Internal Medicine,* Vol. 98., No. 3 (February 1983), 243–247.

Canterbury v. Spence, "The Information Desired by a Reasonable Patient"
(464 F.2d 772).

Alexander Capron, "The Subjective Standard: Canterbury Can Require Too Little"
reprinted by permission of the author and the publisher from A. Capron, "Informed Consent," University of Pennsylvania Law Review, Vol. 123, 1974, 404–409, 413–414, 416–418. Copyright by A. Capron.

Jewish Compendium on Medical Ethics, "The Best Interest of the Patient"
reprinted with permission of the publisher from *Compendium on Medical Ethics,* eds. David M. Feldman and Fred Rosner, Federation of Jewish Philanthropies, New York, 1984, pp. 18–23.

Philip E. Devine, "The Species Principle and the Potentiality Principle"
reprinted from Philip E. Devine, *The Ethics of Homicide.* Copyright © 1978 by Cornell University. Used by permission of the publisher, Cornell University Press.

L. W. Sumner, "The Criterion of Sentience"
from L. W. Sumner, *Abortion and Moral Theory,* excerpt pp. 142–146. Copyright © 1981 by Princeton University Press. Reprinted by permission of Princeton University Press.

Baruch A. Brody, "The Criterion of Brain Functioning"
from Robert Baker and Frederich Elliston (eds.), *Philosophy and Sex.* (Buffalo, N.Y.: Prometheus Press, 1975.) Reprinted by permission of Prometheus Press.

Michael Tooley, "The Criterion of Awareness of Self as a Continuing Entity"
reprinted from Joel Feinberg, *The Problem of Abortion,* pp. 122–130. © 1983 by Michael Tooley.

H. Tristram Engelhardt, Jr., "Multiple Concepts of Personhood"
reprinted by permission of the publisher from William B. Bondeson and others, eds., *Abortion and the Status of the Fetus.* Copyright © 1983 and 1984 by D. Reidel Publishing Company, Dordrecht, The Netherlands.

Germain Grisez and Joseph M. Boyle, "The Morality of Killing: A Traditional View"
reprinted with permission of the authors and the publisher from Germain Grisez and Joseph M. Boyle, Jr., *Life and Death with Liberty and Justice: A Contribution to the Euthanasia Debate* (Notre Dame, Ind.: University of Notre Dame Press, 1979), pp. 393–94, 407–8, 410, 412–13, 415–19. Copyright © 1979 by University of Notre Dame Press.

H. Tristram Engelhardt, Jr., original contribution combined with a selection from John P. Kenny, "Principle of Double Effect"
reprinted by permission of the Paulist Press, Ramsey, N.J. from *Principles of Medical Ethics* (Westminster, Md.: Newman Press, 1962), pp. 5–6.

Baruch A. Brody, "A Non-Consequentialist Argument for Active Euthanasia" from M. Kohl (ed.), *Beneficent Euthanasia*. (Buffalo, N.Y.: Prometheus Press, 1975.) Reprinted by permission of Prometheus Books.

Peter Singer, "A Consequentialist Argument for Active Euthanasia" reprinted by permission of the publisher from Peter Singer, *Practical Ethics* (Cambridge University Press, 1979), pp. 147–153.

President's Commission, "The Traditional Distinctions Are Unhelpful" from The President's Commission for the Study of Ethical Problems, *Deciding to Forego Life-Sustaining Treatment*, pp. 60–62, 66–67, 73–79, 82–83, 89–90 (Government Printing Office: Washington, D.C.), 1983.

Law Reform Commission of Canada, "Roots of the Belief in the Sanctity of Life" reprinted by permission of the Commission from the publication *Sanctity of Life or Quality of Life*, pp. 10–18.

Jewish Compendium on Medical Ethics, "A Jewish Statement on the Sanctity of Life" reprinted by permission of the publisher from *Compendium on Medical Ethics*, eds. David M. Feldman and Fred Rosner (Federation of Jewish Philanthropies: New York) 1984, pp. 12–13 and 106–108.

President's Commission, "Life Is Sometimes a Modest Benefit" from The President's Commission for the Study of Ethical Problems, *Deciding to Forego Life-Sustaining Treatment*, pp. 174–177 and 181–186 (Government Printing Office: Washington, D.C.), 1983.

H. Tristram Engelhardt, Jr., "Some Qualities of Life Are Not Worth Living" from M. Kohl (ed.), *Beneficent Euthanasia*. (Buffalo, N.Y.: Prometheus Press, 1975.) Reprinted by permission of Prometheus Books.

President's Commission, "The Right to an Adequate Level of Health Care" from The President's Commission for the Study of Ethical Problems, *Securing Access to Health Care*, vol. 1, pp. 18–20 and 32–37 (Government Printing Office: Washington, D.C.), 1983.

Allan Gibbard, "When is the Best Care Too Expensive" reprinted from Allan Gibbard, "The Prospective Pareto Principle and Equity of Access to Health Care," *MMFQ*, Vol. 60 3(1982). © Milbank Memorial Fund. Reprinted by permission.

Norman Daniels, "Health Care as Fair Opportunity" reprinted from Norman Daniels, "Equality of Access to Health Care," *MMFQ*, Vol. 60 1(1982). © Milbank Memorial Fund. Reprinted by permission.

Amy Gutmann, "Equality in Health Care" reprinted from Amy Gutmann, "For and Against Equal Access to Health Care," *MMFQ*, Vol. 59 4(1981). © Milbank Memorial Fund. Reprinted by permission.

Baruch A. Brody, "Liberty and the Purchase of Health Care"

from Baruch A. Brody, "Health Care for the Haves and Have Nots: Toward a Just Basis of Distribution." In Earl Shelp, *Justice and Health Care*, pp. 151–159. Copyright © 1981 by D. Reidel Publishing Co., Dordrecht, The Netherlands.

Carol McCarthy, "The Money We Spend and Its Sources"
from Carol McCarthy, "Financing for Health Care." In Jonas, *Health Care Delivery in the United States*, 2nd ed. (New York: Springer Publishing Co.). Used by permission of the publisher.

Alain Enthoven, "The Consumer Choice Health Plan"
an unpublished HEW report.

Peter Singer, "National Health Plan: Why We Need to Follow the British"
reprinted with permission from R. Veatch and R. Branson, eds., *Ethics and Health Policy*, copyright 1976, Ballinger Publishing Company.

Charles Fried, "The Primacy of the Physician as Trusted Personal Advisor and Not as Social Agent"
combines material published in Charles Fried, *Medical Experimentation* (Elsevier/North Holland), pp. 73–78, and in Charles Fried, "Rights and Health—Beyond Equity and Efficiency," *New England Journal of Medicine*, Vol. 293(5), 1975, pp. 241–245. Reprinted by permission of the publishers and author.

Baruch A. Brody, "Costs and Clinicians as Agents of Patients"
an original essay prepared for this volume.

Oath reprinted with gratitude from *Hippocrates*, trans. W. H. S. Jones (Cambridge: Harvard University Press) 1962, vol. 1, pp. 299, 301

American Hospital Association, "A Patient's Bill of Rights"
reprinted with permission of the American Hospital Association, copyright 1972.

American Medical Association, "Principles of Medical Ethics"
reprinted with permission of the American Medical Association, from *Current Opinions of the Judicial Council of the AMA*, 1984.

American Medical Association, "Current Opinions of the Judicial Council of the AMA— 1984"
reprinted with permission of the American Medical Association, from *Current Opinions of the Judicial Council of the AMA*, 1984.

International Council of Nurses, "Code for Nurses: Ethical Concepts Applied to Nursing" (1973)
International Council of Nurses, 1973, reprinted in part with permission.

American Nurses' Association, "Code for Nurses" (1985)
American Nurse's Association. *Code for Nurses with Interpretive Statements* (Kansas City, Mo.: The Association) 1985, reprinted with permission.

BIOETHICS

Readings & Cases

PART I
Moral Theory

SECTION A
Introduction

The goal of this book is to enable its readers to think in a more critical fashion about the difficult moral problems encountered in the provision of health care. This goal is approached not only through readings but also through an introduction to and a discussion of representative and difficult cases in 39 areas.

This goal itself raises fundamental questions. How can one think in a structured and critical fashion about these many difficult cases? What can we do by way of enabling our discussion to get beyond a mere expression of how we feel about the cases as we confront them? Many people believe that these questions cannot be answered. Others argue that the most that we can do is to articulate our feelings about particular cases. This book presupposes that this widespread view is not accurate and that critical reflection upon more theoretical questions about the nature of personhood, the nature of decision making, and the nature of justice can enable us to approach difficult cases in a principled fashion. In other words, this book presupposes that someone who develops in a coherent fashion a perspective on such important theoretical questions as who ought to be making what types of decisions, what is a person and how sacred is the life of a human being, and what are the rights to health care and how should these be balanced against social needs will be able to do something more than just articulate one's feelings about hard cases. This person will be able to use a theoretical position to clarify what is involved in the hard cases and to resolve them. Because of this presupposition, Part II of this text addresses these theoretical questions. Part III sets forth the difficult cases that invariably arise in the administration of health care. It is hoped and expected that readers will focus on Part II of the text and come to some opinions of their own on these important theoretical questions before looking at the hard cases in Part III.

Saying all of this raises, however, still further questions: What are we to use as our basis for adopting a position on these important theoretical questions? The readings on these questions present alternative viewpoints, but how do we

1

decide which viewpoints are right and which are wrong? Can we do anything more than simply accept whatever instinctively appeals to us as a theoretical position on these questions?

Again, there are many who are skeptical about whether these questions can be answered. We believe this skepticism is unfounded. We also believe that the reader will be aided in coming to a decision about these important theoretical questions by thinking about them from the perspective of fundamental moral theory. By identifying the major moral considerations that we need to take into account, we will be in a better position to evaluate the various viewpoints expressed in Part II of this text and therefore ultimately in a better position to decide what to do about the hard cases presented in Part III. Even if one cannot come to a final resolution of all moral debates in bioethics, rational analyses can at least show that some solutions are untenable and others more plausible.

Our purpose in this part of the book is to provide those readers who have not had much formal training in theoretical ethics with an introduction to that field of inquiry. Although reading this section is no substitute for a more sustained and substantial investigation of ethical theory, it will help those who have not had that training and also provide a quick review of some major points for those who have had such training.

Most introductions to ethical theory center around the presentation of a number of major moral theories such as utilitarianism, Kantianism, social contract theory, and others. The student is taught moral theory as a battleground between a number of major competing theories. We have not adopted this approach. What we present is an overview of a number of considerations (for example, the appeal to consequences, the appeal to rights, the appeal to justice and equality, the appeal to the virtues) that people generally appeal to as they ponder important moral questions. It is only later in Part I that we introduce the major moral theories. Each theory will be presented as a particular approach to weighing the significance of the various moral factors we have discussed. In this way, we hope to point out more clearly how much the various moral theories have in common, even while recognizing the important differences among them.

In short, then, the goal of this introductory part of the text is to present certain major considerations that have been developed by ethicists. These considerations will be used in Part II of the text, which deals with the major theoretical questions in medical ethics, to help illuminate the various positions and to help the reader decide which of them one should adopt. The introduction to each of the readings in Part II of the text will identify explicitly the theoretical presuppositions contained in that selection. Then both basic moral theory and the theoretical considerations in medical ethics will be referred to when we introduce the various hard cases. All of this means that readers will be well advised to work through this text in a systematic fashion so that they can benefit fully from all of the discussions and their interrelationships.

SECTION B
The Major Moral Considerations

1. APPEALING TO THE CONSEQUENCES OF OUR ACTIONS

Let us begin by looking at a simple example of a moral dilemma as a way of seeing not only how we often think about such dilemmas but also as a way of introducing the idea of the *appeal to consequences*. The dilemma is based on a true story: In 1841 the *William Brown*, a ship sailing from Liverpool to Philadelphia, struck an iceberg and began to sink. Two lifeboats, neither very safe, were lowered and then became separated. One was so overloaded with passengers that it was barely able to move. It began to leak and then a squall came up. The captain realized that unless the load was lightened everyone might die, but because no one volunteered to jump overboard, he was faced with a moral dilemma. What should he do? One way of thinking about that decision is this: The first thing the captain must do is consider the alternatives open to him. One, of course, is to do nothing and hope the lifeboat will not capsize. Another is to encourage volunteers to sacrifice themselves but not to force anyone overboard. A third option is to force *some* people overboard. This last choice will have several versions, depending upon what processes are adopted for deciding who should be thrown overboard. Having identified these alternatives, the captain then has to determine the likely consequences of each of them. The probable outcome of the first action (doing nothing) is that the boat will capsize and everyone will die. Still, the captain must take into account the possibility, even though it is unlikely, that this will not happen. The likely consequences of the second alternative (encouraging volunteers to sacrifice themselves) will depend on the people involved, the effectiveness of the encouragement, and so forth. For the third option, the likely consequence is that those thrown overboard will die and the rest will be saved, although we need to be alert to the possibility that this will do no good and everyone will die anyway. In thinking about this dilemma, the captain is required to make sure that he has really considered all of the alternatives. In calculating the consequences, he always has to allow for uncer-

3

tainty. Thus, the captain doesn't know for sure that the lifeboat will capsize if everyone stays on board, nor can he be certain that the boat will not capsize anyway.

This is one way of thinking about such a moral dilemma. One looks at the alternatives available, identifies their consequences, and then performs the action that is most likely to lead to the best consequences. We shall call this the *appeal to consequences.*

There are three major questions that we need to think about very carefully as we discuss the question of the appeal to the consequences of our actions in determining which is the best action to pursue. The first question that needs to be thought about very carefully is the question of which consequences shall be taken into account: the consequences to the person performing the action? to everyone affected? to only some of the people affected? The second question that we need to think about is how we shall evaluate the consequences to which we are appealing. Are the best consequences the ones that produce the most pleasure? Are the best consequences the ones that most satisfy the desires and preferences of the people affected? Are the best consequences the ones that are best for people whether or not they desire them and whether or not they derive pleasure from them? The third question that we need to consider very carefully is how we are going to weigh the gains and losses to those involved. Let us explain more carefully what this question is. Unless we are evaluating only the consequences to one person, we will be looking at the consequences for many who are affected by the actions. In a large number of cases, there will be those who benefit (however benefit is defined) and those who suffer (however suffering is defined). There are going to be very few cases in which we can decide that something is the right action to do just because its consequences are the most beneficial for everyone affected. That being the case, we will need to ask ourselves the question of how we weigh the benefits and losses to those affected by our actions. How shall we decide whether the action that benefits Joe and Mary but causes harm to Frank and Sally is better or worse than the action that benefits Frank and Sally but harms Joe and Mary? Let us look at all three of these questions much more closely.

The first of these questions is whose interests shall we consider as we evaluate consequences. The *thesis of egoism* is the belief that, in deciding which is the right action to perform, one should merely consider the consequences to oneself. In saying this, egoism does not mean to suggest that we should totally disregard the implications our action has for other people. For one thing, we often benefit when good things happen to those whom we love and care about. So we need to look at the consequences of actions for them, even according to egoism, but only insofar as we care about them and derive pleasure from the thought that they are doing well. Another reason why we need to look at the implications for other people is that there will be cases in which, if we do that, and if we choose the action that will benefit some other people, they will do likewise and choose the action that will benefit us. A rational egoist will sometimes choose the action that will lead to the best immediate consequences for others in the hope that this will lead to the best long-range consequences for oneself. In short, then, the egoist says that the right action to perform is the one that leads to the best consequences for oneself in the long run, but that may often mean sacrificing short-range gains and it always means taking into account the interests of others we love and care about.

This thesis of egoism has been rejected by most people who have thought about the question of how we should structure the appeal to the consequences of our actions in evaluating our actions from a moral perspective. They see egoism as a sound account of rational self-interest; they see egoism as giving us a good explanation of how one should look at the consequences of one's actions if one is simply thinking in terms of one's self-interest. Morality, however, is something else. At least part of what is involved in adopting the moral stance is taking into account the consequences for others as one evaluates actions by appealing to their consequences.

Which others? One widespread answer is that we should take into account the consequences for all those affected by the action. Let us call this the *thesis of altruism.* We need to be clear that this thesis does not mean that we should take into account, from the moral perspective, the consequences of our actions for everyone but ourselves. We are among those who are usually affected by our own actions, and the altruist thinks, therefore, that we need to take into account those implications. In fact, we are often the people most affected by our actions, and in those cases the consequences of our actions for ourselves may be the most important consideration that we need to take into account as we evaluate our actions from the perspective of their consequences. What the altruist is saying is that we should not just take into account the consequences to ourselves; we should take into account the consequences for all involved, ourselves included.

There is considerable intuitive appeal to this altruist answer. It seems to express a fundamental notion that all people are important and that we need to think about how our actions affect them before we decide what is the right action to do. Still, we need to think carefully about exactly which groups are included in the altruist answer that we should consider the implications for all of those affected. Should we, for example, count only human beings or should we take into account the implications of our actions for animals? Consider the case of medical experimentation employing animals. The consequences of that experimentation for human beings may be highly desirable, for such experimentation often leads to extremely important knowledge that will help humans to improve the length and quality of their lives. But such experimentation often results in very bad consequences for the animals being experimented on. Do we need to weigh those consequences and decide whether the benefits to human beings outweigh the harm to the animals? Or can we simply say that, in appealing to the consequences of our actions for all those affected, we merely appeal to the consequences for all people affected? Again, what about consequences to future generations not yet born? Consider the ways in which we deplete from the environment certain natural resources for our benefit at the cost of those who will follow us much later on (assuming that there will still be a world for our descendants). Are those actions the right actions because they produce the best consequences for all those right now who are affected by them, or are they wrong because the gains right now may be outweighed by the losses to those humans who will live later on? Still a third question is how we should think about the consequences to fetuses. Abortion might be beneficial to a woman but is harmful to the fetus (leaving aside, for now, the person whom the fetus will develop into). Do we need to balance the gains to the woman and the losses to the fetus? Or should we, in thinking about the consequence of our actions, consider only the consequences to already-born human beings? In short, even if one adopts the altruist answer and says that one needs to consider the consequences to all those affected when we try to evaluate actions from the perspective of the consequences of our actions, we are still left with considerable ambiguities as to which consequences to take into account.

Putting aside for now the ambiguities in the altruist answer, there is still another set of questions that we need to examine very carefully. When we appeal to the consequences of our actions in evaluating their moral rightness or wrongness, we often believe that there are some people to whom we owe great obligations and the consequences to whom we therefore need to take into account more fully than the consequences to other people. Members of families often feel that they are morally obligated to weigh the consequences of their actions to their family members more significantly than the consequences of their actions to other people, even if they cannot, of course, totally disregard the consequences to nonfamily members. Professionals such as doctors or nurses, lawyers or accountants, architects or engineers often feel that they have special responsibilities to their patients or clients, and that in deciding which of their actions lead to the best results, they need to take into account these special obligations and responsibilities and weigh the consequences to their patients or clients more heavily than the consequences to others. All of us seem to feel that we are under a special obligation to those who have helped us in the past or those to whom we have made promises to help. This sense of special obligations leads us in many cases to weigh more heavily the consequences to those to whom we made promises and to those who have helped us than the consequences to others. In short, the altruist answer, however it is understood in light of the ambiguities we discussed above, needs supplementation as we consider this matter of special obligations.

Let us see where we stand. We began by looking at the question of which consequences we need to take into account as we evaluate the moral quality of our actions in light of their consequences. The egoist answer, that we need only to consider the consequences to ourself, seems better as a summary of rational self-interested thinking than as a summary of moral thinking. The altruist answer, that we need to take into account the consequences for all those affected by our actions, is an improvement on the egoist answer, but it suffers from certain ambiguities. It needs to be supplemented because of the fact that we often have special relationships to people and this dictates that we need to weigh the consequences for them more heavily than the consequences of our actions for other people. At this point, that seems to be the most we can say by way of an overview of the question of which consequences we need to take into account as we evaluate our actions from the perspective of the appeal to consequences.

The second question we need to ask is: How should we evaluate consequences? What makes some consequences good and other consequences bad? What is the standard for evaluating consequences of our actions? One classical answer is that given by the hedonist. The hedonist claims that the one and only standard to be used in evaluating consequences is the pleasure produced by our actions. From the perspective of the appeal to the consequences of our actions, pleasure is the one and only good. In stating this, the hedonist is not saying that health isn't good or that knowledge isn't good or that beauty isn't good. The hedonist agrees that these things are good, but only as a means to the consequences that are the real good, namely, pleasure. In short, then, the hedonist argues that the best actions are the ones that produce the most pleasure. This is said while recognizing that the best way to produce the most pleasure often is by first producing something else.

An example may make this clearer. Suppose that a doctor undertakes a course of action that cures a patient. In most cases, this consequence of the action would count as a major reason for thinking that the action was morally right. But what consequences of the doctor's action are the ones that make the action so good? The hedonist would say that the consequence is not that the patient's health was restored and the patient is living a longer life. That consequence is only a means to the patient experiencing more pleasure, and that is what makes the consequences so good.

Hedonism is a position that has had an extensive history, and the world contains many hedonists. Nevertheless, most moral philosophers would object to the hedonistic account of what makes consequences good consequences. There are two reasons for doing so:

1. *Bad pleasures.* Consider the case of a sadist who is beating up a victim. We will probably all agree that the sadist's action is wrong, at least in part because it leads to bad consequences. Why is this so? According to the hedonist, the answer must be that, although there are some good consequences of the sadist's action, namely the pleasure that the sadist gets, these good consequences are outweighed by other bad consequences, namely the pain of the victim. This carries with it the implication that there might be cases in which the sadist gets so much pleasure and the victim experiences so little pain that the consequences are actually better when the sadist beats up the victim. This seems unacceptable. Most of us, objecting to the hedonist, would say that there are some cases (like the case of the sadist) in which pleasure does not count on behalf of the action; there are some pleasant consequences of an action that are not *good* consequences of an action.

2. *Other intrinsic goods besides pleasure.* The hedonist is committed to the view that the only thing that makes consequences good is that they are pleasant. No doubt, pleasant experiences are things that we all desire. There are, however, many other things that we desire besides pleasure and whose realization we would consider to be a good consequence of an action. Why should we not count these things as being other reasons why consequences are good besides the fact that they are pleasant? Why give pleasure this special status?

All of this has led many moral theorists to what has come to be called the *desire-satisfaction theory.* According to this theory, a consequence of an action is good because it satisfies the desires or preferences of the person affected by the action. Conversely, the consequence of an action is bad insofar as it frustrates those desires and preferences of the person affected by the action.

It is easy to see how this theory grows out of our criticism of hedonism. The hedonist, we have shown, pays attention to only one of those things that people desire, namely pleasure. The desire-satisfaction theory evaluates consequences of our actions as good insofar as they lead to any of the things that we want, and not just pleasure. In this way, the theory seems to be an improvement over the earlier hedonist theory. The point is that because we have many other preferences in addition to the preference for pleasure and the absence of pain, the desire-satisfaction theory seems broader and more in tune with human nature than the narrower hedonist approach.

There is an important confusion that often follows when adopting this approach. To say that the evaluation of consequences depends on the preferences of the people affected is not to say that we are supposed to do (other things being equal) what they want us to do. The people affected may want us to act in certain ways because they believe that those actions will lead to the satisfaction of their preferences. We may be in a position to see that alternative courses of action will be the ones that actually lead to the satisfaction of their preferences. In such cases, the appeal to the consequences of our action will lead us to perform those actions that will in fact lead to the best consequences rather than the actions they want us to do. According to the desire-satisfaction theory, the preferences of individuals determine what consequences are good or bad for them. It then becomes a factual question, independent of their preferences, as to which actions will lead to those desirable consequences. It may often be the case that individuals are the best judges of that factual question. Conversely, it may sometimes *not* be the case that they are the best judges. In such cases, if we are thinking simply of the appeal to the consequences of our actions, we may need to conclude that the right thing to do is not what others want us to do for them.

The desire-satisfaction theory is, for the reasons we have already indicated, a clear improvement over the hedonist theory. Nevertheless, it is not a sufficient improvement. To begin with, it will not enable us to deal with situations like the sadist. After all, sadists have a preference for beating up on their victims as much as they take pleasure from beating up on them. If the hedonist is wrong in counting the pleasures that the sadist derives as good consequences of the sadist's actions, then the desire-satisfaction theory is equally wrong in taking into account the fact that the sadist's actions satisfy the preference of the sadist. This point is particularly important in the health-care setting. Sadism is not just a question of physically beating up on other people. Many patients sadistically wish not to be healed so that their illnesses can impose burdens on others. A similar point needs to be made about masochism. There are patients who wish not to be healed so that their illnesses inflict suffering on themselves. Are these preferences to be counted, as the desire-satisfaction theory seems to say? We are all inclined to answer that question by saying no. The same thing can be said outside the medical setting about such preferences as *discriminatory* preferences. There are people who simply have a preference that members of other races and other religions suffer from being discriminated against. Shall we count the satisfaction of their preferences as reasons for supporting discriminatory actions? Shall we say that discrimination is bad only because the losses to the victims are greater than the gains to those who prefer to engage in discriminatory practices? Shall we accept the implication that, from the point of view of the appeal to the consequences of our actions, there are going to be cases where the desire to discriminate is so great that discriminatory actions are the ones leading to the best consequences? We think not.

All of this leads us to a viewpoint that has been suggested by many in recent years, and by others in the history of philosophy, but which has never been satisfactorily worked out. It is the view that only the satisfaction of some preferences counts as a reason for consequences being good, and only the frustration of some preferences counts as a reason for the consequences of an action being considered bad. This view, which we might call the *corrected* desire-satisfaction theory, in effect claims that there are some preferences that we ought not to take into account as we evaluate the consequences of actions.

Although theoretically very attractive, one major question remains that proponents of this view have yet to work out satisfactorily: Which preferences are we to disregard? Examples we gave before are of certain immoral preferences, such as the preference to inflict suffering or the preference to discriminate against others. But how are we to decide when preferences are so morally unacceptable that their satisfaction does not count on behalf of the performance of a given action? Are there other preferences that we ought to rule out: irrational preferences, pathological preferences, and so forth?

Let us see where we stand on this point. The question that we were considering was how we should evaluate the consequences of our actions for whoever it is we are concerned with. The hedonist says that we should simply look at whether our actions produce pleasure or pain. This seems inadequate. The desire-satisfaction theory seems better, because it generalizes beyond what the hedonist takes into account and accepts the fact that there are many things that people have preferences for other than simply pleasure and the absence of pain. But even it is not fully satisfactory because it fails to take into account the fact that there are some preferences whose satisfaction is not a good thing. This leads us to the corrected desire-satisfaction theory and to the recognition that there is much work that needs to be done before that theory will enable us to deal adequately with the many questions surrounding the appeal to the consequences of our actions. For example, one will need to know how to rule out gains and losses correctly.

We now turn to the third and last of our important questions: How do we weigh the gains to some and the losses to others as we evaluate the consequences of our actions? The problem raised by that question is that we often confront choices among actions when the consequences are good for some and bad for others, and the question we need to consider is how we should take into account these gains and losses as we decide, from the perspective of the consequences of our actions, which actions have the best consequences.

One simple suggestion that might be made is that we should judge the actions that benefit the most people and harm the fewest as having the best consequences. The trouble with that simple suggestion is that it fails to take into account the following scenario: Imagine a situation where one person would greatly benefit by an action and many others would be harmed in a *very* limited way. Imagine, moreover, that the benefits to the one person are really so great that we would truly like to say that they vastly outweigh the much more modest losses to the others. In other words, we would intuitively like to say that the action in question has very good consequences, even though there are many who lose and few who gain. Would not such a case serve as a counterexample to our simple suggestion?

There is another way of stating this difficulty with our simple suggestion. The suggestion supposes that we count the number of winners and the number of losers and use the difference to weigh the gains to some and the losses to others as we evaluate the consequences of our actions. That is clearly inadequate. We need to take into account not just how many will gain and how many will lose from our actions, but we also need to take into account how *much* those who gain will gain and how *much* those who lose will lose. The trouble is that we have no way of systematically making such comparisons. In the technical literature of economics and ethics, this problem has come to be called the *problem of the interpersonal comparison of utility,* that is, the problem of comparing the gains and losses to different people as we evaluate the consequences of our actions.

What can we do in the real world as we try to evaluate the consequences of our actions as part of the process of determining which actions we ought to engage in? We can certainly at least try to identify who benefits from and who is harmed by our actions so that we can get some idea of the number of winners and losers. Normally, when we see that there are many who gain and few who lose, we will count that as a strong reason for performing the action in question unless we feel intuitively (even though we cannot spell out the justification of this intuition) that the losses to the losers are far greater than the gains to the winners. Similarly, when we normally see that there are a great many losers and few winners, we will count that as a strong reason for not performing the action unless we intuitively feel that the gains to the winners are really far greater than the losses to the losers. In those cases in which our intuitive feelings tell us to be suspicious of simply counting winners and losers, we need to recognize that—absent an account of how to make interpersonal comparisons of gains and losses—we will often find it very difficult to decide, from the perspective of the appeal to the consequences of our actions, which action is the best action to perform.

We have by now carefully reviewed the three questions raised by the appeal to the consequences of our actions in trying to decide which is the right action to choose. We have tentatively concluded that the altruistic approach, which said that we need to take into account the consequences for all those affected by our actions, is on the right track. It needs, however, to be supplemented, owing to the fact that special relationships may dictate that we count the consequences for some people more than the consequences for others. It also remains ambiguous about the question of counting the consequences for animals, fetuses, and members of future generations. We have tentatively concluded that the desire-satisfaction theory is a better way of evaluating consequences for those we are concerned with, but that we need to find ways to modify it along the lines of the *corrected* desire-satisfaction theory so that we can rule out the satisfaction of some desires as reasons for performing an action. Here we will need to face the problem of which gains and losses should be weeded out. Finally, we have seen that the problem of the interpersonal comparison of utilities makes it very difficult to weigh the gains to some and the losses to others as we try to decide, from the perspective of evaluating the consequences of our action, which is the best action to perform. This will be less of a problem in those cases in which there are many losers and few winners or many winners and few losers. Even then, there will be instances where we will not be satisfied simply by counting the number of winners and losers. In those instances, and in the instance in which the number of winners and losers is far more balanced, it will be very difficult to weigh the gains to some and the losses to others, and it will therefore be very difficult to decide what is right by evaluating the consequences of our actions.

The appeal to the consequences of our actions in trying to decide what is right or wrong is, then, a very complicated appeal, raising many difficult theoretical and practical questions. It is, however, an appeal that must be included in any adequate moral theory, and it is a factor that we will need to take into account throughout this book.

2. APPEALING TO RIGHTS

Let us look at another example of a moral dilemma as a way not only of seeing how we often think about such dilemmas but also as a way of introducing the idea of the *appeal to rights* in helping us to deal with such dilemmas. This particular example illustrates a situation that has perplexed health-care providers for a long time: Mr. Jones is a Jehovah's Witness. Members of that religious sect, who usually seek medical care when dealing with a medical problem, reject the use of blood transfusions on the grounds that this violates their understanding of the biblical prohibition against the eating of blood. Mr. Jones has a severe bacterial infection. As a result, he has developed thrombocytopenia (a decrease in the number of platelets in his blood) and is in great danger of spontaneous bleeding. Normally, patients like Mr. Jones would be treated by controlling their bacterial infection and also with platelet transfusions to help deal with their immediate and significant bleeding problem. He and his family refused all transfusions. What are the health-care providers to do? At least one aspect of their thinking about that question is the feeling on the part of many that, as a competent adult, Mr. Jones has the right to maintain his religious beliefs and refuse the platelet transfusion, even if this really compromises his chances for survival. Another aspect of the case is the feeling on the part of many that he has a right to life, and this means a right to the health care that he needs to keep him alive. There are those who advance these considerations as a reason for transfusing him even against his wishes. In looking at this case, we can see it as a conflict between two major human rights.

This is a second way of thinking about moral dilemmas. One looks at the alternatives open to one, identifies the relevant rights of the parties in question, and then engages in the action that most preserves their rights. We shall call this second way of thinking about a moral dilemma the *appeal to rights*.

What does it mean to claim that someone has a right to something? Many theories have been advanced to answer this question. For our purposes, we shall understand such claims in the following fashion:

> X has a right to Y against Z just in case Z has an obligation to X not to deprive X of Y or not to withhold Y from X.

Thus, in our example, to say that Mr. Jones has a right against the health-care providers to decide whether or not he is going to get a transfusion of platelets is to say that the health-care providers have an obligation to Mr. Jones not to deprive him of the authority to make the decision as to whether he will get the platelets. Again, to say that Mr. Jones has a right to life against the health-care providers is simply to say that they have an obligation to Mr. Jones not to withhold from him the health care that he needs in order to survive.

Throughout the history of moral philosophy, there have been considerable discussions as to whether or not all rights have these correlative obligations. Our definition above assumes, in effect, that that is the case. For our purposes it is sufficient to note that the rights we will be talking about are ones that involve correlative obligations and that we therefore have no difficulty defining rights in terms of corresponding obligations of other people.

Before we turn to a consideration of the specific rights that are significant for our purposes, a number of major points need to be made about rights in general. These concern the relationship between rights and the moral rules that have long been prevalent in the Western tradition, the question of the waiving and the losing of rights, the question of the overriding of rights, the question of who possesses rights, and the distinction between negative and positive rights. Let us review each of these points separately.

Most of the moral and religious traditions of the West have advocated certain fundamental moral rules which they take as being central to morality. Such ways of thinking about morality are called *deontological* approaches, approaches that emphasize that doing the right thing is following the relevant moral rules. Examples of such rules are prohibitions against killing, against inflicting bodily injury on others, and against theft, as well as rules commanding us to come to the aid of those in distress and commanding us to keep our promises. It is not hard to see that there is a close relationship between following these moral rules and respecting the rights of people affected by one's actions. To kill someone is to violate that person's right to life, so insofar as one obeys the moral rule not to commit murder, one is respecting the relevant person's right to life. To break one's promise to someone is to violate that person's right to have a promise made to them kept. Thus, following the moral rule in question is equivalent to respecting the particular right of the party in question. This is not to say that all moral rules enjoin respecting rights; there may be moral rules dealing with other moral questions. It is just that the appeal to moral rights is often a deontological appeal, an appeal to well-known moral rules.

There are those who advance the view that at least some rights are inalienable rights. By that they mean that these rights can never be waived by the party who possesses them nor can they ever be lost by that party. An example that is often given of an inalienable right is the part of the right to life that consists of the right not to be killed. People believe that the right not to be killed is an inalienable right if they also believe that a human being cannot lose that right, no matter how badly one has behaved, and that a human being cannot waive that right, no matter how much that person desires to die. People who believe that the right not to be killed is an inalienable right will therefore believe that this right constitutes a very powerful moral objection both to capital punishment and to voluntary euthanasia. Not all moral theorists accept, however, the idea that there are inalienable rights. Some moral theorists believe that even the right to life, in the sense of the right not to be killed, can be lost by behaving in certain ways and can be waived by competent parties who wish strongly enough to die. Those who accept this notion of the alienability of all rights, including the right not to be killed, will therefore not use an appeal to the right to life as the basis for objecting either to capital punishment or to voluntary euthanasia.

Are rights absolute? An absolute right would be a right whose claim is so strong that it will always be wrong for us to violate that right. An absolute right would be one which, if not lost or waived, must always be respected. Some claim that rights in general, or at least some specific rights (the favored one being the right not to be killed), are in this sense absolute. Others disagree. They point out that the recognition of a right does not suppose that the right in question is absolute. Consider, as an example, the obligation that someone has to repay a loan. Suppose that the borrower on the day the loan is due needs the money for a more pressing purpose, say to buy food for his or her family. The obligation the borrower has to feed his or her family may take precedence over the obligation to repay the debt, in which case the lender has a right to be repaid, a right which the lender has neither waived nor lost but which may legitimately be overridden. Those who believe that rights are not absolute use this as a concrete example to show that rights can always be overridden. Naturally, according to this view, some rights have greater moral force than others and therefore can be overridden on fewer occasions. Even if one does not accept the view that the right not to be killed is an absolute right, one can still see it as a very powerful and fundamental right, and allow the legitimacy of its being overridden, when it has not been waived or lost, in very few cases.

An important point needs to be made about what happens when nonabsolute rights are overridden: These rights do not disappear. Suppose, once more, that my right to have the loan repaid is overridden by the borrower's more pressing obligations. Although the borrower may not have to fulfill his or her obligation and return the money to me now, the failure to do so—the failure to respect my right to the money—means that the borrower has a new obligation, namely the obligation to repay me as soon as possible (say as soon as he or she has the funds and other more pressing obligations are no longer present). When rights and their correlative obligations are overridden because of more pressing obligations, new obligations are created to make up for the failure to carry out these earlier obligations. In short, then, even if one does not believe in absolute rights, one may still believe in very strong rights that can be rarely overridden and which, when overridden, create new rights and obligations.

There is a long tradition that distinguishes between negative rights and positive rights. Negative rights are the rights that X has against Z to not be deprived of Y. Thus, the right not to be killed is a negative right that X has against Z not to be deprived of his or her life. Conversely, positive rights are rights that X has against Z to not withhold Y from X. The right to be aided in life-threatening emergencies is a positive right because it is the right the person whose life is threatened has against someone else not to withhold that which can save another's life. Those who draw this distinction between negative and positive rights often go on to claim that negative rights are more important than positive rights in that there are fewer occasions for overriding a negative right than a positive right. This has often been extended to the claim that negative rights are absolute rights in the sense that they can never be legitimately overridden when not waived or lost, whereas positive rights are less than absolute rights in the sense that, even when not waived or lost, they may still be legitimately overridden. These claims about the strengths of negative and positive rights need to be distinguished from the distinction itself. One may well accept the distinction without necessarily accepting these very strong claims about the difference in the significance of these rights.

One final point needs to be made about rights in general. A tremendous debate has ensued on the question of what entities can have rights. In many ways, this debate parallels the discussion about what are the entities whose interests need to be taken into account as we appeal to the consequences of our action. Some claim that only already-born human beings have rights. That position is sometimes extended to the claim that even some of those human beings (particularly newborns and/or those near death) are not possessors of rights. Others would liberalize the criteria to allow fetuses and/or future human beings and/or past human beings to have rights. Still others would go further and extend rights to members of various animal species.

In short, then, even before we analyze the various rights that are important in the health-care context, we need to keep in mind that the appeal to rights is a very complex appeal. It is the appeal to rights that explains many of the major moral rules that are so widely accepted. But these rights may or may not be inalienable and may or may not be absolute. If not absolute, many important questions arise about when they can be overridden and what further rights are created when the initial ones are overridden. Moreover, considerable doubt exists about what is the domain of rights, and about what are the entities that can have rights. So the logical structure of the appeal to rights is a very complex structure, and that appeal becomes even more complex as we turn to an examination of the particular rights important to health care.

There are seven particular rights that we we need to discuss as we think about the appeal to rights in the health-care setting. Four of these are negative rights: the right not to be killed, the right not to have bodily injury or pain inflicted on oneself, the right not to be deceived by others, and the right not to have one's confidences revealed to third parties. We also will be looking at three positive rights: the right to be aided in times of need, the right to have authority over decisions as to how one will be treated or how members of one's family will be treated, and the right to be respected as a person and be treated as an end rather than as a means. Let us look at each of these rights separately.

The first, the right not to be killed, is part (but only part) of what is normally referred to as the *right to life*. What that means is something like the following:

> X has a right against everyone not to be killed, since everyone has an obligation to X not to deprive X of X's life (where that means not to cause the loss of X's life).

It is important to keep in mind what the right not to be killed means, because our analysis of it already indicates that this right is not going to be relevant to a very large number of cases in medical decision making in which the issue to be decided is whether or not to commence or to continue treating a terminal illness. In all of those cases, if we fail to intervene to delay the death, we are not going to be causing the death of the patient. The cause of the patient's death is the underlying disease disorder—not our failure to intervene—and therefore our failure to intervene cannot be criticized on the grounds that it violates the patient's right not to be killed. All of this is not to say that we may not be obligated to prolong the life of patients in particular cases because of some other right that these patients possess. The one thing we do know is that the right not to be killed cannot be the basis of our obligation to prolong life in those cases.

Is this right an inalienable right, and is it an absolute right? These are important questions about the right not to be killed in general, and several aspects of these questions need to concern us directly in the context of the ethics of health care. The first aspect is the question as to whether this is a right that can be waived. The reason why this question is particularly important in the health-care setting is that there are occasions where the issues of suicide and active voluntary euthanasia arise (cases in which the patient has requested that his or her life be taken). Often people argue against suicide and against voluntary euthanasia on the grounds that it violates the right to life of the patient (the right of the patient not to be killed). If this right can be waived, their argument will be incorrect, because persons attempting to commit suicide or persons requesting active euthanasia have clearly waived their right not to be killed. So the question of whether or not this is an inalienable right is an important one, one that we will return to throughout the discussion of many of the hard cases in Part III of this book.

The second relevant aspect of the questions posed above is whether this right can be lost. In the health-care setting, that question becomes relevant in those cases of contemplated abortions where the fetus poses a threat to the life of the mother. There are some who would argue that even if the fetus has a right to life, if the fetus poses a threat to the life of the mother, this causes the fetus to lose that right, so this aspect of the issue of the inalienability of this right is one to which we will need to return later on in the text.

The second of the negative rights with which we shall be concerned is the right not to have bodily injury or pain inflicted on oneself. That right can be stated thus:

> X has a right against everyone not to have bodily injury or pain inflicted on X since everyone has an obligation to X not to diminish X's current state of bodily integrity and comfort.

Once more, it is important to understand that this is an obligation not to cause a diminution of integrity or comfort. As a result, the right in question and its corresponding obligation can never be the basis for an obligation to continue treatment. If one fails to commence or continue treatment, the underlying disease or disorder, and not one's actions, causes the diminution. There may be other rights that require one to commence or to continue treatment, but this particular right cannot.

What about this right being inalienable or absolute? This clearly is a right that can be waived. After all, there are many cases in which for good reasons we allow providers to perform procedures that inflict pain on us or that diminish our bodily integrity (think of an amputation to save a life). Why are the actions of the providers morally permissible in such cases? Part of the answer to that question is that the patient has given consent, and in doing so has waived this right. A very similar consideration gives us reasons for believing that this right can be overridden. We feel justified in performing many of these very same procedures, even when the patient does not agree because the patient is either incompetent or unconscious. It seems that it is the benefits that would be derived by the patient that override the nonwaived right not to have bodily injury inflicted on oneself. The way in which we treat patients indicates that this particular right, as important as it may be, can be waived by the patient and may be overridden by considerations having to do with the well-being of the patient.

Before turning to the last two negative rights, we need to look for a moment at the question of who possesses these rights. Several special groups need to be considered. We have already alluded to the fact that the issue of the moral permissibility of abortion is connected with, although not settled simply by consideration of, the issue of whether fetuses have a right not to be killed and a right not to be harmed physically. We also need to remember that the question of animal experimentation is at least connected with, even if not settled simply by a consideration of, the question of whether animals have these rights. Finally, some aspects of the question of treating defective newborns and the near-dying are tied up with the question of whether these individuals possess these rights. So the question of who possesses these first two negative rights is an extremely important one, and an entire section of Part II of this book, the section on the concept of a person, is devoted to these questions.

We turn then to the third and fourth negative rights, the right not to be deceived by others and the right not to have one's confidences revealed. Let us begin with the right not to be deceived. What is it to be deceived? To be deceived is to be caused to have false beliefs. How can we cause others to have false beliefs? In two ways. The first is when we make false claims to others, knowing that they will believe us. The second is when we fail to provide people with certain information that we have available, knowing that they will infer false beliefs from our failure. If I say to a patient who I know is dying, "Don't worry; you really do have a good chance of pulling through," then my statement is a clear case of the first type of deception. But if I give patients lots of information about possible ways of dealing with their medical problems, knowing that they will draw the conclusion that they have a good chance of pulling through, and I fail to tell them that their chance is really slim even with all of the care I am providing, then I have deceived them in the second way, because I have caused them to hold false beliefs by not providing them with certain information.

It is important to keep in mind that accepting the existence of these two forms of deception does not mean accepting the view that we are under an obligation to provide all the information that we know to all those who might want to know it. We deceive patients only in those cases in which our failure to provide information causes the patient to hold false beliefs rather than simply not holding beliefs at all. It is only that type of withholding of information that is a form of deception.

Can this right not to be deceived be waived? Can it be overridden? These two questions have provoked considerable discussion. Looking at the first question first, what ought one to do about nervous and concerned patients who say, "If the news is bad, lie to me; I don't really want to know the truth until I have to because I'll do better in the time that remains to me if I don't know the bad news"? Looking at the second question, what ought one to do in those many cases in which one sometimes thinks that the patient will be better off if he or she is deceived? Consider, for example, the case in which the physician believes that the patient's best chance for survival is agreeing to a surgical procedure but also recognizes that, even with this best chance, the patient's chances aren't very good. The physician may believe that the patient is unlikely to consent unless the patient has a more optimistic outlook than is justified, and the physician is therefore tempted to lie to the patient. What ought to be done in this case?

Opinions on this question vary widely. Some hold that this right not to be

deceived is an inalienable and absolute right, and that we are under an obligation, no matter what the patient wants, not to deceive patients in either way.
Others believe that the patient's right to be deceived can never be overridden,
and is in that sense absolute, but can be waived by the patient because the patient
has the right to waive this right not to be deceived. Still others believe that the
right can be both waived and overridden if the resulting benefits to the patient
are sufficiently great. Naturally, people in this third group often disagree about
what are the cases in which the right not to be deceived can be overridden. We
will be returning to these questions in the theoretical readings in Part II and
even more extensively in many of the hard cases in Part III of this book.

We turn finally to the last of the negative rights, the right not to have one's
confidences revealed to others. Put into our usual schematic form, this right can
be stated thus:

X has a right against Z not to to have X's confidences revealed just because Z is
under an obligation to X not to deprive X of control over information regarding X.

There is one point that immediately stands out as we examine this definition of the right to confidentiality. This is that the heart of the right to confidentiality is the patient's right to control information about his or her health status
and about the care the patient is receiving. The health-care provider can supply
that information to others without violating the patient's right to confidentiality
providing that the health-care provider does so with the authorization of the
patient. On the other hand, if the patient has not given that authorization, then
the patient's right to confidentiality is being breached even if the provider gives
that information to family members or close friends of the patient. The right to
confidentiality is, in effect, a right to have control over information.

Can this right be waived or lost? It is clear that the answer to both of these
questions is yes. The right must be one that can be waived because in waiving the
right, the patient is simply authorizing that information about his or her condition and treatment be given to anyone, and how, in light of our definition of the
right, can this be a moral problem? But it is clearly also a right that can be lost.
Consider, for example, the patient whose health-care problems result from a
stabbing incurred in the course of committing a crime. Surely that fact justifies
the information being provided to at least some third parties without the patient's consent. Similar considerations make us recognize that this right can also
be overridden. We expect information about certain communicable diseases, for
example, to be conveyed to the relevant health authorities, even if the patient
does not want the information to be conveyed to them, so that these communicable diseases can be better controlled.

All of these familiar practices indicate that the right to confidentiality is
alienable and nonabsolute. Of the four negative rights, it is the one that most
clearly falls in these categories. However, that is not to say that it is not a significant negative right. It just is perhaps not quite as significant as the first three
negative rights, which are, of course, extremely significant rights.

We turn now to the consideration of our three positive rights: the right to
be aided in times of need, the right of decisional authority, and the right to be
treated with respect as an end and not just as a means. In our usual fashion, we
will examine each of these rights separately.

The first of these rights is the right to be aided in times of need. The claim that there is such a right is highly controversial. Many have argued that this right does not exist. Such theorists, often called *libertarians,* have claimed that whereas it may be a good thing for people to come to the aid of others in life- or health-threatening situations, there is no obligation to do so, not even if one is a health-care provider. Something like this seems to have been the tradition of the common law, which always rejected the idea that health-care providers were obliged to provide emergency aid even in life-threatening situations. Moreover, something like this seems to lie behind the traditional claim that indigent people were not entitled to health care, no matter how much they needed it, but could at best hope for the charity either of the general public or of individual health-care providers. The alternative position, and the one that has come to be far more widely adopted in recent times, is the view that the right to receive aid in life- or health-threatening situations, and the corresponding obligations of individuals and the body politic to provide that aid, definitely does exist. Although this is an increasingly accepted view, the extent of the right and the corresponding obligation are matters of great debate and will be discussed much more fully in Section C–7 of Part II of the book.

What is the nature of this right? It seems to come to the following:

> X has a right to be aided in life- and health-threatening situations against those who are present and capable of aiding X, since those who are both present and capable have an obligation to X to provide this aid to X.

Several points need to be immediately noted about this right. The first is that this is a right that X has against those who are present and capable of aiding X. This helps explain why we primarily think of this as a right that X has against health-care providers, because we suspect that they are usually going to be the only people who are both present and capable of providing that aid to X. However, and this is the second point that needs to be noted, in truth this is not a right that people have only against health-care providers. All people have an obligation to provide the aid if they are present and capable of aiding in life- or health-threatening situations. This right has special implications for health-care providers only because they are often the ones who are most capable of providing that aid and sometimes the *only* ones capable of providing that aid.

Is this right alienable and is this right absolute? Consider first the question of the patient waiving this right. Some argue that this is an inalienable right that cannot be waived. Their view is that this right, like the negative right not to be killed, is one of the components of the right to life, and that the right to life is a right that cannot be waived. Those who hold this view often draw from it the implication that the corresponding obligation to provide aid persists in the health-care setting, even when patients no longer wish this aid. They often draw from this the conclusion that those whose life and health can be significantly improved by health care should receive that health care even if they do not wish it. Others reject this view of the inalienability of this right to be aided. They want to claim that this right, like most or all other rights, can be waived, and when the potential recipient of the aid waives it, then health-care providers are no longer obliged to provide that aid. They may even be forbidden to provide that aid, because their doing so may violate another right to be discussed below, namely, the right of decisional autonomy. This important controversy about the nature of this right, and other issues associated with it, will be discussed in Section A–3 of Part II of this book.

Can this right be lost? Again, this is a matter of considerable controversy. Some maintain that the right to this aid and the corresponding obligation to provide it do not apply to persons who are themselves responsible for their being in a life- or health-threatening situation. According to this view, if someone has engaged in a very dangerous activity, such as exploring deep underground caves, and that person is in serious danger, then no one is under any obligation to aid the person, who must count on those who are prepared to extend themselves beyond the limits of their obligation. Similarly, if someone has become severely ill from cirrhosis due to excessive use of alcohol, there are those who would say that health-care providers in particular, and society in general, have no obligation to help that person face his or her health crisis and the person must count solely on the willingness of others to go beyond their obligations. Others would disagree. They claim that whatever the blame that may lie on the person, the person's right to be aided in times of life- or health-threatening situations, and society's corresponding obligation, is never lost.

Finally, can this right be overridden? Are there considerations that must take precedence over the realization of this right? It seems clear that the answer to this question must be yes. Suppose that someone is seriously ill and the form of aid that is required, say admission to an intensive care unit, can only be provided by withdrawing that aid from someone else who is already receiving it. In this case, whatever decision is made, someone is not going to get the aid and that person's right to be aided is going to be overridden by the right of the other person to get the aid. Many other examples can be given to illustrate this point.

In short, the right to be aided in life- and health-threatening situations is an extremely important right when we consider ethical questions in the provision of health care. Unfortunately, it is surrounded with great controversy. There is a question about whether the right even exists. And even if it is conceded that the right does exist, there is a question of what is the extent of the corresponding obligation, of whether the right can be waived or lost by the potential recipient, and of the conditions under which it can be overridden. Because of the controversy surrounding this right and because of its centrality to all those ethical questions in the provision of health care that involve an appeal to rights to resolve them, we will be returning to an analysis of the right to be aided at many points in both Part II and Part III of this book.

We turn now to the next of our positive rights—the right to decisional authority in cases where the actions decided on affect oneself and the right to decisional authority in cases where the action decided on affects members of one's family. We need to look at each of these separately.

The most crucial step that needs to be taken to define this right of decisional authority properly is to distinguish two types of cases in which it might be invoked. The first case concerns a health-care provider who wishes to treat a patient in a certain fashion and the patient does not wish to receive that form of medical treatment. This is the case in which the claim of the right to decisional authority by the patient has its greatest plausibility. This right is rooted, after all, in the idea that the patient's body is the patient's and not the provider's, and that the patient has a right to determine the forms of treatment that he or she will receive. The second case is one in which the health-care provider is opposed to a form of treatment and the patient requests the treatment despite the opposition of the health-care provider. Here the invocation of the right of decisional authority is far less plausible. After all, the provider, like anyone else, has rights. One of the rights the provider has is the right not to be bound to perform actions simply because someone else wants them performed. The patient is free to seek out some other health-care provider who will be willing to provide those forms of treatment, but the patient presumably has no right to impose a servitude on the health-care provider.

In light of this distinction, we can define this right of decisional authority as follows:

> X has the right against everyone to be the final decision-maker for allowing treatment for X, since everyone is under an obligation to X to give this decisional authority to X.

Defining it this way makes it clear that X's right is the right to decide as to whether the treatment the doctor wishes to provide will be provided to X, but that it does not extend to X's having the right to receive the treatment the physician feels is inappropriate and does not wish to provide.

Is this right alienable and is this right absolute? It seems reasonably clear that this right can be waived. Not everyone, after all, wants to be a decision-maker. This is true in general and is particularly true in a medical context. Patients may feel emotionally incapable of having to confront difficult decisions at a time of illness, and they may have sufficient trust in a health-care provider to wish the provider to assume that authority for them. Patients may feel intellectually incompetent to make some forms of difficult decisions, and they may wish to leave that in the hands of the providers who know better about difficult medical and technical questions. There may be still other motives that lead patients to avoid decisional authority. We may, for a variety of reasons, positively or negatively evaluate decisions on the part of the patient not to be a decision-maker, but we can hardly claim that the health-care provider who decides for the patient at the patient's request violates the patient's rights. After all, as autonomous individuals, patients can authorize the health-care provider to make the decision for them.

The question of this right being overridden is much more controversial. The most plausible cases for its being overridden are those circumstances in which the patient will suffer irreversible losses if the recommended form of treatment is not provided. The case becomes even more plausible when the harm will occur to others as well (such as the patient's family). There are those who would conclude that at least in those cases, the right to be a decision-maker can be overridden. Whether or not this is true will be examined carefully in Section A–3 of Part II of this text.

One final point should be made about this right of decisional authority in one's own case. In order for the patient to use his or her decisional authority effectively, the patient is going to need a wide range of information about the options available, their comparative benefits and costs, etc. The information that the patient is going to need is, for the most part, only going to be available to the patient through the help of the health-care provider. It is this practical reality that has led to the requirement of informed consent, a requirement that is discussed much more fully in Section A–4 of Part II of the text.

What about the right of decisional authority in cases where the actions decided on will impact on members of one's family? This right, which in medical context becomes the right of family members to participate in decisions concerning the treatment of the patient, requires careful analysis.

If the family member who is to be treated is an adult, competent patient, then it seems unlikely that this right exists at all. In fact, the right not to have one's confidences revealed (discussed previously) requires that even providing information to the family, much less giving them a role in decision making, be guided by the patient's wishes. Naturally, the question arises as to who is an adult competent patient, and that question will be explored more fully in Section A–1 of Part II of the text. So let us consider only those cases in which we are dealing either with a minor or with an incompetent patient. Sometimes the patient is no longer competent but was once competent, and the family may have strong evidence about what the patient would have wished. In such cases, decisional authority will rest in the patient's previously expressed wishes. It is in those cases in which the patient is a minor, or has always been incompetent, or was previously competent but never evidenced any wishes, that the family's decisional authority becomes relevant. And most of what has to be said about this right is really analogous to what has been said above. It is presumably a right that can be waived and overridden.

One special question needs to be examined briefly. Is this authority the authority simply to decide in light of what would be in the best interests of the patient? Or is it the authority to decide, taking that into account but also taking into account the interests of other members of the family? Although we will not say anything more about this question at this point, it will become extremely relevant as we look at some of our hard cases in Part III of the book.

We turn, finally, to the last of our positive rights: the right to be treated with respect and to be treated as an end rather than as a means for the realization of other people's ends. Many who have discussed this theme of respect for persons and of treating them as ends, and who have wanted to claim that it is a fundamental human right, have probably meant this as a way of summarizing the appeal to all of the other rights that we have discussed so far. Many have probably believed that to treat people with respect and to recognize them as an end rather than as a means is to respect all of their positive and negative rights to the largest extent possible. However, others have described this theme in ways that suggest that they had something else in mind. But it is very unclear what this "something else" might be. Because such a clear statement is absent in the literature of moral theory, we will, for the purposes of this book, treat the right to respect and the right to be treated as an end rather than as a means simply as a "summation right," summarizing all of the negative and positive rights that we have discussed up till now.

The appeal to rights is obviously a very complex matter. Complexities exist in the logical structure of any appeal to rights, and further complexities arise as soon as we examine each of the particular rights. Our discussion until now, including the examples drawn from the health-care setting, should make it clear, however, that the appeal to rights is very essential to any moral evaluation of questions that arise in the provision of health care. We will see this even more clearly in the remaining parts of this book. So the final conclusion we have to draw from this section is that the moral world is a complex world, and we need to do our best to understand these complexities and to deal with them as we encounter particularly difficult cases.

3.   APPEALING TO THE VIRTUES

Let us begin our discussion by looking at a third example of a moral dilemma, which will help us understand another way of thinking about moral issues. This dilemma is based upon a very common problem germane to the health-care setting, particularly when one is dealing with patients with incurable cancer. A typical example runs something as follows: Mr. Jones presents with an advanced case of cancer of the prostate for which there is little that can be done. His providers are primarily concerned with affording him relief from his symptoms. They feel that they can do so, with the family's concurrence, without telling Mr. Jones about his underlying illness and his inevitable demise. In fact, this is precisely what the family wishes them to do. The family feels that once Mr. Jones's symptoms are relieved, he will be able to live for some period of time with a reasonably high quality of life but only if he is not aware of his impending death from cancer. They feel that it will be cruel to tell him what the underlying disease is and how dim his prognosis is. On the other hand, Mr. Jones often asks about his disease, and one could carry out the family's request only by systematically lying to him. The physicians and the other health-care providers in question are reluctant to engage in this full-scale deception of Mr. Jones because they find themselves uncomfortable with the thought of this dishonesty. What should they do?

At least one way of thinking about this dilemma is to recognize the existence of certain virtues that would lead one to adopt one or another course of action. The honest thing to do is to tell Mr. Jones the truth when he asks about his underlying disease. The compassionate thing might be to withhold that information from Mr. Jones as long as possible so that he does not have to struggle with the knowledge of his inevitable death from cancer.

This is a third way of looking at moral issues. We recognize that there are a number of alternative actions open to us, and we also recognize that each of these actions seems to exemplify one or another virtue. We argue for performing one or another of the actions open to us on the grounds that these are virtuous actions.

Ancient moral philosophy placed great emphasis on the moral virtues. Plato and Aristotle, for example, did not primarily discuss either the question of which action will lead to the best consequences or the question of which action most respects the rights of the parties involved. They focused on questions of what sort of actions we are to take and what sort of people we ought to try to be in terms of the virtues. Modern moral philosophy has paid much less attention to such questions, preferring to focus on the appeal to consequences and the appeal to rights. In light of the spirit expressed at the beginning of this introduction, we will not enter into this conflict, but simply introduce the *appeal to the virtues* as a third type of appeal that needs to take its place along with the appeal to consequences and the appeal to rights in determining what we ought to do in a particular situation.

There are at least four virtues that play a major role as we think about difficult value choices in the provision of health care. These are the virtues of compassion, courage, honesty, and integrity. What we shall be looking at now is a preliminary analysis of what is involved as we appeal to these different virtues.

The first virtue that we shall consider is the virtue of *compassion*. There seem to be many decisions that health-care providers make that are justified at least in part on the grounds that these decisions and the resulting actions show great compassion. In our above example, if the providers decide not to tell Mr. Jones about his underlying disease, they will presumably be doing so on the grounds that it is the compassionate thing to do. Again, the health-care provider who stops to aid an accident victim with whom he or she had no previous professional relation is certainly to be praised at least in part on the grounds that the person is performing a compassionate act of caring for others.

What is compassion? One could define it as a certain way of responding to the suffering of other people. When one feels the suffering of others and responds by attempting to alleviate that suffering, then one is engaged in a compassionate act. Although such actions certainly are compassionate actions, they are not the only type of compassionate action. Consider, for example, the comatose patient who is not suffering any pain because of his or her diminished mental status. Such an individual has nevertheless suffered a great loss. To feel that loss, and to respond to that loss by attempting to care for the patient and restore the patient's functioning, is certainly an act of compassion. We need to understand compassion as a caring attempt to alleviate the losses of others and not merely as a caring response to the suffering of others. There are other losses besides suffering.

There are clearly going to be some cases of compassionate actions where the action performed is one that we have an obligation to perform. Health-care providers caring for patients who are in pain are certainly under an obligation, absent special circumstances, to help alleviate that pain. The action goes beyond a mere obligatory one and becomes a compassionate action as well when the health-care provider does so not merely out of a sense of obligation but also out of a sharing of the suffering and loss and a resulting desire to alleviate them. There are other cases, however, where a compassionate act is, although virtuous, an action that one may have no obligation to perform. Thus, in any of the cases in which we decide that someone does not have a right to be saved, and where the potential health-care provider does not have an obligation to provide that saving care, the provider who nevertheless goes beyond his or her obligations and provides the care in question, and does so out of a desire to alleviate the loss, is certainly performing a compassionate action, even if it is one that is not obligatory.

One additional point needs to be made about the appeal to the virtue of compassion in the health-care setting. One's normal examples of compassionate actions are actions performed by providers. This is not surprising. In the context of health care, it is the recipient who has suffered the loss and the provider who is in a position to perform the compassionate action. But that is not always the case. Very often cases arise in which health-care recipients can engage in compassionate actions toward health-care providers. These are cases in which the recipients can perform compassionate acts of recognizing the humanity and needs of providers and not impose unnecessary and extra burdens on providers. This may be nothing more than not requesting immediate treatment of a problem that could be deferred for another occasion when it is clear that the health-care provider is tired. It may also be something much more substantial. Consider the case of a family who puts the physician in a difficult situation by requesting that the physician heavily sedate a dying patient (where it is understood that the heavy sedation may well result in the death of the patient), when the family knows that such an action would not be compatible with the moral values of the physician. Would it not be a compassionate act on the part of the family to recognize this fact and to avoid placing the physician or health-care provider in a difficult and uncomfortable situation? Thus, compassion can be displayed not only by providers but also by recipients and their families.

The next virtue to which we might appeal in the health-care setting is the virtue of *courage*. It seems that many decisions that both health-care providers and health-care recipients make can be praised, at least in part, on the grounds that the decision and the resulting action show great courage. Any account of the virtues relevant to health care should include this important virtue of courage.

Long ago, Aristotle pointed out that courage is not the same thing as foolhardiness. The foolhardy person is one who seems totally unconcerned with the possibility that his or her action will lead to pain, bodily injury, or death. The foolhardy person will often perform actions that are wildly inappropriate because they risk a great harm for very little gain. The foolhardy person is willing to perform these actions because he or she is inappropriately unconcerned with such losses. Foolhardiness, as Aristotle pointed out, is no virtue. Courage is a virtue precisely because it is not foolhardiness. Courage is a virtue precisely because it consists of performing appropriate actions and not being excessively swayed by these fears.

These fears can be fear of pain, injury, or death, or they can be fears of private guilt or public disapproval afterwards. The person who makes the right choice and is not excessively swayed either by fears of pain, bodily injury, or death, or by a fear of guilt feelings or public disapproval afterwards, is a person who is acting courageously. It is easy to think of many examples of courageous decisions and actions performed by health-care recipients. The patient who consents to an appropriate surgical procedure, for example, even where there is a real risk of pain or injury or even death, is properly described as a courageous patient and properly praised for that courage. Similarly, relatives who have to decide on surgical procedures for family members are also people who can display this type of courage. If, after weighing the various factors, they make the decision that seems best, and are not excessively swayed either by their fears for the patient or by their fears of later guilt feelings or later disagreements with others, they have acted courageously. Finally, health-care providers can also display this form of courage. Although providers do not face an immediate threat of pain, bodily injury, or death, they are often called upon to make decisions knowing very well that they may later regret the decisions or that they may later be criticized for the decisions they made. Courageous health-care providers are those who move forward after careful reflection to make the necessary decisions and are not excessively swayed by such fears.

There is one extremely important difference between courage and compassion that needs to be made explicit. Compassion as a virtue helps explain why certain actions that are not obligatory are nevertheless praiseworthy. In this way, the virtue of compassion generates values for actions that would otherwise have no particular moral value. Courage is not that sort of virtue. After all, the courageous person is one who is performing the otherwise appropriate action without being excessively swayed by certain fears. We praise people for being courageous, but their courage is not the source of value of the actions they perform. Those actions are independently valuable. This is not to downplay the significance of the virtue of courage. All that this does is note that there is a difference between the virtue of courage and the virtue of compassion.

The third of the virtues that we need to consider is the virtue of *honesty*. It seems clear that many communications between providers and recipients are to be praised at least in part on the grounds that they are honest communications. Thus, any full account of the virtues relevant to health care must include this important virtue of honesty.

The first thing we need to note is that there are two different ways in which dishonesty can be exemplified. To begin with, one is dishonest when one makes claims that are known to be false and when one makes those false claims with the deliberate intention of misleading the person receiving the information. If you tell a patient who you know is almost certain to die that he or she has a good chance of recovering, then you have engaged in a dishonest act of communication. Conversely, when a patient tells a provider that he or she does not drink heavily when in fact the patient is a serious alcoholic, then the patient is being dishonest. This is not, however, the only way in which one can engage in dishonest acts of communication. If you withhold information with the expectation and intention that the person from whom you are withholding the information will draw false conclusions, then the withholding of information is also a dishonest act of communication. When a provider is taking a history of a patient and asks the patient about abnormal symptoms and the patient reports some but withholds others—knowing that the provider will draw the inference that he or she has no further symptoms—then the patient is being dishonest in this withholding of information. Similarly, the provider who informs patients of certain side effects of the drug they are being given but fails to inform them of other equally probable and serious side effects, and who does so expecting and hoping that patients will surmise that there are no other side effects, engages in a dishonest act of communication by withholding this information. This is not to say that all withholding of information is automatically dishonest. Rather, it is withholding information with the expectation and intention of misleading others that is dishonest.

It is important to note that there are many arguments, independent of the appeal to the virtue of honesty, for honest acts of communication. There are "rights" arguments for honest communication between health-care recipients and health-care providers. After all, both providers and recipients have the right to make certain decisions based on information, and they are deprived of that right when false information is provided or when information is misleadingly withheld from them. Moreover, there are appeals to consequences, which can justify honest communication between providers and recipients. Providers who engage in honest communication with recipients will build trust and will have greater compliance with their recommendations. Recipients who honestly provide information to their providers are likely to get a better diagnosis and treatment, more concern and care and so forth. Nevertheless, as an additional third consideration, honest communication can be praised on the grounds of the appeal to the virtue of honesty.

This leads one to the conclusion that for the most part honesty as a virtue in the health-care setting is more like courage than like compassion. In most cases, the person who is engaged in an honest act of communication is performing an action for which there are moral reasons independent of the virtue of honesty. There may, however, be a small number of cases in which honesty may lead one to certain acts of communication that are valuable precisely because of their honest character and not because of the other factors such as the appeal to rights and the appeal to consequences. The sort of case that we have in mind is the following: There may be cases in which we are led for one reason or another to make a decision to provide treatment for patients against their wishes. In such a case, should a health-care provider honestly inform the patient and family afterwards what was done? The argument for that cannot be based on the right of patients to be informed decision-makers because decisions are being made independently of their wishes. It is also hard to see that the other factors that we mentioned above (the appeal to consequence factors of building trust and encouraging compliance) are likely to be nurtured by such an act of communication. This is because we are raising conflict rather than building trust by telling the patient and the family what action has been taken. Nevertheless, some moral reasons exist for thinking that it would be appropriate to inform the patient and the patient's family about what was done. The moral reason seems to be precisely that it would be the honest thing to do. If there are some cases in which it is morally appropriate to treat the patient against the wishes of both the patient and the patient's family, and if in those cases it is morally appropriate to communicate what has been done to the patient and family, then it seems as though there will be at least some cases in which the virtue of honesty provides an independent reason for the performance of certain acts of communication. In these limited numbers of cases, honesty may be more like compassion than courage.

We turn, finally, to the last of the virtues that we will be considering, the virtue of *integrity*. Many decisions that health-care providers and recipients make are justified, at least in part, on the grounds that only by making these decisions can they maintain their integrity. For example, providers who refuse certain forms of care that patients request on the grounds that doing so is contrary to their values and judgments can certainly justify their actions on the basis of appealing to the virtue of integrity. Similarly, patients who sometimes refuse to be treated in certain ways because they believe these treatments go against their values and judgments can argue that it would be wrong for them to have that care precisely because having it violates the virtue of integrity.

What does this sense of integrity mean? Certainly, people who do what they are obliged to do even if it would be in their personal gain to do otherwise may correctly say that their doing so is an act of integrity. That appeal to integrity reinforces the appeal to already existing moral obligations. It is an important part of the appeal to integrity. But there is, we believe, an even more essential facet of the appeal to integrity that needs to be understood as well.

In order to grasp this other type of integrity, it is important to keep in mind that not all values are purely moral values. People frame for themselves conceptions of their goals in life that they wish to pursue, conceptions of the things that they care more about and the things that they care less about, and so forth. These conceptions that people form are an essential part of their personhood, and those who lack such personal values may properly be described as lacking a philosophy of life. The appeal to the virtue of integrity is often an appeal to behaving in accordance with these personal values rather than in accordance with basic moral obligations.

Perhaps a few examples will illustrate this point. Consider a patient who has always placed a high value on being mentally alert, being in control of a situation, being capable of making independent decisions, and so forth. Such a patient, when confronting the considerable pain of a terminal illness, might well find the type of pain relief offered to many patients inappropriate precisely because it produces a mental state in which these things would no longer be possible. If that patient chooses to refuse that form of sedation, then we might well praise that choice as reflecting both a deep sense of personal integrity and immense courage. Other patients whose values are very different might well make the choice of ending their life in a sedated state without being open to the criticism that they have failed to display integrity. The crucial point is that decisions that might appropriately be made by one patient would be made inappropriately by another patient precisely because those decisions would be in consonance with the values of the first patient yet not be in consonance with the values of the second. A similar point can be made about the values of providers. There are providers who are particularly sensitive to the value of human life and who seek a practice in which they regularly confront patients whose very life is at stake so that they can find ways to prolong human existence. Such providers may well not want to participate in decisional processes that lead to decisions that sacrifice the value of the prolongation of life in order to promote other values such as the relief of pain. They may rightly feel that their participation in such a decision violates their integrity because it calls on them to abandon their goal and adopt the goals of others. Other providers may have a different conception of their goal in health care. Their primary goal might be providing their patients with what the patients want in order to promote patient goals. Such providers might well participate in the same process without feeling any loss of integrity.

In short, then, particular decisions and actions made by both health-care providers and health-care recipients can be praised on the grounds that they display integrity or be criticized on the grounds that they fail to display integrity. The crucial point is that the very same decision made by one person might be praised, whereas it would be criticized when made by another person. The appeal to the virtue of integrity addresses both providers and recipients and calls on them to stand firm in their values. Because this is so, this type of appeal to integrity, unlike the appeal to integrity that is connected with actions that are morally obligatory, is like the appeal to compassion in the important sense that it creates moral reasons for performing actions that would otherwise be morally neutral.

There is, however, an important difference between the virtue of integrity and the virtue of compassion that should be noted. The virtue of compassion is by its very nature an *other-centered* virtue. The compassionate person is responding to the suffering and losses of others. The virtue of integrity is not in that way necessarily other-centered. The person of integrity may perform certain actions as a way of pursuing goals that are self-oriented rather than other-oriented. To say that there is this distinction between compassion and integrity is not, however, to say that compassion is a more important or more valuable virtue than integrity. We ought not to assume that the most important virtues are other-centered virtues. Assuming this is one component of the failure to understand that there are many aspects of morality, and the other-centered aspects are not the whole story.

We have briefly examined the nature of four virtues that we often need to appeal to in health-care settings in order to evaluate a particular action. This appeal to virtue needs to be added to the appeal to consequences and the appeal to rights as we try to determine what is the morally appropriate thing to do in many complex cases.

4.   APPEALING TO JUSTICE AND EQUALITY

A fourth appeal that we need to take into account as we evaluate moral issues in the delivery of health care is the appeal to *justice and equality*. Although there is wide agreement that this appeal exists, there is disagreement as to exactly what this appeal involves. So we need to examine the appeal to justice and the appeal to equality very carefully and separately. Why is there this disagreement about the nature of these appeals? The disagreement seems to focus on the relation between the appeal to justice and the appeal to equality. There are those, whom we shall call *egalitarians,* who see these two appeals as being essentially the same. For the egalitarian, justice demands that we maximize equality in the distribution of goods and services in society. There are others, whom we shall call *redistributivists,* who see these appeals as being only partially equivalent. According to the redistributivists, justice demands that we redistribute certain goods and services so as to ensure that everyone has equal access to some allotment of them. After this redistribution has taken place, the demands of justice provide no further reasons for pursuing equality. Finally, there are some, whom we shall call *libertarians,* who reject entirely the appeal to equality and who claim that the appeal to justice involves seeing that people have what is due to them, but does not involve any recognition of claims about equality.

In this introduction, we will not attempt to detail these general notions of justice and equality, nor will we attempt to detail the reasons offered for these notions. Instead, we will turn directly to their conception of the nature of the appeal to justice and equality in the health-care setting.

An egalitarian conception of justice and equality in the health-care setting might be the following: What justice demands is that all people receive all the health care from which they would benefit. In this way, whereas some people would get more health care because they have greater health problems and others would get less health care because they have fewer problems, everyone is being treated equally because everyone is equally receiving all the health care from which one would benefit. In the real world, this is rarely the case because the health care that people receive depends on such factors as the amount of money they have to purchase that health care, their physical proximity to physicians and hospitals, and so forth. So at the moment, this picture of justice and equality in the provision of health care is simply an ideal. But even as an ideal, it can lead us to criticize the fact that some people are not getting the health care from which they would benefit.

One crucial point needs to be noted immediately about this egalitarian picture of the equality and justice in the health-care setting. The egalitarian is not demanding that each person receive the same *amount* of health care. That would be a foolish demand, for it would not take into account the fact that some people have fewer health problems and need less health care, whereas others have more substantial health problems and need much more care. What the intelligent egalitarian is saying is that justice demands that all people receive equally an entitlement to all the health care they need.

This view of what justice demands in the provision of health care immediately confronts a major difficulty. Consider the substantial amount of money currently spent in the United States on the provision of health care. As we shall see in Section C–8 of Part II, we currently spend close to 11 percent of our total gross national product on the provision of health care. Despite this heavy expenditure, many Americans are still receiving much less care than what justice demands from this egalitarian account. If we were to meet the stringent demands of this egalitarian claim, we would have to spend even more on the provision of health care, and that would result in our having less available to spend on other important social and individual goods.

Egalitarians have a number of responses open to them. They might argue that many of our current expenditures are wasted expenditures, and that a more appropriate approach to the provision of health care—such as greater emphasis on preventative medicine, on changing conditions that give rise to health-care problems—might enable their egalitarian picture of justice in health care to be met without posing a tremendous financial burden on society. Alternatively, they might recognize that this version of egalitarianism makes too many demands on society, and they might argue that what justice demands is that everybody equally receive some lesser level of health care. Some of the readings in Section C–7 of Part II of this text explore these possibilities.

Not all philosophers would agree, however, that justice demands that every person receive an equal level of health care, whether it be all the health care from which they would benefit or some lesser level of care. Many would argue that justice merely demands that every person receive, whether or not they can afford to pay for it, some appropriate level of health care. Beyond that, individuals who have the capacity to purchase additional health care should be free to do so. This second redistributive picture of justice, unlike any of the egalitarian pictures of justice, is willing to accept the idea that inequality is compatible with justice. It simply demands in the name of justice that some portion of people's health-care needs be equally met. Those who advocate this conception of the appeal to justice and equality insist that it is both morally sound and fiscally responsible even in light of the heavy health-care expenditures discussed in Part II of the text. Naturally, those who hold this view need to develop a conception of what is the level of health care to which all are equally entitled. Different attempts to do this are found in some of the readings in Section C–7 of Part II.

There is an important variation of the redistributive approach to the question of justice and equality in the provision of health care, and it goes further in emphasizing freedom and minimizing equality in the provision of health care. It claims that justice makes no particular demands on the level of health care an individual will receive. The most that justice demands is that the indigent individual receive from society some level of redistribution of money. After that point, it is up to each individual, including those indigents who have received funds from society, to choose the level of health care they will purchase. As long as society meets the demands of justice to redistribute money to those in need, justice makes no further demands on the degree of equality of health care received by members of society.

This last remark suggests another way of looking at the difference between the three positions outlined above. The first two positions insist that justice makes special demands in connection with health care. The egalitarian position insists that justice demands that all people receive a level of health care equally appropriate to their health-care needs. The first redistributive position insists that justice demands that everyone equally receive at least a certain basic minimum of health care. The second redistributive position disagrees with this presupposition. It says that justice only demands that those who are sufficiently indigent receive certain cash redistributions from society. Whether that money is used to purchase health care or to purchase other goods is a decision to be made by the individuals themselves.

Why is this question about the nature of justice and equality in the area of health care so important? For one thing, as we shall see in Part II of this book, the United States is currently spending a great deal of money ensuring that those in need of health care receive some care, even if they cannot afford to pay for it. As we shall also see in Part II, the amount of money we are spending to do this has increased very rapidly in recent years. Many proposals have been put forward concerning the ways in which we might restructure the delivery of this health care, in part to save money but also in part to ensure that the demands of justice and equality are being met. We will not be in a position to think intelligently about all of these proposals until we better understand the nature of the appeal to justice and equality in the provision of health care. This is why the question we have been discussing until now is of great significance as one thinks about American health-care policy.

Thus far in our discussion of the appeal to justice and equality in the health-care setting, we have discussed these issues in the arena of policy making about health care. We will now turn to the appeal to justice and equality in individual clinical decisions.

There seem to be at least two contexts in which questions about justice and equality arise in the clinical setting. The first context is when there is a new medical technology that is currently available on a limited basis so that all those who could benefit from its use cannot obtain that benefit. A classic example is the development of kidney dialysis for patients with end-stage renal disease. Such patients, until the time of kidney dialysis, would inevitably die of their disease. With the development of the technology to treat these patients, it became possible to save those who would otherwise die. Initially, however, not enough dialysis machines were available to meet the demand for dialysis. The question that arose was who should be treated and who should not, knowing that those who were not treated would die. It was literally impossible to treat everyone equally, unless it was decided that no one should be dialyzed until all could be dialyzed. That seemed to be an unattractive alternative, for it would mean that everyone would die instead of only some dying and some being saved. Thus, the question arose as to what would be the just way of allocating this limited new technology until such time that it became available to all.

The second context where questions about justice and equality arise is in the public provision of health care (that is, a county hospital, a VA hospital), where a limited budget is made available to a public institution charged with providing health care to all members of an eligible group. In that context, the budget actually allocated makes it impossible to provide to all those who are eligible all the health care from which they would benefit. Thus, the question arises: What is the just way of allocating resources to provide health care to potential recipients?

There are those who argue that individual clinicians should never consider these questions of the just distribution of health care. Their view is that the responsibility of the individual clinician is to the particular patient who is being treated at any given time and to do what is best for that patient without worrying about other patients who might as a result not receive care. Those who hold such a view will conclude that questions of justice and equality are never relevant clinical questions; such questions are only relevant for policy-makers. Whether that view is correct, and how those who hold it deal with the types of problems that we have just discussed, is a question we will examine in Section C–9 of Part II of this text.

For the moment, let us put aside that claim and see what the various theories of justice would say about our cases, working on the assumption that in fact morally sensitive clinicians will want to appeal to considerations of justice and equality in deciding about the allocation of resources.

What would an egalitarian theory of justice say about such cases? It cannot say that all people should equally receive all of the health care they need, because the facts of our cases rule out that possibility. Still, egalitarians will want to emphasize some notion of an equal right of all. One way of doing that would be to introduce the idea of a random lottery to choose who will get treated. Thus, in the kidney dialysis case, before adequate facilities were available to treat all those in need, there was a widespread view that the just thing to do would be to choose—from among all those who were equally in need and equally likely to benefit—those who would actually receive the care through random selection. What everybody would receive equally was an equal chance to receive the treatment. Not everybody would receive the treatment; that was not possible. But this scheme would at least allow some suggestion of equality in the care of all. A similar notion might be put forward as to what would be the just way to allocate the limited resources of the public facility to all those who are eligible for care. Alternatively, in that second case, where care is not an all-or-nothing matter but can be provided at different levels, one might conclude that the budget of the public facility would be justly allocated, given an egalitarian theory of justice, if the budget was used to set a level of care that all in need could receive, and no one would receive more. Still other schemes are possible. The crucial point is that any egalitarian scheme of justice will insist that we must retain some element of equality in these health-care allocation decisions. (Note, by the way, that the appeal to other moral factors might lead to other conclusions. All that we are analyzing here is what is required by the appeal to an egalitarian understanding of justice.)

What about redistributive theories of justice? How would they deal with such choices? Let us begin with the redistributivist position that justice demands that everyone is entitled to a certain level of health care. Beyond that point, justice makes no demand on us as to how health care should be allocated. When believers in such a redistributive theory of justice turn to the question of how the limited health-care resources are to be allocated, they need initially to decide whether or not the health care in question, which cannot be provided to everyone for physical or fiscal reasons, is part of that health care to which everyone is equally entitled to or not. If it is not, then justice will, according to this version of the redistributivist theory of justice in health care, have nothing to say about the question of how these resources ought to be allocated. Other moral considerations will need to be brought to bear. It may be an appeal to rights or it may be an appeal to consequences or it may be an appeal to various virtues. But if the form of health care in question is not part of that basic minimum to which we are equally entitled, then this version of redistributivism will have to conclude that the appeal to justice is irrelevant to these difficult questions. The situation is very different if the form of health care in question is, according to the redistributive view we are considering, part of that health care to which everybody is entitled. If that is the case, then the redistributivist will have to agree with the egalitarian that we need to find some mechanism for providing everyone with an equal opportunity to obtain that health care.

The appeal to justice is totally irrelevant in these cases, according to the other kind of redistributivism that insists that society's only obligation is to distribute a certain level of funds to indigent individuals. On this account, justice has nothing to say about how health care ought to be distributed. It only has something to say about the distribution of wealth. Believers in this view would presumably want to say that it is perfectly just to allow the physically limited forms of health care to be purchased by those who are able to pay the highest fee. This does not mean that this is the morally right thing to do, for there are many other moral considerations that might mandate an alternative approach. What we are saying is that believers in this form of justice in health care cannot claim that justice mandates something else. Similarly, according to believers in this form of justice, justice has nothing to say about how fiscally limited health-care resources should be allocated in the public provision of health care because considerations of justice would not mandate the existence of such a form of public provision. As far as justice is concerned, once the indigent have received the funds to which they are entitled, they should purchase health care like anyone else rather than receive some allocation of health care from the public sector.

The perceptive reader will undoubtedly have noticed that there is a crucial difference between our discussion of the appeal to justice and equality and our earlier discussions of the appeal to consequences, of the appeal to rights, and of the appeal to virtues. Whereas we noted, in our discussion of each of these earlier appeals, substantial disagreements about the proper understanding of those appeals, there was also substantial agreement about the logical structure and much of the content of those appeals. That agreement is simply not present in the case of the appeal to justice and equality, as there is fundamental and radical disagreement about the structure and content of the appeal in general and in the health-care setting in particular. Readers need to keep these disagreements in mind as they look at more detailed issues in the later sections of this book.

SECTION C

A Brief Introduction
to the Major Moral Theories

In this final section of Part I of the book, we will briefly review four major theories (Aristotle's virtue theory, Bentham's utilitarianism, Kant's categorical imperative, and Rawls' contractual theory of justice) that have been put forward in the history of moral philosophy. As we shall see, each of these theories can best be understood as an attempt to make one of the appeals that we have been discussing the central feature of morality. Having done that, the proponents of those theories will then need either to deny the significance of the other appeals or attempt to show how they can be incorporated into their basic approach. We shall see how this is done in the case of each of the theories.

Aristotle, in the beginning of the *Nicomachean Ethics,* argues that there must be a single goal which each of us desires for its own sake and for which we do everything else. This goal might well be thought of (although Aristotle does not use this term) as the *meaning of our life.* Aristotle goes on to assert that there is a general verbal agreement about what this goal is, namely, happiness. But, he insists, this is just a verbal agreement, and people have very different conceptions of what happiness is. A full moral philosophy must develop some concrete conception of happiness. Aristotle insists that happiness consists in an individual performing excellently those rational activities that are special and distinctive to human beings. Note that for Aristotle happiness is not some state of mind such as pleasure, although it may typically be accompanied by that state of mind. Rather, it is excellence in performing certain actions. For Aristotle, there are two types of excellences in performing rational activities: excellence in pure rational thought and excellence in rational choices in our day-to-day life. Aristotle develops extensive theories of both, especially the latter. He asserts that the main virtues such as courage and temperance are excellences in choosing. The courageous person is the person who chooses well when confronted with fearful things. The temperate person is the person who chooses well when confronted with pleasures. Choosing well (having these virtues) is, for Aristotle, a matter of choosing a mean between two extremes. This is his theory of the *golden mean.*

The courageous person, for example, makes choices that lie somewhere between the choices of the foolhardy person and the cowardly person. The good life for Aristotle—the moral life—consists then in being a certain type of person, a person who excels both in the choices of actions and in capacities of intellectual reasoning. Such a person's life will typically be a life that also has much pleasure in it, but that is not the heart of its excellence.

Many aspects of Aristotle's moral theory are clearly deserving of much further attention than we can give them now. For our purposes, we need to note just several crucial points. They are the following:

1. For Aristotle, the main appeal in thinking morally is the appeal to the virtues. The question that we need to ask ourselves again and again is whether or not the action we are thinking of doing or which we have done is a virtuous action. There is no explicit mention in Aristotle's theory of any appeal to the consequences of our actions or to some notion of individual rights. Aristotle does incorporate into his theory the appeal to justice and equality, but only because he treats justice as one of the virtues, and he gives an account of the relationship between the virtue of justice and equality.

2. There are many virtues that we emphasized in our discussion of the appeal to virtues (honesty, compassion, and integrity) that play no major role in Aristotle's account, and there are some virtues (temperance) that he discusses at some length and that seem less relevant for our purposes. No doubt part of the explanation of this difference is that we are concerned with the virtues that seem particularly relevant to the health-care setting, whereas Aristotle was concerned with the virtues in general. In addition, there is every reason to suppose that the list of the virtues does change over a period of time and from one civilization to another. Still, it seems possible to construct an Aristotelian account of the virtues that we emphasized and that he did not discuss. Consider, for example, compassion. We might think of the compassionate person as the person whose choices lie somewhere between the extremes of cold-hearted lack of concern for others, on the one hand, and excessive indulgence toward those who have gotten themselves into trouble, on the other. So, while our appeal to the virtues may be somewhat different from Aristotle's, there is nothing about our appeal that rules out an Aristotelian account.

3. It is very difficult to see exactly how Aristotle thinks the appeal to the virtues helps us decide what we are to do in a particular case. We are told that the morally correct thing to do is to behave in a virtuous fashion. We are told that the virtuous pattern of choices lies between two extreme patterns of choices. But we are given little additional information as to where between the two extremes is the appropriate pattern of choices. At one point, Aristotle attempts to develop a theory of practical reason, which is no doubt meant to help provide some account of how we are to judge precisely what is the virtuous course of action, but that account is very difficult to follow.

It is easy to be critical of Aristotelian theory. One can conclude, quite correctly, that the theory is inadequate because it fails to take into account certain major appeals, including the general appeal to the consequences of our actions and the appeal to respecting the rights of other individuals, and because its account of the appeal to virtues is inadequate, in part because it leaves out some of the virtues and in part because it gives us no clear indication of how we should understand the meaning of the virtues when we are trying to decide whether a particular action is virtuous. But to say all of this is to miss certain very important points that Aristotle has made. The first is his crucial observation about the happy life, his observation that the happy life is not just a life full of pleasing experiences but rather is a life involving patterns of excellence in action. The second, and for our purposes the more important, crucial observation that Aristotle made is that whatever else we may need to add to develop a full theory of morality, it would be inappropriate to leave out the virtues. Appealing to the virtues is an important part of the moral life.

The second major moral theoretician whose views we wish to briefly present are the views of Jeremy Bentham, one of the leading founders of British utilitarianism. *Utilitarianism,* as Bentham presents it, is a moral theory that places at the heart of all moral appeals the appeal to the consequences of our actions. For a Benthamite utilitarian, the right action is the action that leads to the most pleasure, taking into account the pleasures and pains suffered by all those affected by our actions.

Several features need to be noted about Bentham's theory of morality. They are the following:

1. We assess the rightness and wrongness of any action by looking at its consequences for all those affected. That is the only relevant appeal. Bentham specifically rejects the appeal to rights as an appeal to superstitious fictional notions, and he argues that both the appeal to the virtues and to the character of the person performing the action are irrelevant to our evaluation of the action, however relevant it may be for our deciding what we are to do about the person, given that he or she has performed the action.

2. When Bentham talks about all those affected by the action, he means literally *all* those affected. Because the effect that he is concerned with is pleasure and the absence of pain, he would include animals among those whom we have to take into account as we weigh the consequences of our actions. Bentham sees this aspect of utilitarianism as reflecting the important truth in the appeal to equality, namely, that a particular unit of pain or pleasure counts equally no matter whose pleasure or pain it is.

3. Bentham is very much a hedonist. He thinks that what makes consequences good is that they are pleasant and that what makes them bad is that they are painful. Moreover, Bentham thought that the relevant features of pleasures and pain are their duration and their intensity. The longer the pain, the worse it is; the longer the pleasure, the better it is. The more intense the pain, the worse it is; the more intense the pleasure, the better it is. Bentham even pondered the possibility of developing a utilitarian calculus by which we could literally weigh the pleasures and pains that our actions produce for all those affected in light of their intensity and duration, thereby establishing in a clear-cut scientific fashion what was the right action to perform.

It is easy to see, in view of our previous discussion of the various appeals, that there are many ways to criticize Bentham's theory. One can begin by objecting to the hedonism that is so central to his approach. More fundamentally, one can argue that his approach suffers precisely because it fails to take into account the legitimacy of some of the other appeals we have discussed. These criticisms, while perfectly legitimate, fail to note the important contributions that Bentham's utilitarianism makes to our understanding of moral decision making. It was the utilitarians who brought to the forefront of moral thinking the appeal to the consequences of our actions. Certainly no moral theory that failed to take that appeal into account could be an adequate moral theory. Secondly, in criticizing the appeal to the virtues on the grounds that it doesn't address the question of what are the virtuous actions, Bentham has made the following clear: If the appeal to the virtues is to do some real work in moral theory, it must address itself very clearly, in a way that Aristotle did not, to the question of how we could tell what a person with a particular virtue would do in a particular case. In each of these ways, Bentham's utilitarianism adds to our understanding of moral decision making.

The third major moral theoretician whose ideas we shall briefly review is Immanuel Kant. There are many aspects of Kant's moral philosophy, and we shall only be looking at those that are most relevant to our discussion, particularly his theory of the *categorical imperative*. Imagine a person who is contemplating performing a particular action. We can view that as a way in which he or she proposes a certain maxim or general rule for acting. If the person is going to do this sort of action in this sort of case, then he or she is implicitly suggesting that this is the sort of action that ought to be done in this sort of case in general. The question for moral theory is which of these maxims can legitimately be considered moral laws and which of the actions performed in accordance with these maxims can therefore legitimately be considered a morally appropriate action. Kant's theory of the categorical imperative is a way of testing these maxims. The legitimate maxims are the ones that can meet this test. Kant presents three formulations of this test. We shall focus on two of them. The first is that one should act only on that maxim that one can at the same time consistently will that it become a universal law of action. Breaking your promise because it is convenient to do so, says Kant, cannot be a morally legitimate action because the maxim implicit in it, that one should break one's promises if it is convenient to do so, could not pass that test. It would be inconsistent that one will this as a universal law of nature, says Kant, because the very existence of the institution of promising presupposes that people will normally keep their promises even if it is inconvenient to do so.

Kant's second version of his test is the claim that one should only act in accordance with those maxims that treat humanity as an end in itself and not as a means to something else. Breaking the promise in the above-mentioned case would, according to Kant, fail this test because following this sort of maxim and acting this way in general would be using the other person to whom the promise had been made as a means and not as an end in himself. Kant argues that these two tests are really equivalent tests, but we will not pursue that particular aspect of his theory any further at this point.

There are two ways in which we can see the close connection between these ideas of Kant and the appeal to rights, which we discussed previously. The first is the following: As we saw in our discussion of the appeal to rights, there appears to be, in the case of each right, an appropriate moral rule that commands its respect. Similarly, there seems to be associated with each of the moral rules, which command certain forms of actions or prohibit others, a corresponding right that those rules are protecting. Thus, any moral theory such as Kant's, which places great emphasis on the evaluation of particular actions by the test of whether they are in accord with appropriate moral rules, is automatically a theory that places great emphasis on the appeal to duties and their corresponding rights in the evaluation of actions. To continue with the above example, the person to whom you have made a promise presumably has a right against you that you keep that promise and you presumably have a corresponding obligation to keep that promise. A theory like Kant's, which would give your action of breaking the promise a negative evaluation on the grounds that it fails to satisfy the demands of morally appropriate rules, is a theory that implicitly gives such an action a bad evaluation because it fails to take into account the rights of certain parties adversely affected.

There is, however, still a second way of seeing the connection between Kant's ideas and the appeal to rights. One of the important themes in the rhetoric surrounding the appeal to rights is that this appeal is a moral appeal that recognizes right-holders as ends in themselves and not merely as means to be used by others. We made this point earlier in the text when we decided to view the right to be treated as an end and not just as a means as a summary of all the other rights that people possess. So any theory like Kant's, which emphasizes this notion that appropriate moral actions and the rules with which they are in accord must be respectful of the idea of people as ends, must be a theory that places great emphasis on the appeal to rights.

Several other crucial points need to be noted about Kant's theory:

1. It is not hard to see that a theory like Kant's, which emphasizes evaluating actions in terms of the general maxim upon which they are based, is open to the objection that it fails to take into account the specific circumstances surrounding particular cases. In a particular case, an action that we cannot consistently will to be a universal law of nature might still be appropriate because of the special circumstances in that case. This is a theme that those who appeal to the consequences of actions in evaluating actions would particularly stress. Their point is that they can more easily take into account this specific nature of a particular action because in those special contexts the actions in question will have unusual consequences. Kantians will need to do something about this problem if they are to avoid the charge that their theory is blind to the special settings in which we are often called on to perform unusual actions.

2. If Kantians are to incorporate into their theory of morality the consideration of justice and equality, they are going to face some difficulties. In one sense, of course, there is some equality automatically built into the Kantian theory, because the very demand that the maxim upon which I act be one that could consistently be willed as a universal law of nature is a demand that similar cases be treated equally and that my action is morally appropriate only if it is one that could be appropriately performed in all similar cases. This may not afford a sufficient basis for an entire theory of justice and equality. The Kantian will need to show, in particular, that one or another approach to the allocation of goods in general and of health care in particular is the only approach that could be consistently willed as a universal law of nature and/or is the only one that respects people as ends and not merely as means. If the Kantian fails to do this, then it will be very hard for Kantians to incorporate a substantive theory of justice and equality into their theory of morality.

3. Underlying both of these problems is a more fundamental conceptual problem about the whole Kantian approach, which evaluates actions based on two presuppositions. The first is that when an individual contemplates performing a particular action, there is one and only one maxim that we can identify as the maxim on which the individual is contemplating acting and about which we can ask if it passes Kant's

tests. It seems as though there are an endless number of ways in which one can describe the maxim on which an individual is acting as the individual contemplates performing a particular action. In the above-mentioned case, we can describe it as a person acting on the maxim of breaking a promise when one wants to, or as a person acting on the maxim of breaking a promise when one has considerable need, or as a person doing what he or she wants to do, and so forth. Secondly, the Kantian assumes that once we identify a set of potential and competing maxims, we can see that only one of those maxims will meet the test in question and that only actions in accordance with that maxim are morally correct actions. It is not clear that we have a basis for holding this claim to be true.

It is easy then to criticize the Kantian moral theory on the grounds that both of its fundamental methological assumptions are false and that their falsity leads to the Kantian's inability to take into account the special circumstances of a particular action and the inability to formulate proper substantive theories of justice and equality. Nevertheless, it would be a mistake simply to be critical of the Kantian theory, for it has stressed certain important features that any complete moral theory needs to take into account. The Kantians have provided a strong advocacy for the importance of seeing that our actions are in accord with appropriate moral rules; they have helped explain the significance of the appeal to rights in the evaluation of actions; they have helped identify that fundamental but very difficult theme of respecting persons as ends and not merely as means. There is much to criticize in Kant's moral theory, just as there was much to criticize in the moral theories of Aristotle and Bentham. However, there is also much to learn from Kant's moral theory.

The last of the major moral theories that we shall examine briefly is the theory of justice advanced by the contemporary American philosopher John Rawls. Rawls asks us to think about questions of justice and equality in the fundamental structure of our society by imagining a group of rational self-interested people coming together, without any knowledge of their own strengths and weaknesses and therefore of their likelihood of success or failure in their lives, and asking themselves what rules they would desire to live under. In this way, Rawls is part of a long tradition that emphasizes the idea that the correct moral rules are ones that people would agree to live by if they came together in a state of nature and tried to develop rules they could live with. Rawls puts the question as being what rules they would agree to under "conditions of ignorance" because, given this ignorance, nobody could propose rules that are more likely to benefit themselves rather than others. Thus there is reason to believe that the rules that are agreed to would be rules that are fair. He describes these conditions as the *veil of ignorance*. Rawls argues in his book *Theory of Justice* that the fundamental principles of justice and equality that would be accepted are the following: Each person is to have an equal right to the most extensive basic liberty compatible with a similar liberty for others; social and economic inequalities are to be arranged so that they are both (1) to the greatest benefit of the least advantaged and (2) attached to offices and positions open to all under conditions of fair equality of opportunity.

We shall not now explore the very rich but complicated arguments that Rawls offers to buttress his claim that these are the principles that rationally self-interested people, deciding under a veil of ignorance, would adopt as the fundamental principles governing their society. Instead, several cogent observations need to be made concerning Rawls's theory.

1. Rawls is very clear that this is only meant as a theory of justice for the basic institutions and structural features of society. It is not meant as a full theory of justice, much less as a complete moral theory. In this respect, he has been misinterpreted by many of his followers who would attempt to derive very concrete policy implications from treating these principles as full theories of morality. Nevertheless, this raises the important question of what is the appropriate relationship between considerations of justice and equality (whether they be seen as Rawls's views or otherwise) and other moral considerations. We need to examine carefully the question as to whether a consideration of justice should always take precedence over other moral considerations or whether these other moral considerations—such as those germane to the other appeals that we have discussed—should take precedence over consideration of justice and equality in at least some cases.

2. Very often, when people think about moral rules, they are inclined to be quite enthusiastic about the idea that the appropriate moral rules for us to live by are the ones that we would all agree to live by. This certainly is part of the attraction of Rawls's whole approach and is why many would want to extend it beyond his careful limitations and use it as a foundation of thinking about morality in general. But it is important to keep in mind that Rawls is not saying that these are the moral principles that we have all agreed to live by or even that we would all agree to live by. They are the principles that totally rational and totally self-interested creatures, operating in very unusual conditions, would agree to live by. Even if Rawls is right in that claim, one needs to ponder carefully the question of the relevance of that claim, given that we are not those people whom he is describing.

Where then do we stand after having reviewed these four major moral theories? One conclusion seems clearly to emerge from our review. It is that each of these theories has strengths and weaknesses. Each of them emphasizes, as essential to moral thinking, one of the appeals that we discussed in Section B. This emphasis is their strength. Aristotle taught us about the importance of the appeal to virtues. Bentham showed us the importance of appealing to the consequences of our actions. Kant focused on the importance of appealing to moral rules and to human rights, and Rawls taught us about the appeal to justice and equality. The weakness of each of these theories, however, is that they fail to do justice to the other appeals.

Does this mean that moral theory is impossible? Such a final pessimistic conclusion is unwarranted. What emerges from our analysis is the recognition of the need to develop new and more sophisticated moral theories that integrate all of the appeals that we have been discussing and that enable us to weigh their relevant significance in particular cases.

What do we do in the interim, given that we lack a fully adequate moral theory? In particular, how shall we evaluate the viewpoints that we will be reading in Part II of this book and how shall we think about the cases that we shall confront in Part III? The best that we can do at this point is to see which of the appeals are being properly emphasized in the readings and which are being neglected. The best we can do as we examine the cases is to try to bring all of these appeals to bear on the particular cases. We want a comprehensive theory to do all of this for us, but, unfortunately, we do not have one. We have learned, however, what are the materials that must be incorporated into such an adequate and comprehensive theory, and we must do our best, at the intuitive level, to use all of them appropriately in thinking about the rest of the material in this text. Even if a final, systematic theory is not available at this time, we will still be in the position, on the basis of philosophical arguments, to eliminate certain conclusions as unacceptable and to identify others as more likely. Although the fact that an adequate and complete moral theory has not been developed at this point may support toleration of a diversity of choices, it does not lead to a complete moral skepticism.

PART II
Readings in Bioethics

SECTION A
Decision Making

INTRODUCTION

This first section of the readings is about decision making in the health-care setting. The ethical issues surrounding the process of decision making have come to occupy a central place in the literature of medical ethics. This is not surprising. Questions of what health care should be provided, and questions about who should make those decisions, arise every day in the provision of health care and are a major source of tension between providers and recipients. They cry out for ethical analysis.

To evaluate the question of whether decision making is primarily the responsibility of the providers (the view that has come to be called, for reasons to be discussed below, the *paternalistic view*) or of the patient (the view that has come to be called the *view of patient autonomy*—also discussed below), we must begin by looking at each party separately. The initial set of readings in this section looks at the patients, whereas the second set of readings looks at the providers.

John Stuart Mill, author of the famous work *On Liberty*, was a great believer in individual autonomy. As he states in the selection reprinted: "Over himself, over his own body and mind, the individual is sovereign." Although Mill does not discuss the provider–recipient relation, it is clear where his sympathies on our question would lie. But even he hastens to add that his belief only applies to human beings in the "maturity of their faculties." This is explicitly intended to exclude children.

Why should children be excluded? When does someone stop being a child? Who should make decisions on their behalf and what criteria should they use? All of these questions are discussed is the readings taken from John Locke and Sanford Leikin. Of particular importance is Leikin's attempt to use the findings of developmental psychology to answer the question of the age at which someone is no longer a minor and can meaningfully become a candidate for being a decision-maker.

Locke (in paragraph 60 of "The Status of Children") claims that there are some who are not minors but who are nevertheless incompetent to make decisions for themselves. He describes these people as "defective." Locke probably had in mind those who are so retarded that they lack decisional competence. In the health-care setting, however, there are many recipients whose competence to be a decision-maker is open to challenge. Their very illness may interfere with their decisional capacities at just that point at which very important health-care decisions must be made. The readings by Gert and Culver, by the President's Commission, and by Abernethy are all attempts to provide criteria for understanding this notion of competency.

Gert and Culver identify two classes of patients who are incompetent in very different ways, and readers need to be sure that they can differentiate those two classes. Gert and Culver also make the crucial point that competency or incompetency to make health-care decisions is different from competency or incompetency to make other decisions. Their approach is an instance of what the President's Commission calls the *actual functioning approach* as opposed to the *outcomes approach* or the *status approach*. The President's Commission agrees with this actual functioning approach, and adds (in a crucial footnote) content to Gert and Culver's basic ideas of competency as adequate actual functioning. The reader needs to ask whether there are aspects of adequate functioning (particularly noncognitive aspects) that are left out of even this fuller account. Still another challenge to this approach is posited by Abernethy, who claims that in practice it often degenerates into an outcomes approach. A crucial question, raised by Abernethy at the end of her article, is whether there is a viable alternative.

The second set of readings, by Jamieton, by Winslow, and by Bartlett, looks at the other claimants to decisional authority, namely the health-care providers. All these readings are based on a recognition that in many health-care settings different professionals are part of the team of providers. In particular, there is the crucial split between physicians and nurses. All three readings explore the relation between these two groups of providers, and these readings are essential as a background to our fundamental concern, to be discussed below, of the conflict between providers as decision-makers and recipients as decision-makers.

The authors cited above all begin by recognizing that the traditional view held both by physicians and by nurses is that insofar as providers are decision-makers, it is the physician who is the decision-maker; nurses are there to help the patient by carrying out the physician's orders. This traditional view is, to a considerable extent, defended by Bartlett on the grounds of its importance for the trust that must exist between patients and physicians. The reader needs to examine what sort of moral appeal this is. Is it an appeal to consequences, to rights, or to the virtues? And how does it differ from the argument about loyalty discussed by Winslow? What sort of moral appeal is that? Bartlett does not, however, accept the traditional view completely, and he does offer suggestions about how other professionals (especially nurses) might directly or indirectly be involved in decisional processes.

Winslow, in his article, discusses the emergence of an alternative view, the concept of nurses as patient-advocates, with its view of the nurse as playing a more significant role in decision making. What is this more significant role and what are the moral arguments for it? He refers to Sally Gadow's view that emphasizes the nurse's role in assisting patients to exercise their authentic self-determination. Again, we need to ask what is the nature of the moral appeal alluded to in that view.

In contrast with Bartlett's view, Costello and her colleagues argue that the differences between nurses and physicians result primarily from the ways in which physicians have dominated health care through licensing laws. These laws have given physicians the legal right to practice nearly any form of health care. Other health professionals, in contrast, have been allowed the right to labor in one of the areas open to physicians. As a result, it is not possible, the authors contend, to find a special conceptual or moral integrity that distinguishes nursing or other allied health professions. Instead, the moral problems that characterize the practice of nursing and the other health professions stem from the legally established power relations among these professions. As Costello and her colleagues acknowledge, this view involves a criticism of licensing laws in general and favors instead certification of health-care professionals. Is this a credible way of protecting the public against unskilled health professionals? The authors defend their position by an appeal both to consequences and to rights. In terms of the consideration of consequences, what do you, the reader, judge to be the likely outcome of embracing such a radical reassessment of the rights, powers, and privileges of the various health-care professions?

The next group of three readings focuses on the virtues of health-care professionals. The selection from Hippocrates combines concerns of etiquette and decorum with those of virtue. Such concerns are tied to the physician's interest in attracting patients and being accepted by the local community. Virtue was not being pursued for its own sake. To what extent do such concerns with consequences undermine the very notion of the virtues of a professional? Dietrich von Engelhardt's study of the virtues expected from a physician during the period of the Enlightenment demonstrates a similar mixing of concerns with pursuing virtue for its own sake with those of pursuing virtue because of its consequences for the preservation and restoration of the health of patients. The articulation of the virtues in the Enlightenment shows the marks of both a particular culture and a particular time. Lists of virtues differ from culture to culture. Indeed, as Alasdair MacIntyre argues, what may count as a virtue in one cultural context may turn out to be a vice in another. In this way, MacIntyre raises the question whether the current cultural and technological context of health care does not transform a number of the traditional virtues into vices.

Having looked separately at each of the major claimants to the power of decision making in the health-care setting, we next consider the fundamental question of who should have that authority. Debate over that question is normally seen as a conflict between two major views. One view is a belief in *autonomy,* a belief in the merit of individual self-determination. This leads to the view that, in the case of competent patients, the role of providers is to give patients information about their condition and about alternative ways of dealing with it, whereas the role of patients is to decide which alternative approach to adopt. The other view is a belief in *paternalism,* a belief that decision making rests in the hands of those who know what is best for the individual involved (like parents making decisions for their child). This leads to the view that providers should make decisions about which course of treatment is best for their patients, even when the patient is competent, and it is this decision that should be carried out.

The readings taken from the President's Commission presents two major arguments for allowing competent adult patients to exercise the power of medical decision making. The first argument is that in light of the frequent absence of objective medical criteria and in light of the preferences of patients, such a policy promotes patient well-being. The second argument is that this policy respects the intrinsic value of self-determination. These are two different types of moral appeals, and in assessing them the reader needs to begin by relating them to the appeals we discussed in Part I of this book.

Clements and Sider argue that this emphasis on patient autonomy is fundamentally in error. They see the value of decision making as only one of many values. The more primary value in the health-care setting, they argue, is the concern for the patient's best interest, and this can often be defined by scientifically determinate norms.

It is important in evaluating this dispute that we identify which of the moral appeals recognized by the President's Commission are accepted by Clements and Sider and which are not. Only then can we ask these crucial questions: Are they right in rejecting some of those appeals, particularly the ones having to do with the intrinsic value of self-determination? Why do they differ with the President's Commission on the question of which approach is justified by the appeal to the patient's self-interest?

Several authors have attempted to bridge the two sides of this conflict. Bruce Miller, in one well-known article, defined four different senses of autonomy: autonomy as free action, autonomy as authenticity, autonomy as effective deliberation, and autonomy as moral reflection. He suggested that most cases of legitimate overriding of the wishes of patients are cases in which autonomy in some of these senses is not present. Many questions are raised by this suggestion: What are the moral appeals advanced by Miller that justify respecting autonomy, and why do they require autonomy in all of these senses? What appeals justify overriding autonomy when it is present in only some of these senses? Could they ever justify overriding autonomy in cases (for example, Jehovah's Witnesses) where autonomy is present in all of these senses? David Thomasma takes another approach to resolving this conflict between autonomy and paternalism. He presents a third model that is meant to supersede both traditional approaches. What are the claims of this model? What type of moral appeals does he use to justify it? These are questions that the reader of Thomasma's article needs to ponder.

The belief in patient autonomy has become (at least in the United States) more than just a moral doctrine. It has become a legal requirement that providers obtain the informed consent of their patients before they treat them. The meaning of that requirement, along with its moral basis, has been extensively discussed. A major court decision on this topic (that has, however, only been followed in some jurisdictions) is the decision in *Canterbury* v. *Spence*. The court in that case clearly based the requirement of informed consent on an appeal to the rights of the patient. The court then used that basis to shape the view as to what information must be provided to the patient. The reader needs to be clear about what the court's *objective standard* rule means and how it is supposed to follow from the nature of the moral appeal with which the court justified the doctrine of informed consent. The Canterbury decision also recognized two exceptional cases in which informed consent is not required, namely emergency cases and therapeutic privilege cases. One needs to see how the recognition of these exceptions fits into the moral framework the court applied.

The Canterbury rule for informed consent has been criticized both on the grounds that it requires too little and that it requires too much. Capron argues that the various moral appeals justifying informed consent require that the provider supply additional information responsive to the individual patient's subjective needs. Is he right in this claim? Which moral appeals, if any, require this additional information? The final article in this section, from the Jewish Compendium on Medical Ethics, expresses substantial doubts but also some qualified acceptance of the doctrine of informed consent. What are these doubts? In what ways do the authors accept it? What moral appeals are being made?

We have reviewed in this introduction the main issues raised by the readings in Section A of Part II of this text. The crucial factor that we have stressed and which the reader needs to keep in mind is that one can properly evaluate the readings that follow only if one understands which moral appeals are being employed by the authors of each selection.

1. CAPACITIES AND COMPETENCIES OF PATIENTS

Not All Can Be Free

John Stuart Mill

The object of this essay is to assert one very simple principle, as entitled to govern absolutely the dealing of society with the individual in the way of compulsion and control, whether the means used be physical force in the form of legal penalties or the moral coercion of public opinion. That principle is that the sole end for which mankind are warranted, individually or collectively, in interfering with the liberty of action of any of their number is self-protection. That the only purpose for which power can be rightfully exercised over any member of a civilized community, against his will, is to prevent harm to others. His own good, either physical or moral, is not a sufficient warrant. He cannot rightfully be compelled to do or forbear because it will be better for him to do so, because it will make him happier, because, in the opinions of others, to do so would be wise or even right. These are good reasons for remonstrating with him, or reasoning with him, or persuading him, or entreating him, but not for compelling

him or visiting him with any evil in case he do otherwise. To justify that, the conduct from which it is desired to deter him must be calculated to produce evil to someone else. The only part of the conduct of anyone for which he is amenable to society is that which concerns others. In the part which merely concerns himself, his independence is, of right, absolute. Over himself, over his own body and mind, the individual is sovereign.

It is, perhaps, hardly necessary to say that this doctrine is meant to apply only to human beings in the maturity of their faculties. We are not speaking of children or of young persons below the age which the law may fix as that of manhood or womanhood. Those who are still in a state to require being taken care of by others must be protected against their own actions as well as against external injury. For the same reason we may leave out of consideration those backward states of society in which the race itself may be considered as in its nonage.

Handwritten margin note: children born to, but not in, full state of equality is the duty to care powes of the parents for offspring

The Status of Children

John Locke

55. Children, I confess, are not born in this full state of equality, though they are born to it. Their parents have a sort of rule and jurisdiction over them when they come into the world, and for some time after, but it is but a temporary one. The bonds of this subjection are like the swaddling clothes they are wrapt up in and supported by in the weakness of their infancy. Age and reason as they grow up loosen them, till at length they drop quite off, and leave a man at his own free disposal.

56. Adam was created a perfect man, his body and mind in full possession of their strength and reason, and so was capable from the first instance of his being to provide for his own support and preservation, and govern his actions according to the dictates of the law of reason God had implanted in him. From him the world is peopled with his descendants, who are all born infants, weak and helpless, without knowledge or understanding. But to supply the defects of this imperfect state till the improvement of growth and age had removed them, Adam and Eve, and after them all parents were, by the law of Nature, under an obligation to preserve, nourish and educate the children they had begotten, not as their own workmanship, but the workmanship of their own Maker, the Almighty, to whom they were to be accountable for them.

58. The power, then, that parents have over their children arises from that duty which is incumbent on them, to take care of their offspring during the imperfect state of childhood. To inform the mind, and govern the actions of their yet ignorant nonage, till reason shall take its place and ease them of that trouble, is what the children want, and the parents are bound to. For God having given man an understanding to direct his actions, has allowed him a freedom of will and liberty of acting, as properly belonging

thereunto within the bounds of that law he is under. But whilst he is in an estate wherein he has no understanding of his own to direct his will, he is not to have any will of his own to follow. He that understands for him must will for him too; he must prescribe to his will, and regulate his actions, but when he comes to the estate that made his father a free man, the son is a free man too.

60. But if through defects that may happen out of the ordinary course of Nature, any one comes not to such a degree of reason wherein he might be supposed capable of knowing the law, and so living within the rules of it, he is never capable of being a free man, he is never let loose to the disposure of his own will; because he knows no bounds to it, has not understanding, its proper guide, but is continued under the tuition and government of others all the time his own understanding is incapable of that charge. And so lunatics and idiots are never set free from the government of their parents: "Children who are not as yet come unto those years whereat they may have, and innocents, which are excluded by a natural defect from ever having." Thirdly: "Madmen, which, for the present, cannot possibly have the use of right reason to guide themselves, have, for their guide, the reason that guideth other men which are tutors over them, to seek and procure their good for them," says Hooker. All which seems no more than that duty which God and Nature has laid on man, as well as other creatures, to preserve their offspring till they can be able to shift for themselves, and will scarce amount to an instance or proof of parents' regal authority.

64. But what reason can hence advance this care of the parents due to their offspring into an absolute, arbitrary dominion of the father, whose power reaches no farther than by such a discipline as he finds

Handwritten margin note: excluded from decision making

most effectual to give such strength and health to their bodies, such vigour and rectitude to their minds, as may best fit his children and to be most useful to themselves and others, and, if it be necessary to his condition, to make them work when they are able for their own subsistence; but in this power the mother, too, has her share with the father.

65. Nay, this power so little belongs to the father by any peculiar right of Nature, but only as he is guardian of his children, that when he quits his care of them he loses his power over them, which goes along with their nourishment and education, to which it is inseparably annexed, and belongs as much to the foster-father of an exposed child as to the natural father of another. So little power does the bare act of begetting give a man over his issue, if all his care ends there, and this be all the title he hath to the name and authority of a father. And what will become of this paternal power in that part of the world where one woman hath more than one husband at a time? or in those parts of America where, when the husband and wife part, which happens frequently, the children are all left to the mother, follow her, and are wholly under her care and provision? And if the father die whilst the children are young, do they not naturally everywhere owe the same obedience to their mother, during their minor-ity, as to their father, were he alive? And will any one say that the mother hath a legislative power over her children that she can make standing rules which shall be of perpetual obligation, by which they ought to regulate all the concerns of their property, and bound their liberty all the course of their lives, and enforce the observation of them with capital punishments? For this is the proper power of the magistrate, of which the father hath not so much as the shadow. His command over his children is but temporary, and reaches not their life or property. It is but a help to the weakness and imperfection of their nonage, a discipline necessary to their education. And though a father may dispose of his own possessions as he pleases when his children are out of danger of perishing for want, yet his power extends not to the lives or goods which either their own industry, or another's bounty, has made theirs, nor to their liberty neither when they are once arrived to the enfranchisement of the years of discretion. The father's empire then ceases, and he can from thenceforward no more dispose of the liberty of his son than that of any other man. And it must be far from an absolute or perpetual jurisdiction from which a man may withdraw himself, having licence from Divine authority to "leave father and mother and cleave to his wife."

Minors' Assent or Dissent to Medical Treatment

Sanford L. Leikin

INTRODUCTION

Although the requirement for the consent of minors involved in medical therapy has been addressed previously, this issue should be reconsidered in light of new knowledge in developmental psychology, the evolution of the theory and practice of obtaining informed consent for intervention with adults, changes in medico-legal statutes concerning minors, and the recognition by society that parents neither own their offspring nor do they always act in their best interest. In this article the current medical/legal status and current views of minors' psychological development in relation to health and disease will be reviewed in order to provide a basis for an ethical analysis of the assent or dissent by minors for medical therapy.

MINORS IN THE MEDICO-LEGAL CONTEXT

Historically, there has been a wide variability in the age of majority and in the reasons for establishing that age. The age of majority may have reflected the physical development of young men to bear arms or work farmland or of a woman to bear children, but it also seemed to recognize the mental and emotional maturity and personal independence appropriate to an autonomous individual and the assignment of certain responsibilities. At present, in almost all the states, an individual is legally a minor and presumed incompetent until he/she has reached age 18. In this context incompetence denotes the individual's inability to have a full understanding of and appreciation for the impact of decisions and acts made for himself or others. In this latter situation, a parent or legal guardian is entitled to make decisions and perform certain acts on behalf of the incompetent.

In the medical/legal context, legislatures and courts have recently expanded minors' rights to give binding consent for reasonable medical intervention without parental consent. First, courts have treated some classes of minors as if they were adults. An "emancipated" minor may, in some jurisdictions, consent to medical treatment. They become emancipated by marriage, judicial decree, military service, consent of the parent(s), or failure by the parents to meet their legal responsibilities. In addition, a minor who is self-supporting and lives apart from his parents is often deemed to be emancipated. The minor in military service is clearly emancipated and, among other things, could consent to medical care because it would be impractical to contact parents for injuries occurring on the battlefield. Motherhood is now also considered evidence of emancipation, regardless of biological age, at least for purposes of consenting to medical treatment for oneself and one's baby or when surrendering the baby for adoption.

In many states a teenage mother is emancipated for all purposes.

In addition to liberalization of the concept of emancipation, beginning in the 1950s all states enacted statutes specifically permitting a minor of any age to consent to treatment for venereal disease without parental knowledge. If notification of parents were a precondition of treatment, the teenager would very likely forego therapy rather than have parents find out it was necessary, thus further spreading the epidemic of VD in young people. Most states have also recently developed analogous statutes to include treatment for alcohol and drug abuse. Beyond statutory authority for treatment of these specific conditions, the majority of states provide a specific statutory age (usually 15 or 16, but 14 in at least one state) at which a minor may consent to any medical or surgical care without parental consent.

Even where there is no statute and the minor is not emancipated, however, not a single case has been reported in this country in at least 15 years in which a parent recovered damages from a physician for treating someone age 15 or older without parental consent. If the treatment was appropriate, no claim of malpractice is proven, and the teenage patient was as capable of giving informed consent as an adult; courts have allowed that consent to prevail over parental objections raised after the fact. This trend in case law is known as the "mature minor rule."

A teenager, as well as an adult, also has the constitutional right of privacy in some circumstances involving medical care. The Supreme Court has held that parents have no veto over their daughter's decision to have an abortion. The courts have also held that minors do have a right of privacy in obtaining contraception. In contrast, a parent's consent is still necessary for nonurgent treatment of a young child; and the courts have made clear that parents have the right to refuse to allow most elective medical interventions.

minors are now allowed to
consent to a lot of medical
intervention even if
they're under 18

From the foregoing, it appears that the law has intuitively begun to modify informed consent standards concerning medical treatment for minors. But, it has been based on a number of different social and medical situations and not necessarily on the basis of the patient's needs, values, or competence. As Annas, Glantz, and Katz have stated:

> It would be most helpful to know at what age a child obtains a true sense of his body and mind, knows what it means to take risks, knows what it means to be harmed or suffer discomfort, knows how to balance risks and benefits, and so forth. If we had this knowledge it might be possible to rationally determine an age at which most people could give an informed consent to medical treatment.

This would allow us to fulfill our ethical obligation for respect for persons as embodied in the two major functions of informed consent—the promotion of autonomy and the protection of the individual's well-being.

MINORS' INVOLVEMENT IN INFORMED CONSENT

To determine whether or not minors can participate in the informed consent process, we need to identify those psychological capacities that develop in an individual to render him/her competent for this activity. The major characteristics should be ones that you would expect most adults to demonstrate most of the time. This task is complex since we need to examine systematically which minors are capable of assuming what decisionmaking roles in treatment situations with what consequences for the minor, the family unit, the professional, and society. Our own attempts to respond in an ethical and therapeutic way to minors in treatment require such information, lest in our zeal we unreflectively burden some minors with decisions they cannot make intelligently and bear responsibilities for action (sometimes to their detriment) or deny to some the opportunity to make decisions of which they are sufficiently capable.

Before proceeding with the several factors involved in the development of competence it would be helpful to identify characteristics that are more often found in minors and that may affect their decisionmaking ability as well as that appear to raise questions concerning the individual's rationality. First, a minor's values are more likely to change with time than those of an older individual. His life goals are not well established and adults are likely to somewhat discount his dissent or assent because of the expected changeability of these values and goals. Second, because of a lack of personal experience or development the minor is less likely to recognize and take into account the possibility of a change in his values over time and is thus less reflective about his choices. It is only in adolescence that a sense of identity develops (that is, a perception of what one might become or want in the future), so that any future consequences of current actions take on a different meaning than they previously might have. In addition, because of their newfound awareness of bodily appearance, teenagers are particularly concerned with any treatments that will affect it in an adverse manner. It should be emphasized that these characteristics of "immaturity" are found in older individuals as well, but less frequently and less strikingly. Although they may modify a minor's decisions, they are not in themselves sufficient indication of a lack of competence to consent.

There are several different levels of involvement of minors in informal consent. First, some have argued that certain broad classes of minors or minors with certain medical conditions should be allowed by law to consent to treatment independent of their parents' consent or knowledge (as in the case of abortion or the treatment of VD). It must be realized, however, that if parents can be held responsible for their minor's financial debts, they may come to know about the condition and this may affect minors' decisions about their medical treatment.

The second type of consent has both legal and ethical connotations. Should minors be provided by law, or be provided by ethical principle, the power to nullify parental consent? There is a third sense to the involvement of minors in the consent process. This is primarily the individual's need to know or participate when treatment is being decided, but not in the sense of a contract or veto power. Here the issue of a minor's competence is not as critical as in the other two, since what is proposed for the professional is an ethical responsibility rather than a legal obligation to justify overriding a child's consent or dissent.

Competence to Provide Independent Consent

To determine whether or not broad classes of children can be viewed as competent to provide independent consent, we must examine the development of the elements of informed consent. These are (understanding, rationality, and voluntariness.)

Understanding. In the context of consent situations, understanding is the match between the information given to the patient and the patient's own paraphrase of that of which he/she has been informed. The adequacy of the match depends in part, of course, on the way the information is communicated and needs to be appropriate to each individual. But certain capacities of the patient—for example, general intellectual capacity, the patient's familiarity with the content area, and the patient's linguistic background—are expected to influence a match as well. Furthermore, some disorders and treatments are simpler to conceptualize than others and, therefore, easier to describe than others.

Psychological studies of normal children show that their conception of illness—their understanding of its cause and cure—is closely related to the sequence of cognitive developmental levels as described by Piaget and Warner. According to Piaget, the first level, prelogical thinking, is typical of children between two and six years of age. It is characterized by children's inability to distance themselves from their environment and results in explanations accounting for the cause-effect relationship in terms of the immediate spatial and/or temporal cues that dominate their experience. In both types of prelogical explanation of illness—phenomenonism and contagion—we see children being overly swayed by the immediacy of some aspects of their perceptual experience. Phenomenonism represents the most developmentally immature explanation of illness. The cause of the illness is an external concrete phenomenon that may occur with the illness but that is spatially and/or temporally remote. Children at this stage are unable to explain the manner in which these events cause the illness. Bibace and Walsh give the following example of this stage of conceptualization:

> "How do people get colds?"—"From the sun."
> "How does the sun give you a cold?"
> "It just does, that's all."

Contagion is the most common explanation of illness offered by the more mature children in the prelogical stage. The link between the cause and the illness is accounted for only in terms of mere proximity or magic. Thus, a kindergarten or second-grade child defines illness only when he is told or is given external signs of his illness, such as, "You have to stay in bed." He believes he gets sick because of a concrete action he does or fails to do, thinks he might keep from getting sick by obeying a set of rigid rules associated with illness, and expects to recover from illness either simply automatically or by rigidly adhering to another set of rules such as staying in bed and drinking chicken soup.

Concrete-logical reasoning is manifested by children roughly between seven to ten years of age. In this stage the major developmental shift is in the accentuation of the differentiation between self and others. Contamination characterizes the explanation of younger children in this stage. The cause is perceived as a person, object, or action external to the child that has an aspect or quality that is bad or harmful for the body. Such a cause brings on illness through the child's body physically contacting the person or object (e.g., through touching, rubbing), or through the child's physically engaging in a harmful action and thus becoming contaminated. An example of this, excerpted from Bibace and Walsh, follows

"What is a cold?"
"It's like in the wintertime."
"How do people get them?"
"You're outside without a hat and you start sneezing. Your head would get cold, the cold would touch it, and then it would go all over your body."

Internalization is a type of illness explanation typically offered by older children in the concrete-logical stage. The external cause, usually a person or object, is linked to the external effect of illness through a process of internalization—for example, swallowing or inhaling. Many children of this age believe an illness to be caused by germs whose very presence is sufficient to make the child sick.

According to Piaget, children who are approximately 11 years of age or older manifest formal-logical thinking. At this stage, there is the greatest amount of differentiation between the self and the other. There is now an understanding that there are multiple causes of illness, that the body may respond variably to any combination of agents, and that host factors within the body interact with the agent to cause or cure the illness. Again, there are two forms of explanation within this stage. Physiological explanations are usually preferred by the younger children in this stage. Although the cause may be triggered by external events, they believe the source and nature of the illness lie in specific internal structures and functions. The cause is usually described as the nonfunctioning or malfunctioning of an internal organ or process, explained as a step-by-step internal sequence of events culminating in that illness.

Psychophysiological explanations express the most mature understanding of illness. As in physiological explanations, the illness is described in terms of internal physiological processes, but the child now perceives an additional or alternative cause of illness—a psychological one. The person is aware that a person's thoughts or feelings can affect the way the body functions. This sequence of development of understanding about illness parallels conceptual development in other content areas, such as physical causality (e.g., what causes rain or wind) although it seems to lag a bit.

Initial studies in the medical setting revealed that in comparison with their healthy counterparts, younger ill children give less mature, objective, well-articulated explanations of illness. Hospitalized children often ascribe the cause of their illness to disobedience of parental commands and may interpret their hospitalization as rejection or punishment. Younger children also perceive medical treatment as a form of punishment for being bad. Older minors with chronic illness, however, understand illness better than healthy children of the same age. This is probably due to the actual experiencing of illness and hospitalization rather than to a basic difference in cognitive function between healthy and sick children.

Reasoning. Giving consent rationally requires several cognitive capacities. These include abstract reasoning, inductive and deductive logical processes, and cognitive complexity, and they correspond with the capacities that Piaget has associated with the emergence of the formal operations stage of cognitive human development. First appearing at about age ten, this stage includes the development of increased cognitive capacity to bring certain operations to bear on abstract concepts in problem solving situations. For example, although a child at the previous concrete operational stage can think logically, it is questionable whether prior to the formal operations stage he or she can perform inductive and deductive operations or hypothetical reasoning at a level of verbal abstraction that would be needed in many consent situations involving treatment alternatives and risks. What is particularly pertinent to the informed consent process is that with the development of the formal operation stage the child is now capable of differentiating between the self and the environment and of understanding that the sources of illness are located within the body, even though the external agent is often described as the ultimate cause.

Further, emergence of the formal operations stage allows a child to become sufficiently flexible in thinking to attend to more than one area of a problem at once—for example, to entertain alternative treatments and risks simultaneously. The sequence in which these categories are ordered empirically is important, not only in terms of cognitive development, but in defining the kind and extent of personal control exerted by the person over what he or she believes to be the cause of the illness. There is now good evidence that by age 14, a substantial percentage of minors have attained the cognitive development stage of formal operations that is associated with the psychological elements of rational consent. There is, however, a wide variability in the age of attainment of the formal operation reasoning, indicating that we cannot equate this cognitive stage with a definite age period.

It should be mentioned that not all adult subjects attain the formal operational level. Therefore, it may not be warranted to consider formal operational reasoning as the sole standard for participation in informed consent. Further, it has been argued that "practical reasoning" involves such elements as judgment, self-knowledge, and character,

which require a long period of moral apprenticeship or paternalistic intervention in the child's decisionmaking. As commendable as these attributes may appear, they are so unpredictable in their attainment and so changeable in a person's life that their use as a criterion for involvement in informed consent is questionable.

In relation to specific clinical situations, a recent study by Whitehorn attempted to address empirically the question of minors' competence to consent. Minors aged 9 and 14 were compared with subjects aged 18 and 21 to test for developmental differences. A measure of competence to render informed decisions was developed to assess "competency" according to four standards: (1) capacity to express a treatment preference, (2) capacity to reach a "reasonable" or "responsible" decision, (3) capacity to reason "rationally" and "logically," and (4) capacity to demonstrate "understanding" of the relevant information regarding treatment alternatives. Four hypothetical medical and psychological treatment dilemmas were used for testing. The findings of the study were consistent with the cognitive developmental theory previously mentioned and suggest that 9 year olds are less competent than adult or 14 year olds with respect to their ability to reason "logically" and to "understand" the treatment information provided. These results indicate that adolescents 14 years of age or older may be developmentally competent to render autonomous treatment decisions. This experiment, however, was performed on healthy individuals and therefore is not exactly the same as in many medical settings with sick or hospitalized individuals, in whom it has been suggested that there is a regression in cognitive development during illness.

What, then, can be concluded about the first two elements of informed consent? Based on this review of developmental psychology of well and ill minors, a child's inability to conceptualize disease and to reason about it prior to the formal operational state means that usually children less than

10 years old are not competent. Thus, any consent that is obtained based on an advanced (physiologic or psychophysiologic) explanation to minors who are at the preconventional or concrete operational conceptual levels cannot be considered what might be called "valid" consent. Although a minor of these ages understands that he is being asked for consent, he lacks the ability to freely understand and appreciate the information given.

Further investigations are needed to determine whether explanations can be provided to children who are at preconventional or concrete operational conceptual levels that will enhance their understanding and will be scientifically accurate. From the standpoint of understanding and reasoning, minors aged 11 to 14 appear to be in a transition period in the development of important cognitive abilities, but there may be circumstances that would justify the sanction of independent consent by these minors for limited purposes when competence can be demonstrated in individual cases. On the other hand, there appears to be no psychological grounds for maintaining the general assumption that minors 15 years or older cannot provide competent consent.

The Logic of Competency

Bernard Gert and Charles Culver

The sentences "John is competent" and "John is incompetent" do not express complete statements. Of course, the context may make it clear what is meant. For example, if we are discussing whether or not to hire John to design a house, it is quite clear that the sentence "John is incompetent" means that John is incompetent to design a house. But not all incompetence is attached to offices or positions or jobs. Someone can be incompetent in what might be regarded as a more fundamental sense, namely, incompetent to do some activity that almost all normal adult human beings can perform. This is not really a different sense of incompetence. Rather, the person is incompetent to do more fundamental activities than those involved in a specific office or job. For example, a person may be incompetent to feed himself. He may simply be unable to figure out what or how to eat. The incompetence shown here is the same kind involved in designing a house. In both cases, there is a specific task to be performed and a person who is unable to perform it. The only difference—a big practical difference—is that only those who occupy some position involving the designing of houses are considered incompetent when they cannot do so, whereas anyone who cannot understand how to feed himself is regarded as incompetent.

As noted before. to say of someone that he is incompetent demands a context. A person is not simply incompetent; he is incompetent to do x, or x and y, or x, y, and z. It is possible for someone to be incompetent to do any of the things that a normal adult human being can do; newborn infants are incompetent in this total way, and so are some adults. Philosophical problems arise when someone is competent to do some kinds of things, but is incompetent to do some others. How is one to decide if such a person is competent to do some particular type of activity? The more precisely described the activity, the more likely it is that one can decide whether or not someone is competent to perform it. Suppose that we are wondering whether someone is competent to make a will. To be competent to do this, one must know what is involved in making a will; one must understand, at least in a practical sense, what a will is. If one is not aware of what is involved in making a will, then one is incompetent to make a will. In general, to be competent to do x, one must have at least a practical understanding

a)
b)
of what it is to do x. One must also understand when one is doing x. It is not enough to know what wills are; one must also be able to understand when one is making a will. Thus two necessary features for being competent to perform an activity are that one understands what that activity is and knows when he is performing it. *Incompetence*

We tentatively define incompetence in the following way: a person is incompetent to do x if it is reasonably expected that any person in his position, or any normal adult human being, can do x, and this person cannot (and his inability to do x is not due to a physical disability). In this account of incompetence, nothing is implied about how one ought to treat a person who is incompetent to do x, except, of course, that if one wanted to get x done, one should not entrust the job to someone who is incompetent to do it. Even with regard to someone who is incompetent to do something that every normal adult human being is expected to be able to do, nothing more is implied than that it would be unreasonable to entrust that person with the task of doing x. Thus if someone is incompetent to handle money, it would be unreasonable to give him some task that involved handling money. However, if he has money of his own, nothing follows about prohibiting him from spending it, or giving it away, or doing anything else he may want to do with it. We are not automatically justified in preventing someone from doing something simply because he is incompetent to do it. If someone is an incompetent poker player, for example, and does not know what hand beats another, it does not follow that anyone is justified in prohibiting him from playing poker if there are others who are willing to play poker with him. As we will see . . . if the consequences of his playing are serious enough, one might be so justified. Similarly, if someone is incompetent to make a decision about some medical treatment, it does not follow that someone else is thereby justified in making that decision for him. It may be that someone is justified, but this does not follow

solely from the fact that the person is incompetent to make the decision himself; it depends upon other matters as well.

VALID CONSENT

Let us now apply these general considerations regarding competence and incompetence to the problem of valid consent. What is involved in saying that someone is incompetent to give valid consent? We believe there are two levels of such incompetence and that it is useful to distinguish clearly between them.

simple consent

1. There is a category of patients who are unable to give or refuse consent at all. Some patients in this category are completely unaware of their surroundings and are not able to understand any question that might be asked of them—for example, infants, patients in a coma, or patients who are severely retarded or senile. For such patients, nothing that they say or do could even count as consent or refusal of consent. They may be called "totally incompetent," and it is universally acknowledged that it is justified, even morally required, for someone else to make decisions for them and on their behalf.

   However, there are other patients in this first category who are less than totally incompetent. They may have very limited cognitive abilities, may be able to ask for food, or for relief from pain, and yet be unable to understand any questions not directly related to present stimuli. Therefore, they do not understand at all the request for consent to a medical procedure. They do not know what is being asked of them and do not realize in fact that they are being asked to give consent. For these patients, as for those who are totally incompetent, it seems appropriate and morally justified for someone else to be authorized to give or withhold consent on their behalf.

   We will refer to both types of patients in this category as being *incompetent to give* (even) *simple consent.* The concept of "simple consent" is explained in the description of the next category of patients. *valid consent*

2. This second category of incompetent patients we refer to as being *incompetent to give valid consent.* They are, however, competent to give simple consent; that is, they understand that they are being asked to consent to a medical

don't understand info

treatment and can give consent or refuse to do so, but they lack the ability to understand or appreciate the information that is necessary to give a valid consent. The clearest example of someone who fits in this category is a patient who is moderately delirious or demented and is aware of only some aspects of his situation. He may perfectly well understand that he is being asked for consent to perform some medical procedure, but may not know where he is, who is asking for his consent, or why they are asking for it; or he may disbelieve most or all of what he is told about the consequences of his giving or refusing that consent. This person differs from the persons discussed in the first category in that he may give his consent to a treatment, or vigorously refuse to give it. But neither the refusal nor the granting of consent count as valid, for such a person does not possess sufficient information to give valid consent. We will say of such a patient that he is competent to give or refuse simple consent but is incompetent to give or refuse valid consent.

Another interesting example of patients in this category are those who have delusions which are relevant to the giving or withholding of consent. Suppose that someone has the paranoid delusion that all of his doctors are part of a plot to take over his body and that regardless of what his doctors are saying, if he gives his consent they will perform some procedure that will give them complete control over his thoughts and actions. He believes this even though consent is being requested only for a diagnostic procedure completely unrelated to his delusion, for example, a biopsy to determine if a tumor is malignant. We maintain that such a person is competent to give simple consent but is incompetent to give valid consent, because he is unable to understand or appreciate the information that is necessary for valid consent. This does not mean that we are thereby justified in performing the biopsy independent of his valid consent. For this to be true, one must apply the justification procedure that we alluded to earlier. . . .

A patient may also have a delusion which results in his giving rather than withholding consent. Suppose a man believes that he has been given superhuman powers and that nothing done to him can harm him in the slightest way. Thus, when he is asked for his consent to undergo a serious and risky experimental operation he readily gives it, for he does not believe that there is any risk for him. In such a case, his simple consent is not valid, for he is incompetent to give valid consent. We say this for the same reason we gave above: he is unable to understand or appreciate the information necessary for valid consent.

competence vs incompetence

Who Is Incapacitated and How Is It To Be Determined?

President's Commission

One of the conditions for health care decisionmaking is the capacity to make such decisions. . . . The components of decisional capacity were delineated there as possession of a set of values and goals, the ability to communicate and understand information, and the ability to reason and deliberate. This Chapter goes beyond that conceptual framework to discuss more fully three aspects of incapacity: the identification of those who are incapacitated,[1] the means for making such assessments, and the relationship between professionals, institutions, and the state in this process.

INCAPACITY

IDENTIFICATION OF INCAPACITY

In light of the presumption that most patients have the capacity to make health care decisions, on what grounds might a person be found to lack such a capacity? Three general criteria have been followed: the outcome of the decision, the status or category of the patient, and the patient's functional ability as a decisionmaker.

The outcome approach—which the Commission expressly rejects—bases a determination of incapacity primarily on the content of a patient's decision. Under this standard, a patient who makes a health care decision that reflects values not widely held or that rejects conventional wisdom about proper health care is found to be incapacitated.

Using the status approach, certain categories of patients have traditionally been deemed incapable of making treatment decisions without regard to their actual capabilities. Some of these categories of patients—such as the unconscious—correspond closely with actual incapacity. But other patients who are presumed to be incapacitated on the basis of their status may actually be capable of making particular health care decisions. Many older children, for example, can make at least some health care decisions, mildly or moderately retarded individuals hold understandable preferences about health care, and the same may be true in varying degrees among psychotic persons.

The third approach to the determination of incapacity focuses on an individual's actual functioning in decisionmaking situations rather than on the individual's status. This approach is particularly germane for children above a certain age (variously described as from seven to mid-teens). For example, rather than considering children under the age of majority incompetent to decide unless they come within one of the exceptions created by the statutory and common law, these patients could be regarded as competent unless shown to lack decisionmaking capacity.[2] Similarly, a senile person may have been declared incompetent by a court and a guardian may have been appointed to manage the person's financial affairs, but the functional standard would not foreclose the need to determine whether the senility also negated the individual's capacity to make health care decisions. What is relevant is whether someone is in fact capable of making a particular decision as judged by the consistency between the person's choice and that individual's underlying values and by the extent to which

the choice promotes the individual's well-being as he or she sees it.

The Commission recommends that determinations of incapacity be guided largely by the functional approach, that individuals not in certain basic categories (such as under the age of 14, grossly retarded, or comatose) should be assumed to possess decisionmaking capacity until they demonstrate otherwise, and that incapacity should be found to exist only when people lack the ability to make decisions that promote their well-being in conformity with their own previously expressed values and preferences.[3] The fact that a patient belongs to a category of people who are often unable to make general decisions for their own well-being or that an individual makes a highly idiosyncratic decision should alert health care professionals to the greater possibility of decisional incapacity. But it does not conclusively resolve the matter.

Rarely—again, the unconscious patient is the main exception—will incapacity be absolute. Even people with impaired capacity usually still possess some ability to comprehend, to communicate, and to form and express a preference. In such cases, even when ultimate decisional authority is not left with a patient, reasonable efforts should be made to give the person relevant information about the situation and the available options and to solicit and accommodate his or her preferences.

ASESSSMENTS OF INCAPACITY

The objective of any assessment of decisional incapacity is to diminish errors of mistakenly preventing competent persons from directing the course of their own treatment or of failing to protect the incapacitated from the harmful effects of their decisions. Health care professionals will probably play a substantial role, if not the entire one, in the initial assessment and the finding may never be reviewed by outside authorities. Nonetheless, since assessment of an individual's capacity is largely a matter of common sense, there is no inherent reason why a health care professional must play this role.

"Decisionmaking incapacity" is not a medical or a psychiatric diagnostic category; it rests on a judgment of the type that an informed layperson might make—that a patient lacks the ability to understand a situation and to make a choice in light of that understanding. Indeed, if a dispute arises or a legal determination of a patient's competence is required, the judge empowered to make the determination will consider the situation not as a medical expert but as a layperson. On the basis of the testimony of health care personnel and others who know the individual well, and possibly from personal observation of the patient, the judge must decide whether the patient is capable of making informed decisions that adequately protect his or her own interests.

Health care professionals are called upon to make these assessments because the question of incapacity to make health care decisions usually arises while a person is under their care. Particularly within institutions such as hospitals, a treating physician often involves colleagues from psychiatry, psychology, and neurology who have ways to accumulate, organize, and analyze information relevant to such assessments.[4] These examinations can yield considerable information about the patient's capabilities. The sources of useful information to be collected include discussions of the situation with relatives and other care-givers, particularly those in close contact with the patient, such as nurses. Ultimately, whether a patient's capabilities are sufficiently limited and the inadequacies sufficiently extensive for the person to be considered incapacitated is a matter for careful judgment in light of the demands of the situation. If the patient improves (or worsens) or if the decision to be made has different consequences, a reassessment of the individual's capacity may be required.

Finally, in any assessment of capacity due care should be paid to the reasons for a particular patient's impaired capacity, not because the reasons play any role in determining whether the patient's judgment is to be honored but because identification of the causes of incapacity may assist in their remedy or removal. The Commission urges that those responsible for assessing capacity not be content with providing an answer to the question of whether or not a particular patient is incapacitated. Rather, in conjunction with the patient's health care team (of which the assessor may be a member), they should to the extent feasible attempt to remove barriers to decisional capacity.

---

1. The terms "incapacity" and "incapacitated" as used in this Report are shorthand labels for patients who lack the capacity to make a particular health care decision. . . . These terms are not synonymous with either mental or physical incapacity. Though decisional incapacity ordinarily results from mental or physical infirmity, all persons with such infirmities are not *ipso facto* "incapacitated" as that term is used here.

2. Law has traditionally viewed people under a specified age—long set at 21 years and more recently at 18—as precluded from making decisions about any contractual matters, including their own health care. In effect, there has been a presumption of *incompetency*, contrary to the usual presumption of competency accorded adults. Some exceptions of a loosely functional nature have been created for "emancipated" or "mature" minors, in recognition that some children under some circumstances in fact have the capacity to make health care decisions and that for reasons of social policy such decisions ought to be sufficient. This system, based on a general rule of incompetence with an ever-expanding number of statutory exceptions, has meant that children are more often presumed competent to make health care decisions, or has at least brought about an implicit lowering of the age of presumed incompetence.

The Commission endorses this general trend, recognizing that there is an age, below about 14 years old, at which the traditional presumption of incompetence still ought to govern. The presumption, however, is merely a starting point for inquiry. Even when children lack the capacity to make decisions, their involvement in the decisionmaking process not only acknowledges their individual status but also may enhance their cooperation in and compliance with therapeutic procedures. The variations in children's capabilities could appropriately be recognized by providing that for certain interventions, a practitioner should obtain both the *consent* of a child's legal guardian and the *assent* of the child. The latter would be insufficient by itself to authorize the intervention, but the intervention could not go ahead without it.

3. When efforts to communicate with a patient and learn his or her preferences would jeopardize the patient's well-being because of an urgent need for treatment, it is appropriate for health care providers to treat the patient as incapacitated and to turn to a surrogate decision-maker or, when none is available, to care for the patient without consent, as permitted by the "emergency" exception.

4. The "mental status examination" is perhaps the best example of how professional expertise can be enlisted in making assessments of incapacity. Such an evaluation is intended, among other things, to elicit the patient's orientation to person, place, time, and situation, the patient's mood and affect, and the content of thought and perception, with an eye to any delusions and hallucinations; to assess intellectual capacity, that is, the patient's ability to comprehend abstract ideas and to make a reasoned judgment based on that ability; to review past history for evidence of any psychiatric disturbance that might affect the patient's current judgment; and to test the patient's recent and remote memory and logical sequencing.

Compassion, Control, and Decisions About Competency

Virginia Abernethy

The definition of mental competency is elusive. To define it is a compelling quest, nonetheless, because a patient's right to exercise autonomy with respect to decisions about his or her medical care is conditional on the patient's competency.

> The root premise is the concept, fundamental in the American jurisprudence system, that "every human being of adult years and sound mind has a right to determine what shall be done with his own body. . . ."

The patient has the right to

> . . . forego treatment or even cure if it entails what for him are intolerable consequences or risks, however warped or perverse his sense of values may be . . . so long as any distortion falls short of what the law regards as incompetency.

There is a legal presumption, but of uncertain magnitude, in favor of finding that an individual is competent; that is, the burden of proof is on those who allege that the patient is not competent. The standard required to overcome the presumption of competency in civil cases was stated, in one decision, to be "clear, cogent and convincing evidence." Similarly, disorientation, mental illness, irrationality, or commitment to a mental institution are not conclusive proof of incompetency.

Although the courts and the medical profession are frequently required to make judgments about competency, there is often great difficulty in implementing the concept. Real complexity in evaluating patients' mental function may be further clouded by conflicts over value systems. To the extent that the outcome of saving life is raised above alternative values such as autonomy, the patient who makes decisions that appear contrary to his best medical interests is likely to be seen as not deciding in a cognitively rational manner and, therefore, as incompetent. In this paper I explore competency in the context of an actual case and recommend conditions that must be met before finding that a patient cannot decide for himself.

CASE REPORT

Ms. A was 72 years of age at the time her story became front-page news. She was described as athletic looking, as appearing much younger than she actually was, and also as dirty and soot-covered. She lived with her six cats in one garbage-strewn room heated by a wood fire in the formerly luxurious house in which she was raised.

In January, a fire in Ms. A's house led to her

being escorted to a hospital by the police. The emergency room doctor noted that she was "mentally competent for her age [and] a very self- and strong-willed individual, very determined-minded person and definitely was not insane."

Ms. A insisted on returning home after spending only the night of the fire with neighbors. Both they and a mayoral aide, who earlier had become aware of Ms. A's life style, became concerned as January temperatures dipped toward zero. On one occasion when the neighbors brought food, they noted that Ms. A's feet were black, blistered, and bleeding. She rejected offers of aid or shelter (she had once met a social worker with a shotgun and refused him entry). Ms. A refused even food unless she was allowed to pay for it.

Finally, the mayoral aide used her influence to mobilize the police. With the aide's repeated urgings and under a broad interpretation of the principle that police can intercede when a person is harming herself, the police made four visits, eventually broke down doors, physically overwhelmed Ms. A, and transported her against her will to the hospital.

Once hospitalized, Ms. A was treated for pneumonia. One week later, gangrene was recognized, and the surgeons advised bilateral, below-the-knee amputations, citing a 50% chance for life with amputation and a 5%–10% chance without the operation. Ms. A adamantly refused amputation. At the surgeons' request, hospital social workers called in the state human services department to assist in persuading her to have the operation. Ms. A still refused, allegedly saying that her feet were just black from soot, so the department sought guardianship under a state law covering protective services for the elderly. (In October 1981 a similar statute became law in New York state.) Grounds for the custody petition were that she was "in imminent danger of death" and "lacked capacity to consent" to treatment.

The case evolved into an effort to determine whether Ms. A was competent to refuse amputation and was heard subsequently at four judicial levels. The state appeals court held an unprecedented hearing at Ms. A's bedside. This yielded the only transcript of evidence or of Ms. A's own words. On this occasion, she was willing to discuss her feet and at no time claimed that their color was attributable to soot. Instead, she pointed out

that the feet and legs had been a cause of concern, and she marshalled evidence of improvement. The following material is from the transcript.

JUDGE: I understand that you had a little problem of getting too cold out there at your house.

MS. A: Yes. It's a point of this, the swelling in my foot was . . . very dangerous looking. . . . So that's what caused most of the trouble. It's starting to go down. Give it a chance; it is starting to go down and it's almost. . . .

JUDGE: You remind me of my mother. She's a good deal older than you are, and she lives by herself, but I go by and see her every morning and sometimes every afternoon.

MS. A: Yes.

JUDGE: Keep mighty close watch on her.

MS. A: Well, these ankles and along these legs have gone down wonderfully.

In addition, Ms. A noted that she could move her toes. Several years before, she had experienced natural recovery from blackening and ulceration of her feet secondary to winter freezing; the experience also contributed to her conviction that the feet would recover.

An account of a similar discussion was reported in the narrative, a reconstruction of lower court proceedings. The guardian *ad litem* appointed by the court to represent Ms. A described the first interview with her client:

[She told me that] the swelling in her feet was going down, she was getting better, and the doctors were wrong about her situation. [Ms. A] said that she felt it was a terrible thing when they can take a person's two feet with the person being denied the right to make that decision.

The surgeons did not dispute the reality of the physical signs to which Ms. A called attention, and the appeals court was, in addition, aware of her repeated experiences with frostbite. Nevertheless, the court accepted both 1) the surgeons' formulation that the only significant chance for life lay with amputation and 2) the idea that a competent person should be willing to make a choice between dying and amputation.

The judges' attempt to force a decision within this surgically defined, two-choice world emerges in the following dialogue.

JUDGE: . . . should we let you die, or would you rather live your life without your feet?

Ms. A: I am giving my feet a chance to get well.

JUDGE: If the time comes that you have to choose between losing your feet and dying, would you rather just go ahead and die than to lose your feet? If that time comes?

Ms. A: It's possible. It's possible only if I . . . just forget it. You are making me sick talking.

JUDGE: I know. I am sorry. You'd be willing to say to me that you just don't want to live if you can't have your feet. Is that the way you feel?

Ms. A: I don't understand why it's so important to you people, why it's so important.

JUDGE: I believe, [Ms. A], that you have made your point that you don't want to live if you can't have your feet. Isn't that it?

Ms. A: That's possible. It's possible to see it that way, to have that opinion.

JUDGE (frustrated):   She wants to live and have her feet.

Ms. A's FRIEND: That's exactly what she wants.

Ms. A: This is ridiculous. I am tired. Ridiculous, you know it is.

In other circumstances, Ms. A's avoidance of the key question might have been seen as canny. The guardian *ad litem* later noted,

> She was not going to let them put her in the position of saying, "Yes, when I become unconscious, you can do it." This was a smart lady. I've seen people on a witness stand say things that hurt them worse. This woman was being cross-examined by an appellate judge, and she wasn't going to give him what he wanted.

Nonetheless, Ms. A's failure to appreciate or accommodate to what was wanted inspired the judge to write:

> The patient has not expressed a desire to die. She evidences a strong desire to live and an equally strong desire to keep her dead feet. She refuses to make a choice.

The mutual frustration and misunderstanding are palpable. In the parting moments, one judge gave Ms. A a final opportunity to consent to amputation, asking to leave her with a "little thought." He started the parable "If thine eye offend thee. . ."; she correctly completed it, and the judge suggested that she apply the moral to her feet. Ms. A thanked him appropriately and added her metaphor:

> Let me leave you with one. Of spirits and ancient inspiration. Well, they're all my facts yet, and I am not going to throw my inspirations and everything away.

Her rejection of the two-choice model became the grounds, finally, for concluding that Ms. A was not competent to refuse amputation. Her hope for a third outcome, that the feet might recover, became the primary evidence of denial and, *ipse dixit,* her incompetence:

> If, as repeatedly stated, this patient could and would give evidence of a comprehension of the facts of her condition and could and would express her unequivocal desire in the face of such comprehended facts, then her decision, however unreasonable to others, would be accepted and honored by the courts and her doctors. The difficulty is that she cannot or will not comprehend the facts.

The court wrote that Ms. A did not "comprehend the facts," although it had heard contrary testimony from a surgeon.

QUESTIONER: Has she ever by statement to you indicated that she comprehends that, in your opinion, her feet are dead and that her life is threatened?

SURGEON: She understands it very well, but I don't think she believes it.

The judges' appreciation of this evidence was apparently dulled by their fixation on a forced choice between amputation and death. Moreover, they chose to ignore both their own observation that the ". . . respondent is an intelligent, lucid, communicative individual . . . and apparently of sound mind generally" and their awareness of a logical problem: Ms. A's alleged incompetence was linked to her refusal of amputation; that is, had Ms. A consented, it was generally agreed that she would have been competent to consent. A judge held the following sworn interchange with the psychiatric consultant:

JUDGE: Please don't think I am trying to make you appear ridiculous because I am not. I want to point out a problem that you have and we have, too.
In some aspects, she has the capacity to consent and she is competent if she consents?

PSYCHIATRIST: That is correct.

JUDGE: But in her very refusal to consent, she is not competent; isn't that really the unusual conclusion we reach from the unusual circumstances?

PSYCHIATRIST: I think that's correct.

The appeals court upheld the lower court custody award to the human services department but conditioned amputation on the written statement of two physicians that Ms. A was "in imminent danger of death." Those letters never were forthcoming because she survived the gangrene. The case rose finally to the United States Supreme Court as a challenge to the constitutionality of the state law, but before it was heard, Ms. A died of a pulmonary embolus. A contributing factor may have been her refusal of medication (heparin sodium) to control blood clot formation in her still unhealed (but nongangrenous) feet.

THE DECISION PROCESS

The court concluded that Ms. A was incompetent because she refused to choose between death and amputation. This decision relied heavily on testimony of mental health professionals that Ms. A was using denial as a psychological defense against reality. One psychiatrist wrote, and a second psychiatrist and a social worker apparently concurred, that Ms. A was employing "psychotic denial."

The greater part of the first psychiatric consultant's written report to the lower court described an alert, intelligent, logical and [initially] pleasant woman but concluded that Ms. A was, after all, using a psychotic defense mechanism:

Nonetheless, I believe that she is functioning on a psychotic level with respect to ideas concerning her gangrenous feet. She tends to believe that her feet are black because of soot or dirt. She does not believe her physicians about the serious infection. There is an adamant belief that her feet will heal without surgery, and she refused to even consider the possibility that amputation is necessary to save her life. . . . My impression is that she does not appreciate the dangers to her life. I conclude that she is noncompetent to decide this issue. A corollary to this denial is seen in her unwillingness to consider any future plans. Here again I believe she was utilizing a psychotic mechanism of denial.

In the appeals court hearing, the psychiatrist testified further: "She can [consent] but she won't. She won't because there is a tremendous amount of emotional investment going on here."

Other evidence for incompetence brought out at the lower court level was a social worker's opinion that Ms. A was "[not] capable of making the decision regarding surgery on her feet [because] . . . she refused to discuss the question and did not believe the doctors' reports [but] felt that they were making it more serious than it really was." On questioning, he said that she was not senile and was ". . . generally capable of making decisions regarding herself except with regard to the decision involving her feet." A second psychiatrist was retained by an amicus curiae but made no official report because he concurred with the negative evaluation of Ms. A's competence.

In brief, to the extent that examiners focused on the feet and on saving life, the patient was placed in a "no win" situation. She was competent so long as she consented to amputation and incompetent if she refused. Under either circumstance, the patient would lose her feet. Even the more sophisticated formulation picked up by the judges allowed Ms. A a choice only so long as she agreed to deal with predetermined categories: amputation or death.

The controversial nature of the ultimate decision suggests that forces other than dispassionate objectivity may have been at work. Three aspects of the case heighten skepticism. There was, first, an aura of medical emergency that pervaded the psychiatric consultations and the judicial process. In addition, Ms. A herself was quick to anger and clearly regarded most interactions with medical personnel as adversarial. Last, one might ask if her hostility engendered reactive anger in those charged with evaluating her competence.

The aura of medical emergency is easily documented. The lower court judge later noted:

> I believe I was misled, and I'm sure not intentionally, but misled in the way the human services department presented the case to us. This was as something that has to be done right now. I constantly was led to believe that the doctor was waiting with his scalpel in his hand by the telephone. That is what was presented to me. I was asking about calling the surgeons to see if we could get a little more time. I set the first hearing early in the morning before court opened.

The psychiatric consultant also believed that a medical emergency existed. He pressed through a snowstorm to see Ms. A (as did the judge on the following morning to personally collect the psychiatric evaluation) and later stated that so long as Ms. A refused amputation, the doctors should decide because,

> . . . we were faced with a life-threatening situation. We have to make a decision on the basis of the facts at hand now.

In court, the psychiatrist, when asked if he had "adequately evaluated her," replied:

> No. I felt I was under the crunch of time. . . . I still feel that her denial of the problem with her feet is a denial of psychotic proportions.

The second disruptive factor was Ms. A's anger. Her sense of being under attack dated realistically to a year earlier when efforts had been made to condemn her home. Her fears and outrage could not have been lessened by the police breaking in and taking her to the hospital. The news that she must have her feet amputated was met with refusal and then, as attempts to persuade her mounted, with increasing anger. Both psychiatrists, one nurse, and a surgeon were among those summarily turned out of her room on at least one occasion. Her angry feelings were manifested on various levels, including the slight alteration of one surgeon's name to "Dr. Tacky."

Such wit and sarcasm are documented features of Ms. A's communication style, but in the context of an emergency psychiatric evaluation and her (by then) adversarial response to anyone appearing to coerce her into consent, the sometimes fanciful dismissal of problems with her feet facilitated misunderstanding. The psychiatrist later recalled an interchange that occurred near the stormy end of the evaluation:

> She ignored, or denied, that there was anything wrong with her feet at first. Then when I said, "Well, you know, that doesn't seem to be the case," she said, "Well, there's just some soot on them."

Finally, one may ask whether the evaluation process was disrupted because Ms. A's anger sparked a like emotion in those she berated. Professionals who think of themselves as altruistic, or at least benevolently motivated, may be particularly sensitive to hostility because they feel deserving of gratitude. Did it, therefore, make a difference that the social worker was the same person whom she once had run off with a shotgun? Similarly, the psychiatrist considered himself ". . . pretty good at interviewing folks that other people have trouble with, [but] forty-five minutes was all the time that she gave me before she verbally threw me out." The second psychiatrist to see Ms. A had a quicker exit. He was dismissed almost immediately but continued the interview from behind the door, using as intermediary Ms. A's trusted friend. Could any negative affect have influenced their evaluations?

This background at least supports a question about the objectivity of professional decision making. Part of the disruptiveness here is attributable to Ms. A's personality and part to social and health care systems that demand acquiescence from even the shanghaied client or patient. It is also no small matter that the courts became the agent of the health care system in its coercive rush to do good.

DISCUSSION

An alternative conclusion to that reached by the courts is that Ms. A's conversation (as recorded in the extensive transcript), other testimony and the judges' own description of her as an "intelligent, lucid, communicative individual . . . of sound mind generally . . ." reveal Ms. A to have been competent, entitling her to make the one decision that mattered most to her, for whatever reason or guiding inspiration she might have had. Hoping for recovery even against great odds is not a criterion of incompetence in this schema.

That judgment requires one to accept that hope (disbelieving the physicians' pessimistic prognosis) is not a criterion of psychotic denial. Hackett and Cassem suggest that denial of the seriousness of medical illness is common among dangerously ill patients, and they do not call this defense mechanism psychotic. Indeed, they note a convergence of psychoanalytic formulations in which denial is seen as the goal of assorted defense mechanisms and tactics. Moreover, they report that, at least for coronary patients, denial is associated with better outcomes during the course of hospitalization.

The possibility still may be raised that the patient is delusional on the issue of the medical decision only, while demonstrating apparent organization in other domains. It is this very problem that the paper has attempted to address: The criterion of a focal delusion is dangerously liable to error because a patient can easily be seen as delusional in an emotionally charged interchange, when in other circumstances he addresses the same issue appropriately. This contrast is clear in the verbatim transcript in which Ms. A gives a cogent account of her feet, their "dangerous" look, and their visible improvement.

If it is granted that Ms. A was competent, discussion of those logical contortions seen in the decision process has been appropriate. It is legitimate to ask why mental health professionals repeatedly stated that Ms. A was incompetent to decide about her feet but only for so long as she refused amputation. Similarly, why did the appeals court formulation make competence depend on choosing between predetermined categories?

It is not self-evident that a patient should be required to address any particular question as a test of competence. On the contrary, the opposite can be inferred from the dubious constitutionality of using the substance of a decision, or outcome, as the criterion that determines the competence of the decision maker. A 1964 opinion by Judge Warren Burger, later to be Chief Justice of the United States Supreme Court, speaks to this point:

> Mr. Justice Brandeis, whose views have inspired much of the "right to be let alone" philosophy, said . . . : "The makers of our Constitution . . . sought to protect Americans in their beliefs, their thoughts, their emotions and their sensations. They conferred, as against the government, the right to be let alone . . . the most comprehensive right and the right most valued by civilized man." Nothing in this utterance suggests that Justice Brandeis thought an individual possessed these rights only as to sensible beliefs, valid thoughts, reasonable emotions, or well-founded sensations. I suggest he intended to include a great many foolish, unreasonable and even

absurd ideas which do not conform, such as refusing medical treatment even at great risk.

The implications of the Brandeis-Burger formulation may be difficult to accept precisely because many health care professionals are outcome oriented. Doing the best for the patient is a mandate that makes it repugnant to allow a patient to self-destruct in the name of the ofttimes conflicting value, autonomy. Yet, declaring Ms. A incompetent because of what she decided might have been seen as a violation of her constitutionally protected rights had the case reached the United States Supreme Court. The thrust of evolving law suggests that autonomy will be protected.

This issue is further brought into perspective by considering that, in practice, the competence of marginally delirious or demented patients who consent to a treatment is rarely challenged. The invisibility of these consenting patients raises an awkward ethical question, and, practically, makes it difficult to think about what level of mental function, or understanding, is consistent with a challenge to competency.

Thus, the complexities of evaluating competence are imposing even in the absence of value conflicts. When there is, in addition, the latent tension between an outcome orientation and a commitment to honor the autonomy of persons, the judiciousness of the system appears overly strained. This case demonstrates the fragility of both clinical and legal processes.

If decisions about competence are in reality so vulnerable to extraneous circumstance, it becomes important to specify strict criteria for determining that a patient is incompetent so that the constitutionally protected right not to be touched is safeguarded. Thus, I recommend that the presumption of competence should be overcome only when significant dysfunction in an array of cognitive and interpersonal domains can be demonstrated. Good overall cognitive skill would be incompatible with a judgment of incompetence, no matter how (by what intrapsychic process) or what the patient decided about medical interventions. A patient who was informable and cognitively capable of making ordinary decisions on matters unrelated to the crisis at hand would be held competent to refuse or accept medical interventions.

Competence is presumed and does not have to be proved. Incompetence must be proved. A high standard of proof is needed as a safeguard of the right to be let alone, because patient autonomy is too easily thrust aside by the double-barreled salvo of medical crisis and interpersonal conflict. A patient may have hope, or may have quality of life priorities that outweigh life itself, and a competent patient should have the scope to express these idiosyncrasies.

2. THE ROLES AND VIRTUES OF DIFFERENT PROFESSIONALS AS PROVIDERS

Physicians and Nurses: A Historical Perspective

Andrew Jameton

It is easy to discern in nursing an expression of the first two criteria of professionalism: competence and dedication to an important social good. The third criterion of professionalism, autonomy, has been a center of struggle since the late nineteenth century.

This chapter discusses some of the major obstacles to the independent practice and self-government of nurses and suggests that a better understanding of the concept of autonomy could help to overcome these obstacles.

HISTORY OF THE STRUGGLE

Nursing has a strong tradition of ethics teaching. No decade has passed since 1900 without publication of at least one basic text in nursing ethics. The *American Journal of Nursing* published an article on ethics in its first volume (1901), and in the 1920s and 1930s it carried a regular column of nursing ethics cases. Ethics courses were often part of the nursing curriculum until they were pushed aside after World War II by burgeoning courses in sciences and health care technology. By contrast, the tradition of ethics teaching in medicine is weaker. Even the development of bioethics as a teaching subject in medical schools in the late 1970s resulted in large part from outside pressure. Why has there been such a difference?

Three plausible explanations are at hand. First, women have carried the humane tradition in modern Western cultures: they educate children, soften the blows of the world, nurture others, and humanize modern life. Nursing and medicine have reified this stereotype. Nurses stereotyped as "feminine" were expected to be concerned with ethics and humanism while physicians stereotyped as "masculine" toiled with diagnostic tests, science, and instruments. An open concern for ethics was not masculine.

Second, medical ethics has been strongly individualistic. Physicians have not enjoyed being told how to behave; typically, they balked at any suggestion that they did not already know what to do. This attitude is reflected by the introduction to the 1972 American Medical Association Code:

Ethical principles are basic and fundamental. Men of good conscience inherently know what is right or wrong, and what is to be done or to be avoided. Written documents attempt to express for the guidance of all what each knows to be true.

Third, nursing has carried a tradition of deference. Thus, it has not seemed strange for textbook authors to instruct nurses in their duties. In her 1901 text *Nursing Ethics:*

For Hospital and Private Use, Isabel Hampton Robb placed obedience at the center of nursing virtues:

Above all, let her remember to do what she is told to do, and no more; the sooner she learns this lesson, the easier her work will be for her, and the less likely will she be to fall under severe criticism. Implicit, unquestioning obedience is one of the first lessons a probationer must learn, for this is a quality that will be expected from her in her professional capacity for all future time. Some learn it with more or less difficulty; others never wholly master it; the happy few, who have been fortunate enough to have been trained to it from childhood, accept it naturally and never find it irksome.

Obedience to supervisors and physicians remained a central focus of nursing ethics teaching until the rebirth of feminism in the 1970s. For example, in a 1917 text we find:

There would be no possible excuse for the nurse to act on her own responsibility in the hospital, as there is always a doctor within calling distance; . . .

A 1947 text includes, among "some good rules,"

Carry out the doctor's orders.

In a 1955 text, the author writes:

Whether the hospital or the patient or the physician employs the nurse, she works *under the instruction of the physician.* . . . In accepting the position, the nurse makes at least an implicit contract to carry out the orders of the physician in charge.

These injunctions, although commonplace, have never been absolute. Nurses have never been called on by these texts to obey physicians making obvious mistakes. Moreover, we can find in nursing history many objections to obedience as a major nursing obligation. As early as 1916 Isabel M. Stewart wrote:

The traditional virtues of the good nurse are: obedience, the spirit of self-sacrifice, courage, patience, conscientiousness, and discretion. These are good, but under the newer conditions they are not alone sufficient. I think we have not placed enough emphasis on the more positive and vigorous qualities, such as self-reliance, the power of leadership, and initiative.

The struggle against obedience reached an important turning point when the ICN dropped from its 1973 code a point that had lingered in its 1965 version:

The nurse is under an obligation to carry out the physician's orders intelligently and loyally.

Instead, the ICN confined itself to the more neutral principle:

The nurse sustains a cooperative relationship with co-workers in nursing and other fields. (ICN, 1973)

The textbook tradition in nursing ethics thus reflects a strong tradition of deference in conflict with the concept of professionalism. In contrast, early nursing leaders were vigorous and outspoken women, improbably cast in a deferential role. This legacy of deference is thus best seen as a price early nursing leaders chose to pay, rightly or wrongly, in order to advance nursing.

At that time, society created many obstacles to leadership by women in health care: Women were supposed to stay in the home; skilled nursing care was confused with unskilled family care; education of women was a new idea for Americans. Other efforts by women to enter health care as professionals were largely defeated. By 1910 only a few women had been able to enter medical practice. Six percent of physicians were women—a number that declined steadily until the 1950s. Midwives, who attempted to practice health care independent of physicians, were driven almost completely out of business by obstetricians and gynecologists.

Midwives lost this struggle around the turn of the century even though their patients had lower mortality rates than physicians'. Nursing was the only form of health practice which women at that time were able to enter in large numbers. They became the workers that allowed the modern hospital to expand. They did so by avoiding direct conflict with physicians. They stayed within the medical model and used deference to avoid threatening physicians.

Many of the historical influences that once made obedience a prudent choice still operate today, and we should look at them in detail. These include hospitals, physicians, nurses, sexism, and the concept of autonomy.

OPPOSITION FROM HOSPITALS

The late nineteenth century was a period of rapid industrialization in the United States. Products previously of handiwork, crafts, small business, and home industry became the products of large organizations. Women who once wove cloth in their homes found themselves weaving and sewing in assembly lines with a consequent degradation in their quality of life and social standing. Early hospitals represented a similar industrialization of the craft industry of health care. At first, hospitals mainly cared for the poor, but soon people recognized the economic advantages of hospitalization for the well-off sick. As homes became urbanized, the hospital appeared as a convenience for the sick and a "home away from home" in which to be cared for.

Early hospitals followed closely the Victorian concept of the home. The early nurse functioned as "mother." She worked inside the home, in other words, the hospital, and took charge of housekeeping and hospital finances. Cleanliness, orderliness, and frugality were thus major nursing virtues. The nurse as mother also bore direct responsibility for patient care. Like children, patients were the central figures and intended beneficiaries of the hospital family. At the same time, patients were expected to have little say-so in the conduct of hospital affairs. The nurses cared for, cleaned up after, managed, and educated their "children." The physician, to complete this all-too-real image, functioned as "father." Like the typical urban male worker, he spent much of his time absent from home. He only visited briefly to leave instructions with "mother" for care of the "children." In addition, he took major responsibility for the conduct of hospital affairs, was the head of the "household," and often owned the hospital, just as the patriarchal male owned the home. As owner, the physician was the primary financial beneficiary of this arrangement, while nurses made financial sacrifices to support the industrialization of health care.

"Owners" of hospitals have changed since the early foundations, and a large portion of hospital-generated revenue now goes to insurers, investors, builders, suppliers, managers, regulators, and so on. Meanwhile, nurses have taken on many functions initially performed only by physicians: injections, diagnosis, physical exams, medication, drawing blood, record keeping, administration, and so on. Although nurses have acquired these new tasks, control over them has remained mostly with physicians, and the organization of autonomy in the hospital is for the most part unchanged. The main obstacles now facing the autonomy of nurses in hospitals are bureaucratic forms of management and the attending-physician system.

Bureaucracies give authority to their personnel through a top-downward *vertical* mode of authority. Each participant has a limited range of activities and discretion. Each is answerable to someone above, and an administrator or board of directors sits at the top of the pyramid. The legal background of hospital care tends to support this bureaucratic conception of nursing. Under the doctrine of *respondeat superior,* hospitals can be held legally responsible for the actions of nursing staff. Along with an employer's interest in controlling em-

ployees' work, this makes hospitals anxious to control the actions of nurses and to discourage autonomy. In contrast, professionals draw their power from a *horizontal* or *collegial* mode of organization. Professionals normally regard each other as having equal authority and do not supervise each other except as teachers. A professional tends to see herself as answerable primarily to the commitments of her profession. Professionals claiming increased autonomy can thus be seen by hospital administrators as potential sources of friction and disloyalty.

Professionalism and bureaucracy are different strategies for allocating decision making. The two strategies can be integrated in the hospital by having nursing representatives sit on management and policy committees. The most striking compromise, however, is that between physicians and hospitals. Here, professional autonomy is reconciled with bureaucracy by giving physicians a central place in management and submerging the conflict between professionalism and bureaucracy in medical dominance. In most U.S. hospitals this reconciliation operates through the *attending physician* system. In this system, the physician, not the patient, is the primary client of the hospital. The hospital provides services to physicians who admit patients. Physicians instruct hospitals via orders to provide selected services to these patients. From an institutional point of view, attending physicians do not give orders to individual nurses. They give orders to the hospital, and through its administrative bureaucracy, it directs individual nurses to fill them. Meanwhile, the hospital has its own contract with patients to provide nursing, dietary, and other services independent of but coordinated with services ordered by physicians.

This dual system of authority places conflicting demands on nurses. The hospital may expect one thing of nurses (conserving supplies, ensuring that all patients receive basic services), while physicians expect another (unstinting devotion to their patients). If nurses had a recognized sphere of discretion adequate to reflect their abilities and professional responsibility, then this dual system might not be such an obstacle to autonomy. But the combined tasks of filling physician orders and completing hospital duties exhaust energy that might be used to initiate nursing care plans, bedside care, and patient teaching.

The rewards and sanctions of bureaucracies combine with the dual system of organization to place nurses in a disadvantageous negotiating position with regard to physicians. While physicians are *clients* of hospitals and therefore cannot be fired for their mistakes, nurses are *employees* of hospitals and hold their jobs at the will of the hospital. In negotiations with physicians, nurses are usually more vulnerable than physicians.

The dual system of authority makes it difficult to establish a nurse-patient relationship. In order to define a realm of professional discretion, nurses need a well-defined relationship with their clients, but definition is hard to achieve in the hospital setting. A nurse may work with many patients during a day, and these patients will have different physicians responsible for special medical aspects of their care. Moreover, a nurse may have only certain duties with respect to each patient. It may be the case that no nurse has the overall duty for the nursing care of a patient. Each patient during a shift may receive the care of many nurses, and on each shift, another set of nurses will look after the patient. The patient does not necessarily have one nurse to look to for nursing services. In some hospitals, a mass of nurses thus has a relationship to a mass of patients. The coordination required by this system fragments the provider-client relationship underlying traditional conceptions of professional autonomy. Particularly in large teaching hospitals, intricate divisions of responsibility obscure the physicians' scope of autonomy as well.

These dynamics are not without secondary advantages. The nurse can appeal to hospital duties in reply to physician demands, and to physician duties in reply to hospital demands. The nurse's own decisions can be presented to the patient with the weight of hospital policy or physician orders as he or she chooses. Nurses skillful in manipulating such responsibilities may gain power or autonomy by keeping hostile forces in balance in the fashion of a nineteenth-century European diplomat. But this mode of gaining power only offers a cynical and covert autonomy. Full autonomy requires that one's power to make decisions be recognized openly and regarded as legitimate.

These problems with autonomy are not present to the same degree in all nursing settings. In "primary care" systems of nursing, a nurse may have primary responsibility for a certain group of patients, or in intensive care settings, responsibility for just one patient. Nurses on the night shift may act without consultation more than nurses in the day: As one nurse remarked, "To physicians, I am a genius at night, and an idiot by day." Nurse practitioners and private duty nurses may also have a clear nurse-client relationship: one nurse practitioner specializing in cancer chemotherapy exclaimed: "At last, I have a doctor-patient relationship!" Outside the hospital in less bureaucratic settings, nurses may also be able to operate with more autonomy. Public health and registry nurses sometimes have this experience. Acute care hospitals tend to be the settings in which nurses, especially staff nurses, experience the most acute autonomy conflicts.

OPPOSITION FROM PHYSICIANS

Medicine became organized as a profession in the United States in the mid-nineteenth century. In an earlier part of that century it had suffered from a populist movement that supported self-care and damaged the physician monopoly over health care services. With this experience fresh in their history, newly organized physicians were assiduous during the last half of the nineteenth century in protecting their position by limiting entry to their profession and by attacking competing professions. Nursing's growth in the face of this competition has placed the two professions in an intimate relationship of cooperation and conflict. The profession of medicine continues to exercise its decreasing but continuing dominance over the profession of nursing through institutionalized gender discrimination and hospital bureaucracy. To patients and the public, the entire health care organization appears as the doctor writ large.

The use of "medical care" to refer to health care uses the name of a small part to stand for the whole. This language, like the use of "he" to refer to both men and women, tends to conceal less powerful practitioners from view. For example, people use such phrases as "new medical technology" to refer to a variety of machinery and equipment usually operated by nonphysicians. Many procedures and forms of care—using a social worker, getting a hearing aid, administering many medications, creating discharge plans, and others—must be done over a physician's signature even though virtually all of the work, quality control, and decision making is done by nonphysicians. Thus, the successes and failures of health care are often attributed to physicians as though they worked alone when in fact hospital care represents the combined work of a variety of specialists. Some physicians even seem to think of themselves as owning the nurses they work with. Some use such phrases as "I look out for my nurses," or "My nurses are very competent." A physician would never refer to his or her colleagues as "my doctors," nor do nurses often speak of "my doctors."

Medicine has been powerful enough to define its practice on its own terms. This has meant that the standard legal definitions of medicine are so broad that it is very difficult to provide any health care without falling within the meaning of "medicine." Consider, for example, a typical legal definition of medical practice:

> . . . judging the nature, character, and symptoms of disease, in determining the proper remedy for the disease, and in giving or prescribing the application of the remedy to the disease; but the system or method employed, or its efficacy, is immaterial.

Sometimes the definition is not limited to "disease" but includes references to "pain, injury, deformity, or physical condition." In one court decision, the judge said:

> In its broadest sense, the term "physician" includes anyone exerting a remedial or salutary influence.

These broad definitions make it hard to consider any clinical approach to human disorders as outside the province of medical practice. Jack Geiger made humane use of this generality when he prescribed food for hungry patients in Mississippi. But medicine's breadth has been used in attempts to block health insurance programs, fluoridating water, midwifery, and holistic health practitioners.

Some of the older statutes give nurses the dubious honor of being the only profession expressly prohibited by law from practicing medicine.

> This chapter confers no authority to practice medicine or surgery or to undertake the prevention, treatment or cure of disease, pain, injury, deformity, or mental or physical condition in violation of any provision of law.

This statute was revised in 1974 with "the legislative intent also to recognize the existence of overlapping functions between physicians and registered nurses and to permit additional sharing of functions. . . ."

By practicing many years alongside medicine so broadly and flexibly defined, nursing has existed largely at the discretion of physicans, and the definition of nursing has proven to be a vexing task. Part of the difficulty in defining nursing comes simply from the size, breadth, and variety of nursing practice. But the broad definition of medicine stands as an obstacle to a similarly broad definition of nursing, since it would inevitably overlap the definition of medicine. As nurses have become more conscious of their own roles, they have been redefining nursing more broadly without such care to avoid areas of medical practice. Yet caution is sounded in such phrases as "nursing diagnosis" and "observing signs and symptoms."

Missing from these efforts is an effort by *nurses* to define *medicine*. Nonphysicians do much of what the definition of medicine says physicians do. Moreover, there are broad areas of health maintenance mostly untouched by medicine, to say nothing of the disease conditions which are engendered by social factors. By observing what physicians actually do, as distinguished from what other health practitioners do, nurses can support a definition of their own profession. Not only is this step needed for clarity, but it also meets a principle of fairness. Physicians have been assiduous in defining the role of nurses for years; it would now be suitable for nurses to make public their reflections upon medicine. Until this work has been done, the work of nurses is likely not to be credited to them, and they may continue to be dimly discernible to outsiders, just as contributions of women to the household have often been in the background of the outsider's gaze.

The invisibility of nurses is maintained in part by cooperative interactions between nurses and physicians. One of the classical varieties of such interactions has been analyzed as the *doctor-nurse game*. It is a gender-role game translated into occupational terms. In it, the nurse makes covert suggestions for patient care to the physician. The physician cooperates by giving the order the nurse suggests without seeming to accept her suggestion. Leonard I. Stein,

who named the game, renders the following example:

Case Example

The medical resident on hospital call is awakened by telephone at 1:00 A.M., because a patient on a ward, not his own, has not been able to fall asleep. Dr. Jones answers the telephone:

"This is Dr. Jones."
"Dr. Jones, this is Miss Smith on 2W—Mrs. Brown, who learned today of her father's death, is unable to fall asleep."
"What sleeping medication has been helpful to Mrs. Brown in the past?"
"Pentobarbital mg 100 was quite effective night before last."
Dr. Jones replies with a note of authority in his voice: "Pentobarbital mg 100 before bedtime as needed for sleep; got it?"
Miss Smith ends the conversation with the tone of a grateful supplicant: "Yes, I have, and thank you very much doctor."

In this dialogue, Dr. Jones asks for and accepts Miss Smith's recommendation. At the same time, the two maintain the verbal forms of the doctor giving orders.

This act of finesse represents a skillful solution to a moral dilemma. The nurse traditionally has both the duty of patient care and the duty of following the physician's orders. How is he or she to meet both duties where physicians are likely to need advice? By these conversational gambits, the nurse can gain influence over the treatment plan by paying the price of deference. When such gambits fail, nurses commonly have the feeling of being "in the middle" since they must either give care they judge inferior or disagree openly with the physician.

Is the nurse who plays the doctor-nurse game any less autonomous than the nurse who makes direct suggestions? It could be argued that the nurse who plays the game is more autonomous than the nurse who does not. The nurse who makes open suggestions runs the risk of a rebuke or loss of influence over some physicians. (Nurses make an effort to know which physicians they can be open with and which not.) So, the more effective control may come from the nurse whose power remains invisible. Invisibility is thus not necessarily identical with powerlessness. It may then seem that the main moral difficulty with the doctor-nurse game is that it uses pretense to solve a moral dilemma. However, a mutual acceptance of pretense in a world imperfect as this one is a peccadillo. In their interaction, Miss Smith and Dr. Jones both recognize in their behavior the importance of Miss Smith's judgment and the need for her recommendation. Why then do they not admit it openly? Because they both believe that it is important to maintain Miss Smith's subordinate position. By using pretense to maintain an appearance of subordination, they give stronger expression to their belief in the system of subordination than they would had Miss Smith's deference been genuine. The game also damages the argument for nursing autonomy. For many years nursing advice about patient care has not been on the record. Thus, the evidence for the consequences of increased nursing discretion has been hidden. The advantage of invisibility is illusory and ephemeral.

A powerful argument for physician dominance is the belief that it is required by the nature of hospital work. Nurses sometimes agree that physicians should be a central source of authority. In discussion, a physician may convincingly claim,

> I am like a captain of a ship or a pilot of an airplane. Someone must have the ultimate authority for decisions here.

There is something right and something wrong about this claim. It is correct that present legal and organizational structure of health care places "ultimate authority" upon physicians for a variety of decisions. A physician facing a malpractice suit would likely not fare well who defended himself

or herself by saying, "I know what I did was contrary to standard medical practice, but I thought it better to follow the nurse's judgment in this case." The physician is expected to make decisions. But this does not mean that we *must* organize our decision-making processes in this way. For example, a small group operating by consensus could equally well take responsibility for decisions. In cases of bad judgments, the law could hold the whole group accountable.

Physicians sometimes argue that since they are *authorities on medicine,* they have a responsibility and a right to direct other health care workers. Again, they are both right and wrong. Physicians are correct when they say that they have special expertise. They are unquestionably authorities on medical diagnosis and therapy. But this kind of authority is simply the authority of expertise; it does not give them the right to order people around. The world is full of experts—engineers, philosophers, seamstresses, roofers, and so on—who do not claim that they therefore have a right or obligation to tell others what to do. Since physicians are the foremost experts on medical diagnosis and therapy, we must take what they have to say on their authority. But this is not the same thing as taking orders. As clients, we can make up our own minds how to use medical information. The physician's expertise is perfectly consistent, theoretically, with the dominance of the nurse over the physician. We only need to see the nurse as deciding upon a treatment plan and coordinating the work of the hospital after taking into account the physician's diagnosis and recommendations for therapy.

Sometimes it is argued that for reasons of efficiency there must be a single decision-maker. Where time is critical and many persons must act in close coordination, someone may be needed to orchestrate a performance, as during cardiopulmonary resuscitation or surgery. But these time-pressured activities do not generalize well. Moreover, even though a surgeon has important authority during surgery, this is consistent with the authority of a nurse over proper sterile procedure and with the authority of the patient over whether the operation should be done in the first place.

The traditional nurse-physician relationship is a hindrance to nursing autonomy. But nurses who focus most of their anger, bitterness, and frustration with hospital care on physicians reinforce medical dominance by keeping physicians in the center of the picture. Resentment can also direct attention away from the process of self-examination and analysis of the system that places physicians in power. Moreover, many physicians are aware of these problems and support nursing autonomy. There are many strains among physicians over what medicine should be, and nursing has some influence over the future directions physicians take. Nurses can also work with other health care personnel who have similar autonomy conflicts with physicians.

From Loyalty to Advocacy: A New Metaphor for Nursing

Gerald R. Winslow

Nurses are by far the largest group of health care professionals, numbering well over one million in the United States today. They are often the professionals with whom patients have the most sustained contact. And because of the profession's perceived tradition of holism and "care more than cure," nursing is often upheld as a hopeful paradigm for the future.

But the paradigm is changing. For over a decade, professional nursing has been engaged in profound revision of its ethic. The evidence is abundant: revised codes of ethics, new legal precedents, a flood of books and articles on nursing ethics, and, what may be more significant than any other attestation, a shift in the central metaphors by which nursing structures its own self-perception.

The metaphors associated with nursing are numerous. Two examples that have received considerable attention recently are the nurse as traditional-mother substitute and the nurse as professional contractor. As substitute mother, the nurse cares for sick children (patients) and follows the orders of the traditional father (the physician). As professional contractor, the nurse negotiates a plan for the care of clients (patients) and consults with other contractors (other health care professionals).

Such metaphors are not mere niceties of language. Rather, they interact with the more explicit features of nursing ethics, such as stated rules and principles, in ways that tend to be either mutually supportive or productive of change. The power of metaphors is due in part to their capacity to focus attention on some aspects of reality while concealing others. For example, thinking of the nurse as a parent may highlight certain functions, such as nurture, protection, and domination, while hiding the patient's responsibility for decisions about his or her own care. The metaphor has the ability to create a set of expectations and make some forms of behavior seem more "natural" than others. Thus, if both nurse and patient begin to use the metaphor of nurse as contractor and its associated forms of expression, such as "negotiations," they may come to expect actions in keeping with a "businesslike" relationship.

This article examines the developing changes in nursing ethics by considering two basic metaphors and the norms and virtues consonant with them. The first is nursing as military effort in the battle against disease, a metaphor that permeates many of the early discussions of nursing ethics. It is associated with virtues such as loyalty and norms such as obedience to those of "higher rank" and the maintenance of confidence in authority figures. The second metaphor is nursing as advocacy of patient rights, an essentially legal metaphor that has pervaded much of the literature on nursing ethics within the past decade. The metaphor of advocacy is associated with virtues such as courage and norms such as the defense of the patient against infringements of his or her rights. I did not select these two metaphors for analysis randomly, but, in part, because they have played a prominent role in the formation of ethics within nursing's own literature. More than most others, these metaphors have been espoused by the leaders of nursing, and have had obvious effects on nursing education and practice. Metaphors such as the nurse as surrogate parent, nun, domestic servant, or "handmaiden of the physician" have often been discussed. But these discussions have been almost entirely intended to reject such metaphors and not to uphold them as representative of nursing ideals. Indeed, such metaphors have been used most often to serve as foils for images considered more adequate. On the other hand, the military metaphor, with its language of loyalty and obedience, and the legal metaphor, with its language of advocacy and rights, have served as basic models of ideal nursing practice as proposed in nursing literature.

THE MILITARY METAPHOR

It would be surprising if professional nursing had *not* early adopted the metaphor of military service. Modern nursing is generally acknowledged to have begun with the work of Florence Nightingale, superintendent of nurses in British military hospitals during the Crimean War in the 1850s. Upon her return to England, she continued her work with the military and was instrumental in founding the British Army Medical School. Whatever else Nightingale was, she most certainly was a practitioner and proponent of strict military discipline. And

though some have criticized Nightingale's work, the idealization of the "Lady with the Lamp" continues, with rare exceptions, in professional nursing to this day. As two nurses very recently declared: "We think of ourselves as Florence Nightingale—tough, canny, powerful, autonomous, and heroic."

Not only was modern nursing born in a military setting, it also emerged at a time when medicine was appropriating the military metaphor: medicine as war. It has now become difficult to imagine a more pervasive metaphor in contemporary medicine (unless, perhaps, it is medicine as economic enterprise). Disease is the *enemy*, which threatens to *invade* the body and overwhelm its *defenses*. Medicine *combats* disease with *batteries* of tests and *arsenals* of drugs. And young staff physicians are still called house *officers*. But what about nurses?

Perhaps even more than medicine, nursing explicitly chose the military metaphor. It was used to engender a sense of purpose and to explain the training and discipline of the nurse. In the fledgling *American Journal of Nursing,* Charlotte Perry, an early leader, described the education required to produce the "nursing character." Upon entering training, wrote Perry, the student "soon learns the military aspect of life—that it is a life of toil and discipline. . . ." Such discipline, the author asserted, is part of the "ethics of nursing," and it should be evidenced in the "look, voice, speech, walk, and touch" of the trained nurse. The nurse's "whole being bristles with the effect of the military training she has undergone and the sacrifices she has been called upon to make. A professional manner is the result."

The goal of the military discipline was to produce trained nurses with many of the qualities of good soldiers. The military imagery was neither subtle nor unusual, as a passage from an early book on nursing ethics illustrates:

[An] excellent help to self devotion is the love a nurse has for the stern strife of her constant battle with sickness. . . . "The stern joy which warriors feel, in foemen worthy of their steel," should inspirit the valiant heart of the nurse as it does the heart of the brave soldier who bears long night watches, weary marches, dangerous battles, for the love of the conflict and the keen hope of victory. The soldier in a just war is upheld by this keen joy of battle. So will the nurse be spurred on to devotion by the love of conflict with disease.

The moral force of the metaphor is obvious. Nurses should be prepared for the hardships of night duty, personal danger, weary walking, and so forth. And there can be little doubt that the military metaphor supported a number of nursing behaviors. A minor example is the uniform. Early discussions of nursing ethics almost always included sections on propriety regarding dress. The uniforms of different schools had characteristic differences, reminiscent of the differences signifying various military units. And as nurses progressed up the ranks, stripes were added to their caps and insignia pins to their uniforms. The uniform was always to be worn while "on duty" but never while "off duty." And ordinary clothing was even referred to as "civilian dress."

Some traits are more important to good soldiers than the proper wearing of uniforms. More central, for example, is suitable respect for those of higher rank. Such respect is evidenced both in obedience and in various symbolic gestures of deference. Commenting on nursing ethics, Perry urged her fellow nurses to have proper respect for rank:

Carrying out the military idea, there are ranks in authority. . . . "Please" and "Thank you" are phrases which may be exchanged between those of equal rank. The military command is couched in no uncertain terms. Clear, explicit directions are given, and are received with unquestioning obedience.

Later, Perry added that there are "necessary barriers" between those of different ranks and "familiarity" should not be allowed to dismantle these barriers. The ideal of military obedience was applied often to the nurse's work with physicians. Physicians were the commanding officers. In a published lecture to nurses, one physician did not hesitate to use the military metaphor in explaining why there must be discipline in the hospital "just as in the regiment, [where] we have the captains, the lieutenants, and the sergeants. . . . Obedience to one's superiors is an essential duty of all." The author acknowledged that some of the rules are bound to "appear captious and unfair." Nevertheless, they must be obeyed. And such obedience should be not in a spirit of fear but rather in a spirit of "loyalty."

Loyalty was one of the key virtues of the ideal nurse. In the words of the Nightingale Pledge: "With loyalty will I endeavor to aid the physician in his work. . . ." Nearly every early discussion of nursing ethics includes a major section on loyalty, and the link between loyalty and the military metaphor was strong. For example, the physician just quoted reminded nurses of their obligation: "As in the hospital loyalty to her superior officers is the duty of the nurse, so in private nursing she must be loyal to the medical man who is in attendance on her patient." This sentiment is echoed in Charlotte Aikens's 1916 book on nursing ethics, a standard text for over twenty years:

Loyalty to the physician is one of the duties demanded of every nurse, not solely because the physician is her superior officer, but chiefly because the confidence of the patient in his physician is one of the important elements in the management of his illness, and nothing should be said or done that would weaken this faith or create doubts as to the character or ability or methods of the physician. . . .

What, then, did it mean for the "trained nurse" to be loyal? It meant, to be sure, faithful and self-sacrificial care of patients. But most of the discussions of loyalty were occupied more with another concern: the protection of confidence in the health care effort. Loyalty meant refusal to criticize the nurse's hospital or training school, fellow nurses, and most importantly, the physician under whom the nurse worked.

Ideally, all these loyalties should harmonize. And nurses were often reminded that being loyal to the physician by preserving the patient's confidence was the same as being loyal to the patient. As one doctor put it: "[L]oyalty to the physician means faithfulness to the patient, even if the treatment is not always in line with what [the nurse] has been taught in the training school.... Loyalty to the physician and faithfulness to the patient do not form a twofold proposition, but a single one." The reasoning was supposed to be obvious: the patient's recovery could be aided powerfully by trust in the doctor and the prescribed regimen. Worry over the doctor's competence was likely to worsen the patient's condition not only because of the wasted energy but also because of the lost power of suggestion and the patient's failure to comply with the treatment. The author of a text on nursing ethics summed up the idea:

> Confidence and skepticism are both contagious, and we know very well how important it often is for a patient's cure that he should have the attitude of faith and confidence in his physician. . . . [It] is unkind indeed to destroy a confidence which is so beneficent and comforting.

The moral power of this reasoning should not be overlooked. Nurses accepted as their solemn obligation assisting in the patient's recovery. And nurses were taught repeatedly that the "*faith* that people have in a physician is as much a healing element as is any medical treatment." Thus, even if the physician blundered, the patient's confidence should usually be maintained at all costs. To quote an early nursing text:

> If a mistake has been made in treating a patient, the patient is not the person who should

know if it can be kept from him, because the anxiety and lack of confidence that he would naturally feel might be injurious to him and retard his recovery.

But what if the nurse finally concluded that the confidence in the physician simply was not merited? It is one of the myths of a later generation that nurses of the past never questioned loyalty to the physician. In speeches, journals, and books, leading nurses complained that loyalty to the physician often was not deserved and even more often was not returned in kind. And the difficult moral dilemmas faced by nurses were usually discussed in terms of conflicts of loyalties. For example, in an earlier editorial titled "Where Does Loyalty End?" the author claimed that many letters from nurses asked essentially the same questions: "Where does the nurse's loyalty to the doctor end? And is she required to be untruthful or to practice deceit in order to uphold the reputation of the physician at her own expense or that of the patient?"

The published letters revealed the kinds of cases troubling nurses. One told how a physician inserted a catheter too far into the patient's bladder—a mistake that, according to the nurse, required surgery to correct. The nurse reported that she was blamed in order to protect the doctor's reputation. Another nurse told how a physician failed to remove a surgical sponge, causing the patient great suffering and near-death. When the problem became apparent, the nurse was unable to keep the truth from the family. Later, the doctor chastised the nurse for failure to conceal the truth. The writer claimed that "nurses are taught that they must stand by the doctor whether he is right or wrong." But, she concluded, if this means lying to the patient in order "to defend the doctor then I don't care for the profession. . . ."

Such letters (and many similar discussions in early nursing literature) indicate that conflicts of loyalties tended to focus on two main issues: truth-telling and physicians' competency. Obviously, these two were often linked. Nurses felt obliged to protect doctors even if the care seemed deficient and the truth suffered. But in many cases the truth was concealed because physicians did not want their patients to know their diagnoses. In her text on ethics, Aikens complained: "From the beginning of her career [the nurse] is impressed with the idea that . . . it is an unpardonable sin to lie to a doctor about a patient but perfectly pardonable, and frequently very desirable, to lie to a patient about his own condition." So, although lying was often roundly condemned, clearly it was often the "order" of the day. Dissonance was the inevitable result. Nurses were pleased, as Lena Dietz put it, to "enjoy a confidence such as is placed in no other women in the world. . . . The fact that they are nurses is accepted as an unquestionable guarantee of honesty." But, at times, loyalty to the "superior officers" left the guarantee more than a little tattered.

In all likelihood loyal protection of the physician often was motivated, in no small measure, by the nurse's desire for self-protection. In the early years of nursing, the goal of most graduate nurses was to leave the hospital and become "private duty nurses." The names of those available for this work were obtained from the local "registry" (kept variously by hospitals, nurses' associations, or medical associations) or simply by word of mouth. Technically, such nurses were hired directly by the patient. But in reality the attending physician was highly influential in the selection of the private nurse and, if need be, in the nurse's dismissal. Understandably, this arrangement led at times to conflicting interests and loyalties. One doctor grumbled: "Paid by the patient, or someone close to him, and not by the physician, [the nurse] sometimes seems to think that it is safest to 'stand in' with the patient, and actually obey him, rather than the physician." The patient paid the wages of the nurse, but the doctor was supposed to be in charge. The financial implications of this arrangement were not lost on nurses.

Aikens wrote: "Not infrequently, a nurse is torn between her desire to be loyal to the patient's interests, and not disloyal to the doctor, who has it in his power to turn calls in her direction, and influence other doctors to do the same, or the reverse."

Troubled at times by conflicting loyalties and worried about employment, nurses advocated a number of strategies for coping with some doctors' apparent ineptitude. Of these strategies, four stand out.

First, the nurse could faithfully obey all orders and simply assume that the doctor knew best. Isabel Robb, in the first American book on nursing ethics, wrote: "Apart from the fact that [the nurse] may be quite wrong in her opinions, her sole duty is to obey orders, and so long as she does this, she is not to be held responsible for untoward results." On this, the prevailing view, the nurse was supposed to be absolved from guilt so long as she followed orders. The doctrine of *respondeat superior* generally did offer nurses legal protection. But moral protection is not always so easily secured, hence the additional strategies.

Second, the nurse could gently question the doctor's orders. Sara Parsons suggested to her nursing colleagues that when the nurse "becomes sufficiently experienced to detect a mistake, she will, of course, call [the doctor's] attention to it by asking if her understanding of the order is correct." This approach of nurses making what amounts to recommendations in the form of questions is apparently long-lived. Recent work indicates that it is still an expected part of the "doctor-nurse game."

A third maneuver was consultation with some other authority figure. In the hospital, the nursing supervisor was the most likely candidate. But the private duty nurse had no such recourse. This difficulty led one author to propose that the nurse call the family's "religious advisor" in a confidential attempt to engineer a change of physicians.

Finally, the nurse could withdraw from the case, or refuse the physician's patients from the beginning. If the doctor was intolerably deficient, Robb counseled, the nurse could "always find some means of refusing to take charge of the nursing of his patients. . . ." Robb added, however, "[O]nce having put herself under [the doctor], let her remain loyal and carry out his orders to the letter." And in his lecture to nurses, a physician put the same point bluntly: "Better to be an honest deserter than a traitor in the camp."

Better than deserter or traitor, however, was the nurse as loyal soldier. Then the world changed. Or at least the metaphors did.

THE LEGAL METAPHOR

It would be foolish to set a date to the changing of nursing's self-image. The process has been gradual, the way tortuous. As was noted earlier, nurses' criticism of the "one-sided loyalty" expected of them dates back nearly to the beginning of the profession. And by 1932, Annie Warburton Goodrich, an acknowledged leader, could speak of nursing's "militarism, that splendid drilling in subordination of self to the machine" as a feature that the profession was attempting to "modify, if not abolish."

Even if the abolition has come slowly, some major events can be identified. For example, a significant blow to nursing's ethic of military loyalty occurred in an unlikely place in 1929. In Manila, a newly graduated nurse, Lorenza Somera, was found guilty of manslaughter, sentenced to a year in prison, and fined one thousand pesos because she followed a physician's order. The physician had mistakenly called for the preparation of cocaine injections (he meant procaine) for a tonsillectomy patient. Witnesses agreed that the physician ordered the cocaine, that Somera verified that order, and that the physician administered the injections. But the physician was acquitted and Somera found guilty because she failed to *question* the orders. The Supreme Court upheld the lower court's decision.

Nurses around the world (and especially in the United States, because the Philippine Islands were under U.S. jurisdiction) were at first stunned and then incensed. A successful protest campaign was organized, and Somera was pardoned before serving a day of her sentence. But the whole affair left an enduring impression on nurses. The doctrine of *respondeat superior* turned out to be thin security. Never again could nurses be taught simply to follow doctors' orders. Even now, over fifty years later, nursing texts still refer to *Somera* as proof of nurses' independent accountability.

But, despite *Somera* and later similar cases, the tradition of loyalty to the physician retained considerable power. This strength was illustrated by the first codes of nursing ethics. Nurses had been calling for a code of ethics before the turn of the century. But not until 1926 was the first "suggested code" for nurses proposed. By present standards this proposed code must be judged remarkably enlightened. It speaks of broad principles and, with regard to nurses' relationship to physicians, it says that "neither profession can secure complete results without the other." When the proposed code discusses loyalty, it says that "loyalty to the motive which inspires nursing should make the nurse fearless to bring to light any serious violation of the ideals herein expressed." Perhaps not surprisingly, the code failed to gain acceptance. The next attempt came in 1940. This proposal was much more similar to what later became the accepted tenets. Obligations to the physicians were central. For example, the code adopted by the American Nurses' Association (ANA) called for nurses to verify and carry out the physician's orders, sustain confidence in the physician, and report incompetency or unethical conduct "only to the proper authority." A similar code, approved by the International Council of Nurses in 1953, spelled out the nurse's obligation to follow the physician's orders "loyally" and to maintain confidence in the physician.

In the 1960s and 1970s the image of the loyal nurse began to be significantly revised.

The forces for change in health care delivery during the past two decades are too numerous and complex to analyze here. In his social history of medicine, Paul Starr describes the "stunning loss of confidence" sustained by medicine during the 1970s. The formerly unquestioned mandate of the "sovereign profession" was challenged with increased frequency. Consumerism was strengthening. And the ever-higher costs of medical care along with the perceived arrogance of many in the medical profession irritated large numbers of consumers. Moreover, medicine was viewed increasingly as a large, impersonal institution, a privileged and protected castle constantly resisting needed modifications. For nursing, a profession populated almost entirely by women, the growth of feminism also proved a highly important development. These forces, and many others, achieved sharp focus in the patients' rights movement which, in Starr's words, "went beyond traditional demands for more medical care and challenged the distribution of power and expertise." Few in the health care system seemed more eager for the challenge to succeed than nurses. It was hardly surprising, therefore, that leaders of the patients' rights movement turned to nurses in the search for "patient advocates." For example, George Annas, an attorney and author of *The Rights of Hospital Patients,* called for nurses to accept the new role of patient advocacy. It is worthy of note that Annas prefaced his appeal to nurses by explicitly attacking the military metaphor. Nurses who accepted such traditional images would be poorly equipped to be patient advocates. At times, orders would have to be challenged. But, Annas argued, properly retrained nurses had the potential to play a "key role" in patient advocacy.

In rejecting the metaphor of nurse as loyal soldier, Annas offered a replacement—the nurse as courageous advocate. The image was essentially legal. As a significant part of their retraining, for example, nurses needed "some clear understanding of the law" relating to patients' rights. "*The powers of the advocate would be precisely the legal powers of the patient.*" Acceptance of the advocacy role entailed a readiness to enter disputes. Patients needed assurance that their advocate was "someone who could be trusted to fight for their rights." Included in Annas's list of rights are those that become the standards of the patients' rights movement: the right to adequate information about proposed medical procedures, the right to refuse or accept any or all such procedures, the right to full information about prognosis and diagnosis, the right to leave the hospital, and so forth. To these canons, Annas added the right of the patient to around-the-clock access to a patients' rights advocate. Clearly, the assumptions were that patients' rights were often being threatened and someone was needed continually to contend for patients. Annas hoped that nurses would be among those to take up the fight. He was not to be disappointed—not, that is, if the volume of nursing literature promoting the role of nurse as patient advocate is a measure of success.

From the mid-1970s to the present, literally scores of nursing books and articles have appeared advocating advocacy. It is now not at all uncommon for nurses to argue, as one recently did, that "the nurse is the ideal patient advocate!" And at least two thoughtful nurse-philosophers have argued that the concept of advocacy is the most appropriate philosophical foundation for the nursing profession. After all, nurses usually have the most regular contact with the patient. And more than any other health care professionals, nurses tend to be concerned with the well-being of the *whole* patient. Moreover, nurses have a long tradition of educating patients, so it is entirely natural for nurses to accept responsibility for assuring that patients are properly informed. Finally, nurses and patients should make obvious and genuine allies since both groups have often suffered the indignities of powerlessness in the modern health care system. Who, then, could function better as a patient advocate than a nurse?

So the arguments go. And, the result has been more than a flurry of words. The metaphor has had a way of "working into life." For example, one school of nursing now requires all of its advanced students to devise and carry out an "Advocacy Project." A student might discover, for instance, that elderly patients in a nursing home feel a need for legal advice. The student would develop a plan for securing such advice and then attempt to put the plan into action.

During the 1970s, the concept of advocacy was also incorporated into nursing's codes of ethics. In its 1973 revision, the International Council of Nurses' code dropped all mention of loyal obedience to the physician's orders. Instead, the code said that the "nurse's primary responsibility is to those people who require nursing care," and the "nurse takes appropriate action to safeguard the individual when his care is endangered by a co-worker or any other person." Even more striking, in some respects, are the 1976 revisions of the ANA code. The revised code requires nurses to protect "the client" from the "incompetent, unethical, or illegal practice of any person." In the interpretive statements on this point, the code makes explicit use of the language of advocacy: "[I]n the role of client advocate, the nurse must be alert to and take appropriate action regarding any instances of incompetent, unethical, or illegal practice(s) by any member of the health care team or the health care system itself, or any action on the part of others that is prejudicial to the client's best interests." The revised ANA code is revealing not only because of this addition but also because of its subtractions. Gone are the rules obliging nurses to maintain confidence in physicians or obey their orders. In fact, "physician" does not even appear in the revised code.

Nursing's adoption of the ethic of advocacy has brought to life a whole new genre of nursing literature: the nurse-as-advocate short story. In a recent example, a nurse detailed her attempts to become an "advocate for the clients." While employed as director of nursing in a county health department, she became aware of the very poor record of maternity care at one hospital. The postpartum infection rate was nearly three times higher than the national average. And the Apgar scores of many newborns were lower than should have been expected statistically. But the hospital resented having the problems called to public attention and resisted any suggested changes. For her efforts, the nurse was ostracized by the health care community. Finally, she resigned before she could be fired. In her view, the theories about advocacy were fine, but "the problem lies in putting these theories into action." Unfortunately, this account is typical of most published nurse-as-advocate stories. They usually describe a nurse's attempt to defend a patient or group of patients against mistreatment. Most often, the endeavor fails because the system overpowers the nurse. The patient suffers or dies. The nurse gets fired or resigns in outrage. The system goes on. As literature, the stories tend to have the features of tragedy (though the flaw is in the character of the system rather than the advocate).

Of such stories, none has been more widely publicized as an example of patient advocacy than the case of Jolene Tuma. In March 1976, Tuma, a clinical instructor of nursing, was asked by a cancer patient about alternatives to chemotherapy. The patient was apprehensive about the therapy. She did not want to question her physician further, however, because he had already indicated his conviction that chemotherapy was the only acceptable treatment. Tuma knew that discussing options with the patient would be risky. In fact, she told the patient that such a conversation would not be "exactly ethical." Nevertheless, Tuma proceeded to discuss a number of alternatives about which the patient had questions, including nutritional therapy and Laetrile. The patient then decided to continue chemotherapy. But, in spite of the efforts, she died two weeks later. One of the patient's children informed the attending physician about Tuma's discussion with the patient. The physician protested to Tuma's employing college and to the Board of Nurse Examiners of Idaho. As a result, Tuma lost her job and her nursing license. The state's nursing board concluded that Tuma had interfered unethically with the physician-patient relationship. During the conflict, Tuma wrote to a nursing journal and described her predicament:

> Does the nurse have the right to assist the patient toward full and informed consent? Litigation against nurses already shows us we have the responsibility when we do not properly inform the patient. But do we have the authority to go along with this responsibility as the patient's advocate?

Tuma's case might have ended like so many other nurse-as-advocate stories except for the fact that she appealed the state board's ruling. Three years later, the Supreme Court of Idaho ruled that the nursing board had been wrong in suspending Tuma's license. It is difficult, however, to assess the extent of Tuma's victory. She did not regain her teaching position, she suffered through three years of legal appeals, and it was too late to change the outcome for the patient. Certainly, the physician and at least some of the patient's family were displeased by her actions. Still, Tuma believes that her actions were justified. She feels that her personal sacrifice has been repaid not only by the assurance that the patient's rights were defended but also by the public attention directed toward the rightful role of nurses as patient advocates. And a recently published poll of 12,500 nurses reveals that Tuma has strong support from her colleagues. Over 80 percent of the respondents agreed that a nurse who acted as Tuma did would be doing the "right thing."

The response of nurses to the Tuma case is a clear indication of the profession's changing self-perception. The new metaphor of nurse as advocate has risen to power. Indeed, if the profession's literature during the past decade is taken as primary evidence, then it can be said safely that no other symbol has so captured imagination or won acceptance within nursing as that of the advocate.

ASSESSING THE ADVOCACY METAPHOR

It is generally easier to criticize the metaphors of an earlier age than to evaluate those now regnant. But further criticism of the military metaphor is hardly in order. The nurse as loyal soldier is dead. Among nurses, mourners of the metaphor's passage are either nonexistent or well hidden. Meanwhile, the metaphor of nurse as patient advocate has nearly achieved the status of a slogan. Criticism of patient advocacy in nursing literature is virtually unknown.

But those who hope that the rise of advocacy is a positive sign of a maturing profession (and I am among them) should give careful attention to the ambiguities and potential criticisms of the advocacy role. I mention only five:

1. *The meaning of advocacy needs clarification.* Metaphors tend to be unruly. Part of their richness is their capacity to generate new and at times surprising perspectives. Thus, referring to nurses as advocates opens apparently boundless possibilities for new understandings. And, as might be expected, a survey of the nursing literature on advocacy soon reveals that the metaphor is invoked in a variety of ways, some of which may be incompatible. At times, advocacy is construed so broadly that it seems to mean something like "doing the best for the patient." But most supporters of advocacy have in mind more specific actions such as helping the patient to obtain needed health care, assuring the quality of health care, defending the patient's rights (such as the right of informed consent), serving as a liaison between the patient and health care professionals, and counseling the patient in order to alleviate fear.

In one of the few thorough discussions, Sally Gadow proposes a model of "existential" advocacy. In her view, the idea is "that individuals be *assisted* by nursing to *authentically* exercise their freedom of self-determination." Gadow argues for a type of advocacy that avoids paternalistic manipulation of the patient on the one hand and reduction of the nurse to a mere technician who is unwilling to recommend alternatives on the other hand. Whether most nurses would agree entirely with Gadow's interpretation, most discussions of the nurse as advocate would benefit both from Gadow's example of careful analysis and from her thesis. In my view, the central, moral significance of the advocacy metaphor lies in its power to shape actions intended to protect and enhance the personal autonomy of patients. Further clarification of this significance is essential if the metaphor is to rise above the level of a simple slogan.

2. *The states' nurse practice acts need revision.* Since 1971, states have been revising practice acts to allow for newly expanded nursing roles. But changes in the laws generally have not kept pace with nursing's adoption and understanding of advocacy. And, as *Tuma* illustrates, the legal limits are often unclear. What does it mean, for example, to interfere with the physician-patient relationship? Does unacceptable interference include suggesting a second medical opinion? What about recommending a change of physicians? As a result of such uncertainties, nurses who set out to be patient advocates may find themselves needing a lawyer. One nurse recently reported just such an experience. She was present when a surgical resident botched a tracheotomy and severed the patient's carotid artery. The patient bled to death. The nurse decided that for the sake of other patients she should report the resident. But the medical director cautioned the nurse not to pursue the matter unless she hired an attorney. As the nurse put it: "Dr. X kills the patient and I need a lawyer." The threat of retaliation and the loss of professional and economic security are bound to have a chilling effect on nurses' willingness to function as patient advocates.

To be effective, the calls for nurses to become patient advocates must be accompanied by political action aimed at needed revision of the states' laws. But when it comes to politics, a more apt metaphor for nursing might be that of slumbering giant. Nursing's status as the largest health care profession generally has not translated into commensurate political strength. As the profession has adopted the ethic of advocacy, however, nurses have begun to pay more attention to the need for political action. We should hope that the effect of such action will be to make patient advocacy a less dangerous activity.

3. *Patients (or their families) are often unprepared to accept the nurse as advocate.* In at least one important respect, nurses are unlike many other professionals whom the patient might engage for services. The patient is usually free to accept or reject the efforts of, say, a physician or an attorney. But in most instances the patient is not involved in the selection of his or her nurse. Thus, the nurse who functions as a patient advocate usually does so for one who has not chosen the nurse's services and who does not *expect* the nurse to serve as an advocate.

There is abundant evidence that society generally accepts a more traditional role for nurses. On this subject, nursing literature is peppered with analyses, laments, and calls for change. But old metaphors die hard. And it is a frustrating fact that vestigial images of the nurse as loyal soldier, substitute parent, assistant physician, or even handmaiden will probably remain in the minds of the public long after most nurses have rejected them. For patient advocacy to be fully successful, further attention must be given to the mechanisms for appropriate public education.

4. *Advocacy is frequently associated with controversy.* It would be a rare advocacy story that did not include a measure of discord. The patient who needs an advocate is often being mistreated by someone's action or inaction. The nurse accepts the responsibility of contending for the rights of the patient, work that may involve conflict.

Some people may thrive on controversy. Many do not. Nursing educators who share the ethic of advocacy must ask how well the nursing curriculum prepares nurses to cope with the potential conflicts. They should also ask how an ethic that makes advocacy central avoids the risk of being *unduly* contentious.

5. *As advocate, the nurse is bound to be torn, at times, by conflicting interests and loyalties.* Metaphors

can conceal as well as reveal facets of reality. The advocacy metaphor may hide the depths of potential conflicts by leaving the impression that only loyalty to the patient counts. But as Susan Thollaug, a nurse interested in patient advocacy, put it: "We can easily underestimate the difficulty of being a patient advocate, forgetting how divided our loyalties tend to be." Patients come and go; the nurse's employing institution and professional colleagues tend to remain. To admit this is not merely to say that nurses may be tempted, along with other mortals, to place self-interest ahead of professional or moral obligations. The issue is more complicated morally. Most of us would acknowledge loyalty to associates as a virtue. An unwillingness to expose a colleague's shortcomings to public view and a desire to preserve confidence in one's institution are among the characteristic features of loyalty. Deeming such loyalty a vice would be a mistake likely to produce detrimental results for both the health care providers and their patients. The obvious difficulty is deciding when the role of advocacy must take precedence over the legitimate concerns of loyalty. Borderline cases, which bring us to the edges of our ability to reason morally, are inevitable. But no ethic of advocacy could be called adequate without a place for the virtue of loyalty.

These five concerns illustrate the impediments that must be overcome if nursing's new ethic of advocacy is to be most effective. But my discussion of these difficulties is in no way intended to suggest that nursing's adoption of advocacy is meaningless, undesirable, or impossible. I believe that nursing's change of images is a hopeful sign for a developing profession. Of course, no metaphor can convey fully the complexities of the profession's moral virtues and obligations. But the season for the nurse as advocate has arrived. Nursing is still a relatively new profession, and one that has often experienced the indignities of powerlessness. The language of advocacy provides a new way to express a growing sense of professional responsibility and power. Once an ethic of "good soldiers," with loyal obedience at its core, made sense to nurses. But nursing has been moving away from a heteronomous morality of constraint and toward a more autonomous morality of cooperation. An ethic of advocacy, with a concern for rights and the virtue of courage at its center, is an important development in this process of change.

Why Physicians Need to Maintain Control of Health Care Delivery

Robert H. Bartlett

Let me reduce the case example to an issue, and propose an immediate solution. We have a sick patient, under the care of a doctor, and another informed person thinks the care is incorrect. The other informed person could be another doctor, or a physical therapist, or a consultant, or a nurse, anyone. That's the problem. In the circumstance we are to discuss today the informed person is responsible for carrying out the directions of the doctor who is in charge. That relationship might exist between an intern and a resident, a resident and a consultant, a nurse and a physician, a LPN and an RN; whoever it is, there is someone who is in charge, and there is someone who disagrees

with what is going on, but is charged with carrying out that particular aspect of care. The solution to the problem, as Mila has already pointed out, is to sit down and talk about it, discuss it. Communication virtually always resolves the problem. The only thing I would add is, it is important to resolve the problem in a way that does not interfere with what you might call the doctor/patient relationship, or the interplay between the physician who is in charge and the patient and the patient's family. Those of you who do not work in this milieu every day should know that disagreement is exceedingly uncommon in relation to the total number of medical care transactions. The vast majority of patients, doctors, and nurses work together very smoothly. So when a disagreement occurs, it is an unusual circumstance; hence we tend to focus on it.

There are three categories of disagreement. The first is a simple lack of communication. The second is a scientific disagreement over what is or is not the correct way to proceed. The third, and the thorniest, is a philosophical or ethical disagreement over a value system. A communication problem can be resolved, or at least clarified, by simple discussion. It does require the ability and the willingness to talk about the disagreement, which requires an action on the part of both parties. The scientific category is one in which the doctor has embarked on a course of action and the nurse thinks he knows a better way. (Please indulge me if I assign a gender to personal pronouns.) The third, the philosophical or ethical disagreement, simply boils down to discussion of value systems. The discussion is, "We have made different value judgments; we should pursue what I think is the correct set of values in behalf of this patient." Of course, these categories might overlap, but usually a problem can be reduced to one of these three.

Since the majority of the audience here are students who have not yet become directly involved in these interrelationships (except, perhaps, as the patient) we should define the background for potential disagreement.

First someone gets sick. He contacts a doctor saying, in essence, "Will you care for me?" The doctor makes a decision. She may say, "No, I don't do that"; or, "I suggest you find another doctor"; that is her prerogative. But as soon as the doctor says, "Take two aspirin and call me in the morning", she has initiated a contract. She is committed to undertake the care of the patient for the duration of the illness, perhaps for a lifetime. The patient and the patient's family may break the agreement at any time. Anywhere along the line they can say, "I think you are not doing the right thing. I

would like someone else to do it." The patient very rarely does, however, because of a normal human desire to believe that the doctor is doing her best in any situation. The patient proceeds on that assumption, and that is a fair assumption. The doctor is obligated, morally, legally, ethically, and for every other reason, to do what she feels is best for the patient. That doesn't necessarily mean all that is absolutely medically *possible* for the patient; sometimes the best treatment is not the maximum treatment.

That trust which is shared between the doctor and the patient is, in fact, the doctor/patient relationship. It is a first principle when considering disagreements over care. Even the cynical pessimist who takes it upon himself to generalize that doctors are money-grubbing people who don't care about patients, or that nurses are lazy and presumptuous, even such a pessimist will usually say, "But *my* doctor is a dedicated physician, or *my* nurse is a compassionate person."

This relationship lasts over a long time, in and out of the hospital, and is important to keep in mind when we get down to discussing specific facts. To disrupt that trust has far-reaching psychological implications on the patient and the family which may interfere with recovery from the disease process. A person who disagrees with the course of treatment must consider all the negative and positive factors of intervening before approaching the patient or family.

The hospital-based nurse and other paramedical people get involved in that relationship when the patient is admitted to the hospital. Although a professional dedicated nurse (or physical therapist, or resident, or whoever) is absolutely committed to the best in scientific and humanistic care of the patient, that person's responsibility is essentially to carry out the job as defined by the hospital and by the physician who is directing the care. His contract lasts for the duration of the time clock. When the shift is over, he can go home. If he doesn't like what is going on, he can take a different patient the next day. He doesn't carry a beeper. He doesn't follow the patient over months or years. He doesn't get calls from the patient's relatives or lawyer or insurance company. He has a different level of commitment.

Now those are the cold hard facts, but those of you who are nurses or physical therapists may well say, "Don't tell me that, fella, I care. I take my patients home. I spend more time with them than the doctor. I stick with them until they live or die." Of course you do. That is the mark of a professional. In practice, nurses develop incredible loyalty to their nursing unit, to patient care, to patients personally, and to the families of the patients personally. This is especially true in critical care units, where the emotional intensity is high and the care is highly specialized. The nurse derives a great sense of satisfaction from combining expert science and compassionate care. In practice, the wise doctor recognizes that and views care of the patient as a team effort. By inviting discussion, the doctor encourages everyone to act as a professional in caring for the patient. Nonetheless, the doctor is "where the buck stops." She makes the decision in an authoritarian democracy. We don't decide on treatment by a show of hands— there is one person who has to call the shots. The patient and the family have their relationship with that one person, so you can see how it comes full cycle.

That's a long-winded explanation of the background, but if you don't work in this field every day, it is important that you understand it. Some nurses and other health care professionals would not like my description of the background. It might be called paternalistic, or onesided, or insensitive. If doctors abuse the system and ignore their counterpart professionals, those adjectives do apply. But, like it or not, that is the system under which we currently operate.

Now, the topic is, what happens when a doctor and nurse disagree?

Poor communication, as I have said, is far and away the most common problem. One classic definition comes from the movie, *Cool Hand Luke,* in which Paul Newman plays the prisoner and the stubby red-necked warden of a little Southern jail says, "What we have heah is a failure to communicate." What the warden means is, "I say what to do and you do it. If you don't do it, that is a failure to communicate." This should never happen in medical practice, but it does. The physician's responsibility is to never be in the position of the warden who considers communication a strict one-way directive. The communication we are talking about has to start with the nurse, because the disagreement starts with the nurse. If the nurse doesn't say, "Why are we doing this?", the communication never begins. The doctor may not spontaneously say, "Today we are doing this because of that." Usually she will walk in, review the patient's condition, write a set of orders and say, "Here are the orders. I'll be back in six hours. Tell me if anything happens." She won't initiate a dialogue unless the person who disagrees asks, "Why are the orders the way they are?" Usually any disagreement will be resolved by just talking about it.

The second category is scientific or medical disagreement. It arises when the nurse thinks he knows (or does know) more than the doctor in a given circumstance. This occurs in highly specialized intensive care units. In a burn unit, or a neonatal intensive care unit, or an emergency room, for example, a nurse or a resident may know much more about what is going on than any particular physician who happens to have a patient in that unit at that time. Such disagreements are rarely problems, because somewhere up the line there is a physician director of that unit or that particular activity who knows at least as much as the nurse knows, and they can agree on a procedure or protocol. The prophylaxis for scientific disagreement, then, is previously prepared protocols. If serious disagreements still arise, the first step is communication. The nurse should ask the prescribing physician why she is doing what she is doing. The insecure physician might react negatively to such a question. If so, perhaps the suggestion would be better directed to the physician who is in charge of the unit. The second step, then, is going to the physician who is ultimately in charge of the case (if the disagreement is with a resident, as in the case example) and/or to the physician in charge of the unit, and moving the scientific discussion to that level. The solution to a scientific dilemma is not, certainly, to go to the family or the patient. They have a relationship established with the doctor. To say to them, "You know, your doctor has prescribed this, but it really would be much better to do this, from a scientific point of view," obviously is going to disrupt that relationship, and may have much more devastating effects than any particular choice in treatment.

For example, suppose a lady has breast cancer. She and her family and her surgeon discuss treatment. After considering the alternatives, the patient decides on the treatment her surgeon recommends, let us say, a partial mastectomy and axillary node dissection. The patient is admitted to the hospital and some well-meaning person says, "You know, the results are better with a radical mastectomy"; or "Local radiation is just as good but less disabling"; or "Don't have a node dissection, it doesn't improve your chances." All these statements are scientifically correct, but to present such opinions directly to the patient is simply meddling with the patient's psychological well-being. It *is* appropriate for a concerned nurse (or radiation therapist or social worker) to ask the surgeon why she and the patient decided on a particular course of treatment, if the question is motivated by a desire to help the patient cope with her disease.

The last category is philosophical disagreement, and this is the most difficult. For example, suppose a patient has meta-

static colon cancer. The doctor and the patient and the family talk about chemotherapy. Chemotherapy might extend the patient's life for a few months. It doesn't have any effect on ultimate survival. It has unpleasant side effects. The doctor asks, "What would you like to do?" The patient always says, "What would you suggest?" He doesn't want to make the choice, nor should he have to. He has not seen 80, or 100, or 600 people who have colon cancer and what happens to them, nor has he seen 600 people who have had chemotherapy and its complications, so he must rely on the doctor's judgment. The doctor knows that she can relate what she would suggest, what she would do for herself, and she also knows that the patient will grasp for any hope. Generally speaking the patient and family will say, "If there is something to do let's do it." Laetrile, herbs, wishful thinking, Cytoxan, all fit into the same category in that particular disease. If the doctor says to the patient, "I think you ought to just go home or take a trip to Europe and forget the chemotherapy," that is very honest and very sincere advice but it may not answer the patient's quest for support. The patient will probably find another doctor who says, "I think we ought to give you a full course of chemotherapy. It costs 60 dollars a day but it might prolong your life."

I paint that background, and ask you to imagine what might happen three months later if the patient has elected chemotherapy and has developed complications. He has a low white count, pneumonia, is bleeding from every orifice and feels miserable. He comes into the hospital, where the nurse enters the scene. The nurse may say, "This is torture. What are we doing this for?" What the nurse is really saying is, "I've made a judgment about the quality of life. I judge that this patient's quality of life isn't as good as I would like to see it, therefore, why don't you stop what you are doing?" On the other hand, suppose the patient did not elect chemotherapy, and comes into the hos-

pital three months later with metastatic cancer in the lung, jaundice, bleeding from
every orifice, and miserable. A nurse might
say, "Why isn't this patient on chemotherapy? What is going on here? I've seen patients on chemotherapy and they do fine.
I've made a judgment about this person's
quality of life and I feel it would be better if
you put him on chemotherapy. I have a big
disagreement."

Now I point out those situations as examples of philosophical value judgment dilemmas, which the people involved may perceive as scientific dilemmas. Although the
nurse says, "There has been a scientific decision here regarding chemotherapy and I
disagree with it," it is actually a value judgment; a discussion about the quality of life
or the longevity of life.

The case example falls into this category.
The nurse is saying that her opinion regarding the patient's quality of life should take
precedence. She presumes that the husband
has not been fully informed and if he were
he would favor withdrawing treatment. It is
a common but presumptuous condition of
mankind—to assume that our own value
system is more correct than others simply
because we believe in it.

The prophylaxis for this kind of dilemma
is discussion, group meetings, getting together the physicians, nurses, therapists,
residents and families involved. If we em-
bark on a course, and everybody knows the
rationale, then there is less likelihood of ar-
riving at philosophical dilemmas.

When the situation does arise, again, I
would advise the person who disagrees with
what is being done to ask the physician first.
If that does not solve the disagreement, go
to the physician who is ultimately in charge
of that particular discipline or arrange a
group meeting. If the dilemma persists, and
you think your opinion must be stated to the
family, the way to do it is to be sure that the
family knows that they can opt for another
physician. Now, the patient and family
should know that from day one. They have
been given a description of the "patient's bill
of rights" on admission to the hospital. They
have been told that they may refuse care or
change physicians, but they forget it because
of the doctor/patient relationship. Most patients don't want to think, "Maybe this doctor is not doing it right, and anytime I want
to I can shift to someone else." They think,
"This person is doing the best she can for
myself, or my wife, or whomever it happens
to be." Occasionally, it is useful to remind
the family that they can select any physician
or hospital they wish, but consider all the
consequences first.

The final solution for the professional
who has a value judgment disagreement is
to withdraw. In the case example the nurse
is urging termination of treatment because
she thinks the patient and her husband
would prefer it. Her unstated frustration is,
"This circumstance is emotionally uncomfortable for me and my staff and we have to
be at the bedside eight hours at a time."
Everyone in medicine experiences this feeling, and a decision to be excused from a case
should always be honored. In this case withdrawing is the best solution and will not
change the ultimate outcome. If the nurse
were urging more vigorous treatment (with
dialysis, or a liver transplant, for example)
which might alter the outcome, the disagreement becomes a scientific one, for
which a scientific answer could be provided.

Licensing, Certification, and the Restraint of Trade:
The Creation of Differences Among the Health Care Professions

Susan Costello, H. Tristram Engelhardt, Jr., and
Mary Ann Gardell

In the delivery of health care, there are often conflicts between health care professionals. These conflicts at times are personal conflicts stemming from individual disagreements about the interpretation of facts and moral principles. They can also be interpreted as conflicts among different health care professions with different stakes in patient care. At times, physicians seem to be in conflict with nurses while at other times both nurses and physicians seem to be in joint conflict with one of the other health professions. These conflicts lead to disputes about the proper organization of the health care team and about how to acknowledge the professional integrity of its members. In the context of such disputes, medicine, nursing, occupational therapy, and the other health care professions are often portrayed as disciplines with distinguishing and distinct foci of attention and skill, as well as special presuppositions of knowledge and ability.

In this essay we will challenge many of the background assumptions of such portrayals. We will not challenge the view that different practitioners have complementary understandings of health care that need to be taken into account in framing successful treatment plans. We will presume that health care practitioners, given their specialized training and opportunities, have contributions to make to health care, which must be acknowledged and should not be overridden by a rigid health care hierarchy. In short, we will not take issue with the important moral questions involved in coordinating individuals with different abilities and insights regarding the care of patients. What we will challenge is the fact that the character of the conflict springs from the assumption that the health care professions are conceptually distinct disciplines with special and distinct intellectual integrities of their own. We will argue that there is no greater gulf of professional integrity and distinctness between nurses and physicians than between surgeons and internists.

I. INTRODUCTION

It is tempting to hold that the health care professions are arranged in terms of special bodies of knowledge. Thus, medicine would be based on the medical sciences, nursing on the nursing sciences, and dentistry on the dental sciences. This assumption is reinforced by the fact that each profession has its own professional licensing boards and professional associations. It would seem that each profession protects society by making sure that no one practices who has not been adequately trained in a profession and by examination shown to have an acceptable level of knowledge and skills.

There are a number of reasons to be skeptical about such a portrayal. First, a closer study of the issues suggests that there are no clear conceptual lines between medical science and nursing science and the knowledge bases of the other allied health professions. For example, the claim that separate medical and nursing sciences exist as discrete bodies of knowledge represents at least in part an attempt by nursing to buttress its position in the academic world with a scientific base that corresponds to the range of practice open to nurses on the basis of licensing laws. But it is the pattern of practice opportunities (legally controlled) that has created the divisions among the health-care professions, rather than discrete conceptual borders that mark different domains of knowledge and skills. Medicine encompasses everything from psychoanalysis to surgery, from internal medicine to public health. Though physicians and surgeons were once organized as separate professions, physicians of today do everything from counseling and comforting patients to prescribing drugs, from performing surgery to engaging in preventive health care. Within the arena of health care delivery, physicians more or less provide whatever care they believe they are competent to offer, while others, such as nurses, must be sure that they do not violate the legally established prerogatives of physicians. Physicians tend to be able to encompass within their authority to practice nearly every area of health care, while podiatrists, anesthetists, occupational therapists, and physical therapists, to name a few, are given a privilege to practice in only a circumscribed area of health care.

If one inspects what takes place in any one area of medical practice, one discovers that expertise overlaps. For example, the lines between psychiatry and psychiatric nursing or between obstetrics and obstetrical nursing are arbitrary in terms of the wide range of usual psychiatric and obstetrical practice. For many of the common, routine problems in psychiatry and obstetrics, both nurses and physicians may possess a similar range of relevant skills. It is for this reason that Health Maintenance Organizations (HMOs) often hire nurse-practitioners to provide much of the routine diagnostic and other interventions performed by physicians. So, too, physicians hire physician-assistants (PAs) to perform a wide range of diagnostic and therapeutic interventions routinely undertaken by physicians. When one looks at how physicians, nurses, physician-assistants, and other allied health care practitioners engage in the practice of their professions, one finds no clear dividing lines based on differences in knowledge, skill, or scientific presuppositions. The stark difference between the health care professions derives from legal definitions of proper areas of practice that secure financial and social perquisites.

We do not intend to suggest that most physicians do not possess knowledge and

expertise not possessed by most nurses and other allied health professionals. The more extensive education and training of physicians usually puts them in a better position to make complicated diagnoses and engage in complicated, involved treatment of patients' problems and diseases. Instead, we are arguing that the professions grade one into another and overlap in ways denied by the sharp differences established by licensing laws. Licensing laws reify and compartmentalize the differences among the health care professions. They suggest false distinctions and clear lines where they do not exist. In addition, they lead, as has already been suggested, to the assumption that there exist discrete bodies of knowledge, distinct from the biomedical sciences that are needed for the practice of podiatry, respiratory therapy, psychology, or nursing.

This point is made by the history of competition between optometrists and ophthalmologists. In many states both are allowed to fit patients for glasses and diagnose ophthalmological diseases, though optometrists are not allowed to prescribe medications.[1] These limitations reach so far as to prevent optometrists from using drugs to dilate the eye. Whether an optometrist can use such drugs varies from state to state and is the result of gaining one of the traditional perquisites of ophthalmologists and of overcoming one of the traditional, legally-established restraints of trade. When one compares the skill and knowledge bases of ophthalmologists and optometrists, one discovers that they both share a wide range of diagnostic and therapeutic abilities.[2] They differ insofar as ophthalmologists are trained in the treatment of systemic medical diseases, e.g., diabetes, and in the surgical treatment of ophthalmological disorders. They differ also in terms of the fees charged by optometrists versus ophthalmologists.

Similar conflicts have occurred elsewhere. The dispute between dentists and denturists, the individuals who manufacture dentures, also provides a good example.

For most of this century, the dental profession has successfully staved off efforts by denturists to legalize their independent practice. State dental practice acts have defined the making of dentures as part of the practice of dentistry, allowing the laboratory fabrication of dentures by non-dentists *only on direct order from and through dentists*. Denturism has therefore been illegal; and the dental profession has campaigned vigorously to keep it that way.[3]

Evidence has accumulated that cooperation between dentists and denturists saves costs while meeting the needs of the public.[4] One finds, in short, a geography of the health care professions defined as much by legal restraints as by differences in skill and knowledge. Moreover, one finds that this geography is for the most part established to the benefit of the dominant health care professions.

II. NURSING AS AN INDEPENDENT PROFESSION AND THE DEVELOPMENT OF PHYSICIAN-ASSISTANTS

Until the early 1960s, nurses functioned in great measure as physician-extenders. In the nontechnical sense, they were physician-assistants. This fact was reflected in early codes of nursing ethics, which stated, for example, that "[t]he nurse is under an obligation to carry out the physician's orders intelligently and loyally and to refuse to participate in unethical procedures."[5] This statement suggests that, though there may be moral disagreements, the physician is the presumed expert regarding patient care. This relationship between physician and nurse (and other health care professions) stems from the circumstance that not only is the physician *an* authority regarding proper health care, but the physician is *in* authority, an authority which is secured by licensure laws. Earlier statements in nursing ethics indicated an even more subordinate role for nurses: "The head-nurse and her staff should stand to receive the visiting physi-

cian, and from the moment of his entrance until his departure, the attending nurses should show themselves alert, attentive, and courteous, like soldiers on duty."[6] The relationship of physicians to other health care professionals was hierarchical with the physician at the top of the hierarchy.

Changes in the position of nurses came with both the development of women's liberation movements, as well as the attempt by nurses to gain an independent professional and academic status. The nursing profession, predominantly represented by women, found itself under dual pressures to develop into a profession that would not be subservient to another profession and in particular to secure independence from the predominantly male profession of medicine. As a result, organized nursing rejected the American Medical Association's offer that the nursing profession include under its aegis the profession of physician-assistants.[7] Such a rejection is understandable given the view of nursing as an independent, academically recognized profession. The aspirations of academia and the status offered by independent licensure made the role of physician-assistant seem less than inviting. Academic nursing prepared nurses to be administrators and coordinators of patient care rather than individuals engaged simply in carrying out medically prescribed care. Many of the traditional day-to-day nursing activities came to be undertaken by practical or licensed vocational nurses, leading to a major gap between professional nursing and those involved in day-to-day nursing care, which often has significant similarities with the undertakings of physician-assistants, both in the strict and the general sense of the term.

The result of all this has been the emergence of a new identity for nurses, which is bound to the academy. Nurses with masters and doctoral degrees now oversee and coordinate health care. They possess a status denied to nurses in the past. "It has been *the universities* which have endowed nursing with a respectability, freedom, and responsibility which embody the self-esteem that nursing has not been able to enjoy in the hospital sickroom despite a century of service."[8] Nurses, in short, have come to see themselves as an independent profession with an integrity that makes them more than simply physician-extenders or physician-assistants. This perception of independence exists despite the overlapping areas of competence among the professions of nurses, physician-assistants, and physicians.

> In contrasting the performance characteristics of PAs and Nurse-practitioners [NPs], most researchers have found that there are many more similarities than differences between these providers. Clinically, they are often used interchangeably. But one important difference is the stance of NPs toward dependent practice. This factor emanates from the philosophical foundations of the respective parent professions: NPs in nursing and PAs in medicine. NPs, since they are part of nursing, insist that they practice collaboratively with physicians, which means that they seek physician consultation whenever they (the NP) deem it appropriate. Some NPs are practicing independently under the aegis of state nurse practice acts. PAs, on the other hand, openly profess dependent practice and legally must always work under physician supervision. This dichotomy holds interesting implications for the future of non-physicians, particularly in light of the forecasted physician excess.[9]

Because of nursing's rejection of the explicit role of being a "physician-assistant," a new profession sprang into life to fill an economic and service environment which nursing could have filled. In response, new laws for certification and control of physician-assistants were fashioned and a new allied health profession took shape.

The history of the development of the profession of physician-assistant underscores the force of professional rivalries and social organizations in the fashioning of the present-day geography of the health care professions. It supports the conclusion that the distinctions among the health care professions are derived as much from political and sociological forces as from underlying conceptual or skill-based differences. Not only do licensing laws shape the boundaries between the professions, but so do academic aspirations and professional orientations. These rivalries also have costs. Evidence is accumulating that PAs can be more effectively used if restrictive medical practice statutes are eased.[10] The point bears on the lifting of restrictions on the activities of non-physician, health care professionals in general.[11] "More Americans will come to realize what certain policymakers and health services researchers already know: that it is possible for trained non-physicians to provide a wide range of medical care tasks safely, effectively, and at a lower cost."[12] Artificial boundaries and constraints may simply not allow people to practice where their skills best enable them.

III. LICENSING VERSUS CERTIFICATION

Given this history of professional jealousies and struggles, one might wonder what the relations of the professions would be like, had licensing laws not allowed particular professions to establish their boundaries firmly. One must observe that there have been periods in the history of health care when little licensing in fact existed.[13] Patients were required to make their own estimation of the expertise of their health care providers on the basis of their own experience and the practitioner's academic credentials, professional associations, and reputation. Even now, patients have few better means of verifying the competency of a particular health care practitioner. In fact, given the character of modern American life, it is no longer the norm to have a long-term relationship with one's primary health care provider, let alone the growing number of specialists that may be involved in providing care. At present, in addition to the traditional criteria, patients rely on the fact that a health care professional has passed a licensing exam (perhaps 20 to 30 years ago) and on whether a practitioner has privileges to admit patients at a hospital or at a hospital of distinction. Were licensing laws to be abandoned and replaced by a process of certification (such exams would certify a particular level of competence without any of the legal implications of licensing exams), patients could still rely on the judgment of peers with regard to whether a practitioner should have admitting privileges or be employed. Additionally, the health care practitioner who had recently passed a certification examination would likely make that known to the patient. Rather than being able to rely on having passed a licensing exam years in the past, practitioners would be under pressure to submit themselves periodically to certification exams in order to remain credible with their patients. It is important to note the extent to which perceived competence and liability laws control the areas in which individuals offer health care in the absence of restrictions due to licensure. For example, in states where the license to practice medicine allows physicians to practice dentistry, few, if any, do without the special training offered by schools of dentistry. Without any formal constraints of licensing, limits are set in terms of skill and ability.

Under a system of certification rather than licensure, patients would be free, should they wish, to seek the care of practitioners who had not been certified recently, just as patients are now free to forego standard medical care and instead seek treatment from various medical cultists or from faith healers. On the other hand, all health care practitioners would be free to take the certification exam usually taken by physicians. It is very likely that some nurse practitioners or physician assistants working in various areas of health care possess knowledge equivalent to that required by many family practitioners in their day-to-day practice of medicine and could in such contexts perform some of the functions of physicians, including writing prescriptions. Much would remain the same: patients

would continue to seek out competent health professionals as they do today. What would be different would be the pressure to take and pass certification exams that assess current knowledge in order to demonstrate competence, since there would not be the authority of licensure to fall back on. In addition, there would be fewer artificial barriers to actual competence and promising innovation.

These suggestions are radical in that they challenge the traditional justification of licensure laws.

Underlying the principle of licensure is the assumption that the public cannot judge whether practitioners of the licensed professions are qualified and competent. In theory, therefore, licensure assures that only those properly qualified are allowed to practice. Licensure requirements . . . prohibit the carrying out of specified tasks by anyone except those expressly licensed to do so. Unlicensed practice can result in criminal prosecution and is punishable by fines, imprisonment, or both.[14]

The foregoing suggests that licensure is not necessarily a better protection than certification. Even if licensure provides some protection, one must decide whether the protection is worth the costs it entails. The abolishment of licensure would, however, involve costs to the dominant health care professions (e.g., physicians and dentists). "An obvious result of licensure is to provide security—in effect a monopoly market position—for members of each licensed profession."[15] This monopoly is not without costs. Michael Pertschuk, who has served as a Federal Trade Commissioner, has argued that: "Study after study has shown that licensing results in higher direct costs to consumers. Indirect costs, in the form of foregone innovation and experimentation, are higher still."[16] This point has been made more generally by Milton Friedman.

I am myself persuaded that licensure has reduced both the quantity and quality of medical practice; that it has reduced the opportunities available to people who would like to be physicians, forcing them to pursue occupations they regard as less attractive; that it has forced the public to pay more for less satisfactory medical service, and that it has retarded technological development both in medicine itself and in the organization of medical practice. I conclude that licensure should be eliminated as a requirement for the practice of medicine.[17]

What Friedman says about medicine can be generalized to the health care professions as a whole.

Even if one does not actually intend to replace licensure with certification, the contemplation of this change can be heuristic. It reminds us of the extent to which the boundaries between the professions are created as compromises fashioned by various professional groups interested in a legally sanctioned restraint of trade. Beyond that, as the last three paragraphs have indicated, certification has the possibility of offering a more efficient means of assessing the expertise of health care professionals and maintaining that expertise throughout the careers of those in practice.[18] Finally, the more one is skeptical of the moral authority of the state to impose artificial restraints on trade counter to the abilities and interests of individuals, the more one will be inclined to conclude that the very process of licensing is itself morally suspect.[19]

IV. SUMMARY

This article supports an unorthodox approach to the problems associated with the traditional medical hierarchy. Much has been made of the fact that health care is dominated by physicians in circumstances where allied health professionals have difficulties in contributing their expertise or maintaining their personal integrity. The image against which much criticism has been directed has been that of the physician as the captain of the ship, a phrase drawn from the law.[20] The response to the model of the health care team based on the physician as the captain of the ship has been the attempt to fashion a team medicine in which each of the team players belongs to an independent profession governed by independent licensing bodies and often presuming an independent body of science and a niche in academia.[21] There are limits to such a refashioning within the constraints of contemporary licensure laws. The physician is the captain of the ship in part because the physician has a near unlimited license to engage in health care endeavors, and all other members of the team have limited licenses. The physicians' controlling position is thus secure by law. Moreover, that position can financially advantage those who work as physician extenders, as physician assistants, insofar as they work under the direction of the physician and the authority of the physician's license. In contrast, we have offered a basis for collegiality, based on the recognition that stark differences in expertise, knowledge, and abilities do not exist between the professions. Rather, they grade one into the other so that often, in fact, nurses may know more about one area of medicine than a physician with whom they find themselves working (consider the young intern just beginning on a hospital service). The current understanding of the relations among the health care professions is based on strategic misperception.

1. *Bluebook of Optometrists* (Chicago: Professional Press, 1980).

2. D. W. Worther, "The Ophthalmologic-Optometric Interface," *Trans. Am. Acad. Ophth. Otolaryn.*, 83 (1) (1971), 155–163; American Optometric Association, *Optometry and the Nation's Health: Recommendations for the Implementation of Congress's National Health Priorities* (Washington, D.C.: American Optometric Association, 1982), pp. 15, 22–26.

3. Herbert M. Hazelkorn and Tom Christoffel, "Denturism's Challenge to the Licensure System," *Journal of Public Health Policy*, 5 (1984), 105.

4. Ibid., p. 113.

5. *International Code of Nursing Ethics*, adopted by the International Council of Nurses (July 1953), #7.

6. Isabel Hampton Robb, *Nursing Ethics for Hospi-*

tal and Private Use, 2nd ed. (Cleveland: Kieckert, 1928), p. 173.

7. A. M. Sadler, Jr., B. L. Sadler, and A. A. Bliss (eds.), *The Physician's Assistant: Today and Tomorrow* (New Haven: Yale University Press, 1972), p. 44.

8. Ibid., p. 63.

9. J. F. Cawley and A. S. Golden, "Nonphysicians in the United States: Manpower Policy in Primary Care," *Journal of Public Health Policy,* 4 (1983), 76.

10. James F. Cawley, "The Physician-Assistant Profession: Current Status and Future Trends," *Journal of Public Health Policy,* 6 (1985), 78–99.

11. James F. Cawley and Archie S. Golden, "Nonphysicians in the United States: Manpower Policy in Primary Care," *Journal of Public Health Policy,* 4 (1983), 69–88.

12. Cawley, "The Physician-Assistant Profession," p. 96.

13. Richard H. Shryock, *Medical Licensing in America: 1650–1965* (Baltimore: Johns Hopkins Press, 1967). Paul Starr has also reexamined this history. See especially pp. 40–45, 57–58, 102–117, and 118–119 in *The Social Transformation of American Medicine* (New York: Basic Books, 1982).

14. Hazelkorn and Christoffel, "Denturism's Challenge," p. 105.

15. Ibid., p. 105.

16. Michael Pertschuk, "Professional Licensure," *Connecticut Medicine,* 43 (1979), 794.

17. Milton Friedman, *Capitalism and Freedom* (Chicago: University of Illinois Press, 1962), p. 158.

18. Charles H. Baron, "Licensure of Health Care Professionals: The Consumer's Case for Abolition," *American Journal of Law and Medicine,* 9 (1983), 335–356.

19. H. T. Engelhardt, Jr., *The Foundations of Bioethics* (New York: Oxford University Press, 1986).

20. McConnel v. Williams, 361 PA. 355, 65 A. 2nd 243 (1959).

21. George J. Agich (ed.), *Responsibility in Health Care* (Dordrecht, Holland: D. Reidel Publishing Company, 1982).

The Virtues of a Physician

Hippocrates

The dignity of a physician requires that he should look healthy, and as plump as nature intended him to be; for the common crowd consider those who are not of this excellent bodily condition to be unable to take care of others. Then he must be clean in person, well dressed, and anointed with sweet-smelling unguents that are not in any way suspicious. This, in fact, is pleasing to patients. The prudent man must also be careful of certain moral considerations—not only to be silent, but also of a great regularity of life, since thereby his reputation will be greatly enhanced; he must be a gentleman in character, and being this he must be grave and kind to all. For an over-forward obtrusiveness is despised, even though it may be very useful. Let him look to the liberty of action that is his; for when the same things are rarely presented to the same persons there is content. In appearance, let him be of a serious but not harsh countenance; for harshness is taken to mean arrogance and unkindness, while a man of uncontrolled laughter and excessive gaiety is considered vulgar, and vulgarity especially must be avoided. In every social relation he will be fair, for fairness must be of great service. The intimacy also between physician and patient is close. Patients in fact put themselves into the hands of their physician, and at every moment he meets women, maidens and possessions very precious indeed. So towards all these self-control must be used. Such then should the physician be, both in body and in soul.

The Enlightenment Picture of the Virtuous Physician

Dietrich von Engelhardt

There is hardly any profession that should be so dependent on virtues, so constructed upon duties, as medicine, according to the belief of the physicians of the Enlightenment. In no situation outside of the military is the mortality so high as it is with physicians. The basis of the medical profession is seen in a philosophical and religious bearing. From this basis true knowledge is shown to be a connection between experience and reason, as well as true action to be a connection between mercy and justice.

Stahl and Storch include, at the beginning of the century, the virtues of piety (*pietas*), erudition (*eruditio*), preparedness (*alacritas, promptitudo*), industry (*diligentia*), courtesy (*humanitas*), patience (*patientia*), courage (*animositas*), wisdom (*prudentia*), truth (*veritas*). A little later Hoffman characterizes humility, generosity, friendliness, and discretion as the essential virtues of the physician. Ploucquet, towards the end of the century, considers patience, philanthropy, sympathy, mildness, modesty, courtesy, industry, and the love of order to be the chief virtues of the physician. They had to be present in the proper measure, but in any case their lack would have worse consequences than their exaggeration. Their foundation is the love of God and neighbour; nevertheless, their psychological basis is not infrequently ascribed to a sanguine-melancholic temperament. Collisions between the different virtues should not be avoided. Intrinsic and extrinsic qualities and virtues are differentiated, divided into physical and spiritual; according to Stark the beautiful figure of the physician is extrinsically physical, his cultural education is extrinsically spiritual. Definitions of virtues are also always definitions of vices, which have been dealt with in essays by physicians. General characteristics of the physician were described by, among others, Stahl and Storch (1728), Hoffman (1738), Unzer (1759), Rübel (1758 and 1766), Mai (1777), Stark (1748), Hildebrandt (1795), and Ploucquet (1797).

The physician's knowledge should include the natural sciences and the clinical subjects, should be extended to philosophy, particularly logic, and even the belles artes; the command of Latin and Greek and some modern languages is necessary, as well as the possession of historical information. Self-knowledge is also essential, and finally a broadening of the consciousness through travel. Reason, knowledge, observation, memory, and discernment are all necessary for the physician. Zimmermann's article "Von der Erfahrung in der Arzneykunst" (1763/64) is the convincing representation of these theoretical qualities. In principle the physician should not overestimate his knowledge and not consider himself above other men: "A physician should be neither courtly nor proud, but rather modest." Erudition should also have an essential fundament in religious belief, without constantly endangering the virtues of the physician.

The quarrel with superstition and charlatanism/chicanery occupies much space, because they are dangerous for the physician as well as for patients; they are the reason medicine is scorned; they are the focus for the battle of physicians from the Enlightenment to the transition into the scientific 19th century. The path of pure experience is dangerous and deceptive, it is chosen by the most varying swindlers, by shepherds, farriers, executioners, pharmacists, surgeons, barber-surgeons, monks, old women, and mid-wives: "the world succumbs to the burden of kind-hearted murderers of life," as Stark complains, who considers no science and art so susceptible to bungling as medical science is. In contrast, the right path is achieved by means of a scientific education at a university and through one's own personal experience; only this will lead to a practice based on reason and make Rousseau's criticism of medicine superfluous. Uncertainty and limitations in medicine must also be recognized; the physician cannot set himself up against time and nature, and he displays his moderation (*temperantia*) when he respects these limits.

The physician also displays the virtues of moderation and modesty in his politeness and self-control, in his refined speech, restrained gestures and mimicry, and his decent clothing. He should avoid gluttony, drunkenness, gambling, and scandalous speech, but also not fall into the habits of greed, pettiness, and taciturnity. The generosity of the 16th and 17th centuries collides with the stronger stress on modesty in the 18th century. The appearance of the physician is also rewritten as 'gallant'; the physician should not be a misanthrope or eccentric, but rather as a social being be in command of the forms of society and possess conduite (the virtue of management and discretion). The physician should be serious about his profession; care, industry, and work receive in medicine the highest esteem: "Intelligence demands that we be hard-working and industrious and abhor indolence." In his practice the physician may not be too hesitant nor too foolhardy; he must adhere to the correct middle way here also, which enables him to act but restrains him from dangerous experiments.

The physician is guided by humanity and helpfulness. As a person he also confronts the person in the sick individual and not only the diseased organs or a defective machine. The author Longolius wrote in 1727 that the physician will "have a steadfast attention to both body and soul in all bodily accidents of a living person." The physician wants to please the patient and tries to win his trust. The sick person must be convinced not only of the knowledge but also of the moral character of the physician. Eminent physicians are said to have healed through trust alone. Faith and hope grow with trust. The physician, however, should defend himself in contrast against, as Ploucquet expressed it, "irritable, impolite behavior of the sick person and his family" if he doesn't want to lower himself to the level of the fawning charlatan. He should not return insults for insults but rather, with Wedekind, recognize the background and show understanding: "thus our passion diminishes, and sympathy with the erring brother takes its

place." What the physician has to suffer in annoyances and resistance is treated in a comprehensive manner in the 'Medicus afflictus' of 1715.

The moral education of the sick person is expected from the physician, he is supposed to influence the sick person, to bring him to a correct attitude concerning the sickness, and to guide him to a sensible manner of living. The physician is responsible for the dietetics of the sick person as well as the healthy person. In the 18th century dietetics still meant the area of the ancient *sex res non naturales* (the six non naturals), the association of air and light, movement and rest, waking and sleeping, eating and drinking, retentions and excretions, passions and emotions. Beginning with the suggestions of Stahl and Hoffman, the range of dietetic writings extends from the impulses of Unzer to Mai's 'medical lenten sermons' (1793/94) and Hufeland's 'art of lengthening human life' (1796). For physicians looking at the plethora of examples, it appears indubitable that virtues lengthen life but vices shorten it: "Virtues promote health and restore it. Vices are evil and unhealthy."

The physician must take care that the patient follows the therapy and also be ready to help when problems arise, as when the patient cannot swallow the medicine because of nausea. The physician's assistance will always be improved by means of psychological knowledge about the power of the passions and their place between physiology and ethics. Vogel relates the *sçavoir faire* of the physician to the association with patients and colleagues; the psychological perspective is dominant, factual knowledge and morality come into play in "the best talents and virtues." The readiness of the physician to help has its basis in love of God and man and basically knows no boundaries. The physician according to Rübel will assist "both day and night his suffering neighbor with help and advice, without regard for class or wealth or person." Views about the attitude towards terminal illnesses differ. Because of the dangers for the physician, Hoffman demands that he "refrain from visiting during the time the patient is dying." The Hippocratic warning is often refused, as it is with Ploucquet: "one still dedicates his strivings even to the dying, should that take place, in order to diminish the sum of his suffering." The physician may not cause the death, whether by his own action or by giving the sick person adequate means. According to the opinion of the physicians, active euthanasia contradicts the explanation of the highest and holiest duty of medicine, to preserve life. Hufeland fears the greatest dangers for the future if this duty is violated: "If the line should be crossed, then there are *no longer any boundaries.*" Faith and morals forbid any active euthanasia, they also demand the highest care with experiments on humans, which should properly be conducted by the physician on himself, according to Hufeland.

The practice of medicine is bound by the duty of confidentiality; Rübel calls discretion the "virtue of not saying the truth when it avails nothing but instead brings certain ill"; discretion refers to the relationship to the sick person as well as to the environment. Physician and priest are bound by the same constraints concerning the knowledge of the secrets of their fellowmen. What the sick person trusts to the physicians, according to Wedekind, should be a "holy deposit" in his breast and may not be related to other persons. The physician should be both discrete and open at the same time; the duty of explanation as well as the duty of silence leads him. Conflicts and compromises cannot be avoided. The obligation of confidentiality ends where other persons come into danger. Prostitution and abortion also place limits on the duty of confidentiality. The physician should explain but at the same time recognize the freedom of the patient, which can lead to a rejection of the truth and even to self-destruction. Illusion and deception touch the physician's understanding of explanation. The physician must conscientiously test to see what the sick person

can bear. Impending death should be concealed from the sick person. According to Stark the patient "often becomes unhappy in body and soul" if this possibility is withheld from him. If the sick person cannot bear this information, the family members at least should be told, even if in many cases restraint should be employed. Other physicians support the belief that patients should be left in ignorance. Hoffman suggests in the case of dangerous diseases, offering a judgment "from which questioners will not know what they should conclude." In general, the physician is reminded that the prognosis of death cannot be given with an absolute certainty regarding time, but a high risk can be indicated.

The physician may expect payment for his services to the sick person. At the same time the payment for him occupies a position of tension relating to the high, nearly holy meaning of medicine, which should not be expressed in financial terms. A Christian physician should practice his profession out of compassion and humanity, not because of the monetary recompense. Therefore, it will also be expected and demanded of the physician that he accept no fee from the poverty-stricken. The physician should not increase his income by means of unnecessary visits; he should base his fee on the ability of the patient to pay.

The physician of the 18th century had to recognize the class differences. Poor and genteel, worldly and spiritual people want to be treated differently. Particularly important are circumspection, discretion, versatility, and stability. The upper class is known for its sensitivity. "Pains are much more suitable for common people," as Rübel reports from his practice and considers this opinion to be correct; people from the lower class simply have a "strong, thick, and less sensitive skin." Stark recommends reserve with genteel persons, which is not the case with simple people, who are themselves so shy and deficient in vocabulary. The duty of confidentiality in respect to the genteel can also be suspended when inferiors contract syphilis; according to Stahl and Storch their superiors should be informed of the disease, since they would experience a greater aversion and disgust than normal people and could even become ill from unexpectedly seeing this disease.

Women and children also demand special attention. They serve as pitfalls for every physician: "There are two difficult things in medicine, namely, to cure children and pregnant women," as Hoffman says. The physician should always stand fast and let himself be led by his knowledge and his humanity—unperturbed by fashion and pity, recompense, flattery and force, never going in contradiction to his conscience. Behind all superficial differences he should always see the person who needs his sympathy and his aid, or in the words of Stark: "He deports himself as a person among other persons, treats them as persons, loves them as his brothers, serves them willingly as friend, tries to ease their fates." The physician in this sense recognizes no differences of class, no differences of religion, sex, or education; for him all men are the same.

During the 18th century the relationship with one's colleagues is repeatedly the theme of discussions concerning virtue and duty. Contentiousness and rivalry among physicians were not without reason a beloved object of the literature and satire of that period. Politeness and respect, camaraderie and aid should characterize the relationships among physicians. Particular attention is paid to the relationship to the surgeon, the apothecary, and the midwife. According to Stieglitz, art and the sick person should compel the physician "to keep the honor of the consultation intact." At the same time the physician is compelled to point out fraudulent colleagues; truth comes before collegiality. If an accusation cannot be proved against a colleague, then he should not be openly scolded or criticized in front of a patient. A discussion of the case at the sick-bed is definitely improper. The physician should seek the advice of his colleagues and always be ready to acknowledge

his uncertainty and mistakes. A consultation protects one from incorrect diagnoses and doubtful therapies, but it serves not only the patient, but also the progress of medicine. Contact with surgeons is necessary on both sides. The physician should not prescribe more medication than is really necessary, so as not to increase the earnings of the apothecary. The prescriptions should conform to the norm. Prescribing by apothecaries should, as far as possible, be circumscribed, since according to Rübel they do not possess "the necessary conditions to practice prudently."

The qualities and capabilities of the physician influence his relationship to the environment of the patient, to other groups in society, and to the state. The duties of silence and explanation reach out from the patient into the life of other people. If the prognosis cannot be related to the patient, the physician must decide whether to tell family or friends. In the case of contagious diseases there is a collision of the duty of confidentiality with the general duty of the physician to protect healthy persons from contagion. According to Rübel, the physician must act cautiously and deliberately, "because not only the welfare of one person but often the health and happiness of an entire republic are dependent on it." There are many points of contact when one considers the clergy. An agreement concerning the care of the soul and particularly the sacrament must be reached. The consequences of the sacrament can in no way be seen as negative only, physicians can even observe emotional calming, which is said to lead to healing. But discretion and circumspection are also repeatedly demanded from priests and ministers, since they have to recognize on principle their lack of medical knowledge. But physicians consider the care of the soul to be important, since sickness and health are always bound with psychic aspects. Dietetics cannot be separated from religion. Finally, the physician must produce expert opinion for the state. On the one hand, careful observation of the facts and rational conclusions are demanded of the physician; on the other hand, he must recognize the limits of medicine and relinquish the final decision; according to Hoffman, he must relinquish "the reasons for decision to the scholars of jurisprudence." The physi-

cian must continually be careful when instructing the public, so that individual honor will be offended as little as possible and society can feel secure as far as possible and not be unnecessarily alarmed.

How Virtues Become Vices

Alasdair MacIntyre

I now want to consider if and how far traditional medical virtues have turned to vices. I want to begin by considering three social presuppositions of the practice of the traditional medical virtues. The first is technological. The practice of medicine has for most of its history been carried on in societies where human life is immensely fragile and vulnerable and where the technical means to safeguard it have been very limited. High infantile mortality rates, low expectations of life for surviving adults, extremely limited predictive powers in framing prognoses, all underlie the ordering of medical priorities embodied in different versions of the Hippocratic Oath. Medicine would have been a quite different form of social practice if *either* life was to be preserved only if health could be restored *or* life was to be preserved only if grave pain and suffering were to be avoided *or* health was to be restored only if in so doing pain and suffering were not to be increased. That ordering of medical priorities which places a supreme value on life is made more intelligible by considering the social background which it originally presupposed.

A second presupposition of the practice of the traditional medical virtues was the existence of a shared and socially established morality. The physician could assume that the patients' attitudes towards life and death would be roughly the same as his own, and vice versa. Hence the patient in putting him or herself into the hands of his or her physi-

cian could feel that he or she was not relinquishing his or her moral autonomy.

A third presupposition of the practice of the traditional medical virtues was that the activities of the physician or surgeon took place within a given social order, but were not themselves able to shape or be responsible for shaping that order. Medicine could not be understood in its traditional perspective as a social practice competing with other social practices for scarce resources and offering debatable criteria for their distribution.

None of these presuppositions is now warranted and it is social change that has destroyed their warranty. Technological change has made of the preservation of human life a very different issue. Moral change has made of the trust which the patient ought to express in the physician a very different issue. Changes in the scale and the cost of medical care as well as political and economic change in society at large have made the distribution of medical care into a very different issue. In each case what was a virtue has become at best problematic, at worst a vice. Consider once more the ways in which virtues become vices.

There is first the case where the effects of a practice change so that the character of the relevant actions change. This is what happened to the medical practice of making the preservation of human life an overriding goal. Consider two kinds of change. It is now the case, as it used not to be, that this goal involves the systematic preservation of the old long after they can function as genuine human beings. It is now the case, as it used not to be, that this goal involves systematically increasing the proportion of hopelessly crippled infants and helplessly decaying old people to healthy adults and children. Any agent who knowingly participates in producing such effects systematically, as many physicians do, does great harm and wrong. What was a virtue has become a vice, but not an unproblematic vice. For the physician now finds himself in a tragic dilemma. Consider the case of recently born crippled infants where heroic efforts may preserve *either* a needless bundle of distorted and suffering nerves and tissues *or*—sometimes against all probable calculation—a human child, physically imperfect but with real potential, perhaps even a Helen Keller. (I consider the case of infants rather than of the old, because the collapse of the extended family has left most of us with a deep inability even to approach the problems of the old, an inability institutionalized in the way we, as a society as well as individuals, treat them.) Any rule which relieves the physician of the burden of extending suffering uselessly imposes on him the burden of taking innocent life wantonly; and no rule would be worst of all.

What has happened to place physicians in this dilemma is the result of the coincidence of two distinct histories of moral change. In the society at large our fragmented inheritance has resulted in abandoning us to a secular, liberal pluralism which leaves us resourceless in the face of moral problems; in the history of medical practice a change in its presuppositions has rendered what was virtuous vicious and what was unproblematic problematic. Thus parts of medical practice became morally problematic precisely at a time when we have minimal resources for the solution of moral problems.

As with the first of the three traditional medical values, so also with the other two. The trust which defines the relationship of patient to physician was based upon the presupposition of a shared, established morality. The physician could have a reasonable assurance that his patients' beliefs about suffering, death and human dignity were much the same as his own; the patient could have a reasonable assurance that his beliefs would be respected. But in a liberal, pluralist moral culture the patient knows, not only that the traditional basis for this assurance is now missing, but that the physician has no special resources for the solution of the moral problems which arise in the course of a relationship to a patient. The parent of a helplessly ill child or a helplessly old person cannot know that the physician wills their good, because they cannot know what his conception of good is. Once again the physician is in a tragic dilemma: the invitation to trust which was once a sign of virtue becomes a sign of something else. The change in the structure of roleplaying has changed the quality of the actions. A virtue has in a characteristic way become a vice. But the physician has no easy way out. The whole nature of medical care is almost unimaginable without a context of mutual trust; to simply abandon that mutual trust, because it is no longer warranted, would be destructive. To try to maintain it in its traditional forms is equally dangerous.

It is of course in this situation that market relations become significantly obtrusive in medical practice. Differential treatment is offered for differential reward; access to medical care is radically unequal. Here again the physician is, like everyone else, in a situation which he cannot escape. The demands of social justice and the demands of the physician for autonomy are in radical conflict. If members of the medical profession choose certain forms of specialization in research or in practice, they thereby determine the availability of certain patterns of medical care. If the freedom of physicians is safeguarded, the equal rights of citizens will be flouted. So the autonomy of the medical profession becomes a social vice, while the freedom of the physician remains an important value. Once again we have a dilemma which is almost intolerable.

3.   THE ROLE OF THE PATIENT AND THE PROVIDER

The Patient as Decision-Maker

President's Commission

What are the values that ought to guide decisionmaking in the provider-patient relationship or by which the success of a particular interaction can be judged? The Commission finds two to be central: promotion of a patient's well-being and respect for a patient's self-determination. Before turning to the components of informed consent (Part Two of this Report) or the means for promoting its achievement (Part Three), these central values will be explored. They are in many ways compatible, but their potential for conflict in actual practice must be recognized.

SERVING THE PATIENT'S WELL-BEING

Therapeutic interventions are intended first and foremost to improve a patient's health. In most circumstances, people agree in a general way on what "improved health" means. Restoration of normal functioning (such as the repair of a fractured limb) and avoidance of untimely death (such as might occur without the use of antibiotics to control life-threatening infections in otherwise healthy persons) are obvious examples. Health care is, in turn, usually a means of promoting patients' well-being. The connection between a particular health care decision and an individual's well-being is not perfect, however. First, the definition of health can be quite controversial: does wrinkled skin or uncommonly short stature constitute impaired health, such that surgical repair or growth hormone is appropriate? Even more substantial variation can be found in ranking the importance of health with other goals in an individual's life. For some, health is a paramount value; for others—citizens who volunteer in time of war, nurses who care for patients with contagious diseases, hang-glider enthusiasts who risk life and limb—a different goal sometimes has primacy.

Absence of Objective Medical Criteria

Even the most mundane case—in which there is little if any disagreement that some intervention will promote health—may well have no objective medical criteria that specify a single best way to achieve the goal. A fractured limb can be repaired in a number of ways; a life-threatening infection can be treated with a variety of antibiotics; mild diabetes is subject to control by diet, by injectable natural insulin, or by oral synthetic insulin substitutes. Health care professionals often reflect their own value preferences when they favor one alternative over another; many are matters of choice, dictated neither by biomedical principles or data nor by a single, agreed-upon professional standard.

In the Commission's survey it was clear that professionals recognize this fact: physicians maintained that decisional authority between them and their patients should depend on the nature of the decision at hand. Thus, for example, whether a pregnant woman over 35 should have amniocentesis was viewed as largely a patient's decision, whereas the decision of which antibiotic to use for strep throat was seen as primarily up to the doctor. Furthermore, on the question of whether to continue aggressive treatment for a cancer patient with metastases in whom such treatment had already failed, two-thirds of the physicians felt it was not a scientific, medical decision, but one that turned principally on personal values. And the same proportion felt the decision should be made jointly (which 64% of the doctors claimed it usually was).

Patient's Reasonable Subjective Preferences

Determining what constitutes health and how it is best promoted also requires knowledge of patients' subjective preferences. In pursuit of the other goals and interests besides health that society deems legitimate, patients may prefer one type of medical intervention to another, may opt for no treatment at all, or may even request some treatment when a practitioner would prefer to follow a more conservative course that involved, at least for the moment, no medical intervention. For example, a slipped disc may be treated surgically or with medications and bed rest. Which treatment is better can be unclear, even to a physician. A patient may prefer surgery because, despite its greater risks, in the past that individual has spent considerable time in bed and become demoralized and depressed. A person with an injured knee, when told that surgery has about a 30% chance of reducing pain but almost no chance of eliminating it entirely, may prefer to leave the condition untreated. And a baseball pitcher with persistent inflammation of the elbow may prefer to take cortisone on a continuing basis even though the doctor suggests that a new position on the team would eliminate the inflammation permanently. In each case the goals and interests of particular patients incline them in different directions not only as to how, but even as to whether, treatment should proceed.

Given these two considerations—the frequent absence of objective medical criteria and the legitimate subjective preferences of patients—ascertaining whether a health care intervention will, if successful, promote a patient's well-being is a matter of individual judgment. Societies that respect personal freedom usually reach such decisions by leaving the judgment to the person involved.

The Boundaries of Health Care

This does not mean, however, that well-being and self-determination are really just two terms for the same value. For example, when an individual (such as a newborn baby) is unable to express a choice, the value that guides health care decisionmaking is the promotion of well-being—not necessarily an easy task but also certainly not merely a disguised form of self-determination.

Moreover, the promotion of well-being is an important value even in decisions about patients who can speak for themselves because the boundaries of the interventions that health professionals present for consideration are set by the concept of well-being. Through societal expectations and the traditions of the professions, health care providers are committed to helping patients and to avoiding harm. Thus, the well-being principle circumscribes the range of alternatives offered to patients: informed consent does not mean that patients can insist upon anything they might want. Rather, it is a choice among medically accepted and available options, all of which are believed to have some possibility of promoting the patient's welfare, including always the option of no further medical interventions, even when that would not be viewed as preferable by the health care providers.

In sum, promotion of patient well-being provides the primary warrant for health care. But, as indicated, well-being is not a concrete concept that has a single definition or that is solely within the competency of health care providers to define. Shared decisionmaking requires that a practitioner seek not only to understand each patient's needs and develop reasonable alternatives to meet those needs but also to present the alternatives in a way that enables patients to choose one they prefer. To participate in this process, patients must engage in a dialogue with the practitioner and make their views on well-being clear. The majority of physicians (56%) and the public (64%) surveyed by the Commission felt that increasing the patient's role in medical decisionmaking would improve the quality of health care.

Since well-being can be defined only within each individual's experience, it is in most circumstances congruent to self-determination, to which the Report now turns.

RESPECTING SELF-DETERMINATION

Self-determination (sometimes termed "autonomy") is an individual's exercise of the capacity to form, revise, and pursue personal plans for life. Although it clearly has a much broader application, the relevance of self-determination in health care decisions seems undeniable. A basic reason to honor an individual's choices about health care has already emerged in this Report: under most circumstances the outcome that will best promote the person's well-being rests on a subjective judgment about the individual. This can be termed the instrumental value of self-determination.

More is involved in respect for self-determination than just the belief that each person knows what's best for him- or herself, however. Even if it could be shown that an expert (or a computer) could do the job better, the worth of the individual, as acknowledged in Western ethical traditions and especially in Anglo-American law, provides an independent—and more important—ground for recognizing self-determination as a basic principle in human relations, particularly when matters as important as those raised by health care are at stake. This noninstrumental aspect can be termed the intrinsic value of self-determination.

Intrinsic Value of Self-Determination

The value of self-determination readily emerges if one considers what is lost in its absence. If a physician selects a treatment alternative that satisfies a patient's individual values and goals rather than allowing the patient to choose, the absence of self-determination has not interfered with the promotion of the patient's well-being. But unless the patient has requested this course of conduct, the individual will not have been shown proper respect as a person nor provided with adequate protection against arbitrary, albeit often well-meaning, domination by others. Self-determination can thus be seen as both a shield and a sword.

Freedom from interference. Self-determination as a shield is valued for the freedom from outside control it is intended to provide. It manifests the wish to be an instrument of one's own and "not of other men's acts of will." In the context of health care, self-determination overrides practitioner-determination even if providers were able to demonstrate that they could (generally or in a specific instance) accurately assess the treatment an informed patient would choose. To permit action on the basis of a professional's assessment rather than on a patient's choice would deprive the patient of the freedom not to be forced to do something—whether or not that person would agree with the choice. Moreover, denying self-determination in this way risks generating the frustration people feel when their desires are ignored or countermanded.

The potential for dissatisfaction in this regard is great. In the Commission's survey, 72% of the public said that they would prefer to make decisions jointly with their physicians after treatment alternatives have been explained. In contrast, 88% of the physicians believe that patients want doctors to choose for them the best alternative. Despite these differences in perception, only 7% of the public reports dissatisfaction with their doctors' respect for their treatment preferences.

Creative self-agency. As a sword, self-determination manifests the value that Western culture places on each person having the freedom to be a creator—"a subject, not an object." Within the broad framework of personal characteristics fixed during the years of development, individuals define their own particular values. In these ways, individuals are capable of creating their own character and of taking responsibility for the kind of person they are. Respect for self-determination thus promotes personal integration within a chosen life-style.

This is an especially important goal to be

nourished regarding health care. If it is not fostered regarding such personal matters, it may not arise generally regarding public matters. The sense of personal responsibility for decisionmaking is one of the wellsprings of a democracy. Similarly, when people feel little real power over their lives—in the economy, in political affairs, or even in their daily interactions with other people and institutions—it is not surprising that they are passive in encounters with health care professionals.

If people have been able to form their own values and goals, are free from manipulation, and are aware of information relevant to the decision at hand, the final aspect of self-determination is simply the awareness that the choice is their own to make. Although the reasons for a choice cannot always be defined, decisions are still autonomous if they reflect someone's own purposes rather than external causes unrelated to the person's "self." Consequently, the Commission's concept of health care decisionmaking includes informing patients of alternative courses of treatment and of the reasoning behind all recommendations. Self-determination involves more than choice; it also requires knowledge.

Types of Autonomy and Their Significance

Bruce Miller

FOUR SENSES OF AUTONOMY

If the concept of autonomy is clarified, we will have a more rigorous understanding of what the right to autonomy is and what it means to respect that right, thus illuminating the problems regarding refusals of lifesaving treatment. At the first level of analysis it is enough to say that autonomy is self-determination, that the right to autonomy is the right to make one's own choices, and that respect for autonomy is the obligation not to interfere with the choice of another and to treat another as a being capable of choosing. This is helpful, but the concept has more than one meaning. There are at least four senses of the concept as it is used in medical ethics: autonomy as free action, autonomy as authenticity, autonomy as effective deliberation, and autonomy as moral reflection.

Autonomy as Free Action

Autonomy as free action means an action that is voluntary and intentional. An action is voluntary if it is not the result of coercion, duress, or undue influence. An action is intentional if it is the conscious object of the actor. To submit oneself, or refuse to submit oneself, to medical treatment is an action. If a patient wishes to be treated and submits to treatment, that action is intentional. If a patient wishes not to be treated and refuses treatment, that too is an intentional action. A treatment may be a free action by the physician and yet the patient's action is not free. If the meningitis victim is restrained and medication administered against his wishes, the patient has not voluntarily submitted to treatment. If the patient agrees to pain relief medication, but is given an antibiotic without his knowledge, the patient voluntarily submitted to treatment, but it was not a free action because he did not intend to receive an antibiotic. The doctrine of consent, as it was before the law gave us the doctrine of *informed* consent, required that permission be obtained from a patient and that the patient be told what treatment would be given; this maintains the right to autonomy as free action. Permission to treat makes the treatment voluntary and knowledge of what treatment will be given makes it intentional.

Autonomy as Authenticity

Autonomy as authenticity means that an action is consistent with the person's attitudes, values, dispositions, and life plans. Roughly, the person is acting in character. Our inchoate notion of authenticity is revealed in comments like, "He's not himself today" or "She's not the Jane Smith I know." For an action to be labeled "inauthentic" it has to be unusual or unexpected, relatively important in itself or its consequences, and have no apparent or proffered explanation. An action is unusual for a given actor if it is different from what the actor almost always (or always) does in the circumstances, as in, "He always flies to Chicago, but this time he took the train." If an action is not of the sort that a person either usually does or does not do, for example, something more like getting married than drinking coffee, it can still be a surprise to those who know the person. "What! Goerge got married?"

A person's dispositions, values, and plans can be known, and particular actions can then be seen as not in conformity with them. If the action is not of serious import, concern about its authenticity is inappropriate. To ask of a person who customarily drinks beer, "Are you *sure* you want to drink wine?" is to make much of very little. If an explanation for the unusual or unexpected behavior is apparent, or given by the actor, that usually cuts off concern. If no explanation appears on the face of things or if one is given that is unconvincing, then it is appropriate to wonder if the action is really one that the person wants to take. Often we will look for disturbances in the person's life that might account for the inauthenticity.

It will not always be possible to label an action authentic or inauthentic, even where much is known about a person's attitudes, values, and life plans. On the one hand, a given disposition may not be sufficiently specific to judge that it would motivate a particular action. A generous person need not contribute to every cause to merit that attribute. If a person's financial generosity is known to extend to a wide range of liberal political causes, not making a contribution to a given liberal candidate for political office may be inauthentic. On the other hand, most people have dispositions that conflict in some situations; an interest in and commitment to scientific research will conflict with fear of invasive procedures when such an individual considers being a subject in medical research. Many questions about this sense of autonomy cannot be explored here, for example, whether there can be authentic conversions in a person's values and life plans.

Autonomy as Effective Deliberation

Autonomy as effective deliberation means action taken where a person believed that he or she was in a situation calling for a decision, was aware of the alternatives and the consequences of the alternatives, evaluated both, and chose an action based on that evaluation. Effective deliberation is of course a matter of degree; one can be more or less aware and take more or less care in making decisions. Effective deliberation is distinct from authenticity and free action. A person's action can be voluntary and intentional and not result from effective deliberation, as when one acts impulsively. Further, a person who has a rigid pattern of life acts authentically when he or she does the things we have all come to expect, but without effective deliberation. In medicine, there is no effective deliberation if a patient believes that the physician makes all the decisions. The doctrine of *informed* consent, which requires that the patient be informed of the risks and benefits of the proposed treatment and its alternatives, protects the right to autonomy when autonomy is conceived as effective deliberation.

Gerald Dworkin has shown that an effective deliberation must be more than an apparently coherent thought process. A person who does not wear automobile seat belts may not know that wearing seat belts significantly reduces the chances of death and serious injury. Deliberation without this knowledge can be logically coherent and lead to a decision not to wear seat belts. Alternatively, a person may know the dangers of not wearing seat belts, but maintain that the inconvenience of wearing them outweighs the reduced risk of serious injury or death. Both deliberations are noneffective: the first because it proceeds on ignorance of a crucial piece of information; the second because it assigns a nonrational weighting to alternatives.

It is not always possible to separate the factual and evaluative errors in a noneffective deliberation. A patient may refuse treatment because of its pain and inconvenience, for example, kidney dialysis, and choose to run the risk of serious illness and death. To say that such a patient has the relevant knowledge, if all alternatives and their likely consequences have been explained, but made a nonrational assignment of priorities, is much too simple. A more accurate characterization may be that the patient fails to appreciate certain aspects of the alternatives. The patient may be cognitively aware of the pain and inconvenience of the treatment, but because he or she has not experienced them, may believe that they will be worse than they really are. If the patient has begun dialysis, assessment of the pain and inconvenience may not take into account the possibilities of adapting to them or reducing them by adjustments in the treatment.

In order to avoid conflating effective deliberation with reaching a decision acceptable to the physician, the following must be kept in mind: first, the knowledge a patient needs to decide whether to accept or refuse treatment is not equivalent to a physician's knowledge of alternative treatments and their consequences; second, what makes a weighting nonrational is not that it is different from the physician's weighting, but either that the weighting is inconsistent with other values that the patient holds or that there is good evidence that the patient will not persist in the weighting; third, lack of appreciation of aspects of the alternatives is most likely when the patient has not fully experienced them. In some situations there will be overlap between determinations of authenticity and effective deliberation. This does not undercut the distinctions between the senses of autonomy; rather it shows the complexity of the concept.

Autonomy as Moral Reflection

Autonomy as moral reflection means acceptance of the moral values one acts on. The values can be those one was dealt in the socialization process, or they can differ in small or large measure. In any case, one has reflected on these values and now accepts them as one's own. This sense of autonomy is deepest and most demanding when it is conceived as reflection on one's complete sets of values, attitudes, and life plans. It requires rigorous self-analysis, awareness of alternative set of values, commitment to a method for assessing them, and an ability to put them in place. Occasional, or piecemeal, moral reflection is less demanding and more common. It can be brought about by a particular moral problem and only requires reflection on the values and plans relevant to the problem. Autonomy as moral reflection is distinguished from effective deliberation, for one can do the latter without questioning the values on which one bases the choice in a deliberation. Reflection on one's values may be occasioned by deliberation on a particular problem, so in some cases it may be difficult to sort out reflection on one's values and plans from deliberation using one's values and plans. Moral reflection can be related to authenticity by regarding the former as determining what sort of person one will be and in comparison to which one's actions can be judged as authentic or inauthentic.

A BRIDGE BETWEEN PATERNALISM AND AUTONOMY

This discussion shows that there is no single sense of autonomy and that whether to respect a refusal of treatment requires a determination of what sense of autonomy is satisfied by a patient's refusal. It also shows that there need not be a sharp conflict between autonomy and medical judgment. Jackson and Youngner argue that preoccupation with patient autonomy and the right to die with dignity pose a "threat to sound decision making and the total (medical, social and ethical) basis for the 'optional' decision." Sound decision making need not run counter to patient autonomy; it can involve a judgment that the patient's refusal of treatment is not autonomous in the appropriate sense. What sense of autonomy is required to respect a particular refusal of treatment is a complex question.

If a refusal of lifesaving treatment is not a free action, that is, is coerced or not intentional, then there can be no obligation to respect an autonomous refusal. It is important to note that if the action is not a free action then it makes no sense to assert *or* deny that the action was autonomous in any of the other senses. A coerced action cannot be one that was chosen in accord with the person's character and life plan, nor one that was chosen after effective deliberation, nor one that was chosen in accord with moral standards that the person has reflected upon. The point is the same if the action is not intentional. When a refusal of treatment is not autonomous in the sense of free action, the physician is obliged to see that the coercion is removed or that the person understands what he or she is doing. Is it possible that coercion cannot be removed or that the action cannot be made intentional? This could be the case with an incompetent patient, not externally coerced, but subject to an internal compulsion, or who lacked the capacity to understand his or her situation. For incompetent patients the question of honoring refusals of treatment does not arise; it is replaced by the issue of who should make decisions for incompetent patients, an issue beyond the scope of this article.

If a refusal of treatment is a free action but there is reason to believe that it is not authentic or not the result of effective deliberation, then the physician is obliged to assist the patient to effectively deliberate and reach an authentic decision. It is not required that everyone bring about, make possible, or encourage another to act authentically and/or as a result of effective deliberation. Whether such an obligation exists depends on at least two factors: the nature of the relationship between the two persons and how serious or significant the action is for the actor and others. Compare the relationships of strangers, mere acquaintances, and buyer and seller on the one hand, with those of close friends, spouses, parent and child, physician and patient, or lawyer and client. To borrow, and somewhat extend, a legal term, the latter are fiduciary relationships; a close friend, parent, spouse, physician, or lawyer cannot treat the other person in the relationship at arms' length, but has an obligation to protect and advance the interests of the other. For example, we have no obligation to advise a mere acquaintance against making an extravagant and unnecessary purchase, though it is an option we have so long as we do not go so far as to interfere in someone else's business. The situation is different for a good friend, a close relative, or an attorney who is retained to give financial advice.

The other factor, the seriousness of the action, is relevant to medical and nonmedical contexts. If, inspired by the lure of a "macho" image, my brother impulsively decides to buy yet another expensive automobile, how I respond will depend on how it will affect him and his dependents. If a patient refuses a treatment that is elective in the sense that it might benefit him if done but will not have adverse consequences if not done, a physician can accept such a refusal even though it is believed not to be the result of effective deliberation. On the other hand, if the refusal of treatment has serious consequences for the patient, the physician has the obligation to at least attempt to get the patient to make a decision that is authentic and the result of effective deliberation. For the patient with meningitis who refuses treatment the consequences of the refusal are indeed serious, but there is no opportunity to determine whether the decision is authentic and the result of effective deliberation and, if not, to encourage and make possible an authentic and effectively deliberated decision.

A crucial issue is whether a refusal of lifesaving treatment that is autonomous in all four senses can be justifiably overridden by medical judgment. It will help here to compare the Jehovah's Witness case with a somewhat fanciful expansion of the meningitis case. The former's refusal is autonomous in three of the four senses and could be judged autonomous in the sense of moral reflection if we knew more about the patient's acceptance of his faith and had a clear idea of the criteria for moral reflection. Though the beliefs of Jehovah's Witnesses are not widely shared, and many regard as absurd the belief that accepting a blood transfusion is prohibited by biblical injunction, their faith has a fair degree of social acceptance. Witnesses are not regarded as lunatics. This is an important factor in the recognition of their right to refuse transfusion. Suppose that the meningitis victim had a personal set of beliefs that forbid the use of drugs, that after years of reflection he came to the view that it was wrong to corrupt the purity of the body with foreign substances. Suppose that he acts on this belief consistently in his diet and medical care, that he has carefully thought about the fact

that refusal in this circumstance may well lead to death, but he is willing to run that risk because his belief is strong. This case is parallel to the Jehovah's Witness case; the principal difference is that there is no large, organized group of individuals who share the belief and have promulgated and maintained it over time. One reaction is to regard the patient as mentally incompetent, with the central evidence being the patient's solitary stance on a belief that requires an easily avoided death. An alternative approach is to not regard the patient as incompetent, but to see treatment as justified paternalism. Finally, the position could be that a refusal of lifesaving treatment that is fully autonomous, that is, in all four senses, must be respected even though the belief on which it is founded is eccentric and not socially accepted. Which approach to take would require an analysis of incompetence, a definition of paternalism, and an examination of when it is justified. Defining paternalism as an interference with autonomy in one or more of the four senses might be an illuminating approach.

The conflict between the right of the patient to autonomy and the physician's medical judgment can be bridged if the concept of autonomy is given a more thorough analysis than it is usually accorded in discussions of the problem of refusal of lifesaving treatment. In some cases where medical judgment appears to override autonomy, the four senses of autonomy have not been taken into account.

Medical Ethics' Assault Upon Medical Values

Colleen D. Clements and Roger C. Sider

The vigorous resurgence of interest in medical ethics during the past two decades has created a large and controversial literature. Especially problematic is the application of medical ethicists' views in clinical settings. Physicians are decidedly ambivalent about

these ethical contributions; on the one hand, they are eagerly searching for assistance in resolving the increasingly complex ethical dilemmas now so common in medical practice. On the other hand, they are wary and disappointed because, until now, the ethicists' contributions have been of dubious value. In this article we will argue that the currently dominant school in medical ethics, that of a patient autonomy-rights model based in rationalist philosophy and liberal political theory, has been used to subvert values intrinsic to medicine, that it has done so without adequately establishing the merits of its case, and that the unfortunate result has been the attempted replacement of the historic medical value system by an ill-fitting alternative.

THE AUTONOMY PRINCIPLE

Because of the hegemony of the rationalist school, any contemporary discussion of medical ethics must begin with an analysis of the concept of autonomy. In everyday use, "autonomy" is a pervasively familiar term. Written into our Constitution (the inalienable right to life, liberty, and the pursuit of happiness) and embodied in our political and legal process (one man, one vote; the right to privacy and bodily integrity), it rings true to all those who have been reared in a democracy. Moreover, the enshrinement of the capacity for freely chosen self-determination in our mental health norms makes autonomy a desirable goal for personal well-being.

In this context, then, it may seem invidious to question such a venerable value. Yet philosophic autonomy must be critiqued, for it goes far beyond the political liberty principle or even the autonomous ego function of which psychiatrists speak. In philosophy, autonomy derives from Kant's attempt to ground ethics upon logical necessity, thereby securing for it universal, unchanging, and absolutely certain status. These goals were achieved at enormous cost, however, in that Kant was forced to separate morality from motivation (no act was good if it was motivated by desire or wish) and cut morality off from the world of experience (no attention could be paid to the consequences of a contemplated act in evaluating its ethical merits). The autonomy principle

is, then, a way of separating ethical thinking from the empirical world and placing it in the rationalist realm of metaethics.

Such a philosophical move has enormous practical consequences. In emptying ethics of content, it makes adherence to procedural matters the test of ethical validity. Philosophic autonomy is based entirely in formal logic and, because it is without content, it reduces to tautology. In clinical medicine this state of affairs becomes concrete in resting the ethical justification for medical care decisions entirely upon the autonomous patient's informed consent. The nature of the patient's reasons are immaterial and the consequences of his decisions practically irrelevant.

Medicine, of course, is not concerned with such formal searches for certainty and has little experience with this style of thinking. Physicians deal inductively in the empirical world of experience and work daily with probabilities, risks, benefits, and harms. Moreover, their ethical orientation is based upon medical health norms that define what interventions are in the patient's interest. But in the autonomy model, such thinking and acting is paternalistic, hence, prima facie, unethical.

It was not long, of course, before it became clear that the application of autonomy ethics to medicine was highly problematic. But such was the appeal of the formalist system that ethicists readily rose to the challenge. Currently, two approaches are apparent. One argues that autonomy properly understood overrides other values. The other questions the primacy of autonomy.

EXPANDING THE DEFINITION
TO MAINTAIN PRIMACY

The first alternative attempts to apply autonomy ethics by developing workable definitions for it in the context of medical practice, although this approach tends to assume the ethical justification for the autonomy principle. To make autonomy a workable principle in medicine, Miller develops four components of its definition that he believes make it an adequate principle for most medical cases. He specifically rejects concerns for the patient's best interest or the patient's condition as ethical grounds on a par with autonomy and argues that if preserving life is allowed to override patient autonomy, the ethical principle of autonomy is forfeited. Since his ethical views require that a proper ethical decision be based on a choice *by* the patient, and not *about* the patient, the autonomy principle cannot be ethically replaced by such considerations as the patient's good. To deal with difficult cases, he suggests autonomy must involve free action, authenticity, effective deliberation, and moral reflection. Authenticity requires coherence of the patient's behavior. Unfortunately, physicians know too well that a nonpsychotic, nondemented (thus legally competent) diabetic patient with a serious character disorder could satisfy all four components of this definition. Such a patient acts as voluntarily and intentionally as any of us; the acts can be consistent with values and character over time; the patient can be quite aware of alternatives and consequences (sometimes painfully aware) and thought processes may not be disordered, although weighting of alternatives may not agree with our weighting. There are, Miller admits, no adequate standards for what constitutes adequate moral reflection. Such patients can meet Miller's criteria, then, and yet be dangerously noncompliant or even self-mutilating, and it seems to the physician peculiar to view their self-destructive choices as ethical. What is missing is precisely any way to appeal to a norm of best interest, health, well-functioning, and development; yet these are the norms that constitute the value base of medicine and verify medical judgment. These medical norms are teleonomic and are therefore valuational in an empirical-normative sense that argues against any fact-value dichotomy. They are not subjective, but they are of course hypothetical (probable) and not categorical (necessary), which the rationalistic

tradition in ethics wishes to define away as not meeting the formalist criteria for ethics.

WHAT HAPPENED TO MEDICAL NORMS?

Somewhere along the way to autonomy ethics, medical norms have been forgotten. And this fundamental oversight is the reason we believe autonomy ethics is inappropriate. Medicine is a profession grounded upon a conviction that norms are discoverable and, when known, give direction to ethical treatment. The simple case of hypertension or hypotension is illustrative. Only by first knowing the norm for blood pressure is the physician able to begin the ethical decision-making process. Moreover, contrary to much current thought, it is the degree of the individual patient's deviation from these norms and not appeal to an autonomy principle that determines the strength of the ethical justification for intervention. Hence, a mildly elevated blood pressure reading calls for a leisurely investigation and discussion of treatment options with the patient. But the presence of hypertensive crisis or hypotensive shock requires emergency intervention. This normative orientation runs so deeply in medical practice that it structures the entire history taking, physical examination, laboratory investigation, and treatment sequence. All data sought are those that can be meaningfully evaluated in the context of known health norms. Where norms are not available, data are irrelevant. And all treatment prescribed is given with reference to these norms. There is no medical practice nor is there any biological science without appeal to biological norms, and there is no ethics appropriate to medicine or to the human organism that is not derivative from such norms. This rootedness of traditional medical values in such a naturalistic ethic is best illustrated in the Table.

TOWARD A CLINICAL ETHIC

We want to make clear that the move from naturalistic ethics to formalist ethics has never been justified sufficiently. Although

The Relationship of Naturalistic Ethics to Medical Values

Natural Law–Naturalistic Ethics	Traditional Medical Values
1. There are empirical norms, standards for well-functioning, adaptive and maladapted responses to the environment, which provide the content and "if-then" forms of ethics.	1. There are scientifically determinable norms, homeostatic mechanisms, and physiological and psychological criteria for functioning of the human organism.
2. "Is" and "ought" are intimately connected. There is no fact-value dichotomy, and certainly no analytic-empirical dichotomy.	2. What "ought" to be done in case management is determined by the "facts" of the situation.
3. There is an obligation to maintain the norm, achieve well-functioning, correct malfunctioning, and adapt if we wish to survive.	3. The physician's role is to restore as far as possible normal functioning.
4. This obligation falls on us as human beings.	4. This role obligation holds in the physician-patient relationship.
5. Doing what is the best in terms of these norms for ourselves and those we are responsibile for is the proper application of ethics.	5. This role obligation involves caring for the patient, in some cases even over his objection, for his best interest.

the philosophic criticism of an absolutist objective ethic is sound, the baby was thrown out with the bathwater. A long tradition from Aristotle through Thomas Hobbes through the Darwinians through William James and John Dewey and now Konrad Lorenz and the sociobiologist E. O. Wilson is not to be discounted easily. And as has become painfully clear to physicians working in medical ethics, the current ethical theories have major problems. Utilitarian and cost-benefit theories confuse the individual patient's choice of good with the choice of the good of efficiency and fairness for the whole medical system, in addition to having numerous technical problems. Patients' rights theories cannot identify the source of these rights. Respect theories based on Kantian ethics create a human nature that is only rational and is divided from the world of experience. These theories, incorporated in a formalist system, leave us with a desocialized, disembodied patient, devoid of affect, or a nonhuman unit in a cost-benefit decision theory assessment, and a confused physician accused of paternalism when he presses for his patient's medical good. Trained to be accountable and partially re-

sponsible for that good, his ethical dilemma is clear. It is also unnecessary.

If we believe the universe is worthwhile, then ethics is possible, ethics that includes the value of decision making as *one* valuable adaptive process but not the only one and certainly not a formal precondition, and that can give a basis for saying that some decisions are wrong. Medicine assumes an affirmation of the world, but then, all ethics does too as stated in an article forthcoming in *Suicide and Life Threatening Behavior*. Excepting suicidal patients, patients visiting a physician's office are also part of this affirming community. And since they are, physicians can construct if . . . then, directive medical advice and care and, in fact, are obliged to if they wish to act within their medical value system. To abandon the value of the patient's well-functioning or best interest in the name of the autonomy system is to abandon the value system of medicine and to act unethically in the physician-patient relationship. Direction and coercion are not, of course, the same. But ethics is primarily a matter of advice and education, not social control by power.

So we suggest that the vocabulary of autonomy, informed consent, and paternalism is an inappropriate lexicon for medical ethics. Although each term is concerned with legitimate issues in medical care, none is primary. Moreover, by casting the debate in such terms, merits of alternative systems are obscured. Choice is one biological function. It is not the only one, or always the overriding one, or a function having preferred formal status.

For an ethic appropriate to medicine, we require a clinical ethic, an ethic that begins with an understanding of the status of norms in medicine. Such norms are discoverable, and, while they are refined by consensus, they are not merely social constructs or subjective choices or minor factors in total well-being. On the contrary, they are basic biological bottom lines. Moreover, within the clinical context, ethical conduct is determined by the facts of the situation, understood in terms of these norms. Thus, clinical ethics is concerned primarily with adaptation, function, and best interest. But such an ethic is also modest. It claims no infallible principles by which treatment decisions may be made. Moreover, medical norms merely set limits on the range of what is adaptive. They do not prescribe with precision. And it is only as normative function is reestablished that the patient as decision maker is truly free to take control of his life.

So although clinical ethics recognizes the importance of respecting the patient's wishes and the value of sharing relevant information with the patient, these issues take their rightful place within a larger context. Such a posture is not arrogant or Godlike paternalism. More consistent with the Hippocratic tradition, it insists that autonomy or formalism is an inappropriate foundation upon which to build medical ethics. When we as physicians act in the best interests of our patients, we do so with the firm hope that, when the time comes, our physicians will do the same for us.

Beyond Medical Paternalism and Patient Autonomy: A Model of Physician Conscience for the Physician-Patient Relationship

David C. Thomasma

The doctor-patient relationship is a rich and varied partnership. No single characterization can properly do justice to this relationship, given the complexity of professional styles, patient expectations and values, and contexts in which the relationship is established. In this essay, I propose a model of the physician's conscience as a means for resolving the difficult problems that arise when a physician adopts either a model of medical paternalism or patient autonomy for the relationship. The core of traditional medicine has been paternalism; the purpose of offering a model of the physician's conscience is to modify this core.

My exploration of this topic is prompted by my dissatisfaction with other models as well: the legalistic model (physician-client); economic model (physician-consumer); contractual model (when the relationship is referred to as a contract between doctor and patient); and religious model (when the relationship is defined as a covenant). The first three models pay insufficient attention to the human factor in the relationship by reducing it to a convenient mode. In fact, the relationship does embody legal, economic, and contractual characteristics, but it is more than that. The religious model, although preserving some of the richness of the relationship, strikes me as too pious, bordering on the sacramental. Although I am in sympathy with religious dimensions that may occur in medicine, I am convinced that medicine is distinct from religion, and that the role of the medicine-man or priest is best left behind us.

There is another reason for my dissatisfaction with these four models. All four have been introduced to attack the traditional paternalistic model of medical practice but, in trying to root out the causes of excessive paternalism, the new models fail to provide a place for medicine's beneficence.

If the newer characterizations seem innocuous, it is important to realize that the mind catalogues reality according to certain visions, and then establishes expectations and roles that follow from these visions. Admittedly, a paternalistic view of medicine is antiquated and better fits the era of the gentleman generalist. But a model excessively focused on patient autonomy is equally absurd. People who are sick need help; their rights to autonomy should not get in the way of their physical needs.

REASSESSMENT

Reassessing the physician-patient relation has been going on since the Second World War. My contribution to this discussion is distinctive only because it is written by a philosopher with over 10 years' experience teaching in the clinical setting. As a result, my proposal is marked by a wariness about claims for patient autonomy not often found among philosophers.

The reassessment was occasioned by three factors. First, the medical profession had been very paternalistic. But the Second World War was the watershed of a rapid rise in higher education and a complex, technologic society. This rise led to a general mistrust of authority. Second, a combination of existentialist and personalist ethics, and a growing civil and individual rights movements undermined the one-sided code of professional standards. Existentialism was a post-war philosophical movement stressing personal development, individual ethical responsibility, and the importance of each gesture in day-to-day life, as opposed to community standards, political authority, and social obligation. Self-determination rather than acting from accepted practice

was encouraged. Pellegrino has written in this regard "Professional ethics derived from the existential situation of the patient are more authentic and more human than the traditional ethics derived from the self-declared duties of the profession."

The third factor is technology itself. Medical technology has its own economic and moral system, requiring more attention to the human values once taken for granted in the physician-patient relationship. Medical technology introduces a fourth party—the machine and its technician—into the physician-patient-insurance triangle. The patient often has more contact with the technician, especially in serious illnesses, than with the physician. Because of the pervasiveness of technology, many moral problems are resolved by technologic solutions, although we are not yet sure whether technology has a true, social good. In effect, we simply postpone the moral question until it becomes unavoidable—when, for example, we must propose criteria for selecting patients for exotic treatment. Finally, the unforeseen consequences of technology often leave the feeling that the future of medicine will take rational control out of human decision making.

The problems associated with technology in medicine show the need to pay more attention to the human factor in the medical relationship. In my opinion, this factor is ignored in the models being proposed for modern medicine.

Before we turn to the proposal being made, there are certain terms that must be defined. The clash between paternalism and autonomy lies at the heart of many medical ethics problems. Questions about the roles of physicians and patients in difficult cases occupy much of our time. Should an aged patient's request to die be honored, or a teenager's refusal of life-saving therapy? In the main, most moral thinkers would agree with Childress that paternalism is wrong, justified only under the most stringent conditions. To understand this claim, it is necessary to agree on definitions of paternalism and autonomy.

Paternalism is an action taken by one person in the best interests of another without their consent. Paternalism is problematic precisely because it is difficult to defend the notion that the physician has better insight into the best interests of the patient than the patient. Paternalism comes in two forms. Strong paternalism is that exercised against the competent wishes of another. For example, the doctor in the Broadway play *Whose Life Is It, Anyway?* gives the main character, a quadriplegic, a sedative against his expressed wishes not to receive it. However, strong paternalism in modern medical practice is not as prevalent as weak paternalism.

Weak paternalism is an action taken by a physician in the best interests of a patient on presumed wishes or in the absence of consent from those who cannot give consent due to age or mental status. In some instances, weak paternalism is practiced when a physician ascertains the best course ahead of time and presents this option to the competent patient. Although the patient could refuse, other options are closed ahead of time in the hopes of persuading the patient to choose what is in his or her best interests. Ackerman has argued that weak paternalism is justified in some instances of research on children. Few other defenses of weak paternalism are found in the literature.

On the other hand, patient autonomy has many champions. The term "autonomy" stems from the Greek for "self-law or rule." Kant made the concept the heart of his moral theory by proposing that the self, through duty, is the ultimate origin of law. Similarly, John Stuart Mill proposed that a person cannot interfere in the freedom of others unless they may cause harm or cannot foresee the consequences of their action (for example, they are acting out of ignorance). In his classic exploration of the concept, Dworkin argued that autonomy entailed authenticity and independence; that is, freedom of action (independence) and the assurance that motives for action were one's own motives (authenticity). These concepts were used by Cassell to argue that the proper object of medicine is to reestablish autonomy.

I have kept my definitions as broad as possible and as close to their everyday understanding in order to encompass the greatest variety of opinions in examining this issue. To narrowly define the terms, as some ethicists have done, is the same as predetermining one's stance on the issue. For example, Culver and Gert note that Childress' definition of paternalism involves conflicting meanings, Buchanan's is too narrow in the kinds of moral rules that are violated, and Dworkin's is too dependent on legal cases and narrower still in its inclusion of coercion and interference with liberty.

Culver and Gert's definition includes the features of my own definition, but with the addition of two qualifiers: that a moral rule must be violated (and thus, paternalism must always be justified), and that the person towards whom one acts beneficially (by preventing an evil) is competent to give consent. I generally agree with the first qualifier, but prefer the distinction between strong and weak paternalism to the second qualifier.

For the purposes of this paper, paternalism should be broadly understood to mean: a medical action taken to benefit a patient; and an action done without full consent of the patient. Although full informed consent is a theoretical ideal, the amount of information patients receive needs to be reasonable, so that they can make a free choice about treatment. Most paternalistic acts violate the reasonableness of the information criterion for two reasons. First, an action may need justification if the patient is competent to give consent, because it violates a moral rule, such as truthtelling (strong paternalism). Or, second, an action may need no justification if the patient is not competent to give consent due to age or mental status (weak paternalism).

Traditional modes of paternalism clash

with that autonomy we normally presume adults possess. However, there are two further considerations that cause some discomfort when concepts of paternalism and autonomy are applied to medicine. First, the moral principle of beneficence, acting for the good of others, is an inherent ethical foundation of medicine. Most often beneficence is expressed by the axiom of nonharm. It is important to preserve beneficence even if its paternalistic aspects are removed. Provider-client and provider-consumer models fail to show the ethics of medical practice in this regard. Second, the conscience of the physician, which I define as prudential judgment, not the superego, is not given sufficient place in the models supposed to correct paternalistic tendencies. Prudential judgment encompassing medical and value factors in the physician-patient relation is a hallmark of professional conduct. Because the model of physician's conscience is designed to correct deficiencies in both the patient autonomy and medical paternalism models, I examine the limitations of these models.

LIMITATIONS OF THE AUTONOMY MODEL

Stressing patient autonomy fails to properly respect the realities of medicine. Newton writes that many proponents of patient autonomy assume that medical paternalism has been part of medical practice since Hippocratic times. As a result, the proposed cure tends to be more radical than may be needed if one properly understands the history of medicine with respect to the physician-patient relationship. Only in more recent times, as medicine became more scientific, and the gap in knowledge between the physician and unlettered patient enlarged out of proportion to the decline in numbers of the patient, did objectionable medical paternalism begin to appear. Care need not be thought of as paternalistic, but neither must patient advocacy be belittled.

Some philosophers who call for more patient autonomy on moral grounds forget that humans are not totally independent from one another. In other words, there is distinct neglect of human relatedness and, especially, the realities of the physician-patient relationship. The source of this atomistic individualism lies in the moral philosophies developed during and after the Enlightenment. One wonders whether these philosophies are valid in our complex, technologic age.

The patient autonomy model ignores the impact of disease on personal integrity. Although one may agree with Cassell that medicine should restore patient autonomy, one cannot assume that autonomy is preserved in cases of serious illness. Bradley formulates a telling objection to the position of Veatch, one of the most prominent philosophers arguing for the patient autonomy model. As Bradley says, "Veatch argues that the relationship between doctor and patient is an equal one, ignoring . . . the fact of illness which places the patient in a potentially vulnerable relationship with his physician. . . . Based as it is on a wrong assumption, this model must be rejected when applied to the traditional doctor-patient relationship."

Even the briefest experience in the clinical setting shows that persons who are ill become angry or fearful, overriding judgments they would make in calmer times. A patient has a new relationship with his body, which is viewed as an object that failed the person. Patients become preoccupied with their disease and their body and are forced to reassess their values and goals. These primary characteristics of disease profoundly alter personal wholeness and should change our assumptions of personal autonomy as well.

The guiding principles of healing as moral components of the physician-patient relationship are not recognized in the autonomy model. At the heart of the physician's task is not just the prevention of harms or evils, the only paternalism Culver and Gert feel is justifiable, but the reestablishment of full or partial biological function. Because this reestablishment is a primary need for patients with some degree of life-threatening disease, we can presume that health is of value to them. Acting for this interest without consent, even in the presence of resistance due to denial, fear, or other personal disruption, is acting altruistically and out of a high moral purpose. For this reason, I hold that weak paternalism, at least, does not need moral justification.

Nor does the patient autonomy model encompass the complicated role of context in medicine and in resolving the quandaries of medical ethics. Although general moral principles and our cherished values work for the most part, there are cases where these values are in conflict and priorities must be set. In such cases I find that thinkers like Childress, who recognizes the occurrence of such clashes, err on the side of autonomy rather than beneficence, for what I can only call an incorrect metaethical view—namely, that rights are always more important than goods. Unfortunately, insisting on rights can sometimes cause death, a presumption that cannot function as an absolute in medicine, which is dedicated to preserving life.

Philosophers often applaud one another for a distinguished tradition of political and ethical libertarianism inconsistent with the everyday realities of human relationships, the impact of disease on persons, and the overwhelming desire patients have for a cure at the expense of normal freedom and routine. Although it is true that occasionally a patient such as a quadriplegic in intensive care will demand rights and recognitions of autonomy over health care, these instances are rare. Most often the medical context permits assumptions of a desire for health as a more primary value to patients than their personal autonomy. Goods, like health, are judged more important than rights.

Finally, patient autonomy models of the physician-patient relationship have their roots in civil and personal rights movements rather than in an ontology of relations. Although no philosopher would disavow the gains made by emphasizing human dignity and rights, it is not surprising that the adversarial presumptions and tone of that movement often are carried over into debates about health care decisions. The vision of doctors as adversaries and the frequent assumptions by medically inexperienced ethicists of sinister practices are simply stereotypes imposed on medicine by the occasional dramatic case, television show, or the civil rights confrontation. In this regard, an ethics of charity, or a religious ethics of compassion for the needy, more closely approximates the ethical nature of medicine than enlightenment-based ethical theories.

LIMITATIONS OF THE PATERNALISM MODEL

Just as formidable objections to the patient autonomy model can be raised, so too can equally important objections to medical paternalism be enumerated. In general, paternalism seems to violate traditional values about persons and their dignity.

The foremost objection is that a physician often cannot heal a person just by curing a disease, especially if the physician systematically ignores or disregards the patient's views. Cassell's argument that restoring function, or curing, should be a secondary aim of medicine, and that medicine's primary aim is to restore autonomy, is well taken. In this sense, healing involves restoring autonomy. For this reason, Culver and Gert are correct, as are Buchanan and Childress, to insist that strong paternalism always demands justification because it violates a moral rule. But Culver and Gert do not seem to plumb the depths of the morality of medicine itself. The reason strong paternalism is objectionable is not only that it violates moral rules but that it violates the aim of medicine itself, which is to heal.

Strong paternalism lacks respect for the civil rights of patients. When strong paternalism appears in medical practice, it violates those rights by assuming that a person cannot manage his or her own affairs. To overturn such rights demands justification.

Medical paternalism fails to capture an essential element of deontological ethics, which is also at the core of medicine. The element is respect for persons. Lack of respect for persons means that medicine does not attend to the needs of others, despite all protestations to the contrary. Acts of medical paternalism, such as failing to discuss all options with a potential bypass patient, can be a form of medical failure as well as ethical failure.

As with the patient autonomy model, medical paternalism also fails to distinguish contexts and their role in medical and ethical decision making. As a consequence, medical paternalism tends to become a stance or style, an authoritarian posture that may have been valid in one context (as in an intensive care unit) and extrapolated to others. Or it may have been suggested by a profound experience in which a physician saved a patient's life by adopting paternalism, and now applies it to all patients. The weakness in this approach lies in the invalid generalization of an experience with one patient or a number of patients into a moral posture.

Perhaps the biggest failure of the medical paternalism model is that it imposes relative values on patients as if these values were absolute. For example, a physician may decide with a surgeon that a bypass operation should be done to save a patient's life, but the patient may have already expressed fears and doubts about the operation, preferring to try calcium inhibitors instead. When the physician tries to talk the patient into having the operation "for his own good," the physician is acting paternalistically, although no coercion or interference in liberty of choice has occurred. The physician is acting as if the values implied or expressed in the discussion with the surgeon—the preservation of life by preventing a possible occlusion—should be taken as absolute and take precedence over the patient's wishes. The patient's wishes may be colored by fear but may also embody

values regarding the body, family, and so on.

The values expressed by medical personnel are often accepted by patients. This does not mean that these values are absolute. When, from time to time, patients object to or reject those values, it does not mean that the physician's competence and dignity is automatically called into question. Instead it should remind us that the values of medicine are relative.

THE CONSCIENCE MODEL

Given the shortcomings of both the patient autonomy and medical paternalism models of medical practice, is there an alternate that is not reductionist or does not unduly stress one or the other model? I suggest there is. I call it the physician's conscience model. If space permitted, this model would be balanced with a comparable model of patient conscience as well; the complexity of the physician-patient relation can never be adequately described in a single model. The purpose of sketching the physician's conscience model is to circumvent the substantial problems with models I have already mentioned, although this is not to claim that the physician-patient relationship has been adequately defined by this model.

There are six major features of the model. First, the aim of medicine should be seen as a form of beneficence. Beneficence, acting for the benefit of another, responds to a plea for help. When medical help is requested, the appropriate response is to offer the best judgment of the patient's condition. There are three elements of medical beneficence. The first is the care of the patient. The patient's problems are the primary concern of the physician: all other concerns must be secondary. Second, do no harm. Beneficence requires the traditional ethical principle of medicine, because a physician cannot care for a patient while attempting to harm them. In other words, ethical judgment is an inherent part of every case in medicine, an essential component of medical judgment. Third, both autonomy and paternalism must take a secondary place to beneficence. That is to say, the choice of a style emphasizing autonomy or paternalism should be based on the needs of the patient rather than the intellectual convictions of the physician.

The second feature of this model is a focus on the existential condition of the patient, as Pellegrino argued, rather than on traditional professional codes. A good example of this focus can be found in Siegler's list of criteria used for deciding the limits of autonomy to be accepted by a physician treating a seriously ill patient. These criteria include the patient's ability to make rational choices about care; the nature and past values of the patient; the age of the patient; the nature of the illness; the values of the physician who must make choices in the care of the patient; and the clinical setting, especially the diffusion of care. Note that the first four items deal with the personal condition of the patient, and the last two only deal with the health care professional and environment.

Third, all elements of the physician-conscience model are recognized as having a value. This model requires the knowledge to identify, rank, and make decisions about values. One of the problems with the autonomy and paternalistic models was that both acquired an automatic quality through the process of extrapolation and generalization. In the physician's conscience model, each patient must be handled individually, not only for the medical but the moral implications as well. No ethical stance is chosen before hand. This is not to say, however, that ethical axioms applied to more than one patient cannot be used, as I will point out.

The fourth feature of the model is consensus. Because there is to be no imposition of values, or decisions made in the best interests of patients without their participation, a consensus with the patient and with other members of the health care team is needed. Admittedly, a consensus model takes time and energy but it also wards off

many agonizing hours of conflict later in the course of a serious illness. In fact, one of the temptations of the autonomy and paternalism models derives from the comparative ease of decision making: either the physician makes all the decisions, or the patient is always thought to be right. Both models abandon the rewards and trials of a mutual exchange between doctor and patient.

Indeed, a consensus reached at the beginning of a patient's care should not be assumed to continue as new developments in the case occur. A mutual exchange of views must continue throughout the treatment. The consensus must be monitored for its continued validity.

The fifth feature is a pragmatic moral object, the resolving of difficult ethical quandries in the treatment of patients by preserving as many values as possible in the case. Ackerman has argued that this moral object should be the goal of bioethics. Whether or not one agrees, it certainly ought to be the goal of a consensus-driven, patient-oriented care approach in which prudential judgment is used to make decisions on a patient-by-patient basis.

Explicit axioms comprise the sixth and last major feature of the physician's conscience model. Just as the physician examines each patient in light of theories or categories of disease and health that span all persons, the prudential judgment used for each patient must adhere to a series of more general ethical axioms, or moral rules. These are necessary to avoid the moral pitfalls of the autonomy and paternalism models. These axioms also function as a summary of the paper.

Axioms of the Physician's Conscience Model

Both doctor and patient must be free to make informed decisions. Because of the necessity to reach a consensus, and to respect the values of both doctor and patient, both must feel free to express their values with sufficient information and freedom from coercion.

Physicians are morally required to pay increased attention to patient vulnerability. There is an imbalance of information due to the technical training of the physician which must be righted by conveying sufficient information to the patient who must make decisions. There is also an imbalance of power between persons who have the ability to care for their own needs and the patient who does not. Physicians must overcome this second imbalance through an almost excessive attention to the dignity and worth of each person, and by supplying what is needed through care of the patient.

Physicians must use their power responsibly to care for the patient. Because of patient vulnerability caused by the assault illness represents on personal integrity, the imbalance of power between patient and physician will always continue to some extent. The power the physician derives from the imbalance must be used to restore as much patient autonomy as is possible. The requirement of self-regulation in the medical profession as a whole is derived from the peculiarities of the physician-patient relationship, and not wholly from the self-professed aims of the profession or the expectations of society.

Physicians must have integrity. The primary quality of a physician must be the ability to make prudential judgments while considering the particulars of a case, the general features of the disease, and universal moral principles. It has become fashionable to downplay the importance of moral character in educating physicians in a pluralistic society, because no one wishes to impose values on others. However, educators may find that in a sea of relativism, there are characteristics of moral and medical judgment that must apply to all physicians. Exhorting physicians to follow this coherence

will depend on training them in it as well. As Aristotle noted, "It is impossible, or not easy, to do noble acts without the proper equipment." To avoid the autonomy-paternalism or the reductionistic models, the interplay between physician and patient in making medical judgments must also occur in making ethical judgments. This skill must be taught, and ought to be the basic objective of all medical ethics and medical humanities programs in medical schools.

The physician must have a healthy respect for moral ambiguity. Respect for ambiguity is difficult, especially when by training and disposition physicians aim for clinical closure and problem solving. But in the model of physician's conscience there is no single answer to the dilemmas a physician will face with patients. Respect for ambiguity would permit a physician to rationally discuss alternatives without the pitfalls so aptly described by Alasdair MacIntyre: "It is a central feature of contemporary moral debates that they are unsettlable and interminable. . . . Because no argument can be carried through to victorious conclusion, argument characteristically gives way to the mere and increasingly shrill battle of assertion with counterassertion."

CONCLUSION

In proposing a model of physician's conscience for the physician-patient relationship, I have tried to show why the consumer, legal, and economic models, as well as the paternalistic and patient autonomy mode, are inadequate visions of modern medicine. But I have also shown why each of the last two models has arisen, and why it is dangerous to medicine and its ethics to accept uncritically either model. In the end the danger lies not only in the models' unreality but also in the severe way that they truncate the moral decision-making responsibility of physicians acting in concert with their patients. The axioms I have proposed for the physician's conscience model are not exhaustive. The axioms are indicative, however, of the kind of education in ethical reasoning and its connections with medicine needed for modern practice if it is not to succumb to false arrangements of its present and future challenges.

4. INFORMED CONSENT

The Information Desired by a Reasonable Patient

Canterbury v. Spence

III

Suits charging failure by a physician adequately to disclose the risks and alternatives of proposed treatment are not innovations in American law. They date back a good half-century and in the last decade they have multiplied rapidly. There is, nonetheless, disagreement among the courts and the commentators on many major questions, and there is no precedent of our own directly in point. For the tools enabling resolution of the issues on this appeal, we are forced to begin at first principles.

The root premise is the concept, fundamental in American jurisprudence, that "[e]very human being of adult years and sound mind has a right to determine what shall be done with his own body. . . ." True consent to what happens to one's self is the informed exercise of a choice, and that entails an opportunity to evaluate knowledgeably the options available and the risks attendant upon each. The average patient has little or no understanding of the medical arts, and ordinarily has only his physician to whom he can look for enlightenment with which to reach an intelligent decision. From these almost axiomatic considerations springs the need, and in turn the requirement, of a reasonable divulgence by physician to patient to make such a decision possible.[1]

A physician is under a duty to treat his patient skillfully but proficiency in diagnosis and therapy is not the full measure of his responsibility. The cases demonstrate that the physician is under an obligation to communicate specific information to the patient when the exigencies of reasonable care call for it. Due care may require a physician perceiving symptoms of bodily abnormality to alert the patient to the condition. It may call upon the physician confronting an ailment which does not respond to his ministrations to inform the patient thereof. It may command the physician to instruct the patient as to any limitations to be presently observed for his own welfare, and as to any precautionary therapy he should seek in the future. It may oblige the physician to advise the patient of the need for or desirability of any alternative treatment promising greater benefit than that being pursued. Just as plainly, due care normally demands that the physician warn the patient of any risks to his well-being which contemplated therapy may involve.

The context in which the duty of risk-disclosure arises is invariably the occasion for decision as to whether a particular treatment procedure is to be undertaken. To the physician, whose training enables a self-satisfying evaluation, the answer may seem clear, but it is the prerogative of the patient, not the physician, to determine for himself the direction in which his interests seem to lie. To enable the patient to chart his course understandably, some familiarity with the therapeutic alternatives and their hazards becomes essential.

A reasonable revelation in these respects is not only a necessity but, as we see it, is as much a matter of the physician's duty. It is a duty to warn of the dangers lurking in the proposed treatment, and that is surely a facet of due care. It is, too, a duty to impart information which the patient has every right to expect.[2] The patient's reliance upon the physician is a trust of the kind which traditionally has exacted obligations beyond those associated with arms-length transactions. His dependence upon the physician for information affecting this well-being, in terms of contemplated treatment, is well-nigh abject. As earlier noted, long before the instant litigation arose, courts had recognized that the physician had the responsibility of satisfying the vital informational needs of the patient. More recently, we ourselves have found "in the fiducial qualities of [the physician-patient] relationship the physician's duty to reveal to the patient that which in his best interests it is important that he should know." We now find, as a part of the physician's overall obligation to the patient, a similar duty of reasonable disclosure of the choices with respect to proposed therapy and the dangers inherently and potentially involved.

This disclosure requirement, on analysis, reflects much more of a change in doctrinal emphasis than a substantive addition to malpractice law. It is well established that the physician must seek and secure his patient's consent before commencing an operation or other course of treatment. It is also clear that the consent, to be efficacious, must be free from imposition upon the patient. It is the settled rule that therapy not authorized by the patient may amount to a tort—a common law battery—by the physician. And it is evident that it is normally impossible to obtain a consent worthy of the name unless the physician first elucidates the options and the perils for the patient's edification. Thus the physician has long borne a duty, on pain of liability for unauthorized treatment, to make adequate disclosure to the patient.[3] The evolution of the obligation to communicate for the patient's benefit as well as the physician's protection has hardly involved an extraordinary restructuring of the law.

V

Once the circumstances give rise to a duty on the physician's part to inform his patient, the next inquiry is the scope of the disclosure the physician is legally obliged to make. The courts have frequently confronted this problem but no uniform standard defining the adequacy of the divulgence emerges from the decisions. Some have said "full" disclosure, a norm we are unwilling to adopt literally. It seems obviously prohibitive and unrealistic to expect physicians to discuss with their patients every risk of proposed treatment—no matter how small or remote—and generally unnecessary from the patient's viewpoint as well. Indeed, the cases speaking in terms of "full" disclosure appear to envision something less than total disclosure, leaving unanswered the question of just how much.

The larger number of courts, as might be expected, have applied tests framed with reference to prevailing fashion within the medical profession. Some have measured the disclosure by "good medical practice," others by what a reasonable practitioner would have bared under the circumstances, and still others by what medical custom in the community would demand. We have explored this rather considerable body of law but are unprepared to follow it. The duty to disclose, we have reasoned, arises from phenomena apart from medical custom and practice. The latter, we think, should no more establish the scope of the duty than its existence. Any definition of scope in terms purely of a professional standard is at odds with the patient's prerogative to decide on projected therapy himself. That prerogative, we have said, is at the very foundation of the duty to disclose, and both the patient's right to know and the physician's correlative obligation to tell him are diluted to the extent that its compass is dictated by the medical profession.

In our view, the patient's right of self-decision shapes the boundaries of the duty to reveal. That right can be effectively exercised only if the patient possesses enough information to enable an intelligent choice. The scope of the physician's communications to the patient, then, must be measured by the patient's need, and that need is the information material to the decision. Thus the test for determining whether a particular peril must be divulged is its materiality to the patient's decision: all risks potentially affecting the decision must be unmasked. And to safeguard the patient's interest in achieving his own determination on treatment, the law must itself set the standard for adequate disclosure.

Optimally for the patient, exposure of a risk would be mandatory whenever the patient would deem it significant to his decision, either singly or in combination with other risks. Such a requirement, however, would summon the physician to second-guess the patient, whose ideas on materiality could hardly be known to the physician. That would make an undue demand upon medical practitioners, whose conduct, like that of others, is to be measured in terms of reasonableness. Consonantly with orthodox negligence doctrine, the physician's liability for nondisclosure is to be determined on the basis of foresight, not hindsight; no less than any other aspect of negligence, the issue of nondisclosure must be approached from the viewpoint of the reasonableness of the physician's divulgence in terms of what he knows or should know to be the patient's informational needs. If, but only if, the fact-finder can say that the physician's communication was unreasonably inadequate is an imposition of liability legally or morally justified.

Of necessity, the content of the disclosure rests in the first instance with the physician. Ordinarily it is only he who is in position to identify particular dangers; always he must make a judgment, in terms of materiality, as to whether and to what extent revelation to the patient is called for. He cannot know with complete exactitude what the patient would consider important to his decision, but on the basis of his medical training and experience he can sense how the average, reasonable patient expectably would react. Indeed, with knowledge of, or ability to learn, his patient's background and current condition, he is in a position superior to that of most others—attorneys, for example—who are called upon to make judgments on pain of liability in damages for unreasonable miscalculation.

From these considerations we derive the breadth of the disclosure of risks legally to be required. The scope of the standard is not subjective as to either the physician, or the patient; it remains objective with due regard for the patient's informational needs and with suitable leeway for the physician's situation. In broad outline, we agree that "[a] risk is thus material when a reasonable person, in what the physician knows or should know to be the patient's position, would be likely to attach significance to the risk or cluster of risks in deciding whether or not to forego the proposed therapy."

The topics importantly demanding a communication of information are the inherent and potential hazards of the proposed treatment, the alternatives to that treatment, if any, and the results likely if the patient remains untreated. The factors contributing significance to the dangerousness of a medical technique are, of course, the incidence of injury and the degree of the harm threatened. A very small chance of death or serious disablement may well be significant; a potential disability which dramatically outweighs the potential benefit of the therapy or the detriments of the existing malady may summon discussion with the patient.

There is no bright line separating the significant from the insignificant; the answer in any case must abide a rule of reason.

Some dangers—infection, for example—are inherent in any operation; there is no obligation to communicate those of which persons of average sophistication are aware. Even more clearly, the physician bears no responsibility for discussion of hazards the patient has already discovered or those having no apparent materiality to patients' decision on therapy. The disclosure doctrine, like others marking lines between permissible and impermissible behavior in medical practice, is in essence a requirement of conduct prudent under the circumstances. Whenever non-disclosure of particular risk information is open to debate by reasonable-minded men, the issue is for the finder of the facts.

VI

Two exceptions to the general rule of disclosure have been noted by the courts. Each is in the nature of a physician's privilege not to disclose, and the reasoning underlying them is appealing. Each, indeed, is but a recognition that, as important as is the patient's right to know, it is greatly outweighed by the magnitudinous circumstances giving rise to the privilege. The first comes into play when the patient is unconscious or otherwise incapable of consenting, and harm from a failure to treat is imminent and outweighs any harm threatened by the proposed treatment. When a genuine emergency of that sort arises, it is settled that the impracticality of conferring with the patient dispenses with need for it. Even in situations of that character the physician should, as current law requires, attempt to secure a relative's consent if possible. But if time is too short to accommodate discussion, obviously the physician should proceed with the treatment.

The second exception obtains when risk-disclosure poses such a threat of detriment to the patient as to become unfeasible or contraindicated from a medical point of view. It is recognized that patients occasion-

ally become so ill or emotionally distraught on disclosure as to foreclose a rational decision, or complicate or hinder the treatment, or perhaps even pose psychological damage to the patient. Where that is so, the cases have generally held that the physician is armed with a privilege to keep the information from the patient, and we think it clear that portents of that type may justify the physician in action he deems medically warranted. The critical inquiry is whether the physician responded to a sound medical judgment that communication of the risk information would present a threat to the patient's well-being.

The physician's privilege to withhold information for therapeutic reasons must be carefully circumscribed, however, for otherwise it might devour the disclosure rule itself. The privilege does not accept the paternalistic notion that the physician may remain silent simply because divulgence might prompt the patient to forego therapy the physician feels the patient really needs. That attitude presumes instability or perversity for even the normal patient, and runs counter to the foundation principle that the patient should and ordinarily can make the choice for himself. Nor does the privilege contemplate operation save where the patient's reaction to risk information, as reasonably foreseen by the physician, is menacing. And even in a situation of that kind, disclosure to a close relative with a view to securing consent to the proposed treatment may be the only alternative open to the physician.

---

1. The doctrine that a consent effective as authority to form therapy can arise only from the patient's understanding of alternatives to and risks of the therapy is commonly denominated "informed consent." The same appellation is frequently assigned to the doctrine requiring physicians, as a matter of duty to patients, to communicate information as to such alternatives and risks. While we recognize the general utility of shorthand phrases in literary expositions, we caution that uncritical use of the "informed consent" label can be misleading.

In duty-to-disclose cases, the focus of attention is

more properly upon the nature and content of the physician's divulgence than the patient's understanding or consent. Adequate disclosure and informed consent are, of course, two sides of the same coin—the former a *sine qua non* of the latter. But the vital inquiry on duty to disclose relates to the physician's performance of an obligation, while one of the difficulties with analysis in terms of "informed consent" is its tendency to imply that what is decisive is the degree of the patient's comprehension. As we later emphasize, the physician discharges the duty when he makes a reasonable effort to convey sufficient information although the patient, without fault of the physician, may not fully grasp it. Even though the factfinder may have occasion to draw an inference on the state of the patient's enlightenment, the factfinding process on performance of the duty ultimately reaches back to what the physician actually said or failed to say. And while the factual conclusion on adequacy of the revelation will vary as between patients—as, for example, between a lay patient and a physician-patient—the fluctuations are attributable to the kind of divulgence which may be reasonable under the circumstances.

2. Some doubt had been expressed as to ability of physicians to suitably communicate their evaluations of risks and the advantages of optional treatment, and as to the lay patient's ability to understand what the physician tells him. We do not share these apprehensions. The discussion need not be a disquisition, and surely

the physician is not compelled to give his patient a short medical education; the disclosure rule summons the physician only to a reasonable explanation. That means generally informing the patient in nontechnical terms as to what is at stake: the therapy alternatives open to him, the goals expectably to be achieved, and the risks that may ensue from particular treatment and no treatment. So informing the patient hardly taxes the physician, and it must be the exceptional patient who cannot comprehend such an explanation at least in a rough way.

3. We discard the thought that the patient should ask for information before the physician is required to disclose. Caveat emptor is not the norm for the consumer of medical services. Duty to disclose is more than a call to speak merely on the patient's request, or merely to answer the patient's questions; it is a duty to volunteer, if necessary, the information the patient needs for intelligent decision. The patient may be ignorant, confused, overawed by the physician or frightened by the hospital, or even ashamed to inquire. Perhaps relatively few patients could in any event identify the relevant questions in the absence of prior explanation by the physician. Physicians and hospitals have patients of widely divergent socio-economic backgrounds, and a rule which presumes a degree of sophistication which many members of society lack is likely to breed gross inequities.

The Subjective Standard: Canterbury Can Require Too Little

Alexander Capron

DISCLOSURE AND COMPREHENSION

From the outset, most judges have rejected the notion that there is an "absolute" duty to inform a patient of any and all risks and consequences expectable from an intervention. Instead, the extent of what a physician must tell his patient has usually been stated with the sort of uninformative circularity that the California district court of appeal employed in *Salgo v. Leland Stanford Jr. University Board of Trustees:* "full disclosure of facts necessary to an informed consent." Under the negligence rationale, if a patient asserted that his physician had withheld information from him, the patient-plaintiff was generally obliged to show that the physician-defendant had deviated from what ex-

pert testimony showed to be the established, acceptable medical practice on disclosure in the community. This reliance on a professional standard was supported by the argument that the major reason for nondisclosure would be the physician's conclusion, as a result of his expert judgment, that disclosure would be harmful to the patient.

Courts following the assault and battery rationale were faced with a harder task. Whether information was withheld negligently, wilfully, or otherwise could make no difference under their theory, provided that the gap was sufficient to render nugatory the consent supposedly given by the patient; yet *some* information is perforce always left out by physicians, so liability would always attach if absolute disclosure were required. The courts were thus faced with two choices, neither really satisfactory. On the one hand, they could attempt to narrow the field of battery cases to those in which the operation performed was not the one to which the plaintiff had consented, and leave malpractice theories to cover situations in which information about the operation (for instance, risks) was not disclosed. The difficulty with this dichotomy is plain, however. What makes the physician's conduct objectionable in the first situation—that the patient has given "consent" under a misimpression of the relevant facts—is equally true of the second. At the least, the dividing line between omissions of fact and errors of description that fundamentally change what has been approved and thereby open the physician to liability for battery defies description. The second alternative, which some courts pursued, was to draw on the fiduciary relationship that a physician has to his patient and hold that a battery occurred when the physician wilfully or negligently breached the fiducial duty of disclosing "to his patient all material *facts* which reasonably should be known if his patient is to make an informed and intelligent decision." This led to a groping for some standard of materiality beyond the plainly uninformative "full disclosure."

In three major recent opinions in this area, the courts seemed to take both routes. Most notably, the California supreme court in *Cobbs v. Grant* clearly adopted negligence rather than battery as the theory of recovery in that state, but at the same time rejected the "reasonable medical practice standard" which formed the backbone of the negligence theory. Paraphrasing the holding handed down earlier in 1972 by the Court of Appeals for the District of Columbia Circuit in *Canterbury v. Spence,* the California court held that "the patient's right of self-decision is the measure of the physician's duty to reveal. . . . The scope of the physician's communications to the patient, then, must be measured by the patient's need, and

that need is whatever information is material to the decision."

Without explicitly so declaring, the California court appears to have adopted a "subjective" standard for determining whether the information withheld from the patient should have been disclosed: the measure of materiality is "the patient's need," whatever the particular plaintiff needed to make up his or her own mind about whether to permit the medical intervention. The two other courts which have taken the lead in redefining consent, the Supreme Court of Rhode Island and the federal appellate court in the District of Columbia, approached the issue of materiality "from the physician's point of view," as two commentators had urged. In holding that the materiality of information is to be judged by what the law's mythical "reasonable person" would want to know, these courts retreated from the logic of their own reasoning.

The courts thus adopted an "objective" standard, rather than keying the definition to what information the *actual* patient needed for his or her personal decisionmaking process. The judges, like the commentators, recognized the subjective standard as "optimal" or "the ideal rule" to protect the interests that prompt the concern with "informed consent" in the first place, but then they backed away from this result for pragmatic reasons. It is not hard to understand the motivation for this outcome; for it might seem harsh to judge the materiality of information by "the patient's need," since a physician "obviously cannot be required to know the inner workings of his patient's mind." But an objective standard shares the basic fault of the "medical community" standard which these courts were abandoning. Adherence to what a group in the lay community believes to be "reasonable" may rob the patient of "the undisputed right . . . to receive information which will enable him to make a choice" as surely as will adherence to a judgment of the medical community.

Whatever the merits of an "objective" standard of disclosure in highly routine interventions—when the very ordinariness of the medical procedures would suggest that a particular patient would be satisfied with information sufficient to satisfy the average, reasonable person, and where jurors would generally be better able to draw on their own experiences in applying the standard—it has no place in the case of the major and often experimental interventions used to treat catastrophic diseases. Since the purpose of requiring informed consent is to allow patient-subjects to participate in the course of therapy and research as informed decisionmakers, concern should focus on whether the patient-subject in question understood what the physician-investigator was proposing to do as compared with other ways of proceeding. To eliminate the "subjective" elements that relate to the particular patient-subject (which lead him, for example, not to be "reasonable" in deciding about certain kinds of interventions) is to make the informed consent doctrine an engine of depersonalization rather than personalization. The after-the-fact application of this rule in the courtroom need cause no greater difficulty. Jurors are not fools; they know when to credit, and when not, a plaintiff's testimony that he needed to know a particular fact in order to reach an informed judgment.

If this subjective standard of materiality places an additional burden on physician-investigators to inquire specially about the attitudes and biases, strengths and weaknesses of the persons whom they propose to treat, that would seem all to the good. Indeed, this might provide encouragement to physicians, and hence to courts, to make the patient's comprehension of the information conveyed the hallmark of a determination of valid consent. The mere relaying of information is not, in itself, more than a necessary precondition to the patient-subject's capacity to give *informed* consent. Although commentators have usefully observed that the doctrine has two parts, information and consent, "information" and "informed" are not equivalents. It would be more accurate to say that its two parts are first, disclosure and comprehension, and second, voluntary consent. Information may, in the manner in which it is conveyed, even be used to decrease the likelihood that the choice is made with insight and understanding. One study suggests that untutored subjects' comprehension is inversely correlated with how elaborately the information is presented.

Even when the information presented is adequate, therefore, the consenting process may be nothing more than a "ritual" if the patient-subject remains "uneducated and uncomprehending." To avoid this result, the physician could be held responsible for taking reasonable steps to ascertain whether the information presented has been understood, so that if it has not he may supplement it as needed or may convey the same information in a manner more comprehensible to the particular patient. Such a process might also be expected to reveal additional factors whose materiality could not have been suspected before the physician questioned the patient. The continual exchange of information between patient and physician which the comprehension-testing requirement is likely to produce gives substance to the idea of mutuality in the catastrophic disease process.

The very factors which led the courts to base the disclosure requirement on "the patient's need" would seem to make necessary the inclusion of some measure of how well that need had been met as an element of the new cause of action. It was suggested previously that the courts might do well to complete the movement from disclosure only at the will of the medical community through standard negligence to a legally established duty. This development made sense in establishing an easily measured, and one hopes easily followed, rule of divulgence, free from the constraints of a negligence formulation. The focus of attention there was on what the physician-investigator *did* (adequate disclosure *vel non*). In speaking of comprehension, however, the focus is on the patient-subject and whether he was informed when he made his decision to proceed. Thus, policy as well as logic dictates that physician-investigators not be held to determine beyond peradventure the state of patient-subjects' knowledge but only to make reasonable efforts to ascertain that they adequately comprehend what is being proposed, including the risks and alternatives.

The importance of a subjective rather than objective standard of materiality can be seen by comparing how well each standard would serve the functions of informed consent. For example, a physician-investigator's self-scrutiny is likely to be increased if he has to ask, "Is this procedure right for *this* patient, based on what I actually know about him or her?" and not on what is known about the "reasonable patient." The very routine nature of the latter does nothing to promote reexamination on the part of the physician-investigator as he plans how he will explain the proposed intervention to the patient-subject. The requirement that the physician-investigator individualize the informing process is consistent with the obligation to individualize the diagnostic and therapeutic processes. Similarly, the respect for the patient-subject as a full human being is better served by a subjective standard. As the courts have recognized, one reason why a physician might withhold information is a belief that if the patient knew it he would refuse an intervention believed necessary by the physician. Yet such a substitution of judgment, permitted under the negligence rationale if nondisclosure were the professional norm, clearly deprives the patient of his power of self-determination and human dignity. The "objective" test has the same effect, for it asks the jury to decide whether the patient would have wanted to know something, had he been a "reasonable person." The paternalistic judgment that it would have been better not to know is thus shifted from the physician's sole discretion to the jury's. It seems highly dubious to say, in the case of the major and often experimental interventions which occur in the catastrophic disease process, that the right of the patient to say "no" on even the least rational grounds should ever be taken away.

The Best Interest of the Patient: Canterbury Can Require Too Much

Jewish Compendium on Medical Ethics

INFORMED CONSENT

The obligation of a physician to consider "Informed Consent" on the part of his patient is relatively recent. Valid consent has become a legal necessity in contemporary medicine. It generally consists of three elements: information, freedom and competency. In other words, a consent is valid if obtained from a patient who is mentally competent, free from constraint or coercion, and knowledgeable concerning the proposed therapeutic program. The underlying principle of consent is patient self-determination. The numerous instances of malpractice litigation based on the lack of informed consent, and the position of the courts on the matter over the past fifteen years, suggest that the license for the practice of medicine in any of its forms ultimately rests with the patient, the object of medical intervention.

Other traditions of medical ethics generally do not share this premise, and view the question from a variety of other perspectives. In the Jewish tradition, informed consent is not always essential. The principle that the physician acts with Divine license to heal may require him, as well as permit him, to do so. Just as it is his duty to heal, so is it the religious obligation of the patient to seek and receive healing. The patient who refuses a reasonable and appropriate medical regimen, whether through wilfulness, despondency, invincible ignorance or irrational fear, is in violation of his Divine trust. The physician, acting in what he knows to be the vital interests of the patient's physical and mental health, would thus not be subject to religious or ethical sanctions for not obtaining consent.

It goes without saying that all citizens are required to obey the law of the land as adjudicated in the courts. The American physician is thus well-advised, from both a moral and a practical point of view, to obtain informed consent wherever possible, though not to jeopardize the life or health of the patient by undue delay.

"Informed consent" does represent a moral issue in Jewish thinking, though not in the same sense as in Western law. Physicians sometimes have personal biases; their therapeutic decisions may be based on intuition rather than fact. They may feel so strongly about the need for a specific procedure that they are unwilling or unable to adequately consider the alternatives or perceive their merits. The patient with reasonably sophisticated medical knowledge, or who has had competent advice from another source, may disagree with a particular physician's approach. He has the right to hear the views of his physician cogently presented, to weigh the alternatives, and to make his own decision between various courses of therapeutic action. It is not "the right to be wrong" that the patient enjoys, but rather the right to choose the course of therapy in which he has the greatest confidence.

There is an asymmetry of power and risk in the doctor-patient relationship. Patients seek doctors when they are sick and vulnerable, and entrust to them their carefully guarded secrets and fears, as well as access to their bodies. When the patient informs himself as to the nature of his illness and therapeutic regimens, he can lessen the asymmetry and enhance the mutuality of the relationship. The patient should find in his physician both the expertise that is the result of professional training and experience, and the humility of human fallibility.

What recourse does a physician have when he simply cannot convince a patient that a certain form of treatment is in the patient's best interest; when the doctor's certainty is challenged by the patient's stubborn refusal to "see the obvious," to accept facts, or to face realities? It is in precisely such a situation that the trained rabbi/ethicist can assist both the physician and the patient. The rabbi acts under the norms of his commitment to a coreligionist, rather than under the usual legal strictures that govern the medical profession. The rabbi is less suspect of having a detached self-interest; his relationship with the patient has been, and generally is, a more intimate one than that between patient and medical specialist. While paternalism on the part of the physician may be morally suspect except in rare cases, paternalistic counsel is often accepted from a religious teacher. The rabbi is thus in a position to assist in obtaining the necessary consent where warranted, and his aid should be enlisted. At the same time, the rabbi can more objectively evaluate alternatives open to both patient and physician, thus being of service to both.

THE RIGHT ("PRIVILEGE") TO KNOW

Learning of imminent death is one of the most traumatic moments of life. To impart such information to a patient or to his family is a responsibility that must be approached with trepidation. To the extent that this information may cause harm, lead to despair, or endanger the "will to live", it is not a "right" of the patient. No person has the right to endanger himself, whether that risk be mental/emotional or physical. The subject is to be approached, therefore, not from the legal consideration of "right to know" but from the ethical perspective which weighs the wisdom, necessity, and purpose in imparting such information. It follows that the decision is not the exclusive right of any single individual but should be determined by the physician in consultation with the rabbi and/or members of the patient's family.

The problem of informing a patient is not a new one, nor has the technological sophistication of modern medicine made it a less emotion-laden task. Jewish tradition, from the most ancient times, has expounded two principles in this regard:

a) A patient should never be informed of anything that may impair his physical or mental well-being and contribute to the deterioration of either.

b) "When he takes a turn towards death, one says to him: 'Confess. For many have died who did not confess. And many have confessed and did not die. And in the merit of your confession, you will live.'"

In essence, the Jewish view is to maintain the proper balance between these two dicta. On the one hand, the well-being of the patient permits, and even requires, that he be spared the distress and apprehension of being informed. Even members of the family who may inadvertently reveal information, should not be burdened with it. On the other hand, the sophisticated patient is rarely unaware of the seriousness of his situation on his own. One cannot spend days in a coronary care unit, receive radiotherapy or chemotherapy, and remain blissfully unaware that life itself is at stake. Patients emotionally able to appreciate the gravity of the situation should be given opportunity to "set one's house in order" both in the economic as well as the spiritual sense. The counsel of physician, clergyman, social worker, and others should be couched in appropriate euphemism to avoid jarring or disturbing one's sensibilities. In the case of an emotionally strong patient, he may even be able then to console and strengthen other members of his family.

Statistics indicate that most physicians do not favor telling a patient that he is dying, but that most patients want to be told. Nevertheless, despite any statistical findings, the welfare of the patient remains the paramount consideration in determining what should be told, when, and by whom.

It is not the province of medical science to set time limits to life. While it may be possible statistically to predict life expectancy at various stages of a disease, no purpose is served by making a guess and relaying what is tantamount to a "death sentence." The physician has Divine license to heal. While there are circumstances under which general time expectations, or "the normal course of the disease," might be shared with mature members of the patient's family, the element of hope should never be put aside, lest the morale of the patient be weakened. Unnecessary mention of death should be avoided lest the will to live be undermined.

The manner of telling is an art. Time should be given to the patient to come to his own conclusions and let facts sink in. The patient must have an opportunity to talk about his fears, doubts, and frustrations. In keeping with the compassionate role of both rabbi and physician, he should be given all the spiritual and emotional support at their command. Alternative possibilities, other scenarios, straws at which to grasp, assume the proportions of life-support systems.

Kübler-Ross described various emotional "stages" that may be anticipated on the part of the patient: denial and isolation, anger, bargaining, depression, acceptance, and finally hope. Each stage requires the sympathetic understanding of those closest to him. Often the same emotions are experienced by members of the family when informed of the patient's terminal illness.

The decision to inform can therefore never be based merely on "the right to know." It is a carefully weighed decision, whether to inform, and when, and by whom. In all of these, the physician should adhere to "The first rule of Medicine: Never harm the patient."

THE FUTURE

Medical science stands on the edge of uncharted frontiers which go far beyond healing, into areas of life-control that require the gravest moral consideration. The modern physician has always faced problems such as: defining death, determining when experimental theory can be translated into clinical practice, deciding when "not to treat," computing risk-benefit ratios, and making heart-rending decisions of triage, and allocation of scarce resources to vital needs. To these are now added areas which only a generation ago belonged to science fiction: cloning, genetic engineering, *in vitro* fertilization, major organ transplants, and the elusive, often delusive goals of "improving the quality of life."

SECTION B

Persons and Their Lives

INTRODUCTION

One of the crucial decisions that health-care providers often have to make concerns life and death. These are decisions about when it is appropriate to withhold and/or withdraw life-support measures; decisions about when, if ever, it is appropriate to actively end human life; decisions about what is death, and so forth. This section of the readings introduces the basic theoretical issues involved in such decisions, issues that need to be thought-out now before we look at the cases in Part III of the text.

When one begins to think of these issues, one is immediately struck by the need to discuss two separate questions. The first is the question of what is a person. We tend to think that the lives of persons are special, and that a fundamental moral value is the value of protecting the lives of persons. But we are unsure about the scope of that value. Are only members of our species persons or can some animals be considered persons? Are fetuses at some point between conception and birth persons? Are newborns? Are patients whose entire brain has ceased functioning? What about comatose patients? The answer to these questions will obviously be very relevant to the analysis of many of the clinical cases we will be discussing in Part III. We need a theory of personhood to help us deal with these questions, and the readings by Devine, Sumner, Brody, Tooley, and Engelhardt are alternative attempts to develop such a theory of personhood.

The second question we need to ask relates to the nature and strength of the value of protecting the lives of persons. Is there a distinction between the taking of a person's life and the failure to save that life? May a person justifiably take his or her own life, and if so, when may one do so? Can someone else do so at the person's request? When, if ever, may we justifiably fail to provide the health care that would save the life of a person? Does it make a difference what type of care we are failing to provide? Does it make a difference whether we are withdrawing care already provided or withholding care not yet provided? The answer to these questions will also be very relevant to the analysis of many of the clinical cases we will be discussing in Part III. We need a theory of the nature and strength of the value of protecting the lives of persons to help us deal with these questions. The readings in Section B–6 provide us with alternative attempts to develop such a theory.

Devine, who is the first author we encounter in the readings, begins by identifying two principles of personhood that he finds plausible. One is the *species principle,* the principle that persons are all those organisms who are members of the human species. Another is the *potentiality principle,* the principle that any creature who has the potentiality of possessing certain crucial features of a normal adult human is a person. Devine notes that both principles ascribe personhood to fetuses and newborns as well as to reversibly unconscious adults, but that these principles disagree about gravely retarded or permanently comatose human beings. Devine also attempts some synthesis of these principles. What reasons does he offer for each of them? How does he meet objections to them? How does he attempt to synthesize them? These questions require the reader's attention.

Many people are concerned as to whether a species principle of personhood is not unfairly biased against members of other species. An alternative would be a principle advanced by Sumner, the *criterion of sentience,* the criterion that creatures experiencing sensations such as pleasure and pain and emotions are persons. Sumner argues for this view and against a view that would require higher-order cognitive processes. What type of moral appeal does he have in mind when he argues that the nature of morality justifies his principle? He also suggests that some organisms might have more of a claim to personhood than others. How would that compare with Devine's view?

A third attempt to define personhood is found in the selection by Brody, who argues that we ought to use current criteria of death as a basis for understanding personhood. That leads him to two suggestions. One is that a person is an entity with a functioning brain and the other that it is an entity with a functioning heart. Many questions are raised by Brody's analysis. These include: Can we use the criteria of death to understand personhood or don't we need a theory of personhood to understand death? Would we have to extend personhood to many animals if we adopt this theory of personhood? How can we decide between these two theories of personhood?

These three theories of personhood are clearly rather inclusive theories of personhood. The authors themselves point out that most of their theories extend at least some degree of personhood to fetuses and some extend personhood to some animal species. A far less inclusive theory of personhood is advocated by Tooley. Here the relevant notion of personhood (at least insofar as that involves having a right to life) requires that the entity in question possess at some time the concept of itself as a continuing self. Tooley explicitly concludes that it is unlikely that fetuses and even newborns meet this criterion. Like Sumner, Tooley rests his argument upon an analysis of a specific moral appeal. Which moral appeal? Is it the same as Sumner's? Does Tooley's criterion of personhood follow from that analysis? All of these questions require careful thought.

Engelhardt, like many of our other authors, begins with the distinction between human biologial life and personhood. For him, a person is a moral agent, one who has the capacity to reason, to choose freely, to have interests, and to have the capacity to be concerned about the nature of proper conduct. This does not lead him to conclude that humans who are not persons have lives not worthy of some respect, but only that they are not persons, with the strong implications of that status for the value of protecting life. The reader needs to compare carefully Tooley's and Engelhardt's positions and the reasons for their positions, because even though both deny personhood even to newborns, they have different criteria and different reasons for doing so.

One general theme to which we have already alluded in some of our comments certainly deserves careful attention. The value of protecting the lives of persons can be rooted in many different types of moral appeals. Do some of them naturally lead to different theories of personhood than do others? Is there an "appeal to consequences" conception of personhood that is different from an "appeal to rights" conception of personhood, which is still different from an "appeal to virtues" conception of personhood?

We next turn to those readings that discuss the second of our major questions, namely, the question of the nature and strength of the value of protecting the lives of persons. The opening reading by Grisez and Boyle (supplemented by the brief selection from Engelhardt's exposition of Kenny) expresses a very traditional Catholic approach to this question. Grisez and Boyle begin by providing a definition of killing and go on to argue that suicide (but not the decisions of martyrs to die rather than violate their conscience), voluntary and nonvoluntary euthanasia, and certain decisions to withhold care fall under this definition of killing and are morally wrong. They insist, however, that certain decisions to withhold care (cases of triaging or cases of withholding extraordinary means of care) do not fall under their definition and may be morally permissible. Crucial to their definition and to the resulting analysis is the difference between intended results and foreseen but unintended results, and both that distinction and the resulting principle of double effect are explained more fully by Kenny.

Many questions are raised by this traditional analysis, which the reader must consider carefully before looking at alternatives. Among them are the following: What is the moral basis of Grisez and Boyle's absolute opposition to killing and is it justified? In light of their basis, is their definition of killing correct? Can they really allow—given their definition of killing and their moral basis for opposing it—for cases in which one can justifiably withhold life-sustaining care from patients?

Opponents of this traditional approach argue that there are cases in which actively killing other individuals (including patients) is morally justifiable. The readings from Brody and Singer advocate this position, although they offer different reasons and would therefore justify that killing in different cases. Brody's argument rests on the suppositions that killing is wrong just because it deprives the victim of the life to which the victim has a right and that that right, like all other rights, can be waived by the victim. Cases of suicide and voluntary euthanasia cannot therefore be wrongful killings because the "victim" has consented. Given that argument, Brody's justification only applies to cases in which the person wishes that his or her life be taken. It should be noted that Brody has argued elsewhere that religious people might have other religiously based reasons for opposing the taking of life and might therefore have reasons for objecting both to suicide and voluntary euthanasia. Singer's argument is quite different. His claim is that in those cases in which we (and even Grisez and Boyle) are willing to let a patient die, we should sometimes on humane grounds actively end the life of the patient. Because these patients suffer for a considerable time before they die, we should avoid that by ending their life. Singer's argument clearly applies then to cases in which active killing would produce better results, and these are not necessarily the cases to which Brody's argument applies.

These two readings raise many questions: What different moral appeals that explain the usual wrongness of killing form the basis of these very different arguments for active euthanasia? Why do these different appeals lead to very different reasons about when active euthanasia is permissible? Do Grisez and Boyle have some other basis for objecting to killing, one that could be used to object to the arguments offered by Brody and Singer?

The reading by the members of the President's Commission offers another basis for objecting to the traditional views of Grisez and Boyle. They insist that traditional distinctions such as the distinction between acting and omitting to act, between stopping therapy and failing to initiate therapy, between intended and unintended consequences, and between ordinary and extraordinary care are either morally irrelevant or confusing. They conclude instead that a decision to forgo treatment is justifiable when it has been made by qualified decision-makers who judge the risk of death acceptable in the circumstances in question. This leads the Commission to accept the idea that care can be withheld, for example, from persistent vegetative patients on the grounds that continued care provides little if any benefits to them and considerable harm to others (for example, their family, society as a whole).

Many questions are raised by these readings: What moral appeals form the basis of the analyses? Are these analyses justifications of suicide and active euthanasia, or are they merely justifications for many more cases of justifiably allowing patients to die?

We turn finally to the question of the sanctity of human life. That principle, as the Canadian Law Reform Commission points out, is primarily rooted in religious traditions, even if nonreligious bases have been offered for it. The authors of the Jewish Compendium on Medical Ethics reaffirm that principle and use it as a basis for opposing suicide and euthanasia, even when the patient requests that he or she be killed. They also use it as a basis for opposing failing to provide or withdrawing life-saving care, except when "the patient is no longer responsive to his [the physician's] ministration." This is probably an even more restrictive approach than the approach of Grisez and Boyle. It naturally leads us to ask what is the difference between these two moral appeals that lead to different conclusions about when withholding care is permissible?

Finally, Engelhardt, in his discussion of passive euthanasia for certain types of deformed children, argues that there are cases in which the continued existence of the patient is a harm to that patient as well as to others, and he suggests that failing to provide further care can actually be obligatory in such cases. The President's Commission, while not willing to go that far, is willing to say that failing to provide care in such cases is at least permissible, since continued existence is, at most, a modest benefit.

In short, we have seen approaches ranging from the view that the active killing of patients is sometimes permissible to the view that only in very narrowly defined circumstances can the physician even withhold life-saving care. In each case, clearly different moral appeals form the bases for these different approaches. In reference to both of our questions—the question of what is a person and the question of the nature and strength of the value of protecting the lives of persons—one must refer back to the appeals discussed in Part I of this text to understand the positions and to properly evaluate them.

5.   THE CONCEPT OF A PERSON

The Species Principle and the Potentiality Principle

Philip E. Devine

7.   THE SPECIES PRINCIPLE

A first statement of the species principle as it applies to killing is as follows: those creatures protected by the moral rule against homicide are the members of the human species, and only the members of the human species. This version of the principle protects all human organisms, whatever their degree of maturity or decay, including fetuses and embryos, but not robots or non-human animals, whatever the attainments of such beings might be.

The species principle does not mean, as Joseph Fletcher thinks, that "we would be human if we have opposable thumbs, are capable of face-to-face coitus and have a brain weighing 1400 grams, whether a particular brain functions cerebrally or not." Obviously a creature might be morally and biologically human while lacking one of these traits—say a child born without hands (and thus without thumbs)—and it is easy to imagine a species that met the suggested criteria without being in any sense human. Membership in a biological species is a complex matter, but scientists are now well able to recognize biological humanity in the fine structure of an organism, without reference to such things as opposable thumbs. Jérôme Lejeune puts the point nicely:

> Let us take the example of trisomy 21 [a chromosome disorder], observed by amniocentesis. Looking at the chromosomes and detecting the extra 21, we say very safely "The child who will develop here will be a trisomic 21." But this phrase does not convey all the information. We have not seen only the extra 21; we have also seen all the 46 other chromosomes and concluded that they were human, because if they had been mouse or monkey chromosomes, we would have noticed.

In other words, even a human defective is a defective *human,* and this biological humanity is recognizable in the genetic structure of the organism even when the genetic structure itself is defective.

Some vagueness does afflict the species principle when it comes to deciding precisely when—at conception or shortly thereafter, when the unity and uniqueness of the nascent creature is secured—a human organism comes into existence, as well as how much breakdown is necessary before we say that a human organism has ceased to be. Ape-human hybrids and the like also pose a knotty problem. But none of these zones of vagueness render the principle unusable, nor do they provide any grounds for refusing to use the principle to condemn killing where the victim is unambiguously a human organism.

Finally, the species principle provides an adequate answer to the "acorn" argument, which has a surprising persistence in disputes about abortion. Whatever may be the case with dormant acorns, a germinating acorn is, while not an oak *tree,* still a member of the appropriate species of oak. If oaks had a serious right to life in their own right, so would oak saplings and germinating acorns. And the same reply can be made to those who would argue about abortion from the premise that a caterpillar is not a butterfly.

A more troubling charge is that of species chauvinism: the charge, that is, that the giving of a higher moral status to members of one's own species than to those of others is akin to regarding members of other races as subhuman. It would not be chauvinism in the strict sense to argue that between two intelligent species, members of one have no rights which members of the other are bound to respect, while each agent is morally required to respect the rights of members of his own species, in particular not to kill them unless he has a very compelling justification. It is, after all, considered worse (all other things being equal) to kill one's brother than a stranger, not because one's brother in himself is morally more worthy than the stranger, but because the relationship between brothers is itself morally significant. Nonetheless we would certainly want intelligent Martians to respect our rights, and might be prepared to respect theirs in return. And, if Martians were enough like human beings that the notion of human individuality could be extended to them, this respect for their rights would naturally take the form, *inter alia,* of regarding Martians as protected by our moral (and quite possibly our legal) rules against homicide.

But this line of thought can be accommodated by a modification of the species principle which does not alter its essential structure. According to this modification, what the moral rule against homicide protects is all members of intelligent species, including, but not limited to, the human. On this account determining whether a given creature is protected by the moral rule against homicide is a two-step process: first, identifying the species to which the creature belongs, and second, deciding whether this species is in fact intelligent. For members of the human species, the human species continues to play a somewhat paradigmatic role, in setting the standard of intelligence which must be approached or exceeded for a species to be considered intelligent, and the same is true for members of other intelligent species. A human being will ask whether Martians as a species are intelligent enough by human standards to be regarded

as persons, and an intelligent Martian will make the corresponding inquiry concerning human beings. In any case, all creatures protected by the original species principle are protected by the modified species principle as well.

Three problems of application arise for the modified species principle, of particular importance in assessing the claims which might be made on behalf of chimpanzees, whales, and dolphins. First, supposing one member of a species reaches the human level, what effect does this achievement have on the status of the other members of the species? Second, what kind of standards are to be employed in determining whether a given species is to be regarded as intelligent? Since we cannot, in answering these questions, rely on the considerations of lineage which settle nearly all questions of species membership, they will require very careful examination.

It seems that we want to regard an individual cat which has, through some chance or other, attained human intelligence as protected by the moral rule against homicide. To do so consistently with the species principle requires the adoption of one of two strategies: (1) the existence of such a cat renders the entire species *Felis domestica* an intelligent species, and all of its members protected by the moral rule against homicide (consider the plea such a cat might make on behalf of its less intelligent brethren) or (2) the intelligence of our super-cat might be considered as producing a different species, consisting of him alone, although he is still capable of breeding fertilely with other, less favored, cats. (He may wish to disassociate himself from other cats, and feel humiliated by his bodily likeness to subhuman creatures.) The first of these strategies would be plausible for the claims of dolphins and the like, all of which at least come somewhat close to human intelligence. The second would be more plausible for the claims of cats and dogs.

The second question is what traits are decisive for regarding a given individual as rendering his species intelligent. Self-consciousness (or consciousness of oneself as a subject of conscious states) might be suggested, as a necessary condition of the desire to live. Moral agency is another contender, since moral agents are presupposed by moral discourse as such. Finally, the use of language is the key to the rich kind of life enjoyed by human beings, so that it may be taken as what distinguishes the human from the subhuman. An attractive blend of these last two possibilities is participation in moral discourse: if we discover that Martians argue about the issues discussed in this book, we should be obliged to regard them for moral purposes as human.

The question of which traits are crucial is less important for the species than for other interpretations of the moral rule against homicide, since no attempt is made to draw lines within the human species. But even here it may be crucial—especially on some interpretations of what it is to speak a language—to the status of some nonhumans such as chimpanzees. What seems to be the case is that the distinction between human and nonhuman rests not on any one trait, but on an interlocking set of traits, which will wax and wane as a whole.

Finally, we need to ask (supposing that the relevant traits admit of degree) how much of them is required to make a species one of the human level. (If they do not, we will still have to adjudicate borderline cases.) It is worth noticing that our standards can be more demanding here than for either of the species principle's two rivals. In order to reach minimally tolerable results, the present enjoyment principle will have to demand very little of a creature before treating it as a person; the potentiality principle can ask for more, since what the creature will attain in due course, not what it attains now, is the standard. But the species principle can demand the production of saints, philosophers, musicians, scientists, or whatever else is thought to be the highest embodiment of human nature, since the bulk of the species

can gain their morally privileged status through the achievements of their best members, so long as there is not a sharp break between the capacities of the best of a species and members of that species generally.

14. THE POTENTIALITY PRINCIPLE

The case just made for regarding the fetus or embryo as a human person does not depend on identifying a person with a human organism. One could ascribe personhood to members of other intelligent species, and deny it to so-called human vegetables, while ascribing it to the (normal) fetus. The underlying premise of such an ascription is what has been called the potentiality principle.

Like the species principle, but unlike the present enjoyment principle, the potentiality principle accounts quite without difficulty for our ascription of humanity to infants and the unconscious and requires ascribing humanity to fetuses as well. According to this principle, there is a property, self-consciousness or the use of speech for instance, such that (*i*) it is possessed by adult humans, (*ii*) it endows any organism possessing it with a serious right to life, and (*iii*) it is such that any organism potentially possessing it has a serious right to life even now—where an organism possesses a property potentially if it will come to have that property under normal conditions for development. It is often convenient to speak of those who are regarded as persons under the potentiality principle, but not under the present enjoyment principle, as "potential persons." But this usage is misleading. For even a normal, awake adult can be thought of as a person for essentially the same reasons as an embryo: both are capable of using speech and so on, although the embryo's capacity requires the more time and care before it is realized.

Notice that, whereas the potentiality principle extends a right to live to all creatures potentially possessing self-consciousness or the use of speech, it could be narrowed to require that such organisms also possess certain additional properties $P_l \ldots P_n$ (e.g., exclusion of twinning, the presence of brain activity, or existence outside the uterus) to have a right to live. A defender of a narrowed version of the principle would, of course, have to show that the additional properties $P_l \ldots P_n$ provided a morally relevant reason to ascribe rights to those having them and to deny rights to those not possessing them. I have had occasion to consider the merits of some suggestions along these lines above.

The basis of the potentiality principle is quite simple: what makes the difference between human beings and other life is the capacity human beings enjoy for a specially rich kind of life. The life already enjoyed by a human being cannot be taken away from him, only the prospect of such life in the future. But this prospect is possessed as much by an infant or fetus as by a full-grown adult. But it is not possessed by the irreversibly comatose, and thus they are morally speaking dead from the standpoint of the potentiality principle.

Finally, a word about the logic of the potentiality principle is in order. The potentiality principle relies heavily on the distinction between what happens in the ordinary course of events, as opposed to by miracle, freak accident, or extraordinary human intervention. Philosophers have sometimes expressed considerable difficulty with such distinctions, and if such difficulties were allowed to prevail, the potentiality principle would collapse, since anything that could be given self-consciousness or other distinctively human traits by some extraordinary manipulation would then be a person. But most of us can understand that a kitten's growing up into a rational being—even if it should happen without human intervention once in a million years—would not be part of the normal course of events, whereas the similar maturation of a human fetus or infant is. Although I have cited the case of a very rare occurrence, the distinc-

tion I have in mind is only in part statistical. Pregnancy for instance is a normal result of coitus, even though it results from coitus with relative infrequency. Hence also statistics on infant mortality and fetal loss are of little relevance to the question of what the normal development of a human infant or fetus is.

Nonetheless, the distinction between a potential person and something which might become a person under extraordinary conditions is dependent on the prevailing conditions of human experience and would change its complexion if these conditions were to be drastically altered. Joel Feinberg observes:

> If we lived in a world in which every biologically capable human female became pregnant once a year throughout her entire fertile period of life [without external intervention], then we would regard fertilization as something which happens to every ovum in "the natural course of events." Perhaps we would regard every unfertilized ovum, in such a world, as a potential person even possessed of rights corresponding to its future interests. It would perhaps make conceptual if not moral sense in such a world to regard deliberate nonfertilization as a kind of homicide.

What the ethics of such a world might be is a matter concerning which it is only possible to speculate. (The case for drawing the line at the beginning of recognizably human form rather than at "conception" would probably be much strengthened.) In any case, it should be possible to acknowledge that changes in human experiences, purposes, and techniques could produce changes in the application of concepts like "right" without regarding every new biomedical development as altering the parameters of moral discourse so fundamentally as to render all older ideas irrelevant. Hence we have good reasons to use the potentiality principle to ascribe personhood to immature human organisms, such as fetuses and infants, and not to spermatozoa and ova.

15. THE POTENTIALITY AND SPECIES PRINCIPLES

The potentiality and species principles both protect all normal human infants and unborn children, along with the reversibly unconscious and, of course, normal, awake adults. They differ importantly as to scope, however. According to the potentiality principle, a gravely retarded human (unable, let us say, ever to communicate with us at all as a person), and an irreversibly comatose human organism whose heart beats of its own accord are not persons, whereas they are members of the human species and as such are protected by the species principle. (The status of someone whose heart beats on only because it is artificially stimulated is unclear even on the species principle.) While generous impulses and an unwillingness to take the moral risk of acting on the narrower principle may predispose us to adopt the species principle, a surer foundation for choice is greatly to be desired.

In what follows, I shall offer a tentative synthesis of the two principles, which I hope will be at least to a minimum degree intuitively acceptable. I shall use the potentiality principle to specify the extension of the expression "person," while continuing to use "human being" as a morally significant expression. That is to say, I shall distinguish two classes of creatures, delimited by the two versions of the moral rule against homicide: persons, that is, creatures having the capacity or potentiality of doing distinctively human things; and human beings, that is, members of the human species. (What is true of human beings could also be true of members of other intelligent species.) I shall suggest that a prima facie obligation to abstain from killing both kinds of creature exists, but the obligation to abstain from killing persons is both primary and more stringent.

Respect for persons is morally fundamental. To deprive a person of his capacity to perform personal acts—to reduce a person to a thing, or displace him by one—is an act that can only be justified under the most stringent conditions. And killing is precisely such a reduction of the victim from personhood to thinghood or the annihilation of a person in favor of a thing. It is unclear whether the language of reduction, or the language of annihilation and replacement, is more appropriate here, because of the suggestion that someone whose existence as a person has ceased may yet survive as a human being. For most purposes, reduction of a person to a thing may be taken as a portrayal of death which, while somewhat mythical, since it supposes that a person is somehow identical with his corpse, is a good enough approximation that ethical conclusions can be drawn from it.

But the principle of respect for persons also extends, by what might be called the "overflow principle," to things closely associated with persons. Thus corpses ought not to be treated as ordinary garbage, and one might also argue that a modicum of reverence should be accorded the processes by which persons come to be. This line of thought explains the (otherwise quite bewildering) expression "the sanctity of life" (as opposed to the sanctity of the living individual), as well as the connection many have seen between questions of homicide and such questions as artificial insemination. Nothing more is claimed for the overflow principle here than that it helps explain a number of our intuitions, and helps suggest a way of bringing together the species and potentiality principles in a way that appears to do justice to the claims of each.

Human beings who are not persons (the expression "person" being used in the semi-technical sense explained above) are entitled to a degree of respect because of their close association with persons. First, all human beings are entitled to be presumed to be persons until it is absolutely clear that they have no capacity for personal activity. Second, even those human beings who clearly have no such capacity ought not to be killed except where the reasons for so doing are very strong and the resulting danger to the principle of respect for persons very small. Thus, for instance, even the most severely mentally retarded ought not to be killed, since to do so would endanger those (the majority of the retarded) who can, with effort, be brought to a human level of existence (roughly, can be taught to talk). On the other hand, one might perhaps allow an abortion to be performed upon fetal indications, to avoid great suffering on the part of the parents, in cases of grave and irremediable mental defect (not, it deserves emphasis, on grounds of physical defect: an oddly shaped human being is no less a person for that reason). For fetuses are not very closely imaginatively linked with born persons. On these premises, disorders like Tay-Sachs disease, which by killing in early childhood prevent the development of significant human capacities, provide (given certainty of diagnosis) just enough justification for abortion on fetal indications. Down's syndrome (mongolism), on the other hand, does not. For some mongols at any rate manage to attain the capacity to speak to us as persons.

Again, an irreversibly comatose human being ought not to be hurried into the grave in order to advance the hospital schedule. But if his heart is needed to save the life of another, it might be taken from him for that end. (Notice, however, that all comas are, in the absence of very clear evidence, to be presumed reversible: one might, of course, terminate life-support systems on grounds of futility somewhat before the point of certainty, though the decision is a very grave one.) Where the body is kept going only by massive artificial aid, one might, indeed, conclude that what one has here is not even a human organism but a corpse with a beating heart.

The Criterion of Sentience

L. W. Sumner

A criterion of life (or teleology) is too weak, admitting classes of beings (animate or inanimate) who are not suitable loci for moral rights; being alive is necessary for having standing, but it is not sufficient. A criterion of rationality (or moral agency) is too strong, excluding classes of beings (human and nonhuman) who are suitable loci for rights; being rational is sufficient for having standing, but it is not necessary. A criterion of sentience (or consciousness) is a promising middle path between these extremes. Sentience is the capacity for feeling or affect. In its most primitive form it is the ability to experience sensations of pleasure and pain, and thus the ability to enjoy and suffer. Its more developed forms include wants, aims, and desires (and thus the ability to be satisfied and frustrated); attitudes, tastes, and values; and moods, emotions, sentiments, and passions. Consciousness is a necessary condition of sentience, for feelings are states of mind of which their owner is aware. But it is not sufficient; it is at least possible in principle for beings to be conscious (percipient, for instance, or even rational) while utterly lacking feelings. If rationality embraces a set of cognitive capacities, then sentience is rooted in a being's affective and conative life. It is in virtue of being sentient that creatures have interests, which are compounded either out of their desires or out of the experiences they find agreeable (or both). If morality has to do with the protection and promotion of interests, it is plausible conjecture that we owe moral duties to all those beings capable of having interests. But this will include all sentient creatures.

Most animal species, like all plant species, are (so far as we can tell) utterly nonsentient. Like consciousness, sentience emerged during the evolutionary process as a means of permitting more flexible behavior patterns and thus of aiding survival. Biologically it is marked by the emergence in the first vertebrates of the forebrain (the primitive ancestor of the human cerebral hemispheres).[1] As far as can be determined, even the simple capacity for pleasure and pain is not possessed by invertebrate animals. If this is the case, then the phylogenetic threshold of moral standing is the boundary between invertebrates and vertebrates.

Like rationality, and unlike life, it makes sense to think of sentience as admitting of degrees. Within any given mode, such as the perception of pain, one creature may be more or less sensitive than another. But there is a further sense in which more developed (more rational) creatures possess a higher degree of sentience. The expansion of consciousness and of intelligence opens up new ways of experiencing the world, and therefore new ways of being affected by the world. More rational beings are capable of finding either fulfilment or frustration in activities and states of affairs to which less developed creatures are, both cognitively and affectively, blind. It is in this sense of a broader and deeper sensibility that a higher being is capable of a richer, fuller, and more varied existence. The fact that sentience admits of degrees (whether of sensitivity or sensibility) enables us to employ it both as an inclusion criterion and as a comparison criterion of moral standing. The animal kingdom presents us with a hierarchy of sentience. Nonsentient beings have no moral standing; among sentient beings the more developed have greater standing than the less developed, the upper limit being occupied by the paradigm of a normal adult human being. Although sentience is the criterion of moral standing, it is also possible to explain the relevance of rationality. The evolutionary order is one of ascending intelligence. Since rationality expands a creature's interests, it is a reliable indicator of the degree of moral standing which that creature possesses. Creatures less rational than human beings do not altogether lack standing, but they do lack full standing.

An analysis of degrees of standing would require a graded right to life, in which the strength of the right varied inversely with the range of considerations capable of overriding it. The details of any such analysis will be complex and need not be worked out here. However, it seems that we are committed to extending (some) moral standing to all vertebrate animals, and also to counting higher animals for more than lower. Thus we should expect the higher vertebrates (mammals) to merit greater protection of life than the lower (fish, reptiles, amphibia, birds) and we should also expect the higher mammals (primates, cetaceans) to merit greater protection of life than the lower (canines, felines, etc.). Crude as this division may be, it seems to accord reasonably well with most people's intuitions that in our moral reasoning paramecia and horseflies count for nothing, dogs and cats count for something, chimpanzees and dolphins count for more, and human beings count for most of all.

A criterion of sentience can thus allow for the gradual emergence of moral standing in the order of nature. It can explain why no moral issues arise (directly) in our dealings with inanimate objects, plants, and the simpler forms of animal life. It can also function as a moral guideline in our encounters with novel life forms on other planets. If the creatures we meet have interests and are capable of enjoyment and suffering, we must grant them some moral standing. We thereby constrain ourselves not to exploit them ruthlessly for our own advantage. The kind of standing that they deserve may be determined by the range and depth of their sensibility, and in ordinary circumstances this will vary with their intelligence. We should therefore recognize as equals beings who are as rational and sensitive as ourselves. The criterion also implies that if we encounter creatures who are rational but nonsentient—who utterly lack affect and desire—nothing we can do will adversely affect such creatures (in morally relevant ways). We would be entitled, for instance, to treat them as a species of organic computers. The same obviously holds for forms of artificial intelligence; in deciding whether to extend moral standing to sophisticated machines, the question (as Bentham put it) is not whether they can reason but whether they can suffer.

A criterion of sentience also requires gentle usage of the severely abnormal. Cognitive disabilities and disorders may impair a person's range of sensibility, but they do not generally reduce that person to the level of a nonsentient being. Even the grossly retarded or deranged will still be capable of some forms of enjoyment and suffering and thus will still possess (some) moral standing in their own right. This standing diminishes to the vanishing point only when sentience is entirely lost (irreversible coma) or never gained in the first place (anencephaly). If all affect and responsivity are absent, and if they cannot be engendered, then (but only then) are we no longer dealing with a sentient creature. This verdict accords well with the contemporary trend toward defining death in terms of the permanent loss of cerebral functioning. Although such patients are in one obvious sense still alive (their blood circulates and is oxygenated), in the morally relevant sense they are now beyond our reach, for we can cause them neither good nor ill. A criterion of life would require us to continue treating them as beings with (full?) moral standing, whereas a criterion of rationality would withdraw that standing when reason was lost even though sensibility should remain. Again a criterion of sentience enables us to find a middle way.

Fastening upon sentience as the criterion for possession of a right to life thus opens up the possibility of a reasonable and moderate treatment of moral problems other than abortion, problems pertaining to the treatment of nonhuman animals, extraterrestrial life, artificial intelligence, "defective" human beings, and persons at the end of life. We need now to trace out its implications for the fetus.

---

1. Psychologists and physiologists tend to use the term "consciousness" to cover perception and such higher-order cognitive processes as thought and language use, rather than sensation. In this sense conscious activities in human beings are localized in the cerebral cortex, an area of the brain that we share with most mammals. Sensation (pleasure/pain) and emotion are rooted in the limbic system, an evolutionarily more ancient part of the brain present in most vertebrates.

The Criterion of Brain Functioning

Baruch A. Brody

FETAL HUMANITY AND BRAIN FUNCTION

The question which we must now consider is the question of fetal humanity. Some have argued that the fetus is a human being with a right to life (or, for convenience, just a human being) from the moment of conception. Others have argued that the fetus only becomes a human being at the moment of birth. Many positions in between these two extremes have also been suggested. How are we to decide which is correct?

The analysis which we will propose here rests upon certain metaphysical assumptions which I have defended elsewhere. These assumptions are: (a) the question is when has the fetus acquired all the properties essential (necessary) for being a human being, for when it has, it is a human being; (b) these properties are such that the loss of any one of them means that the human being in question has gone out of existence and not merely stopped being a human being; (c) human beings go out of existence when they die. It follows from these assumptions that the fetus becomes a human being when it acquires all those characteristics which are such that the loss of any one of them would result in the fetus's being dead. We must, therefore, turn to the analysis of death. . . .

We will first consider the question of

what properties are essential to being human if we suppose that death and the passing out of existence occur only if there has been an irreparable cessation of brain function (keeping in mind that that condition itself, as we have noted, is a matter of medical judgment). We shall then consider the same question on the supposition that Ramsey's more complicated theory of death (the modified traditional view) is correct.

According to what is called the brain-death theory, as long as there has not been an irreparable cessation of brain function the person in question continues to exist, no matter what else has happened to him. If so, it seems to follow that there is only one property—leaving aside those entailed by this one property—that is essential to humanity, namely, the possession of a brain that has not suffered an irreparable cessation of function.

Several consequences follow immediately from this conclusion. We can see that a variety of often advanced claims about the essence of humanity are false. For example, the claim that movement, or perhaps just the ability to move, is essential for being human is false. A human being who has stopped moving, and even one who has lost the ability to move, has not therefore stopped existing. Being able to move, and *a fortiori* moving, are not essential properties of human beings and therefore are not essential to being human. Similarly, the claim that being perceivable by other human beings is essential for being human is also false. A human being who has stopped being perceivable by other humans (for example, someone isolated on the other side of the moon, out of reach even of radio communication) has not stopped existing. Being perceivable by other human beings is not an essential property of human beings and is not essential to being human. And the same point can be made about the claims that viability is essential for being human, that independent existence is essential for being human, and that actual interaction with other human beings is essential for

being human. The loss of any of these properties would not mean that the human being in question had gone out of existence, so none of them can be essential to that human being and none of them can be essential for being human.

Let us now look at the following argument: (1) A functioning brain (or at least, a brain that, if not functioning, is susceptible of function) is a property that every human being must have because it is essential for being human. (2) By the time an entity acquires that property, it has all the other properties that are essential for being human. Therefore, when the fetus acquires that property it becomes a human being. It is clear that the property in question is, according to the brain-death theory, one that is had essentially by all human beings. The question that we have to consider is whether the second premise is true. It might appear that its truth does follow from the brain-death theory. After all, we did see that that theory entails that only one property (together with those entailed by it) is essential for being human. Nevertheless, rather than relying solely on my earlier argument, I shall adopt an alternative approach to strengthen the conviction that this second premise is true: I shall note the important ways in which the fetus resembles and differs from an ordinary human being by the time it definitely has a functioning brain (about the end of the sixth week of development). It shall then be evident, in light of our theory of essentialism, that none of these differences involves the lack of some property in the fetus that is essential for its being human.

Structurally, there are few features of the human being that are not fully present by the end of the sixth week. Not only are the familiar external features and all the internal organs present, but the contours of the body are nicely rounded. More important, the body is functioning. Not only is the brain functioning, but the heart is beating sturdily (the fetus by this time has its own completely developed vascular system), the stomach is producing digestive juices, the liver is manufacturing blood cells, the kidney is extracting uric acid from the blood, and the nerves and muscles are operating in concert, so that reflex reactions can begin.

What are the properties that a fetus acquires after the sixth week of its development? Certain structures do appear later. These include the fingernails (which appear in the third month), the completed vocal chords (which also appear then), taste buds and salivary glands (again, in the third month), and hair and eyelashes (in the fifth month). In addition, certain functions begin later than the sixth week. The fetus begins to urinate (in the third month), to move spontaneously (in the third month), to respond to external stimuli (at least in the fifth month), and to breathe (in the sixth month). Moreover, there is a constant growth in size. And finally, at the time of birth the fetus ceases to receive its oxygen and food through the placenta and starts receiving them through the mouth and nose.

I will not examine each of these properties (structures and functions) to show that they are not essential for being human. The procedure would be essentially the one used previously to show that various essentialist claims are in error. We might, therefore, conclude, on the supposition that the brain-death theory is correct, that the fetus becomes a human being about the end of the sixth week after its development.

There is, however, one complication that should be noted here. There are, after all, progressive stages in the physical development and in the functioning of the brain. For example, the fetal brain (and nervous system) does not develop sufficiently to support spontaneous motion until some time in the third month after conception. There is, of course, no doubt that that stage of development is sufficient for the fetus to be human. No one would be likely to maintain that a spontaneously moving human being has died; and similarly, a spontaneously moving fetus would seem to have become human. One might, however, want to claim that the fetus does not become a human being until the point of spontaneous movement. So then, on the supposition that the brain-death theory of death is correct, one ought to conclude that the fetus becomes a human being at some time between the sixth and twelfth week after its conception.

But what if we reject the brain-death theory, and replace it with its equally plausible contender, Ramsey's theory of death? According to that theory—which we can call the brain, heart, and lung theory of death—the human being does not die, does not go out of existence, until such time as the brain, heart, and lungs have irreparably ceased functioning naturally. What are the essential features of being human according to this theory?

Actually, the adoption of Ramsey's theory requires no major modifications. According to that theory, what is essential to being human, what each human being must retain if he is to continue to exist, is the possession of a functioning (actually or potentially) heart, lung or brain. It is only when a human being possesses none of these that he dies and goes out of existence; and the fetus comes into humanity, so to speak, when he acquires one of these.

On Ramsey's theory, the argument would now run as follows: (1) The property of having a functioning brain, heart, or lungs (or at least organs of the kind that, if not functioning, are susceptible of function) is one that every human being must have because it is essential for being human. (2) By the time that an entity acquires that property it has all the other properties that are essential for being human. Therefore, when the fetus acquires that property it becomes a human being. There remains, once more, the problem of the second premise. Since the fetal heart starts operating rather early, it is not clear that the second premise is correct. Many systems are not yet operating, and many structures are not yet present. Still, following our theory of essentialism, we should conclude that the fetus becomes a human being when it acquires a functioning heart (the first of the organs to function in the fetus).

There is, however, a further complication here, and it is analogous to the one encountered if we adopt the brain-death theory. When may we properly say that the fetal heart begins to function? At two weeks, when occasional contractions of the primitive fetal heart are present? In the fourth to fifth week, when the heart, although incomplete, is beating regularly and pumping blood cells through a closed vascular system, and when the tracings obtained by an ECG exhibit the classical elements of an adult tracing? Or after the end of the seventh week, when the fetal heart is functionally complete and "normal"?

We have not reached a precise conclusion in our study of the question of when the fetus becomes a human being. We do know that it does so sometime between the end of the second week and the end of the third month. But it surely is not a human being at the moment of conception and it surely is one by the end of the third month. Though we have not come to a final answer to our question, we have narrowed the range of acceptable answers considerably.

The Criterion of Awareness of Self as a Continuing Entity

Michael Tooley

How can one determine what properties endow a being with a right to life? An approach that I believe is very promising starts out from the observation that there appear to be two radically different sorts of reasons why an entity may lack a certain right. Compare, for example, the following two claims:

(1) A child does not have a right to smoke.
(2) A newspaper does not have a right not to be torn up.

The first claim raises a substantive moral issue. People might well disagree about it, and support their conflicting views by appealing to different moral theories. The second dispute, in contrast, seems an unlikely candidate for moral dispute. It is natural to say that newspapers just are not the sort of thing that can have any rights at all, including a right not to be torn up. So there is no need to appeal to a substantive moral theory to resolve the question whether a newspaper has a right not to be torn up.

One way of characterizing this difference, albeit one that will not especially commend itself to philosophers of a Quinean bent, is to say that the second claim, unlike the first, is true in virtue of a certain *conceptual* connection, and that is why no moral theory is needed in order to see that it is true. The explanation, then, of why it is that a newspaper does not have a right not to be torn up, is that there is some property P such that, first, newspapers lack property P, and secondly, it is a conceptual truth that only things with property P can be possessors of rights.

What might property P be? A plausible answer, I believe, is set out and defended by Joel Feinberg in his paper, "The Rights of Animals and Unborn Generations." It takes the form of what Feinberg refers to as the *interest principle:* ". . . the sorts of beings who *can* have rights are precisely those who have (or can have) interests." And then, since "interests must be compounded somehow out of conations," it follows that things devoid of desires, such as newspapers, can have neither interests nor rights. Here, then, is one account of the difference in status between judgments such as (1) and (2) above.

Let us now consider the right to life. The interest principle tells us that an entity cannot have any rights at all, and *a fortiori*, cannot have a right to life, unless it is capable of having interests. This in itself may be a conclusion of considerable importance. Consider, for example, a fertilized human egg cell. Someday it will come to have desires and interests. As a zygote, however, it does not have desires, nor even the *capacity* for having desires. What about interests? This depends upon the account one offers of the relationship between desires and interests. It seems to me that a zygote cannot properly be spoken of as a subject of interests. My reason is roughly this. What is in a thing's interest is a function of its present and future desires, both those it will actually have and those it could have. In the case of an entity that is not presently capable of any desires, its interest must be based entirely upon the satisfaction of future desires. Then, since the satisfaction of future desires presupposes the continued existence of the entity in question, anything which has an interest which is based upon the satisfaction of future desires must also have an interest in its own continued existence. Therefore something which is not presently capable of having any desires at all—like a zygote—cannot have any interests at all unless it has an interest in its own continued existence. I shall argue shortly, however, that a zygote cannot have such an interest. From this it will follow that it cannot have any interests at all, and this conclusion, together with the interest principle, entails that not all members of the species *Homo sapiens* have a right to life.

The interest principle involves, then, a thesis concerning a necessary condition which something must satisfy if it is to have a right to life, and it is a thesis which has important moral implications. It implies, for example, that abortions, if performed sufficiently early, do not involve any violation of a right to life. But on the other hand, the interest principle provides no help with the question of the moral status of human organisms once they have developed to the point where they do have desires, and thus are capable of having interests. The interest principle states that they *can* have rights. It does not state whether they *do* have rights—

including, in particular, a right not to be destroyed.

It is possible, however, that the interest principle does not exhaust the conceptual connections between rights and interests. It formulates only a very general connection: a thing cannot have any rights at all unless it is capable of having at least some interest. May there not be more specific connections, between particular rights and particular sorts of interests? The following line of thought lends plausibility to this suggestion. Consider animals such as cats. Some philosophers are inclined to hold that animals such as cats do not have any rights at all. But let us assume, for the purpose of the present discussion, that cats do have some rights, such as a right not to be tortured, and consider the following claim:

(3) A cat does not have a right to a university education.

How is this statement to be regarded? In particular, is it comparable in status to the claim that children do not have a right to smoke, or, instead, to the claim that newspapers do not have a right not to be torn up? To the latter, surely. Just as a newspaper is not the sort of thing that can have any rights at all, including a right not to be destroyed, so one is inclined to say that a cat, though it may have some rights, such as a right not to be tortured, is not the sort of thing that can possibly have a right to a university education.

This intuitive judgment about the status of claims such as (3) is reinforced, moreover, if one turns to the question of the grounds of the interest principle. Consider, for example, the account offered by Feinberg, which he summarizes as follows:

Now we can extract from our discussion of animal rights a crucial principle for tentative use in the resolution of the other riddles about the applicability of the concept of a right, namely, that the sorts of beings who *can* have rights are precisely those who have (or can have) interests. I have come to this tentative conclusion for two reasons: (1) because a right holder must be capable of being represented and it is impossible to represent a being that has no interests, and (2) because a right holder must be capable of being a beneficiary in his own person, and a being without interests is a being that is incapable of being harmed or benefited, having no good or 'sake' of its own. Thus a being without interests has no 'behalf' to act in, and no 'sake' to act for.

If this justification of the interest principle is sound, it can also be employed to support principles connecting particular rights with specific sorts of interests. Just as one cannot represent a being that has no interests at all, so one cannot, in demanding a university education for a cat, be representing the cat unless one is thereby representing some interest that the cat has, and that would be served by its receiving a university education. Similarly, one cannot be acting for the sake of a cat in arguing that it should receive a university education unless the cat has some interest that will thereby be furthered. The conclusion, therefore, is that if Feinberg's defense of the interest principle is sound, other more specific principles must also be correct. These more specific principles can be summed up, albeit somewhat vaguely, by the following, *particular-interests principle:*

> It is a conceptual truth that an entity cannot have a particular right, R, unless it is at least capable of having some interest, I, which is furthered by its having right R.

Given this particular-interests principle, certain familiar facts, whose importance has not often been appreciated, become comprehensible. Compare an act of killing a normal adult human being with an act of torturing one for five minutes. Though both acts are seriously wrong, they are not equally so. Here, as in most cases, to violate an individual's right to life is more seriously wrong than to violate his right not to have

pain inflicted upon him. Consider, however, the corresponding actions in the case of a newborn kitten. Most people feel that it is seriously wrong to torture a kitten for five minutes, but not to kill it painlessly. How is this difference in the moral ordering of the two types of acts, between the human case and the kitten case, to be explained? One answer is that while normal adult human beings have both a right to life and a right not to be tortured, a kitten has only the latter. But why should this be so? The particular-interests principle suggests a possible explanation. Though kittens have some interests, including, in particular, an interest in not being tortured, which derives from their capacity to feel pain, they do not have an interest in their own continued existence, and hence do not have a right not to be destroyed. This answer contains, of course, a large promissory element. One needs a defense of the view that kittens have no interest in continued existence. But the point here is simply that there is an important question about the rationale underlying the moral ordering of certain sorts of acts, and that the particular-interests principle points to a possible answer.

This fact lends further plausibility, I believe, to the particular-interests principle. What one would ultimately like to do, of course, is to set out an analysis of the concept of a right, show that the analysis is indeed satisfactory, and then show that the particular-interests principle is entailed by the analysis. Unfortunately, it will not be possible to pursue such an approach here, since formulating an acceptable analysis of the concept of a right is a far from trivial matter. What I should like to do, however, is to touch briefly upon the problem of providing such an analysis, and then to indicate the account that seems to me most satisfactory—an account which does entail the particular-interests principle.

It would be widely agreed, I believe, both that rights impose obligations, and that the obligations they impose upon others are *conditional* upon certain factors. The difficulty arises when one attempts to specify what the obligations are conditional upon. There seem to be two main views in this area. According to the one, rights impose obligations that are conditional upon the interests of the possessor of the right. To say that Sandra has a right to something is thus to say, roughly, that if it is in Sandra's interest to have that thing, then others are under an obligation not to deprive her of it. According to the second view, rights impose obligations that are conditional upon the right's not having been waived. To say that Sandra has a right to something is to say, roughly, that if Sandra has not given others permission to take the thing, then they are under an obligation not to deprive her of it.

Both views encounter serious difficulties. On the one hand, in the case of minors, and nonhuman animals, it would seem that the obligations that rights impose must be taken as conditional upon the interests of those individuals, rather than upon whether they have given one permission to do certain things. On the other, in the case of individuals who are capable of making informed and rational decisions, if that person has not given one permission to take something that belongs to him, it would seem that one is, in general, still under an obligation not to deprive him of it, even if having that thing is no longer in his interest.

As a result, it seems that a more complex account is needed of the factors upon which the obligations imposed by rights are conditional. The account which I now prefer, and which I have defended elsewhere, is this:

A has a right to X

means the same as

A is such that it can be in A's interest to have X, and *either* (1) A is not capable of making an informed and rational choice whether to grant others permission to deprive him of X, in which case, if it is in A's interest not to be deprived of X, then, by that fact alone, others are under a prima facie obligation not to de-prive A of X, *or* (2) A is capable of making an informed and rational choice whether to grant others permission to deprive him of X, in which case others are under a prima facie obligation not to deprive A of X if and only if A has not granted them permission to do so.

And if this account, or something rather similar is correct, then so is the particular-interests principle.

c) What I now want to do is apply the particular-interests principle to the case of the right to life. First, however, one needs to notice that the expression, "right to life," is not entirely happy, since it suggests that the right in question concerns the continued existence of a biological organism. That this is incorrect can be brought out by considering possible ways of violating an individual's right to life. Suppose, for example, that future technological developments make it possible to change completely the neural networks in a brain, and that the brain of some normal adult human being is thus completely reprogrammed, so that the organism in question winds up with memories (or rather, apparent memories), beliefs, attitudes, and personality traits totally different from those associated with it before it was subjected to reprogramming. (The pope is reprogrammed, say, on the model of Bertrand Russell.) In such a case, however beneficial the change might be, one would surely want to say that *someone* had been destroyed, that an adult human being's right to life had been violated, even though no biological organism had been killed. This shows that the expression, "right to life," is misleading, since what one is concerned about is not just the continued existence of a biological organism.

How, then, might the right in question be more accurately described? A natural suggestion is that the expression "right to life" refers to the right of a subject of experiences and other mental states to continue to exist. It might be contended, however, that this interpretation begs the question against certain possible views. For someone might hold—and surely some people in fact do—

that while continuing subjects of experiences and other mental states certainly have a right to life, so do some other organisms that are only potentially such continuing subjects, such as human fetuses. A right to life, on this view, is *either* the right of a subject of experiences to continue to exist, *or* the right of something that is only potentially a continuing subject of experiences to become such an entity.

This view is, I believe, to be rejected, for at least two reasons. In the first place, this view appears to be clearly incompatible with the interest principle, as well as with the particular-interests principle. Secondly, this position entails that the destruction of potential persons is, in general, prima facie seriously wrong, and I shall argue, in the next section, that the latter view is incorrect.

Let us consider, then, the right of a subject of experiences and other mental states to continue to exist. The particular-interests principle implies that something cannot possibly have such a right unless its continued existence can be in its interest. We need to ask, then, what must be the case if the continued existence of something is to be in its interest.

It will help to focus our thinking, I believe, if we consider a crucial case, stressed by Derek Parfit. Imagine a human baby that has developed to the point of being sentient, and of having simple desires, but that is not yet capable of having any desire for continued existence. Suppose, further, that the baby will enjoy a happy life, and will be glad that it was not destroyed. Can we or can we not say that it is in the baby's interest not to be destroyed?

To approach this case, let us consider a closely related one, namely, that of a human embryo that has not developed sufficiently far to have any desires, or even any states of consciousness at all, but that will develop into an individual who will enjoy a happy life, and who will be glad that his mother did not have an abortion. Can we or can we not say that it is the embryo's interest not to be destroyed?

Why might someone be tempted to say that it is in the embryo's interest that it not be destroyed? One line of thought which, I believe, tempts some people, is this. Let Mary be an individual who enjoys a happy life. Then, though some philosophers have expressed serious doubts about this, it might very well be said that it was certainly in Mary's interest that a certain embryo was not destroyed several years earlier. And this claim, together with the tendency to use expressions such as "Mary before she was born" to refer to the embryo in question, may lead one to think that it was in the embryo's interest not to be destroyed. But this way of thinking involves conceptual confusion. A subject of interests, in the relevant sense of "interest," must necessarily be a subject of conscious states, including experiences and desires. This means that in identifying Mary with the embryo, and attributing to it her interest in its earlier nondestruction, one is treating the embryo as if it were itself a subject of consciousness. But by hypothesis, the embryo being considered has not developed to the point where there is any subject of consciousness associated with it. It cannot, therefore, have any interests at all, and *a fortiori*, it cannot have any interest in its own continued existence.

Let us now return to the first case—that of a human baby that is sentient, and which has simple desires, but which is not yet capable of having more complex desires, such as a desire for its own continued existence. Given that it will develop into an individual who will lead a happy life, and who will be glad that the baby was not destroyed, does one want to say that the baby's not being destroyed is in the baby's own interest?

Again, the following line of thought may seem initially tempting. If Mary is the resulting individual, then it was in Mary's interest that the baby not have been destroyed. But the baby just *is* Mary when she was young. So it must have been in the baby's interest that it not have been destroyed.

Indeed, this argument is considerably more tempting in the present case than in the former, since here there is something that is a subject of consciousness, and which it is natural to identify with Mary. I suggest, however, that when one reflects upon the case, it becomes clear that such an identification is justified only if certain further things are the case. Thus, on the one hand, suppose that Mary is able to remember quite clearly some of the experiences that the baby enjoyed. Given that sort of causal and psychological connection, it would seem perfectly reasonable to hold that Mary and the baby are one and the same subject of consciousness, and thus, that if it is in Mary's interest that the baby not have been destroyed, then this must also have been in the baby's interest. On the other hand, suppose that not only does Mary, at a much later time, not remember any of the baby's experiences, but the experiences in question are not psychologically linked, either via memory or in any other way, to mental states enjoyed by the human organism in question at *any* later time. Here it seems to me clearly incorrect to say that Mary and the baby are one and the same subject of consciousness, and therefore it cannot be correct to transfer, from Mary to the baby, Mary's interest in the baby's not having been destroyed.

Let us now return to the question of what must be the case if the continued existence of something is to be in [its] own interest. The picture that emerges from the two cases just discussed is this. In the first place, nothing at all can be in an entity's interest unless it has desires at some time or other. But more than this is required if the continued existence of the entity is to be in its own interest. One possibility, which will generally be sufficient, is that the individual have, at the time in question, a desire for its own continued existence. Yet it also seems clear that an individual's continued existence can be in its own interest even when such a desire is not present. What is needed, apparently, is that the continued existence of the individual will make possible the satisfaction of some desires existing at other times. But

not just any desires existing at other times will do. Indeed, as is illustrated both by the case of the baby just discussed, and by the deprogramming/reprogramming example, it is not even sufficient that they be desires associated with the same physical organism. It is crucial that they be desires that belong to one and the same subject of consciousness.

The critical question, then, concerns the conditions under which desires existing at different times can be correctly attributed to a single, continuing subject of consciousness. This question raises a number of difficult issues which cannot be considered here. Part of the rationale underlying the view I wish to advance will be clear, however, if one considers the role played by memory in the psychological unity of an individual over time. When I remember a past experience, what I know is not merely that there was a certain experience which someone or other had, but that there was an experience that belonged to the *same* individual as the present memory beliefs, and it seems clear that this feature of one's memories is, in general, a crucial part of what it is that makes one a continuing subject of experiences, rather than merely a series of psychologically isolated, momentary subjects of consciousness. This suggests something like the following principle:

> Desires existing at different times can belong to a single, continuing subject of consciousness only if that subject of consciousness possesses, at some time, the concept of a continuing self or mental substance.

Given this principle, together with the particular-rights principle, one can set the following argument in support of a claim concerning a necessary condition which an entity must satisfy if it is to have a right to life:

(1) The concept of a right is such that an individual cannot have a right at time *t* to continued existence unless the individual is such

P₁ - Indiv cannot have right to exist unless it has an interest in that right

P₂ - The person cannot have an interest in continued existence unless that person wants to exist as a subject of consciousness or that the person can have desires @ other times

that it can be in its interest at time t that it continue to exist.

P₂ (2) The continued existence of a given subject of consciousness cannot be in that individual's interest at time t unless *either* that individual has a desire, at time t, to continue to exist as a subject of consciousness, *or* that individual can have desires at other times.

P₃ (3) An individual cannot have a desire to continue to exist as a subject of consciousness unless it possesses the concept of a continuing self or mental substance.

P₄ (4) An individual existing at one time cannot have desires at other times unless there is at least one time at which it possesses the concept of a continuing self or mental substance.

Therefore:

C (5) An individual cannot have a right to continued existence unless there is at least one time at which it possesses the concept of a continuing self or mental substance.

This conclusion is obviously significant. But precisely what implications does it have with respect to the morality of abortion and infanticide? The answer will depend upon what relationship there is between, on the one hand, the behavioral and neurophysiological development of a human being, and, on the other, the development of that individual's mind. Some people believe that there is no relationship at all. They believe that a human mind, with all its mature ca-

pacities, is present in a human from conception onward, and so is there before the brain has even begun to develop, and before the individual has begun to exhibit behavior expressive of higher mental functioning. Most philosophers, however, reject this view. They believe, on the one hand, that there is, in general, a rather close relation between an individual's behavioral capacities and its mental functioning, and, on the other, that there is a very intimate relationship between the mind and the brain. As regards the latter, some philosophers hold that the mind is in fact identical with the brain. Others maintain that the mind is distinct from the brain, but causally dependent upon it. In either case, the result is a view according to which the development of the mind and the brain are necessarily closely tied to one another.

If one does adopt the view that there is a close relation between the behavioral and neurophysiological development of a human being, and the development of its mind, then the above conclusion has a very important, and possibly decisive implication with respect to the morality of abortion and infanticide. For when human development, both behavioral and neurophysiological, is closely examined, it is seen to be most unlikely that human fetuses, or even newborn babies, possess any concept of a continuing self. And in the light of the above conclusion, that means that such individuals do not possess a right to life.

Multiple Concepts of Personhood

H. Tristram Engelhardt, Jr.

This point can be seen by examining the force of the definition of death. The development of the brain-oriented definitions of death can be interpreted as the acquisition of a rather straightforward ontological conviction: when there is no longer the possibility of sapient action in the world, one is no longer in the world. This point can be extended to human ontogeny. It would appear that before one is sapient, one is not *yet*

in the world. Or more simply, one is not yet in existence. The distinction between human biological and human personal life which these realizations presuppose can be put more graphically by way of an illustrative parable. Consider, for example, being confronted by a neurologist's diagnosis that one has a disease that will destroy one's entire brain, but that the powers of modern science will allow one to live a nor-

P₃— A person cannot want to exist as a subject of consciousness unless the person knows what a continuing self or mental substance is

P₄

mal lifespan. A reasonable response would be that it would not just be senseless to continue living under such circumstances, but that one would not in fact be *there* as the supposed beneficiary. One would no longer exist.

This parable can lead further. The neurologist can revise the initial diagnosis and say that at least the lower parts of the brain, such as the medula, pons, and cerebellum (which are involved in reflexes, posturing, and complex motions), can be preserved. However, the higher brain associated with consciousness will be destroyed. If one still concluded that not only would it be senseless to preserve one's life under those circumstances, but that one would not in fact 'be' there, one has then taken firm possession of the notion of drawing a line between human biological and human personal life.

Such a set of considerations will, however, argue for a neocortically oriented, not simply a whole-brain oriented, definition of death. Since all tests have risks of both false positive and false negative determinations, one may still accept a whole-brain oriented definition of death. One may be willing to act as if certain dead individuals are alive in order to avoid the risks of false positive determinations, though conceptually one holds a neocortically oriented definition of death to be correct. Such concerns regarding false positive determinations of death may account in part, at least, for the reason why individuals such as Karen Quinlan are not declared dead. Though it would be very difficult to hold that there is any person such as Karen Quinlan still existing in the world, one might still be reluctant to establish canons for a definition of death that would allow her to be declared dead, because one has an interest in avoiding criteria for the declaration of death with unproven risks of false positive determinations of death. Further, one would need to consider the emotional trauma involved in disposing of a living body, even though it is no longer the body of a person. We persons treat with respect many objects in the world that are

not persons. For all these reasons one might then be willing to declare individuals dead only when easily determinable, necessary conditions for the possibility of persons being in the world are absent, even when it might be fairly certain that all of the sufficient conditions for being present in the world have not been fulfilled. This consideration should remind us why the presence of EEG activity in a fetus does not indicate the presence of a person, though the absence of these findings may indicate the absence (i.e., death) of a person. There is a difference between necessary and sufficient conditions for persons being present. It should also suggest why entities that are not persons strictly are treated as if they are persons strictly. Here one might think not only of the ways in which infants, but also the severely mentally retarded, and the senile, are treated with respect as if they were persons in the strict sense, though they can be the bearers only of rights, not of duties. In short, examining the distinction between human biological and human personal life will disclose further ontological complexities including the fact that we employ more than one concept of person in our moral practices.

In drawing a line between human biological and human personal life, one is presupposing a concept of person. The concept of person is, one should note, not simply biological. One can see this when one considers what would be involved, for example, in asking whether an intelligent being from another planet is a person. One would be asking how to identify beings who are morally equivalent to us: we who write books on philosophy or read them. Persons are important in moral discourse because they are the origin of moral questions and answers. They are in the end the moral judges of the significance of the universe. One might think here, for example, of John Rawls's characterization of persons:

Moral persons are distinguished by two features: first, they are capable of having (and are assumed to have) a conception of their good (as expressed by a rational plan of life); and second, they are capable of having (and are assumed to acquire) a sense of justice, a normally effective desire to apply and act upon the principles of justice, at least to a certain minimal degree. We use the characterization of the person in the original position to single out the kind of beings to whom the principles chosen apply.

This is a point that has been made clearly since Kant: persons are the sustainers of the world of moral concerns, and they are rational, self-determining entities. What we will count as persons will need to possess at least the capacity to reason, to choose freely, to have interest in goods, and to have the capacity to be concerned about the nature of proper conduct.

This sense of person stands out if one considers the minimum notion of ethics. Though it may be very difficult to establish by reason alone the correctness of one particular, concrete view of the good life, still, the very enterprise of resolving moral disputes by reasons and peaceably forwarded considerations, not force, presupposes mutual respect among the participants in such disputes. Only moral agents can be participants in such disputes. They must be respected as a condition for the possibility of ethics as an alternate to force, before and beyond any ability to discover or create a particular view of the good life. Killing, imprisoning or hurting innocent moral agents, as a result, count as paradigm evil acts, whether or not the beings are human. The relevant ontological concept of person is thus found through an inquiry as to the nature of beings who would ground the very possibility of moral interests.

These considerations have application at the beginning of human life. Though it is usually possible to speak of what one did at the age of six, it requires use of metaphor to speak of what one did at, say, the age of one month. We were not there, much less doing something. There was surely an organism

present from which we would come. But we, as moral agents, as the person known to ourselves and others, did not yet exist. It is only later that we appeared and united in a stream of memories and actions the enterprises which are our lives. Early in human development, there is in fact less of 'someone' there, than in the case of adult non-human mammals. This would suggest that treating infants as persons is a conservative compromise, between restricting abortions and allowing infanticide—somewhat like employing whole brain oriented definitions of death rather than neocortically oriented definitions. Yet in the case of possible death, one can know for certain that there at least had been a person. One is concerned about mistakenly declaring that person dead. In the case of the one-month-old infant, however, there is no evidence that a person in a strict sense is present. The organism shows none of the mental capacities of a mature non-human primate.

Zygotes, embryos, and fetuses, like brain-dead but otherwise alive human beings, give no evidence of being persons. Nor will it help to say that they are potential persons. *Ys* that are potential *Xs* are *a fotiori* not *Xs*. If fetuses are to be treated with respect greater than that accorded to non-human animals of similar development, it will be because of the value of such a practice, not because of the intrinsic value they possess (at least insofar as general, secular arguments are concerned). One will have to determine whether the competing moral issues at stake in abortion are in any fashion similar to those that would allow (or forbid) infanticide of children up to a week of age.

The distinction between being a human and being a person, which these considerations presuppose, should not appear arbitrary. Being a human is a biological designation. It indicates membership in the genus *homo*, or perhaps more narrowly in the species *homo sapiens*. What is of prime moral interest is not species membership, as the above indicates, but whether an entity is in fact a person.

How human fetuses will be valued will depend on such issues as a society's interest in having more persons, or more persons of a particular sort. Thus the fact that many zygotes do not implant is likely to be celebrated by individuals or communities impressed by the present over-population of the earth. Similarly, the fact that most chromosomally defective zygotes do not survive to term is likely to be considered a fortuitous happening by individuals insofar as it is less difficult and less costly to raise persons free of handicaps than those who are not so blessed. The view would be that it is better to prevent the birth of excess numbers of persons, or of handicapped persons, for once such persons come into existence, they have strong rights to forebearance and can make persuasive claims upon our beneficence. By avoiding such births, one avoids a needless moral test of one's virtues, and some of the tragedies of human life. Such avoidance (i.e., through abortion) is much more on a par with a couple deciding to postpone initiating a pregnancy until the circumstances are more fortuitous, than it is with an interference with the rights of a person. Further, to abort a fetus does not harm the person the fetus would have become, any more than those possible persons are harmed who will not be brought into existence due to the fact that the readers of this article are not mating, but are instead engaged in philosophical reflection. (I do not wish to claim that such a conjunction of activities is formally or even materially impossible, only unlikely.) Which is to say, in abortion no one (i.e., no person) is killed, though a human organism is extinguished. This may involve an evil in addition to what is involved in a choice not to reproduce, however, not the evil of murder.

What are we to make of the status of infants, the severely mentally retarded, the severely senile, and the severely brain-damaged? It would appear, all else being equal, that killing them would be equivalent to killing an animal of a similar level of sentience. Although this would be a serious act, it would in itself not have the seriousness of killing, for example, an adult higher primate. However, all else is not equal in the case of infants, the severely mentally retarded, etc., for they play important moral roles within particular communities of persons. A plausible reconstruction of this state of affairs is that our settled practices presuppose more than one concept of person. The first would involve the strict sense of a moral agent, an entity that could be a member of a moral community. It is through appeals to such a notion that we would understand certain entities to have strong, through abstract, natural rights to forebearance, so that it would be an equally heinous moral act to slay for sport and without consent an innocent human person or an innocent extra-terrestrial person. Our treatment of instances of human life that are not also persons must be explained in terms of general practices established to secure important goods and interests, including the development of kindly parental attitudes to children, concern and sympathy for the weak, and protection for persons in the strict sense when it is not clear that they are still alive. This practice of imputing personhood thus depends upon the moral geography of a particular moral community. For example, one may wish to treat infants as persons in order to secure attitudes of love and attention to children. In addition, one will wish to ensure that the person the infant will become will be secure against injuries that would antedate his or her personhood. Again, because one might fear false positive determinations of the fact that one was no longer a person strictly, one might, for example, treat individuals such as Karen Quinlan as if they were persons strictly, though all the available evidence suggests the contrary (i.e., their status is the consequence of a false negative test for death). That is, one would establish operational criteria for deciding in a conservative fashion what was a person strictly.

6. THE SANCTITY OF THE LIVES OF PERSONS

The Morality of Killing: A Traditional View

Germain Grisez and Joseph M. Boyle, Jr.

In the strict sense one kills a person when, having considered bringing about a person's death as something one could do, one commits oneself to doing it by adopting this proposal instead of some alternative and by undertaking to execute it. By definition killing in the strict sense is an action contrary to the good of life. The adoption of a proposal to bring about someone's death is incompatible with respect for this good. Thus every act which is an act of killing in the strict sense is immoral. No additional circumstance or condition can remove this immorality.

This definition and moral characterization of killing in the strict sense make no distinction between intent to kill, attempt to kill, and the consummation of the undertaking by successful execution. These distinctions, which are legally significant, are morally irrelevant. If one commits oneself to realizing a certain state of affairs, by the commitment one constitutes oneself as a certain type of person. If one commits oneself to killing a person, one constitutes oneself a murderer. This remains true even if one is prevented from attempting to execute one's purpose—for example, if someone else kills the intended victim first. Even more obviously it remains true if one attempts to execute one's purpose but fails—for example, if one shoots to kill but misses the intended victim.

Although everything which is an act of killing in the strict sense is immoral, not every deadly deed is an act of killing in this sense. As we have explained, some deadly deeds carry out a consciously projected design, but the performance is not the execution of a proposal adopted by the actor's choice to bring about the death of a human individual. The examples of the enraged wife and the dutiful soldier belong here. In what follows we call this type of performance a "deadly deed" to distinguish it from a killing in the strict sense.

Finally, there are other cases of causing death, such as some killing in self-defense, which are neither killing in the strict sense nor deadly deeds as here defined. The proposal adopted or the consciously projected design carried out by persons defending themselves might not extend beyond incapacitating the attacker, but this can result in the attacker's death if the only available and adequate means to incapacitate the attacker also will result in mortal wounds.

We turn now to the consideration of cases in which one brings about one's own death. Even in ordinary language some ethically significant distinctions are made in speaking of this, for one does not call "suicide" all cases in which someone causes his or her own death. Most people who consider suicide immoral do not class martyrs and heroes as suicides, since "suicide" suggests an act of killing oneself. Yet not all who commit suicide do a moral act of killing in the strict sense.

In cases in which suicide is an act of killing in the strict sense the proposal to kill oneself is among the proposals one considers in deliberation, and this proposal is adopted by choice as preferable to alternatives. For example, a person who for some reason is suffering greatly might think: "I wish I no longer had to suffer as I am suffering. If I were dead, my suffering would be at an end. But I am not likely to die soon. I could kill myself. But I fear death and what might follow after it. I could put up with my misery and perhaps find some other way out." One thinking in this way is deliberating. In saying "I could kill myself" suicide is proposed. If this proposal is adopted, one's moral act is killing in the strict sense. As in other instances this act is incompatible with the basic good of human life, and it cannot morally be justified, regardless of what else might be the case.

One can propose to kill oneself without saying to oneself "I could kill myself." One might say something which one would accept as equivalent in meaning: "I could destroy myself," "I could rub myself out," or something of the sort. Again, one might say something which one would admit amounts to "I could kill myself" although not equivalent in meaning to it, such as "I could shoot myself," when what one has in mind is shooting oneself in the head and thereby causing death, not merely shooting oneself to cause a wound.

There are still other cases in which individuals contribute to the causation of their own deaths by acts which are morally significant but which in no way execute proposals which are properly suicidal. Typical martyrs lay down their lives. The death could be avoided if the martyr were willing to do something believed wrong or to leave unfulfilled some duty which is accepted as compelling. But the martyr refuses to avoid death by compromise or evasion of duty. Such persons do only what they believe to be morally required; the consequent loss of their own lives is willingly accepted by martyrs, neither sought nor chosen as a means to anything.

The martyr reasons somewhat as follows: "I would like to please everyone and to stay alive. But they are demanding of me that I do what I believe to be wrong or that I omit doing what I believe to be my sacred mission. They threaten me with death if I do not meet their demands. But if I were to comply with their threat, I would be doing evil in order that the good of saving my life might follow from it. This I may not do. Therefore, I must stand as long as I can in accord with my conscience, even though they are likely to kill me or torture me into submission."

Someone who does not understand the martyr's reasoning is likely to consider the martyr a suicide. But martyrs who reason thus do not propose to bring about their own deaths. The martyr bears witness to a profound commitment, first of all before the persecutors themselves. The latter can and in the martyr's view should accept this testimony and approve the rightness of the commitment. The martyr's refusal to give in does not bring about the persecutor's act of killing; the martyr only fails to win over the persecutor and to forestall the deadly deed.

Of course, we hold that suicide which is killing in the strict sense is necessarily immoral simply because it violates the basic good of human life. One who deliberately chooses to end his or her own life constitutes by this commitment a self-murderous self. But considerations, which tell against even nonsuicidal acts which bring about a person's own death also argue against the moral justifiability of suicidal acts, which execute a proposal to destroy one's own life.

Considering matters from a moral point of view and from the side of the one whose life is to be ended, voluntary euthanasia is not significantly different from other cases of suicide. The proposal is to bring about death as a means to ending suffering. This proposal, if adopted and executed, is an instance of killing in the strict sense. It can never be morally justified.

Of course, a person who is in severe pain and who seeks death to escape it is likely to have mitigated responsibility or even to be drawn into acceptance without a deliberate choice, just as is the case with others whose suffering drives them to a deadly deed against themselves.

However, if an individual plans to seek euthanasia and arranges for it well in advance of the time of suffering, then the pos-

[handwritten:] v. concerned about domino effect

sibility that the demand for death is not an expression of deliberate choice is greatly lessened. The conditions which from the point of view of proponents of euthanasia are optimum for making a decision about the matter are precisely the conditions in which the decision is likely to be a morally unjustifiable act of killing in the strict sense.

Considering voluntary euthanasia from the point of view of the person who would carry out the killing, matters seem no better from a moral viewpoint. The performance can hardly fail to be an execution of a deliberate choice; the one carrying out the killing can hardly be driven to it, nor can anyone in the present culture accept the duty unquestioningly.

Nonvoluntary euthanasia also clearly proposes death as a treatment of choice. The act hardly can fail to be killing in the strict sense. And in addition to the violation of the good of life, the rights of those to be killed also will be violated—for example, by denial to them of equal protection of the laws. Nonvoluntary euthanasia would violate both life and justice.

It clearly is possible to kill in the strict sense by deliberately letting someone die. If one adopts the proposal to bring about a person's death and realizes this proposal by not behaving as one otherwise would behave, then one is committed to the state of affairs which includes the person's death. This commitment, although carried out by a nonperformance, is morally speaking an act of killing. It involves the adoption and execution of a proposal contrary to the basic good of human life. Thus, any case in which one chooses the proposal that a person die and on this basis allows the person to die is necessarily immoral.

[handwritten arrow] For example, if a child is born suffering from various defects and if the physicians and parents decide that the child, the family, and society will all be better off if the burdens entailed by the child's continued life are forestalled by its death, and if they therefore adopt the proposal not to perform a simple operation, which otherwise would be done, so that the child will die, then the parents and physicians morally speaking kill the child—"kill" in the strict sense clarified at the beginning of this chapter. The fact that there is no blood spilled, no poison injected, that the death certificate can honestly show that the child has died from complications arising from its defective condition—none of this is morally relevant. The moral act is no different from any other moral act of murder.

The same thing will be true in every instance in which a judgment is made that someone—whether oneself or another—would be better off dead, the proposal to bring about death by not causing or preventing something is considered and adopted, and this proposal is executed by outward nonperformance of behavior which one otherwise might have attempted.

Michael Tooley and others also have criticized those who hold that there is a significant moral difference between killing a person and letting the person die. Their criticism is that if one considers a case of killing and a case of letting die between which there is no difference except that in the one the death is brought about by a performance which causes it while in the other it is brought about by not causing or preventing something, then there is no moral difference between the two cases.

We agree. Both actions are killing in the strict sense; neither can ever be moral. However, not every instance in which someone deliberately lets another die is an action shaped by the proposal that the person whose death is accepted should die or die sooner than would otherwise be the case. We turn now to the consideration of such deliberate omissions which, considered from a moral point of view, are not acts of killing.

The fundamental point about these omissions is that one can omit to do some good or prevent some evil without adopting any proposal which either is opposed to the good or embraces (as means) the evil whose occurrence one accepts. This possibility is most obviously instantiated when one must forgo doing a certain good or preventing a certain evil because one has a duty, incompatible with doing the good or preventing the evil, to do some other good or prevent some other evil.

For example, in an emergency situation in which many people are seriously injured and the medical resources—including time and personnel—are limited, those making decisions must choose to treat some and put off the treatment of others, perhaps with fatal consequences to those not treated first. The nontreatment of those who are not treated is deliberate; even their deaths might be foreseen as an inevitable consequence and knowingly accepted when the decision to treat others is made. Yet plainly the nontreatment of those who are not treated need involve no proposal that these people should die or die more quickly than they otherwise would. Provided there is no partiality or other breach of faith with those not treated, the execution of a proposal to save others does not embrace the death of those who die, and no immorality is done.

There is another type of reason for forgoing doing good which involves no disrespect for the good which would be realized by the action. One might notice that doing the action good in itself will in fact bring about many undesirable consequences. And one might choose not to adopt the proposal to do the good in order to avoid accepting these various bad consequences. This situation is exemplified in a very important way in many instances in which potentially life-prolonging treatment is refused, withheld, or withdrawn—even in the case of a patient who is not dying—because of the expected disadvantages of accepting, carrying out, or continuing treatment.

We have articulated grounds on which someone might reasonably consider treatment undesirable: if the treatment is experimental or risky, if it would be painful or otherwise experienced negatively, if it

would interfere with activities or experiences the patient might otherwise enjoy, if it would conflict with some moral or religious principle to which the patient adheres, if it would be psychologically repugnant to the patient, or if the financial or other impact of the treatment upon other persons would constitute a compelling reason to refuse treatment.

The moral legitimacy of refusing treatment in some cases on some such grounds certainly was part of what Pius XII was indicating by his famous distinction between ordinary and extraordinary means of treatment. The Pope defined "extraordinary means" as ones which involve a "great burden," and he allowed that one could morally forgo the use of extraordinary means.

The conception of extraordinary means clearly is abused, however, when the proposal is to bring about death by the omission of treatment, and the difficulties of the treatment are pointed to by way of rationalizing the murderous act. If it is decided that a person would be better off dead and that treatment which would be given to another will be withheld because of the poor quality of the life to be preserved, then the focus in decision is not upon the means and its disadvantageous consequences. Rather, what is feared is that the means would be effective, that life would be preserved, and that the life itself and its consequences would be a burden.

Moreover, even when treatment is refused, withheld, or withdrawn because of an objection to the means—and without the adopting of a proposal to bring about death—there still can be a serious moral failing.

A person who refuses lifesaving or life-prolonging treatment, not on a suicidal proposal but because of great repugnance for the treatment itself, might have an obligation to maintain life longer in order to fulfill duties toward others.

For example, someone on dialysis might wish to give up the treatment because of the difficulties it involves, and some persons in this situation could discontinue treatment and accept death without moral fault. But a parent with children in need of continued care, a professional person with grave responsibilities, and many other persons who can prolong their lives at considerable sacrifice to themselves are morally bound to do so, even by this extraordinary means, because they have accepted duties which others are entitled to have fulfilled, and persons who love the goods as one ought will faithfully fulfill duties toward others at considerable cost to themselves.

Similarly, if one refuses, withholds, or withdraws lifesaving or life-prolonging treatment for another because of the grave burdens entailed by such treatment, the burdens must be grave indeed. This is especially clear in cases in which the patient is not dying—for example, cases of defective infants. One must be quite sure, at the least, that with no suicidal proposal one would in the patient's place not wish the treatment. Otherwise, one accepts moral responsibility for a very grave wrong toward the patient.

Principle of Double Effect

H. Tristram Engelhardt, Jr., and John P. Kenny

The *principle of double effect* is an acknowledgment that there is a moral difference in many circumstances between foreseeing an outcome and intending an outcome. A devout Roman Catholic woman who has just married and who desires children may accept a hysterectomy for cancer of the cervix, not with the intent of being sterilized (in fact, she really would have wanted to have children), although she foresees that the operation will, in fact, sterilize her. Interventions in medicine may have numerous effects, only one of which is intended, although the others must be tolerated. This notion is captured in the term *side effects*, which identifies foreseen but not intended consequences of a drug, operation, or other medical intervention. Father John P. Kenny has provided a very useful summary of this principle:

Moral Principle: It is lawful to perform an action having two effects, one good and the other evil, when the following conditions are present:

a. *The act must be good in itself or at least indifferent.* This means that any action which is evil in itself may never be performed, even though good may result. An act is judged good or indifferent by viewing the moral object, i.e.,

that to which the act is immediately ordained by its nature. Note that it is a question of the moral object, not the physical object. The same physical act may have a different moral object, e.g., the taking of another's life.

b. *The good effect must follow as immediately from the cause as the evil effect.* Otherwise the good effect would be caused by the evil effect. We may never do evil in order that good may result.

c. *The intention of the individual must be good.* Even a good action becomes bad if done with an evil intention. The evil effect must not be desired in itself; it may, however, be permitted if all conditions are fulfilled. To intend the evil effect is wrong.

d. *There must be a proportionately grave cause for performing the action.* It is unreasonable to permit a very great evil in order that a minor good may result. There must be a proportion between the good intended and the evil permitted.

The principle of double effect plays a role throughout medicine even when it is not explicitly invoked. The principle underscores the complex consequences of actions and enjoins the actor to take them all into consideration. If one does not intend the evil "foreseen side effects," one must still ensure that enough good consequences also follow to justify the costs of the action. Finally, one should note that the principle forbids certain interventions when the action is intrinsically evil. An example here in the Roman Catholic tradition would be masturbation in order to secure a sperm sample. No positive balance of good outcomes can justify the act, nor would the principle of intending, but not foreseeing, help either, for the character of the act (masturbation) according to the Catholic tradition is intrinsically immoral.

A Non-Consequentialist Argument for Active Euthanasia

Baruch A. Brody

I

An act of euthanasia is one in which one person (I shall refer to him as A) kills another person (B) for the benefit of the second person, who does actually benefit from being killed. This definition emphasizes two features of acts of euthanasia. The first is that they involve one person killing another. It is, of course, this feature that raises serious doubts about the moral permissibility of such acts. The second is that they involve A's acting from benevolent motives and in so doing benefitting B. It is this feature (a mixture of subjective and objective factors) that suggests that such acts may be morally permissible.

Let us look more carefully at each of these features. The first feature distinguishes acts of euthanasia from suicides, on one hand, and mere omissions to save others, on the other hand. Suicides are not acts of euthanasia because they do not involve killings of others. More importantly, omissions are not (usually) acts of euthanasia because they do not (usually) involve killings. Therefore, the question of the moral permissibility of one must be distinguished from the question of the moral permissibility of the other. This is an important point. In a recent, much-publicized case in Maine in which parents refused to authorize an operation needed to save the life of their seriously deformed child, much of the public discussion was marred by a failure to distinguish the omission of medical efforts to save a life from an act of euthanasia.

There are those who challenge this second distinction, who maintain that it is a distinction without a difference. According to them there is no morally relevant difference between A's killing B and A's failure to save B. Thus, Joseph Fletcher writes: "What, morally, is the difference between doing nothing to keep the patient alive and giving a fatal dose of a painkilling or other lethal drug? The intention is the same either way. A decision not to keep a patient alive is as morally deliberate as a decision to end a life." Fletcher's arguments are very weak. That both decisions are morally deliberate does not entail that there are no morally relevant differences between them. And the same is true of the fact that the two actions are performed in order to accomplish the same result (this is, presumably, what Fletcher means when he says that "the intention is the same either way"); after all, the means chosen, as well as the end pursued, count in the moral evaluation of an action. More importantly, Fletcher's position seems untenable for two reasons. First, it seems that we have an equally strong obligation not to kill anyone, but the existence and strength of our obligation to save others depends, to a considerable degree, upon our relationship to that person. Fletcher would, I am sure, agree that a father has a greater obligation to save his starving child than to save a starving stranger who lives thousands of miles away. Second, there are many things that would relieve us from our obligation to save another but that would not relieve us from our obligation not to kill another. Thus, if someone threatens to take my life (a limb, or my life's-savings) unless I

[handwritten margin notes: "Interesting, or true" "depend obviously" "degree protecting of it is" "'saving' too" "p = diff btwn active killing and passive not saving"]

refrain from saving you, that seems to relieve me of my obligation to save you, but if he threatens to take my life (a limb, or my life's-savings) unless I kill you, then it would seem as though I still have an obligation not to kill you. So, on two counts, we have a distinction that does make a difference.

All of this is perfectly compatible with a realization that the boundary between killing someone and failing to save him is not always precise. Has one killed someone or has one merely refrained from continuing to save him when one turns off the life-supporting machine that is keeping him alive? *[margin: O.k.]* My point is that one can distinguish clear-cut cases of killing from clear-cut cases of failure to save and that the moral considerations relevant to an evaluation of the one act are not necessarily relevant to an evaluation of the other act.

So much for the first feature of euthanasia cases. We turn now to the second feature: that A is killing B for the benefit of B and B does actually benefit from being killed. Before commenting on this point, let me add that if B consents to A's killing him or requests that A kill him, we have a case of voluntary euthanasia.

In such cases of voluntary euthanasia, there are three different factors that might justify A's killing B: A's benevolent motives, B's gain, and B's consent or request. Proponents of voluntary euthanasia have to be clear on the precise weight that they ascribe to each of these features. To be sure, if we have a case in which B is suffering from the terminal stages of an incurable disease and would be better off dead, in which B requests that A kill him, and in which A does so to save B from his terrible suffering, all of these factors are present, and the proponents of voluntary euthanasia need not decide which is most important. But there are obviously cases in which these differences become important. (1) Suppose that A kills B, in the above case, to gain a legacy. Is A's act permissible if done for a bad motive, or does A's motive turn his act into an act of murder? (2) Suppose that A kills B, in the *[margin: who decides this? & B?]*

above case, but B has never requested or consented to euthanasia and is now incapable of doing so. Is A's act permissible because of his motives in performing it and because of its benefits, or does the lack of consent turn A's act into an act of murder? (3) Suppose that A kills B, in the above case, but because of special circumstances the act results in a loss to B. Is A's act permissible because of his motives and B's consent, or does the resulting harm to B turn A's act into an act of murder? *[margin: what loss?]*

This point can also be put as follows: Proponents of euthanasia have to decide which of the three factors, or which disjunction(s) of them, is (are) necessary for A's act to be permissible and which of these three factors, or which conjunction(s) of them, is (are) sufficient for A's act to be permissible. Their decision on this point will determine whether they are proposing euthanasia, voluntary euthanasia, or killing for benevolent motives.

I will be arguing only for voluntary euthanasia, since I will only be arguing that B's consent or request justifies A's killing him. I *[margin: Prem]* will also try to show that there are cases in which, by extension, euthanasia is permissible even if it has not been consented to or requested. For reasons that will emerge below, I will treat A's motives and the benefit to B as neither necessary nor sufficient.

My argument will be based upon certain assumptions about killing and about the right to life. These are: (1) A's killing B is wrong—when it is wrong—only because it involves A's wrongfully depriving B of that life to which, in those cases, B has a right; (2) there should be laws prohibiting A's killing B only because of the law's function of protecting our possession of that to which we have a right. I shall try to show that these assumptions lead to the conclusion that voluntary euthanasia is permissible and should be legalized. Without entering into a full-fledged defense of these assumptions, I shall defend them against some standard objections. In any case, since these assumptions are both plausible and widely believed, *[margin: P&C]*

I think that the assertion that they lead to these consequences will be of interest.

II

Let us begin by considering a case in which B requests that A kill him. Can A do so without wrongfully depriving B of something to which he has a right? In order to answer this question, we must first remind ourselves of an elementary point concerning the possession of rights.

Suppose that B has the right to some property. Normally, this entails that A has a duty to refrain from taking the property away from B and that A would act wrongly (unless there were special circumstances) if he took it away from B. But now suppose that B consents to A's taking it. Then, although A has no duty to do so (unless there are special circumstances), A does not wrongfully deprive B of the property if he does take it away. Although A is depriving B of that to which B has a right, A is not doing so wrongfully, because of B's consent.

This point can be generalized. If A takes from B something to which B has a right, then A has not wrongfully deprived B of that thing if B consents to A's doing so. Notice that this claim is weaker than the claim that A has wrongfully deprived B of the thing in question only if B positively wants it; A will have wrongfully deprived B of that to which he has a right, even if B does not positively want the thing in question, so long as B does not actually consent to A's taking it.

This general principle about rights leads to an argument for the moral permissibility of voluntary euthanasia. According to assumption 1, A's killing B is wrong only when it involves A's wrongfully depriving B of that life to which B has a right. But in cases of voluntary euthanasia, B consents to A's taking his life. Therefore, by our general principle about rights, A has not wrongfully deprived B of that life to which he has a right. So, by assumption 1, A's killing B is

not wrong when it is an act of voluntary euthanasia.

But does our general principle about rights hold in all cases? Consider a person's right to be free: Is it permissible for A to deprive B of that right by enslaving him even if B consents to A's doing so? If not, doesn't this show that there are some rights that a person can be wrongfully deprived of even when he consents to the deprivation? Perhaps the right to life is another example of such a right.

I do not find this objection convincing. That it is wrong for A to enslave B does not entail that A has wrongfully deprived B of that freedom to which he has a right. It may be wrong for other, independent reasons, most notably because it may be wrong for us to treat another person as a thing to be used. Moreover, even if one insists that A has wrongfully deprived B of his right to freedom, the case is not like the case of euthanasia because, unlike the case of euthanasia, the person deprived of his right goes on existing without that right. In short, then, it is not clear that the right to freedom does serve as a counter-example to our principle, and in any event, it is significantly different from the right to life; I am therefore inclined to treat the right to life analogously to all other rights.

There are three points about our argument that should be noted: (1) this argument is also an argument for the moral permissibility of suicide. After all, if B kills himself, then he has consented to his being killed, and he has therefore done nothing wrong. Indeed, from the perspective of this argument, there is no significant difference between suicide and voluntary euthanasia; (2) the question of A's motive and the benefit to B is irrelevant: our argument shows that A's act is permissible as long as B consents. Consent is a sufficient condition and neither benevolent motives nor beneficial consequences are necessary conditions; (3) there are limitations on our argument, growing out of general limitations upon the efficacy of consent. There are, after all, cases in which B's consent does not count, cases in which A wrongfully deprives B of that to which B has a right even though B consents. These include, among others, cases in which B (because of his youth or insanity) is incompetent to consent and cases in which B's consent is obtained by duress or fraud. It would be wrong, therefore, for A to kill B despite B's consent if B is incompetent or if his consent is obtained by fraud or duress. But one must not overemphasize this last point. There are those who claim that by consenting to being killed B has shown that he is incompetent and that his consent does not count. This claim should be accepted only if one also accepts the claim that consenting to being killed is so irrational in all circumstances that anyone so consenting could do so only by virtue of mental incompetence. But this last claim seems implausible; it would be hard to show that so consenting is always irrational. We must therefore reject the view that anyone who consents to being killed has thereby shown that he is incompetent to consent.

I have argued for voluntary euthanasia on the grounds of B's consent. There is, however, an additional, and perhaps more significant, point to consider. B also requested that A kill him, and this seems to provide another basis for the permissibility of A's killing B, namely, that A is acting as B's agent. After all, if it is permissible—and I have argued that it is—for B to kill himself, why should not it also be permissible for his agent, A, to do it? This argument rests upon the assumption that if it is permissible for B to do something, then it is also permissible for B to appoint A as his agent to perform the action in question and it is also permissible for A to perform that action. But this assumption is incorrect. If, for example, B is a judge, then it is permissible for B, in certain circumstances, to sentence a criminal, but it is not permissible for B to appoint an agent to do so. Or, while it is permissible for B to have intercourse with his or her spouse (providing that the spouse

has consented), it hardly follows that it is permissible for A to do so as B's agent. Still, our argument can be saved. After all, in these cases, B's privileges result from the permission of someone else (society, the spouse), and that permission has been granted only to B personally. But since B's right to kill himself does not derive from the permission of others, our general principle about agency holds.

We have so far considered the case in which B both consents to A's killing him and requests that A kill him. This is the paradigm case of voluntary euthanasia. But there are other, more perplexing, cases to consider. One is that in which B is no longer competent to consent and/or request (for example, if he is doped with pain-killing drugs), but in which, at some earlier time, he requested that A kill him if certain conditions—the ones that actually do obtain now—were to exist. In short, this is the case of euthanasia arranged for in advance. Is this also a case of permissible voluntary euthanasia?

Those who emphasize the importance of A's benevolent motives and the benefit to B would not find such cases perplexing. They would say that it is still permissible for A to kill B, even when B does not consent, so long as B benefits and A has benevolent motives. They would concede that our earlier argument showed that neither factor was necessary to justify A's killing B; but, they would claim, either (or, perhaps, just both) is sufficient.

I find this argument, with its supposition about what is sufficient to justify A's killing B, problematic. Suppose that A kills B for B's benefit, it is beneficial for B, but B objects. Or suppose that B does not object because he cannot, but would object if he could. Would we say in such cases that it is permissible for A to kill B? And if we would not, then we must reject the view that even A's benevolent motives joined with the benefit to B is sufficient to justify A's killing B; so this argument collapses.

It must be conceded that the case we are considering—euthanasia arranged for in advance—is different because B has previously consented to, and authorized, A's killing him. But this suggests that we consider that factor, and leave aside for now A's motives and the consequences for B. Does B's previous action suffice to justify A's killing him?

There are two lines of argument for concluding that it does: (1) one's privilege to waive one's right, to consent to others' taking what is yours, is not limited to doing so at the actual time in question; one can, and often does, consent in advance and conditionally. Similarly, one can, and often does, appoint agents in advance and conditionally. So, concludes this argument, as long as B does not revoke his earlier conditional consent and/or request, there is no morally significant difference between the paradigm case of voluntary euthanasia and the extended case of euthanasia arranged for in advance; (2) what justifies A's killing B in such cases is the consent that B would now give, and the request that B would now make, if he could. All that B's previous arrangements do is to serve as evidence as to what B would do now.

There are two difficulties with this second hypothetical approach. Practically speaking, it is hard to be sure what B would do now, even in light of his previous actions, since people do change their minds. Theoretically speaking, it rests upon a stronger, and perhaps more dubious, principle than any we have employed until now, namely, that if A takes from B something to which B has a right, then A has not wrongfully deprived B of that thing if B would consent if he could. On the other hand, this approach might allow more cases of permissible euthanasia if B's hypothetical consent were evidenced by something other than his earlier consent and/or request.

In conclusion, then, considerations of consent and agency, independent of any considerations of motives and benefit, seem sufficient to justify, on the assumptions outlined in section one, voluntary euthanasia, both in the paradigm case and in the extended case of consent in advance. They may even do so in cases in which B has never consented.

A Consequentialist Argument for Active Euthanasia

Peter Singer

ACTIVE AND PASSIVE EUTHANASIA

The conclusions we have reached in this chapter will shock a large number of readers, for they violate one of the most fundamental tenets of Western ethics—the wrongness of killing innocent human beings. I have already made one attempt to show that our conclusions are, at least in the area of defective infants, a less radical departure from existing practice than one might suppose. I pointed out that we are prepared to kill a fetus at a late stage of pregnancy if we believe that there is a significant risk of it being defective; and since the line between a developed fetus and a new-born infant is not a crucial moral divide, it is difficult to see why it is worse to kill a newborn infant known to be defective. In this section I shall argue that there is another area of accepted medical practice that is not intrinsically different from the practices that the arguments of this chapter would allow.

I have referred to the birth defect known as spina bifida, in which the infant is born with an opening in the back, exposing the spinal cord. Until 1957, most of these infants died young, but in that year doctors began using a new device, known as a

Holter valve, to drain off the excess fluid that otherwise accumulates in the head with this condition. In some hospitals it then became standard practice to make vigorous efforts to save every spina bifida infant. The result was that few spina bifida infants died—but of those that survived, many were severely handicapped, with gross paralysis, multiple deformities of the legs and spine, and no control of bowel or bladder. More than half were mentally retarded. Keeping the valve working properly and free from infection required repeated operations. In short, the existence of these children caused great difficulty for their families, strained the available medical resources, and was often a misery for the children themselves.

After studying the results of this policy of active treatment a British doctor, John Lorber, proposed that instead of treating all cases of spina bifida, only those who have the defect in a mild form should be selected for treatment. (In fact, he proposed that the final decision should be up to the parents, but parents nearly always accept the recommendations of the doctors.) This principle of selective treatment has now been widely accepted, and in Britain has been recognized as legitimate by the Department of Health and Social Security. The result is that fewer spina bifida children survive beyond infancy, but those that do are, by and large, the ones whose physical and mental handicaps are relatively minor.

The policy of selection, then, appears to be a desirable one: but what happens to those defective infants not selected for treatment? Lorber does not disguise the fact that in these cases the hope is that the infant will die soon and without suffering. It is to achieve this objective that surgical operations and other forms of active treatment are not undertaken, although pain and discomfort are as far as possible relieved. If the infant happens to get an infection, the kind of infection which in a normal infant would be swiftly cleared up with antibiotics, no antibiotics are given. Since the survival of the

infant is not desired, no steps are taken to prevent a condition, easily curable by ordinary medical techniques, proving fatal.

All this is, as I have said, accepted medical practice. In articles in medical journals, doctors have described cases in which they have allowed infants to die. These cases are not limited to spina bifida, but include, for instance, babies born with Down's syndrome (mongolism). According to testimony given to a United States Senate sub-committee in 1974, several thousand mentally and physically defective children are allowed to die each year.

The question is: if it is right to allow infants to die, why is it wrong to kill them?

This question has not escaped the notice of the doctors involved. Frequently they answer it by a pious reference to the nineteenth-century poet, Arthur Clough, who wrote:

Thou shalt not kill; but need'st not strive
Officiously to keep alive.

Unfortunately for those who appeal to Clough's immortal lines as an authoritative ethical pronouncement, they come from a piece of verse—"The Latest Decalogue"—the intent of which is satirical. The opening lines, for example, are:

Thou shalt have one god only; who
Would be at the expense of two.
No graven images may be
Worshipped except the currency.

So Clough cannot be numbered on the side of those who think it wrong to kill, but right not to try too hard to keep alive. Is there, nonetheless, something to be said for this idea? The view that there is something to be said for it is often termed "the acts and omissions doctrine." It holds that there is an important moral distinction between performing an act that has certain consequences—say, the death of a defective child—and omitting to do something that has the same consequences. If this doctrine is correct, the doctor who gives the child a lethal injection does wrong; the doctor who omits to give the child antibiotics, knowing full well that without antibiotics the child will die, does not.

What grounds are there for accepting the acts and omissions doctrine? Few champion the doctrine for its own sake, as an important ethical first principle. It is, rather, an implication of one view of ethics, of a view which holds that so long as we do not violate specified moral rules which place determinate moral obligations upon us, we do all that morality demands of us. These rules are of the kind made familiar by the Ten Commandments and similar moral codes: Do not kill, Do not lie, Do not steal, and so on. Characteristically they are formulated in the negative, so that to obey them it is necessary only to abstain from the actions they prohibit. Hence obedience can be demanded of every member of the community.

An ethic consisting of specific duties, prescribed by moral rules which everyone can be expected to obey, must make a sharp moral distinction between acts and omissions. Take, for example, the rule "Do not kill." If this rule is interpreted, as it has been in the Judaeo-Christian tradition, as prohibiting only the taking of innocent human life, it is not too difficult to avoid overt acts in violation of it. Few of us are murderers. It is not so easy to avoid letting innocent humans die. Many people die because of insufficient food, or poor medical facilities. If we could assist some of them, but do not do so, we are letting them die. Taking the rule against killing to apply to omissions would make living in accordance with it a mark of saintliness or moral heroism, rather than a minimum required of every morally decent person.

An ethic which judges acts according to whether they do or do not violate specific moral rules must, therefore, place moral weight on the distinction between acts and omissions. An ethic which judges acts by their consequences will not do so, for the consequences of an act and an omission will

often be, in all significant respects, indistinguishable. For instance, omitting to give antibiotics to a child with pneumonia may have consequences no less fatal than giving the child a lethal injection.

Which approach is right? I have argued for a consequentialist approach to ethics. The acts/omissions issue poses the choice between these two basic approaches in an unusually clear and direct way. What we need to do is imagine two parallel situations differing only in that in one a person performs an act resulting in the death of another human being, while in the other she omits to do something, with the same result. Suppose that a road accident victim has been in a coma for several months. Large parts of her brain have been destroyed and there is no prospect of recovery; only a respirator and intravenous feeding are keeping her alive. The parents of the victim visit her daily, and it is obvious that the long ordeal is placing a great strain on them. Knowing all this, the victim's doctor notices one day that the plug of the respirator has worked loose. Unless she replaces it the victim will die. After thinking about the situation she decides not to replace it.

The second case is exactly like the first, except that the respirator has a tight-fitting plug and so the situation will go on indefinitely unless the doctor does something. After thinking about the situation, the doctor gives the patient a lethal injection.

Comparing these two cases, is it reasonable to hold that the doctor who gives the injection does wrong, while the doctor who decides not to replace the plug acts rightly? I do not think it is. In both cases, the outcome is the swift and painless death of the comatose patient. In both cases, the doctor knows that this will be the result, and decides what she will do on the basis of this knowledge, because she judges this result to be better than the alternative. In both cases the doctor must take responsibility for her decision—it would not be correct for her to say, in the first case, that she was not responsible for the patient's death because she did nothing. Doing nothing, in this situation, is itself a deliberate choice and one cannot escape responsibility for its consequences.

One might say, of course, that in the first case the doctor does not kill the patient, she merely allows the patient to die; but one must then answer the further question why killing is wrong, and letting die is not. The answer that most advocates of the distinction give is simply that there is a moral rule against killing (innocent human beings, that is) and none against allowing to die. This answer treats a conventionally accepted moral rule as if it were beyond questioning; it does not go on to ask whether we should have a moral rule against killing (but not against allowing to die). But we have already seen that the conventionally accepted principle of the sanctity of human life is untenable. The moral rule against killing cannot be taken for granted either.

 I suggest that reflecting on these cases leads us to the conclusion that there is no *intrinsic* moral difference between killing and allowing to die. That is, there is no difference which depends solely on the distinction between an act and an omission. (This does not mean that all cases of allowing to die are morally equivalent to killing. Other factors—extrinsic factors—will sometimes be relevant.) Allowing to die—"passive euthanasia"—is already accepted as a humane and proper course of action in certain cases. If there is no intrinsic moral difference between killing and allowing to die, active euthanasia should also be accepted as humane and proper in certain circumstances.

Indeed, because of extrinsic differences—especially differences in the time it takes for death to occur—active euthanasia may even be the *only* humane and morally proper course. Passive euthanasia can be a slow process. In an article in the *British Medical Journal,* John Lorber has charted the fate of 25 infants born with spina bifida on whom it had been decided, in view of the poor prospects for a worthwhile life, not to operate. It will be recalled that Lorber freely grants that the object of not treating infants

is that they should die soon and painlessly. Yet, of the 25 untreated infants, 14 were still alive after one month, and 7 after three months. In Lorber's sample, all the infants died within nine months, but this cannot be guaranteed. An Australian clinic following Lorber's approach to spina bifida found that of 79 untreated infants, 5 survived for more than 2 years. For both the infants, and their families, this must be a long-drawn-out ordeal; nor should the burden on the hospital staff and facilities be disregarded.

Or consider those infants born with Down's syndrome, better known as mongolism. Most mongoloid infants are reasonably healthy, and will live for many years. A few, however, are born with a blockage between the stomach and the intestine which, if not removed, will prevent anything taken into the stomach from being digested, and hence bring about death. These become candidates for passive euthanasia. Yet the blockage is easy to remove and has nothing to do with the degree of mental retardation the child will have. Moreover, the death resulting from passive euthanasia in these circumstances is, though sure, neither swift nor painless. The infant dies from dehydration or hunger. It may take two weeks for death to come.

It is interesting, in this context, to think again of our earlier argument that the fact that a being is a member of the species *homo sapiens* does not entitle it to better treatment than a being at a similar mental level who is a member of a different species. We could also have said—except that it seemed too obvious to need saying—that the fact that a being is a member of the species *homo sapiens* is not a reason for giving it *worse* treatment than a member of a different species. Yet in respect of euthanasia, this needs to be said. We do not doubt that it is right to shoot a badly injured or sick animal, if it is in pain and its chances of recovery are negligible. To "allow nature to take its course," withholding treatment but refusing to kill, would obviously be wrong. It is only our misplaced respect for the doctrine of the sanctity of human life that prevents us from seeing that what it is obviously wrong to do to a horse it is equally wrong to do to a defective infant.

To summarize: passive euthanasia often results in a drawn-out death. It introduces irrelevant factors (a blockage in the intes-tine, or an easily curable infection) into the selection of those who shall die. If we are able to admit that our objective is a swift and painless death we should not leave it up to chance to determine whether this objective is achieved. Having chosen death we should ensure that it comes in the best possible way.

The Traditional Distinctions Are Unhelpful

President's Commission

REEXAMINING THE ROLE OF TRADITIONAL MORAL DISTINCTIONS

Most patients make their decisions about the alternate courses available to them in light of such factors as how many days or months the treatment might add to their lives, the nature of that life (for example, whether treatment will allow or interfere with their pursuit of important goals, such as completing projects and taking leave of loved ones), the degree of suffering involved, and the costs (financial and otherwise) to themselves and others. The relative weight, if any, to be given to each consideration must ultimately be determined by the competent patient.

Other bases are sometimes suggested for judging whether life-and-death decisions about medical care are acceptable or unacceptable beyond making sure that the results of the decisions are justified in the patient's view by their expected good. These bases are traditionally presented in the form of opposing categories. Although the categories—causing death by acting versus by omitting to act; withholding versus withdrawing treatment; the intended versus the unintended but foreseeable consequences of a choice; and ordinary versus extraordinary treatment—do reflect factors that can be important in assessing the moral and legal acceptability of decisions to forego life-sustaining treatment, they are inherently unclear. Worse, their invocation is often so mechanical that it neither illuminates an actual case nor provides an ethically persuasive argument.

In considering these distinctions, which are discussed in detail in the remainder of this chapter, the Commission reached the following conclusions, which are particularly relevant to assessing the role of such distinctions in public policies that preclude patients and providers from choosing certain options.

- The distinction between acting and omitting to act provides a useful rule-of-thumb by separating cases that probably deserve more scrutiny from those that are likely not to need it. Although not all decisions to omit treatment and allow death to occur are acceptable, such a choice, when made by a patient or surrogate, is usually morally acceptable and in compliance with the law on homicide; conversely, active steps to end life, such as by administering a poison, are likely to be serious moral and legal wrongs. Nonetheless, the mere difference between acts and omissions—which is often hard to draw in any case—never by itself determines what is morally acceptable. Rather, the acceptability of particular actions or omissions turns on other morally significant considerations, such as the balance of harms and benefits likely to be achieved, the duties owed by others to a dying person, the risks imposed on others in acting or refraining, and the certainty of outcome.

- The distinction between failing to initiate and stopping therapy—that is, withholding versus withdrawing treatment—is not itself of moral importance. A justification that is adequate for not commencing a treatment is also sufficient for ceasing it. Moreover, erecting a higher requirement for cessation might unjustifiably discourage vigorous initial attempts to treat seriously ill patients that sometimes succeed.

• A distinction is sometimes drawn between giving a pain-relieving medication that will probably have the unintended consequence of hastening a patient's death and giving a poison in order to relieve a patient's suffering by killing the patient. The first is generally acceptable while the latter is against the law. Actions that lead to death must be justified by benefits to the patient that are expected to exceed the negative consequences and ordinarily must be within the person's socially accepted authority. In the case of physicians and nurses, this authority encompasses the use of means, such as pain-relieving medication, that can cure illnesses or relieve suffering but not the use of means, such as weapons or poisons, whose sole effect is viewed as killing a patient.

• Whether care is "ordinary" or "extraordinary" should not determine whether a patient must accept or may decline it. The terms have come to be used in conflicting and confusing ways, reflecting variously such aspects as the usualness, complexity, invasiveness, artificiality, expense, or availability of care. If used in their historic sense, however—to signify whether the burdens a treatment imposes on a patient are or are not disproportionate to its benefits—the terms denote useful concepts. To avoid misunderstanding, public discussion should focus on the underlying reasons for or against a therapy rather than on a simple categorization as "ordinary" or "extraordinary."

The analysis of these four distinctions in this chapter need not be repeated in decisionmaking for each individual patient. Rather, the Commission intends to point to the underlying factors that may be germane and helpful in making decisions about treatment or nontreatment and, conversely, to free individual decisionmaking and public policy from the mistaken limitations imposed when slogans and labels are substituted for the careful reasoning that is required.

Action Versus Omission

The moral significance of the difference. Actual instances of actions leading to death, especially outside the medical context, are more likely to be seriously morally wrong than are omissions that lead to death, which, in the medical context, are most often morally justified. Usually, one or more of several factors make fatal actions worse than fatal omissions:

(1) The motives of an agent who acts to cause death are usually worse (for example, self-interest or malice) than those of someone who omits to act and lets another die.

(2) A person who is barred from acting to cause another's death is usually thereby placed at no personal risk of harm; whereas, especially outside the medical context, if a person were forced to intercede to save another's life (instead of standing by and omitting to act), he or she would often be put at substantial risk.

(3) The nature and duration of future life denied to a person whose life is ended by another's act is usually much greater than that denied to a dying person whose death comes slightly more quickly due to an omission of treatment.

(4) A person, especially a patient, may still have some possibility of surviving if one omits to act, while survival is more often foreclosed by actions that lead to death.

Each of these factors—or several in combination—can make a significant moral difference in the evaluation of any particular instance of acting and omitting to act. Together they help explain why most actions leading to death are correctly considered morally worse than most omissions leading to death. Moreover, the greater stringency of the legal duties to refrain from killing than to intervene to save life reinforces people's view of which conduct is worse morally.

However, the distinction between omissions leading to death and acts leading to death is not a reliable guide to their moral evaluation. In the case of medical treatment, the first and third factors are not likely to provide grounds for a distinction: family members and health professionals could be equally merciful in their intention—either in acting or omitting—and life may end immediately for some patients after treatment is withdrawn. Likewise, the second factor—based on the usual rule that people have fairly limited duties to save others with whom they stand in no special relation—does not apply in the medical context. Health professionals have a special role-related duty to use their skills, insofar as possible, on behalf of their patients, and this duty removes any distinction between acts and omissions.

Only the final factor—turning the possibility of death into a certainty—can apply as much in medical settings as elsewhere. Indeed, this factor has particular relevance here since the element of uncertainty—whether a patient really will die if treatment is ceased—is sometimes unavoidable in the medical setting. A valid distinction may therefore arise between an act causing certain death (for example, a poisoning) and an omission that hastens or risks death (such as not amputating a gangrenous limb). But sometimes death is as certain following withdrawal of a treatment as following a particular action that is reliably expected to lead to death.

Consequently, merely determining whether what was done involved a fatal act or omission does not establish whether it was morally acceptable. Some actions that lead to death can be acceptable: very dangerous but potentially beneficial surgery or the use of hazardous doses of morphine for severe pain are examples. Some omissions that lead to death are very serious wrongs: deliberately failing to treat an ordinary patient's bacterial pneumonia or ignoring a bleeding patient's pleas for help would be totally unacceptable conduct for that patient's physician.

Not only are there difficult cases to classify as acts or omissions and difficulties in placing moral significance on the distinction, but making the distinction also presupposes an unsound conception of responsibility, namely (1) that human action is an intervention in the existing course of nature, (2) that not acting is not intervening,

and (3) that people are responsible only for their interventions (or, at least, are much more responsible for deliberate interventions than for deliberate omissions). The weaknesses of this position include the ambiguous meaning of "intervention" when someone takes an action as part of a plan of nonintervention (such as writing orders not to resuscitate), the inability to define clearly the "course of nature," and the indefensibility of not holding someone responsible for states of affairs that the person could have prevented.

Withholding Versus Withdrawing Treatment

A variation on the action/omission distinction sometimes troubles physicians who allow competent patients to refuse a life-sustaining treatment but who are uncomfortable about stopping a treatment that has already been started because doing so seems to them to constitute killing the patient. By contrast, not starting a therapy seems acceptable, supposedly because it involves an omission rather than an action.

Although the nature of the distinction between withholding and withdrawing seems clear enough initially, cases that obscure it abound. If a patient is on a respirator, disconnecting would count as stopping. But if the patient is on a respirator and the power fails, does failure to use a manual bellows mechanism count as "stopping" a therapy (artificial respiration) or "not starting" a therapy (manually generated respiration)? Many therapies in medicine require repeated applications of an intervention. Does failing to continue to reapply the intervention count as "stopping" (the series of treatments) or as "not starting" (the next element in the series)? Even when a clear distinction can be drawn between withdrawing and withholding, insofar as the distinction is merely an instance of the acting-omitting distinction it lacks moral significance.

Adopting the opposite view—that treatment, once started, cannot be stopped, or that stopping requires much greater justification than not starting—is likely to have serious adverse consequences. Treatment might be continued for longer than is optimal for the patient, even to the point where it is causing positive harm with little or no compensating benefit. An even more troubling wrong occurs when a treatment that might save life or improve health is not started because the health care personnel are afraid that they will find it very difficult to stop the treatment if, as is fairly likely, it proves to be of little benefit and greatly burdens the patient. The Commission received testimony, for example, that sometimes the view that a therapy that has been started could not be stopped had unduly raised the threshold for initiating some forms of vigorous therapy for newborns. In cases of extremely low birth weight or severe spina bifida, for example, highly aggressive treatment may significantly benefit a small proportion of the infants treated while it prolongs the survival of a great number of newborns for whom treatment turns out to be futile. Fear of being unable to stop treatment in the latter cases—no matter how compelling the reason to stop—can lead to failure to treat the entire group, including the few infants who would have benefited.

Intended Versus Unintended But Foreseeable Consequences

Since there are sound moral and policy reasons to prohibit such active steps as administering strychnine or using a gun to kill a terminally ill patient, the question arises as to whether physicians should be able to administer a symptom-relieving drug—such as a pain-killer—knowing that the drug may cause or accelerate the patient's death, even though death is not an outcome the physician seeks. The usual answer to this question—that the prohibition against active killing does not bar the use of appropriate medical treatment, such as morphine for pain—is often said to rest on a distinction

between the goals physicians seek to achieve or the means they use, on the one hand, and the unintended but foreseeable consequences of their actions on the other.

One problem with assigning moral significance to the traditional distinction is that it is sometimes difficult to determine whether a particular aspect of a course of action ought to be considered to be intended, because it is an inseparable part of the "means" by which the course of action is achieved, or whether it is merely an unintended but foreseeable consequence. In medicine, and especially in the treatment of the critically or terminally ill, many of the courses that might be followed entail a significant risk, sometimes approaching a certainty, of shortening a patient's life. For example, in order to avoid additional suffering or disability, or perhaps to spare loved ones extreme financial or emotional costs, a patient may elect not to have a potentially life-extending operation. Risking earlier death might plausibly be construed as the intended means to these other ends, or as an unintended and "merely foreseeable" consequence. Since there seems to be no generally accepted, principled basis for making the distinction, there is substantial potential for unclear or contested determinations.

Even in cases in which the distinction is clear, however, health care professionals cannot use it to justify a failure to consider all the consequences of their choices. By choosing a course of action, a person knowingly brings about certain effects; other effects could have been caused by deciding differently. The law reflects this moral view and holds people to be equally responsible for all the reasonably foreseeable results of their actions and not just for those results that they acknowledge having intended to achieve. Nevertheless, although medication is commonly used to relieve the suffering of dying patients (even when it causes or risks causing death), physicians are not held to have violated the law. How can this failure to prosecute be explained, since it does not rest on an explicit waiver of the usual legal rule?

The explanation lies in the importance of defining physicians' responsibilities regarding these choices and of developing an accepted and well-regulated social role that allows the choices to be made with due care. The search for medical treatments that will benefit a patient often involves risk, sometimes great risk, for the patient; for example, some surgery still carries a sizable risk of mortality, as does much of cancer therapy. Furthermore, seeking to cure disease and to prolong life is only a part of the physician's traditional role in caring for patients; another important part is to comfort patients and relieve their suffering. Sometimes these goals conflict, and a physician and patient (or patient's surrogate) have the authority to decide which goal has priority. Medicine's role in relieving suffering is especially important when a patient is going to die soon, since the suffering of such a patient is not an unavoidable aspect of treatment that might restore health, as it might be for a patient with a curable condition.

Ordinary Versus Extraordinary Treatment

In many discussions and decisions about life-sustaining treatment, the distinction between ordinary and extraordinary (also termed "heroic" or "artificial") treatment plays an important role. In its origins within moral theology, the distinction was used to mark the difference between obligatory and nonobligatory care—ordinary care being obligatory for the patient to accept and others to provide, and extraordinary care being optional. It has also played a role in professional policy statements and recent judicial decisions about life-sustaining treatment for incompetent patients. As with the other terms discussed, defining and applying a distinction between ordinary and extraordinary treatment is both difficult and controversial and can lead to inconsistent results,

which makes the terms of questionable value in the formulation of public policy in this area.

CONCLUSIONS

Good decisionmaking about life-sustaining treatments depends upon the same processes of shared decisionmaking that should be a part of health care in general. The hallmark of an ethically sound process is always that it enables competent and informed patients to reach voluntary decisions about care. With patients who may die, care givers need special skills and sensitivities if the process is to succeed.

A number of constraints on the range of acceptable decisions about life-sustaining treatment have been suggested. They are often presented in the form of dichotomies: an omission of treatment that causes death is acceptable whereas an action that causes death is not; withholding treatment is acceptable whereas withdrawing existing treatment is not; extraordinary treatment may be foregone but ordinary treatment may not; a person is permitted to do something knowing that it will cause death but may not aim to kill. The Commission has concluded that none of these dichotomies should be used to prohibit choosing a course of conduct that falls within the societally defined scope of ethical medical practice. Instead, the Commission has found that a decision to forego treatment is ethically acceptable when it has been made by suitably qualified decisionmakers who have found the risk of death to be justified in light of all the circumstances. Furthermore, the Commission has found that nothing in current law precludes ethically sound decisionmaking. Neither criminal nor civil law—if properly interpreted and applied by lawyers, judges, health care providers, and the general public—forces patients to undergo procedures that will increase their suffering when they wish to avoid this by foregoing life-sustaining treatment.

Roots of the Belief in the Sanctity of Life

Law Reform Commission of Canada

A. THE ROOTS IN THEOLOGY

The sanctity of life principle clearly has religious origins, both in Eastern religions (especially Hinduism) and in the Judeo-Christian traditions. Inasmuch as Western law was shaped to a large degree by Judaism and Christianity it is arguable that the centrality of the sanctity of life principle in law is largely religious in origin and orientation. Recalling here these now largely forgotten and seldom articulated religious links between religion and law, therefore seems appropriate in a paper directed to, among others, law makers and law reformers. Ideally we can best make rational choices about which values we choose to continue protecting in any new formulation of the sanctity of life principle only by recalling and articulating the religious and secular values and insights which shaped and shape that principle.

1. The Two Major Themes

Confining ourselves to recent and present-day theologians and/or religious arguments we find a number of frequently recurring themes, and a general agreement between Protestant and Catholic analyses of the sanctity of life principle. There are two major and related "root" themes.

Man's dignity, worth and sanctity are from God, and not due to some quality or ability in man.

Moral theologians and others who argue this theological point in our time base their views in large part on Karl Barth's theology of creation, redemption and "respect for life" (the latter expression being one Barth borrows from Albert Schweitzer). For Barth life is sacred and worthy of respect not because of something in life itself by itself, but because of what God has done, a God who is Himself holy. Barth puts it this way: "Life does not itself create this respect. The command of God creates respect for it. When man in faith in God's Word and promise realizes how God from eternity has maintained and loved him in his little life, and what he has done for him in time, in this knowledge of human life he is faced by a majestic, dignified and holy fact. In human life itself he meets something superior. He is thus summoned to respect because the living God has distinguished it in this way and taken it to Himself."

The Protestant moral theologian Paul Ramsey makes the same point, and contrasts the religious position to the secular or modern one when he writes: ". . . in modern world views the sanctity of life can rest only on something inherent in man. . . . One grasps the religious outlook upon the sanctity of human life only if he sees that this life is asserted to be surrounded by sanctity that need not be in a man; that the most dignity a man ever possesses is a dignity that is alien to him. . . The value of a human life is ultimately grounded in the value God is placing on it. . . . That sacredness is not composed by observable degrees of relative worth. A life's sanctity consists not in its worth to anybody. . . ."

Life is a gift in trust, it is on loan, man does not have dominion over it.

This too is a theme which recurs constantly in both Protestant and Catholic analyses. An example is Norman St. John-Stevas, a Catholic: "The value of human life for the Christians in the first century A.D., as today, rested not on its development of a superior sentience, but on the unique character of the union of body and soul, both defined for eternal life. . . . Its other aspect is the emphasis on the creatureliness of man. Man is not absolutely master of his own life and body. He has no dominion over it, but holds it in trust for God's purposes."

Paul Ramsey (a Protestant) puts it this

way: "Every human being is a unique, unrepeatable opportunity to praise God. His life is entirely an ordination, a loan, and a stewardship."

But just before moving on and looking for another, more secular basis, let us at least attempt to distil some conclusions from the theological roots of the sanctity of life principle, putting aside the particular tenets of faith which nurture those roots. In doing so we might in part find that, though the arguments advanced by the theological and secular perspectives differ, there is at least a roughly equivalent investment in the centrality and meaning of the principle. One could say that the religious roots I have sketched can be distilled into these three statements:

(i) The sanctity of human life is not the result of the "worth" a human being may attribute to it—either to one's own life or that of others. Considerations such as "degrees of relative worth," "functional proficiency," or "pragmatic utility" which humans may acquire or have are in no sense appropriate yardsticks for determining or measuring sanctity of life.

(ii) Human life may not be taken without adequate justification, nor may human nature be radically changed.

(iii) The sanctity of life principle is basic to our society, and its rejection would endanger all human life.

B. THE ROOTS IN EXPERIENCE AND INTUITION

The roots of the sanctity of life principle are clearly religious. But not even theologians normally claim that theology is the only basis of important moral principles. In this regard one could hardly do better than cite the observations of the theologian James Gustafson. While acknowledging that theology is significant to believers, he adds, "For most persons involved in medical care and practice the contribution of theology is likely to be of minimal importance, for the moral principles and values can be justified without

reference to God, and the attitudes that religious beliefs ground can be grounded in other ways. . . . Functional equivalents of theology are present in the patterns of actions and the ethical thought of persons who find theology to be a meaningless intellectual enterprise."

Gustafson is no doubt correct in general but at least on the subject of the sanctity of life principle not many of those "functional equivalents of theology" have in fact been articulated and argued in any detail. One of the few such efforts is that of Edward Shils.

1. Roots of the Principle in the Nature of Things

Shils builds his position on the "common experience" of mankind. Despite waning theological belief, many of the actual or prospective interventions of biomedicine give rise to a "deep abhorrence or revulsion." Why is this? Not just because those who are no longer believers are still unconsciously motivated by vestigal traces of religious belief. On the contrary, "The source of the revulsion or apprehension is deeper than the culture of Christianity and its doctrine of the soul. Indeed, it might be said that the Christian doctrine was enabled to maintain its long prosperity and to become effective because it was able to conform for so many centuries to a deeper protoreligious 'natural metaphysic.'"

There we have it. Both for those who are and are not religious the experience of a deep respect for human life (as recognized for instance in law by the *Bill of Rights*) can be traced ultimately to the nature of things, to the way things are—a protoreligious, natural metaphysic. He goes on to say,

The chief feature of the protoreligious "natural metaphysic" is the affirmation that life *is* sacred. It is believed to be sacred not because it is a manifestation of a transcendent creator from whom life comes: it is believed to be sacred because it is life. The idea of sacredness is generated by the primordial experience of being alive, of experiencing the elemental sensation of vitality and the elemental fear of its extinction. Man stands in awe before his own vitality, the vitality of his lineage and of his species. The sense of awe is the attribution and therefore the acknowledgment of sanctity. All else man feels to be sacred derives its sanctity because it controls or embodies that sacred vitality of the individual, the lineage and the species.

Though he does not use the expression "sanctity of life," P. D. Medawar's writing on the subject of genetic options makes much the same point when he writes: "At what point shall we say we are wantonly interfering with nature and prolonging life beyond what is proper and humane? In practice the answer we give is founded not upon abstract moralizing but upon a certain natural sense of the fitness of things, a feeling that is shared by most kind and reasonable people even if we cannot define it in philosophically defensible or legally accountable terms."

There is nothing in Shils of the "alien dignity" version of sanctity proposed by the theological perspective we noted above. Quite the contrary. For Shils, as for the "secular" perspective in general, dignity, worth and sanctity are inherent in man, grounded in the way things are, not given and maintained by God. Nevertheless, it is worthy of note that when it comes to the "bottom line" the religious and secular views may not be so far apart.

Barth and Shils are both able, from their quite different perspectives, to speak about our "standing in awe" before human life. Shils wrote (above) that "man stands in awe before his own vitality." Barth wrote that, "Respect [for life] is man's astonishment, humility and awe at a fact in which he meets something superior—majesty, dignity, holiness, a mystery which compels him to withdraw and keep his distance, to handle it modestly, circumspectly and carefully."

And Shils is very close to the view we noted above of St. John Stevas, when he writes that if sanctity of life goes, ". . . then nothing else would be sacred."

It may not, however, be entirely correct

to characterize the "secular" perspective, as opposed to the "religious" perspective, as one which always sees sanctity as inherent in man, intrinsic to man. For instance, Danner Clouser, though he has serious reservations about the usefulness of the concept, yet acknowledges that sanctity could be seen as at least a "derived" property of life given the prior acceptance of religious propositions such as creation. But, he argues, apart from the religious context, "There is no universally accepted theory—if any at all—that entails a property called 'sanctity.'" He therefore concludes that sanctity of life "is more something we pledge ourselves to, a commitment, than it is an objective property that demands acknowledgment."

C. CONCLUSIONS: SOME AGREEMENTS

So much for the roots of the principle in theology and experience. There remain and will remain vast differences between the two perspectives. We have indicated some of them. No one has yet managed to satisfactorily reconcile the two approaches in theory. But there are also agreements, and I have indicated some of them as well. The most important point of practical agreement, of practical consensus, is of course in the affirmation of the principle itself, at least in its general lines and orientation, as the fundamental one and the starting point for all biomedical decision making. That in itself is no small matter. We are thus able to say that, ". . . the concept is an expression of a basic intuition about human life that can be had by men who are not religious in the narrow sense of the term. . . the intuition that gives rise to the concept of the sanctity of life is somehow related, in an intrinsic and positive way, to the mystery that overhangs all finite existence. Religious concepts and myths specify the nature of this mystery, but such specification is not necessary to recognize its existence and the fact that it must be taken into account somehow (at least in terms of reverence, caution and humility) when we deal with persons."

One does not want to suggest that everyone accepts the principle, or applies it in the same way. But it or some equivalent principle is widely affirmed, implicitly or explicitly. Commentators tend to agree that the principle includes at least these three points:

(i) Human life is precious, even mysterious, and is worthy of respect and protection.

→is just a natural good.

Human worth is not determined merely by subjective or utilitarian concerns.

(ii) Human life may not be taken without adequate justification, and human nature may not be radically changed. ↳genetics research?

✳ (iii) The sanctity of life principle (or an equivalent principle) is basic to our society and its rejection would endanger all human life.

A Jewish Statement on the Sanctity of Life

Jewish Compendium on Medical Ethics

HUMAN LIFE

I Our first principle, as stated above, is that every human life is of infinite value. From this all-encompassing tenet stem numerous practical rulings, such as:

a) The duty to heal the sick, seen as a religious precept;

b) The suspension of almost all ritual requirements in the face of any danger to life;

c) The prohibition of acts such as suicide and euthanasia;

d) Opposition to unethical, hazardous or uncontrolled experimentation on living humans.

II This principle is the indispensable foundation of a moral society. If a person with only a few moments to live were to be considered less valuable than one with many years of life ahead, the value of every human being loses its absolute character. It becomes relative to life expectancy, to state of health, to intelligence, or usefulness to society, or to any other arbitrary criterion. Such reduction of human value from absolute to relative standards could well be the wedge that allows us to divide humanity into people of superior and inferior value; into those with a greater and those with a lesser claim to life. It leads to the catastrophic conclusions that sought to liquidate so-called "inferior races." The moment any human being is toppled from the high pedestal on which he stands, the whole fabric of a moral society is endangered. The erosion of the moral ethic begins when the nearly-dead are equated with the dead; this value judgment is then extended to encompass the inferior individual, the mentally retarded, the disabled or the incurably ill. The undesirable, the unproductive or the alien are then also excluded from their inalienable right to life. domino effect

Judaism never condones the deliberate destruction of human life, except in judicial execution for certain criminal acts, in self-defense, or in time of war. Nor may one sacrifice a life to save another one, even if the saved person is granted many years of constructive living; this too is murder. cuts off many questions in making judgement

Euthanasia

The Jewish attitude towards euthanasia as well as towards suicide is based on the premise that "Only He Who gives life may take it away." In this regard, the Jewish ethical stance is not different from the common law view now prevalent in most civilized countries: that euthanasia is not a legal act. This view is contrary to the attempts of some modern writers on medical ethics to relax the strictures on euthanasia in the name of "death with dignity" or "right to die." Any deliberate induction of death, even if the patient requests it, is an act of homicide. Only when pt stops responding to all treatments

For Judaism, human life is "created in the image of God." Although all life is considered to be God's creation and good,

domino effect.

human life is related to God in a special way: It is sacred. The sanctity of human life prescribes that, in any situation short of self-defense or martyrdom, human life be treated as an end in itself. It may thus not be terminated or shortened because of considerations of the patient's convenience or usefulness, or even our sympathy with the suffering of the patient. Thus euthanasia may not be performed either in the interest of the patient or of anyone else. Even individual autonomy is secondary to the sanctity of human life and, therefore, a patient is not permitted to end his or her life or be assisted in such suicide by anyone else, be he or she a health care professional, family member, friend, or bystander. In Judaism suicide and euthanasia are both forms of prohibited homicide. No human life is more or less sacred.

Euthanasia is prohibited whether it involves an overt act to terminate life, or withholding life saving measures. Active euthanasia is obviously forbidden, i.e., to administer any drug, or institute any procedure which may hasten death, unless such drugs or procedures have significant therapeutic potential, or are meant to reduce unbearable pain.

More perplexing is the question of passive euthanasia. This term has been used to describe a wide range of medical practices, from the well-intentioned prescribing of maximum dosages of barbiturates or narcotics—despite the knowledge that these may physiologically compromise the patient—to the withholding of antibiotics where bronchopneumonia has set in. These actions would bring a speedier end to an ebbing life force, though they are passive and/or indirect.

A child born deformed but in need of lifesaving surgery exemplifies the problem for pediatric surgeons and others. Should the consummate skill of the surgeon be used to preserve a life of dubious "quality"? The question surely transcends pure medicine. Centuries of ethical concern have alerted humanity to a "domino theory" in social ethics. One seemingly innocuous inroad into the inviolate sanctuary of human life may threaten the entire ethical structure of society. Defining a deformed child's life as qualitatively of less worth than that of a healthy child, undermines the foundations of a society based on the proposition of the infinite worth of man. At the other end of life, hastening the dying process of a pain-wracked patient would have the physician make a value judgment on the preservation of life based on quality alone.

The physician is committed to prolong the life of his patient and to cure him of his illness. Acting in any other capacity, he forfeits his special character and must be judged like any layman who decides to hasten the death of a deformed or critically ill patient.

Active euthanasia is an act of homicide running counter to the great philosophical and ethical values which ascribe infinite worth to even residual life. Passive euthanasia, the omission of necessary treatments, support systems, or medical procedures, is likewise a failure of the technician to fulfill his oath of office. When the physician can in good conscience declare the patient no longer responsive to his ministration, the physician is then beyond his ability to serve. At that point, and with due consideration of the risk-benefit ratios of possible further intervention, the physician may withdraw from specific therapeutic interventions and leave life in the hands of God.

Life Is Sometimes a Modest Benefit

President's Commission

IDENTIFYING PATIENTS

Unconsciousness. No one can ever have more than inferential evidence of consciousness in another person. A detailed analysis of the nature of consciousness is not needed, however, when considering the class of patients in whom *all* possible components of mental life are absent—all thought, feeling, sensation, desire, emotion, and awareness of self or environment. Retaining even a slight ability to experience the environment (such as from an ordinary dose of sedative drugs, severe retardation, or the destruction of most of the cerebral cortex) is different from having no such ability, and the discussion in this chapter is limited to the latter group of patients.

Most of what makes someone a distinctive individual is lost when the person is unconscious, especially if he or she will always remain so. Personality, memory, purposive action, social interaction, sentience, thought, and even emotional states are gone. Only vegetative functions and reflexes persist. If food is supplied, the digestive system functions and uncontrolled evacuation occurs; the kidneys produce urine; the heart, lungs, and blood vessels continue to move air and blood; and nutrients are distributed in the body.

Exceedingly careful neurologic examination is essential in order for a diagnosis of complete unconsciousness to be made. Application of noxious stimuli to the nerve endings of an unconscious patient leads to simple, unregulated reflex responses at both the spinal and the brain stem levels. Reflexes may allow some eye movement, grimacing, swallowing, and pupillary adjustment to light. If the reticular activating system in the brain stem is intact, the eyes can open and close in regular daily cycles. The reflex activity can be unsettling to family and other observers, but the components of behavior that produce this appearance are "accompanied by an apparent total lack of cognitive function." In order to have awareness, a person must have an integrated functioning of the brain stem's activating system with the higher "thinking" functions from the thalamus and cerebral hemispheres. Many patients whose brain dysfunctions cause unconsciousness nevertheless have a fairly intact brain stem and, if provided extensive nursing care, are able to remain alive without respirator support for many years.

Permanence. The other essential property of this category of patients is that their unconsciousness is permanent, which means "lasting . . . indefinitely without change; opposed to temporary." Three sources of uncertainty should be acknowledged about any judgment that a particular patient's unconscious state is permanent.

The first uncertainty affects any scientific proposition about as-yet-unobserved cases. No matter how extensive the past evidence is for an empirical generalization, it may yet be falsified by future experience. Certainty in prognosis is always a matter of degree, typically based upon the quantity and quality of the evidence from which a prediction is made.

Second, this empirical qualification is especially serious in predictions about unconsciousness because the evidence relevant to a prognosis of permanence is still quite limited. The overall number of such patients is small, and most cases have not been carefully studied or adequately reported. Furthermore, the number of variables affecting prognosis (for example, the cause of unconsciousness, the patient's age and other diseases, the length of time the patient has been unconscious, and the kinds of therapy applied) is large and imperfectly understood.

Finally, any prediction that a patient will not regain consciousness before dying, regardless of the treatment undertaken, contains an implicit assumption about future medical breakthroughs. Since some such patients can be maintained alive for extended periods of time (often years rather than days, weeks, or months), this assumption about treatment innovations can be a long-range one. At the moment, however, it introduces only a very small uncertainty, since the possibility of repairing the neurologic injuries that destroy consciousness is exceedingly remote.

Given these three qualifications on the meaning and basis of any judgment regarding permanence, such a judgment is always a matter of probability about whether a particular patient will remain unconscious until he or she dies despite any treatment that might be undertaken. Nevertheless, the Commission was assured that physicians with experience in this area can reliably determine that some patients' loss of consciousness is permanent.

REASONS FOR CONTINUED TREATMENT

Physicians arrive at prognoses of permanent unconsciousness only after patients have received vigorous medical attention, careful observation, and complete diagnostic studies, usually over a prolonged period. During this time when improvement is thought to be possible, it is appropriate for therapies to be intensive and aggressive, both to reverse unconsciousness and to overcome any other problems. Once it is clear that the loss of consciousness is permanent, however, the goals of continued therapy need to be examined.

The interests of the patient. The primary basis for medical treatment of patients is the prospect that each individual's interests (specifically, the interest in well-being) will be promoted. Thus, treatment ordinarily aims to benefit a patient through preserving life, relieving pain and suffering, protecting against disability, and returning maximally

effective functioning. If a prognosis of permanent unconsciousness is correct, however, continued treatment cannot confer such benefits. Pain and suffering are absent, as are joy, satisfaction, and pleasure. Disability is total and no return to an even minimal level of social or human functioning is possible.

Any value to the patient from continued care and maintenance under such circumstances would seem to reside in the very small probability that the prognosis of permanence is incorrect. Although therapy might appear to be in the patient's interest because it preserves the remote chance of recovery of consciousness, there are two substantial objections to providing vigorous therapy for permanently unconscious patients.

First, the few patients who have recovered consciousness after a prolonged period of unconsciousness were severely disabled. The degree of permanent damage varied but commonly included inability to speak or see, permanent distortion of the limbs, and paralysis. Being returned to such a state would be regarded as of very limited benefit by most patients; it may even be considered harmful if a particular patient would have refused treatments expected to produce this outcome. Thus, even the extremely small likelihood of "recovery" cannot be equated with returning to a normal or relatively well functioning state. Second, long-term treatment commonly imposes severe financial and emotional burdens on a patient's family, people whose welfare most patients, before they lost consciousness, placed a high value on. For both these reasons, then, continued treatment beyond a minimal level will often not serve the interests of permanently unconscious patients optimally.

The interests of others. The other possible sources of an interest in continued care for a permanently unconscious patient are the patient's family, health care professionals, and the public. A family possessing hope, however slim, for a patient's recovery shares that individual's interest in the continuation of treatment, namely, the possibility that the prognosis of permanent unconsciousness will prove wrong. Also, families may find personal meaning in attending to an unconscious patient, and they have a substantial interest in that patient's being treated respectfully.

Health care professionals undertake specific and often explicit obligations to render care. People trust these professionals to act in patients' best interests. This expectation plays a complex and crucial part in the professionals' ability to provide care. Failure to provide some minimal level of care, even to a permanently unconscious patient, might undermine that trust and with it the health care professions' general capacity to provide effective care. Furthermore, the self-identity of physicians, nurses, and other personnel is bound in significant ways to the lifesaving efforts they make; to fail to do so is felt by some to violate their professional creed. Consequently, health care providers may have an interest in continued treatment of these patients.

Finally, society has a significant interest in protecting and promoting the high value of human life. Although continued life may be of little value to the permanently unconscious patient, the provision of care is one way of symbolizing and reinforcing the value of human life so long as any chance of recovery remains. Moreover, the public may want permanently unconscious patients to receive treatment lest reduced levels of care have deleterious effects on the vigor with which other, less seriously compromised patients are treated. Furthermore the public has reason to support appropriate research on the pathophysiology and treatment of this condition so that decisions always rely upon the most complete and recent data possible.

There are, on the other hand, considerations for each of these parties—the family, health care professionals, and society—that argue against continued treatment of permanently unconscious patients. As mentioned, long-term treatment commonly imposes substantial financial burdens on a patient's family and on society and often creates substantial psychological stresses for family members and providers. Health care professionals must devote scarce time and resources to treatment that is nearly certain to be futile. Any alternate useful allocation of the resources and personnel is likely to benefit other patients much more substantially.

In sum, the interests of the permanently unconscious patient in continued treatment are very limited compared with other patients. These attenuated interests in continuing treatment must be weighed against the reasons to choose nontreatment in order to arrive at sound public policy on the care of the permanently unconscious.

Some Qualities of Life Are Not Worth Living

H. Tristram Engelhardt, Jr.

There is another viewpoint that must be considered: that of the child or even the person that the child might become. It might be argued that the child has a right not to have its life prolonged. The idea that forcing existence on a child could be wrong is a difficult notion, which, if true, would serve to amplify the foregoing argument. Such an argument would allow the construal of the issue in terms of the perspective of the child, that is, in terms of a duty not to treat in circumstances where treatment would only prolong suffering. In particular, it would at least give a framework for a decision to stop treatment in cases where, though the costs of treatment are not high, the child's existence would be characterized by severe pain and deprivation.

A basis for speaking of continuing existence as an injury to the child is suggested by the proposed legal concept of "wrongful life." A number of suits have been initiated in the United States and in other countries on the grounds that life or existence itself is, under certain circumstances, a tort or injury to the living person. Although thus far all such suits have ultimately failed, some have succeeded in their initial stages. Two examples may be instructive. In each case the ability to receive recompense for the injury (the tort) presupposed the existence of the individual, whose existence was itself the injury. In one case a suit was initiated on behalf of a child against his father alleging that his father's siring him out of wedlock was an injury to the child. In another case a suit on behalf of a child born of an inmate of a state mental hospital impregnated by rape in that institution was brought against the state of New York. The suit was brought on the grounds that being born with such historical antecedents was itself an injury for which recovery was due. Both cases presupposed that nonexistence would have been preferable to the conditions under which the person born was forced to live.

The suits for tort for wrongful life raise the issue not only of when it would be preferable not to have been born but also of when it would be *wrong* to cause a person to be born. This implies that someone should have judged that it would have been preferable for the child never to have had existence, never to have been in the position to judge that the particular circumstances of life were intolerable. Further, it implies that the person's existence under those circumstances should have been prevented and that, not having been prevented, life was not a gift but an injury. The concept of tort for wrongful life raises an issue concerning the responsibility for giving another person existence, namely, the notion that giving life is not always necessarily a good and justifiable action. Instead, in certain circumstances, so it has been argued, one may have a duty *not* to give existence to another person. This

concept involves the claim that certain qualities of life have a negative value, making life an injury, not a gift; it involves, in short, a concept of human accountability and responsibility for human life. It contrasts with the notion that life is a gift of God and thus similar to other "acts of God," (that is, events for which no man is accountable). The concept thus signals the fact that humans can now control reproduction and that where rational control is possible humans are accountable. That is, the expansion of human capabilities has resulted in an expansion of human responsibilities such that one must now decide when and under what circumstances persons will come into existence.

The concept of tort for wrongful life is transferable in part to the painfully compromised existence of children who can only have their life prolonged for a short, painful, and marginal existence. The concept suggests that allowing life to be prolonged under such circumstances would itself be an injury of the person whose painful and severely compromised existence would be made to continue. In fact, it suggests that there is a duty not to prolong life if it can be determined to have a substantial negative value for the person involved. Such issues are moot in the case of adults, who can and should decide for themselves. But small children cannot make such a choice. For them it is an issue of justifying prolonging life under circumstances of painful and compromised existence. Or, put differently, such cases indicate the need to develop social canons to allow a decent death for children for whom the only possibility is protracted, painful suffering.

I do not mean to imply that one should develop a new basis for civil damages. In the field of medicine, the need is to recognize an ethical category, a concept of wrongful continuance of existence, not a new legal right. The concept of injury for continuance of existence, the proposed analogue of the concept of tort for wrongful life, presupposes that life can be of a negative value such that the medical maxim *primum non nocere* ("first do no harm") would require not sustaining life.

The idea of responsibility for acts that sustain or prolong life is cardinal to the notion that one should not under certain circumstances further prolong the life of a child. Unlike adults, children cannot decide with regard to euthanasia (positive or negative), and if more than a utilitarian justification is sought, it must be sought in a duty not to inflict life on another person in circumstances where that life would be painful and futile. This position must rest on the facts that (1) medicine now can cause the prolongation of the life of seriously deformed children who in the past would have died young and that (2) it is not clear that life so prolonged is a good for the child. Further, the choice is made not on the basis of costs to the parents or to society but on the basis of the child's suffering and compromised existence.

The difficulty lies in determining what makes life not worth living for a child. Answers could never be clear. It seems reasonable, however, that the life of children with diseases that involve pain and no hope of survival should not be prolonged. In the case of Tay-Sachs disease (a disease marked by a progressive increase in spasticity and dementia usually leading to death at age three or four), one can hardly imagine that the terminal stages of spastic reaction to stimuli and great difficulty in swallowing are at all pleasant to the child (even insofar as it can only minimally perceive its circumstances). If such a child develops aspiration pneumonia and is treated, it can reasonably be said that to prolong its life is to inflict suffering. Other diseases give fairly clear portraits of lives not worth living: for example, Lesch-Nyhan disease, which is marked by mental retardation and compulsive self-mutilation.

The issue is more difficult in the case of children with diseases for whom the prospects for normal intelligence and a fair lifestyle do exist, but where these chances are remote and their realization expensive. Children born with meningomyelocele present this dilemma. Imagine, for example, a child that falls within Lorber's fifth category (an IQ of sixty or less, sometimes blind, subject to fits, and always incontinent). Such a child has little prospect of anything approaching a normal life, and there is a good chance of its dying even with treatment. But such judgments are statistical. And if one does not treat such children, some will still survive and, as John Freeman indicates, be worse off if not treated. In such cases one is in a dilemma. If one always treats, one must justify extending the life of those who will ultimately die anyway and in the process subjecting them to the morbidity of multiple surgical procedures. How remote does the prospect of a good life have to be in order not to be worth great pain and expense? It is probably best to decide, in the absence of a positive duty to treat, on the basis of the cost and suffering to parents and society. But, as Freeman argues, the prospect of prolonged or even increased suffering raises the issue of active euthanasia.

If the child is not a person strictly, and if death is inevitable and expediting it would diminish the child's pain prior to death, then it would seem to follow that, all else being equal, a decision for active euthanasia would be permissible, even obligatory. The difficulty lies with "all else being equal," for it is doubtful that active euthanasia could be established as a practice without eroding and endangering children generally, since, as John Lorber has pointed out, children cannot speak in their own behalf. Thus, although there is no argument in principle against the active euthanasia of small children, there could be an argument against such practices based on questions of prudence. To put it another way, even though one might have a duty to hasten the death of a particular child, one's duty to protect children in general could override that first duty. The issue of active euthanasia turns in the end on whether it would have social consequences that refraining would not, on whether (1) it is possible to establish procedural safeguards for limited active euthanasia and (2) whether such practices would have a significant adverse effect on the treatment of small children in general. But since these are procedural issues dependent on sociological facts, they are not open to an answer within the confines of this article. In any event, the concept of the injury of continued existence provides a basis for the justification of the passive euthanasia of small children—a practice already widespread and somewhat established in our society—beyond the mere absence of a positive duty to treat.

SECTION C
Health Care and Justice

INTRODUCTION

The readings in the first two sections of Part II of the text have focused primarily on questions of individual decision making. Section A was devoted to who should make what decisions in particular cases in which health care might be provided. Section B was devoted to the moral principles governing decision making in life-and-death situations. The focus in this section is very different, for the readings here address moral questions in the design of the health-care system as a whole.

Health care costs a great deal of money. Traditionally, those who were indigent had to depend for their health care upon the private charity of individual providers and of groups who funded charity hospitals. More recently, there has arisen a growing acceptance of the idea that there ought to be equitable access to health care for all. The readings by the President's Commission, by Gibbard, by Daniels, by Gutmann, and by Brody offer alternative analyses of this concept of equitable access or alternatives to it.

Equitable access, according to the President's Commission, does not mean that everyone receives the same level of health care, for that would deprive the affluent of their legitimate ability to use their money to seek better care. Neither does it mean that all people would receive all the health care from which they would benefit, for that would require an excessive outlay of public funds for health care. The Commission claims that equitable access should be understood as everyone having access to some adequate level of health care, and that an obligation of society to provide that level of care can be defined independently of some theory of a right to health care.

Several crucial questions are raised by such an analysis. The first has to do with the nature of the moral appeals that would justify the claim that society has an obligation to provide all people an adequate level of health care but not all the health care from which they could benefit. The second has to do with the very difficult question of how to define that adequate level of care. The third question is one raised by the Commission itself, namely, how we should judge costs and benefits in deciding what care should be part of that adequate level.

Gibbard and Daniels provide differing approaches to the attempt to define this idea of equitable access to an adequate level of care. Gibbard's view is that there may be some forms of care that are so expensive and that offer such modest benefits that it would be irrational for individuals and society to want (in advance of needing that care) to have that care at that cost. Such forms of care, Gibbard concludes, should not be part of the adequate level of care. Daniels' view is that the adequate level of care to which everyone should have equal access is that care required to ensure equality of opportunity by providing services needed to maintain, restore, or compensate for the loss of normal functioning. Other forms of care should not be part of the adequate level of care to which all are entitled.

Both of these authors clearly base their proposals on a conception of the moral basis for the demand that everyone receive an adequate level of care. What are their different bases and how do these lead to their different views? Which of their proposals leads to including more health care in the adequate level of care? These are some of the questions that require attention.

Gutmann and Brody reject the idea that justice in health care should be structured around this concept of ensuring equal access to an adequate level of care. Gutmann argues that we would do better to seek to realize the ideal of complete equality in access to health care, even at the cost of limiting the freedom of the affluent to purchase better care. Brody argues that we should drop the whole idea of justice in health care, create appropriate programs for distributing money to the indigent, and allow them and everyone else to purchase in the market the level of health care they choose. We might view Gutmann as emphasizing equality at the cost of freedom and Brody as emphasizing freedom at the cost of equality. These authors, like all the others we have examined, base their approaches on special moral appeals. The reader needs to identify those appeals to see why they lead Brody and Gutmann to disagree radically with the views of the President's Commission.

Ensuring equity in access to health care is only one of the desiderata of a health-care system. We also want good health care at a reasonable cost provided in a fashion we find pleasant and sensitive to our needs. Does our current health-care system meet these goals? Could it be restructured so as to better meet these goals? These are the questions raised in the readings from McCarthy, Enthoven, and Singer.

McCarthy's main goal is to describe the American health-care system from an economic perspective. As she points out, the money to pay for health care comes from the government (primarily to pay for health care for the elderly, the indigent, and veterans), from private insurance companies, and from individuals receiving the care. That money is used to pay fees to providers and to hospitals and to purchase medications and health-care devices (wheelchairs, prosthetic devices, etc.). Physicians have traditionally been paid by a fees-for-service approach, an approach according to which a separate fee is paid for each service provided. Some physicians (those working in public hospitals, for example) are paid salaries and a few receive an annual payment per patient in return for which they provide the care the patient needs. Hospitals have traditionally also been paid for each service provided, but recently it has been suggested that hospitals be paid a fee set in advance for each patient of a given type served, regardless of the amount of services the patient receives. This approach, called *prospective reimbursement,* has been adopted by the federal government—since the publication of McCarthy's article—as a way of paying hospitals for medicare patients.

As one reads McCarthy's account, one is struck by the extent to which we have a fragmented health-care system, one which arose through a series of historical accidents rather than a systematic plan. It is not surprising then that many people criticize the system, some on the grounds that it fails to provide equitable access to an adequate level of care, and others on the grounds that it costs too much money (in 1984, about 10.6 percent of the gross national product went for medical care) and is threatening to bankrupt our society. The readings from Enthoven and Singer represent two very different approaches to restructuring the nation's health-care-delivery system.

Singer advocates a national health system similar to the one in Great Britain. Such a system of health care is financed by general tax revenues and provides everyone with an equal level of care. Physicians are paid an annual fee for each patient for whose care they are responsible, and hospitals receive an annual budget to cover the costs of providing acute care. Singer offers several arguments for his approach; the reader needs to identify each of them and see the nature of the moral appeal inherent in each. Enthoven's approach is clearly meant as an alternative to the development of a national health system, although it is also an attempt to rationalize and systematize the delivery of health care in America. Enthoven envisions a system in which competing groups of physicians would offer plans of providing all health care to consumers and in which consumers would choose which system to sign up for based upon cost and level of care. The group of physicians would receive a set fee per person enrolled. Those who are too poor to pay for membership in such a group would receive a voucher from the government to pay for their membership. Again, Enthoven offers several arguments for his approach, and the reader needs to identify each of them and their presupposed moral appeal.

It is tempting to say that Enthoven emphasizes competition because he is primarily concerned with rising health care costs while Singer advocates a national health system because he is primarily concerned with ensuring equitable access to health care. That analysis is too simplistic, however, because both authors insist that they are concerned with both efficiency and equity. The reader needs to analyze their arguments and their moral presuppositions very carefully to find the basis of the difference between the two authors.

To what extent should individual providers caring for individual recipients take these social issues into account as they make decisions concerning the care of their patients? The traditional answer, carefully articulated by Charles Fried, is that they should not take these issues into account at all. The integrity of the physician–patient relation, argues Fried, requires that doctors do the best they can for their patients, independent of the general needs of society. The relation demands complete and unstinting devotion. Bureaucrats should structure health-care institutions to meet social needs; providers working within those institutions should attend to the needs of their patients. Brody argues that this view is simplistic. He claims that providers have multiple obligations in any context and additional obligations in special contexts, and these other obligations need to be attended to by any morally sensitive provider. Again, the reader needs to see what moral appeals lead to these differing conclusions.

7.   THE RIGHT TO HEALTH CARE

The Right to an Adequate Level of Health Care

President's Commission

THE CONCEPT OF EQUITABLE ACCESS TO HEALTH CARE

The special nature of health care helps to explain why it ought to be accessible, in a fair fashion, to all. But if this ethical conclusion is to provide a basis for evaluating current patterns of access to health care and proposed health policies, the meaning of fairness or equity in this context must be clarified. The concept of equitable access needs definition in its two main aspects: the level of care that ought to be available to all and the extent to which burdens can be imposed on those who obtain these services.

Access to What?

"Equitable access" could be interpreted in a number of ways: equality of access, access to whatever an individual needs or would benefit from, or access to an adequate level of care.

Equity as equality. It has been suggested that equity is achieved either when everyone is assured of receiving an equal quantity of health care dollars or when people enjoy equal health. The most common characterization of equity as equality, however, is as providing everyone with the same level of health care. In this view, it follows that if a given level of care is available to one individual it must be available to all. If the initial standard is set high, by reference to the highest level of care presently received, an enormous drain would result on the resources needed to provide other goods. Alternatively, if the standard is set low in

order to avoid an excessive use of resources, some beneficial services would have to be withheld from people who wished to purchase them. In other words, no one would be allowed access to more services or services of higher quality than those available to everyone else, even if he or she were willing to pay for those services from his or her personal resources.

As long as significant inequalities in income and wealth persist, inequalities in the use of health care can be expected beyond those created by differences in need. Given people with the same pattern of preferences and equal health care needs, those with greater financial resources will purchase more health care. Conversely, given equal financial resources, the different patterns of health care preferences that typically exist in any population will result in a different use of health services by people with equal health care needs. Trying to prevent such inequalities would require interfering with people's liberty to use their income to purchase an important good like health care while leaving them free to use it for frivolous or inessential ends. Prohibiting people with higher incomes or stronger preferences for health care from purchasing more care than everyone else gets would not be feasible, and would probably result in a black market for health care.

Equity as access solely according to benefit or need. Interpreting equitable access to mean that everyone must receive all health care that is of any benefit to them also has unacceptable implications. Unless health is the only good or resources are un-limited, it would be irrational for a society—as for an individual—to make a commit-ment to provide whatever health care might be beneficial regardless of cost. Although health care is of special importance, it is surely not all that is important to people. Pushed to an extreme, this criterion might swallow up all of society's resources, since there is virtually no end to the funds that could be devoted to possibly beneficial care for diseases and disabilities and to their prevention.

Equitable access to health care must take into account not only the benefits of care but also the cost in comparison with other goods and services to which those resources might be allocated. Society will reasonably devote some resources to health care but re-serve most resources for other goals. This, in turn, will mean that some health services (even of a lifesaving sort) will not be devel-oped or employed because they would pro-duce too few benefits in relation to their costs and to the other ways the resources for them might be used.

It might be argued that the notion of "need" provides a way to limit access to only that care that confers especially important benefits. In this view, equity as access ac-cording to need would place less severe de-mands on social resources than equity according to benefit would. There are, how-ever, difficulties with the notion of need in this context. On the one hand, medical need is often not narrowly defined but refers to any condition for which medical treatment might be effective. Thus, "equity as access according to need" collapses into "access ac-cording to whatever is of benefit."

On the other hand, "need" could be even more expansive in scope than "benefit." Philosophical and economic writings do not provide any clear distinction between "needs" and "wants" or "preferences." Since the term means different things to dif-ferent people, "access according to need" could become "access to any health service a person wants." Conversely, need could be

interpreted very narrowly to encompass only a very minimal level of services—for example, those "necessary to prevent death."

Equity as an adequate level of health care. Although neither "everything need-ed" nor "everything beneficial" nor "every-thing that anyone else is getting" are defen-sible ways of understanding equitable access, the special nature of health care dic-tates that everyone have access to *some* level of care: enough care to achieve sufficient welfare, opportunity, information, and evi-dence of interpersonal concern to facilitate a reasonably full and satisfying life. That level can be termed "an adequate level of health care." The difficulty of sharpening this amorphous notion into a workable foundation for health policy is a major problem in the United States today. This concept is not new; it is implicit in the public debate over health policy and has man-ifested itself in the history of public policy in this country. In this chapter, the Commis-sion attempts to demonstrate the value of the concept, to clarify its content, and to ap-ply it to the problems facing health policy-makers.

Understanding equitable access to health care to mean that everyone should be able to secure an adequate level of care has several strengths. Because an adequate level of care may be less than "all beneficial care" and because it does not require that all needs be satisfied, it acknowledges the need for set-ting priorities within health care and signals a clear recognition that society's resources are limited and that there are other goods besides health. Thus, interpreting equity as access to adequate care does not generate an open-ended obligation. One of the chief dangers of interpretations of equity that re-quire virtually unlimited resources for health care is that they encourage the view that equitable access is an impossible ideal. Defining equity as an adequate level of care for all avoids an impossible commitment of resources without falling into the opposite error of abandoning the enterprise of seeking to ensure that health care is in fact available for everyone.

In addition, since providing an adequate level of care is a limited moral requirement, this definition also avoids the unacceptable restriction on individual liberty entailed by the view that equity requires equality. Provided that an adequate level is available to all, those who prefer to use their resources to obtain care that exceeds that level do not offend any ethical principle in doing so. Finally, the concept of adequacy, as the Commission understands it, is society-relative. The content of adequate care will depend upon the overall resources available in a given society, and can take into account a consensus of expectations about what is adequate in a particular society at a particular time in its historical development. This permits the definition of adequacy to be altered as societal resources and expectations change.

A Right to Health Care?

Often the issue of equitable access to health care is framed in the language of rights. Some who view health care from the perspective of distributive justice argue that the considerations discussed in this chapter show not only that society has a moral obligation to provide equitable access, but also that every individual has a moral right to such access. The Commission has chosen not to develop the case for achieving equitable access through the assertion of a right to health care. Instead it has sought to frame the issues in terms of the special nature of health care and of society's moral obligation to achieve equity, without taking a position on whether the term "obligation" should be read as entailing a moral right. The Commission reaches this conclusion for several reasons: first, such a right is not legally or Constitutionally recognized at the present time; second, it is not a logical corollary of an ethical obligation of the type the Commission has enunciated; and third, it is not

necessary as a foundation for appropriate governmental actions to secure adequate health care for all.

Legal rights. Neither the Supreme Court nor any appellate court has found a constitutional right to health or to health care. However, most Federal statutes and many state statutes that fund or regulate health care have been interpreted to provide statutory rights in the form of entitlements for the intended beneficiaries of the program or for members of the group protected by the regulatory authority. As a consequence, a host of legal decisions have developed significant legal protections for program beneficiaries. These protections have prevented Federal and state agencies and private providers from withholding authorized benefits and services. They have required agencies and providers to deliver health care to eligible individuals—the poor, elderly, handicapped, children, and others.

In addition, Federal statutes protecting the civil rights of all citizens and the constitutional provisions of equal protection and due process have been interpreted to apply both to governmental agencies and to private health care providers in certain circumstances. Decisions affecting beneficiaries and providers must be made through orderly and fair processes, and there can be no discrimination based on race, sex, handicap, or age in the allocation of resources and operation of the health care programs. A recent study by the Institute of Medicine presents evidence showing the continuing existence of distinctive, separate, or segregated patterns in the sources of care and the amount of care received. These patterns were found to be influenced by such factors as patient income, source of payment for care, geographic location, race, and ethnicity.

Moral obligations and rights. The relationship between the concept of a moral right and that of a moral obligation is complex. To say that a person has a moral right to something is always to say that it is that person's due, that is, he or she is morally entitled to it. In contrast, the term "obligation" is used in two different senses. All moral rights imply corresponding obligations, but, depending on the sense of the term that is being used, moral obligations may or may not imply corresponding rights. In the broad sense, to say that society has a moral obligation to do something is to say that it ought morally to do that thing and that failure to do it makes society liable to serious moral criticism. This does not, however, mean that there is a corresponding right. For example, a person may have a moral obligation to help those in need, even though the needy cannot, strictly speaking, demand that person's aid as something they are due.

The government's responsibility for seeing that the obligation to achieve equity is met is independent of the existence of a corresponding moral right to health care. There are many forms of government involvement, such as enforcement of traffic rules or taxation to support national defense, to protect the environment, or to promote biomedical research, that do not presuppose corresponding moral rights but that are nonetheless legitimate and almost universally recognized as such. In a democracy, at least, the people may assign to government the responsibility for seeing that important collective obligations are met, provided that doing so does not violate important moral rights.

As long as the debate over the ethical assessment of patterns of access to health care is carried on simply by the assertion and refutation of a "right to health care," the debate will be incapable of guiding policy. At the very least, the nature of the right must be made clear and competing accounts of it compared and evaluated. Moreover, if claims of rights are to guide policy they must be supported by sound ethical reasoning and the connections between various rights must be systematically developed, especially where rights are potentially in con-

flict with one another. At present, however, there is a great deal of dispute among competing theories of rights, with most theories being so abstract and inadequately developed that their implications for health care are not obvious. Rather than attempt to adjudicate among competing theories of rights, the Commission has chosen to concentrate on what it believes to be the more important part of the question: what is the nature of the societal obligation, which exists whether or not people can claim a corresponding right to health care, and how should this societal obligation be fulfilled?

MEETING THE SOCIETAL OBLIGATION

The relationship of costs and benefits. The level of care that is available will be determined by the level of resources devoted to producing it. Such allocation should reflect the benefits and costs of the care provided. It should be emphasized that these "benefits," as well as their "costs," should be interpreted broadly, and not restricted only to effects easily quantifiable in monetary terms. Personal benefits include improvements in individuals' functioning and in their quality of life, and the reassurance from worry and the provision of information that are a product of health care. Broader social benefits should be included as well, such as strengthening the sense of community and the belief that no one in serious need of health care will be left without it. Similarly, costs are not merely the funds spent for a treatment but include other less tangible and quantifiable adverse consequences, such as diverting funds away from other socially desirable endeavors including education, welfare, and other social services.

There is no objectively correct value that these various costs and benefits have or that can be discovered by the tools of cost/benefit analysis. Still, such an analysis, as a recent report of the Office of Technology Assessment noted, "can be very helpful to decisionmakers because the process of analysis gives structure to the problem, allows an open consideration of all relevant effects of a decision, and forces the explicit treatment of key assumptions." But the valuation of the various effects of alternative treatments for different conditions rests on people's values and goals, about which individuals will reasonably disagree. In a democracy, the appropriate values to be assigned to the consequences of policies must ultimately be determined by people expressing their values through social and political processes as well as in the marketplace.

When Is the Best Care Too Expensive?

Allan Gibbard

According to the Ex Ante Pareto Principle, then, we may settle at least some questions of social ethics as follows. Given a choice between two policies, we ask for each affected person: "What prospects for an intrinsically rewarding life does each policy present him?"; "Which policy is the better one, simply in terms of how desirable it leaves his prospects in life?" If the answer is the same for each person, then the policy that gives each person a better prospect is Pareto-superior ex ante, and hence, according to the Ex Ante Pareto Principle, the better policy ethically speaking. If the answer differs from person to person, the Ex Ante Pareto Principle offers no moral guidance.

APPLICATIONS: EXTRAORDINARILY EXPENSIVE TREATMENTS

What constitutes just or equitable access to health care? There is an answer that is sometimes accepted as so obvious as to need no comment. What justice requires, it is often supposed, is that every person have available to him the best health care that could possibly be provided, given the current state of medical knowledge.

However, if the Ex Ante Pareto Principle is valid, then justice cannot demand so much—or so I shall argue in this section. In this and the following two sections, I should stress, I shall not be asking whether the Ex Ante Pareto Principle indeed is valid. That will come later. Rather, I shall be examining the kinds of ethical conclusions that can be drawn from the principle, on the assump-

tion that it is valid. The conclusions here will not follow deductively from the principle taken alone; they are conclusions, rather, in that they follow from the principle in combination with what, I take it, we know about the human condition in a society like ours—a moderately wealthy society, capable of high medical technology.

Does justice or equity, then, require that everyone receive the finest medical care that money can buy? In so unqualified a form, the claim seems thoughtless. In the first place, it might be technologically infeasible to provide everyone with the best medical care that could be provided to anyone. Resources may be too scarce. If a kind of treatment draws extensively on scarce resources, then although it may be that the resources of a society are sufficient for such treatment to be provided to a few, the resources of that society, or indeed of the world, are insufficient for the treatment to be provided to all. Equity cannot require the impossible, and if the demands of equity are demands on governmental policy alone, then they cannot require what is economically infeasible.

A more modest version of the demand that all receive the best is this: If it is economically feasible for all to receive the best care known to medical science, then equity demands that such care be provided to all. In this formulation, the principle is quite narrow, in that it says nothing about what equity demands when "the best known treatment for all" is economically infeasible. Before we examine the demand even in this narrow version, though, a further revision is needed. Some health care discussions address conditions that are not serious—conditions that do not threaten life and do not threaten to become debilitating. That all must receive the best feasible health care seems most plausible in questions of life or death, or questions of serious impairment. Can we at least say this: If it is economically feasible for all to receive the best care known to medical science, then at least when life itself is at stake, or when care may prevent serious, long-term debilitation, equity demands that all receive the best care known to medical science.

I take equity here simply to mean acceptability from an ethical point of view. A virtue of the Ex Ante Pareto Principle is that it transforms some questions of equity into questions of prudence under conditions of risk; questions of equity in retrospect become questions of unanimous prudence in prospect.

There is a limit to what it is rational to pay to avoid risks of catastrophe. When one crosses a busy street, one runs a small risk of death or crippling injury, usually for a small gain; but if one crosses prudently, the small likely gain, all of us seem to think, outweighs the risk of catastrophe. Suppose, then, that certain life-saving medical treatments are extraordinarily expensive. If a person faced a private choice of whether to insure against the need for such treatment, his choice would be, in effect, one of whether to accept the risk of needing expensive medical treatment and not being insured for it, for the small benefit of saving on the insurance premium to buy something else. If the treatment is sufficiently expensive and the chances of needing it are small, then the prospect of going uninsured may be the more desirable one, prudentially speaking. That may be so for the same reason as the prospect of crossing a street is often more desirable than the alternatives, despite a small risk to life and limb. Just as there is a limit to what it is rational to pay, on prudential grounds, to avoid other risks,

there is a limit to how much it would be rational for an individual to pay for a guarantee of whatever expensive, vital health care he might turn out to need.

In the first place, of course, some medical care is of no benefit to a person whatsoever; it is hard, for instance, to see why anyone should want to be kept alive if he should fall into an irreversible coma, and it would be unreasonable to sacrifice an iota for an assurance that one would be kept alive in that eventuality. Other assurances of expensive treatment may be worth something, but not as much as the assurances themselves would cost. A possible example is the assurance that kidney dialysis will be available if needed. It may be a better prospect—rationally to be preferred, that is, on prudential grounds—to enjoy what the premium will buy if one is healthy and risk needing the treatment and not being able to get it, than to live less well if healthy and get the treatment if one needs it.

Whether an assurance is worth its price is a matter of the risk of needing the treatment, the value of the treatment if it is needed, and the cost of the assurance. The social cost of the assurance will be a matter of the risk of the disease and the resources diverted to treatment from other uses to which they might be put. What the assurance costs a given person, in comparison to a specific alternative economic arrangement without that assurance, is a matter of how the social cost of the assurance is distributed. The import of the Ex Ante Pareto Principle is this. Suppose a scheme is proposed for assuring and financing an expensive kind of medical care. Suppose the cost is distributed in such a way that each person, in advance of knowing whether he will need that kind of care, faces a worse prospect on balance given the scheme and his share of its cost than he would face without the scheme and keeping his share of the cost. Then it is better, ethically speaking, not to have the scheme. True, those who turn out to need the care are, as it turns out, substantially worse off without the scheme than with it. On the other hand, the many who do not need the care are better off having their share of the cost to spend on other things. These are the considerations that need to be weighed against each other, and the rest by desirability of individual prospects shows us how, from an ethical point of view, they balance out.

There must be a limit, then, to what we ought, from an ethical point of view, to be willing to pay for life-saving treatment. More precisely, if the Ex Ante Pareto Principle is valid, then there are ways of allocating economic burdens that are so onerous that it would be better, ethically speaking, for no one to receive certain kinds of lifesaving treatment, than for the burdens to be imposed and for everyone to be assured of getting those treatments if in need of them. The Ex Ante Pareto Principle gives a sufficient condition for an assurance of treatment not to be worth its cost.

Applying the principle requires both extensive knowledge and careful reflection. One must be broadly knowledgeable of what life can be like under various conditions, and one must engage in carefully thoughtful experiments about the risks worth taking in life. Are such thoughtful experiments practicable? They are surely impossible to perform with any precision, but I think they can be of value. In the first place, I maintain, such thoughtful experiments can reassure us on matters that seem obvious in health care policy, but that we might begin to doubt when we realize how insecurely based is much of received wisdom regarding health care. We can reassure ourselves that when effective treatments of debilitating or life-threatening ailments are known, the assurance that those treatments will be available, if needed, may be of great value. The shock of current medical costs may hide that from us. The proportion of the gross national product devoted to health care has approximately doubled in recent

decades, reaching nearly 10 percent. These facts in themselves, though, do not show that anything has gone wrong, and the Ex Ante Pareto Principle can help us see why not. As medical treatment becomes more effective, and as expensive, effective treatments are discovered for serious conditions that were previously untreatable, it may become rational, from a prudential point of view, to pay more for assurances of medical treatment. That can easily be seen in an extreme case. If, at one time, there are no known effective treatments, it is then irrational to pay anything for the assurance of treatment. If, later, effective treatments are discovered, then it is clearly rational to pay something, at least, for the assurance of receiving them if one needs them. There is no reason why further advances in medical knowledge should not further increase what it is rational to pay for to ensure access to treatments one may need. The Ex Ante Pareto Principle extends this conclusion to the society at large.

On the other hand, if the Ex Ante Pareto Principle is valid, then there is no defense for a universal precept: "Where life is at stake, cost is no object." That precept may apply in specific circumstances, where the cost of the best treatment is moderate and the treatment is effective in saving life and restoring health. What counts for these purposes as moderate cost may indeed seem horrendously high. It may be, for all I have said, that there are now no serious ailments for which effective treatments are known, where the most effective known treatment is not worth the cost. The Ex Ante Pareto Principle and considerations of rational prudence, however, tell us that the best known treatment for a serious ailment might not be worth the cost, ethically speaking; I leave it open whether, at present, there is, in fact, any serious ailment, the best known treatment for which is not worth the cost.

Health Care as Fair Opportunity

Norman Daniels

TOWARD A DISTRIBUTIVE THEORY: THE FAIR EQUALITY OF OPPORTUNITY ACCOUNT

Is Health Care "Special"?

My suggestion that the notion of a "decent basic minimum" is inadequate to support the moral weight it bears in the "market" approach is best supported by the proposal of an alternative account. It is possible to give a more perspicuous, if still abstract, account of what equitable access should be access to. My account is an attempt to answer the question: what is so special or important about health care compared to other social goods? Many people in many societies believe it is especially important, for they often insist health care be more equally, actually equitably, distributed than various other social goods. What might explain this special importance?

We need to back up a bit and consider more carefully the *function* of health care. Such an analysis is what was missing in the use-per-need account. Suppose we adopt a rather narrow, if not uncontroversial, view of disease: diseases will be departures from normal species functioning. Health care needs, broadly construed, concern things we need to prevent, maintain, restore, or compensate for—departures from normal species functioning. Why are such departures from normal functioning of social importance? One initially plausible answer is that, whatever else we need or want, we need normal functioning—it is a necessary condition for happiness, say. But this answer seems less plausible when we note that happiness or satisfaction in life does not so clearly require normal functioning. Many people "cope" well with significant impairments.

A more plausible answer, I believe, is that normal species functioning is an important component of the *opportunity range* open to individuals in a society. The opportunity range is the array of life plans that it is reasonable to pursue within the conditions obtaining in a given society. This range is, of course, relative to various social facts about the society—its stage of technological development, material well-being, and so on. Thus, similar impairments of normal species functioning might have different effects on opportunity ranges in different societies. But within a society, it becomes possible to give at least a crude ranking to the effects of different impairments of normal functioning in terms of their effects on the normal opportunity range. In turn, this gives us a crude ranking of the importance of different health care needs. Moreover, on this account, some uses of health care services— for example, some cosmetic surgery or some kinds of counseling—do not meet health care *needs*, but only certain other wants and preferences.

I am suggesting that we can account for the special importance ascribed to health care needs by noting the connection between meeting those needs and the opportunity range open to individuals in a given society. This suggests that the principles of justice governing the distribution of health care should derive from our general principles of justice guaranteeing fair equality of opportunity. Specifically, health care institutions will be among a variety of basic institutions (for example, educational ones) which are important because they insure that conditions of fair equality of opportunity obtain. I cannot argue here the issues in the general theory of justice that would support the view that fair equality of opportunity is a requirement of justice. But if I am granted the assumption that it is, we have the foundations for important social obligations in the distribution of health care. Moreover, a concern for fair equality of opportunity—in theory if rarely in practice—has a long historical tradition in this country.

There are, to be sure, worries with my approach. For example, the notion of opportunity has to be age-relativized or it seems to embody a significant age bias—like productivity measures of the value of life-saving technologies. Similarly, I must show that these requirements of justice do not open a bottomless pit into which we are required to pour endless resources in quest of an unreachable egalitarian goal. But this is not the place to consider even such important details, and I have discussed them elsewhere.

Implications for Access

The fair equality-of-opportunity account of distributive justice for health care has several important implications for the issue of equitable access we have been discussing. First, the account is compatible with, though it does not imply, a multi-tiered health care system. In contrast, the "market" approach requires at least a two-tier system. Thus, my account shares with the market approach the view that health care services serve a variety of functions, only some of which may give rise to social obligations to provide them. The basic tier in my account would include health care services that meet health care needs, or at least important health care needs—as judged by their impact on opportunity range. Other tiers, if they are allowed, might involve uses of health care services to meet less important health care needs or to meet other needs and wants. My account leaves open the possibility that other tiers of the system might also be important enough to be given special precedence over other uses of social resources; but if they are, it will be for reasons different from those which give such precedence to the basic tier.

Second, the fair equality-of-opportunity account provides a way of characterizing the health care services that fall in the social-ly guaranteed tier. They are the services needed to maintain, restore, or compensate for the loss of normal functioning. In turn, normal functioning constitutes a central component of the opportunity range open to individuals. This account is, to be sure, abstract. It requires moral judgment in its application. Still, it provides a principled basis for argument about what is included in the basic tier, a basis we found lacking in the notion of a decent basic minimum and in Fried's gloss on the notion of "tolerable life prospects."

Third, whichever way the upper tiers of the health care system are to be financed, there should be no obstacles—financial, racial, geographical, and so on—to access to the basic tier. The importance of such equality of access follows, I think, from basic facts about the sociology and epistemology of the determination of health care needs. The "felt needs" of patients are at best only initial indicators of the presence of real health care needs. Structural and other process barriers to initial access—for example, to primary care—compel people to make their own determination of the importance of the symptoms they feel. Of course, every system requires some such assessment, but financial, geographical, and other process barriers (waiting time, for example) impose the burden for such assessment on particular groups of persons. Indeed, where it is felt that sociological and cultural barriers exist preventing people from utilizing services, positive steps are needed (in the schools or through relevant community organizations) to make certain that decisions are informed.

The Aday and Andersen approach may be helpful here. Their utilization-per-need criterion, or a refinement of it, gives us a way of telling when a potential access factor is likely to be affecting opportunity through its impact on utilization rates. Moreover, whereas their unqualified assumption about the homogeneity of health care was problematic for the health care system as a whole, it is not problematic in this context. Indeed, my account characterizes that function in a perspicuous way, enabling us to see why it has special moral importance. In addition, my account permits "suspect" variations in utilization-per-need rates to be explained away as informed choice where this is plausible. (Aday and Andersen also leave room for such modifying explanations.) In short, I think the account I offer takes what is reasonable from the argument from function which underlies the utilization-per-need-account and provides a clearer moral rationale for it.

Fourth, the fair equality-of-opportunity account remains silent on what to make of demands for strict equality in process variables ("amenities"), that is, independently of their effect on utilization-per-need rates. It also remains silent on equity of access requirements for the upper tiers, if such there be. It also needs to be carefully applied if it is to answer the kinds of problems that I raised concerning the marker approach with regard to variations in quality—that is, efficacy and protection from risk. These are not issues I am prepared to take a direct stand on here.

Equality in Health Care

Amy Gutmann

There is a fairly widespread consensus among empirical analysts that access to health care in this country has become more equal in the last quarter century. Agreement tends to end here; debate follows as to whether this trend will or should persist. But before debating these questions, we ought to have a clear idea of what equal access to health care means. Since equality of access to health care cannot be defined in a morally neutral way, we must choose a definition that is morally loaded with a set of values. The definition offered here is by no means the only possible one. It has, however, the advantage not only of clarity but also of having embedded within it strong and commonly accepted liberal egalitarian values. The debate is better focused upon arguments for and against a strong *principle* of equal access than disputes over definitions, which tend to hide fundamental value disagreements instead of making them explicit.

An equal access principle, clearly stated and understood, can serve at best as an ideal toward which a society committed to equality of opportunity and equal respect for persons can strive. It does not provide a blueprint for social change, but only a moral standard by which to judge marginal changes in our present institutions of health care.

My purpose here is not only to evaluate the strongest criticisms that are addressed to the principle, ranging from libertarian arguments for more market freedom to arguments supporting a more egalitarian principle of health care. I also propose to examine the sorts of theoretical and practical problems that arise when one tries to defend an egalitarian principle directed at a particular set of institutions within an otherwise inegalitarian society. Since it is extremely unlikely that such a society will be transformed all at once into an egalitarian one, there ought to be room within political and philosophical argument for reasoned consideration and advocacy of "partial" distributive justice, i.e., of principles that are directed only to a particular set of social institutions and whose implementation is not likely to create complete justice even within those institutions.

THE PRINCIPLE DEFINED

A principle of equal access to health care demands that every person who shares the same type and degree of health need must be given an equally effective chance of receiving appropriate treatment of equal quality so long as that treatment is available to anyone. Stated in this way, the equal access principle does not establish whether a society must provide any particular medical treatment or health care benefit to its needy members. I shall suggest later that the level and type of provision can vary within certain reasonable boundaries according to the priorities determined by legitimate democratic procedures. The principle requires that if anyone within a society has an opportunity to receive a service or good that satisfies a health need, then everyone who shares the same type and degree of health need must be given an equally effective chance of receiving that service or good.

Since this is a principle of equal *access,* it does not guarantee equal *results,* although it probably would move our society in that direction. Discriminations in health care are permitted if they are based upon type or degree of health need, willingness of informed adults to be treated, and choices of lifestyle among the population. The equal access principle constrains the distribution of opportunities to receive health care to an egalitarian standard, but it does not determine the total level of health care available or the effects of that care (provided the care is of equal quality) upon the health of the population. Of course, even if equality in health care were defined according to an "equal health" principle, one would still have to admit that a just health care system could not come close to producing an equally healthy population, given the unequal distribution of illness among people and our present medical knowledge.

PRACTICAL IMPLICATIONS

Since the equal access principle requires equality of effective opportunity to receive care, not merely equality of formal legal access, it does not permit discriminations based upon those characteristics of people that we can reasonably assume they did not freely choose. Such characteristics include sex, race, genetic endowment, wealth, and, often, place of residence. Even in an ideal society, equally needy persons will not use the same amount or quality of health care. Their preferences and their knowledge will differ as will the skills of the providers who treat them.

A One-Class System

The most striking result of applying the equal access principle in the United States would be the creation of a one-class system of health care. Services and goods that meet health care needs would be equally available to everyone who was equally needy. As a disincentive to overuse, only small fees for service could be charged for health care, provided that charges did not prove a barrier to entry to the poorest people who were needy. A one-class system need not, of course, be a uniform system. Diversity among medical and health care services would be permissible, indeed even desirable, so long as the diversity did not create differential access along nonconsensual lines such as wealth, race, sex, or geographical location.

Equal access also places limits upon the market freedoms of some individuals, especially, but not exclusively, the richest members of society. The principle does not permit the purchase of health care to which other similarly needy people do not have effective access. The extent to which freedom of the rich must be restricted will depend upon the level of public provision for health care and the degree of income inequality. As the level of health care guaranteed to the poor decreases and the degree of income inequality increases, the equal access standard demands greater restrictions upon the market freedom of the rich. Where income and wealth are very unevenly distributed, and where the level of publicly guaranteed access is very low, the rich can use the market to buy access to health care goods unavailable to the poor, thereby undermining the effective equality of opportunity required by an equal access principle.

The restriction upon market freedoms to purchase health care under these circumstances creates a certain discomforting irony: the equal access principle permits (or is at least agnostic with respect to) the free market satisfaction of preferences for non-essential consumer goods. Thus, the rigorous implementation of equal access to health care would prevent rich people from spending their extra income for preferred medical services, if those services were not equally accessible to the poor. It would not prevent their using those same resources to purchase satisfactions in other areas—a Porsche or any other luxurious consumer good. In discussing additional problems created by an attempt to implement a principle of equal access to health care in an otherwise inegalitarian society, I return later to consider whether advocates of equal access can avoid this irony.

Hard Cases

As with all principles, hard cases exist for the equal access principle. Without dwelling upon these cases, it is worth considering how the principle might deal with two hard but fairly common cases: therapeutic experimentation in medicine, and alternative treatments of different quality.

Each year in the United States, many potentially successful therapies are tested. Since their value has not been proved, there may be good reason to limit their use to an appropriate sample of sick experimental subjects. The equal access principle would insist that experimenters choose these subjects at random from a population of relevantly sick consenting adults. A randomized clinical trial could be advertised by public notice, and individuals who are interested might be registered and enrolled on a lottery basis. The only requirement for enrollment would be the health conditions and personal characteristics necessary for proper scientific testing.

How does one apply the principle of equal access when alternative treatments are each functionally adequate but aesthetically or socially quite disparate? Take the hypothetical case of a societal commitment to adequate dentition among adults. Replacement of carious or mobile teeth with dentures may preserve dental function at relatively minor cost. On the other hand, full mouth reconstruction, involving periodontal and endodontal treatment and capping of affected teeth, may be only marginally more effective but substantially more satisfying. The added costs for the preferred treatment are not inconsiderable. The principle would seem to demand that at equal states of dental need there be equal access to the preferred treatment. It is unclear, however, whether the satisfaction of subjective desire is equivalent to fulfillment of objective need.

In cases of alternative treatments, proponents of equal access could turn to another argument for providing access to the same treatments for all. A society that publicly provides the minimal acceptable treatment freely to all, and also permits a private market in more expensive treatments, may result in a two-class system of care. The best providers will service the richest clientele, at the risk of inadequate treatment for the poorest. Approval of a private market in alternative treatments would rest upon the empirical hypothesis that, if the publicly funded level of adequate treatment were high enough, few people would choose to short-circuit the public (i.e., equal access) sector; the small additional free market sector would not threaten to lower the quality of services universally available.

Most cases, like the one of dentistry, are difficult to decide merely on principle. Proponents of equal access must take into account the consequences of alternative policies. But empirical knowledge alone will not decide these issues, and arguments for or against a particular policy can be entertained in a more systematic way once one exposes the values that underlie support for an equal access principle. One can then judge to what extent alternative policies satisfy these values.

SUPPORTING VALUES

Advocates of equal access to health care must demonstrate why health care is different from other consumer goods, unless they are willing to support the more radical principle of equal distribution of all goods. Norman Daniels provides one foundation for distinguishing between health care and other goods. He establishes a category of health care needs whose satisfaction provides an important condition for future opportunity. Like police protection and education, some kinds of health care goods are necessary for pursuing most other goods in life. Any theory of justice committed to equalizing opportunity ought to treat health care as a good deserving of special distributive treatment. Equal access to health care provides a necessary, although certainly not a sufficient, condition for equal opportunity in general.

A precept of egalitarian justice that physical pains of a sufficient degree be treated similarly, regardless of who experiences them, establishes another reason for singling out certain kinds of health care as special goods. Some health conditions cause great pain but are not linked to a serious curtailment of opportunity. The two values are, however, mutually compatible.

A theory of justice that gives priority to the value of equal respect among people might also be used to support a principle of equal access to health care. John Rawls, for example, argues that without self-respect "nothing may seem worth doing, or if some things have value for us, we lack the will to strive for them. . . . Therefore the parties in the original position would wish to avoid at almost any cost the social conditions that undermine self-respect."

Conditions of Self-Respect

It is not easy to determine what social conditions support or undermine self-respect. One might plausibly assume that equalizing opportunity and treating similar pains similarly would be the most essential supports for equal respect within a health care system. And so, in most cases, the value of equal respect provides additional support for equal access to the same health care goods that are warranted by the values of equal opportunity and relief from pain. But at least some kinds of health care treatment not essential to equalizing opportunity or bringing equal relief from pain may be necessary to equalize respect within a society. It is conceivable that much longer waiting time, in physicians' offices or for admission to hospitals, may not affect the long-term health prospects of the poor or of blacks. But such discriminations in waiting times for an essential good probably do adversely affect the self-respect of those who systematically stand at the end of the queue.

Some of the conditions necessary for equal respect are socially relative; we must arrive at a standard of equal respect appropriate to our particular society. Universal suffrage has long been a condition for equal respect; the case for it is independent of the anticipated results of equalizing political power by granting every person one vote. More recently, equal access to health care has similarly become a condition for equal respect in our society. Most of us do not base our self-respect on the way we are treated on airplanes, even though the flight attendants regularly give preferential treatment to those traveling first class. This contrast with suffrage and health care treatment (and education and police protection) no doubt is related to the fact that these goods are much more essential to our security and opportunities in life than is airplane travel. But it is still worth considering that unequal treatment in health care, as in education, may be understood as a sign of unequal respect even where there are no discernible adverse effects on the health or education of those receiving less favored treatment. Even where a dual health care system will not produce inferior medical results for the less privileged, the value of equal respect militates against the perpetuation of such a system in our society.

Liberty and the Purchase of Health Care

Baruch A. Brody

Health care seems to be a basic need of all individuals. It goes with such other basic needs as food, clothing, and shelter. This may help explain our national commitment (in such programs as Medicaid and Medicare) to providing adequate health care for the indigent. Despite this commitment, and the great costs incurred in trying to meet it, the problem of providing adequate health care for the medically indigent (the have-nots) at an affordable cost to the taxpayers (the haves) seems to be unsolved. Some see the problem as being one of excessive costs. Some see the problem as being one of inadequate coverage; too many Americans who are medically indigent are not assured of adequate medical care. Some see the problem as being one of quality control; the medically indigent are receiving second-rate medical care. In truth, all of these problems are present. We are providing inadequate health care to an insufficient number of people at an excessive and rapidly increasing cost.

All of these issues have led many to reassess this national commitment, to ask whether we are doing too much or too little. This essay is part of this process of reassessment. Its goal is to seek out the roots of our national commitment. The hope is that such an analysis will lead us to structure our programs so that we may at least alleviate some of these problems.

In the first section of this essay, I will argue that the programs in question have to be viewed in the context of programs of redistribution aimed at promoting greater equality. In the second section, I will outline a theory to justify such redistributions. In the final section, I will develop some of the policy implications of adopting this justificatory theory.

I

I would like to begin by making two crucial points about programs of providing medical care for the indigent, viz., that they are programs of distributive justice and that they could in theory be made unnecessary by the direct provision of adequate funds to the indigent. Let us look at each of them separately.

The first point is that these are programs of taking funds from better-off taxpayers to provide health care for the indigent on the grounds that justice demands this equalization of capacity to obtain basic needs. Several implications follow from this point: (a) the problem of providing health care should not be separated from other problems of distributive justice; it should not be separated from other problems concerning the taking of funds from better-off taxpayers to provide other basic needs to the indigent. Some of these other basic needs (e.g., food and housing) are obviously related to health care, while others (e.g., education) are less so. Still, all must be supplied through funds raised from the same taxpayers, so we need to consider all of these needs together; (b) since the justification for these programs is that they are providing a basic need to those who are in need, the programs should apply to all who are medically indigent, to all who cannot pay for their medical care. There is no reason why certain indigent individuals (e.g., the aged, or children with only one parent living at home) should be covered while others are not.

The second major point which I wish to make in this section is that programs for providing medical care for the indigent would be unnecessary if we simply redistributed sufficient funds to the indigent so that they could pay for their basic needs including health care. I am not now saying either that distributive justice requires such a redistribution of wealth or that such a redistribution is better than the in-kind provision of health care. All that I want to claim for now is that if we did have such a redistributive program, the macro-problem of justice in the provision of health care would disappear.

The following case, it seems to me, both explains this second point and justifies it: suppose that we had distributed to the indigent sufficient funds so that they could pay for their basic needs including health care. Suppose, moreover, that one such recipient then used this aid for other purposes, became ill and was unable to pay for health care, and came to ask for more help. Would we be compelled as a matter of justice (as opposed to private mercy) to aid that person? I think not, and for two reasons. Aiding that person would be requiring those who had already paid for the just distribution to pay for it again, and that seems unfair. Moreover, an autonomous decision-maker can hardly claim a right to protection from the unfortunate consequences of his own freely chosen errors.

In fact, our own society has, for the most part, chosen a different technique for providing health care to the indigent. We have provided them with a medical insurance policy. One of the crucial policy questions with which we will have to grapple in Section III is whether this was a wise choice.

II

Let us now turn to the question as to whether justice demands the provision of health care to the medically indigent. I shall treat that question as equivalent to the question as to whether the medically indigent have a right to health care.

There are those who derive the existence of the right to health care from the assumption that we all equally need that care. Their argument runs roughly like this: we all equally need health care; therefore, we all have an equal right to health care; but the operations of the market result in some not having that care; therefore, society must redistribute wealth so that health care (or at least the means to purchase it) is available to everyone. I have never seen the force of this argument. After all, even if we do equally need health care, an equal right to health care follows only if one assumes that the need generates a right. This crucial assumption is left totally unsupported by the argument.

There are those who derive the existence of the right to health care from the assumption that the existence of transfers adequate to insure health care maximizes general welfare. Their argument runs roughly like this: any reasonable assumptions about the diminishing marginal utility of money, even when combined with assumptions about the need of monetary incentives to maximize production, lead to the conclusion that utility will be increased by the distribution of funds to purchase health care to the indigent. Therefore, the indigent have a right to this redistribution. I have never seen the force of this argument either. Its crucial difficulty is its move from maximizing utility to rights. Despite the ingenuity of Mill and those who have followed his theory of rights, it would seem as though rights are moral considerations independent of considerations of general utility, in that policy *A*'s leading to the maximization of utility does not entail that there is a right to the carrying-out of policy *A*.

There are those who derive the existence of the right to health care from the existence of other rights. Their argument runs roughly like this: the effective enjoyment of these other rights (e.g., political rights) presupposes the possession of a certain basic set of goods. Since everyone has these other rights, it follows that everyone also has a right to the possession of this basic set of goods. But not everyone possesses these basic goods. Therefore, society must distribute wealth so that these basic goods (or at least the means to purchase them) are possessed by everyone. Health care is one of these goods, so society must provide it for the indigent. Again, I have never seen the force of this argument. Its crucial difficulty is the assumption that if everyone has certain rights, it follows that they also have the right to what is required for the effective enjoyment of these rights, an assumption left unsupported by the argument.

I do, nevertheless, think that an argument can be mounted from the theory of justice for a program of redistribution that certainly has implications for the right to health care. Let me now sketch that theory of justice and redistribution, a theory on which I am currently working, and which I have tentatively called quasi-libertarianism. It is best understood by first considering libertarianism.

The popular image of the libertarian is that of someone who is opposed to extensive government activity, someone who believes that the only legitimate functions of the state are the watch-dog functions of protecting us against force, theft, and fraud. This image is, as far as it goes, correct, but it leaves out what is truly fundamental in the libertarian picture of man and society.

To the libertarian, the fundamental fact about man is that he is a rational agent who often chooses to act in certain ways, from among the alternatives open to him, because of his beliefs that these actions are either intrinsically best or best in leading to what he does desire intrinsically. Not all of these choices are deliberative, but many are. To the libertarian, man's freedom to act this way without being restrained or coerced by his fellow human beings is of fundamental importance and one of the fundamental human rights is the right not to be constrained or coerced from so acting by others. It is this which provides a foundation for the libertarian's opposition to most of the activities of the welfare state. The welfare state, in pursuing its goals of maximizing general welfare, of redistributing wealth, etc., constantly passes laws and regulations which are coercive in that they impose substantial penalties upon our acting in certain ways.

In theory, these basic libertarian views are independent of any views about the institution of private property and of any views about an individual's right to property. In fact, however, most writers in this tradition from Locke on have held that besides our right to life and bodily integrity and our right of freedom from coercion, we also have a right to the 'fruit of our labor,' to the value produced by our labor. The contemporary libertarian puts that in the form of a right to the value of any unowned commodity upon which we have worked (initial property rights) or to the value that others freely agree to give to us either in exchange for our giving them something else, e.g., our labor-power for a certain period of time, or gratuitously (transferred property rights). Because libertarians hold these additional views about property and the right to property, they have a second objection to the welfare state. The welfare state, in order to finance its programs of maximizing general welfare, of redistributing wealth, etc., takes the property to which we have a right, and this is another reason for its illegitimacy (libertarians, in fact, have to do a lot of work to explain how even the minimal state is to finance its activities).

Naturally, a lot more has to be said by

way of explaining and justifying all of these claims, and I cannot do this in the context of this paper. What I do want to say is that (a) it seems to me that libertarianism, understood this way, is an important doctrine embodying certain correct perceptions about the relation between man and the state but that (b) it requires modification. Let me elaborate upon one crucial modification, for it leads to the quasi-libertarianism and the theory of distributive justice which I wish to advocate.

The modification which I would introduce into the libertarian account has to do with the question of the distribution of wealth. From the strict libertarian point of view, the only wealth to which an individual is entitled is that wealth which he has acquired by his labor on unowned commodities or that wealth which has been freely transferred to him by others already entitled to it. There is no special pattern of distribution about which individuals can claim that they have a right to get what they would have under this pattern. I would suggest, however, that there are libertarian grounds for modifying this strict conclusion.

The crucial idea behind the libertarian theory of property, going back to Locke, is that initial property rights are ultimately grounded in entitlements to the value produced by labor, and that all property rights arise from these initial entitlements. But some wealth which exists is simply the initial value of natural resources, and neither Locke nor anyone else in the libertarian tradition has ever really explained why anyone should have an entitlement to that wealth. My argument suggests that the simultaneous existence both of property rights and rights to redistributive welfare arises out of the difference between labor-created wealth and the wealth which is the value of natural resources. To see how this works, let us imagine an initial position of a social contract. All those forming the contract recognize the existence of equal libertarian rights not to be prevented or coercively threatened

from using the natural resources of the earth. They also recognize that allowing exclusive property rights, which must be over natural resources as well as labor-created values, is economically efficient. What I claim is that such people would agree (a) to allow for the formation of exclusive property rights over natural resources as well as added values, (b) to compensate those who would lose the rights to use the natural resources assigned to property values, and (c) to provide that compensation in the form of socially-recognized welfare rights, socially-recognized rights to a minimum level of support.

I have found it useful, in thinking out the implications of this approach, to imagine the terms of the social contract running something like this: the natural resources of the earth are leased to those who develop them, or to those to whom they transfer those leases. In return, they owe a rental to everyone. That rental is collected as taxes and paid into a social insurance fund which covers everyone equally. The social insurance fund insures us against destitution, and it pays payments to those who are destitute. Like all insurance funds, while all are equally covered, not all receive payouts much less equal payouts.

Several crucial points follow even on the basis of this sketch: (a) most property rights are rights over a mixture of natural resources and added values. They can exist, therefore, only if the conditions agreed to in the initial social contract are met. Consequently, legitimate private property rights presuppose some redistribution of wealth; (b) the theory of social justice which is the heart of quasi-libertarianism leads to a theory of redistribution of wealth and not to special rights to any particular basic need. This provides a theoretical justification for the claim made in the last section that the problem of health care should not be separated from other problems of distributive justice. It should not be separated because what justice gives rise to is a right to certain redistributions. The right to health care is at best derivative from that more general distributive right; (c) since the fundamental right generated by this theory of justice is the right of the indigent to payments from the social insurance fund, all of the demands of justice would be satisfied by such a redistribution. So our theory provides a theoretical justification for a generalized version of our other main claim in the last section, viz., that there would be no macroproblem of justice in the provision of health care if there were in effect an adequate general system of redistribution.

III

Suppose that one were to agree that the demands for just redistribution are properly grounded in the sorts of considerations that were sketched in the last section. What would follow for the question of medical care for the indigent, viewed, as it should be, as a problem of distributive justice?

In order to answer this question, two corollaries of the theory must first be mentioned, corollaries having to do with the level of payments from the social insurance fund. In general, those who have argued that the indigent have rights either to cash payments or to in-kind benefits have not adequately considered the question of the level of payments or benefits demanded by justice, and yet that is obviously a crucial question. On our account, the level is determined by two factors—the amount paid to the insurance fund by the taxpayers, and the number of recipients drawing benefits. The amount paid to the insurance fund should be a fair rental for the natural resources, and the number of recipients will depend upon eligibility requirements. Both of these points need extensive elaboration which we cannot give here; all that I want to do for now is to draw out the two corollaries: (a) since a fair rental will be a function of the possible uses of the resource, and since these will normally be greater in an affluent society, an affluent society should,

all other things being equal, provide a higher level of payments or benefits than a poor society; (b) since, for any given society at any given time, the amount in the insurance fund is set independently of the number of recipients, the level of payments or benefits will vary in proportion to the number of recipients.

All of this means that we cannot say, in advance, whether the redistribution of wealth called for by the theory of justice will be sufficient to cover the cost of providing all basic needs for all who are indigent. It will depend upon the level of affluence of the society and upon the number of indigents. Suppose then that you were one of the original contractors, trying to decide whether or not you should receive your insurance payments, if you need them, in the form of a cash payment or in the form of in-kind services. This problem will be of special importance to you in the many cases (probably the vast majority of cases in the actual history of mankind) in which the insurance payments will not fund all of your basic needs. It seems to me that you would have a powerful argument for asking for cash payments rather than in-kind services. Choices will have to be made as to which needs are going to be satisfied and at what level. Which choice is best for you is probably different than which choice is best for anyone else. If the insurance payments are in the form of provisions of in-kind services, the choice is not likely to reflect the best mixture for you. If, however, the insurance payments are in the form of cash benefits, you can use that cash to pay for a mixture that seems best for you. So, it would seem that the initial contractors would, as rational agents, agree to the insurance payments as cash payments.

If this argument is correct, then most of our current redistributive programs including Medicare and Medicaid are not properly structured. To begin with, they all suffer from not being part of an integrated redistributive program. We cannot determine the level of funding appropriate for each, for the level of funding is, if our theory is correct, only determinable for the whole of our social insurance program. Not surprisingly, then, some Americans find a particular program too costly, while others find it inadequate. Secondly, the largest of them (the medical programs and the food programs) provide in-kind services, and there is no reason to suppose that the mix of current services provided is the best for the people in question. For example, many of the recipients would probably be better off with a less elaborate medical program and a better housing program. Finally, many of the eligibility requirements reflect prejudices and

misconceptions rather than any notions of justice.

Our society has consistently preferred piecemeal categorial programs to any program of social insurance for all the needy. If my arguments are correct, then the theory of justice would seem to suggest that this preference is mistaken. Actual experience seems to second this suggestion, but that is an additional argument. I conclude for now with the claim that there is only the general problem of the haves and the have-nots, and that we've gotten into trouble by thinking that there are more specialized problems such as that of justice in health care.

8. FINANCING AND DELIVERY OF HEALTH CARE

The Money We Spend and Its Sources

Carol McCarthy

WHERE THE MONEY COMES FROM

Ultimately, of course, the people pay all health care costs. Thus, when we say that health care monies come from different sources, we really mean that dollars take different routes on their way from consumers to providers of care. The three major routes are direct payment from consumer to provider; through government; and through private insurance companies, profit and nonprofit. In 1978, approximately 33% of expenditures were directly out of pocket ($55.3 billion), the public share was about 39% (about $65 billion), with the federal government bearing almost three-fourths of that; and 27% was paid through insurance companies (over $45 billion). The balance, 1.3% ($2.2 billion), was provided by philanthropy and by industry for in-plant health services.

Public Outlays

The amount transferred by the public sector in 1978 ($65 billion, 39% of the total) compares with 24.8% in 1966, 22.4% in

1950, 14.7% in 1935, and 9% in 1929. The increase is largely due to greater federal expenditures. Proportionately, state and local government outlays have remained rather constant over time, in the 11%–13% range. They accounted for 11% of the total in 1978. In contrast, the federal share of outlays rose from 12.9% in 1966 to 20.8% in 1967, to almost 28% in 1978. This significant rise in federal spending is accounted for by the Medicare and Medicaid programs, Titles XVIII and XIX, respectively, of the Social Security Act.

Medicare. Medicare was inaugurated on July 1, 1966. It provided a limited range of medical care benefits for persons aged 65 and over who were covered by the Social Security system. In July 1973, benefits were extended to the disabled and their dependents, and those suffering from chronic kidney disease. Part A of the program, financed by payroll taxes collected under the Social Security system, provides coverage for care rendered in a hospital, an extended care facility, or the patient's home. Part B, a voluntary supplemental program that pays certain costs of doctors' services and other medical expenses, is supported in part by general tax revenues and in part by contributions paid by the elderly. Neither Part A nor Part B of Medicare, however, offers comprehensive coverage. Built into the program are deductibles (set amounts the patient must pay for each type of service each year before Medicare begins to pay) and co-payments (a percentage of charges paid by the patient). Limitations on the amount of coverage exist as well. Hospital benefits cease after 90 days if the patient has exhausted his lifetime reserve pool of 60 additional days; extended-care facility benefits end after 100 days. Home health care visits are limited to 100.

In brief, Medicare provides the elderly with some protection in time of illness but does not pay the whole bill. Spending under Medicare rose from $3.2 billion in 1967 to $18.3 billion in 1977, but only 44.3% of the $41.3 billion that went for personal health care for the aged in fiscal 1977 was paid for by Medicare. Nor was coverage uniform: 74% of hospital care costs was covered; 56% of physicians' charges; 52% of "other professional services," and only 3% of nursing home expenses. Even after other government programs and supplementary private health insurance were taken into account, 1977 per capita out-of-pocket expense for the elderly was $613, approximately 35% of costs. The dimensions of the problem emerge when data from the 1970 census are presented: 58% of elderly individuals were in families with less than $5,000 income; only 18% had family incomes over $10,000.

Medicaid. Unlike Medicare, Medicaid is a program run jointly by federal and state governments: the name is more or less a blanket label for 49 different state programs. (Arizona has no Medicaid program.) Designed specifically to serve the poor, Medicaid provided, as of January 1967, federal funds to states on a cost-sharing basis (according to each state's per capita income), so that welfare recipients could be guaranteed medical services. Payment in full was to be afforded to the aged poor, the blind, the disabled, and families with dependent children if one parent was absent, unemployed, or unable to work. Four types of care were covered: (1) inpatient and outpatient hospital care; (2) other laboratory and X-ray services; (3) physician services; and (4) skilled nursing care for persons over 21. By July 1970, home health services and early and periodic detection and treatment of disease for persons under 21 were also covered.

The 1972 Social Security Act amendments added family planning to the list of "musts." Prescriptions, dental services, eyeglasses, and care in an "intermediate facility" (institutions that do not qualify as skilled nursing homes or those serving the mentally retarded) are allowable "optionals," as is coverage of the medically indigent (those who are self-supporting except for medical care costs). Under the 1972 amendments, coverage of the medically indigent is, by law, tied to their payment of monthly premiums, the amount being graduated by income. Deductibles and co-payments are also allowed on all services for the medically indigent and on optional services for welfare recipients.

Those who pass a means test proving that their income is below state-established poverty levels must be supplied with the basic services without charge in any state participating in the Medicaid program. Limits on covered benefits are, however, left to the individual state, which, along with the variety of options allowed, has resulted in a wide diversity of operative programs. New York and California, for instance, established such broad programs that in 1976 they received 34% of total Medicaid expenditures.

There has been a continuing increase in spending for Medicaid. In 1968, federal outlays for the program totaled $1.8 billion. By 1978, total federal, state, and local expenditures under Medicaid had reached

$18.4 billion, about 56% of it federal. These monies provided services for approximately 23 million American eligible poor. Excluded from benefits were most working poor, childless couples, the medically indigent in 27 states, and in 26 states, low-income families with an unemployed father present. Estimates made in 1974 by the Office of Research and Statistics of the Social Security Administration indicate that 9 million persons officially designated as "poor" were still excluded from Medicaid coverage.

In 1978, Medicaid and Medicare accounted for two-thirds of public outlays for personal health care services. The next-largest expenditure category, state and local government dollar support for their own hospitals, totaled $5.5 billion in 1978—up 6% from the previous year. Included here are funds used to operate psychiatric hospitals and other long-term care facilities, as well as acute-care general hospitals at the county and municipal levels.

Other public expenditures. There are four remaining significant personal health care categories for which government monies are spent: (1) federal outlays for hospital and medical services for veterans ($4.9 billion in 1978, 7.6% of public personal health care expenditures); (2) provision of care by the Department of Defense for the armed forces and military dependents (in 1978, $3.6 billion, 5.6%); (3) workmen's compensation medical benefits ($3.1 billion, 4.7%); and (4) other federal, state, and local outlays for personal health care ($3.5 billion, 5.4% in 1978), including support for maternal and child health programs, vocational rehabilitation, Public Health Service and other federal hospitals, the Indian Health Service, temporary disability insurance, and the Alcohol, Drug Abuse, and Mental Health Administration.

Private Health Care Expenditures

The bulk of private health care expenditures comes from two sources: the individual receiving treatment and the private insurer making payment on his behalf. In 1978, their combined contributions totaled $100.6 billion, 59.9% of all personal health care expenditures. In 1965, prior to the advent of Medicare and Medicaid, their share was 76.9%; in 1935, 82.4%; in 1929, 88.4%. This decline in the private share of total expenditures is due primarily to the sharp drop in out-of-pocket payments that is associated with increased federal spending. In 1965, for example, 53% of personal health care expenditures was paid directly by the patient; in 1978, only 33%. Unfortunately, however, because of inflation and other factors, the per capita dollar amount paid directly in 1978 was 2½ times what it was in 1965.

Private insurers have paid between 20% and 28% of personal health care costs since 1965. Their share was $45.3 billion in 1978, 27% of the total. But it is not the dollar figure alone that focuses attention on the private insurance industry. Medicare, and Medicaid to a limited extent, utilize the industry in a middle-man capacity, as a "fiscal intermediary." Several of the major national health insurance plans proposed are based on the private insurance mechanism.

Health care utilization is not a rare occurrence. On the average, each person in the United States visits a physician five times a year. One out of every seven Americans is admitted to a hospital at least once a year. Other than coverage for catastrophic illness, a fairly rare event, health insurance has become a mechanism for offsetting expected rather than unexpected costs. The experience of the many is pooled in an effort to reduce expected outlays to manageable prepayment size. Perhaps the term "assurance" more appropriately describes the health care payment system that has evolved. In Britain, "assurance" is used to denote coverage for contingencies that must eventually happen (life assurance); "insurance" is reserved for coverage of those contingencies like fire and theft, which may not occur.

Blue Cross and Blue Shield. The establishment of payment mechanisms to defray in general the costs of illness can be traced to the Great Depression. Previously, hospitals had sought to assure reimbursement for their services through public education campaigns directed at encouraging their users, middle-income Americans, to put money aside for unpredictable medical expenses. When hard times proved the inadequacy of the savings approach, attention turned to the development of a stable income mechanism. A model was at hand in the independent prepayment plan pioneered in 1929 at Baylor University Hospital in Texas to assure certain area schoolteachers of some hospital coverage. Under the plan, 1,250 teachers prepaid half a dollar a month to provide themselves with up to 21 days of semiprivate hospitalization annually.

Like Baylor's, most early plans were for single hospitals. Then, in the early 1930s, nonprofit prepayment programs offering care at a number of hospitals were organized in several cities. The American Hospital Association vigorously supported the growth and development of these plans, soon to be named Blue Cross, and the special insurance legislation that was required for their establishment in each state. The AHA set standards for plans and then offered its seal of approval to plans meeting the standards. A provider-insurer partnership was firmly established. Indeed, not until 1972 did national Blue Cross formally separate from the American Hospital Association.

Like Blue Cross, Blue Shield was a child of provider interests born of the Depression. In this instance, the provider was the physician: the professional organization, the state medical society. In 1917, county medical societies in Washington and Oregon had established "medical bureaus" to compete with private doctors and clinics for medical service contracts covering employees of railroads and lumber companies. In 1939, gen-

erally recognized as the year Blue Shield began, state medical societies sponsored plans in California and Michigan. Eight additional states followed suit in the period from 1940 to 1942, and in 1943, the American Medical Association established a Council on Medical Service and Public Relations in order to formulate standards and approve state and local Blue Shield plans. The growth of Blue Shield was less dramatic than that of Blue Cross following the Depression because physicians in general were in less dire financial circumstances than hospitals were. Instead, the period of greatest growth for Blue Shield was between 1945 and 1949, when the medical profession sought to stave off movements for federal and state health insurance.

In other respects, however, Blue Shield mirrors Blue Cross. For example, both are local or statewide undertakings organized for the most part under special state enabling acts. They are incorporated as not-for-profit charitable organizations and therefore relieved of the obligations facing stock and mutual insurance companies—namely, the maintenance of substantial cash reserves and the payment of state and federal taxes. In most states, the Department or Commissioner of Insurance supervises the Blues, issuing or approving their certificates of incorporation, reviewing their annual income and expenditure reports, monitoring the rates subscribers pay into the program and the rates the programs pay to the providers.

In line with their not-for-profit status, both programs, at least initially, were committed to "community rating." Under such a policy, a set of benefits is offered at a single rate to all individuals and groups within a community, regardless of age, sex, or occupation of community members. In essence, the rate represents an averaging out of high- and low-cost individuals and groups so that the community as a whole can be serviced with adequate benefits at reasonable cost. When commercial for-profit insurance companies entered the field, however, they did so with a policy of "experience rating," charging different individuals and population subgroups different premiums based on their use of services. Low-risk groups could secure benefits at a lower premium. As a result, the Blues also decided to offer a multiplicity of policies with differing rate and benefit structures, and often had to go to experience rating. Had they not, adverse risks alone would have comprised their health insurance portfolios.

Finally, it is the Blues that, by and large, serve as the fiscal intermediaries between the federal and state governments in the Medicare and Medicaid programs. The role of intermediary is a key one. Under Medicare, for example, the intermediary: (1) determines how much the provider is to be paid; (2) makes the payment, (3) audits the provider's books; and (4) assists in the development and maintenance of utilization review systems designed to check unnecessary costs. In 1977, 68 Blue Cross/Blue Shield plans served as fiscal intermediaries under Medicare. In contrast, only five private health insurance companies were intermediaries for Part A of Medicare and only 12 for part B.

Commercial insurance. The profit-making commercial insurance companies entered the general health insurance market cautiously. They had realized losses on income-replacement policies during the Depression; they were leery of the Blues' initial emphasis on comprehensive benefits. However, a Supreme Court decision recognizing fringe benefits as a legitimate part of the collective bargaining process, following as it did upon the freezing of industrial wages during World War II, proved too much of a temptation. Business was shopping for insurance carriers, and the commercials responded. By the end of 1977, over 700 for-profit companies were offering insurance of one sort or another against the cost of illness.

In the main, Blue Cross offers hospitalization insurance; Blue Shield, coverage of in-hospital physician services and a limited amount of office-based care. The commercials offer both. As in the case of the Blues, commercial hospital and hospital physician coverage is primarily provided to groups through employee fringe-benefit packages negotiated through collective bargaining. Individual coverage can be purchased, but it is usually quite expensive or has limited coverage. The commercials also sell major-medical and cash-payment policies. The former, directed primarily at catastrophic illness, pay all or part of the treatment costs beyond those covered by basic plans. They are sold on both a group and an individual basis. (Blue Cross and Blue Shield also sell group major-medical policies. In 1977, they had more than a third of such coverage.) Cash-payment policies pay the insured a flat sum of money per day of hospitalization, and are usually sold directly to individuals, often through mass advertising campaigns. Although the daily cash-payment sum is usually small, it can help defray costs left uncovered by other insurance.

Like the Blues, the commercials are subject to supervision by state insurance commissioners, although such supervision does not include rate regulation. The one requirement is that commercials establish premium rates high enough to cover claims made under the insurance they provide. Solvency of the insurer is the principal aim of insurance commission surveillance.

The independent plans. In addition to Blue Cross/Blue Shield and the commercials, a number of so-called independent insurance plans have been established. Kaiser-Permanente, located primarily on the West Coast; the Health Insurance Plan of Greater New York; and the Group Health Cooperative in Washington State are among them. Most combine a prepayment mechanism with a captive medical group practice, although Independent Practice Associations and Group Health Insurance in New York use individual practices. Some plans cover inpatient and ambulatory services; some, ambulatory services alone. Sponsors may be industry, employees/unions, community groups, or providers.

In sum, most independent plans combine to some extent the functions of insurance carrier and provider: in exchange for premium payments, plan enrollees are entitled to medical services provided by physicians contracting with or employed by the plan. At times, care is provided at sites owned or leased by the plan or in institutions with whom the plan has contracted for services for its enrollees.

HOW THE MONEY IS PAID OUT

Paying Providers

Health care is a labor-intensive industry. About 70% of all expenditures are for personnel. The vast majority of health workers are paid by wages or salary. However, about 500,000 dentists, physicians, osteopaths, optometrists and opticians, chiropractors, psychologists, social workers, speech pathologists, and physical and occupational therapists, among others, are paid on a fee-for-service basis by their patients or third parties—private insurers or government.

Fee for service. The fee-for-service system has provoked a great deal of controversy. It has been vigorously attacked and just as vigorously defended. Proponents of the fee-for-service system usually argue, especially in relation to fee-for-service reimbursement for physicians, that direct payment cements the necessary bond between provider and patient, a bond on which effective treatment often hinges; that it gives the provider an incentive to work that is not present under any other system; that it is justified by the special life-and-death responsibility that physicians, in particular, must accept.

Opponents claim there is no "natural" justification for the fee-for-service system: it is simply a product of the guild status of physicians, since the majority of health care providers are paid by salary. They point out that the fee-for-service approach creates the two-class system of medical care in the United States about which there is so much complaint. If fees, which some people cannot afford, were not charged at the time of service, then there would be no need to have one set of health care facilities for those who can afford to pay the doctor and a second for those who cannot.

Further, opponents for fee-for-service see the cash exchange as a barrier to utilization and as an interference rather than a help in the provider-patient relationship. As for the argument based on the life-and-death relationship, opponents say that the provider is not usually in a life-and-death relationship with his patient. But even if he were, the airplane pilot does not collect a fee for service, and he certainly has a life-and-death relationship to his passengers. The fireman does not request personal payment before he turns on the water or even after he has put out the fire. Indeed, when a fireman undertakes a life-and-death responsibility for a person in a burning building, he does not ask for a fee, even though he risks his own life, which doctors rarely, if ever, do.

Finally, opponents argue that with fee-for-service reimbursement, costs go up more rapidly than with other payment mechanisms. They point to the national health insurance experience of other countries such as Canada, Australia ("Amendments to Australia's Act"), and Japan. Thinking along the same lines, William Glaser cites the unnecessary work so frequently attendant on the fee-for-service system—encouraging the paying patient to return when he wishes, ordering inpatient rather than ambulatory services, and the like. In addition, he indicates that, given the choice of two or more, the practitioner more often chooses the higher-paid procedure when payment is on a fee basis.

Capitation and salary. The alternative forms of provider reimbursement are capitation and salary. The latter approach is self-explanatory. As indicated earlier, its use as a payment mechanism for health professionals is widespread. Certainly, from the employer's point of view, a salary system has the merit of administrative simplicity. When the employer is the government, there is the added benefit of flexibility: the movement of providers into areas of medical scarcity and unpopular jobs is more easily accomplished under a salary system than under other payment mechanisms. From the provider's point of view, he or she has an income protected from sudden fluctuations in supply and demand, is free of bill collection problems, and, usually, benefits from extensive fringe benefits. In a survey conducted by Goldberg, 40% of the physicians interviewed mentioned shorter work weeks, time off to study, rests or vacations without income loss, liberal pension plans, and paid life, health, and malpractice insurance as significant compensations in a salaried system. Finally, salaried providers tend to utilize less costly diagnostic and treatment procedures and to avoid unnecessary utilization of services.

However, payment by salary is not without drawbacks. The provider, for example, is faced with a limit on his lifetime income. The comparatively high salaries marking his early years of practice are balanced by the fact that his earnings peak more quickly than the fee-for-service practitioner's. In addition, he is subject to administrative constraints on such matters as schedules and vacations and to peer review regarding his performance. Often, he must abandon individual goals in order to conform with his employer's objectives. To the extent that fee-for-service stimulates quality work, the employer, in turn, must increasingly rely upon the individual physician's dedication, his desire to give fully of his attention and skill to all his patients. From the patient's vantage point, the salary system provides few incentives against undertreatment. The physician receives the negotiated salary regardless of the amount of services provided.

Under the capitation arrangement—which is used primarily for physicians providing ongoing care—the physician receives a flat annual fee for each person who agrees to be under his care, again regardless of the frequency with which his services are utilized. Like salary, capitation promotes administrative simplicity—unless, of course, financial incentives are added to base payments to encourage care of the chronic or time-consuming patient. Capitation too removes barriers to care raised by fee requirements for each treatment episode and offers the physician no incentive to undertake more costly rather than less costly medical procedures. In addition, the capitation system advances continuity of care and, thus, an improved provider-patient relationship.

But there are drawbacks in this system too. With barriers to care reduced, the provider may have to cope with unnecessary calls for treatment. There is also an incentive to increase the number of patients served even if such an increase should result in too little time to offer comprehensive care and needed emotional support.

Paying Hospitals

As stated earlier, payments to hospitals constitute the largest single category of national health expenditures. There are four major modes of hospital reimbursement. The first, oldest, and most rapidly disappearing, is that based on *charges*. This method is used by private, profit, and not-for-profit hospitals. A price (which may or may not bear some relationship to the cost of that service) is put on each item of service—a day in bed, use of the operating room, a lab test—and the patient, and/or his insurer under cash-indemnity plans, is billed for that price, usually called a charge.

A more sophisticated reimbursement mode is based on cost. The determination of cost never involves individual patients. It is a matter for negotiation between hospitals and the major insurance companies in their areas. In certain states, the Insurance Department and/or Department of Health may be a party to the negotiations in either an advisory or approval capacity. Cost reimbursement is used when insured patients receive their benefits as services rather than as dollar indemnities. (Almost all group health insurance policies in the United States now provide service benefits rather than dollar indemnities.) In the usual approach, one of several accounting techniques determines the cost of various services per unit of service; the hospital is reimbursed for those costs as it provides the services. Thus, if the agreed bed-day cost figure is $150 for each day of care provided to a patient with Blue Cross insurance, the hospital will receive $150 from Blue Cross. This method is sometimes called "retrospective cost reimbursement."

A still more sophisticated approach, "prospective reimbursement," is used in certain parts of the country. An insurer and/or public agency attempts to predict, on the basis of previous experience and current rates of cost-increase, what costs will be for the coming year. (Hospital influence on the process depends upon the extent to which the process is voluntary or mandated by state law.) The hospital then receives that rate per service (or, in some instances, per hospital stay or even per time-period without relation to the number of units of service actually provided), regardless of its actual cost. There is an obvious stimulus for

hospitals to attempt to control costs, because under prospective reimbursement they receive a given amount of money for providing a given service without regard to the service at the time it is rendered. This method, particularly when applied to the total hospital budget, obviously approaches annual budgeting for hospitals as related to total program, rather than to individual units of service. However, in most cases reimbursement to the hospitals is still based on the number of items of service delivered.

Finally, government hospitals at all levels operate on total annual budgets, and have always done so. The costs of various inputs, salaries, and expenses are determined and a budget is prepared that is not related to units of service in any way. Although some third-party payments, primarily Medicaid/Medicare, are available to them with reimbursement rates calculated on a cost basis, for most government hospitals the proportion is small. The bulk of government hospital monies comes from tax revenues. Thus, government hospital budgets are subject to other considerations besides costs and programs. As health care expenditures, particularly for hospitals, continue to rise at a high rate, and as we move toward national health insurance, it is likely that prospective reimbursement or annual budgeting will be applied to increasing numbers of hospitals outside of the public sector in an attempt to control costs, if nothing else.

The Consumer Choice Health Plan

Alain Enthoven

CONSUMER CHOICE HEALTH PLAN (CCHP)

Main Ideas

Reform through incentives. To achieve good quality comprehensive care for all, at a cost we can afford, we must change the fundamental structure of the health care fi-

nancing and delivery system. Instead of today's fragmented system dominated by cost-increasing incentives, we need a health care economy made up predominantly, though not exclusively, of competing organized systems. In such systems, groups of physicians would accept responsibility for providing comprehensive health care services to defined populations, largely for a prospective per capita payment, or some other form of payment that rewards economy in the use of health care resources.

Today we cannot see very clearly what such an economy would look like. We should seek to find our way there by a fair market test among competing alternatives in which systems that do a better job for a lower cost survive and grow. Many types of systems might succeed in such a competition, including not only Prepaid Group Practices (PGP) and Individual Practice Associations (IPA), the two "official" types of HMOs, but also "Health Care Alliances" as proposed by Ellwood and McClure and "Variable Cost Insurance" as proposed by Newhouse and Taylor in which premiums reflect the cost-control behavior of providers. There would be a substantial role for pure insurance and for traditional fee-for-service practice. CCHP seeks to accomplish this transformation by voluntary changes in a competitive market.

Informed choice among competing alternatives. CCHP is designed to assure that all people have a choice among competing alternatives, that they have good information on which to base their choice, and that competition emphasizes quality of benefits and total cost (as opposed to today's emphasis on preferred risk selection, minimizing only administrative cost, etc.). CCHP would resemble the Federal Employees Health Benefits Program (FEHBP) and other conceptually similar plans. It would extend to the whole population and to all qualifying health plans its proven principles of competition, multiple choice, private underwriting and management of health plans, periodic government-supervised open enrollment, and equal rates for all similar enrollees selecting the same plan and benefits.

Equity and incentives for economizing choices. CCHP seeks to correct inequities

and cost-increasing incentives in the tax laws and Medicare. The present exclusion of employer and deduction of employee premium contributions would be replaced by a refundable tax credit based on actuarial categories. Medicaid would be replaced by a system of vouchers for premium payments, integrated with reformed welfare, and reaching 100 percent of Actuarial Cost for basic benefits in the case of the poor. Medicare would be changed to give each beneficiary the freedom to have his Adjusted Average Per Capita Cost (AAPCC) paid to the qualified plan of his choice as a fixed prospective periodic payment. Thus, CCHP takes money now used to subsidize people's choice of more costly systems of care, and uses it to raise the floor under the least well covered. It gives people an incentive to seek out systems that provide care economically by letting them keep the savings. While Government assures that people have enough money to join a good plan, at the margin people are using their own (net aftertax) money, which should motivate them to seek value for it. These changes would permit continuity of coverage regardless of job status.

Incremental changes. CCHP is not an immediate radical replacement of the present financing system with a whole new one. Rather, it is a set of incremental "midcourse corrections" in the present financing and regulatory system, each one of which is comparatively simple and familiar taken by itself, but whose cumulative impact is intended to alter the system radically, but gradually and voluntarily, in the long run. CCHP corrects the faulty incentives produced by present government programs, and seeks to correct known market imperfections. CCHP preserves flexibility. If these changes do not produce the desired results, after experience has been gained, more corrections can be made. CCHP recognizes that there is no "final solution" to health care financing problems, as experience in countries with NHI clearly demonstrates. CCHP is not necessarily incompatible with some proposed regulation such as health planning, hospital cost controls, and physician fee controls. On the contrary, CCHP would increase the effectiveness of the Heath Systems Agencies by giving them incentives to control costs they now lack. And competing private plans with the right incentives might enforce a fee schedule far more effectively than a government agency could.

The Financing System

Actuarial categories and costs. The flow of funds in CCHP is based on Actuarial Cost (AC), i.e., the average total costs of covered benefits (insured and out-of-pocket) in the base year, updated each year by a suitable index, for persons in each actuarial category. For persons not covered by Medicare, the actuarial categories might be the simple and familiar three-part structure of "individual, individual plus one dependent, and individual plus two or more dependents." However, in a competitive situation, this might give health plans too strong an incentive to attempt to select preferred risks by design of benefit packages (e.g., good maternity benefits to attract healthy young families), location of facilities, or emphasis in specialty mix (strength in pediatrics, weakness in gerontology and cardiology). Carried to a logical extreme, such a system could lead to poor care for high-risk persons (though open enrollment—described below—would always assure the right of high-risk persons to join any qualified health plan). So experience might show that a more complex set of actuarial categories is desirable. For example, the three-part structure might be supplemented by special categories for persons aged 45–54 and 55–64. In the limit, one might go to a structure based on individual age (e.g., in 10-year steps) and sex, though I doubt this would be necessary.

Actuarial Cost would also reflect location, because there are large regional differentials in health care costs. The appropriate

geographic unit would probably be the State. However, regional differences in real per capita subsidies based on AC would be phased out over a decade.

The appropriate index for updating AC would probably be the "all services" component of the Consumer Price Index (CPI).

Assume, for the sake of illustration, that the AC for a "typical" family of four is $1,350 per year. (This happens to reflect the approximate average per capita cost for hospital and physician services for children and working-age persons in FY 1978.)

In CCHP, premiums would be set by each health plan for each actuarial category and benefit package, based on its own costs and its own judgment as to what it can charge in a competitive market. Thus, persons in more costly actuarial categories would pay higher premiums. This is desirable because we want competing plans to be motivated to serve them. This is made socially acceptable by giving such people higher subsidies through the following mechanisms.

Vouchers for the poor. The poor need more subsidy to assure their access to an acceptable plan. CCHP would provide them with a voucher usable only as a premium contribution to the qualified plan of their choice. It should be administered through the reformed cash-assistance system and designed according to the same principles. The voucher's value would be means-tested on the same basis as cash income supplements. The exact choice of formula requires analysis and judgments similar to those that went into welfare reform.

The voucher system can be integrated with the tax system and the unemployment insurance system.

Medicare would be retained for the aged, disabled, and victims of end-stage renal disease (ESRD). Eligibility would be expanded to all legal residents aged 65 and over for Part A (institutional services) and Part B (physicians' services). The benefits should be expanded to conform to the benefits for the rest of the population. The 150-day limit on hospital days should be removed—in effect providing catastrophic coverage. Better still, an annual limit on out-of-pocket expenses on covered benefits by any individual should be enacted.

The most important change needed in Medicare is a "freedom of choice provision" that would permit any beneficiary to direct that the "Adjusted Average Per Capita Cost" (AAPCC) to the Medicare program for people in his actuarial category be paid to the qualified plan of his choice in the form of a fixed prospective periodic payment. If done properly, this would end the Medicare subsidy to those who choose a more costly system of care, and would permit beneficiaries to reap the benefit of their economizing choices in the form of reduced cost-sharing or better benefits.

In addition, about 7.7 million aged, blind, and disabled receive Medicaid supplements to assist with costs not covered by Medicare. CCHP would replace this part of Medicaid, as far as acute care is concerned, with a voucher, comparable to the voucher for the non-aged poor, for premiums for a policy to supplement Medicare. In FY 1978, the average per capita hospital and physician costs for the aged not covered by Medicare will be about $385. This would be an appropriate level for the voucher.

Is health care financing more appropriately organized as a Government monopoly, or through private markets? Much of the case for NHI rests on "private market failure." And there is no doubt that the private market for health insurance, as presently constituted and shaped by numerous government policies, does a poor job of allocating resources. The main idea of CCHP is that the private market needs to be restructured, and that a reconstituted private market can do a better job than a government monopoly of health insurance.

Consideration of private market failure needs to be balanced by an appreciation of

some of the characteristic limitations of government. The following generalizations, while obviously not true in every case, summarize important insights that must be considered in deciding whether NHI should be based mainly on private markets or on a government monopoly. They are stated here baldly and without applicable qualifications to save time. The point of what follows is not to imply that government is "bad" compared to private enterprise, or that government people are better or worse than private enterprise people. Rather, the point is that government has certain limitations that are deep rooted, if not inherent. Government is good at some things such as taking money from taxpayers and paying it to social security beneficiaries, and maintaining competition in many industries; it performs badly at other things. The problem of public policy design is to define the appropriate role for government to achieve desirable social purposes most effectively.

1. Government responds to well-focused producer interests; competitive markets respond to broad consumer interests. People specialize in production, diversify in consumption. They are therefore much more likely to pressure their representatives on their producer interests than on other consumer interests.

2. "The rule of 'Do no direct harm' is a powerful force in shaping the nature of social intervention. We put few obstacles in the way of a market-generated shift of industry to the South . . . but we find it extraordinarily difficult to close a military base or a post-office." (Schultze) Thus, a government-run or regulated system must be very rigid.

3. When every dollar in the system is a Federal dollar, what every dollar is spent on becomes a Federal case. Abortion illustrates the point.

4. Equality of treatment by Government tends to mean uniformity. The uniform product is often a bargained compromise that pleases no one.

5. Government generally does a poor job providing services to individuals.

6. The Government performs poorly as a cost-effective purchaser. Think of the Rayburn

Building, the South Portal Building, Medicaid, and the C-5A. If a government agency gets tough with suppliers, the suppliers can bring pressure to bear to get the rules changed. Government purchasers are surrounded by many complex procedural rules; they cannot use nearly as much judgment as their private sector counterparts. The Government seems addicted to cost-reimbursement despite its notorious record for generating cost overruns. Cost-reimbursement protects providers.

7. The Government has a much harder time than the private sector in attracting and retaining the best operating management talent on a career basis. Government attracts many of the best people—usually for two- to four-year tours. But building an effective, economical operating organization usually takes years of dedicated effort; it cannot be done on revolving two- or four-year stands.

8. The political system is extremely risk averse. This makes it very difficult to innovate in a government-regulated environment.

The financing of individual health care services does not need to be a monopoly. There is no technial or economic factor that must make it a "natural monopoly" like a public utility. Nor is personal health care a "public good" like defense or police protection. The benefits of individual health care services are enjoyed primarily by the individual and his family, and he should be allowed a large measure of choice concerning it. The important public purposes of universal access to good quality care can be pursued most effectively in a decentralized private system guided by an appropriate structure of incentives and pro-competitive regulation.

The "consumer choice" issue. Proposals to rely on consumer choice to guide the health services system are invariably subjected to the attack that "consumers are incapable of making intelligent choices in health care matters." So it seems worthwhile to make clear exactly what is being assumed. Admittedly, the element of ignorance and uncertainty in health care is very large; that is true for physicians and civil servants as well as ordinary consumers. CCHP does not assume that the ordinary consumer is a *good* judge of what is in his own best interest. Consumers may be ignorant, biased, and vulnerable to deception. CCHP merely assumes that, when it comes to choosing a health plan, the ordinary consumer is the *best* judge of it. The theory of optimum allocation of resources through decentralized markets does not assume that every consumer is perfectly informed and economically rational. Markets can be policed by a minority of well-informed rational consumers. And we are seeking merely a good and workable solution, not a theoretical optimum. CCHP provides consumers with substantially better information than they get now and much stronger incentives to use it. If there were a demand for it, much could be done to organize better consumer information. In any case, the key factor is the incentive CCHP gives to providers, i.e., provider systems will get their money from satisfied consumers rather than from the Government. In CCHP, above the tax credit/voucher level, consumers would be working with their own money, not somebody else's.

Critics of the consumer choice position usually are not very explicit about whom they consider to be better qualified than the average American to choose his health plan for him. In reality, the alternative to a consumer choice system is a provider-dominated system.

Presumably *every* NHI scheme under consideration would allow each consumer choice of physician and free choice as to whether or not to accept recommended medical treatment—decisions that could be aided by technical knowledge. *What distinguishes CCHP from the others is that it seeks to give the consumer a choice from among alternative systems for organizing and financing care,* and to allow him to benefit from his economizing choices. The issue then is whether consumers can be trusted to choose wisely when it comes to picking a health plan—some of which cost less than others.

Part of the "consumer choice" issue is resistance to the idea of letting the poor, because of their poverty, choose a less costly health plan that might not meet their medical needs. There is appearance of a conflict here with the principle of CCHP that people must be allowed to benefit from their economizing choices. (There is, of course, an issue as to how much the poor should be forced to accept their share of society's assistance in the form of costly medical technology of doubtful value, as opposed to leaving them free to spend the resources on other things like food and housing known to be good for health.) The problem can be resolved in CCHP by setting the premium vouchers (usable only for health insurance), at a high enough level to assure access to a plan with adequate benefits—always letting plans that do a better job attract members by offering less cost sharing or more benefits.

Equity issues. CCHP uses the most effective way to redistribute income, i.e., directly. It takes money from the well-to-do and pays it to lower-income people in the form of tax credits and vouchers. By this method, the amount of redistribution is clearly visible, and one can be sure the money reaches its intended target. CCHP can thus be used to bring about whatever income redistribution for medical purchases our political process will support. I suspect the reason some will criticize CCHP on equity grounds is because they think that the amount of redistribution Congress will be willing to vote is less than their own personal preferences. So they seek indirect methods of redistribution that may be supported on other grounds. A major trouble with this approach is that third-party insurance systems are an exceedingly ineffective way to redistribute income. Medicare pays more on behalf of rich than poor. In a bureaucratic system, such as would be created under Health Security, individuals and organized groups who are forceful and skillful at getting their way come out ahead.

The equity of CCHP ought to be compared with where we are today and where we are likely to go as a society. It is useless to compare it to some hypothetical egalitarian ideal that has never been attained in any society and is surely not supported by the American people today.

National Health Plan: Why We Need to Follow the British

Peter Singer

A NATIONAL HEALTH SERVICE?

A national health service must be financed by taxation. It does, therefore, limit the freedom of the taxpayer to decide for himself how much he shall spend on health, and how much on other items. Of course, other welfare measures like social security do the same, in their own area. There is, however, a prima facie case against such a restriction. What can be said in defense of the restriction in this case?

First, it may be that the community, acting together, can achieve goods that the individual could not achieve, no matter how much he decided to spend on health care. We have already seen examples of this in respect of obtaining cheap, uncontaminated blood and obtaining medical services that have not been distorted by the threat of malpractice suits. There are many other ways in which the special nature of medical care may make it unsuited to market control. For instance, the market's answer to the uncertainty of an individual's need for extensive medical care is private insurance. Private insurance, however, tends to be extremely expensive for ordinary visits to a doctor, because a doctor, in the privacy of his office, is not subject to supervision from his peers or anyone else, and so might prescribe unnecessary treatment in order to increase his remuneration from the insurance company. One consequence of this is that most people are insured for hospital visits, but not for office visits; and a consequence of this is that some medical care now takes place in hospitals that would be done more economically in the patient's home or the doctor's office. The ultimate consequence is that the consumer pays more for his medical insurance.

This difficulty is not one that can be eliminated simply by a system of national health insurance like those envisaged in recent congressional bills. These proposals would retain the principle of paying the doctor for each treatment, and this would leave the system wide open to abuse if it covered office visits, unless there were a huge and expensive system of inspectors. On the other hand, if the scheme does not cover office visits, it will accelerate the trend to increased hospitalization.

This problem can be avoided under a national health service, by paying the doctor on some basis other than the cost of the treatment he prescribes. In Britain, for example, doctors are paid according to the number of patients on their roll, with a lower payment per patient after a certain figure is reached to discourage excessively large rolls, and an absolute ceiling at a higher point, to prohibit unworkably large practices. Admittedly there are drawbacks to this method too, for a doctor gets paid even if he does very little for his patients. A complaints procedure and the possibility of patients transferring to another doctor may curb this tendency. A more important restraint is the bond of an ethical relationship between doctor and patient that has not been eroded by the commercialization of medical practice.

Another frequently cited drawback of proposals for either a national health service or national insurance is that the patient has no disincentive to prevent him visiting a doctor as often as he likes, since he does not pay for it. In fact, British statistics do not

bear out this fear; although the figures are not comprehensive enough to give a decisive answer, they do not appear to show any rise in demand per patient since the inauguration of the National Health Service. Perhaps the explanation for this is that the overutilization that one might expect from a few people is compensated for by the practice of preventative medicine. Prevention is, as the saying goes, better than cure, and a patient who goes for a regular checkup, or when he first notices something wrong, may in the end be much less expensive to treat than one who puts off a visit to the doctor until he is seriously ill. One thing that is certain is that Britain spends a smaller percentage of its Gross National Product on health than the United States does, despite the fact that health is free to all in Britain. Quite apart from the question of expense, though, it should be asked how many cases of overutilization are needed to offset one case of a patient who dies because he postponed seeking treatment in order to save money.

Another possible justification for a national health service is that it is an effective means of redistributing income, since it may be paid for by a progressively graduated income tax, and distributed to all irrespective of income. The poorest, especially, are assisted, since they will pay little or no tax, and receive essential services that they could not otherwise afford. It is hardly necessary to describe the distress that a person may feel if he requires medical care but is unable to afford it. The security and peace of mind that arises from knowing that one will never be in this situation is one of the greatest benefits that a society can bestow on its poorer citizens. Indeed, the heights that medical expenses have reached in this country recently mean that it is not only the poor, but also those in the middle income bracket, that require this security. Senator Ribicoff, in *The American Medical Machine,* cites the case of a family that received a bill of $4600 for the four and a half days their father had been in the hospital before he died. Medical bills are now a major factor in bankruptcies: in Tulsa, Oklahoma, a survey showed that they account for 60 percent of all bankruptcies.

Conservative economists are not necessarily opposed to some measure of redistribution, especially if it is designed to improve the condition of the very poor. Milton Friedman, in *Capitalism and Freedom,* goes so far as to advocate a negative income tax. This would mean redistribution in cash rather than services. Friedman prefers cash because he thinks it makes for more freedom, leaving it up to the individual to spend his money as he likes. He may choose to spend it on health insurance, or he may choose whatever else he desires.

I have already suggested that the freedom of the individual is limited by the marketplace in subtle ways that Friedman and his likeminded colleagues overlook. Still, we must admit once again that there is *some* truth in what Friedman says here; and if we wish to defend a national health service on redistributive grounds, we should admit that there is an element of paternalism in so doing. If we give benefits to the poor in services rather than cash, it is at least partly because we believe that they will be better off with the services; and that even if they were able to buy adequate medical services with the money we gave them, some at least would spend it less prudently, so as to gain short-term satisfactions at a cost of greater distress and suffering in the long run.

Friedman grants that a paternalist position is internally consistent, but he associates it with dictatorship and insists that "those who believe in freedom must believe also in the freedom of individuals to make their own mistakes." Paternalism, Friedman says, is an arrogant position, while the liberal displays humility in refusing to decide for others what is good for them. The standpoint from which Friedman criticizes paternalism, however, is the same superficial liberalism that we encountered earlier. Friedman does not inquire into the social conditions and circumstances in which the poor decide how

to spend their money. He does not consider the effect of being brought up in a family that never had the habit of providing for the future because there was never more than enough to provide for the present. He does not consider that alcoholism, drug addiction, or gambling may be factors in producing poverty. Is the alcoholic free to choose whether to invest his money in health insurance? He is not; and there are many others who for a variety of reasons are scarcely more able to make an informed, carefully considered, long-term choice. How often do we have to watch people do something that they come to regret bitterly when it is too late to do anything about it, before we can say to the next person about to do the same thing that he is making a mistake? Is it really arrogant to claim that we may sometimes know what is in another person's interests better than he does himself? Or is it merely an honest appreciation of a fact that stares us in the face, a fact that could hardly be denied were it not for a prevailing mythology that demands that we do deny it?

The final justification for overriding the freedom of each to spend his income as he prefers is one that relates to a theme that has run through this chapter: the nature of the community that we live in. Here we must consider whether it is not desirable that a community be integrated in certain fundamental areas of life, rather than being divided along lines of class or race. As Brian Barry has noted, the promotion of this value distinguishes a national health service from a system of universal insurance that provides standard sums of money for given treatments, while leaving doctors and hospitals to charge what they will, and the patient to make up the difference if he selects a doctor or hospital that charges above the standard amount. This insurance system would provide a basic level of care for everyone. I do not agree with Barry that this value is the *only* one that distinguishes these two systems of providing health care (I have suggested others in this chapter); but it is true that universal insurance would provide many of the benefits of a national health service, including redistribution and the provision of security for all against the threat of ruinous expenditures on medical care. What the insurance proposal could not do, however, is provide an integrated health service that is used by people of all classes and races. We would still have one standard of care for the wealthy and another for the poor.

How important is integration in the area of medicine? It does not seem to be as important as in education, for it does not determine a person's opportunities for the whole of his life to the extent that education does (although medicine may do this in exceptional cases). Still, there are important reasons for desiring integration in medicine too. As Barry says, "so long as those with money can buy exemption from the common lot the rulers and the generally dominant groups in a society will have little motive for making sure that the public facilities are of good quality." In other words, if we want good public facilities, we have to ensure that those who can complain effectively when standards are allowed to drop use the facilities.

A more fundamental aspect of integration is that it makes a substantial difference to the image that we have of our community. The knowledge that when it comes to vital things like medical care we are all in it together, and your money cannot buy you anything that I am not equally entitled to, may do a good deal to mitigate the effects of inequality in other less vital areas, and create the atmosphere of community concern for all that I have already discussed.

This last consideration is the first one we have encountered that goes beyond even what the British National Health Service has achieved. Private medicine does exist in Britain, and very wealthy people do sometimes get treatment that the National Health Service does not provide. Money may allow one to go down to London and be operated on by an outstanding surgeon, while a person who could not afford this would have to accept the general level of surgery in the area in which he lived. Yet this is not a major problem. Because of the generally high standard of treatment that the National Health Service provides at no cost, and the high costs of private medicine, only a very few people avail themselves of private treatment. Of those who do, by no means all actually do receive treatment that is superior to that offered by the National Health Service. So long as private medicine remains such a minor part of health care as a whole, it does not seem necessary to take the step of prohibiting it altogether. Allowing private medicine to exist, can, as Barry suggests, be seen as a reasonable compromise between the values of freedom and integration.

9. INDIVIDUAL PATIENTS AND SOCIAL NEEDS

The Primacy of the Physician as Trusted Personal Advisor and Not as Social Agent

Charles Fried

In the case of the doctor–patient relation the elements that combine to constitute the significance of that relation include:

— The importance and nature of the interests served by that relation. This suggests that not everything that now falls into that professional ambit necessarily has to. The identification of these interests and of what is distinct about them is discussed in the next chapter.

— The complex of intelligence, knowledge and judgment that is needed to serve these interests. Particularly, as I shall argue, there is the fact that health has different significance for different persons, depending on their life plans and value systems, and the further fact that in some situations the doctor may need to help his patient not so much to realize his life plan as to realize that he must radically revise that plan.

— The expectations and confidence which tradition (maybe only mythology) relates to the role of the physician in our culture. This is not a circular argument: the fact of the expectations is not being used to account for the expectations. Rather my point is that the role of trusted personal adviser and helper is a distinctive and significant one, as a total role and not just for the discrete benefits conferred within it. In different times and cultures the precise outlines and the kinds of functions included within this role may vary. Yet because of the significance of the role it is important that the commitments of that role be honored, even if the role might perhaps have been defined otherwise.

The intuitive notion is one of the integrity of a relationship, and therefore of conduct which meets the conception of that relationship. And so when a doctor does less than he is able for his patient, albeit in the name of the progress of medicine and the welfare of larger numbers of persons, this is disquieting because it does violence to the integrity of a relationship which the patient assumes he is in, and which doctors have traditionally stated they were in. The notion of the integrity of this relationship is, to be sure, a complex one. Even in its most extreme form, I would doubt that it carries with it the expectation that the doctor will do everything conceivable to further the interest of his patient. He will not, perhaps, endanger himself. He will not, perhaps, allow the claims of his patients to overwhelm his whole existence and all other relationships in which he might stand. But these qualifications themselves refer to structures of rights, relations, and expectations of the same form as his relation to the patient, of the same form as the relation of helper to helped. The best way to conceive of the system of these relationships is in terms of adjacent obligations, adjacent relationships. And the technique for resolving conflicts is

not one of weighing up and balancing, but of drawing the boundary lines and the terms of the obligation.

The notion is one of doing unstintingly what it is that one does, though choosing with care the occasions on which one will do it. The notion of doing one's utmost in a system of adjacent relations can be contrasted to a notion in which the doctor conceives of himself as performing only one large scale action, which is acting as the agent of the health care system to the population at large. On this latter view his activity and his target is a population of persons, while in the former case his activity has as its object a sequence of discrete objects who are individual patients. And in that latter case, it is his responsibility not to exhaust his resources before he has attended to the totality of his object, which is the population at large, while in the former case if he has exhausted his resources (or himself) on a particular patient, then those with whom he has not entered into this relationship and to whom he is no longer available have no complaint.

How these integral actions and relations come about, what their contents are, in what their integrity consists, and the relationships between them are deep problems of psychology and ethics. I will not, because I cannot, offer a general theory for such problems here. At best in the course of this essay I will offer certain partial solutions to specific problems. Nevertheless it is important to give some sense of the notion of integrity in actions and relations, because it is that notion which captures the special dimension of the subject before us. And as a general concept it suggests an important criticism of the standard classical utilitarian view of ethics. On the utilitarian view, what a person does, the relationships he enters into, and the choices he makes are all made with an eye towards a distant global end, which is furthering the greatest good of the greatest number or some such optimizing goal. But, I am arguing here that the ethical life of human beings, the values they perceive and follow, inhere in the concrete actions they perform and the concrete relationships into which they enter. It is these which allow a man to live in the present and to give ultimate, intrinsic value to the things that he does. Traditionally the doctor has seen himself as a person who stands to his patients in a relation that is at least analogous to that of friend or lover. To be sure the relation is less intense and pervasive, but it is analogous because it has its own integrity, and it demands, at least within its more circumscribed ambit, complete and unstinting devotion. Moreover, being a relationship its value is a value for *both* parties to it, doctor and patient, and both parties have rights that arise out of it. Although I have been focusing on the interests of patients in the ideal of personal care, it should be clear that this ideal implies an interest and a right on the part of the doctor as well to maintain the integrity of his activity, to work not as a tool or as the bureaucratic agent of a social system, but as one whose professional activity is a personal expression of his own nature, the relationships he enters into being freely chosen, the obligations freely assumed, not imposed.

The reciprocal of this relation may be better seen if we recall some of the other relationships that make this demand of integrity: friendship, love, family relationships, the relation to one's self are all examples I have mentioned. Nor are all such instances to be found in the realm of relations between persons. The relationship of an artist to his art or a scholar to truth has this quality. It is evident that the artist gives to his art an unstinting devotion which is analogous to the care a doctor gives his patient. And the relation between the artist's art and his other concerns, his concerns as a person, citizen, parent, and so on, are relations of adjacent demands, whose structure must be adjusted in some systemic way, rather than the relation of factors of supply whose price and productivity determine the optimum mix of products from the artist, as if from a business firm. There may not be

many other professional relationships which have this quality; some think that the lawyer owes his client that degree of concern, and that the lawyer, like the doctor, is not to be viewed as a businessman selling a product or a bureaucrat allocating a scarce resource.

What the foregoing argument shows is that the concept of personal care is a pervasive one, which grows out of a relation that people can create only in the context of more or less direct contact, and that the actions and ends pursued in the context of such relations are qualitatively different from those pursued outside of them. Finally, we have seen that the distinct character of those relations, actions and values gives rise to interests not only in those who benefit from them—in this case the patient—but in the benefactor, here doctors, as well. For doctors, like others entering into relations of personal care, achieve in that relation the capacity to perform a distinct kind of service and to pursue a distinct kind of value. And the structure of these relations and values presupposes that they are deliberately entered into, chosen, assumed as obligations.

RIGHTS TO HEALTH CARE AND RIGHTS IN HEALTH CARE

Positive Rights

More difficult than these rights not to be used are the rights to the fulfillment of whatever obligations are implicit in the relation of care itself. These rights are the most difficult because they are rights to benefits, rather than rights that certain kinds of harms and impositions not take place. And as soon as we speak of a right to a benefit, economic considerations appear to take over. Yet they need not. The benefits I am speaking of are benefits that arise out of a relation that is created, obligations that are undertaken in providing medical care so that the denial of these benefits is in fact a kind of breach of faith.

The physician who withholds care that it

is in his power to give because he judges it is wasteful to provide it to the particular person breaks faith with his patient. Examples would be the refusal to treat recurrent pneumonia in an aged and debilitated patient or to admit to an intensive-care unit an infant who over his life is likely to need frequent, elaborate medical attention. Similarly, a physician who undertakes new obligations knowing that they will disable him from fulfilling obligations that he has already contracted also breaks faith. He is like somebody who makes a second promise that he knows he can only keep if he breaks an earlier promise.

These are simple notions, but they are all that can be or need to be opposed to the equipment maintenance or triage models. They express the sound intuition that the right to health care goes beyond the right to one's fair share of health care. Beyond one's fair share, one is entitled to be treated decently, humanely, personally and honestly in the course of medical care, and since medical care is often provided in situations of desperation and vulnerability, the demands of decency and humanity may run high.

It will be objected that recognizing these rights in health care will conflict with both efficiency and equity, and undoubtedly it will. The overall efficiency of the health-care system may well be decreased if physicians do not subject their patients to experimentation without their consent, if they do not lie to them, do not withhold care from unpromising cases, or refuse to take on new patients when doing so would conflict with their existing obligations. Recognizing these rights in health care will often be hard to square with equity as well. Refusing to withhold care from one person may deprive another person distinguishable from the first only by his place in the queue. But why should this possibility be surprising? The fact that respecting rights in medical care will conflict to some extent with efficient and just distribution of medical care simply argues against the easy assumption that effi-

ciency and equity exhaust our moral universe. It is my precise point that persons have rights that go beyond the one single right to whatever would be allotted to them under a just overall distribution of benefits and burdens in society. Consider, for instance, the forced incarceration and treatment of persons who have committed no offense but have what appear to be dangerous dispositions. This preventive action may be very efficient, and no concept of distributive justice is detailed enough to preclude such an imposition. Yet there is a violation of rights nonetheless.

BUREAUCRATS AND PHYSICIANS: TWO LEVELS OF OBLIGATION

A further objection would have it that recognition of rights in medical care would make the job of budget officers impossible. For if personal rights are allowed to supersede efficiency and equity, do we not undermine the sole guides for rational policy? Not necessarily. Since the department of health, the legislature, and maybe even the director of the hospital do not have the kind of personal relations with patients that call into being the rights in personal care, respecting these rights is not a constraint upon persons at that level. Since administrators and bureaucrats are dealing in large, impersonal statistical groups, the primary moral norms applicable to relations with such abstract entities are precisely those of efficiency and justice. To be sure, planners and bureaucrats must not direct individual physicians to violate personal rights, but questions about the enjoyment of those rights can only be determined rationally on norms of efficiency and equity. Thus, the personal physician must respect the rights of his patient, and the department of health (although it may not on efficiency or equity grounds direct that he violate those rights) must determine on efficiency and equity grounds how many people, and in what circumstances, will be the beneficiaries of such care.

Take, for instance, the well-worn example of dialysis. The physician would violate his obligation to his patient and the patient's right to the physician's fidelity, if he withheld dialysis on the grounds that it is inefficient to devote these kinds of resources to this kind of patient. In much the same way a physician would violate his obligations to an elderly patient with pneumonia if he withheld antibiotics on the grounds that further medical care of such patients is inefficient. (I put to one side the question whether in some cases the physician fulfills his obligations to his patient by not engaging in heroic measures.) But there is no such violation if the state determines to build only a certain number of dialysis machines, and the state provides procedures and mandatory guidelines regarding their availability. Whatever the patient's rights to personal care, and whatever the physician's obligation to his patients, they do not extend to having his doctor engage in political manipulation so that the patient can leapfrog the line or obtain a government benefit that is not properly available to him. Once again, this resolution of the dilemma only seems odd to those who expect a unitary solution in terms solely of equity and efficiency. The doctor is responsible to his patient only for what he can accomplish, and it is with that responsibility that rights in medical care are concerned.

CONFINING THE CONCEPT OF EMERGENCY

Finally, it will be objected that the content of a doctor's obligation to his patients is itself the product of convention and that the conventions are in turn defined by overall social judgments of equity and efficiency. Thus, it may be agreed that personal care is simply what efficiency dictates in the relatively affluent normal situation of middle-class medical care, whereas triage is what is dictated by the battlefield or emergency situation. Therefore, it is the situation that defines in each context the content of the doctor's obli-

gation to the particular patients. This objection seems to me to exemplify yet another error in social and ethical philosophizing. One might call it the fallacy of the lowest common denominator. It assumes that because certain things are true of what might be called emergency or unusual situations, we should therefore be able to generalize from them to the normal or all situations, and define our principles from that vantage. But I would suggest that one might think of rights in medical care in much the same way that John Rawls has asked us to think about the priority of liberty: liberty takes priority over all material advantages only when a certain level of material development has been reached. But this fact does not mean that even after that development level has been reached, our earlier willingness to compromise liberty shows that liberty does not truly have priority at that later stage. Similarly, I would acknowledge that triage is an appropriate concept on the battlefield and in emergencies, without being willing to generalize from that to the proposition that the rights in medical care that we posit for the more usual situation are no better than special cases of the same principles that dictate triage in an emergency.

To be sure, a characteristic of a nonemergency situation is that one can recognize rights to the prejudice of efficiency and equity without producing extreme distortions. This admission does not prove that efficiency and equity are our sole moral principles after all. For it is our very willingness to sacrifice rights, to think only in starkly economic terms, that gives emergencies some of their unusual and potentially dehumanizing quality. The concept of emergency is only a tolerable moral concept if somehow we can truly think of it as exceptional, if we can truly think of it as a circumstance that, far from defining our usual moral universe, suspends it for a limited time and thus suspends usual moral principles. It is when emergencies become usual that we are threatened with moral disintegration, dehumanization.

Costs and Clinicians as Agents of Patients

Baruch A. Brody

A traditional view of the patient–physician relation and of the question of medical costs runs something like this:

a. The job of the physician is to do that which is best for the patient without regard to any financial costs that might be imposed upon other people or upon society. The physician is the agent of the patient.

b. It is permissible to take the cost of medical care into account only to the extent that those costs impose burdens upon the patient. A paternalistic physician might withhold some care if the costs to the patient were too high, whereas a patient-rights–oriented physician might ask the patient about whether the extra care is worth the extra money.

Claim (b) is meant, of course, to follow from claim (a).

What are the roots of this view? I think that there are three moral arguments for it. The first is a *consequentialist* argument. It claims that the patient–physician relation flourishes and patient-care is improved when patients trust their physicians, and that trust is promoted when patients recognize that their physicians are their agents and not the agents of society in general. The second is a *contract-based rights* argument. It claims that patients employ physicians with the understanding that the physician is looking out for the interests of the patient. A physician who does not follow that policy is breaking his or her contract with the patient and is therefore violating that patient's right to have the contractual understanding followed. The third argument claims that view (a) simply represents the intrinsic nature of the patient–physician relation.

I think that there is a point to each of these arguments, but that the second and third points are undercut in certain settings of the modern public provision of health care, and the first may be outweighed in those settings by other consequentialist considerations. Let me begin by explaining what forms of health care I have in mind.

The forms of health care with which I am concerned are most fully exemplified in the United States by the county hospitals that provide health care for the indigent (even when they are not covered by Medicare and/or Medicaid) and the Veteran's Administration medical system. In England, the National Health Service exemplifies the sort of system with which I am concerned. The crucial features of these systems are: (1) there are individuals who are eligible to receive care in these systems but not funds to purchase health care in some private health-care system; (2) the funds for running these systems are provided from tax revenues rather than from payments by the recipients; (3) the level of funding for the system is not high enough to provide all of the health care from which the eligible individuals can benefit.

Not all cases of the public provision of health care meet these three criteria. Medicare and Medicaid do not meet the first criterion because they provide funds rather than health care. And one could imagine a scheme (although I don't know of any) in which enough financing was provided so that all those eligible could receive all the care from which they could benefit. Our examples, however, do meet qualifications (1) through (3).

My argument is going to be that these forms of health care are ones in which an entirely different account of the patient–physician relation is required. I would identify the major claims of that account as follows:

(a¹) The job of the physician in these forms of health care is to do that which best promotes the health of that class of eligible patients for whose care the physician is responsible. The physician is both the agent of society, which is paying to protect and promote the health of that class of people, and the agent of the entire class of eligible patients.

(b¹) It is required in these settings that one take into account the cost of providing health care to any given patient. In particular, the physician in these settings must allocate the health-care resources over which he or she has control so that resources are used to provide the maximum benefit for the class of eligible patients.

Claim (b¹) is, once more, meant to follow from claim (a¹).

It is easy to see why some of the arguments for the traditional views (a) and (b) have no relevance for the settings which I am discussing. Because of features (1) and (2) of these settings (set forth previously), the patients do not employ the physicians. It is society that employs them and imposes upon them such contractually based obligations as exist. That being the case, the argument that the physician is bound by his or her contract with the patient to be the patient's agent simply does not arise for the particular settings I am discussing.

One word of preaching at this point: Given point (3) regarding the level of funding, society, if it were honest with itself, would make explicit that the traditional patient–physician relation has been redefined for these settings. It never has, neither in the United States nor in England. Attempts are always made to pretend that the budget limitations highlighted in point (3) limit waste and perhaps some amenities, but not useful health care, and that physicians in these public settings can really act without thinking about costs and about the needs of other patients. We need to stop pretending. The point remains that physicians in such settings cannot be bound by contractual relations with their patients who have hired them to be their agent.

What about the third argument drawn from the very nature of the patient–physician relation? Such an argument depends upon the existence of some accepted account of the intrinsic nature of the patient–physician relation, a nature that is set independently of anybody's agreement, and which binds physicians and patients in all settings. One might be very dubious about any such views of the intrinsic nature of any relation. But there are special reasons for being skeptical here. It seems perfectly plausible to hypothesize that the view of the physician as the patient's agent arose in more traditional settings and was turned into a view of the intrinsic nature of the relation without any argument.

This leads us to the first of the arguments for the traditional views (a) and (b), the consequentialist argument that only by acting as the patient's agent can the physician build the trust relation that is essential for good patient care. That is a powerful argument, and I fully agree that giving up (a) and (b) in the settings that I am discussing leads to certain real losses in that trust and in the resulting quality of care. But, I would submit, keeping (a) and (b) leads to even worse consequences. In the settings we are discussing, providing all the care that would benefit one's current patients would, given the number of those eligible and the budget limits, result in others not getting care from which they would benefit even more. The net result is that we must go to (a¹) and (b¹), even if we pay some price in doing so.

Thus far we have been arguing that the traditional arguments for (a) and (b) fail in the settings we are discussing. We have also seen one consequentialist reason for moving to (a¹) and (b¹), namely, that it will use the limited resources in ways that maximize the benefits produced. But there are other reasons for adopting (a¹) and (b¹). The most important of these are considerations of fairness and equity. All of the members of the eligible class equally have rights to health care (that usually is why society is trying to provide that care), and, in any case, they have had those rights equally granted by those who are providing the funds. Physicians who follow (b¹) recognize all these claims and try to allocate the limited resources fairly to all those eligible and in need by allocating them so as to produce the maximum benefit, equally taking into account the health-care needs of all the eligible. Physicians who follow policy (b) are allocating on a first come, first served basis, allocating to those who come first whatever they benefit from and leaving over for others only the remaining resources. That seems unfair. I am not claiming that (b^1) represents the fairest way of allocating the limited resources; all I am saying is that it is fairer than (b) and the most plausible step in the right direction.

Several final points need to be made before my argument is complete. They are the following: (I) it is an open question as to whether or not any particular budget limit set by society for this form of the public provision of health care is or is not fair. Whether it is fair or not cannot be decided independently of some theory about redistributive justice in general and justice in the delivery of health care in particular. I have not attempted to say anything about these issues in this paper. All that I have been discussing is the question of how physicians ought to allocate the resources that are made available; (II) moving from (a) and (b) to (a^1) and (b^1) is a profoundly revolutionary step. It involves major systems questions for physician-administrators about allocating funds for preventive and primary care as opposed to funds for treating catastrophes. It also involves day-by-day decisions about admissions to hospitals and to ICUs, about referrals and tests, etc.; (III) an important question that arises is the extent to which patients entering into such systems should be made aware of the extent of these special features of the patient–physician relation. The British, we are told in recent reports, make a real effort to avoid informing the patient about these matters. Is that really appropriate? Should we be more open, and how should we do that? Can we count on the patients coming to understand what is going on? These are all questions that deserve further study; (IV) I have argued that certain special settings require a redefinition of certain aspects of the patient–physician relation. But can that redefinition really be confined just to those settings? What happens as society pays for more and more of the medical care provided in the private sector, either directly through Medicare and Medicaid or indirectly via subsidies for health insurance? These too are questions that deserve further study.

PART III

Case Areas

SECTION A

Reproductive Issues

1. DECISIONS TO REPRODUCE

The theologian and philosopher St. Augustine of Hippo argued in A.D. 400 that the goods of marriage were offspring, fidelity, and the sacramental value of marriage (*proles, fides,* and *sacramentum*). The decision to marry was tantamount to the decision to have children. The Christian West came to condemn any separation of the social and convivial dimensions of sexuality from the reproductive dimensions. From as early as the first-century Christian document the *Didache,* or *Teachings of the Twelve Apostles,* contraception was forbidden. In addition, pleasure in sexual intercourse, even in marriage, was held by many authorities, including Pope Gregory the Great (540–604), to be sinful.[1] The reasons for these attitudes were complex. They were articulated within an understanding of natural law drawn both from Aristotle and from Stoic sources, which held that there were rules intrinsic to nature that one could discover by reason and that one was morally forbidden to violate. As a result, within this tradition it was very difficult to speak of decisions to reproduce in the way that they are currently understood. It was considered sinful and immoral even to entertain the notion of marrying while planning to use contraception or not to reproduce at all.

Although the tradition was pronatalist, it forbade activities to enhance reproductive possibilities if these fell outside of the bounds of marriage or violated natural law. Artificial insemination was condemned because it required masturbation, which was held to be unnatural.[2] In addition, artificial insemination from a donor compounded an unnatural act with the sin of adultery. The result of these teachings was a tension between the rationally chosen reproduc-

---

[1] *Epistles* 11.64.
[2] St. Thomas Aquinas, *Summa Theologica* II,II, 154.

tive goals of individual men and women and the supposed constraints of natural law.

In the twentieth century many Western religions retreated from a strong "exceptionless" condemnation of contraception and sterilization, and the philosophical arguments supporting such understandings of natural law tended not to be widely accepted outside of Roman Catholic religious circles. However, a powerful onus remained against decisions to curtail reproduction. These views were bolstered by a paternalistic attitude toward requests by patients to be sterilized or to receive contraceptives. Until the 1950s, and in some places the 1960s, a patient's request for sterilization was not honored until the age of the patient multiplied by the number of children equalled a numerical score, often 150. Moreover, the consent of both spouses was usually required. In contrast with the current views of the President's Commission, which sees the patient as the central decision-maker, the physician was seen as obliged to protect the patient against prematurely foreclosing reproductive opportunity, which the patient might regret, should an offspring die or the patient remarry. The more children the patient had and the older the patient became, the less interest in future reproduction was at stake to be protected by the physician. In addition, laws remained that restricted the availability of contraceptives, even for married couples. Such laws reflected the traditional Christian view that the use of contraceptives violated divine law and natural law. There was also the view that the widespread availability of contraceptives would encourage fornication and other forms of sexual license. Both law and accepted medical practice thus tended radically to restrict opportunities for reproductive decision making. Children were considered to be the gifts of God, not the outcomes of deliberate and responsible human choices.

Current law and public policy have developed around a concept of a right to privacy that secures the opportunity for individuals to decide when and under what circumstances they will reproduce. This understanding was articulated in the Supreme Court ruling of *Griswold v. Connecticut* (1965) in which the Court held that the state must show a compelling interest in order to restrict the access of married couples to contraceptives. Justice Goldberg argued that a right to privacy in marital relations was fundamental and basic and that it was one of the rights "retained by the people" within the meaning of the Ninth Amendment to the Constitution. In 1972 the Supreme Court, in *Eisenstadt v. Baird,* extended the constitutional right of access to contraceptives to unmarried persons. It held that if the right to privacy was to mean anything, it is the right of an individual, married or single, to be free from unwarranted governmental intrusion into decisions whether to bear or beget a child. This right to privacy in reproductive decision making was further bolstered in 1973 in the Supreme Court abortion decision of *Roe v. Wade* and *Doe v. Bolton.*

The result of these court decisions is a constitutionally protected right to decide whether to conceive a child or to carry a child to term. Before people could easily choose to reproduce or not to reproduce, the area of reproductive responsibility was arguably diminished. However, given a constitutionally recognized right to decide one's reproductive destiny, one can then begin to speak of moral responsibility in reproductive decision making. Once the procreative and convivial elements of human sexuality can be effectively separated, and children become the products of free choice, the question then arises as to the circumstances under which reproduction is irresponsible. Unlike fornication with the benefit of effective contraception, sexual intercourse with the possibility of reproduction involves an unconsenting third party, namely the child who may be produced. Even Engelhardt and Tooley, who set limits to the moral standing of fetuses and young infants, acknowledge that such entities may develop into persons to whom one will have moral obligations. Indeed, following Brody's suggestion that physicians ought to be agents of the social good, one might ask whether physicians and other health-care professionals are obliged to discourage or refuse to cooperate with irresponsible reproduction? Or should they simply be advocates of the patient's interest and eschew imposing particular views of proper reproduction. Do considerations such as those raised by Clements and Sider in the readings suggest that judgments about the best interests of patients may conflict with autonomous patient choices regarding reproduction? Under what circumstances would a patient's requests violate a physician's integrity?

These issues have been complicated by the fact that indigent individuals have often been sterilized without adequate consent. The result of such abuses has been federal regulations that required that individuals receiving sterilizations through federally funded programs give consent 30 days in advance of the procedure. What sort of view does this presuppose concerning the circumstances and capacity of the poor to make reproductive decisions in an effective and competent manner? Do such paternalistic restrictions collide with concerns such as those of Norman Daniels regarding access to health care as an element of fair opportunity? What implications does the President's Commission's analysis of the patient as decision-maker have for such regulations? How ought one to balance considerations of conflicting rights and responsibilities in reproductive decision making?

Case A

A 32-year-old lesbian lawyer requests that her gynecologist artificially inseminate her so that she might have a child. As she indicates to the physician, she is a successful attorney and, even as a single parent, can provide at least as much support and care as occurs with many working couples. In addition, there are many single-parent families headed by women. She would hope to raise the child, whether male or female, with an openness to being either heterosexual or homosexual. The physician is hesitant, in part because the woman is unmarried and would be raising the child alone, and in part because of her committed homosexual lifestyle.

Case B

A 19-year-old college sophomore in the top 10 percent of his college class consults a urologist and requests a vasectomy. He states that he has reflected on the condition of the world and judges it is not a place to raise children. In addition, he does not want to expose women to the possibility of unwanted pregnancy, nor ask them to expose themselves to the risks involved with effective contraception. He states that he understands that a vasectomy is usually irreversible, and he is willing to take the risk that, should he change his mind, he might not be able to reverse the procedure. He states that he has stored semen in a local sperm bank. Here, too, he recognizes that the long-term potency of frozen sperm is questionable. The physician is appalled and refuses to perform the sterilization, indicating that the student is too young and will very likely regret this choice. On the other hand, the student argues that society respects other choices fraught with risk, such as hang-gliding or joining the Armed Forces. He pleads that the physician's attitude is inconsistent.

Case C

A 36-year-old unmarried welfare mother with ten children asks the physician at the local clinic to remove her IUD (intrauterine device) so she can have another child. She remarks that it was a mistake to have had it inserted a year before because she misses the pleasure of being pregnant and having a young child around the house. Her two oldest children, 22 and 21, are currently serving jail sentences for armed robbery; her three oldest daughters, ages 19, 17, and 15, have a total of six children among them. The woman has never had a stable relationship with any man, nor held a job in the last ten years. The physician believes it would be best for society and for her children still at home, who range in age from 12 to 3, if she had no additional children. The physician wishes to advise strongly that it would be improper to continue having children. In fact, the physician feels inclined to tell the woman that if she wishes the IUD removed, she will need to find some other physician in the clinic to do it. The physician judges that the woman is acting irresponsibly, both with respect to society and to her already living children.

Case D

On admission for her seventh delivery, a 28-year-old mother of six children is informed that she will need to have the seventh child delivered by a Caesarean section. She consents, but insists that at the same time the physicians perform a tubal ligation. She explains that she lives in a rural part of the state and, given the need to take care of the other children as well as to help her husband on the small farm where they are sharecroppers, she will not have a chance to come in later to be sterilized. Past history reveals that she has not been able to use contraceptives effectively and that she once attempted to use an IUD but complications led to its being removed. The physicians explain that they are not able to honor her request because the sterilization is federally funded and, under such circumstances, consent must be acquired 30 days in advance of the sterilization. She, however, protests that such a policy will commit her to having more children and to more poverty, and she insists that she be sterilized.

Case E

A 38-year-old woman and her 38-year-old husband consult their family physician. They have been married for seven years and the woman had a hysterectomy at the age of 30 for cancer of the uterus. They want the physician to inseminate artificially the woman's best friend, age 33, with the husband's sperm. The friend has agreed to provide her services as a surrogate mother, and the couple have agreed to pay for the medical and hospital expenses associated with the pregnancy and delivery and to accept the child under all circumstances, even if the child has serious birth defects. Although there are no laws in the state precluding such activities, the physician is concerned about the morality of such an arrangement. The physician is of the opinion that the couple should not consider a biological link between the child and the father to be that important, and the couple should instead seek to adopt a child.

Under what circumstances may a physician express his or her views to a patient regarding what counts as responsible reproduction? How sure must the physician be that the view expressed does not represent a mere prejudice but is instead a well-founded judgment based on the regard for the best interests of the child or society? What are the moral limitations on a person's reproductive choices? Is there a moral right to reproduce if others must pay for the costs of raising that child? To what extent ought physicians, clinics, or societies establish policies that either encourage or discourage certain reproductive choices, or that would protect individuals from choices they might later regret, as, for example, in the case of the young student. Are there any reproductive choices or means for controlling reproduction that are intrinsically immoral?

2. NEW REPRODUCTIVE TECHNOLOGIES

It is a cliche that modern technology has transformed the lives of men and women. This has been no less true of sexuality and reproduction. As the last section indicated, effective contraception and sterilization procedures have separated the social and convivial dimensions of sexuality from the reproductive dimensions. But the separations have been more extensive. At least since the report of the Royal Society of London of the artificial insemination of a draper's wife in the eighteenth century, it has been possible to separate reproduction from sexual intercourse. Modern medical technology has increased the possibilities for this separation and for the direct control of the processes of reproduction. Research in this area began with a focus on transferring fertilized embryos from one animal to another. In 1890, Walter Heap, working in Cambridge, England, performed the first successful embryo transfer involving the embryos from an angora rabbit, which were placed into the oviduct of a Belgian hare. Finally, in 1959, after a number of disputed reports of in vitro fertilization and embryo transfer, M.C. Chang of the Worcester Foundation in Massachusetts documented a successful procedure.

These technologies not only have implications for animal husbandry but also provide a technique for the study of early human development. The fertilization of human ova in the laboratory and the observation of the development of human embryos under controlled circumstances offer a means for better understanding the effect of noxious agents on early embryos, the mechanisms by which chromosomal abnormalities are produced, and the processes of normal and abnormal cell growth and differentiation, including the development of hydatidiform moles. In addition to their implications for research in the basic sciences, these techniques have clinical significance. The procedures of removing ova from a woman whose oviducts are blocked, fertilizing the ova in the laboratory, and then transferring the embryo to her uterus offer a means for overcoming one of the major causes of sterility.

At least 250,000 reproductively active American women are sterile because of surgically irreversible pathology of their oviducts (fallopian tubes). Also, women who have been surgically sterilized by tubal ligation may wish again to become fertile and find that surgical repair is not possible. For such individuals, in vitro fertilization offers the only means to reproduce. The initial major locus of research was at Cambridge University, England, where on July 25, 1978, research conducted by Patrick Steptoe and Richard Edwards led to the birth of Louise Brown by in vitro fertilization and embryo transfer. Subsequently, in vitro fertilization clinics have developed throughout the United States and the world, reflecting a considerable demand by couples to have children of their own and a desire by women to experience a pregnancy leading to the birth of their child.

Although most of the cases have involved married couples where the wife seeks to have her ova fertilized by her husband's sperm, the procedure allows not only the use of donated sperm but also donated ova. As a result, a woman who is unable to ovulate but whose uterus is intact could receive an embryo produced from donated ova and her husband's sperm. Or, a woman who could ovulate but lacked a uterus could have the embryo produced from her ovum and her husband's sperm but carried by a surrogate mother. The effectiveness of an ovum donation can be maximized if the ovum is fertilized in vivo and then transferred to the woman (presumably the wife of an infertile couple) who will carry the embryo to term. A form of in vivo fertilization may also be used, to counter some of the objections of the Roman Catholic Church, by removing an ovum or ova from a woman whose oviducts are blocked and then placing it in the uterus and seeking fertilization through normal intercourse.

Despite this last conservative possibility, the implications are generally radical. These technologies not only make paternity uncertain but also maternity. One must distinguish between the mother as the donor of the ova used, versus the mother as the woman who carries the embryo to term. One can imagine circumstances under which woman A donates her ova to be fertilized by the sperm of man B, which will be implanted in the uterus of woman C in order to provide a child for a married couple D and E. Under such circumstances, who has the traditional rights of mothers and fathers regarding a fetus? Can a woman acting as a host-mother for an embryo, resulting from the sperm and ovum of the couple for whom she has contracted to bear the child, refuse to give up the child after birth? If fetal surgery must be performed, who ought to be consulted, and in what order? The question also arises of whether one should fertilize all ova that are harvested and whether those fertilized should all be implanted or only a few and the rest frozen. By freezing embryos, one can (1) avoid acquiring further ova for fertilization, should the first attempt be unsuccessful, and (2) forgo fertilizing and implanting all available ova in the hope of maximizing the chance for a successful implantation, despite the risk that this procedure will lead to the birth of triplets or other multiple births. The moral and legal implications are thus considerable.

In response to the moral and legal uncertainties raised by the prospect of in vitro fertilization and embryo transfer, the Secretary of the U.S. Department of Health, Education, and Welfare asked the Ethics Advisory Board in 1978 to consider the ethical, legal, and social aspects of these procedures. The board's report was published in the *Federal Register* on June 8, 1979. It included the following conclusions:

> The ethics advisory board finds that it is acceptable from an ethical standpoint to undertake research involving human in vitro fertilization and embryo transfer provided that:
>
> A. If the research involves human in vitro fertilization without embryo transfer, the following conditions are satisfied:

1. The research complies with all appropriate provisions of the regulations governing research with human subjects (45 CFR 46);

2. The Research is designed primarily: (a) to establish the safety and efficacy of embryo transfer and (b) to obtain important scientific information toward that end not reasonably attainable by other means;

3. Human gametes used in such research will be obtained exclusively from persons who have been informed of the nature and purpose of the research in which such materials will be used and have specifically consented to such use;

4. No embryos will be sustained in vitro beyond the stage normally associated with the completion of implantation (14 days after fertilization); and

5. All interested parties and the general public will be advised if evidence begins to show that the procedure entails risks of abnormal offspring higher than those associated with natural human reproduction.

B. In addition, if the research involves embryo transfer following in vitro fertilization, embryo transfer will be attempted only with gametes obtained from lawfully married couples.[3]

Despite the lapse of time and the further development of in vitro fertilization techniques in the United States, no final regulations have been issued. Certain states have regulations bearing on fetal research, which may have implications for basic science investigations with human embryos; however, no general national policy exists.

Numerous studies and reports have come from many sources. The "First Report by the National Health and Medical Research Council Working Party on Ethics in Medical Research" of Australia (August 1982); an interim report of the Committee to Consider the Social, Ethical and Legal Issues Arising from In Vitro Fertilization, Victoria, Australia (September 1982); "Human Fertilization and Embryology" by The Royal Society (March 1983, London); "In Vitro Fertilisation: Morality and Public Policy" issued by the Catholic Bishops' Joint Committee on Bio-Ethical Issues (March 1983, United Kingdom); and the "Report of the Committee of Inquiry into Human Fertilization and Embryology" (the "Warnock Report") by the Department of Health and Social Security (July 1984, London) are among the reports that have addressed these issues. The Warnock Report recommended a new statutory authority to license both research and infertility services, including not only in vitro fertilization and embryo transfer but also artificial insemination by donor. The report endorsed the clinical use of frozen embryos and would allow research on human in vitro embryos under licensing procedure. However, it would forbid maintaining an embryo beyond 14 days after fertilization.

This proliferation of reports reflects the uncertainties and moral problems raised by these reproductive technologies. First, what is the morality of experimenting on early embryos? The federal regulations concerning research on fetuses apply only to the product of conception, "from the time of implantation"

---

[3] *Federal Register* 44 (June 18, 1979), 35056.

(45 Code of Federal Regulations 46.203[c]) and therefore would appear not to govern work with zygotes and very early embryos. What form of permission from sperm and ova donors should be required to meet the criteria for free and informed consent? Which contributors to this book regard fetuses, zygotes, and early embryos as persons? When they are not persons, what sort of respect is due to them? Devine argues that "human beings who are not persons are entitled to a degree of respect because of their close association with persons." He holds that such entities should not be killed in the absence of very strong reasons, even when they have none of the capacities of persons. Should such reasoning apply so early in human gestation? Second, if one discards or otherwise does not implant a zygote or early embryo, does this count as an abortion? How, if at all, can one balance the rights of embryos and fetuses with those of persons wishing to use in vitro fertilization in order to reproduce? Do such entities have rights? Finally, does the non-natural character of in vitro fertilization raise any special moral issues? For example, in most cases sperm for the procedure must be procured through masturbation, which is forbidden by Roman Catholic moral theology. Does the separation of human procreation from expressions of conjugal and marital love threaten important values in our culture?

Case A

A scientist at a private in vitro fertilization clinic applies to a private foundation for funds in order to do basic research with early human embryos. The scientist wishes to study the genetic similarities between humans and other great apes by mixing human gametes with those from other primate species and then following the development of the embryo for at least 14 days. The scientist argues that this research will contribute to a better understanding of our relationship to other species of primates.

Case B

Physicians who are in charge of a university-based in vitro fertilization clinic wish to institute a policy of fertilizing all ova harvested from women participating in the program and freezing those ova not implanted in order to have them available for implantation should the first attempt fail or the couple wish to have further children. Should the frozen embryos not be used by the couple, the physicians propose making them available to couples where both partners are infertile, but where the woman is capable of bringing a fetus to term. If no one is able or willing to receive the embryos, they would then be discarded.

Case C

Mr. and Mrs. C are accepted by an in vitro fertilization clinic. Six ova are harvested from Mrs. C, three are implanted in Mrs. C, and the other three frozen. On the way back from the clinic, after implantation, Mr. and Mrs. C are killed in an automobile accident. The next of kin who would inherit in the event that Mr. and Mrs. C failed to have children ask to be declared heirs and have the remaining three frozen embryos discarded. However, three women volunteer to receive the embryos.

Case D

On an island in the West Indies, with the approval of the local government, a number of American entrepreneurs form "Offshore Embryos Unlimited." The corporation offers all-expense-paid, round-trip vacations plus $500 for college females who, after meeting rigorous physical requirements, agree to be inseminated and have the fertilized embryo lavaged from their uteruses and frozen, to be kept for sale. The corporation intends to market these embryos, underscoring the excellent genetic and physical background of both the ova and sperm donors. The embryos will be sold either for implantation or for research.

Case E

Mr. and Mrs. E contract with Miss F that she will bring to term an embryo produced by the Es' sperm and ova. After embryo transfer to Miss F, her mother dies and she begins to smoke and drink in a fashion that the Es find excessive. The Es ask her either to desist from this behavior, which is likely to be damaging to the child, or to secure an abortion. She refuses. The child is born prematurely and underweight for its gestational age, which the Es and their physician attribute to Miss F's excessive consumption of alcohol. The Es refuse to accept the child, arguing that Miss F failed in her contractual responsibility to be a responsible host-mother, and that they will not therefore accept a child who may have been damaged by Miss F's behavior.

What ought laws and regulations to say concerning each of these cases? Should the decision in Case A be left to the private funding agency, or should there be federal or state laws restricting what basic science research may be undertaken with zygotes and early embryos? What ought the character of such laws to be? What regulations, if any, should apply to frozen embryos? Is it a matter of prudence, so that individuals and clinics should ask donors of sperm and ova to determine what should be done with the products of conception? Should the decision be made by those who contract for the use of such sperm and ova? Should states provide for couples who die without having specified what should be done with the embryos they have frozen? To what extent ought embryos to be considered property under the contractual control of others or open to sale?

3. ABORTION

Although the Hippocratic Oath requires that "I will not give to a woman a pessary to cause abortion," abortions were widely performed in the ancient world. This tension between the Oath and actual practice stems in part from the fact that the Hippocratic Oath may have been written by a group of Pythagorean physicians and did not represent the general sentiments of physicians in the ancient world. In fact, Soranus of Ephesus (second century A.D.), in his textbook on gynecology, notes that the Hippocratic corpus includes suggestions on how to abort a fetus and that a great number of the physicians at the time, given proper indications, would perform an abortion. Abortion was also seen, at least by some, to be a part of reasonable public policy, as shown by Aristotle's recommendation of first-trimester abortions as a method of population control.[1]

Western public policy has been influenced by the fact that, from the beginning, Christians were opposed to both contraception and abortion, often failing to distinguish between the two. Many forms of contraception appear to have been interpreted by the early Christians as *abortifacients*. A Christian toleration of abortion in the Middle Ages developed through a reading of Exodus 21:22–23, which distinguishes punishment due for killing the fetus versus killing the woman:

> If men strive, and hurt a woman with child, so that her fruit depart from her, and yet no mischief follow: he shall be surely punished, according as the woman's husband will lay upon him; and he shall pay as the judges determine. And if any mischief follow, then thou shalt give life for life.

Medieval philosophers and theologians depended not on the original Hebrew text but on the Septuagint, a Greek translation made in Alexandria in the second century B.C., which distinguished between a formed and unformed (ensouled and unensouled) fetus. This distinction resonated with Aristotle's contention that animation of the human fetus occurred at 40 days for male fetuses and as late as 90 days for female fetuses.[2] Under the influence of Aristotle, St. Thomas Aquinas argued for a three-stage ensoulment, through which first the vegetative, then the animative, and finally the rational soul entered the fetus.[3] St. Thomas still held that early abortion was not the taking of the life of a person, although it was a seriously evil act similar to contraception.

This understanding became part of public policy. From the thirteenth century until 1869, except for a period between 1588 and 1591, canon law made a distinction between early and late abortions and provided the full punishment of murder only for the latter. In fact, the Jesuit Tomas Sanchez (1550–1610) argued that early abortions could be permitted to save the life of the mother and included circumstances such as when a girl feared that her father would severely beat her if he found her pregnant and unmarried. The distinction between ensouled and unensouled fetuses had its analogue in the traditional common law distinction between a *quickened* and *unquickened* fetus. Significant punishments for abortion were applied only after quickening. More stringent prohibitions of abortion developed through statutes passed in the nineteenth century. The British Parliament adopted a law in 1803 and Connecticut one in 1821. By 1860, 20 states and territories of the United States had statutes forbidding abortion at all stages of pregnancy, and by 1965 all 50 states forbade abortion during all stages of pregnancy. Most of the statutes provided for abortion only for therapeutic reasons, such as to save the life of the mother. However, the 1960s were marked by a growing interest in moderating such laws by allowing social reasons for

---

[1] Aristotle, *Politics* 7.16.15.

[2] *Historia Animalium* 7.3.583b.

[3] Thomas Aquinas, *Summa Theologica* I.118.2.

abortion, such as forcible rape or incest. In addition, states such as Arkansas, Colorado, Delaware, and Georgia revised their laws prior to 1970 to permit abortion on a number of grounds, including fetal deformity. The most dramatic change occurred with the Supreme Court rulings in *Roe v. Wade* and *Doe v. Bolton* on January 22, 1973, which established a constitutional right of women to access to abortion independently of medical or special social considerations.

The 1973 decisions held that there existed a constitutional right to privacy, which included a woman's right to decide, in consultation with her physician, whether to terminate her pregnancy. The Court held that, during the first trimester, there could be no state restrictions beyond requiring that those who performed abortions be physicians. However, in the second trimester, safety regulations such as the licensing of abortion clinics were allowable, and the state was permitted from the point of viability to forbid abortions except when they were undertaken on the basis of the woman's life or health. Subsequent court decisions further outlined the character of the right to procure an abortion by striking down requirements of spousal and/or parental consent (*Planned Parenthood of Central Missouri v. Danforth,* 1976; *Bellotti v. Baird,* 1979; and *City of Akron v. Akron Center for Reproductive Health Inc.,* 1983) except in the case of immature, unemancipated minors (*H.L. v. Matheson,* 1981).

Even though the courts have supported the right of access to abortion, they have not required federal or state support of abortion (*Williams v. Zbaraz,* 1980, and *Harris v. McRae,* 1980). Consequently, federal and state funds to pay for abortions for the indigent have been greatly restricted. Indeed, the funding of abortion and attempts to reverse the ruling of the Supreme Court, either through a constitutional amendment or through appointments to the Court, have become central elements of American politics. The political debate has had a markedly philosophical character. Those who oppose liberal abortion policies argue that embryos are persons from the moment of conception and that obligations to such persons preclude taking their lives for the mere convenience of the pregnant woman. Many pro-choice advocates argue either that human life is not the equivalent of human biological life or that obligations to intrauterine persons do not include being forced to bring them to term. The latter have argued that the obligation not to kill does not entail the obligation to be the host of a person in utero. Arguments of the first sort may grant that human life begins at conception but hold that such life becomes the life of a person only later.

Would the contributions to this volume by Devine and Sumner support the view that embryos must be respected from the moment of conception? According to Devine, even if zygotes and early embryos would not yet count as persons, they would still be protected by the potentiality and species principle. How strong should such protections be? Would zygotes and early embryos meet the level of sentience required by Sumner? Will such positions lead to forbidding not only abortion but also the use of intrauterine devices (IUDs), which may work by preventing the implantation of the early embryo? There are also utilitarian considerations, such as the avoiding of unwanted children and defective newborns, as well as the contrary consequentialist considerations that too easy access to abortion may blunt respect for defenseless life and for children. To what extent can positions such as Engelhardt's and Tooley's take into account such utilitarian considerations? What are the implications of intermediate positions such as Brody's for abortion policy?

Case A

A 14-year-old honor student from a strict Roman Catholic family who emigrated from Mexico ten years ago consults her mother's gynecologist and requests an abortion. The girl is in the upper 5 percent of her ninth-grade class and is highly motivated. She explains to the physician that a pregnancy would totally disrupt all of her plans and that she had not used contraception, given her family's religious views. She adds that she received no sex education and now understands the importance of her responsibility to avoid pregnancies in the future. She asks that her mother not be informed of the pregnancy. The physician is also a Roman Catholic and is strongly opposed to providing non-therapeutic abortion.

Case B

A 35-year-old lawyer who is pregnant for the first time consults her obstetrician. She wishes to have an abortion, explaining that she will come up for partner in her firm in the next four years and does not wish to have anything jeopardize this important step in her career. The time lost for a pregnancy and a delivery would mean that she could not continue with her full workload. This is her first marriage. For her 44-year-old husband of three years, this is his second marriage, his first marriage having ended when his wife and two children were killed in an automobile accident six years before. He insists that his wife not terminate the pregnancy, for he is afraid that there may not be another opportunity for her to conceive and carry a child to term.

Case C

A 40-year-old mother of four requests that her physician perform an amniocentesis to determine whether the child she is bearing has Down's syndrome (mongolism). She is a resident of a small rural town. An amniocentesis is performed at 16 weeks, the material is mailed to a laboratory in a distant city, and the physician waits for the report. After three weeks, it is determined that the sample has been lost and the patient is scheduled for a second amniocentesis. The report of the second amniocentesis is finally available two weeks later, when the patient is in the 21st week of her pregnancy. The report shows that the fetus does indeed have Down's syndrome. The patient requests that the physician use an abortion technique such as hypertonic saline in order to ensure that the fetus will be killed and not be born alive.

Case D

A 25-year-old theology student who is completing her doctoral dissertation on the influence of John of Leiden upon sixteenth-century Protestantism, finds that she is pregnant by a close friend, also a graduate student, who is completing his dissertation on seventh-century Sanskrit love poetry. Ms. D consults her physician, seeking an abortion. She explains that a pregnancy at this time would interrupt her graduate work and complicate that of her boyfriend, whom she expects eventually to marry. The nurse who is present while Ms. D is being examined by the physician believes she should interrupt Ms. D's conversation with the physician and ask Ms. D whether in all of her theological studies she has reflected on the notion of responsible sexual activity. The nurse believes that health professionals should raise such issues when they are likely to have a bearing on the need for further medical services (for example, repeat abortions).

What ought the physician in Case A to do? Would it be proper to refer the girl to a clinic that will provide abortion at a reduced cost? Since the physician is morally opposed to abortion, would such a referral be morally inappropriate? May the nurse add her opinions? Must she first ask the physician's permission? If the physician informs the nurse that she must either be quiet or quit, is that fair? Is it proper for a nurse or physician to lecture patients desiring an abortion about the morality of "proper" sexual behavior? What moral obligations, if any, does the woman in Case B have to her husband? What ought the physician to say to the woman? How directive ought any counseling to be? In Case C, is it proper to seek out the most effective means for killing a fetus, or is a woman only entitled to expel the fetus from her uterus? If arguments that fetuses are not persons succeed, then the matter of killing the fetus may be less serious than in the case where the argument for the permissibility of abortion turns on the limits of the duty of a woman to maintain a fetus in utero. The woman in Case D is within her legal rights to have an abortion for matters of convenience. But is she within her moral rights? What ought her physician to suggest, if anything?

4. GENETIC AND PRENATAL COUNSELING

The contemporary practices of genetic and prenatal counseling must be understood in terms of the moral issues explored in the previous three sets of case studies. Insofar as genetic counseling forms the basis for reproductive decisions, it presupposes, at least for most couples, access to effective contraception and sterilization. In many cases, it presumes the availability of abortion as well. The legal and public policy foundations were established for the freedom to choose when to reproduce or to carry a fetus to term. At the same time there arose major scientific and technological advances in the capacity to diagnose genetic diseases. Opportunity and knowledge were thus intertwined so as to make the screening both of carriers of genetic diseases and of embryos a feasible practice for both individuals and society. At present, approximately 100 genetic and chromosomal defects can be determined through amniocentesis, a process by which fluid is withdrawn from the amniotic sac within which the fetus lies, and which is usually carried out in the 15th to 17th gestational week. A new technique—biopsying the chorionic villi (a part of the fetal sac)—has allowed determinations in the late first trimester (8th to 10th week of gestation). Recombinant DNA techniques promise to extend the capacity to diagnose genetic defects through both amniocentesis and chorionic villus biopsy.

The ability to identify individuals carrying genetic diseases has also increased. This has led to the development of screening programs and to the provision of genetic counseling for couples considering reproduction. Individuals who are carriers of recessive genetic diseases and who are considering having a child can be informed that they risk a one-out-of-four chance of having an affected child. (The actual percentage may be somewhat lower because affected fetuses are eliminated through spontaneous abortions; in other cases, the disease may not fully express itself, even if the affected individual is homozygous for the trait, that is, has inherited it from both parents.) If one partner carries a dominant trait, the chance of an affected offspring will be one out of two, and if both carry a dominant trait, the odds are three out of four. In the case of sex-linked traits, women will be carriers and males who inherit the gene will tend to have the disease. One-half of the male offspring of carrier women will tend to be affected (the qualifications regarding recessive genes apply as well to dominant and sex-linked traits).

This combination of freedom and knowledge provides a new understanding of reproductive responsibilities. Because people today have easy access to contraception and abortion, children cease to be simply the gifts of God. They are even more the products of human choice, but here the choice is weighted with the consequences of reproducing when one has information indicating a good chance that a child will suffer from a disease. The choice to reproduce, as has already been noted in the case studies of decisions to reproduce, involves a third and unconsenting party, the child-to-be. Even if one holds, as do Engelhardt and Tooley, that fetuses are not persons, still, if one injures a fetus and does not abort the fetus, one will then injure the future person the fetus will become.

Genetic screening techniques do not have implications only for the decision to reproduce or to abort. They can also reveal information about carriers, which bear on the carrier's own health status. Genetic screening can indicate that an individual will be more susceptible to certain chemicals in the workplace. Indeed, over 50 major corporations have investigated the feasibility of genetic screening programs that could indicate which individuals are more likely to develop occupational diseases due to their inherited susceptibility to chemicals and other hazards in the work environment. Genetic information can disclose the likelihood of developing a serious and fatal disease later in life, such as Huntington's chorea. Newborn screening programs can also identify children as having inherited diseases for which early treatment may be crucial (for example, phenylketonuria, or PKU). Such information may affect an individual's chances for admission to professional school, employability, and insurability. Major issues of confidentiality and truth-telling are raised as well.

The availability of access to abortion and contraception, along with the possibility of acquiring information concerning the risks to possible future children, have led to suits on the part of both children and parents against physicians and others for not providing adequate or correct information for reproductive decision making. Parents have argued that, had they had sufficient information, they would either not have conceived the child or, had they conceived the child, they would not have brought it to term. Some individuals have been successful in such tort-for-wrongful-birth suits. Some children have also succeeded in tort-for-wrongful-life suits, where the allegation has been that the child was harmed by having been allowed to be born under such circumstancs. Even if the law does not recognize fetuses as persons, it can recognize that an injury to a fetus can lead to an injury to a future person, if the injury is not avoided by abortion. But what of detriments that are integral to the very conception of the fetus and the existence of the future person? Although awards have not set a value on existence itself, could that be done?

One such case, *Curlender v. Bio-Science Laboratories* (165 C 477 [Cal App 1980]), involved a child born with Tay-Sachs disease, an autosomal recessive disorder that is incurable. The disease leads to a decerebrate state, with death occurring usually before four years of age. The court not only awarded damages to the parents and to the child, but held that the child could have sued the parents, had the parents brought the child to term in the face of information concerning serious risks to the child. The possibility of recovery from parents was not sustained on appeal to the California Supreme Court in another case, *Turpin v. Sortini* (643 P2d 954 [Cal 1982]), and the state of California precluded such recovery by statute (Cal Civ Code §43.6). Still, the legal responsibility of physicians and other health care workers to give adequate and accurate advice remains intact. In addition, the moral issue raised with respect to parental obligations is a serious one.

Testing for carriers and for individuals affected with genetic diseases occurs under a number of circumstances. Many are voluntary programs, such as sickle cell testing that was established by Dupont at the request of black employees in 1972. In other cases, screening is standard practice or is mandated by law at birth. A number of states, for example, require all newborns to be tested for metabolic genetic diseases, which can seriously impair the development of the newborn.

Concerns regarding genetic screening and counseling led to the publication in 1983 of a report by the President's Commission for the Study of Ethical Problems in Medicine and Biomedical and Behavioral Research (*Screening and Counseling for Genetic Conditions: The Ethical, Social, and Legal Implications of Genetic Screening, Counseling, and Education Programs*). The report emphasizes the need to maintain confidentiality, to respect the autonomy of the individuals involved, to convey accurate and appropriate amounts of knowledge concerning genetic disorders, to protect the well-being of those influenced by screening programs, and to ensure equity in the development and operation of screening programs. In particular, the report notes that "Professionals should generally promote and protect patient choices to undergo genetic screening and counseling, although the use of amniocentesis for sex selection should be discouraged"[1] and that "Genetic information should not be given to unrelated third parties, such as insurers or employers, without the explicit and informed consent of the person screened or a surrogate for that person."[2]

Under what circumstances would programs of genetic screening and counseling, which incorporate prenatal diagnosis and amniocentesis, be acceptable to individuals such as Devine, Sumner, and Brody? Concerns with genetic screening raise the issue of the amount of defect or suffering that would defeat an obligation to bring a fetus to term either by appeal to the suffering of the child, the anticipated burden to the parents, or on the basis that the defect is so serious as to render the fetus something less than fully human (or precluded from ever becoming a person). What extent of suffering or defect should be a sufficient

---

[1]President's Commission, *Screening and Counseling for Genetic Conditions*, 1983, p. 6.
[2]Ibid, p. 6.

reason for aborting a fetus according to an analysis such as that offered by Devine? What would the position of Sumner and Brody be with respect to a fetus determined in utero to be anencephalic, that is, to have no brain? Can a position such as that advocated by Clements and Sider help one to discover biological norms that can guide individuals and public policy with respect to what traits should be avoided through genetic counseling? (Is color blindness a defect, the transmission of which should be avoided?) Should genetic counseling and selective abortion for defective fetuses be part of an adequate level of health care, as described by the President's Commission? Does the provision of such services have any special relationship with ensuring fair opportunity or equality in a society? How would one develop an account of the proper provision of services in these areas in terms of the arguments of Gutmann and Daniels? How do rights-oriented versus consequence-oriented moral analyses aid us in answering these questions?

Case A

Mr. and Mrs. A are a young couple in their twenties who met at a retinoblastoma (a dominant autosomal trait leading to cancer of the retina) awareness day held by a local hospital in a large metropolitan area. It was attended by affected individuals, their families, and other interested parties. Both Mr. and Mrs. A have each lost an eye to cancer. Mrs. A informs her family physician that she and her husband intend to have children, even though the odds are that three out of four children will inherit the trait and therefore be at high risk of developing cancer of the eye. The physician is disturbed by the proposal not only because of what it would mean for the A's children but because it means spreading a serious genetic disease in the gene pool.

Case B

A women's group in a large California city develops a television and newspaper campaign in an attempt to endow a women's clinic to provide amniocentesis and, if necessary, abortion for indigent women over 35. As the group emphasizes, the risk of a woman giving birth to a child with Down's syndrome increases with age and becomes approximately one out of 100 at age 40 and one out of 40 at age 45. A right-to-life group opposes the funding drive, arguing that such a program would constitute simply another attack on the poor and underprivileged. The women's group rejoins that the provision of such services is integral to equity and fairness.

Case C

A 43-year-old Atlanta man is diagnosed as having amyotrophic lateral sclerosis, or ALS, a motor neuron disease. A careful history reveals that the man's father and two uncles also developed the disease in their early forties. There appears to be additional evidence that the man's grandfather died of ALS as well. The neurologist concludes that the patient is suffering from a form of ALS that is transmitted as an autosomal dominant with nearly complete penetrance. The patient reveals that, about 20 years before, he lived in California, was married, and had one child by that union. Since then he has had little contact with the family. However, he knows that his one son, a product of that marriage, is now 21 and a premed student in the process of applying for medical school. The neurologist believes that the son should be informed that he has a fifty-fifty chance of developing ALS, most likely by the time he is in his late forties. The father insists that the son not be informed until he has been accepted to medical school. He does not want the son to have to make refer-

ence to this possible difficulty in his application form. In addition, he believes that the stress will affect his son's attitude and therefore his chance to be accepted to medical school. The son plans to be married within six months.

Case D

A large chemical company plans to introduce a test for glucose-6-phosphate dehydrogenase deficiency among its workers. This trait, which occurs in 10 percent of American black males and a higher percent of Mediterranean Jews, is associated with an occupational risk of a hemolytic crisis lead-

ing to anemia on exposure to certain chemicals such as naphthalene. No new workers with this trait will be hired, and current workers who have the trait will be transferred to jobs where there is little likelihood of exposure to such chemicals.

Do Mrs. and Mrs. A have a moral right to reproduce? What obligation do the As have to their future children? What role should the eugenic concern about the gene pool play, if any? How should the law respond, if at all? Should affected children who develop cancer of the eye be able to sue their parents for having been born with such a trait? Should such programs as those supported by the women's group be underwritten by public funds? Is the right-to-life group correct in its argument? What do equity and fairness require in such circumstances? The issue of confidentiality is explored further in a subsequent case study in this volume. In genetic counseling one finds special examples of the tension between the relationship of physician and patient, and the concern for third parties. When and how, if at all, should the physician inform the patient's son about his risk of developing amyotrophic lateral sclerosis? Does a company have a right to refuse to hire individuals who have an increased risk to workplace pollutants, or should such companies instead be required to control the amount of pollutants so that risks do not exist, even given a genetic predisposition to risk? Under what conditions may workers be transferred? What if the new jobs are not as interesting or pay less? In short, the very existence of new and more accurate knowledge about the genetic transmission of diseases and the predispositions to develop diseases raises difficulties for moral reasoning and public policy.

SECTION B

Perinatal Issues

5. FETAL TREATMENT

Advances in medical technology have made it possible not only to identify high-risk conceptions and fetuses affected by genetic and congenital disorders, but also to treat fetuses in utero. For the most part, such interventions are still largely experimental. However, they foreshadow an area of future interventions that will offer benefits both for fetuses and parents who hope to have healthy children. They raise as well a new area of conflict. The previous sections addressed moral problems involving decisions not to reproduce or to terminate a pregnancy. Here the difficulties are encountered when a woman does not wish to be subjected to the morbidity and low risk of mortality involved in treating the fetus in her uterus, even if it offers a possible benefit for the fetus. The physicians involved in such circumstances encounter a conflict between their commitment to two different patients who are, at least for the time being, biologically intertwined.

One finds repeated here an issue raised by the discussion of abortion: When and under what circumstances does a fetus become an entity to be respected and, in part at least, to be regarded as a patient? The question of the standing of the fetus, it should be noted, does not go away, given the Supreme Court rulings in *Roe v. Wade* and *Doe v. Bolton* (1973). As was indicated in the case studies concerning genetic and prenatal counseling, once a woman has decided not to discontinue a pregnancy, one then faces the issue of injuries to the future person the fetus may become. In fact, easy access to abortion may increase the moral obligation to make use of fetal surgery and other forms of fetal treatment if fetal deformities are diagnosed in time to terminate the pregnancy and the woman does not avail herself of that opportunity (a point that has been made by Prof. Judith Areen). One can argue that the woman had an opportunity to terminate the pregnancy, had she desired, and, failing to do so, she has committed herself to securing the life and health of the fetus. It will be necessary to determine limits to this obligation. How much of a risk to her life or inconvenience in terms of pain or suffering does a woman assume by foregoing an abortion when she learns that the fetus she carries has defects that are surgically correctable in utero?

The answers to such questions are unclear, in part because the technologies themselves are so new. It is only beginning to be possible to envision reliable surgical interventions on the behalf of the fetus outside of a very few institutions. As such interventions become more feasible, there will need to be a balancing among (1) traditional concerns to respect the rights of individuals (in this case the pregnant woman) to refuse bodily invasion, (2) emergent concerns to protect the persons fetuses will become, and (3) developing concepts of maternal responsibility to maximize the health of the fetus.

The case studies of the moral and legal issues raised by seeking a cesarean section against the wishes of the pregnant woman (see below) suggest similarities with the issue of fetal surgery. To what extent is the fetus, who may benefit from in utero treatment, analogous with the fetus who may benefit from being delivered by cesarean section? Both involve invasions of the mother's body.

On this point, policy statements, insofar as they exist, strike a balance in favor of the woman's right to free and informed consent and therefore of the right of refusal by the woman. The Council on Scientific Affairs of the American Medical Association, in addressing in utero fetal surgery,[1] applied the AMA's policy regarding fetal research to in utero fetal surgery.

> In fetal research primarily for treatment of the fetus: (A) Voluntary and informed consent, in writing, should be given by the gravid woman, acting in the best interest of the fetus. (B) Alternative treatment or methods of care, if any, should be carefully evaluated and fully explained. If simpler and safer treatment is available, it should be pursued.[2]

The AMA's approach to the issue suggests that its stance is predicated on the fact that the treatment is experimental. But what ought to happen once such surgical interventions can promise reliable benefits for the fetus with minimal risks to the mother? How ought law and public policy to respond to the conflicts that will surely emerge between the mother as the patient and the fetus as the patient? If the mother is seen to have an obligation to submit to treatment on behalf of the fetus, what becomes of the doctrine of free and informed consent, especially as developed in the excerpt from *Canterbury v. Spence* in this volume? Are woman simply to be informed regarding what will take place but not to be at liberty to consent or refuse? What balancing of benefits and risks should take place, and what should the physician's role be in deciding on the correct balance? What would need to be added to the views of the President's Commission, reprinted in this volume, with regard to the patient as decision-maker in order to come to terms with conflicts such as these? What are the implications of positions such as those of Engelhardt and Tooley for these questions, since neither holds fetuses to be persons? Remember—even if fetuses are not persons, they will

---

[1]Resolution 73[1–81], JAMA 250 (Sept. 16, 1983): 1443–1444.

[2]Current Opinions of the Judicial Council of the American Medical Association, 1984, section 2.09[8].

become persons if they are not aborted. How ought one to regard the rights of future persons? What are the consequences of having different policies regarding fetal treatment?

These concerns, which result from recent advances in technology, raise issues very similar to those already present through our current knowledge of the effects of the environment and the lifestyle of the pregnant woman on the health of her future child. In addition to the question of the ways in which the fetus may be treated in utero by medicine, there is also the question of the kind of treatment owed to the fetus by the woman. The questions of responsibility raised by in utero surgery must thus be seen within a broader context of responsibility of the pregnant woman to her future child.

Case A

A 25-year-old woman who works as a bartender is told by her physician that she is pregnant. The woman has been married for three years, has never been pregnant, and did not plan this pregnancy. She does not want an abortion, but she is angry about the pregnancy and the complications it will impose on her life and that of her husband, who plays in a local band. In taking a history, the physician finds that the woman smokes two packs of cigarettes a day and consumes the equivalent of four to five ounces of alcohol a day. He informs the woman that this lifestyle is likely to be injurious to the fetus. Smoking, the physician states, has been implicated in studies to be correlated with decreased birth weight, and that even smoking ten cigarettes per day is associated with perinatal death. Some follow-up studies of children born to smokers have shown an increase in deaths, hospital admissions, and physical and mental impairments. In addition, significant alcohol intake (even one to two ounces of alcohol per day) has been associated with a 10 percent to 20 percent instance of anomalies including growth retardation and mental deficiency. The woman states she is not concerned and that the fetus should be happy it is not being aborted. The physician, in frustration, consults the husband, who turns out to be a heavy smoker and drinker and adds to the history that the couple regularly uses marijuana and cocaine. The physician believes that this behavior is immoral because it exposes the future child to an avoidable set of serious risks, and the physician wants to consult a lawyer in an attempt to have the woman committed for the rest of the pregnancy.

Case B

Mrs. B is a 36-year-old mother of four who, during her last delivery, suffered a tear in the opening of the cervix. At that time, the physicians told her, should she want to have another child, she would need to have a "purse string" or cerclage operation, by which the cervix is sutured to give it sufficient structural strength so as to avoid a spontaneous abortion. Mrs. B declined, saying that she wished to have no further children and therefore did not need to have the operation. Two years later the woman's physician finds that Mrs. B is again pregnant. The physician recommends that the woman have a cerclage operation, and the husband concurs, insisting that he does not want the fetus to be aborted. The husband hopes it will be the son for whom he has long waited. The dispute continues into the fourth month of the pregnancy, at which point a sonogram shows that the fetus is a boy. The woman still refuses the cerclage operation, arguing that it is her right to have an abortion until the fetus is viable, and it should not concern anyone how she goes about getting it done, either by medical intervention or because of the structural weakness of her cervix.

Case C

Mr. and Mrs. C are in their thirties, having been married for ten years, before Mrs. C becomes pregnant for the first time. The marriage has for the most part been a good one, although it has been marred in the last three years by the fact that Mrs. C has converted to a religion that eschews the use of surgery. Mr. C is a conservative Jew who is very concerned that the child not only be born but born healthy. The Cs live in a large metropolitan area, and Mrs. C consents at least to medical monitoring of her pregnancy. Mrs. C's physician determines that the fetus she is carrying is suffering from congenital hydronephrosis, secondary to urethral obstruction, a blockage of the duct that passes urine from the bladder out of the body. The physician informs Mr. and Mrs. C that a team at the hospital has successfully intervened in cases such as this in six out of eight times attempted. The physician is convinced that without intervention the child will suffer serious irreversible damage to the kidneys. On the other hand, with the procedure the physician believes there is a 75 percent chance of assuring good kidney function. There appears to be no evidence of any other defects. The woman still refuses the surgery. The husband is frantic and wishes to consult a lawyer in order to force surgery through a court order.

> How ought the following conflicting concerns be balanced: (1) respect for the freedom of women to determine their own lifestyles and the integrity of their bodies and (2) regard for the health of the future child? Under what circumstances, if any, may governmental force be used to protect the best interest of the fetus? Does the answer depend in part on (1) how significant and (2) how certain the risk or benefit? What if the woman in Case A smoked only three or four cigarettes and had an occasional beer? Or in the case of Mr. and Mrs. C, would the answer be different if physicians had been successful in only two of the eight previous attempts to correct urethral obstruction in utero? To what extent does the issue of viability play a role? May one only intervene with a court order once the fetus is viable? Once again, concerns about the developing status of the fetus are important. The situation is complicated by the fact that a woman might claim that she will get a late second-trimester abortion, continue to harm the fetus or fail to get treatment for it, and then decide afterwards to bring the fetus to term.

6. ALTERNATIVE BIRTH SETTINGS

Generally, in traditional societies, women are delivered by other women and without the benefit of specialized medical care. Birth under such circumstances usually requires the active participation of the woman. Medical care has been introduced primarily by the problems associated with difficult births. In medieval Europe, though most deliveries were performed by midwives, special expertise from the medical profession was at times available where the birth was complicated and the patient could pay. Ibn Sina (980–1037), known as Avicenna in the West, describes the use of forceps. In the West, the use of the forceps were introduced by the Chamberlens, a family of obstetricians and surgeons. William Chamberlen, a Huguenot refugee, fled to England in 1569. His son Peter the Elder (1560–1631) was probably the inventor of the forceps that the family used as a secret device for a century. Peter the Elder aided the wives of James I and Charles I in childbirth, and Hugh Chamberlin assisted the wife of Charles II. Hugh Chamberlin also unsuccessfully attempted to sell the secret of the forceps to the French government for 10,000 thalers in 1670.

The technique of using forceps, along with developing medical knowledge, began to shape obstetrics as a medical specialty that would in time come to be distinguished from the techniques practiced by nonphysician midwives. For a while, however, the line between physician and nonphysician practitioners was unclear. For instance, Louise Bourgeois (1563–1636) functioned as accoucheuse (midwife) to the French court and wrote three important treatises. However, from the eighteenth century on, physicians assumed the functions once held by midwives alone. During the process, women became ever more the passive recipients of medical care—patients—and pregnancy became a sort of disease to be treated by anesthesia, episiotomies, and careful medical management.

The result was the "medicalization" of childbirth. As a result, by the mid–twentieth-century in America, few women delivered at home or without benefit of medical assistance. Midwives were employed for the most part by the poor in rural areas, where traditional medical care was not available. Most children were delivered in the antiseptic environment of hospitals, which were geared to respond to the complications of labor and delivery that had cost the lives of women in childbirth in the past.

A revolution in attitudes took place during the 1960s and 1970s, when fathers wished to be present at the birth of their children and women began to voice objections to the controlled and sterile atmosphere of most delivery units. Various groups also argued that natural forms of childbirth were to be preferred because of the psychological and physical benefits they conferred on the mother and the child. In short, a constellation of forces, including growing notions of (1) individual rights, (2) women's rights, (3) the rights of fathers, (4) a desire to have birth as a social experience for the family, and (5) arguments about the benefits of natural childbirth, led to a rejection of the usual and customary medical approach to childbirth. These ideas combined with the concept of natural childbirth, which had been developed in the 1940s by Grantly Dick-Read, a British obstetrician. His approach to natural childbirth minimized the use of surgery and anesthesia and concentrated on recruiting the mother's cooperation in the process of childbirth. Dick-Read postulated that fear causes tension, which causes pain, which can then retard the process of the delivery and increase the discomfort associated with it. His approach, as well as those of the Lamaze and Leboyer methods, emphasizes preparation on the part of both the mother and the father for the delivery. The Leboyer method stresses the importance of bonding and recommends that the mother at once cuddle, stroke, and nurse the infant.

The result was not only the restructuring of labor and delivery units to incorporate labor rooms where family members could be present—and delivery rooms where fathers were allowed entry—but also to a demand that childbirth occur in as natural a setting and circumstance as possible. Various groups developed programs in which prospective fathers and mothers prepared for a delivery where a minimal amount of anesthesia would be used and where there would be maximum participation by the father. This led to a demand on the part of some that childbirth again take place in the home where the event could be a part of the life of the family. The disinclination of obstetricians to participate under such circumstances, coupled with independent forces within nursing, led to a rebirth of the profession of midwifery.

In response to these concerns, numerous states began licensing nurse-midwives in significant numbers. In addition, programs in nursing and medical schools were established for the training of midwives. With this rebirth of the profession of nonphysician midwives, the medical profession has voiced concern that pregnant women who are likely to face serious medical complications may not receive sufficient or timely care if they are delivered in the home or in other nontraditional settings. These concerns also address the welfare of future children who might not be able to receive emergency care, should it be needed.

The issue of alternative birth settings thus raises issues similar to those raised in the case studies regarding fetal treatment and cesarean sections: To what extent may women choose in ways that do not maximize the health prospects of their future children or which do so in non-traditional ways? May women choose to be delivered at home, even though that will deprive their future infants of medical support, should it be needed, in order to achieve the goal of a more satisfying birth process for themselves and their husbands? Is it proper for a woman to value the ways in which she will bond with the child at home over the possible needed contributions of emergency hospital services for her child?

Fundamental philosophical issues are raised here regarding the status of children and their relationship with their parents. To what extent may parents expose their children to risk in order to achieve goals of their own or special values embraced by a family? Locke, in the reading contained in this volume, argues that "The power, then, that parents have over their children arises from that duty which is incumbent on them, to take care of their offspring during the imperfect state of childhood." Are choices of alternative birth settings compatible with this duty? The issues raised here are similar to those raised in the section concerning fetal treatment, because in consenting to a form of treatment, the mother exposes the child to risk. To what extent may women decline medical advice that urges childbirth take place in a hospital? Here again one may see limitations on the doctrine of free and informed consent as it is presented in the readings in this volume.

The issue can be approached in a different way. To what extent do the disputes regarding alternative birthing settings reflect professional competition between physicians and nonphysician midwives? To what extent do the appeals of physicians to possible risks to the mother and the infant mask an interest on the part of physicians to maintain control of an area of health care? The development of nurse-midwives offers a case study of the attempt to create a new, or reestablish an old, autonomous health profession. What are the implications of the article by Costello, Engelhardt, and Gardell for this issue?

The questions here also turn on who should determine the proper ranking of best interests and harms for others. Thus, the question of paternalism and individual autonomy is joined. What is the proper role for medical and societal paternalism in restricting the freedom to choose alternative birth settings, when such a choice would entail significant risks to either the woman or the infant? How much of a risk must be at stake to override the choice of women to use an alternative birth setting? How does one balance the rights of women with those of the children who will be born? How ought one to compare the consequences of different policies regarding access to alternative forms of birthing?

Case A

Mr. and Mrs. A are in their early thirties and already have two children, who were delivered in a Boston hospital with Mr. A present. Although neither parent participated in Lamaze classes, they both found it rewarding to share the experience together. In the seventh month of her third pregnancy, Mr. A was transferred by his electronics company to a small southwest college town. The As were very pleased with the transfer because it allowed them to live outside of town in a rural village. They made arrangements with a physician there to have their child delivered in that small town's hospital.

With all of the turmoil of the move, they did not explore issues further. When labor began and Mr. A brought Mrs. A to the hospital, he was informed that he should remain in the waiting room. There was no provision at the hospital for husbands to be present during labor, much less be in the delivery room. The As were aghast, and Mrs. A at once requested a transfer to the hospital in the nearby college town. The hospital where she had been admitted refused, on the basis that delivery was imminent and transfer could not be made safely.

Case B

Mr. and Mrs. B, who are 28 and 26, respectively, moved from West Virginia to a southwest oil town, where Mr. B, up until two years ago, was employed by an offshore drilling company. After being laid off, the Bs have been employed in various low-paying jobs and have no medical insurance. They have a significant equity in their home and own two cars, which disqualifies them from receiving care through the local charity hospital. In addition, they find the hospital dirty and unacceptable. On the other hand, they do not have the funds available to pay for a

physician or hospital care. Mrs. B's mother, who is back in West Virginia, volunteers to come out and help her deliver the child. She has had some experience working as an amateur midwife, and she argues that Mrs. B is in good health, her first delivery was quick and without complication, and there is no reason to suspect that Mrs. B will not be able to give birth without complications. Mrs. B sees no reason why her daughter should be forced to deliver her child in a hospital. She adds that Mrs. B was in fact delivered at home, as was she.

Case C

Mrs. C is a 25-year-old prima gravida who has been a diabetic since the age of 12. Her husband also worked for the oil exploration firm that employed Mr. B. Mr. C has been laid off and the Cs are in financial circumstances similar to the Bs. Emboldened by the example of the Bs, they decide to deliver at home as well. Initially, they have consider-

able difficulty in finding a midwife willing to accept the case, because most are concerned with the problem of managing Mrs. C's diabetes, and also because they recognize that there is increased neonatal morbidity and mortality associated with an ill-managed delivery of a diabetic mother. For example, infants of diabetic mothers may suffer from hypoglycemia, which can lead to death. Mr. and Mrs. C say they are willing to accept such risks. They point out that, after all, they are no more than 20 minutes from a good hospital.

Do hospitals have the right to exclude fathers, as in the case of Mr. A? What if the exclusion is based on inadequate space in the labor rooms? What would be proper grounds for such a policy? What of couples B and C? What amount of risk to the fetus can override the right of parents to determine the circumstance under which their children will be born? What if B's and C's choices had not been based on financial need, but on a commitment to delivery in the home? At present there are no clear guidelines to resolve such issues. Should there be public policies that would require the use of force to constrain women to deliver in hospitals when a home delivery would constitute a risk to the infant?

7. CESAREAN SECTIONS

The term *cesarean section* is improperly held to be derived from Julius Caesar's delivery from his mother's womb through an abdominal incision. Instead, the term may be derived from the *lex caesarea,* a decree held to have been made by Numa Pompilius (715–673 B.C.), which continued to the time of the Caesars and required that the fetus be removed from any woman dying in late pregnancy. Alternatively, it may simply be derived from the past participle, *caesum,* of the verb to cut, *caedere.* In any event, this procedure has been practiced on dead pregnant women from very ancient times. It is recorded as a procedure in the Sanskrit medical text, *Sushruta Samhita,* which dates from before the fourth century B.C. Requirements similar to those of ancient Rome were enacted in Renaissance Europe: A 1608 decree of the Venice senate required all physicians to perform a cesarean section when a woman died late in pregnancy.

Beginning in the sixteenth century, cesarean sections were at times attempted on living women, in the hope of saving both the mother and the infant. In the early half of the nineteenth century, the mortality rate from this procedure was about 50 percent. The development of new techniques at the end of the nineteenth century led to significant improvements in mortality rates. By the beginning of the twentieth century, with advances in both surgery and antisepsis, maternal morbidity was about 3 percent, and 95 percent of the infants were born healthy. In short, the procedure ceased to be a heroic medical intervention of extraordinary proportions and became part of the usual and customary means for maximizing the health and well-being of both the mother and the child.

Cesarean sections now have become a frequent occurrence, increasing from about 5 percent of all deliveries in the late 1960s to about 15 percent of all deliveries in the mid-1980s. Cesarean sections are performed not only for such indications as cephalopelvic disproportion, placenta previa, and a previous cesarean section (because a cesarean section weakens the walls of the uterus), but also for fetal distress, malposition, and malpresentation. The maternal morbidity rates associated with cesarean section range from about 4 to 8 per 10,000, and in one study the risk of death from a cesarean section was found to be 26 times greater than that associated with a vaginal delivery. Outside of cases of significant fetal difficulties, it is disputed whether the current level of cesarean sections conveys a benefit on either the fetus or the woman. However, one author even suggests that all pregnant women be offered the opportunity of having a cesarean section in order to minimize risks to their child.

The problems of conflict between mother and fetus already explored in the case studies of genetic counseling, fetal treatment, and alternative birth settings repeat themselves here. The difference is that the conflict more frequently takes place in a hospital setting where the woman is more readily placed under the control of both physicians and the court. Individuals may more easily gather data and ask for an injunction to require women to submit to a cesarean section. In addition, cesarean sections, unlike fetal surgery, are not experimental. As a result, a plausible argument may be made for intervening to save the life of the mother and of the fetus.

Recent American case law has provided a number of interventions to protect the life of both the mother and the fetus. Most of these have not involved a court of record. However, in 1981 the Georgia Supreme Court, in *Jefferson v. Griffin Spalding County Hospital Authority* (274 SE2d 457), required that a woman with placenta previa (that is, the placenta is implanted in the lower uterine segment in the area where the fetus would pass through the cervix) in the 39th week of her pregnancy submit to a cesarean section, despite her refusal on religious grounds. The decision of the court was made on the basis of information indicating that, without a cesarean section, the fetus stood a 99 percent chance of dying and the woman a 50 percent chance. Although the woman in fact successfully delivered vaginally, the case underscored the willingness of physicians and hospitals to go to court and of the courts to grant requests for a cesarean section over the protest of the woman involved.

Given the frequency with which cesarean sections are performed, these decisions raise a considerable moral and public policy issue with regard to the circumstances under which women are at liberty to give free and informed consent to, and therefore also to refuse, cesarean sections. Again, one must ask how certain one must be of what level of danger to the fetus that may be avoided through a cesarean section so as to justify overriding the wishes of the woman. One finds here a development in technology that is restricting the ability of women to choose the circumstances under which they will deliver a child. Developments here conflict with those associated with the alternative birthing movements discussed in the previous set of case studies. One is forced once more to explore the issue of whether the failure to terminate a pregnancy commits a woman to employing all means necessary to secure the health of the child the fetus will become.

As in the other sections involving choices by women affecting their fetuses, issues are involved regarding the status of fetuses and the liberty of women to consent to or refuse treatment. One must recognize that even individuals such as Engelhardt and Tooley, who argue that fetuses are not persons, still may recognize that choices affecting fetuses can harm the persons such fetuses may become. Here also the selections from *Canterbury v. Spence* and the President's Commission regarding the patient as decision-maker must be reconsidered when a third party, namely the future child, is so intimately involved. How ought one to balance conflicting rights and assess consequences in order to determine the proper policy with regard to the use of cesarean sections?

Case A

Miss A, a 15-year-old pregnant girl, after much consideration, decides not to have an abortion but instead to bring the pregnancy to term and give the child up for adoption. As the pregnancy has continued, it has become very important for her to have the pregnancy over and to return to her high school studies, where she was in the upper fourth of her class. She wishes as soon as possible to forget the entire incident completely. However, in the 26th week of gestation, labor begins and the amniotic sac ruptures. Because the fetus must be delivered at this juncture and because of its prematurity, a cesarean section is recommended. Miss A absolutely refuses. She does not want the scar to remind her of her pregnancy, and she argues that she would have had an abortion had she known that anything like this would take place. The fetus should be grateful for being born at all, the girl reasons, and she should not be obliged to suffer further to maximize its chances. The physicians are unclear as to the proper course. One physician argues that the girl appears to be dilating well and that a vaginal delivery may be possible without too much risk to the fetus. Two other physicians disagree. They wonder whether they should consult the hospital lawyer and/or a court. The girl pleads for them simply to attempt a vaginal delivery.

Case B

Ms. B, a 30-year-old unmarried mother of one, is admitted to the hospital in the 39th week of her pregnancy. The membranes had ruptured about three hours before she came to the hospital. The amniotic fluid was found to be meconium stained, the fetal heart rate was increased and fluctuation in the heart rhythm was absent, all indicating fetal distress. A cesarean section was indicated. However, the woman refused. When asked why, she explained that surgery was too much of a hassle and she did not really care what happened to the child. The physicians involved in her care want to obtain a court order to require her to submit to a cesarean section.

Case C

Mrs. C is the mother of three children, all delivered by cesarean section. During the last birth, she nearly suffered a rupture of her uterus prior to delivery. Her physician warned her that future pregnancies would present a risk to her and that she would surely need to have a cesarean section for all future deliveries. Pregnant once again, she is admitted to the hospital in the 40th week of her pregnancy in the first stages of labor. She is somewhat agitated, belligerent, and uncooperative. When informed that she will again need a cesarean section, she refuses. It is explained to her that without the procedure she will run a very high risk of death, as will the fetus. She still refuses. The physicians involved are not convinced that she is competent, given her belligerent behavior. However, they do not have a medical or psychiatric explanation for the behavior. Her husband insists that she be given a cesarean section. He adds that she is acting peculiarly and he, too, cannot explain it. The physicians and the husband wish to obtain a court order to require her to submit to a cesarean section.

Should Miss A's wishes be respected? Some might think that her young age and the fact that she decided to go through with the pregnancy bolster her right to refuse a cesarean section, especially when it is not clear that the infant will die or be seriously harmed without the section. How much of a risk of death or injury to the child would need to exist before she would be required to submit to surgery? One must bear in mind that the surgery involves not only the issue of the scar but also that it poses an increased risk to the girl over that of a vaginal delivery. Do matters change in the case of Ms. B because she is older and she advances less of a considered argument for why she should be allowed to refuse a cesarean section? The case of Mr. and Mrs. C is complicated, as are many actual medical cases. Not only is there the issue of Mrs. C's right to refuse treatment, but one has also to consider the husband's wishes, Mrs. C's possible incompetence, and the risk that the refusal poses for her. Should one's judgment of the case change if the husband agrees with his wife and it is clear that the woman is, in fact, competently refusing surgical intervention? What if the risk to Mrs. C is less significant?

One must assess the issue of forced cesarean section not only in terms of individual women and their fetuses but also in terms of the rights of women to make decisions regarding themselves during pregnancy. The advent of relatively safe cesarean sections and the recognition of very liberal indications for the performance of cesarean sections have dramatic implications for the rights of pregnant women. Because nearly all activities of women carry some risk for their fetuses, how all-encompassing should the control of the lives of pregnant women become?

8. DEFECTIVE NEWBORNS

In many ancient cultures, deformed infants were allowed to die. Even Aristotle in his *Politics* recommended that there be a law that no *deformed* child shall live. The Greek physician Sextus Empiricus wrote, "Solon gave the Athenians the law 'concerning things immune' by which he allowed each man to slay his own child. . . ."[1] So, too, Table IV of the ancient Roman Twelve Tables (circa 450 B.C.) gave the father similar prerogatives. Cicero remarked in his *De Legibus,* "A dreadfully deformed child ought to be killed quickly, as the Twelve Tables ordain."[2] The Romans made their choices on the basis of quality-of-life and cost considerations. They did not possess a notion of the sanctity of life.

The Judeo-Christian tradition introduced a notion of the sanctity of life into public policy and attempted with some success to suppress infanticide, although midwives and others often did not give full attention to children with severe anomalies or with little promise of thriving. This traditional problem of deciding when to treat a deformed or defective child or when to let it die becomes acute in modern societies with advanced medical technology. The use of such technology can involve not only considerable cost but can also preserve the lives of infants with severe physical and mental handicaps, who would otherwise have died in the past. When these technologies developed in the 1960s and 1970s, there grew a widespread acceptance of the notion that parents, in consultation with their physician, should have the right to decide whether or not to treat such children. Raymond S. Duff, M.D., and A.G.M. Campbell, M.B., re-

---

[1] *Outlines of Pyrrhonism*, III. 211.
[2] Cicero, *De Legibus*, III, 8, 19.

ported in the October 25, 1973, *New England Journal of Medicine* that of the 299 consecutive deaths occurring in a special-care nursery, 43 (14 percent) were related to withholding treatment. Articles reviewing such cases were published with the view to suggesting which children should be treated and which should not, on the basis of the future quality of life and productive capacities of the child. Research was also undertaken—such as that by John Lorber, who reviewed 524 cases of myelomeningocele (the hernial protrusion of part of the spinal cord and its covering through a defect in the vertebral column)—in order to provide possible selection criteria for treatment. The view of many writers was that it was not enough to save life, but that it was necessary to determine with as much accuracy as possible whether that life was worth saving. An attempt was made to balance the notions of the quality and the sanctity of life.

The character of current regulations and controversies was shaped by the birth in April 1982 in Bloomington, Indiana, of a baby known as Infant Doe. The child suffered from Down's syndrome complicated by esophageal atresia (that is, there was no passage from the mouth to the stomach), and tracheal esophageal fistula (a connection between the windpipe and the gullet). There was a suggestion that the child also suffered from cardiovascular and perhaps intestinal problems. The parents refused surgery, and their right to do so was upheld by the Indiana Supreme Court in an informal hearing. In response to this case, President Ronald Reagan instructed Richard Schweiker, then-Secretary of the Department of Health and Human Services (DHHS), to notify healthcare providers that Section 504 of the 1973 Rehabilitation Act "forbids recipients of Federal funds from withholding from handicapped citizens, simply because they are handicapped, any benefit or services that would ordinarily be provided to persons without handicaps." As a result, the DHHS issued a "Notice to Health Care Providers" on May 18, 1982, informing American hospitals that they risked losing federal funds if they withheld treatment or nourishment from handicapped infants. Formal regulations were published in the *Federal Register* on March 7, 1983, providing for a toll-free number for individuals anonymously and confidentially to report possible violations. Federal teams (so-called Baby Doe squads) were available to investigate such allegations. These regulations were overturned by a federal court on technical grounds, and newly proposed regulations were published in the *Federal Register* on July 5, 1983; finally, on January 12, 1984, regulations were implemented. These were challenged in court, which led to a new law and final regulation on April 15, 1985. The result has been a conflict between a view on one part of the medical profession, which allows parents to refuse treatment for children with severe mental and physical handicaps, and a governmental policy supported by other parts of the medical profession that has as its goal the elimination of quality-of-life judgments leading to selective nontreatment.

Consider the following three policy statements. The first is from the *Current Opinions of the Judicial Council of the American Medical Association—1984:*

> Quality of life: In the making of decisions for the treatment of seriously deformed newborns or persons who are severely deteriorated victims of injury, illness or advanced age, the primary consideration should be what is best for the individual patient and not the avoidance of a burden to the family or to society. Quality of life is a factor to be considered in determining what is best for the individual. Life

should be cherished despite disabilities and handicaps, except when the prolongation would be inhumane and unconscionable. Under these circumstances, withholding or removing life-supporting means is ethical provided that the normal care given an individual who is ill is not discontinued.[3]

In contrast with the AMA's endorsement of quality-of-life choices, the American Academy of Pediatrics, in its Joint Policy Statement, "Principles of Treatment of Disabled Infants," categorically rejects such considerations:

> When medical care is clearly beneficial, it should always be provided. When appropriate medical care is not available, arrangements should be made to transfer the infant to an appropriate medical facility. Considerations such as anticipated or actual limited potential of an individual and present or future lack of available community resources are irrelevant and must not determine the decisions concerning medical care. The individual's medical condition should be the sole focus of the decision. These are very strict standards.[4]

This view of the American Academy of Pediatrics approximates that of the January 12, 1984, federal regulations, which allow the non-treatment of newborns who are unlikely to survive but forbid non-treatment on the basis of quality-of-life considerations. The federal regulation states:

> (i) Withholding of medically beneficial surgery to correct an intestinal obstruction in an infant with Down's syndrome when the withholding is based upon the anticipated future mental retardation of the infant and there are no medical contraindications to the surgery that would otherwise justify withholding the surgery would constitute a discriminatory act, violative of section 504.
> (ii) Withholding of treatment for medically correctable physical anomalies in children born with spina bifida when such denial is based on anticipated mental impairment, paralysis, or incontinence of the infant, rather than on reasonable medical judgments that treatment would be futile, too unlikely of success given complications in the particular case, or otherwise not of medical benefit to the infant, would constitute a discriminatory act, violative of section 504.
> (iii) Withholding of medical treatment for an infant born with anencephaly, who will inevitably die within a short period of time, would not constitute a discriminatory act because the treatment would be futile and do no more than temporarily prolong the act of dying.
> (iv) Withholding of certain potential treatments from a severely premature and low birth weight infant on the grounds of reasonable medical judgments concerning the improbability of success or risks of potential harm to the infant would not violate section 504.[5]

Because of court challenges, the Congress passed and on October 9, 1984, President Reagan signed into law, amendments to the Child Abuse Prevention and Treatment Act, which provided that withholding medically indicated treatment would constitute child abuse to be prevented by the states. Withholding treatment was to be understood as the following:

---

[3]Current Opinions of the Judicial Council of the American Medical Association—1984, 2, 14.
[4]*Pediatrics* 73 (April 4, 1984), 559.
[5]*Federal Register* 49 (January 12, 1984), 1654.

. . . the failure to respond to the infant's life-threatening conditions by providing treatment (including appropriate nutrition, hydration, and medication), which, in the treating physician's or physicians' reasonable medical judgment, will be more likely to be effective in ameliorating or correcting all such conditions, except that the term does not include the failure to provide treatment (other than appropriate nutrition, hydration, or medication) to an infant when, in the treating physician's or physicians' reasonable medical judgment, (a) the infant is chronically and irreversibly comatose; (b) the provision of such treatment would (i) merely prolong dying, (ii) not be effective in ameliorating or correcting all of the infant's life-threatening conditions, or (iii) otherwise be futile in terms of the survival of the infant; or (c) the provision of such treatment would be virtually futile in terms of the survival of the infant and the treatment itself under such circumstances would be inhumane. [Public Law 98–457]

Final regulations were issued by the Department of Health and Human Services on the basis of this law on April 15, 1985.[6]

These controversies turn on major philosophical and ethical questions. If newborns are not persons in a strict sense, as Tooley and Engelhardt argue, why is it not permissible to stop treatment as did the Greeks and Romans? If they are persons, as Devine, Sumner and Brody argue, why should it be permissible? Is it because some qualities of life would be so dim as to constitute an injury to the child, as Engelhardt contends? Would a believer in the sanctity of life accept such a claim? Are there any limits on the duty of beneficence to treat deformed children other than futility? If the costs are very high, can such duties be defeated? What do such cases say about the President's Commission's concept of an adequate level of health care? Would Gibbard and Daniels see these forms of health care as required under the right to health care? Should individual physicians be concerned with this question of cost, as Brody argues, or should they not, as the policy statements assert and as Fried argues? And what of parental integrity? Would Locke allow parents to decide to withhold care in such cases? If so, must parents be put in the position of showing that their decision not to treat is justified, or must the burden be borne by the state? Moreover, what information ought to be provided to parents as informed decision-makers under the *Canterbury* ruling? And if the state orders treatment against parental wishes, ought the state to sustain all costs?

Case A

A 25-year-old mother of two children gives birth in an outlying hospital to a premature infant, weight 600 grams, in approximately the 26th week of gestation. The hospital, which does not have facilities to care for such a premature infant, transfers the child by ambulance to the closest neonatal intensive care unit. On the second day after arrival the child is found to suffer from severe intracranial hemorrhage. Though it appears possible to save the child's life with considerable cost, the child is likely to suffer from cerebral palsy, severe mental deficiency, convulsions, and hydrocephalus (accumulation of fluid in the cranial vault). The parents wish to discontinue all treatment, in part because of the child's dim future promise and in part because of the cost they must sustain, which would bankrupt the family.

---

[6]*Federal Register* 50 (April 15, 1985), 14878–14901.

Case B

A couple in their early thirties return home with their first child, who appears to be normal. On the 14th day after delivery, the infant develops lesions similar to chicken pox, which are diagnosed on the 16th day as herpes. By the time the child is admitted to the hospital, it has developed herpes encephalitis with seizures, difficulty in breathing, and a slowed heart rate. The physicians inform the parents that, although the child could likely be saved, it would probably be severely mentally retarded (an IQ lower than 50), would suffer from seizures and spasticity, and would need long-term institutional care. The physicians recommend that treatment should be discontinued but the parents believe that life must be saved at all cost. All costs of treatment will be borne by Medicaid and the local county hospital budget.

Case C

Baby Jane Doe was born in October 1983, in Port Jefferson, New York, with multiple birth defects, including hydrocephalus, microcephaly (an abnormally small head), and myelomeningocele. The parents initially chose not to perform surgery that might prolong the child's life and protect it against other disabling conditions in order to avoid the risks of surgical treatment, including increasing the weakness of the child's lower extremities. The federal government attempted to intervene to force surgical treatment.

What would the authors of each of the policy statements say about what should be done in each of these cases? Whom would they have making the decisions in each case? In light of the implications of the policy statements for these cases, what do you think about the merit of the statements? About their theoretical backing?

Ought the wishes of the parents in Case A be respected? Is your answer influenced by the fact that they are considering the quality of the life and the costs to them of the treatment? Are the parents in Case B correct in supposing that considerations of sanctity of life require treatment? Is society required to sustain the long-term cost of that treatment? Should treatment continue if the child's condition worsens and its chance for survival lessens? When does it become so futile that the parents' wishes could be disregarded? Is this the concept of futility presupposed by the DHHS regulations? In Case C, do the parents have the right to choose a conservative medical treatment, at some risk to the child's survival, in order to increase its quality of life? Should such choices be made instead by courts, by governmental regulatory authorities, or by ethics committees?

9.   TRIAGE IN THE NEONATAL INTENSIVE CARE UNIT (NNICU)

Ever since the early 1960s, special nurseries have developed for the purpose of coordinating high-intensity care of newborn infants (neonates) born with severe disorders. Such nurseries employ specially trained physicians and nurses, have a very low staff-to-patient ratio (sometimes approaching 1:1), and have available a wide variety of advanced monitoring and therapeutic equipment.

It has been extensively documented that the existence of such units significantly reduce (up to 50 percent) infant mortality rates for very sick neonates. Admission of neonates to these units is therefore of great significance, and the inability to secure a place would be for many a sentence of death. For this reason, physicians managing such newborns will insist upon admitting them to such a unit.

All of this progress comes at great expense. A 1981 study showed a national expenditure of $1.5 billion on neonatal intensive care. This represents both a significant number of admissions and a very high daily cost for each patient admitted. Thus, powerful economic reasons exist for limiting both the number of such units and the number of patients admitted. As a result, cases often arise in which neonates would benefit from admission to such a unit, but there seems to be no place available in many of the nearby neonatal intensive care units (NNICU). The cases in this section raise the issue of what should be done in those circumstances.

It is sometimes suggested that we think of such cases as being analogous to the types of problems that often arise in wartime where military medical staff confront more casualties than they can manage and must choose whom to care for and whom not to care for. This problem was first explicitly introduced by Baron Dominique Jean Larrey, Napoleon's chief medical officer, who first sorted patients out and insisted that the more seriously ill receive care before the less seriously ill. Similar but more complicated schemes were introduced during the American Civil War, the First World War, and the Second World War. By then, it had become clear that there were really three major categories of patients: the slightly injured, who could be treated quickly or whose treatment could be postponed until later; the very badly wounded, who would probably not survive and whose treatment needed to be deferred even if it meant that they would certainly die; and the seriously wounded, who had a good chance of responding to treatment and whose extensive care should get the highest priority. Those who draw this analogy suggest that neonatologists employ a similar scheme.

Many questions are raised by such a suggestion. The first is the question of the responsibility of providers discussed by Fried and Brody in Section C9 of the readings. Can an individual provider responsible for the care of an individual patient accept such a *triaging* scheme, in the name of justice, even if that means neglecting the best interests of one's own patient, or must the provider focus on what is best for the individual patient and resist any triaging considerations? The second is the question of what is the appropriate system of allocating these scarce resources. The triaging system is best understood as being based upon an appeal to its consequences. Advocates of triaging claim that it saves the most lives and in that way produces the best results. But what would be the implications of other appeals, particularly the appeal to rights, to the virtue of compassion, and to equality? What alternative schemes would they support? The third question is whether or not this problem should be eliminated by society developing more extensive systems of neonatal intensive care. Is this type of expensive but efficacious care something that we have a social obligation to provide to everyone, regardless of one's ability to pay? What would the President's Commission, Gibbard, Daniels, Gutmann, and Brody have to say about that issue? Moreover, there is the question of who should be involved in that decision. Is this a decision to be made just by the providers or is there some role for the families of the competing candidates for a place in the neonatal ICU? How, for example, would the view of the President's Commission, as found in Section A3 of the readings, apply to this type of decision making? Finally, there is the question of whether or not this type of triaging involves an impermissible violating of the sanctity of human life. Would it be acceptable to Grisez and Boyle? Would it be acceptable to the Jewish Compendium on Medical Ethics?

What are the alternatives in neonatology to a policy of triaging? Few alternatives have been advocated in this setting, in part because of the relative newness of these issues and in part because many alternative approaches (for example, judging social worth) are less applicable here. Still, at least two other alternatives can be identified. One is the principle of caring for those neonates who come first and never neglecting the care of one of them on triaging grounds in order to produce care for someone who comes later. Such a principle (usually called a "first-come, first-served" principle) was advocated in another triaging context by Charles Fried, who wrote:

> So far as the doctor is concerned, there is a queue for his services. And since it is better that some receive personal care than that none do, and since he is in the relationship that he is to those patients who are already before him, then he must let those at the end of the queue take care of themselves. True, it is not their fault that they are at the end of the queue; but it is not the doctor's fault either.[1]

Fried's argument clearly rests on his view of the patient–physician relation. But what other appeals can be used as additional justifications for the first come, first served principle? Are there any appeals to consequences that would justify it? Any appeals to rights? Any appeals to justice and equality? A second principle (sometimes mistakenly identified with the first) is a principle of *random selection*. Thus, James Childress has written:

> It [random choice] preserves a significant degree of personal dignity by providing equality of opportunity. Selection by chance more closely approximates the requirements established by human dignity than does utilitarian calculation.[2]

Again, the reader needs to consider these questions: What are the major differences between random selection approaches and first-come, first-served principles? What moral appeal is Childress making and how do they differ from Fried's? How do you balance these moral appeals against the appeal to consequences, which speaks so strongly in behalf of triaging?

With this background in mind, let us turn to our cases:

Case A

Several days before the birth of this child, the mother was admitted to the hospital because of low cardiac output. When this resulted in fetal distress, a cesarean section was performed. It was discovered that there was a 60 percent disruption of the placenta, which explained why this baby was not breathing at birth. Resuscitative efforts began and the baby was placed on pulmonary support. Later that day, the child developed

---

[1]Charles Fried, *Medical Experimentation* (North Holland: Amsterdam, 1974).

[2]James Childress, "Who Shall Live?" *Soundings* 53 (Winter 1970), 339–355.

seizures, which were treated with phenobarbital. The child's neurological situation deteriorated, but it did not have a flat EEG. Even if it had, it could not have been declared dead because of the uncertainty of that test in light of the use of phenobarbital. The attending physicians were not sure if they should continue any treatment for that child in light of its poor prognosis, so they consulted the father (later, when she was better, the mother as well). Both parents were very firm in their insistence that everything possible be done for this child despite its very dim prognosis, and the child was kept in the unit on full support until it died. Even before the child was admitted, the unit was beyond its official capacity, and the level of care for every patient was being compromised. Moreover, during the time the child was in the unit, at least six more promising patients were denied transfer from outlying hospitals. Many felt that it had been wrong to admit the patient to the NNICU, in light of its being overcrowded, and to keep it there at the cost of not admitting the other patients.

Case B

This child was born in an outlying hospital. The mother had genital herpes and it was a very premature birth, so it was clear in advance that there could be serious problems; despite that fact, the local obstetrician delivered the child by cesarean section without attempting to transfer the mother to a large hospital with a neonatal intensive care unit. Only after birth, when the extent of the child's problems became clear, did the physician attempt to transfer the neonate to a local NNICU. This attempt was fully supported by the family. Three of the local units were entirely full and refused admission. The fourth had a few spaces left, but it had only six nurses on duty for the 21 children already there (way above the normal staffing ratio) and there were equipment shortages. It also refused admission although the neonatologist in charge agreed (1) that he would have admitted the child if it had been born in his hospital because "then he would be our problem"; (2) that there were several very sick children in the unit whose chances of survival, while not nonexistent, were very low; and (3) that the child's chances without intensive care were much worse (although not certainly fatal) than if he were admitted.

Case C

This baby was born weighing 525 grams (a little more than a pound). Such babies rarely survive, and in this particular unit, such babies are not normally resuscitated. This baby was an exception. It had a strong heart beat and it managed for a while to breathe on its own. Finally, when it required help, it received full resuscitative efforts. The child's history in the hospital involved many crises. Sometimes it required high amounts of oxygen-rich air (up to 80 percent), and this resulted in its developing blindness (retinopathy of prematurity). It stayed in the neonatal ICU for many months, and in the hospital for over a year. But the staff seemed content to work with it because it was "fighting so hard" and because the parents and their entire family wanted so much for this baby to survive, were always present, and were so appreciative. Ultimately, to everyone's surprise and delight, the baby was able to go home after the longest stay ever for a patient in that hospital. The bill for its care was way over $1 million; the baby is blind, and its future prospects are uncertain. Many times during the course of this child's treatment the unit was full and outside transfers were turned away. Thus, the money spent on this infant could have provided intensive care for many other children. Was it an appropriate allocation of resources?

Case A raises in a very concrete fashion all of our questions. Should this child have been admitted to the neonatal intensive care unit, as the parents insisted, or should it simply have been allowed to die? What would the principle of triaging say in this case? What would a first-come, first-served approach say? What would a random-selection approach say? How is all of this influenced by the wishes of the family? Once the baby was admitted, and once he deteriorated, should he have been allowed to stay in the unit when other infants were denied admission? What would our three approaches say to that question? What is the importance of the continued parental insistence upon further treatment? Would Grisez and Boyle allow one to discontinue support and transfer the child out of the unit to make place for others? Would the Jewish Compendium on Medical Ethics allow that? Finally, does a case like this show us that we need more neonatal intensive care units? Does it show us that such units are misused? What light does this case shed on the right to health care? Did this child have a right to the care it received?

Case B presents an interesting contrast to Case A, for it has an emphasis on the child denied admission, not on the child admitted. An additional factor present is the significance of the question of where the child was born. Review the arguments of Brody and Fried in the readings in Section C9. What are the implications of their views for the relevance of this fact to the decision in question? Putting that aside, what would a policy of triaging, a policy of first-come, first-served, and a random-selection policy say about this case? Another important issue was whether there was an appropriate decisional process in this case. Note that in Case B the wishes of the parents were disregarded, whereas in Case A they were central. Could that difference be justified in light of the position of the President's Commission on decision making? Would an alternative theory of decision making, such as the views of Clements and Sider, be more helpful here? Note, moreover, that the nurses were not consulted although a shortage of nursing care was a central reason for the neonatologist's decision. Should they have been consulted, and should the child have been admitted if they agreed to the extra burden? What would Bartlett say about that? What would the adherents of Winslow's various models say?

Many of the questions raised by the previous Cases A and B are raised by Case C as well. But it also raises two special questions. One is the difficult question of the extent of the right to health care. The parents in this case were dependent upon public funds to pay for the care of their child. Does that child (and its parents) have a right to such extensive care? The reader needs to review again the theories of Brody, Daniels, Gibbard, Gutmann, and the President's Commission to see what their implications are for such a case. But Case C also raises in a very special way questions of triaging. At the time this baby was admitted to the neonatal ICU and full intensive care began, everyone knew that (1) its chance of survival was low; (2) it would, if it survived, use up tremendous resources during its care; and (3) there would be children who could benefit from admission to the unit but who would not be admitted because of this baby. What would a triaging approach say about such a case? What would a random-selection approach say? What would a first-come, first-served approach say?

SECTION C

Pediatric Health Care

10. ASSENT AND CONSENT TO PEDIATRIC TREATMENT AND EXPERIMENTATION

One of the fundamental principles of modern medical ethics is that patients must give informed consent before they can receive treatment. That requirement, and the many issues that arise in connection with it, was extensively analyzed in the readings in Sections A3 and A4. That general requirement is even more important when a provider is carrying out an experiment on a patient. In such cases, society has felt an even greater need to ensure that the rights and best interests of the patient are being considered. One way in which it has done so is by imposing very strict requirements for informed consent. Those very strict requirements and other related ways of protecting experimental subjects will be discussed in case area 15 later in the text.

What happens in situations in which the patient is a minor? Who must consent for a minor's treatment? Who must consent before a minor can be experimented on? Are there any limits on the treatments and experimentation to which these people can consent? What importance, if any, shall we give to the wishes of pediatric patients? Does this change as that patient gets older? These are the many questions with which we shall be concerned. After reviewing some of the current legal analyses of these issues, and after comparing these analyses to the ideas found in the readings in Sections A1, A3, and A4, we shall look at some hard cases that deserve careful examination.

The general common-law rule has always been that minors cannot consent to medical or surgical treatment, and that physicians must obtain the consent either of their parents or of some other guardian. This traditional rule applies to all patients under the age of majority (now defined as 18) and was meant to apply in all cases except for medical emergencies. Physicians who treated minors in non-emergency situations were guilty of battery (an intentional touching without consent), and suits could successfully be brought against them by the parents of the child. Thus, in a 1920 Texas case—*Moss v. Rishworth*—an 11-year-old girl was taken by one of her adult sisters to a doctor. The doctor performed a tonsillectomy with the sister's consent, but without attempting to obtain the parents' consent. The doctor was held liable for unauthorized surgery.

Two important exceptions to this traditional rule have emerged in recent years. The first is the "emancipated minor rule." An emancipated minor is usually one who is not living at home and is self-supporting. He or she may in addition be married and/or in the military. The precise definition of emancipation varies from state to state. The crucial point is that such minors can consent to their medical care. Some states have added age as part of the definition for emancipation. Thus, a 1979 Colorado statute (13–22–103) states:

> A minor fifteen years of age or older who is living separate and apart from his parent, parents, or legal guardian, with or without the consent of his parent, parents, or legal guardian, and is managing his own financial affairs, regardless of the source of his income . . . may give consent.

The other exception is the "mature minor rule." This allows the physician to proceed with the consent of the minor patient if the minor has demonstrated sufficient maturity of understanding and intelligence. This rule, like the emancipated minor rule, is usually applied to adolescents aged 15 to 18, although both have occasionally been applied to younger adolescents.

In addition to these general exceptions, the law has also made special exceptions allowing for medical treatment of minors without parental consent for venereal disease, for contraception and abortion, and for drug and alcohol abuse. These special exceptions will be covered in case area 12 of the text.

One useful way of looking at these exceptions is to see them as a way of dealing with the questions raised by the readings from Locke and from Leikin in Section A1. The common-law rule seems to be an expression of Locke's idea about parental authority. Leikin, as we saw in the readings, raises the question of the legitimacy of those ideas when we are dealing with adolescents. Are these legal exceptions, some of which he discusses, sufficient to meet Leikin's concerns? If not, what alternatives could do a better job?

We turn from the question of the medical and surgical treatment of children to the question of medical experimentation involving children. Our focus now needs to be on federal regulations rather than on the common law or on state legislation. This is because the federal government has taken a major role, primarily through regulations issued by the Department of Health and Human Services, in regulating all research.

The crucial question the federal regulations had to address was the role of parents and of children in consenting to research. The issue was sufficiently controversial that proposed regulations first suggested in 1978 were not finally implemented by the DHHS until 1983. The new regulations identify four major classes of research studies, three of which are relevant for our purposes: (1) studies involving no more than minimal risk, (2) studies involving more than minimal risk but which hold out the prospect of direct benefit to the child, and (3) studies involving more than minimal risk and no direct benefit to the child but which hold out the prospect of generalizable knowledge. In each of these cases, permission of both parent and child (when the child is capable of giving permission) is required. In cases (2) and (3), even that is not sufficient. Cases of type (2) require determination by an outside board that the risk to the child is justified by the anticipated benefits to the child and that there is no alternative approach with a more favorable risk/benefit ratio. Cases of type (3) require determination by an outside board that the knowledge is of vital importance and that the risk is not that great.

Several questions are raised by these regulations. The first goes back to our earlier discussion of when children are old enough to play a role in decision making. The regulations say that the child's permission (called "its assent") is required

> . . . when in the judgment of the IRB [the outside board] the children are capable of providing assent. In determing whether children are capable of assenting, the IRB shall take into account the ages, maturity, and psychological state of the children involved.[1]

Compare this approach to the approach embodied in the exceptions to the traditional common-law rules discussed above. Which better meets Leikin's concerns about the traditional approach? Which, if either, would be acceptable to Locke?

The second question before us concerns the fact that these regulations place a limitation on the authority of the parent even when the child is a young minor whose assent is not required. Parents cannot allow their children to be experimental subjects unless an independent outside board agrees that the risks are appropriate. Locke, in his discussion of parental authority, also suggests at several points that parental authority can and should be limited. Would the limitations found in the federal regulations be covered by Locke's suggestion? Are they too limiting or too generous in granting parental authority? Shall we instead adopt the view of the Medical Research Council of Great Britain, which said in a 1963 report that

> In the strict view of the law parents and guardians of minors cannot give consent on their behalf to any procedure which are of no particular benefit to them and which may carry some risk of harm.

These are questions which the reader must carefully consider.

With this general background in mind, we turn now to a consideration of cases that raise these issues. More specialized cases involving organ donations, adolescent sexuality, and religious objections to treatment will be covered in case areas 11, 12, and 13.

Case A

This child was diagnosed at the age of four as having acute lymphoblastic leukemia. He was treated with a three-drug regimen of prednisone, vincristine, and L-asparaginase, and a complete remission was obtained. Un-fortunately, a relapse occurred about nine months later. Several other remissions were induced, but as expected, the period of re-mission in each case was smaller and small-er. The last attempt was particularly un-

---

[1]*Federal Register* 48 (March 8, 1983), 9819.

pleasant. The child developed GI toxicity, non-focused infections, terrible nausea, and respiratory problems. At this point, the physicians decided to stop attempting to induce a remission because they had very few chemotherapy options open, saw little hope for any of them, and were afraid of causing more pain and suffering for this six-year-old dying child. They were strongly supported in this by the nurses who suffered terribly with the child. The parents saw it very differently. They had two older children (19 and 17) and this child was a late, unplanned child who, they felt, had given great meaning to their middle years. They didn't want to give up because (1) "he is too dear to us" and (2) "further care is his only chance." What should be done?

Case B

This child was diagnosed at the age of ten as having nasopharyngeal carcinoma. He was treated with local radiation and chemotherapy and initially responded very well. Within a year, however, his condition worsened and he required radical neck surgery followed by postsurgical chemotherapy. After that time, he was essentially symptom free until shortly after his 13th birthday, when he presents with headaches, nausea, vomiting, and other symptoms. There is clear evidence of a recurrence of his cancer. At that point, the only options left are several experimental chemotherapy protocols. The physicians are clear that the child's long-term prognosis is very poor, but they believe they can buy this child some good time. This is a very close family. The parents have only this one child and have been very much involved at all stages of his care. Now, for the first time, real conflict has broken out. The parents concur with the physicians' recommendation, saying that it offers a real prospect of some good prolongation of life. The 13-year-old patient disagrees. He says that he is tired of all that he has gone through and just wants to be left alone. Several conferences involving the physicians, the entire family, and various counsellors have been held, but the conflict has not been resolved. The real tension in a previously close family confronting a great crisis is a source of terrible anguish to all concerned.

Case C

The child in question is a 16-year-old severely retarded girl who began menstruating at 13 but has been incapable of looking after her personal hygiene. She lives in an institution and has been found having sexual relations with other residents on several occasions. Standard forms of contraception seem unlikely to be successfully used by this girl. The parents are very concerned about the possible problems to their daughter if she becomes pregnant, and they see no hope (their physicians concur) of their daughter ever being able to care for a child. The physicians and the parents would prefer to sterilize this child, but they wonder whether or not it would be appropriate to do so in light of the daughter's inability to participate in the decision and to give her consent.

Case A is an extremely difficult case because it raises questions from a difficult and unexpected direction. The traditional discussion focused on cases in which physicians wanted to treat a minor patient but in which they needed someone's consent, and the crucial question was: Whose consent? This case poses the opposite problem. The parents wanted the child to be treated, but the physicians saw further care as inappropriate and didn't wish to provide it. Shall we apply the legal principles of parental consent discussed above to this case, and conclude that the physicians are required to provide the care in question? Would a moral appeal to consequences or to the virtues of compassion and integrity lead to a different conclusion? What about an appeal to Locke and the right of parental authority? Still further questions are raised by Case A. The remaining chemotherapy protocols are all experimental in nature. They can only be provided for this child as part of medical research, and they would presumably fall in research class (2), since they are studies involving more than minimal risks (all of the horrendous side effects) but which hold out the prospect of direct benefit to the child (the possible prolongation of his life). We saw above that such research is currently allowed only if these risks are outweighed by the anticipated benefits. Who is to decide that, the providers who say that the risks outweigh the benefits or the parents who say just the opposite? And if that question is submitted to an outside board, how should it settle that question?

Suppose we begin by looking at Case B from the traditional common-law perspective. That would seem to imply that the parental wishes should be respected unless this 13-year-old falls under one of the new exceptions. Clearly it cannot be the emancipated minor exception. But could he be treated as a mature minor for this decision? What criteria would you use in deciding that? Would Leikin's arguments suggest that he should fall under this exception? Unfortunately, there is a complication. The treatment that the doctors propose and which the parents wish is an experimental treatment, one which falls under class (2) of the federal regulations. The child's assent is required by those regulations as long as the IRB judges that he is of the appropriate age, maturity, and psychological state. If it judges that the child's assent is required, then the parental wishes cannot be respected. Again, how would you decide that question? Finally, there is still another set of issues. Given that there is hope for prolonging the life of this minor, would a failure to do so be permissible according to Grisez and Boyle, according to the President's Commission, according to the Jewish Compendium on Medical Ethics?

If we simply look at Case C from the common-law perspective, it seems non-problematic. The parents are consenting to a medical procedure which the physicians wish to perform on their minor child, and the child is neither emancipated nor mature. Nevertheless, even they seem to hesitate about this decision. Why? It is probably because Case C forces us to think about what we mean by health care, the care for which parental consent is sufficient. Does it cover this proposed sterilization? More generally, what sort of authority is Locke talking about when he speaks about parental authority over children? Does it extend to sterilization of a severely retarded child who will never be able to make that decision for itself?

11. PEDIATRIC DONATION OF ORGANS

Few areas of medicine have attracted as much attention as have organ transplantation and donation. A lot of this attention represents fascination with the idea of one person being able to live with the use of another person's organs. A lot of this attention also represents general fascination with such outstanding progress in medicine. But some of this attention reflects concern with important ethical and legal issues raised by these developments, and it is those issues that will be the focus of our attention in this area of cases.

Some of the ethical questions arise with the use of organs taken from cadavers for transplantation. These issues (especially the definition of death and the use of parts from cadavers) will be discussed below in case areas 38 and 39. But there are other very different issues raised by the use of organs, primarily kidneys and bone marrow, taken from live donors for transplantation. These issues, especially questions of consent, will be our focus in this area of cases when we discuss issues of pediatric donations of organs, and in case area 26, when we discuss issues of adult donations of organs.

The fundamental issue here is that of consent. All of the standard requirements of informed consent, discussed above in Section A4 of the readings, apply here, and we will need to analyze what informed consent means in these situations. But we also need to focus on a different set of questions. Who can give consent if the donor is a minor? Can anyone give consent if the donor is a minor given that the procedure is not for the benefit of the donor? To what extent should the donor be involved in the decision? A historical survey of cases will best enable us to approach these issues.

Transplantation of kidneys began as an experimental procedure in the mid-1950s. By 1959, three cases developed in Boston where counsel for the hospital performing transplantations sought court approval to allow minors, with parental consent, to donate kidneys to save the lives of their siblings. The ages of the minors ranged from 14 to 19. The Massachusetts courts gave that permission, and have since routinely allowed kidney or bone marrow transplants from minors. Courts in many other states have followed that principle as well, but in the 1970s, in two important decisions, state courts refused to allow retarded adolescents and retarded adults to donate organs. Let us look at those two decisions, and at other important decisions allowing such transplants, to get an idea of the issues.

In 1973, in the case of *In re Richardson,* a Louisiana court refused permission for a retarded 17-year-old, with a mental age of three or four, to donate a kidney to his 32-year-old sister suffering from acute glomerulonephritis. The 17-year-old was the best candidate for donor, but he was not the only possible donor. The Louisiana court refused to allow the boy to be used as a donor on the grounds that it was against his best interests to donate the kidney. A similar decision, involving an adult incompetent estimated to have the intelligence of a 12-year-old, was handed down by the Wisconsin Supreme Court in 1975 in the case of *In re Pescinski.* That case also involved a woman suffering from acute glomerulonephritis, but in that case the *only* suitable candidate for a donor was her 39-year-old brother institutionalized as a chronic catatonic schizophrenic. The argument of the court was clear. Neither the parent, nor the guardian, nor the court could consent in such a case:

> A guardian of the person had the care of the ward's person and must look to the latter's health, education, and support. The guardian must act, if at all, loyally in the best interests of his ward. There is absolutely no evidence here that any interests of the ward will be served by the transplant. . . . In the absence of real consent on his part, and in a situation where no benefit to him has been established, we fail to find any authority . . . to approve this operation (*In re Pescinski* 226 NW2d 180 C1975).

What are the arguments on the other side? What arguments would allow the use of organs from minors or incompetents? Our argument was suggested by the Court of Civil Appeals of Texas in the 1979 case of *Little v. Little*. Anne Little, the prospective donor, was a 14-year-old girl suffering from Down's syndrome. Her mother sought permission to use one of her kidneys for Anne's brother, Stephen, who suffered from end-stage renal disease. Anne's own willingness to donate was judged irrelevant, but in light of of her close relation to her brother and her evident discomfort when he was away, and in light of her ability to understand helping others, the Texas court concluded that it was in her best interest to allow the organ donation. Given that it was, the court concluded that it could accept the mother's request:

> ... there is ample evidence to the effect that she understands the concept of absence and that she is unhappy on the occasions when Stephen must leave home for hours, when she journeys to San Antonio for dialysis. . . . The testimony is not limited to the prevention of sadness. . . . The record before us indicates that Anne is capable of experiencing such an increase in personal welfare from donating her kidney (*Little v. Little* 576 S.W2d 493 C1979).

Another argument was used by a Kentucky court in the 1969 case of *Strunk v. Strunk*. That case involved a 27-year-old with a mental age of six who was the only possible donor of a kidney to save the life of his brother, who was increasingly ill because of his chronic glomerulonephritis. The court, in allowing the transplant, appealed to the so-called substituted judgment principle, the principle that guardians may consent if they judge that their wards would have consented if they were competent. That view is also vigorously presented in Justice Day's dissent in the Wisconsin case of *In re Pescinski* cited above.

> The majority opinion would forever condemn the incompetent to be always a receiver, a taker, but never a giver. For in holding that only those things which financially or physically benefit the incompetent may be done by the court, he is forever excluded from doing the decent thing, the charitable thing. The British courts have not so held . . . by the device known as "substituted judgment" where the court in effect does for the incompetent what it is sure he would do for himself if he had the power to act. This approach gives the incompetent the benefit of the doubt, endows him with the finest qualities of his humanity, assumes the goodness of his nature instead of assuming the opposite (*In re Pescinski* 226 NW2d 180 C1975).

As one looks over this debate, one is struck by a number of major questions. The first is the question of the extent of the authority of parents or guardians who must decide for those who cannot decide for themselves. Must they only consider the best interests of their child or ward, as supported by the courts of Louisiana, Wisconsin, and Texas? Or may they also consider the interests of others (as is implicitly suggested under the guise of "substituted judgment" by Justice Day)? If we think of that question from the perspective of someone like John Locke, it becomes the question of what is the authority that Locke postulates for parents over minor children or over children who never reach maturity?

Our second question is how do we define the best interests of the child or ward. In discussing the appeal to consequences, we looked at hedonistic, desire-satisfaction, and corrected desire-satisfaction views of the good. Which one, if any, was employed by the Texas court in *Little v. Little?* Which one should we employ when defining the best interests of minor children or of an incompetent who will never reach maturity? The third question relates to the scope of the discussion itself. All of the legal discussions have focused on the right of decision making. But what about an appeal to the right to be saved on the part of the person needing the organ? And what about an appeal to the consequences? Would those distinguish the case of Richardson, where there were other less satisfactory donors, from the case of Pescinski, where there were none, so that a decision against allowing the transplant might be a decision resulting in the death of the potential recipient? All of these questions are ones that the reader needs to think about as we look at our cases.

Case A

This case involves a 15-year-old potential donor of a kidney. The potential recipient is his brother, who is a severely retarded, institutionalized 11-year-old suffering from end-stage renal failure. Although the recipient could live with regular dialysis treatments, his physicians believe that he would be much better off medically with a transplant. They also believe that he would not be able to understand the need for regular dialysis, and it would be psychologically undesirable to impose that upon him, especially if he could get a kidney transplant. The parents and the potential donor have had little to do with the severely retarded child since he was institutionalized many years earlier. Nevertheless, the brother is willing to donate his kidney; he feels very strongly that it would be wrong for him to refuse in light of his brother's need. The parents are not willing to consent. Their view is that however modest the risks, they do not want to impose any risks on their healthy normal child for the sake of their other child. When the institution's physicians suggest to the parents that they are abandoning their sick and severely retarded child, they respond very honestly by saying that they made that decision many years ago and that they resent any attempt to force this child back on them or on their healthy child. What should be done in this case?

Case B

A 12-year-old boy was diagnosed as having idiopathic aplastic anemia. He has been treated with androgens and corticosteroids, but these have not been successful. He is in a catabolic state, is septic, and is bleeding from multiple sites. He and his parents are certainly very willing that he receive a bone marrow transplant. The only issue is whom to use as a donor. There are five siblings, but only two are compatible. One is a retarded 17-year-old son and the other a normal 10-year-old daughter. The daughter says that she is willing to be a donor, but is clearly very frightened about the prospects, even though she seems to understand that the risks to her are really very small. The prospects of an hour in an operating room and the large number of aspirations frighten her. The 17-year-old retarded child also agrees to be a donor and does not seem frightened, but it is very unclear whether he understands very much about what is proposed because he can or will not answer even simple questions about what has been told to him. The parents are very unsure as to which child should be used as the donor and even as to whether it would be appropriate in light of one sibling's fears and the other's inability to understand. What should be done in this case?

Case C

This case involves a 16-year-old potential donor of bone marrow for a younger sibling suffering from acute lymphoblastic leukemia who is now in a second remission. The parents agree to allow the bone marrow transplant, but the potential donor is unwilling to make that donation. The minimal risks and discomforts have been explained to him, but this seems to make no difference. The parents have explained that this son has been a serious problem for years. He has run away from home on several occasions, is a terrible truant from school, and is constantly in minor trouble with the police. They do feel that they can get him to agree, but only by threatening to withdraw all types of privileges from him. They are willing to do so in part because they are so angry about his unwillingness to help his brother, but also in part because they really care more about their younger child. Several members of the treating team wonder whether it would be appropriate to accept such a coerced donation from this 16-year-old, even if it is so desirable and even if he is such an unpleasant adolescent. The younger sibling is, after all, in remission, and while his chances are much better with the transplant, it isn't absolutely required.

One suggestion for handling Case A would be to wait three years until the donor is 18. Then, under the principles discussed in case area 10, the donor will be able to consent on his own, and the wishes of the parents will be irrelevant. The physicians caring for the institutionalized child are reluctant to follow that path, in part because they fear the consequences, physical and psychological, of leaving the 11-year-old on dialysis for the next three years, and in part because they wonder whether their appeal to the brother will be as successful three years from now. They would like to invoke the mature minor rule as a basis for allowing this 15-year-old to consent to donating his organ. Is that a legitimate use of that role or would it be an inappropriate infringement on the rights of the parents? How would Justice Day analyze this case? How would his colleagues, who were the majority in the Pescinski case? How would the Texas court analyze it?

Several different questions are raised by Case B. The first has to do with whether this case should even be analyzed analogously to the kidney transplant cases. The procedure in question, aspirating bone marrow, is certainly less dangerous than taking one healthy kidney from a body. Moreover, there is less risk afterwards to the donor. Is there any basis for the parents' concern about the legitimacy of their consenting on behalf of one of the siblings to donate the bone marrow? What would the Supreme Court of Wisconsin, which refused in the Pescinski case to allow the parents to consent to donating a kidney, say in this case? Putting that question aside, which sibling should be employed as the donor? Is it more appropriate that we use a frightened but understanding and willing minor donor or that we use a willing but retarded minor donor who does not really comprehend what is going on?

In all of the court cases we examined earlier, and in our first two cases here, there was no question of coercing the minor donor to go along with the transplant. Case C is different precisely because it involves that aspect. Would Justice Day have to agree that it would be wrong to perform the transplant, because no appeal to "substituted judgment" could justify it in this case? On the other hand, would the court in the Richardson and Pescinski cases allow this transplant on the basis of the parental consent because of the minimal risks to the donor and the great need of the recipient? Finally, would an appeal to consequences justify accepting the parentally coerced consent of the potential donor in order to improve the chances of the recipient?

12.   CONFIDENTIALITY AND ADOLESCENT SEXUALITY

The problem of physician–patient confidentiality in matters of adolescent sexuality is a recent one. First and foremost, adolescence is a relatively modern phenomenon. In most nonindustrialized societies, individuals marry soon after they become able to reproduce. In traditional societies, there are rarely prolonged postponements of reproduction and/or marriage, especially on the part of women. It is rather in societies such as ours where it is important to acquire complex intellectual and technical skills that marriage and childbearing are often postponed for a decade and a half beyond puberty. Where such postponement is the rule, complex strategies must be developed to prevent children from being born before marriage.

In the case study of decisions to reproduce, it was noted that the law has recently recognized not only the right of married couples but also unmarried individuals to have access to contraception (*Eisenstadt v. Baird,* 1972). But a question remains regarding unmarried adolescents, for they are still considered in many respects to be under the control of their parents. Here law and public policy reflect an old tradition in which children were under parental sovereignty, in the hand (*in manu*), of their parents until emancipated. Parents or guardians must generally be consulted and their consent must be obtained before non-emergency treatment is provided. In many circumstances, treatment that would benefit a minor cannot be provided, even if the minor wants it, if it is against the wishes of the parents. One might think here of cosmetic surgery to remove a birthmark that evokes teasing from classmates.

The question of parental authority becomes complex as a child develops into a teenager mature enough to appreciate the consequences of at least certain medical choices. Generally, emancipated minors (for example, a self-supporting minor over 16 living independently) have been allowed to consent to medical treatment. However, unemancipated minors may possess the same intellectual and emotional maturity as emancipated minors. In addition, there may be public policy considerations not to discourage minors from seeking prompt treatment through requiring parental consent, as may occur with venereal diseases. Finally, because decisions to use contraception or to terminate a pregnancy through an abortion bear on the entire future life of the minor, the minor's claim to choose has substantial weight. Because a minor is generally obliged to support his or her children, it is plausible that the minor should be able to choose whether he or she wishes to have such duties of support.

One finds a tension among a set of important social goals. Concepts of family sovereignty and the ideal of an open parent–child relationship collide with the child's developing capacities as an individual to understand and appreciate the consequences of his or her own decisions. Public policy interests in controlling venereal disease and avoiding unwanted pregnancies strengthen the claims for confidential relationships between physician and adolescent in matters bearing on sexuality. Yet some raise countervailing public policy interests, arguing that making contraceptives easily accessible under circumstances undisclosed to parents encourages teenage promiscuity and, in fact, exacerbates the twin plagues of teenage pregnancies and venereal disease.

The right of minors to have access to contraception was sustained in *Carey v. Population Services International* (481 U.S. 678). The court struck down a New York statute that made criminal the sale or distribution of non-prescription contraceptives to minors under 16. This ruling established a right of privacy for procreative decision making by minors. Other courts have upheld the non-notification of parents regarding the prescription of contraceptive devices and medication to their minor children (see, for example, the ruling of the U.S. Court of Appeals for the Sixth District that involved a Michigan family planning clinic: *Doe v. Irvin* [615 F 2d 1162]). In addition, the Supreme Court has acknowledged a constitutional basis for the right of mature minors to have access to abortion without parental consent (*Planned Parenthood of Kansas City, Mo., Inc. et al. v. John Ashcroft, et al.*).

Initially, Congress supported easy access to family planning programs. Title X of the Public Health Services Act specified that the patient alone was authorized to consent to medical care and that fees for services would not be based on parental income.[1] This direction was underscored in 1978 when Congress amended Title X legislation to require specifically that adolescents in need of family planning be served.[2] In 1981, a change of direction occurred when Congress again amended Title X legislation, but this time to require that "to the extent practical, entities which receive grants and contracts shall encourage family participation. . . ."[3] On February 22, 1982, the Department of Health and Human Services proposed regulations requiring family planning clinics funded under Title X to notify the parents of unemancipated minors (that is, those under age 18, unmarried, without children, not in the armed forces, and not self-supporting) when prescription contraceptives were provided.[4] This requirement was popularly termed the "squeal rule." Final regulations were published on January 26, 1983, and became effective on February 25, 1983.[5] These rules were immediately challenged in the courts, and in two jurisdictions they were barred from taking effect. As a result, a major controversy regarding public policy in this area remains unresolved.

The issue of parental notification raises the question of the status of children and the status of parental authority, a point explored by Locke in the readings. How ought one to balance the rights of parents and children? This question raises as well an issue allied to the point that Charles Fried makes with respect to a physician being a trusted personal adviser, not a social agent. Insofar as physicians are required to report to others what transpired within the physi-

---

[1]P.L. 91–572, Sec. 2 (1).

[2]P.L. 95–613 (a) (1).

[3]P.L. 97–35, Sec. 931 (b) (1).

[4]"Parental Notification Rule," *Federal Register* 47 (Feb. 22, 1982), 7699–7701.

[5]Parental Notification Requirements Applicable to Projects for Family Planning Services; Final Rule, *Federal Register* 48 (Jan. 26, 1983), 3600–3614.

cian–patient relationship, they become instruments of particular social policies. What are the likely consequences of different policies regarding confidentiality about adolescent sexual behavior? One must also ask whether the provision of contraceptives is not an element of that part of health care that is integral to what Norman Daniels sees as undergirding fair opportunity. If a girl becomes pregnant in high school, her chances of completing her education and of learning sufficient job skills to be an effective member of society will likely be compromised in a way that will dramatically influence her range of opportunity in society. How do considerations of justice and equity bear on the analysis of these issues?

Case A

Miss A is a 17-year-old high school senior. In the last semester of her senior year, she makes an appointment for a physical required for admission to the college where her 20-year-old boyfriend is completing his sophomore year. He is a premed student and doing very well. She plans to attend the school. Though they have not informed their parents, they intend to live together. Miss A wants her physician to prescribe the Pill for her. The physician, who has a long-time relationship with the As going back at least 20 years and who delivered Miss A, is shocked by the proposal. He disapproves of her living with her boyfriend and disapproves even more of the request for the Pill. He insists that Miss A discuss the issue with her parents. Miss A says that she does not intend to inform her parents, and if the physician is not willing to prescribe the Pill for her, she will go elsewhere. She remarks that she is disappointed in his reaction. After their long-standing physician–patient relationship, she had expected him to support her.

Case B

Youth B is a 15-year-old tenth grader in a rural town of 10,000, where there are two drugstores. At the last school dance, he engaged in heavy petting with his 14-year-old girlfriend. After much soul-searching, he enters one of the drugstores and waits until there are no other customers. He then approaches the pharmacist and asks to purchase a package of prophylactics. The druggist is shocked. He asks B what his parents or the local minister would say if they found out that he was planning to be sexually active. The boy, abashed but undaunted, insists that the druggist sell him the prophylactics. He explains that if he does not get some condoms, he is sure that he will end up getting a girl pregnant. The druggist at that point chases the boy out of the drugstore.

Case C

Miss C is 13 years old, the youngest child of a family of five children. The mother is divorced and must work to support the family. The family lives in an apartment complex and the children are unsupervised until the mother returns from work at around 6:30 each evening. Miss C makes an appointment at a neighborhood clinic and is first seen by a nurse-practitioner. She informs the nurse that she wants to be put on the Pill because she and some of her girlfriends have begun to have sex parties with boys in the complex after they return from school. They smoke marijuana and then have sex. She is afraid that she will get pregnant during high school, as did one of her older sisters. That sister terminated the pregnancy with an abortion. The nurse consults the clinic's physician. She tells the physician that she really believes the mother should be informed about both the marijuana smoking and the sex parties. The

nurse emphasizes that the future of not only Miss C but of all the boys and girls involved in these parties is at stake.

Case D

After the local paper in a Midwest town with a population of 100,000 runs a story about the local family planning clinic providing contraceptives to minors without parental notification, the town council passes an ordinance making parental notification man-

datory. The ordinance also requires that notice be given to parents whose children received contraceptives through the clinic during the last 12 months. The director and board of trustees of the family planning clinic decide to fight the matter in court.

Should parental notification be required (or allowed) in any of the above cases? Does it make a difference that in Case A the girl is soon to reach her majority and leave home? Does the druggist have a right to decide whether he will sell contraceptives to minors? What if the pharmacists in both drugstores refuse to provide contraceptives to teenagers? Even if one were to decide that such a decision is within one's right as a druggist, would it still be wrong in the sense of not being a beneficent choice? Does the fact that Miss C is 13 years old bear on what the policy should be with respect to her request? What should take place if the nurse and physician disagree? Does it matter who takes the side of affirming confidentiality? If you think that notification should be given to the parents if contraceptives are prescribed, do you also believe that the substance of the girl's communication should be given to the mother, even if the clinic does not make contraceptives available? To answer these questions, one will need to examine the conflict among individuals, the rights of adolescents, the rights of parents, and the rights of communities. The last point is emphasized in Case D. Does a community have the moral right to employ governmental force in setting a particular moral standard? Is it morally proper for the community in Case D to require parental notification if contraceptives are provided to minors? Even if the answer is yes, should such a requirement be retroactive?

13.   RELIGIOUS OBJECTIONS TO TREATMENT OF MINORS

In case area 10 we discussed the fundamental principle governing pediatric treatment and experimentation, the principle that parental consent is required before treatment can normally be provided to a minor. This principle carries with it the clear implication that a parental refusal of permission is sufficient to block the provision of medical care.

Unfortunately, cases exist in which respecting this parental authority (which Locke described in the reading in Section A1) would lead to terrible results for the minor. The child in question may need a particular form of treatment in order to survive or to avoid a terrible disability or suffering, and the parents in question may refuse their consent because of ignorance or malice. Are we bound to accept that parental refusal? In general, the courts have been willing to overrule parental refusal. To quote the Texas court in the 1947 decision of *Mitchell v. Davis:*

> Medicines, medical treatment, and attention are in a category with food, clothing, lodging and education as necessities from parent to child, for which the former is held legally responsible. . . . An omission to do this is a public wrong which the state, under its police power, may prevent.

The general procedure for overruling parental refusal is for the health personnel or institution to petition a court either for temporary guardianship of the child so that they can consent on the child's behalf or simply for permission to proceed without parental consent.

If we look at the argument offered by the Texas court, it is clearly based on the idea that there are parental responsibilities to a child as well as parental rights of authority over the child, and that a failure of the parents to perform the former leads to a parental loss (at least temporarily) of the latter. Would Locke agree with this claim? The reader needs to review carefully Locke's theory of why parents have authority over children in order to answer that question.

This is not to say that courts will always compel minors to undergo whatever care is recommended by the physicians in question. If the care refused by the parents is risky, or unlikely to succeed, or a response to a problem that is not immediate and/or grave, the court is less likely to order care and override the parental refusal. It is most likely to do so when there exists an immediate and grave threat to the health and/or life of the child, when there is a treatment with a good success rate, and when the risks of the treatment are modest when compared to the threat to the life and/or health of the child.

It is against this background that we need to examine the question of parental refusal of health care for minor children on the grounds of religious objections to the treatment. It is probably helpful to divide such cases into three different categories:

1. Parents who regularly refuse on religious grounds all forms of standard health care for their minor children—The classic example of such parents would be Christian Scientists. Members of this religious sect believe that illnesses, like all other physical evils, are illusions attributable to a lack of faith, illusions that can be dispelled through prayer which strengthens faith. Thus, they seek no standard medical care.

2. Parents who regularly refuse on religious grounds certain specific forms of standard health care for their minor children while accepting all other forms of standard health care—The classic example of these parents would be Jehovah's Witnesses. Members of this sect believe that blood transfusions are prohibited by the biblical commandment prohibiting the eating of blood. Therefore, while they seek out standard medical care (including surgery), they do so only on the condition that they not receive any blood products as part of that treatment.

3. Parents who regularly accept standard health care for their minor children but who on a special occasion refuse on religious grounds a major portion of standard health care—An example of such parents would be those few Pentecostalists who refuse permission to treat their child when the child is diagnosed as having a serious illness and who believe that God has revealed to them that the child will be saved only through the parent's faith, a faith that must be demonstrated by their relying on the power of prayer and by their refusing standard medical care.

It is customary to say that our society is not willing to accept parental refusal of required medical care for minor children even if that refusal is based on their deeply held religious beliefs. Thus, writing about a Jehovah's Witness father who refused permission for a life-saving transfusion for his 12-day-old infant suffering from erythroblastic anemia, a Missouri court in 1952 wrote:

> The fact that the subject is an infant child of a parent who, arbitrarily, puts his own theological belief higher than his duty to preserve the life of this child cannot prevail over the considered judgment of an entire people, in a case such as this (*Morrison v. State* 252 SW2d 97 (1952)).

But there clearly are some exceptions to this rule. The most notable exception is that which allows Christian Scientists to refuse standard treatment for their children. Typical of this exception, found in many states, is an Idaho statute, which allows the court to take into consideration

> any treatment being given the child by spiritual means alone, if the child or his parent, guardian, or legal custodian are adherents of a bona fide religious denomination that relies exclusively on this form of treatment in lieu of medical treatment (Idaho Code 16–1616).

Many questions are raised by these standard legal doctrines. The first is the obvious question of whether the law is right in dismissing the idea that parental refusal of treatment for minors is justifiable if it is based on religious conviction rather than on malice or ignorance. The second is whether it is right to treat Christian Scientists differently.

Case A

A child was born with hypoplastic left heart syndrome. In this condition, which has been uniformly fatal until very recently, the left ventricle of the heart fails to develop. Thus, after birth, when the heart must take on the task of pumping oxygenated blood to the rest of the body, the child succumbs, partly as a result of a lack of blood to the rest of the body and partly as a result of a building up of fluids in the lung. In 1983, William Norwood and his colleagues reported a successful two-stage surgical procedure to allow the body to function with only one functioning ventricle. Other successes but many failures have been reported since then. As a result of these successes, the physicians managing the child in this case approached the parents with the idea of performing Dr. Norwood's surgical procedures (familiarly called the *Norwood shunt*) on this child in the hope of saving its life. The parents were quite receptive until they learned that such surgery could not be undertaken with a commitment not to use blood products as required. At that point, the parents began to disagree between themselves. Both were Jehovah's Witnesses. The father wanted to give permission for the surgery, saying that he couldn't deprive his child of its only chance to live, even if the chance was admittedly not that good. The mother disagreed, insisting that they needed to stick to their religious beliefs and not condemn both themselves and their child to eternal damnation by agreeing to the use of blood products as required. The staff was unable to get these parents to resolve their dispute. What should be done for the child at this point?

Case B

A 13-year-old girl was diagnosed as having Ewing's sarcoma, a small cell tumor of the bone that was localized in her leg but without any signs that the tumor had spread. At the time of diagnosis, her main complaints were pain and localized swelling and tenderness. Her physicians wished to treat this tumor as aggressively as possible, and they recommended surgical resection of as much of the tumor as possible, radiation therapy to the entire bone, and multiple-drug chemotherapy. They correctly pointed out to the parents that this offered a very high chance of short-term control and a good chance of long-term survival. The parents were initially very receptive to this suggestion, as was the child, although they were appropriately concerned with side effects and the possibility of long-term failure. The next day, however, they responded quite differently. Both parents and daughter were deeply religious people who studied the Bi-

ble and prayed regularly. The daughter, in her prayer the previous night, had become convinced that God was testing her faith with this illness, and that if she rested all of her faith in Him and did not seek out therapy, He would cure her. After a long discussion that morning with their minister, and after much praying, the family had agreed to support their daughter's wishes. The parents withdrew their consent to all of the recommendations and made it clear that they wished their daughter to go home as soon as possible. The physicians involved suggested a combination of prayer and medical therapy, but the daughter explained that God wanted her total faith in Him and that was incompatible in her mind with using medical therapy. Some of the nurses who had become attached to the girl felt strongly that these views were based on her deep convictions and reflected her knowledge of the risks she was taking by refusing medical care.

Case C

An 11-year-old boy has been suffering from birth with von Recklinghausen's disease, which has caused a massive deformity of the right side of his face and neck. There is a large overgrowth of facial tissues that causes the whole right side of his face to droop, giving him a grotesque and repulsive look. Fortunately, this has not affected his sight or hearing. However, he clearly suffers from problems with his relations with peers, who shun him, and although a psychiatrist reports no outstanding psychiatric disorders, the youngster is described as demonstrating excessive depression, low self-esteem, and a tremendous sense of inferiority. Problems in school have adversely affected his learning skills and he is underachieving. These results

reinforce his psychological feelings. Everybody feels that the child would benefit from plastic surgery, although his condition is for now in no way life-threatening and there are risks involved in the surgery. The mother and father would agree if the surgery could be performed without the use of blood products, but no surgeon will agree to that because there will be too much loss of blood during surgery. The child's mother and father are both Jehovah's Witnesses, and they refuse permission in light of the need for blood transfusions. The child expresses no strong feelings either way, and everyone sees this as a reflection of the child's dependency and low self-esteem. What should be done in this case?

There are many issues raised by Case A. The first thing that it forces us to recognize is that there is a fundamental ambiguity in the legal requirement of parental consent. How many parents need to consent and what happens when the parents disagree? We don't normally have to resolve that ambiguity, but this case forces us to try to do so. The reader needs to review the various arguments about parental authority and parental responsibilities, beginning with Locke's discussion, to see how this issue might best be resolved. There is, however, a second and even more difficult question. Suppose that we decide that the refusal of one parent is sufficient to block parental consent. Or suppose that the mother persuades the father to retract his consent. Is this a case in which the physicians and nurses caring for this child should seek a court order to get custody so that they can authorize the surgery? On the one hand, the courts have been reluctant to interfere with parental judgments when the prospects of success are not that high. On the other hand, this is the child's only hope, and early reports of the successes are quite optimistic about the ultimate prognosis if the surgery is successful. How do we balance these considerations as we try to decide whether to seek custody of the child? And how do we take into account compassion for the parents and respect for their integrity, which leads many to think that we should just let them alone to carry out their views, especially since we don't have anything that great to offer to their child?

Case B is different from Case A in two crucial respects. We are dealing in Case B with proven therapy rather than with radically new surgical procedures. That certainly must weigh in favor of disregarding the family's wishes and seeking a court order to authorize the surgery. On the other hand, we are dealing in Case B with more than just parental refusal. This adolescent patient is the one really refusing the care, and both her parents and some of the professionals who are closest to her feel that her wishes should be respected. That certainly must weigh on the side of accepting the family's decision. How do we balance these conflicting factors in deciding whether to follow the parental refusal? Does her refusal fall under the mature minor rule, in which case we have a different reason, based on her right of decision making, for respecting the refusal of treatment? Shall we adopt an appeal to consequences, and if we do, how do we weigh the medical benefits of treatment to her against the psychological harm of treatment to her and her family? Shall we view her decision as courageous and full of integrity, demanding respect, or shall we question her competency and the competency of her parents, wondering about their psychological abilities to make sound decisions during a time of crisis? What would the President's Commission say about that? What would Abernethy? Would Clements and Sider see this as a case in which medical values must take precedence? How would Miller and Thomasma respond?

Case C presents new issues. Until now, we have been concerned with parental refusal on religious grounds to consent to medical treatment required by a minor child to save its life. Here there is no such threat to the child's life. But the unanimous professional opinion is that this child would benefit psychologically and socially from the surgery. The parents do not disagree with this assessment. What they argue is that their religious beliefs rule out this surgery in light of the need for blood transfusions. Is this one of those cases in which parental authority can legitimately be overridden? Are the benefits to the child sufficient to justify seeking a court order?

SECTION D

Adult Patients: General Issues

14. CONSENT OF ADULTS TO TREATMENT

Although the question of free and informed consent does not have a long history in Anglo-American law, the concern with disclosure to patients goes back at least to the time of ancient Greece. Plato in the *Laws* distinguishes between two kinds of physicians: those who treat slaves and those who treat free people. The first, he says, are usually slaves themselves and treat their patients "in the brusque fashion of a dictator." In contrast, the free practitioner treats patients "by going into things thoroughly from the beginning in a scientific way, and takes the patient and his family into his confidence. . . . He does not give his prescriptions until he has won the patient's support. . . ."[1]

The literature in bioethics has emphasized that free and informed consent to treatment depends on a number of factors, only a few of which are indicated in the passage from Plato. First, the consenting individual must be competent to decide, a point that is emphasized in the readings from the President's Commission's analysis of the problem involved in identifying incapacity. Sufficient information must be transmitted, and the patient must be free of coercion. Finally, as has been alluded to in the case study of pediatric assent and consent to treatment and experimentation, and with respect to confidentiality and adolescent sexuality, the status of a patient as a minor may undercut the legal significance of a patient's consent. In short, for consent to be fully valid, the individual consenting must have (1) decision-making capacity, (2) adequate information, (3) freedom from coercion, and (4) legal capacity to give consent.

In the Anglo-American tradition, the law of battery held individuals secure against the unauthorized touchings of others. The problem in medicine has been

---

[1]*Laws* 4.720 b–e, in E. Hamilton and H. Cairns (eds.), *The Collected Dialogues of Plato*, Princeton: N.J.: Princeton University Press, 1961.

to balance the obligation to respect the autonomy of the patient with the often-conflicting obligation to achieve the health of the patient. As the selection in this text from the President's Commission regarding "The Patient as Decision-Maker" suggests, there may be a conflict between respecting the self-determination of a patient and causing a patient's well-being. There has always been the fear that blunt disclosures are likely to dissuade patients from needed treatment, if not, in fact, so to distress them as to make their condition worse. Still, there has been an acknowledgment of a duty to inform the patient about the nature of the treatment to be undertaken. There is a King's Bench decision as early as 1767, *Slater v. Baker and Stapleton,* affirming that "It is reasonable that a patient should be told what is about to be done to him, that he may take courage and put himself in such a situation as to enable him to undergo the operation" [2 Wils. 359, 95 Eng. Rep. 860 (King's Bench 1767)]. In American law, the first bold finding in favor of that right is in *Schloendorff v. Society of N.Y. Hospital* in 1916, when Justice Benjamin Cardozo held that "every human being of adult years and sound mind has a right to determine what shall be done with his own body; and a surgeon who performs an operation without his patient's consent commits an assault, for which he is liable in damages" [211 N.Y. 125, 105 N.E. 92, 93 (1914)].

Even with the principle of informed consent in place, the issue still remains of how much information ought to be given to the patient. Justice Oliver Wendell Holmes (1841–1935) stated that ". . . the patient has no more right to all the truth than he has to all of the medicines in the physician's saddlebags." The traditional standard of disclosure, the professional standard, reflected this viewpoint. The Supreme Court of Missouri declared in 1965:

> The question is not what, regarding the risks involved, the juror would relate to the patient under the same or similar circumstances, or even what a reasonable man would relate, but what a reasonable medical practitioner would do. Such practitioners would consider the state of the patient's health, the condition of his heart and nervous system, [and] his mental state. This determination involves medical judgment as to whether disclosure of possible risks may have such an adverse effect on the patient as to jeopardize success of the proposed therapy. [*Aiden v. Clary,* 396 S.W.2d 668, 674–675 (Mo. Sup. Ct. 1965)]

This view represented the traditional approach of physicians and made the standards for disclosure to patients dependent on the standards of the community of physicians.

American law began to depart from the professional standard with the articulation of the so-called objective standard, the duty of the physician to explain to a patient enough about the procedure to be undertaken so as "to warn him of any material risks or dangers inherent in or collateral to the therapy, so as to enable the patient to make an intelligent and informed choice about whether or not to undergo such treatment" [*Sard v. Hardy,* 397 A 2d 1014, 1020 (Md. 1977)]. To discharge this duty according to the objective standard, physicians must acquaint a patient with all the material risks involved in the treatment, where a material risk is understood as a risk that "a reasonable person, in what the physician knows or should know to be the patient's position, would be likely to attach significance to in deciding whether or not to forego the proposed therapy" [*Canterbury v. Spence,* 464 F.2d 772, 797 (D.C. Cir. 1972)]. The accent falls on what would influence a reasonable patient in his or her decision making. The selection in this volume from *Canterbury v. Spence* illustrates this approach to the disclosure of information.

In addition to the objective standard, which is being used in ever-more jurisdictions in the United States (but not in a majority of jurisdictions), some commentators such as Capron in this volume have defended a subjective standard of disclosure. A subjective standard would require disclosing not what a reasonable and prudent patient would require, but what would influence any particular patient in deciding to accept or refuse treatment.

Even with the acceptance of the objective standard, certain qualifications and exceptions have been recognized by a number of courts. In emergency circumstances when it is not possible to gain consent from the patient or the next of kin, physicians may act to save life and limb. Also, a remnant of the professional standard survives as the therapeutic privilege. Physicians are excused from giving full information when, on the basis of facts that would convince a reasonable person, the disclosure would likely render the patient "so ill or emotionally distraught on disclosure as to foreclose a rational decision, or complicate or hinder the treatment, or perhaps even pose psychological damage to the patient" [*Canterbury v. Spence,* 464 F. 2d 772, 789 (D.C. Cir. 1972)]. In such circumstances, disclosure can instead be made to the next of kin. Finally, some courts have recognized that the physician is not obliged to disclose risks where the patient requests not to be informed. The obligation to disclose then becomes the obligation to make information available to the patient, but not to force the patient to accept the information. We will return to this point in the case study of truth-telling.

Here the focus is on the extent to which physicians are required to disclose information to all patients who presumably would want to be fully informed. To what extent will the adverse effect on a patient from disclosure defeat the obligation to provide information on that basis? To what extent is the very notion of the therapeutic privilege incompatible with respect for the autonomy of patients? How "full" must disclosure be? Must physicians tell patients of every adverse reaction reported in the literature associated with the treatment about to be undertaken? The limits here are in part practical limits, for full disclosure of every possible risk would take not only a long lecture but also an introduction into the science and art of medicine. Answers to these questions are part of giving flesh to the notion of the patient as an autonomous agent. How does disclosure bear on the proper understanding of Bruce Miller's four senses of autonomy? Are the arguments of Capron realistic? Can physicians be required to meet a subjective standard of disclosure as Capron argues? In the President's Commission's analysis of the patient as decision-maker, what level of disclosure is morally appropriate? What are the likely consequences of different policies of disclosure for the practice of medicine? What are the implications of the objective and subjective standards for the character of health care? How ought physicians to balance their commitments to honesty and professional integrity when they believe that full disclosure will lead to patients choosing less than optimal care?

Case A

Mrs. A, a 35-year-old secretary, is found after her routine pap smear to have carcinoma of the cervix. The cancer is in an early stage, confined to the cervix, with minor invasion (microinvasion) of the tissue of the cervix (stage 1A). The tumor is still easily treatable by means of a simple hysterectomy. Even though the physician informs Mrs. A that there is a 90 percent chance of complete cure, she is very distraught and apprehensive. When the physician raises the issue of scheduling a time for surgery, Mrs. A is evasive and says she wants to think things over. The physician makes another appointment to speak with her a week later. Mrs. A still is very reluctant to discuss the matter of surgery but agrees that "most likely, it is something I will have to face." She then asks what risks would be involved in a hysterectomy. The physician is concerned that if he describes all of the risks in full detail (for example, injury to the bladder, to the ureter [the tube that connects the kidney and the bladder], injury to the bowel and/or intestinal obstruction, and urinary incontinence, not to mention possible death due to anesthesia), the woman will postpone the surgery even further. He wonders whether he should instead inform the woman's husband of the usual risks and indicate to the woman more globally that things will likely go well and that people are able to return home from the hospital after only a few days.

Case B

Mr. B is a 39-year-old clerk-typist working for a local sheriff's office. Approximately two years ago, he began to experience severe pain between his shoulder-blades. He consulted a number of physicians who prescribed medications, but this failed to control the pain. He was finally referred to a neurosurgeon. A myelogram revealed findings compatible with a ruptured disk at the level of the fifth thoracic vertebra. The physician recommends an exploratory operation likely to lead to a laminectomy. In gaining consent for the procedure, the physician informs the patient that, in addition to the risk of death due to anesthesia, there is also the risk that the operation would not in fact cure the pain, that there could be injury to major blood vessels, that the spine might become unstable, and that he might suffer impaired muscle function. The physician does not indicate that, in rare cases, patients suffer paralysis, incontinence, and impotence. In the physician's judgment, the risk is sufficiently remote not to warrant disclosure.

Case C

Mrs. C brings her 4-year-old son, Johnny, to see his pediatrician. Johnny has been running a fever, has a runny nose, and has been complaining of sore throat. He has also been pulling on his ear and complaining of pain. An examination of the eardrum reveals an absence of the light reflex and impaired mobility. It is diffusely red. The findings establish the diagnosis of otitis media (inflammation of the middle ear). Johnny's throat on examination is beefy-red with a white exudate over the tonsils. On the basis of these findings, the pediatrician decides to prescribe a form of ampicillin. Because Johnny has received ampicillin before with no indications of hypersensitivity, the pediatrician gives no warning concerning the possible side effects of the drug. On returning home, Mrs. C looks up the medication prescribed in a current reference book on drugs. She finds that not only can it cause fatal anaphylactoid reactions but also skin rashes, serum sickness, and, in rare cases, problems with the blood such as anemia, thrombocytopenia, and leukopenia. As the book indicates, these blood problems usually, but not always, disappear when the treatment stops. She asks the pediatrician why she was not informed of these risks. The pediatrician says that perhaps she should have told Mrs. C about the risk of possible allergic reactions, but they were fairly minimal, given the fact that Johnny had taken ampicillin in the past with no difficulties. However, the pediatrician asserts that the other risks are so remote as not to bear mentioning. The woman disagrees and says that she will never come back to that physician again.

In Case A, is the distress that Mrs. A experiences sufficient to warrant her physician invoking the therapeutic privilege and informing her husband, but not her, about all the risks associated with a hysterectomy? Under what circumstances is it proper to use the privilege? In Case B, should Mr. B have been told of the possibility of paralysis? How remote does a serious risk have to be in order to no longer be a material fact? Does a physician need to inform a patient about all of the risks ever reported regarding a drug, as Mrs. C insists? Does Mrs. C have a right to insist on a subjective standard of disclosure as a condition of her remaining with her pediatrician or as a part of any new physician–patient relationship?

15. CONSENT OF ADULTS TO EXPERIMENTATION

Medical research on human subjects is without any doubt essential for medical progress. Whether it be a new drug, a new device, or a new surgical procedure, there comes a point at which it must be tried out on patients who might benefit from it if it works or who might suffer harm from it if it has unforeseen problems. It is even sometimes necessary to experiment on human subjects (healthy or ill) to obtain basic knowledge not otherwise obtainable. This may even be done without having any hope that the experiments will directly benefit the experimental subjects, although it might benefit others at some later time. In a very preliminary fashion, we can see that such experimentation might force us as a society to choose between an appeal to consequences, which would justify it, and an appeal to the rights of the subjects, which would challenge its legitimacy. Moreover, such experiments might lead, on the one hand, to conflicts in the obligations of individual clinicians to their patients, and, on the other hand, to the need for medical knowledge.

There is no doubt but that sensitivity to this problem has greatly increased by an awareness of the medical experiments carried out by the Nazis during the Second World War. Beginning with the outbreak of the war, experiments were conducted on non-German nationals, both prisoners of war and Jewish and other "asocial" civilians. This practice was barbarous. It included everything from placing victims in chambers where the pressure was lowered to simulate an increased altitude to see at what point subjects would die, to freezing people to near-death to test the most effective ways of reviving them, to infecting victims with bacteria in deliberately inflicted wounds to test the effectiveness of drugs, to infecting subjects with typhus to test the effectiveness of proper vaccines, and so forth. Naturally, a large percentage of the subjects died, and most of the others suffered immensely. Those responsible for running these tests were tried at Nuremberg after the war. One of them, Dr. Gerhard Rose, put his defense as follows:

> Without these experiments, the vaccines, which were recognized as useless, would have been produced in large quantities. The victims of this Buchenwald typhus test did not suffer in vain and did not die in vain. There was only one choice, the sacrifice of human lives, of persons determined for the purpose, or to let things run their course, to endanger the lives of innumerable human beings. . . . Aside from the self-experimentation of doctors, which represents a very small minority of such experiments, the extent to which subjects are volunteers is often deceptive. In the majority of such cases, if we ethically examine facts, we find an exploitation of the ignorance, the frivolity, the economic distress, or other emergency on the part of the experimental subjects.[1]

In response to this appeal to consequences combined with a radical cynicism, the Nuremberg court identified ten principles governing appropriate medical experimentation. Some were clearly based on analyzing consequences. Experiments should be designed to minimize risks to subjects, should not be carried out when the risks are too high, and should be justified by the sufficient importance of the knowledge to be obtained. Other principles are clearly based on a consideration of the rights of the subjects. These include the principles that experimenters must obtain the voluntary consent of the subjects involved, based on subjects having adequate information, and that subjects must be free to withdraw in the middle of the experiment if they no longer find it acceptable. Ideas similar to these have been embodied in the World Medical Association's Declaration of Helsinki of 1964.

Interest in regulating human experimentation developed somewhat later in the United States, and the first attempts at regulation began in the 1960s. One set of regulations came from the Food and Drug Administration (FDA). The background to these were the thalidomide-inspired Javits Amendments to the Drug Act of 1962. There had been considerable controversy in the late 1950s over the thalidomide disaster, in which many children were born with under-developed limbs because thalidomide had been taken by their mothers during the first trimester of pregnancy. The FDA, in response to this legislation introduced by Senator Jacob Javits, issued regulations in 1966 requiring informed consent before the use of investigational drugs. At the same time, the National Institutes of Health adopted regulations assigning safety review of human research and review of patient rights to local peer-review committees. Contained in these regulations from the mid-1960s are the two major themes from Nuremberg and Helsinki, namely minimizing risks and obtaining informed consent. By the early 1970s these regulations had come to govern all federally funded research and applied to all research with human subjects. In the meantime, Congress had become very interested in these matters, in large measure because of hearings held on possible legislation to remedy problems discovered in a major federally funded study, the Tuskegee Syphilis Study (1932–1972), where it was alleged that important health care had been withheld from the subjects without

---

[1]Jay Katz, *Experimentation with Human Beings* (New York: Russell Sage, 1972), p. 300.

their knowledge. Congress established in 1974 a National Commission for the Protection of Human Subjects, which issued reports from 1975 to 1978. In large measure, these reports were incorporated into the current regulations for adult research, which were adopted in January 1981.

What is required by these regulations? The crucial requirement is that each institution conducting research has an independent committee, called an Institutional Review Board, which must approve all research on human subjects before it can begin. Approval must be based upon a determination that the research:

1. Minimizes risks to subjects;
2. Has risks that are reasonable in relation to anticipated benefits, if any, to subjects, and the importance of the knowledge that may reasonably be expected to result;
3. Involves an equitable selection of subjects;
4. Involves subjects who have given informed consent;
5. Adequately protects confidentiality and privacy;
6. Contains safeguards to protect subjects vulnerable to coercion or undue influence.

The requirement of informed consent is explained as including information about the nature of the experimental procedure, the reasonably foreseeable risks or discomforts, the benefits to the subjects or others, alternatives, the extent of the confidentiality of the records, possible compensation for injuries, the obligation to contact subjects if problems arise, and the right of subjects to refuse to participate or to withdraw. In addition, there are special protections for pregnant women and for prisoners.

Having reviewed the history of the recent attempts to regulate research with human subjects, we need to stop and ask ourselves some crucial questions about the regulations that have emerged. Some of these questions center around the relative importance of these two themes: ensuring a favorable risk/benefit ratio and ensuring consent of the subjects. What moral appeals justify each of them? Should we allow experiments that contain one but not the other? If not, why not? What moral arguments could be given, for example, to justify not allowing any experiments as long as the subjects truly consent in an informed and free fashion? Other questions focus on who benefits from the research. The regulations allow risk research where the benefits, if sufficient, will accrue to future patients and not to the subjects ("non-therapeutic research"). Review at this point the views of Fried and Brody in Section C9 of the readings. Would either or both agree to the permissibility of such research? Another set of requirements centers around the information required by the federal regulations for informed consent for experimentation. Are they more or less than the requirements imposed on regular therapy by the *Canterbury* decision in the reading in Section A4? What would Capron say about them? What would the Jewish Compendium on Medical Ethics say?

We turn now to cases involving medical research.

Case A

In 1976, the national surgical adjuvant project for breast and bowel cancers launched a multicenter, randomized trial to compare mastectomies (removal of the entire breast) and lumpectomies (removal only of the tumor and the surrounding tissue) in patients with small breast cancers. By 1978, it had become clear that not enough patients were being enrolled. A major difficulty was getting physicians to ask their patients to consent to being randomly assigned to one or another group, thereby admitting ignorance and truly asking patients to have their fate settled in a random fashion. Another major difficulty was getting patients to understand the very detailed information presented in the consent form required by the relevant Institutional Review Boards (IRBs). To meet this problem, the study adopted a new approach called prerandomization. It was designed to eliminate not all of the above-mentioned problems but at least one of them, namely, having to obtain the patient's consent to being "randomized," to participate without knowing in advance what treatment will be administered. This technique involves having physicians randomly assign patients to one or another treatment before discussing the study, then asking patients to participate if they will accept that treatment, but allowing them in the end to be treated in any way they prefer. With this change, the study was able to move forward. Still, many people were concerned that the physician's knowledge of the assigned treatment resulted in conscious or subconscious tailoring of the study presentation to dispose the patient to accept the assigned therapy.

Case B

The role of blood clots in coronary arteries in the development of a heart attack has, in recent years, come to be seen as very central. Therefore, there is now increasing interest in administering to patients medications that dissolve clots (thrombolytic agents) as soon as possible after their heart attack begins. In 1984, a study began to test the merits of two such medications: streptokinase and recombinant tissue plasminogen activator. The former was often (but by no means usually) used before the study; the latter was a promising alternative. Patients who consented to participate in the study were randomized to receive one or the other of these medications intravenously. The goal of the study was to see which medication produced a quicker and fuller dissolution of the clot with fewer side effects.

Case C

In 1972, the National Health, Lung, and Blood Institute funded a study called the Multiple Risk Factor Intervention Trial (MRFIT) designed to see whether proper treatment and counseling could lower the incidence of coronary heart disease in high-risk patients, patients with combined histories of cigarette smoking, elevated serum cholesterol, and elevated blood pressure. Half the subjects were randomized to receive special interventions including stepped-care treatment for hypertension, counseling for cigarette smoking, and dietary advice for lowering blood cholesterol. The other half were simply invited to return annually for physical and laboratory studies, the results of which were sent to their physicians with an explanation of the study. These subjects received no special interventions. A crucial point to be noted is the study's claim that "Ethical consideration prompted notification of these physicians of the findings from each annual visit, although the MRFIT centers made no recommendation regarding intervention for usual care men."[2] It is this issue that we need to examine carefully.

2"Multiple Risk Factor Intervention Trial," *JAMA* 248 (September 24, 1982), 1475.

Many questions are raised by Case A. Before considering them, however, it is worth pointing out that this example once more illustrates the importance of research on human subjects. In the 1970s, when this study began, we really did not know whether or not the less disfiguring lumpectomies would be as good for saving lives as the more disfiguring mastectomies. The only way to find out was to run a randomized trial. This appeal to consequences to justify human experimentation must always be kept in mind. We turn now to the questions raised by Case A. The first of these has to do with the amount of information to be provided to the subjects. In truth, there is tremendous uncertainty about the best way of managing early breast cancer. Meeting the requirements of the federal regulations involved providing very complete information, information that many physicians felt was too much for patients having to make a difficult and emotion-laden choice without background information. Physicians therefore chose to get consent for their favorite approach, using, no doubt, a lesser standard of information. Just how much and what type of information do the federal regulations require in such a case? Would *Canterbury* require less information if the physician was just obtaining consent for a patient's usual treatment? Are both of these standards too high, and would some lesser standard be more appropriate? A second question has to do with the prerandomization approach. Is it a viable solution to the problems raised by such important studies? Does it meet the federal requirements? Are there any other ethical problems with it? Is the fear of bias any worse than the bias involved in obtaining ordinary consent?

In Case B we are dealing once more with a very important study whose implications for the management of patients shortly after their heart attack are great. The information to be obtained is significant, the patients themselves may benefit from the study (if they get the better medication), and the risks were carefully minimized by the study group. So most of the federal regulations were certainly met. But what about the requirement of obtaining informed consent, a requirement that was so central to the Nuremberg Code, the Declaration of Helsinki, and the current federal regulations? Can one meaningfully talk about obtaining informed consent (using a two-page, single-spaced detailed information form) from a scared and medicated patient so quickly after a heart attack? If not, should informed consent be obtained from the family? Are family members in any better position to assess the issues and give their consent? It is interesting to go back to the *Canterbury* decision in Section A4. That court allowed therapeutic interventions in emergency situations without informed consent. Might we not legitimately extend that emergency exception to cover very important research whose benefits might well accrue to the experimental subject?

Case C raises still further questions. By 1972 sufficient evidence indicated that these risk factors contributed significantly to coronary heart disease. Interventions that could lower these risk factors promised much benefit to the subjects receiving them. Would it be morally appropriate to withhold those interventions from the control group? The MRFIT study compromised by withholding those interventions but also by notifying the subjects' usual physicians about the findings (knowing very well that they might initiate the interventions). Was that compromise a fair and just solution to this problem? Note that the federal regulations and the Declaration of Helsinki say nothing about risks to the control group, which does not receive the interventions in question. Is that a serious gap? How should it be met?

16. CONFIDENTIALITY

The Hippocratic oath stresses confidentiality as one of the cardinal obligations of physicians ". . . [W]hatsoever I shall see or hear in the course of my profession, as well as outside my profession in my intercourse with men, if it be what should not be published abroad, I will never divulge, holding such things to be holy secrets." (W.H.S. Jones' translation). This attitude has persisted in medicine. In 1803 Thomas Percival stated that "Secrecy and delicacy, when required by peculiar circumstances, should be strictly observed."[1] This work influenced the development of the first code of medical ethics of the American Medical Association, which was adopted in Philadelphia in May 1847. According to Article I, Section 2, "The obligation of secrecy extends beyond the period of professional services:—none of the privacies of personal and domestic life, no infirmity of disposition or flaw of character observed during professional attendance, should ever be divulged by him [the physician] except when he is imperatively required to do so." Although the Hippocratic oath would suggest that there are no exceptions to the obligation to maintain confidentiality, in the modern Western world various exceptions have been recognized. These have concerned for the most part testimony in court and the reporting of communicable diseases. However, various threats to confidentiality have developed as more physicians have become employees of corporations and as medical records have been computerized and disseminated to insurance companies and regulatory agencies.

The result is a tension between the role of the physician as custodian of the health and best interests of patients and a competing role in which physicians are also cast as custodians of the public health or employees of companies or agencies. This conflict has similarities with those within other professions that maintain client confidentiality. One might think here of the tension between attorneys as advocates of a client and as officers of the court. American law has recognized a near-absolute privilege for the attorney–client relationship, reasoning that only in this fashion can an adequate defense be mounted on behalf of a client. If clients are fearful that their lawyers will disclose information, an appropriate defense will not be possible in an adversary system of justice. So, too, it has been argued that a defendant needs at least one individual in whom he or she can confide when confronted with the force of the state. Still, this role may conflict with the attorney's role as an individual committed to truth and to the service of justice.

A similar argument has been made for the obligation of physicians to keep communications confidential and for a legal privilege to be secure against having to disclose confidential information to third parties, including the courts. In most cases, physicians do not enjoy such a privilege. The conflict between physicians as advocates of a patient's health versus physicians as citizens with the duty to testify in court or as agents of public health with a duty to report communicable diseases or warn third parties tends to be resolved in favor of exceptions to the physicians' duties of confidentiality. Further conflicts arise when a physician is hired by a company or school in which the patient is either employed or studies. So, too, physicians in the military find that they face special conflicts between their role as officers and their role as physicians. A corporation, a

[1]Chauncey Leake (ed.), *Percival's Medical Ethics* (Huntington, N.Y.: Krieger, 1975).

school, or the military may wish to have information that has been disclosed by a patient to a physician, which would under other circumstances remain confidential.

Generally, physicians are required to report gunshot wounds, communicable diseases, child abuse, and similar findings. Moreover, physicians' records can be subpoenaed and revealed in criminal and civil court proceedings. Outside of such legally compelled disclosures, records are usually confidential in the sense that physicians are obliged not to disclose them to third parties without the permission of the patient. This general state of law and public policy is well summarized by the American Medical Association in its statement of the physician's duties of confidentiality.

> The information disclosed to a physician during the course of the relationship between physician and patient is confidential to the greatest possible degree. The patient should feel free to make a full disclosure of information to the physician in order that the physician can most effectively provide needed services. The patient should be able to make this disclosure with the knowledge that the physician will respect the confidential nature of the communication. The physician should not reveal confidential communications or information without the express consent of the patient unless required to do so by law.
>
> The obligation to safeguard patient confidences is subject to certain exceptions, which are ethically and legally justified because of overriding social considerations. Where a patient threatens to inflict serious bodily harm to another person and there exists a reasonable probability that the patient may carry out the threat, the physician should take reasonable precautions for the protection of the intended victim, including notification of law-enforcement authorities. Also, communicable diseases and gunshot and knife wounds should be reported as required by applicable statutes or ordinances.[2]

One might note that a proposed "Ethics Guidelines for Sex Therapists, Sex Counselors, and Sex Researchers" suggests that it will not be unethical under certain circumstances to refuse to divulge legally required information. "A sex therapist who believes that an unjustified violation of the confidentiality and trust of the therapist–client relationship would occur if such material were divulged under legal edict in response to a subpoena may properly refuse to comply and will not be viewed as acting in other than an ethical manner within the context of these guidelines."[3]

The moral justification for confidentiality and its exceptions depends in part on the contention that, if physicians come to possess information that would be divulged to them only if strict confidentiality were offered, no one is harmed if the physician then does not divulge the information required. The physician would not have acquired that information had assurance of confidentiality not been offered. Third parties are not in any worse position as a result of strict physician–patient confidentiality in such circumstances. Indeed, if confidentiality encourages effective treatment of conditions that pose a danger to third parties, and effective persons would come to treatment only later or not at all in

---

[2]*Current Opinions of the Judicial Council of the American Medical Association—1984*, 5.05, p. 19.

[3]*Ethical Issues in Sex Therapy and Research*, Vol. 2, W.H. Masters, V.E. Johnson, R.C. Kolodny, S.M. Weems (eds.). (Boston: Little, Brown, 1980), p. 411.

the absence of the assurance of strict confidentiality, then the assurance of strict confidentiality will in general benefit third parties. On the other hand, it may be difficult to contemplate the fact that physicians may know information that would benefit third parties, who are at risk for serious harm, without disclosing that information.

These questions raise moral issues of a general sort regarding the extent to which the physician is a trusted adviser, as Charles Fried describes the role, or in fact is closer to being a social agent, as Baruch Brody contends. Decisions will depend in part on the consequentialist considerations raised in the preceding paragraph regarding when a practice of assuring strict confidentiality will lead to the greatest good for the greatest number. It will depend as well on questions of when duties of beneficence to particular individuals who are at risk will override consequentialist considerations to keep confidentiality. In addition, one will need to be clear to patients about the extent to which confidentiality can be assured. If a physician promises strict confidentiality, there may be a special obligation to preserve it, even when there is no legal recognition of the strict confidentiality that has been assured. Here the virtue of honesty has an important expression. In short, the practice of confidentiality raises questions about the consequences of practices, conflicts of rights, and the problem of balancing consequence-oriented and rights-oriented approaches to bioethics.

Case A

Mr. A is a 33-year-old salesman. He consults his family physician the day after returning from a convention and reports that he is concerned that he may have contracted gonorrhea. Although he has not yet informed the physician of his symptoms, he suffers pain and burning on urination, has noted some puslike discharge from his penis, and has experienced a need to urinate frequently, though he produces very little urine. He informs the physician that he will not provide a history of his symptoms or allow the physician to examine him unless he can be assured of strict confidentiality. He does tell the physician that he had sex with a prostitute on the first night of the convention and five days prior to consulting the physician. The salesman explains to the physician that he has not yet had intercourse with his wife and that there is no way to track down the prostitute to have her treated. Thus, no good will be served by reporting his case should he have gonorrhea.

Case B

Because of their concern for the increasing number of child-abuse cases in the large metropolitan area where they practice, one pediatrician and two psychiatrists decide to establish a special clinic for child abusers. They have data to support the view that their therapeutic technique is remarkably effective in extinguishing this behavior. These physicians are convinced that, unless they are able to offer strict confidentiality, parents will not come for care until they have significantly abused their children. They wish, as a result, to offer strict confidentiality, even though this violates the reporting laws of the state in which they practice. Such strict confidentiality, they argue, would be beneficial because the cases of child abuse that would come to their attention would not be those discovered in the ordinary practice of medicine.

Case C

Mr. C is a 55-year-old pilot who has three months left before retiring with maximum pension benefits. If he is removed from his duties as an active pilot prior to that time, his retirement benefits will be diminished. He is not due for a required physical for another six months. Mr. C goes to see a private cardiologist and informs her that he is a pilot and wishes to discuss a matter with her in absolute confidentiality. Mr. C has experienced substernal pain and tightness in his chest, which occurs after eating a large meal. The pain is initially mild but increases in severity and never lasts more than about ten minutes. Mr. C says that he does not know whether it might involve his heart or might simply be indigestion, in that it is often accompanied by the desire to belch. Mr. C wants the physician to determine whether he might be suffering from angina, but he wants assurance that the physician will not report the matter to the airline for which he works. As he points out, a physical is not required for another six months, and everyone is better off if he has the matter confidentially explored at this juncture. Moreover, there is always a co-pilot when he flies.

Under what circumstances should physicians offer strict confidentiality? Should physicians be morally bound to obey all legal requirements for reporting diseases and other circumstances that come to their attention? Are physicians morally excused if honoring the requirement will deter a patient from timely treatment, and violating the requirement will not only bring prompt treatment but aid third parties? What should one make of the case of the child-abuse clinic? Given the data of the case, such a clinic can be given a very plausible utilitarian justification. On average, the chance of children being subjected to child abuse should diminish in that community because of the presence of the clinic. What should the physicians do, however, if in a particular case they have grounds to believe that a child is at significant risk? How would one develop the proper moral rules for a child-abuse clinic that offers proper confidentiality to child abusers? Finally, what should the cardiologist do in Case C? It may very well be that Mr. C is only suffering from indigestion. On the other hand, the lives of a great number of people could be jeopardized.

17. ACCESS TO HEALTH CARE

The provision of health care for the poor through both charitable organizations and through county-level support has a long history. In the nineteenth century, the development of democratic and social ideals, movements for improved public hygiene, and the increasing efficacy of medicine led to proposals to provide more comprehensive systems of health care for those unable to pay privately. The state provision of health care can be understood as a form of social insurance against the loss of the natural and social lotteries. All individuals, in running a risk of developing a disease or physical disability, are subject to the natural lottery. Also, whether one will have sufficient funds to purchase adequate health care when needed can be seen as a result of the social lottery. The creation of public policy to provide health care for those in need when they cannot pay can be seen as the fashioning of a particular societal insurance policy with certain levels of protection and with specified exceptions.

One of the original models for socialized medicine evolved out of the health insurance program developed in Germany in 1883. Today, West Germany provides a comprehensive health-care system in which over 99 percent of the population is covered. All individuals under a certain level of income are required to be covered, and additional coverage is available through private carriers. This additional coverage, for the most part, provides for the difference in costs between care in a ward (third-class care) versus a semiprivate room (second-class care). Hospitalization in a private room (first-class care) is available as well. Under the West German system there is considerable freedom in selection of physicians, and the income of physicians is closer to that of American rather than British doctors.

Another influential model for state provision of health care derives from the British National Health Service. The National Health Service Act, which went into effect in July 1948, consolidated and expanded on some 35 years of social legislation, which provided for health care in a piecemeal fashion. By 1950, 95 percent of the population was enrolled on the lists of doctors participating in the service, and 88 percent of physicians participated. Under the British system, patients enroll with a local general practitioner. When necessary, patients are referred to specialists who also may see private patients on a fee-for-service basis. In addition to all citizens being covered by the National Health Service, a small but growing percentage has directly or through their employers purchased private health-care insurance, which allows greater ease of access to elective procedures, such as inguinal hernia repairs. Under the National Health Service, an individual may wait for months before receiving an inguinal hernia repair. The British system has succeeded in keeping health-care costs to below 7 percent of the country's gross national product (GNP), whereas the percentage of the GNP in both the United States and West Germany has risen above 10 percent.

Britain has achieved cost containment by erecting barriers to access to the full range of high-technology treatments available in the United States and West Germany. Some costs are saved through discouraging treatment sought on an elective basis through long queues for admission to a hospital. In addition, high-cost, high-technology interventions that promise marginal benefits are discouraged. As a result, the United States performs many more coronary bypass operations than does the United Kingdom. Moreover, Britain, through various informal means, discourages individuals over 50 or 55 from receiving hemodialysis if they develop end-stage renal disease. However, Britain provides a wide range of social services. When a health-care system provides all-encompassing care with easy access to high-technology medicine, a higher percentage of that nation's GNP is committed to health care.

Although some provision of health care on a state and county basis existed in the United States from very early times, a large proportion of the services provided to the indigent was on a charity basis. This occurred either through hospitals associated with religious communities or through physicians providing care gratis to the poor, often by an arrangement with the county medical society or the local charity hospital. As medicine became more established as a successful science, interest increased in providing a comprehensive basis for the provision of health care to the poor. In 1916 the American Association for Labor Legislation began a campaign for national health insurance for individuals with low incomes. With the passage in 1935 of the Social Security Act, funds were made available for certain categories of indigent persons. These monies could be applied to medical expenses. By 1960, 40 states had established programs under a 1950 law allowing federal participation in the provision of medical services by states. In 1960 a bill sponsored by Senator Robert Samuel Kerr and Representative Wilbur Mills offered to expand state vendor payment programs to include aged persons who were not poor enough to qualify for cash assistance, but who did not have sufficient funds for adequate medical care.

The year 1965 saw passage of legislation creating both Medicare and Medicaid. Through Medicaid the federal government in cooperation with the states supported the provision of health care for the indigent. Each state determines its own eligibility criteria. In contrast, Medicare provided an insurance system with uniform eligibility and benefit structure throughout the United States for individuals over 65, and it covered both hospital bills and physician's bills, without an appeal to a means test. In 1972, coverage was extended to include persons with chronic renal disease and to individuals under 65 receiving disability benefits for two or more years. However, co-payments and other restrictions have been adopted. In April 1983, legislation was passed to establish a prospective reimbursement system for hospital costs covered by Medicare based on 468 diagnostically related categories (DRGs). Depending on the diagnosis, a set reimbursement was established so that costs in addition to those provided—with a certain allowance for "outliers" (patients whose treatment costs exceeded what was expected under the DRG)—had to be absorbed by the hospital. Various mechanisms have also been established to control the rising costs of Medicaid, such as Professional Standard Review Organizations (PSROs), and peer-review organizations (PROs). Limits have also been set on the amount of days reimbursable for the hospitalization of Medicaid patients.

The result is a tension among a number of important health-care goals: (1) providing the best health care, (2) providing equal care for all, (3) maximizing provider and consumer choice, and (4) cost containment. According to the *President's Commission Report on Securing Access to Health Care,* at present about 90 percent of Americans usually have some form of health-care insurance, whereas 8 percent to 11 percent have none. An additional 11 million individuals have lost insurance because of unemployment. Those who are not covered may, if they are sufficiently indigent, quality for free care at local county or other charity hospitals.

Any attempt to provide health care for those who do not receive all the health care they need or from which they can benefit raises the questions addressed in the section in this text on health-care and justice. To what extent and at what cost ought a society attempt to provide equal health care for all? Attempts to ensure equitable health care or to ensure cost containment will place restrictions on the freedom of both consumers and providers to expend resources of time and money as they freely choose. Do considerations of justice and equity constrain us to choose a particular pattern of health-care distributions for society, as is suggested both by Gutmann and Daniels? Are such choices best made by individuals, as argued by Brody? What principles of justice and of ownership are presupposed in answering such questions? Do you agree with Singer's argument that one must have a one-tier system of health care in order to ensure quality of care for the indigent? Does the pursuit of such a goal violate rights to property and free association? Does Enthoven offer a convincing means for restructuring the health-care system? In all of these considerations, how ought one to balance social goals with individual rights?

Case A

Mr. A, a 48-year-old electrical engineer, was laid off a year ago. Although his wife has been able to secure a job as a checker at a local grocery store and he a position in a fast-food restaurant, neither of them is at present covered by health insurance. After noticing a mass in his scrotum, he is brought by his wife to the emergency room of the local county hospital. The physician informs him that he has an inguinal hernia and is able to reduce it. Mr. A is told to return, should intestines again appear in his scrotum. It is determined that their income, as well as the fact that they own a home and two cars, disqualifies them from receiving surgery at the county hospital. However, Mr. A does not have enough money available to afford a hernia repair while still keeping up the payments on their mortgage. The physician suggests that Mr. A wear a truss and postpone a surgical repair either until he has saved enough money or until he has a job with insurance benefits.

Case B

Mrs. B is the common-law wife of a sharecropper and lives in a rural area where there is no easy access to physicians who will accept Medicaid patients. She has become quite concerned about the health of her five-year-old boy who seems to be very susceptible to colds and earaches and often runs high fevers. Twice he has developed convulsions due to the high fever and has ruptured his eardrum because of a middle-ear infection. The closest charity hospital is 50 miles away and is accessible only if someone gives Mrs. B a ride to a bus route into town where she can then catch a city bus and reach the hospital. The trip takes at least three hours, and then she usually has to wait several more hours before she is seen by the clinic.

Case C

Mr. and Mrs. C are in their late seventies. Mrs. C had worked as a librarian and Mr. C had been a professor at a small liberal arts college. They own their modest two-bedroom house and have small pensions in addition to Social Security. When Mrs. C notices that the professor has become even more forgetful than usual, she insists that he be evaluated by a local physician. The physician determines that Professor C is suffering from Alzheimer's disease. As the disease progresses, it becomes increasingly difficult for Mrs. C to care for her husband. She is able to have his hospitalization for acute crises reimbursed through Medicare. However, she is informed that they are not eligible for Medicaid payments to reimburse nursing home care. In order to put her husband in a nursing home, she would need to mortgage her house to secure the funds to pay for these costs. A lawyer has suggested that all of their assets be placed in Mrs. C's name and that she then divorce her husband and render him indigent and therefore eligible for Medicaid. She has heard that her state will soon be taking steps to prevent such schemes to circumvent Medicaid eligibility requirements. She finds the prospect of divorcing her husband more than she can bear, yet she does not know how to come to terms with the present circumstances of their lives.

How ought society to respond to these sorts of cases? Is it improper to force Mr. A to wear a truss and wait until he has saved sufficient funds for a hernia repair? Do the burdens to Mr. A violate Norman Daniels' principle of health care as integral to fair opportunity? What does this principle have to say with respect to the young son of the sharecropper? Should one allow such inequalities in access to health-care resources? Or, instead, is Brody correct in arguing that it would be best to give individuals funds so they could make their own choices, rather than simply provide them with a right to health care? Consider how, for example, the well-being and health of the sharecropper family in Case B might be improved if they had funds to buy a used car instead of simply possessing a right to health care. The case of Mr. C raises the issue of how society should set aside resources for the care of individuals dying of diseases such as Alzheimer's. As presently structured, the system provides funds for high-technology ICU treatment to prolong Mr. C's life, but not nursing-home care.

18. PREVENTIVE MEDICINE

It is often thought that the major improvements in life expectancy and morbidity rates experienced in Europe and America during the nineteenth and twentieth centuries were attributable to advances in medicine. As Rene Dubos and others have shown, this appears not to be the case. The mortality and morbidity rates for the major infectious diseases such as tuberculosis, scarlet fever, and diphtheria declined independently of the introduction of antibiotics or immunizations. The changes appear to have been due to improvements in the standard of living as well as the elimination of disease-carrying agents in the water and food supply through innovations such as pasteurization. One could eliminate all personal health care in America and Europe and still have a life expectancy much in excess of many parts of the third world, as well as that of America and Europe in the nineteenth century.

Preventive medicine and public health measures have traditionally been a part of medicine. Hippocrates and the Greeks generally understood that the incidence of disease was in part dependent on the quality of the environment (see the Hippocratic treatise "Airs, Waters, and Places") and on personal health habits (see the Hippocratic treatise "Regimen"). Such a view suggested that individuals are in great measure accountable for their illnesses, insofar as they could influence the mixture of their "humors." In contrast, modern scientific, high-technology medicine brought with it the notion that specific causes of disease can be treated by medicine in ways that would remove the need for patients to engage in health regimens or for societies to control deleterious environmental influences. Consider the statement of Paul Ehrlich in 1906 regarding the search for magic bullets to destroy diseases: "Substances able to exert their final action exclusively on the parasite harbored within the organism would represent, so to speak, magic bullets which seek their target of their own accord." Preventive medicine fails to convey the excitement of new scientific breakthroughs requiring the accoutrements of high technology. In addition, preventive medicine carries the quasi-moralistic message that people and societies are responsible for their health and must shoulder certain disciplines in order to avoid disease.

Because the most significant public health measures may not be the doing of physicians but rather of industrialists who raise the standard of living or regulators who require milk to be pasteurized, preventive medicine is not clearly medical. As a result, it does not fall within the charge of a powerful scientific establishment, as do, for example, the development of organ transplantation programs and intensive care units. It may falsely appear more important for the health of a developing country to have funds set aside for more high-intensity-care medicine rather than for the accumulation of capital, which will provide more and better-paying jobs, which will in turn increase health and well-being.

One of the difficulties in fashioning public health policy is that its claims and impacts are statistical. One is forced to make choices not on the basis of aiding particular identifiable individuals, but rather in terms of which programs are likely to have the greatest benefit for statistical lives. However, as the economist Guido Calabrezi has indicated, we tend to favor identifiable lives over statistical lives. We are more willing to invest $100,000 rescuing identifiable individuals trapped in a collapsed mine than to invest the same amount of money in mine safety, an investment that over the long run would save more lives. In medicine, this means that societies tend more readily to provide funds for heart transplants than funds to encourage good diets and discourage smoking. In addition, some of the choices in preventive medicine entail balancing the number of lives that are likely to be lost with one public health policy versus the number of lives likely to be lost with another. When smallpox vaccinations were still required, it was known that between one out of 4,000 to one out of 100,000 individuals vaccinated would develop encephalitis from the vaccine and that about half of those would die. The judgment was that a policy of vaccination, even though it would kill individuals, would prevent a greater loss of life by preventing smallpox epidemics.

Despite all these difficulties, preventive medicine is most easily amenable to equal distribution. Because of its pervasive effects, it also has the most significant impact on fair equality of opportunity. Would arguments such as these of Norman Daniels, as a result, lead to favoring preventive medicine over personal health care? What forms of preventive medicine should be a part of the "adequate level" of health care described by the President's Commission? Who is in authority to choose among the comparative advantages of proposed public health measures and with respect to the allocation of resources for public health interventions versus personal health care? One must determine what sort of consent should be required for those involved in public health programs. Under what circumstances may individuals refuse vaccinations or veto the chlorination or fluoridation of public water supplies?

Case A

A women's group intends to develop a free clinic for indigent women in a large metropolitan area. The organizers of the group meet to decide what services will be provided. The question arises of how often routine Pap smears should be offered. A number of recent studies suggest that providing a test every three years is sufficient. However, on closer examination of the literature, they find that this reflects a cost-benefit judgment. They calculate that the difference between providing Pap smears every year and every three years results in an identification of a woman with cancer at the cost of $50,000 worth of investments in Pap smears, given the age of the women likely to be using the clinics. The women ask them-selves: Is it worth $50,000 to offer a woman a chance of an early and complete cure of cancer of the cervix? Obviously, the cost is worth it to the woman who has her cancer identified early, even if she has to pay for her own Pap smear. The question is, is it worth it for the clinic, which must decide between yearly Pap smears and providing adequate contraception for young teenagers?

Case B

At the two-month checkup for her first-born child, Mrs. B is told by her pediatrician that it is now time to give Johnny the first of his series of DPT immunizations. Mrs. B says that she has read newspaper stories about serious side effects, including permanent mental retardation and death due to such shots. In fact, the article suggested that much of the current low incidence of whooping cough is not due to the availability of the vaccine, but to other factors such as better nutrition. For example, the mortality rate linked to whooping cough dropped from 12.5 per 100,000 in 1920 to 4.8 per 100,000 in 1930, even though immunization was not introduced until 1940. The pediatrician replies that, yes, such a decrease did take place independently of immunization, but that now, after the use of vaccination, the mortality rate is around 0.1 per 100,000. However, one must bear in mind that about one out of every 180,000 vaccinated will develop encephalitis, which may lead to permanent brain damage and death. The woman states that she does not want her child vaccinated; she will trust that enough other parents will have their children vaccinated so that she will get protection without risking her child's life. The pediatrician disagrees, pointing out that if everyone attempts to be a free rider like Mrs. B, soon there will be serious epidemics.

Case C

In a large metropolitan area, a group of concerned citizens band together to raise funds to provide education about diet to grammar school and high school students. They are impressed by recent studies that suggest that a 1 percent reduction in blood cholesterol will yield approximately a 2 percent reduction in heart disease rates. Just before they are ready to start a television campaign for contributions, supported in part by time that will be donated by local television stations, another group of citizens initiates a campaign to raise $100,000 to cover the costs of a heart transplant for a 38-year-old car mechanic living in the same city. The second campaign captures the media's attention, and the television stations inform the first group that they do not have enough time now to set aside gratis to support the group's effort and it will be at least another six months before they can do so.

Case D

Representative D is appalled by the health-care costs attributed to diseases associated with smoking. He decides to introduce into Congress an amendment to require higher contributions by smokers to Social Security. Representative D argues that this is the only way in which smokers can be made to pay their fair share of the costs they engender. A smokers' group rejoins that, if one grants that smoking may cause heart disease and lung cancer, it may be the smokers who are owed a rebate from Social Security. They point out that everyone must die of something sometime, and it benefits the Social Security fund if smokers die before they draw their Social Security benefits and/or become eligible for Medicare. A major polit-

ical debate ensues regarding the ways in which the state should discourage smoking and the extent to which smokers should be made to pay for the health costs attributable to smoking. The issue is raised of the impact of cigarette smoke on nonsmokers in closed rooms.

How should the women's group decide to expend its resources? Is there any single correct choice? Are group members forced to choose among a number of plausible alternatives, each with its own advantages and disadvantages? What of Mrs. B? Is it immoral for her to allow her son to be a free rider in order to maximize his chances? Under what circumstances, if any, would it be proper to compel Mrs. B with state force to have her child vaccinated? Is it morally proper to make such immunizations a condition for attending public school? In Case C, have the television stations chosen improperly in favoring the campaign for the transplant over the diet-education program? What are the moral principles to which one can appeal in choosing to invest resources in saving statistical lives rather than individual lives? Finally, one must observe that, as Case D suggests, the final costs and benefits for a society of any health practice are complex. As with all utilitarian analyses, one will need to assess all the consequences, not just some, that are likely to follow from a policy or a set of actions.

19. OCCUPATIONAL SAFETY AND THE SOCIAL RESPONSIBILITY TO PREVENT JOB-RELATED ILLNESS AND DEATH

The previous class of cases involved value questions that arise when we recognize that individuals can lower the likelihood of suffering from certain illnesses or of dying prematurely by modifying their individual behavior (for example, the way they drive, what they eat or drink, whether they smoke). We will now look at value questions that arise when we consider other ways of preventing illness or death, ways that cannot be adopted by an individual acting in isolation because they require social decisions and joint action. Such ways can be thought of as *public health measures,* using that term in its broadest sense. They include traditional public health measures such as providing safe drinking water, properly disposing of human wastes, vaccinating against certain diseases, and so forth. They also include more recent public health measures designed to prevent illness or death by modifying the environment in general, or the work environment in particular, so as to lessen certain risks. Because of considerations of space, we will focus on occupational safety.

It has long been recognized that the work environment, especially in an industrialized society, poses many hazards to the health and/or life of workers. In the latter half of the nineteenth and the first half of the twentieth century, attention focused on responding to these hazards by developing ways to compensate workers who had suffered traumatic sudden injuries (for example, losing an arm caught in a machine) or to compensate the family of those who died in such industrial accidents. Anglo-American common law had developed several legal doctrines that stood in the way of workers receiving this compensation. These included the doctrine of *assumption of risk* (workers assumed the risks of the job when they took it, presumably because it paid a higher salary than if the worker had a less-risky job); the *fellow-servant rule* (workers could not collect from their employers for harm caused by a fellow worker, because fellow workers are responsible for watching out for each other's negligence); and *contributory negligence* (the worker does not deserve compensation if the accident is at least partly the worker's fault). To avoid these problems, America introduced in the first part of this century a worker's compensation scheme designed to compensate employees for lost wages and for medical expenses due to industrial accidents. These schemes have their own shortcomings, but they were effective enough to blunt the problem of compensation for accidents in those states (40 by 1920, all the states by 1948) which developed them.

There are two major gaps in worker's compensation schemes. First, because they are designed to address industrial accidents, they do little to address the question of injuries to health or death caused by slow-acting exposure to toxic substances. Secondly, and perhaps more importantly, they do nothing to mitigate these health problems; they merely compensate the victims.

These issues came to the forefront in the 1960s and 1970s. To begin with, certain well-known examples attracted considerable public attention. It was discovered that coal workers suffered from "black lung" disease (pneumoconiosis), which produced considerable disability and even death. In addition, prolonged inhalation of asbestos particles, it was discovered, results in severe pulmonary fibrosis and respiratory disability, which continues to progress even after the exposure is discontinued, and which also leads to cancer of the lung and the pleura (mesothelioma). Exposure to cotton dust, it was learned, leads to chronic bronchitis and emphysema. All of these cases involve particles inhaled by the worker. Other well-known examples involved exposure to toxic fluids and metals. Low-level chronic exposure to benzene, it was discovered, produces a higher risk of leukemia as well as many other less life-threatening problems. Cancer of the lung is common in fishermen whose nets are preserved by the use of tar. (Interestingly, this discovery parallels Potts' discovery in 1775 that London chimney sweeps, exposed to coal tar in chimneys, exhibited a high rate of scrotal cancer.) Moreover, several books on worker safety and health were published, some of which blamed the problem on a conspiracy (the Ralph Nader task force report *Bitter Wages*), some of which blamed it on a lack of any incentive for managers to be safety-conscious (Roy Davidson's *Peril on the Job*), and some of which blamed the problem on a lack of understanding (Franklin Wallick's *The American Worker: An Endangered Species*). All of these discoveries and controversies led to the passage of the Occupational Safety and Health Act of 1970.

What are the main provisions of this act? The crucial point to understand in answering this question is that this law was intended to prevent occupational disease, not to provide compensation. Its goal is

> to assure so far as possible every working man and woman in the nation safe, healthful working conditions.

Employers are required to comply with health and safety standards promulgated under the act, and each employer shall furnish to each of his employees employment and a place of employment which are free from recognized hazards that are causing or are likely to cause death or serious physical harm to his employees.

Crucial to this law is the requirement that the Secretary of Labor, in pomulgating standards dealing with toxic materials,

> shall set the standard which most adequately assures, to the extent feasible, on the basis of the best available evidence, that no employee will suffer material impairment of health or functional capacity even if such employee has regular exposure to the hazard . . . for the period of his working life.

The development of these standards has turned out to be a very complex matter, illustrating many of the issues to which we need to turn our attention. Let us focus on one example, namely, the development of a standard for vinyl chloride, one of the first standards developed under the OSHA legislation. Vinyl chloride is a gas that is the primary component in the production of polyvinyl chloride, a white resin used in the manufacture of more than half of all plastic products. It has been known for some time that exposure to vinyl chloride could produce health hazards, and there were industrywide standards limiting such exposure. In early 1974, the B.F. Goodrich Chemical Company discovered that three employees working with vinyl chlorine in their Kentucky plant had died from a rare cancer—angiosarcoma of the liver. The Occupational Safety and Health Administration (OSHA) issued in April of that year a temporary standard restricting exposure to 50 ppm. Then, further animal tests revealed that angiosarcoma *might* be caused even at that level. But no one was sure. OSHA, backed by organized labor, issued as a final standard a "no detectable level" rule, a rule that set the upper limit of exposure at 1 ppm. Strict monitoring standards and extensive medical surveillance standards were also introduced. The chemical industry challenged these standards, saying that evidence for their need was insufficient, that there were major technological problems in their implementation, and that the cost would be prohibitive. It lost the court challenge. As a result, several plants closed, and the remaining plants spent $200 million to $300 million to meet the standards. One conservative estimate is that the cost per year of lives saved will be in the range of $400,000 to $500,000.

The first question raised by this early example of OSHA regulation is the question of cost per year of lives saved. The cost is paid, of course, by society as a whole (in the increased costs of plastic products) rather than by those whose lives are saved. In this respect, the adoption of this standard needs to be viewed as part of the increasing cost of health care discussed in the readings in Section C8. In a world of limited resources, is it an appropriate expenditure? What would defenders of the sanctity of life say? What would the President's Commission say? Is this type of protection part of what we are required to provide to all people, regardless of the fact that they do not pay for it? What would Gibbard say? Daniels? The President's Commission? The second question relates to the standard resulting in certain plants closing because it would be very expensive for these plants to meet the standard. Workers in those plants were given no choice about that decision. Should they have been given the option of taking the risks involved to preserve their jobs? Is that part of the autonomy advocated by the President's Commission and others in the readings in Section A3? If not, why not? If so, how can these standards be defended? The final questions relate to the issue of uncertainty in this case. Should we always err on the side of safety? How should decisions involving levels of safety take into account the question of uncertainty?

Case A

For years, industrial-health experts knew that exposure to benzene might lead to various nonmalignant diseases. This led to an industrial policy of limiting exposure to 10 ppm averaged over an 8-hour period, with a maximum at any one time of 25 ppm. Studies began to show that benzene, at high doses, led to leukemia. It was not known how low an exposure to benzene produced that result. It was also not clear how much it would cost to lower the exposure for all workers to 1 ppm. Nevertheless, OSHA decided to introduce regulations limiting the exposure to 1 ppm. Was that desirable?

Case B

Exposure to certain toxic substances produced considerable risks for fetuses. To avoid that problem, a major chemical plant announced that women of childbearing age would be removed from jobs where they, and possibly their fetuses, would be exposed to these toxic substances. They would be given other jobs if that were possible, but, in fact, many would be laid off entirely. To avoid that problem, five women arranged to be sterilized. What should we do in this case?

Many questions are raised by Case A. How much should we spend to produce some further safety in the workplace? Would we be better off spending that money on other more traditional public health measures or on other forms of health care? Who should make that decision? On what basis? Suppose some workers are thrown out of work by this regulation. Should they be allowed to choose to work at a higher level of exposure, especially since the risk is unclear? These questions need careful consideration. The reader needs to compare Case A to the vinyl chloride case to see if these questions, raised by each case, can be answered differently in the two situations.

Case B raises many difficult additional questions. To begin with, we need to decide what protection society as a whole and potential mothers owe to fetuses. This raises in a special way all of the issues of personhood discussed in the readings in Section B5. But it also raises the very different question of equality in society. If a job is unsafe for a woman of childbearing age, should we allow men to hold these jobs in their place? Should we instead limit exposure to toxic substances for all workers? Finally, Case B raises a special problem for the physicians who were asked by the women that they be sterilized in order to keep their jobs. Was that request, made for the above reason, a legitimate exercise of autonomy? Would it depend on their age, their marital status, or the number of children they already had? How would the President's Commission reply? How would Thomasma, Miller, and Clements and Sider answer?

20. ALTERNATIVE FORMS OF CARE

Modern medicine appears to many as a uniform, encompassing, and generally accepted body of scientific theories, facts, and scientifically based treatments. This has not always been the case, nor is it without exception the case today. There have always existed numerous and competing accounts of diseases and treatment, many of which are still represented by practitioners today. These include *homeopaths,* whose theories were developed by Friedrich Samuel Christian Hahnemann (1755–1843). He summarized his theory of medicine in the maxim, *Similia similibus curantur* (likes are cured by likes), as opposed to the maxim of orthodox medicine, *Contraria contrariis curantur* (dissimilars are cured by dissimilars). Hahnemann argued against the use of cupping, blistering, repeated bleeding, powerful emetics, and strong purgatives. His philosophy of restraint offered his patients in many cases more benefit than did the orthodox medicine of the time (which homeopaths termed *allopathy*). Homeopathy commits itself to the use of medications at great dilutions, as well as to supporting the vital forces of the patient so as to restore health.

The nineteenth century saw the developments of a number of non-standard approaches, many of which have survived into the twentieth century. *Hydrotherapy,* or the water cure, was developed as a system of medicine by individuals such as Vincenz Priessnitz (1799–1851) and the nineteenth-century German-born philosopher of technology, Ernst Kapp, who made his home in Texas. Many of the "baths" of Europe recall this popular mode of treatment. The nineteenth century also gave us *osteopathy,* whose founder A.T. Still (1828–1917) established the American School of Osteopathy in Kirksville, Missouri, in 1892. Although Still decried the use of drugs and supported a new system of healing based on an account of "structural derangements," modern osteopathy is nearly indistinguishable from orthodox medicine. There are numerous schools of osteopathy, and many physicians have a D.O. degree rather than an M.D. degree. Among the systems that have remained apart from orthodox medicine is *chiropractic,* which was founded by Daniel David Palmer in 1895 in Davenport, Iowa, and developed further by his son, B.J. Palmer. They propounded a theory of treatment based on a system of adjusting vertebrae of the spinal column. Currently, not only are there a number of degree-granting schools of chiropractic, but many insurance policies provide for chiropractic treatment.

Physicians in the nineteenth century and early twentieth century were generally held to the standards of their school. In this fashion, law and public policy acknowledged the existence of widely different approaches to medical theory and medical treatment. The law did not require patients to choose any particular theory; rather, it required physicians to meet the standards of care and treatment of the school to which they were allied. Some of this tolerance toward the diversity of medical theories weakened as the views of orthodox medicine became established and accepted as the standard scientific account.

The nineteenth century also saw a continued emphasis on religious approaches to the cure and treatment of diseases. The Christian West traditionally erected shrines at various sites where miracles and healing occurred. Such shrines are often filled with crutches, braces, and other tokens of grateful pilgrims and petitioners. This faith in miraculous cures remains prominent, as attested not only by Lourdes but by television programs where evangelists demonstrate their healing powers. A unique nineteenth-century synthesis of these religious concerns with a system of treatment was *Christian Science,* founded by Mary Baker Eddy, who propounded a "scientific system of divine healing." Christian Science, according to Mary Baker Eddy, teaches its adherents "to forsake and overcome every form of error or evil on the basis of its unreality." Error and evil are interpreted to include disease, which can be overcome through Christian Science. Currently, reimbursement for Christian Science practitioners is provided by Medicare.

The twentieth century has produced its own wide range of nonstandard approaches to the cure of diseases and the promotion of health. Advocates of laetrile, vitamin C, and various diets continue to vie with orthodox medicine for the attention of patients. As a consequence, there are many well-established nonstandard forms of medical treatment. In the past, before orthodox medicine could in fact effectively treat disease and postpone death, it probably made very little difference whether one relied on standard treatments or not. In many cases, patients probably fared better if they relied on other than the heroic interventions of orthodox medicine. The difficulty is how to regard such alternative forms of treatment now that medicine can often make a decisive difference in curing disease and postponing death. How should physicians and others respond when patients choose other than a standard form of treatment, especially when it appears that such a choice involves a serious risk to the patient? How ought one to react when patients rely on prayer rather than on medicine, especially given the traditional American right to act on one's own religious convictions? These problems are complicated when the decisions involve not only adults but also children, who may not fully appreciate the significance of their rejection of standard forms of medical care.

In analyzing the rights of individuals to choose for themselves or their children non-standard forms of treatment, one returns to the fundamental issues raised by the selections in this text concerning informed consent and the role of the patient. The more that one takes autonomy seriously, the more one is forced to conclude that individuals have a right to do things that are wrongheaded. The purchase price of freedom is often tragedy. Even if one agrees with this point, one must confront the issues that Locke raises with regard to the status of children. To what extent may parents influence or constrain their children's choice of non-standard forms of treatment, particularly when such treatment involves a significant risk or when a serious disease or disability is involved that could be cured by standard treatment? How ought one to compare the competing claims of orthodox and non-standard forms of health care? To what extent ought the state to forbid the practice of non-standard forms of medicine that do not have the efficacy of standard forms? Costello and colleagues argue against licensure and in favor of certification. This would allow a wide range of free choice to forms of non-standard care. Costello and colleagues define their position in terms of rights considerations and the consequences of alternative policies. Do you agree with either of their arguments? How would you apply Miller's and Thomasma's analyses of patient autonomy to choices of non-standard forms of medical care?

Case A

Mr. A, 44, decides to start a vigorous exercise program. He consults his family physician for a workup prior to beginning jogging and a general fitness program. Changes on the electrocardiogram during a stress test suggest that Mr. A may be suffering from mild coronary artery disease. He is referred by his physician to a cardiovascular surgeon who thoroughly evaluates Mr. A and determines that he has coronary artery disease involving one of his coronary arteries. The surgeon suggests coronary bypass surgery and Mr. A agrees. On the day he is hospitalized prior to the surgery, he begins to talk freely about his history and the findings with one of the nurses. This nurse is usually assigned to the internal medicine service but has for this month been working on the cardiovascular surgery service instead. The nurse has spent a great deal of time listening to discussions by internists concerning cases such as Mr. A's, who they believe are best treated by a conservative medical approach rather than a surgical approach. The nurse realizes that many internists believe that the surgical procedure offers no increase in life expectancy and, because Mr. A has no angina, probably no improvement in morbidity. In fact, the surgery may involve useless pain and suffering. She asks Mr. A whether he ever considered getting a second opinion from an internist. He replies no. She wonders whether she should inform him that he might very well wish to reconsider a conservative medical approach instead of the surgical approach.

Case B

Mr. B is a 67-year-old retired waiter who is diagnosed as having cancer of the head of the pancreas after a CAT scan is performed as part of a workup for unexplained painless obstructive jaundice. His physicians tell him that an operative intervention to treat the disease will likely itself involve one chance in five of dying. In addition, the best treatment can probably offer him no more than a 15 percent five-year survival rate. He is asked on a Thursday to consider over the weekend what he wants to do and then to come back and inform his physician the following Monday morning. On Monday Mr. B returns. He has decided to go to a cancer clinic outside of the United States. The clinic's cancer therapy consists of laetrile and a diet high in vitamins and free of artificial additives. The clinic claims that at least 50 percent of individuals with cancer of the head of the pancreas can be cured with this therapy. Mr. B's physicians are outraged and state that he would simply be wasting his money. If he does not want to take the long-shot chance of being cured by surgery, Mr. B should at least rely on standard medical support in order to make his last days as comfortable as possible.

Case C

Mrs. C is a 22-year-old secretary who is apparently in excellent health. Ten days after seeing her physician for a routine Pap smear, she is asked to return when the results are positive. A careful examination of her cervix reveals a small ulcerated lesion; a punch biopsy is taken and read as microinvasive carcinoma of the cervix. She is informed that she has Stage IA cancer of the cervix, which is easily treatable by a simple hysterectomy. Chances of a permanent cure are over 90 percent. Mrs. C is visibly overwhelmed by the news, thanks the physician very much, and begins to leave the office. The physician emphasizes that Mrs. C must have a hysterectomy, otherwise the cancer will spread and she will die. She says she does not believe that is the case. She has read a book that has convinced her that current radical treatments for cancer do more harm than good, and she intends to treat the problem with a new high-vitamin, all-vegetarian regimen. The physician is appalled by this response and calls Mr. C to inform him of his wife's decision. Mr. C tells the physician that he agrees with his wife and believes that medicine's invasive procedures are uncalled-for. The physician is distressed that this woman who could be easily cured will likely return for treatment only when her cancer has spread, at which time it will be incurable.

Case D

Mr. and Mrs. D are a devoutly religious Roman Catholic family who have six sons and four daughters. Their 12-year-old daughter suffers a fracture of her right femur just above the knee while playing football. The treating physician, when examining the fracture, concludes from the X ray that the daughter, Miss D, may have osteogenic sarcoma of the leg. Miss D and her parents are referred to a physician at a university medical center. That physician confirms that it is very likely that she does have a sarcoma and that it will be necessary to amputate her leg and to provide chemotherapy for her to have any hope of survival. The physician indicates that Miss D has a greater than 50 percent chance of a complete cure. The parents and the daughter are shocked by this news and indicate that they first want to discuss the matter with their priest. They return three days later to inform the physician that they do not intend to allow amputation but will instead take their child to Lourdes. The physician asks why they would ever do such a thing. The parents quite calmly respond that they have faith in God, and they have heard of a recent case of a similar cure. Moreover, the daughter does not want to live without a leg, and the priest informs them that her strong aversion to the amputation makes the intervention an instance of extraordinary care.

Case E

The executive committee of a union has been petitioned by members to ask that future insurance coverage for workers also reimburse for chiropractic care. The state medical society, upon learning of this proposal, asks to send physician representatives to meet with the executive committee to indicate that, in its opinion, individuals should seek medical, not chiropractic, care. The physicians offer evidence to establish the scientific superiority of standard medical diagnoses and treatment. One of the members of the union's executive committee points out that he once had back pains that his physician could not cure and that an orthopedic surgeon said justified an operation. He consulted a chiropractor who cured the pain and has been without difficulties during the five years since. He visits the chiropractor at least once every six months. Another member of the executive committee says that he has heard that orthodox medicine is now incorporating some of the manipulative procedures of chiropractic and that this is especially the case in rehabilitative medicine. He wonders whether orthodox medicine's opposition might be economically motivated.

What are the nurse's responsibilities, if any, to acquaint Mr. A with the data that she believes justify a conservative medical rather than a surgical approach to Mr. A's coronary artery disease? Is she bound to respect what she believes to be the wishes of the treating surgeon, or is she bound to act in a way to benefit the patient? To what extent and under what circumstances may a nurse acquaint a patient with alternative treatments, which the treating physician has forgotten to mention or does not wish to mention? What if this were a cancer patient and the nurse was of the opinion that laetrile was useful as a treatment for cancer? Would the hospital or surgeon have a right to fire the nurse in either case, or only in the case of raising the possibility of laetrile treatment?

If you were brought in as a consultant psychiatrist to speak with Mr. B, what would you say? Would there be grounds for saying he is making an irrational choice? Is an irrational choice different from an incompetent choice? One might conclude that, given the dim prognosis, it will not much matter what Mr. B chooses and therefore there is not much harm in humoring him. Yet one would wish to protect patients against being exploited. In addition, there is in fact a one out of six chance of curing Mr. B. Mrs. C makes the issue more difficult, in that there is a very high probability of effecting a total cure. The longer one waits, the less likely such a cure becomes. How would you go about trying to convince the Cs that Mrs. C should have a hysterectomy? What if Mr. and Mrs. C explain that the real reason they do not want a hysterectomy is that they are just married and want to have a child? What if she were already three months pregnant and wished to bring the pregnancy to term, even though that involves a high probability of costing her life?

The Ds raise a number of bothersome questions. First, their grounds for rejecting treatment are based on a mainline religious belief. In fact, they interpret their case as standing within the general moral theological tradition to which they are committed, even though it is very likely that a great number of theologians might disagree with their conclusions in this particular case. If you believe that a court order should be sought to mandate treatment, what would your position as a judge be if the daughter agrees with her parents and explains that she wishes to refuse treatment because she does not want to live as a cripple and that she does trust in God to cure her.

Finally, to what extent ought insurance policies to provide for only that form of medical care accepted as standard by the orthodox medical community? One must recognize that there has been a long history of rivalry between orthodox medicine (allopathy) and so-called sectarians. This rivalry is not simply based on conflicting scientific views but on conflicting economic interests. What is wrong, if anything, with allowing patients to decide on their own which form of treatment they want to receive for an illness? Are there grounds for paternalistically restricting the options for reimbursement so as to encourage the use of orthodox medical procedures? If non-orthodox approaches cheaply relieve minor complaints, would this alter your view in the matter?

Adult Patients: Special Issues

21. CHRONIC PAIN AND CHRONIC PROBLEMS

It is difficult for modern medicine to address the treatment of "mere symptoms." Contemporary medicine developed through the triumph of anatomy, physiology, and pathology by which it became possible to demonstrate the underlying causes of diseases and disabilities. Bona fide complaints became those that had a demonstrable pathoanatomical or pathophysiological truth value. True diseases came to be seen as those for which demonstrable lesions could be adduced. Scientific medicine became that medicine that aimed at the underlying causes of diseases. One hoped to find specific treatments aimed at underlying causes so as to be able to avoid engaging in merely symptomatic treatment. The very structure of modern medicine emphasizes this organ-oriented, lesion-oriented approach. Medical students and residents are trained in hospitals where there is a heavy accent on high-technology medicine and where patients are treated by specialists whose expertise is focused on particular organs or organ systems. On the one hand, this training reinforces the notion that complaints, pains, and difficulties should have demonstrable causes. On the other hand, patients who have complaints without such demonstrable causes are viewed with suspicion. Lacking a pathophysiological or pathoanatomical truth-value, such complaints are seen as mala fide and the patients are regarded as "crocks" or are otherwise deprecated.

This circumstance contrasts with the fact that a great proportion of the individuals coming to see general practitioners and family physicians do not have specific complaints. Traditionally, individuals consulted physicians with vague concerns, worries, anxieties, and pains for which medicine is still unable to provide specific therapeutic responses. Prior to the nineteenth century, a greater receptivity existed to patients complaining of such vague problems. In fact, many classifications of diseases were symptom- or complaint-oriented. For example, Francois Boissier de Sauvages (1707–1767), in his *Nosologia Methodica*

Sistens Morborum Classes Juxta Sydenhami Mentem et Botanicorum Ordinem (1763), organized some 2,400 diseases under ten classes, including the class *dolores* or pains. In this fashion, Sauvages directed medical attention to a major cluster of patient problems, which are now seen simply as symptoms. Under the class *pain* he included the genus *dolores vagi, qui nomen a sede fixa non habent* (wandering pains that do not take a name from a fixed site). This genus embraced lassitude, stupor, itching, and anxiety.

Unlike Sauvages, modern medicine has a difficulty in deciding what to do with individuals who present with vague complaints or pains for which a physical basis cannot be discovered. Such individuals are likely to receive minor tranquilizers on a long-term basis or eventually to be subjected to an operation in the desperate hope to remove the lesion or offending organ. This view of diseases and symptoms has also made it difficult to treat individuals with chronic pain and has led to the necessity of developing special pain clinics in which the difficulties of coming to terms with irremediable and at times inexplicable pain can in part be overcome. Such clinics have rediscovered what Sauvages and others knew, namely, that medicine must often treat pain as a disease in its own right.

Such an approach leads to construing diagnoses not so much as discoveries of underlying pathoanatomical or pathophysiological disorders, but rather as therapy dictates. To make a diagnosis of a particular kind allows the physician to use a particular range of treatments. A symptomatic diagnosis is a successful one if there are useful symptomatic treatments for the patient's problems. In such a case, making a complaint-oriented diagnosis will warrant a set of reliable medical interventions, even if one does not know the underlying cause of the complaints.

Should the treatment of vague pains and anxieties be a part of the minimal decent or adequate level of health care provided to all citizens? Or, instead, should such treatment be available only to those who have the funds to pay for it, restricting free care to those in need, where there is a clear physical or standard psychiatric diagnosis? In short, to what extent are such problems truly medical problems and to what extent is the provision of treatment for them integral to the demands of justice? How would you apply the arguments of Daniels, Gutmann, and Singer to the allocation of resources for the treatment of vague patient complaints? To what extent do patients with such complaints seek to override the autonomy of the physician as a scientist and transform the physician into someone who simply fulfills needs defined by the patient? Would such a transformation violate the integrity of physicians? Is there anything wrong with this more complaint-oriented role for physicians? How would you apply the arguments of Clements and Sider here where patients may more easily direct the focus of medical care?

Case A

Mr. A is a 35-year-old real estate agent who, three years ago, consulted his family physician with the complaint of chest pains. He was sent to a cardiologist; an electrocardiogram and treadmill test indicated no pathology. Mr. A continued to complain and was referred to a gastroenterologist to assess the possibility of an ulcer or perhaps an esophageal hernia. All evaluations were normal, but the symptoms persisted. At this point he was again reevaluated by a cardiologist, who performed a cardiac catheterization. The results were negative. Mr. A was then referred to a psychiatrist and entered therapy. The psychiatrist tells Mr. A that he uses the pain to gain the sympathy of his wife and children and to assume a dependent role when at home. After a year with the symptoms unabated, he begins to shop around for physicians who might be able to treat his problem. Finally, one physician simply prescribes 5 mg of a popular tranquilizer four times a day. The result has been that the complaints have greatly subsided and Mr. A generally feels better. He has been taking the tranquilizer and keeping to a dosage of some 20 mg to 30 mg a day. Recently, he consults his original family physician about a complaint of gastrointestinal flu, which was self-limited and easily treated. The family physician becomes concerned that Mr. A is committed to taking the tranquilizer indefinitely without having any demonstrable basis for his problem. The family physician warns that even the use of minor tranquilizers can lead not only to physical and psychological dependence but also possible difficulties with the liver and the blood. The family physician does not believe that one should take such risks when there is no actual disease being treated. Mr. A disagrees. He says that the tranquilizers are really treating his problem.

Case B

Mrs. B is a 37-year-old housewife and mother of three children, ages 15 to 7. She has always had profuse and painful periods, but over the last seven years her complaints have increased and her periods have become at times irregular, sometimes occurring every 20 days. She is a tense, somewhat anxious individual and is concerned that she may develop cancer of the cervix, as did her first cousin, who died of the disease eight years ago at the age of 37. After routine examination by a physician in her Health Maintenance Organization, she is referred to a gynecologist. Pap smears and all routine examinations, including a dilation and curettage, are normal. Mrs. B is then referred to an endocrinologist who performs further workup, again producing negative results. The complaints of Mrs. B continue, and she now wishes to find a physician who will perform a simple vaginal hysterectomy.

Case C

Mr. C is a 32-year-old accountant who was without major physical or mental complaints until last year. In January, five months after having root-canal work on a right upper molar, he developed an aching, deep-throbbing pain on the right side of the face. He describes the pain as spreading into the region of the ear and down the neck. After examinations by both his dentist and his family physician—which reveal no source for the pain—he is referred to a neurologist. The neurologist also is not able to determine the cause of the problem. It is now late March and the accountant says that it is impossible for him to meet all the deadlines associated with tax preparations for his clients unless he is given sufficient pain medication to control his complaints. He insists he be given whatever is necessary, even narcotics, because the pain is incapacitating. All evidence, in fact, demonstrates that the pain is significantly interfering with his capacity to work.

Case D

Mr. D is a 29-year-old construction worker who is referred to a neurologist for evaluation of persistent pain in his right leg. A year ago Mr. D was involved in a motorcycle accident in which the right leg was broken. But from all objective signs, healing has been complete. Mr. D has continued to complain of episodic pain in the right leg when he walks, for which no clear origin is demonstrable. Mr. D also has a suit pending for the injury.

How ought the physicians to respond to such cases? Is there anything wrong with providing Mr. A with minor tranquilizers indefinitely, as long as this helps him control his pain? Does he have a real medical problem, or is he just using his complaints in order to attract sympathy and gain access to a tranquilizer? How could one tell, and would it matter, as long as the complaints are controlled? Should a physician provide Mrs. B with a hysterectomy if she is willing to pay, even in the absence of demonstrable physical indications for the surgical procedure? What if her anxiety about developing cancer increases? Is it proper to provide surgical treatment for what in all likelihood is an emotional difficulty? Mr. C presents the problem of many individuals with chronic, intractable pain. There may very well be a physical cause, but it is not easily discoverable. However, their problems are likely to be seen as psychological problems because of the impact the pain has on their personal and mental lives. The demand for pain-killing medication is understandable. However, it is likely to make them prime candidates for addiction. What amount of disability merits what amount of risk of addiction? Mr. D, along with Mr. A, illustrates how medical complaints can also have social significance in terms of various forms of secondary gain from symptoms. How should physicians "treat" the ways in which patients use their symptoms for gain? At what point should physicians discourage further interventions, either through surgery or medication, and instead provide general supportive care? Finally, one must recognize that even further evaluation of complaints carries with it not only financial costs but also risks of morbidity and even mortality.

22. RELIGIOUS OBJECTIONS TO TREATMENT BY ADULT PATIENTS

One of the most difficult problems that any society must confront is the question of how to accommodate the religious beliefs of some members of that society when these beliefs are radically different from those of the majority. At least in modern times, that problem is less difficult when the question is simply one of belief. Enshrined in the American Constitution and in the fundamental values of most modern societies is the freedom of individual citizens to believe whatever they choose to believe in the area of religion. The problem is more difficult when we confront people turning their unusual religious beliefs into action. Here the state must balance the religious freedom of individuals against other state interests that are affected by the actions in question.

In a series of cases ranging back to the nineteenth century, the U.S. Supreme Court has struggled with this question of how to balance these conflicting interests of religious freedom and other state goals. In 1879, in the famous case of *Reynolds v. United States,* the Supreme Court upheld a conviction of a Mormon for the crime of bigamy despite the fact that the person convicted argued that his bigamy was based on his religious beliefs. The court held that the state's compelling interest in regulating marriage and the family was of greater significance than the individual's need to carry out his religious beliefs by engaging in bigamy. In similar decisions from the 1940s, the states were allowed to enforce compulsory vaccinations that were contrary to certain religious beliefs and were allowed to stop ritualistic snake handling. In both cases, the argument was that the state's interest in promoting health, safety, or welfare outweighed the interests of the individuals concerned.

In other decisions, the courts have looked at conflicting interests and decided that the religious freedom of the individual should take precedence. Thus, in the famous case of *Wisconsin v. Yoder* (1972), the Supreme Court allowed Amish parents not to send their children to regular high schools as a way of preserving the beliefs and values of the Amish religious community. We have here, then, a classical problem of balancing legitimate state interests on the one hand and the rights of individuals to carry out their religious beliefs and practices on the other.

It is against this background that we must understand the issues we are going to examine. In each of the cases that we will be looking at, the patient wishes to refuse some or all medical care on the basis of personal religious beliefs. These patients will argue that their right to religious freedom and to privacy should allow them to refuse the treatment in question. They are opposed by the doctors and the hospitals who argue that other values need to take precedence.

One of the first court cases to raise this issue was one that occurred in a District of Columbia hospital. In that case, a 25-year-old woman with a ruptured ulcer was taken to the hospital for emergency care. She had lost approximately two-thirds of her total blood supply. Nevertheless, she rejected the suggestion of a blood transfusion because both she and her husband were Jehovah's Witnesses and they believed that the taking of blood violates God's law. Physicians attending the patient were alarmed. They believed that death was imminent without such care, and they were particularly concerned because the woman had a seven-month-old child at home. The lawyers for the hospital asked the District Court for an order authorizing the blood transfusion. This request was denied. They then turned to the District of Columbia Circuit Court of Appeals, and Justice Skelley Wright authorized the transfusion. A majority on the Court of Appeals later denied a petition for a rehearing but offered no reason for that denial.

It would be valuable for our purposes to look at the various considerations that Justice Wright offered in his opinion. They are:

1. Justice Wright felt that in light of the fact that this was an emergency situation, and in light of the fact that there were arguments to be weighed on both sides, it would be better to issue such a writ, risking error on the side of life, rather than not to issue a writ, risking error on the side of death. Clearly this argument is appropriate only in a case like this, which raises such questions for the very first time. It would become less appropriate after courts had had the opportunity to examine such cases and come to some general policy.

2. Justice Wright felt that by going to the hospital, the patient indicated that she wanted to live. If the doctors provided her with the transfusion against her wishes, it would not be her responsibility and she would not be opposed to it. This argument is summarized in the following claim:

If the law undertook the responsibility of authorizing the transfusion without her consent, no problem would be raised with respect to her religious practice. Thus, the effect of the order was to preserve for Mrs. Jones the life she wanted without sacrifice of her religious beliefs.[1]

This very subtle argument suggests that compelling the patient to have the transfusion is actually satisfying what the patient wants, namely, that his or her life be preserved without voluntarily consenting to the blood transfusion. It rests on the supposition that what the patient is opposed to is voluntarily being transfused, rather than simply being transfused.

3. Justice Wright was clearly moved by the consideration that the physicians had both a right and a responsibility to treat this patient in accordance with their best professional judgment. To quote Justice Wright:

> It is not clear just where a patient would derive her authority to command a doctor to treat her under limitations which would produce death.[2]

A very similar argument was used by the New Jersey Supreme Court in a similar case in 1971—*J. F. Kennedy Memorial Hospital v. Heston*. The justices' arguments ran as follows:

> When the hospital and staff are involuntary hosts and their interests are pitted against the beliefs of the patient, we think it reasonable to resolve the problem by permitting the hospital and its staff to pursue their functions according to their professional standards. This solution sides with life, the conservation of which is, we think, a matter of state interest.[3]

4. Justice Wright was moved by the consideration that the patient in question had a seven-month-old child at home. He felt that the state had a responsibility to protect this child by seeing to it that the patient was not allowed to die.

The position advocated by Justice Wright has been followed by a number of other courts. We have already mentioned another major decision following it, namely, the decision of the New Jersey Supreme Court in 1971 in the *Heston* case. Heston was a 22-year-old unmarried patient who was severely injured in an automobile accident. She had suffered a ruptured spleen and would die unless operated upon. That would require whole blood. Ms. Heston and her mother, who were Jehovah's Witnesses, were opposed to blood transfusions. She maintained that position in a condition of shock, but her mother maintained it while thoroughly alert and competent. The New Jersey Supreme Court, for reasons already indicated, ordered the operation and the blood transfusions.

One final case advocating this approach is a 1981 Georgia case, *Jefferson v. Griffin Spaulding County Hospital*. In that case, a woman was seen in her 39th week of pregnancy in the hospital's outpatient clinic for prenatal care, and it was determined that she had a complete placenta previa, which would make the risk of fetal mortality during a vaginal delivery as high as 99 percent. The risk of

---

[1] Application of President & Directors of Georgetown College [331 F2d 1000 (1964)].
[2] Ibid.
[3] JFK Memorial Hospital v. Heston [279 A2d 670 (1971)].

maternal mortality was very high as well. The patient nevertheless refused the suggestion of a cesarean section, arguing that God would take care of her problems. The court ruled that the mother was required to have the appropriate cesarean section even against her religious beliefs.

Other courts have adopted alternative positions. As early as the 1960s, courts in New York, in *Erickson v. Dilgard* (1962), and in Illinois, in the case of *In re Estate of Brooks* (1965), had suggested that the religious rights of the patients should take precedence. The arguments for that position were clearly articulated in the extremely important case of *In the Matter of Osborne*, settled by the District of Columbia Court of Appeals in 1972. That case involved a 30-year-old patient suffering from injuries and internal bleeding caused by a tree falling on him. He refused a transfusion because he was a Jehovah's Witness. His wife concurred in his decision. The couple had two children, but the extended family were prepared to help the wife care for them, and their financial future was secure. The court was considering an appeal from a judgment issued by Judge Bacon, who refused to order the transfusion. It concurred with that refusal and argued as follows:

> Thus Judge Bacon and his court was faced with a man who did not wish to live if to do so required a blood transfusion, who viewed himself as deprived of life everlasting even if he involuntarily received the transfusion, and who had, through material provision and family and spiritual bonds, provided for the future well being of his two children. In reaching his decision, Judge Bacon necessarily resolved the two critical questions presented—(1) has the patient validly and knowingly chosen this course for his life, and (2) is there a compelling state interest which justifies overriding that decision? Based on this unique record, we have been unable to conclude that judicial intervention respecting the wishes and religious beliefs of the patient was warranted under our law. Judge Bacon's decision is supported by available evidence to the degree of certainty respecting the two basic questions.[4]

A similar approach was adopted in a New York court's recent charge to a jury in another Jehovah's Witness case, namely, *Randolph v. City of New York* (1984). The charge ran as follows: "A competent adult has a common-law right to decline or accept medical treatment despite the fact that the treatment may be beneficial or even necessary to preserve a patient's life. The patient's right to determine the course of his or her own medical treatment is paramount to what otherwise might be the doctor's obligation to provide needed medical care. Therefore, the defendants cannot be held to have violated any legal or professional responsibilities when they honored the right of Bessie Randolph to decline medical treatment, specifically not to be transfused."[5]

A number of themes emerge as we examine these cases. Some of them have to do with the right to life and the physician's obligation to act always on the side of that right. This is a theme certainly important in the thinking of those courts that ordered medical treatment for patients against their wishes. The reader needs to review the various positions about the sanctity of life and the right to life discussed in Section B6 of the readings to see what the authors of those positions

---

[4]In the matter of Osborne [294 A2d 372 (1972)].

[5]Unpublished opinion.

would say about these cases. Would Grisez and Boyle see a decision not to be transfused as an objectionable act of suicide, and the decision to go along with that refusal as an objectionable act of participating in the wrongful killing of the patient? Would believers in the sanctity of life hold that view? What would the President's Commission have to say about that question? A second theme that emerges in these cases is the right of the individual to make decisions, whether those decisions are based on one's religious beliefs or on any other belief, and the obligation of health-care providers to go along with those decisions. The reader needs to review the readings in Section A3 about the role of patients and providers. What would the President's Commission have to say about the significance of that right in these cases? How would it be assessed by such authors as Miller, Clements and Sider, and Thomasma? Finally, there is the theme of the responsibility of adult patients to dependent children. How far do these responsibilities extend, and do they provide reasons for state interference to force the patients to be transfused?

With all of these issues before us, we are now in a position to turn to several clinical cases that raise all of these issues.

Case A

The patient in this case is a 37-year-old unmarried male who arrived in the hospital emergency room with clear evidence of internal bleeding. The patient was in shock and was quite confused. The physicians felt that he needed transfusions to replace the blood that he was losing, and surgery was needed to deal with his ruptured internal organs. They did their best to explain this to the patient, and they felt that he did understand what they were saying. However, he told them, in a wandering fashion, that he wanted no transfusions. A friend explained that the patient had recently become a Jehovah's Witness, was very firm in his newly found religious beliefs, and that this was the reason why he did not wish to be transfused. What ought to be done for this patient in this case?

Case B

The patient in this case is a 32-year-old male who presented in the hospital's emergency room with severe chest pains. He was admitted to the hospital for monitoring for a possible heart attack. At the time of admission, he signed the hospital's standard form allowing the hospital to perform whatever treatment is required, but in the relevant place, he indicated that he wanted no blood products because of his religious beliefs. The hospital has this on its standard form because its policy is not to transfuse patients against their will. At the time, however, that was only a theoretical question. Later that day, his condition began to worsen. He suffered a cardiopulmonary arrest, was resuscitated, was given oxygen to help his breathing, and was started on medications to help maintain adequate cardiac output. He has been disoriented and lethargic since then. Moreover, he has developed many other problems including a stress ulcer, is bleeding internally, and requires transfusions to replace the lost blood. His wife insists that he receive full treatment. She is not a Jehovah's Witness, and she claims that his allegiance to that religion is only nominal. When confronted with his statement on the admission form, she says that he only said that because he didn't seriously think he would need any blood products. If he knew, he would have given permission. The staff is

unsure of what to make of her claims. Because she is not a Jehovah's Witness, they
think that she may be indicating what she
wants rather than what her husband would
want. What should be done in such a case?

Case A is significantly different from many of the earlier cases that we have
looked at for two reasons. To begin with, the patient's competency is somewhat
questionable. While the physicians feel that he did understand what was said to
him, everyone agrees that his thinking capacity was affected. Thus, there is a
question as to whether we are dealing with a competent patient who is refusing
treatment. Secondly, there is the question of how seriously to take the patient's
refusal based on very recently acquired religious beliefs. Is this type of refusal as
significant a refusal as one based on long-standing religious beliefs? Would the
courts that have argued for respecting the right to refuse treatment based upon
religious beliefs extend their argument to this case? What guidance would they
get about the question of competency from Gert and Culver? From the various
approaches discussed by the President's Commission? From Abernethy's position? What guidance would they get about the question of autonomy from the
views of Miller? From the views of Clements and Sider, and from Thomasma?
On the other hand, what would Justice Wright have to say about this case? There
is certainly nothing here concerning the deserting of a dependent child. Would
that be sufficient to make the judge change his mind? Or would Judge Wright
only be reinforced in his decision by the factors of questionable competency and
newly acquired religious beliefs?

A factor that distinguishes Case B from the others we have examined is that
we cannot at the relevant time ask the patient what he would want, and the
evidence is ambiguous. Would the courts that have allowed Jehovah's Witnesses
to refuse transfusions agree in this case to the wife's request that this patient be
transfused because of the ambiguity of the evidence? Or would they insist that
we should follow what he said at admission? A second factor that distinguishes
Case B is that the patient is very sick anyway and his chance of survival, while
improved by the transfusions, is still not that high. Would judges like Justice
Wright agree to go along with the patient's stated requests, despite the wife's
testimony, because of that dim prognosis? Would judges perhaps say that the
arguments for violating the patient's beliefs are much weaker when the chances
of the patient's survival are less? What would the President's Commission say
about a case like this? What would Miller say? What would Clements and Sider?
Thomasma? What would be the implications of the traditional beliefs expounded by Grisez and Boyle and by the authors of the Jewish Compendium?

23. PSYCHIATRIC PATIENTS

The practice of psychiatry is shaped by the circumstance that mental problems
appear to touch to the core of a person's life. Adequate psychiatric treatment
often requires a detailed examination of a patient's feelings and of the most
intimate areas of one's life. Thus, psychiatrists frequently play the role of secular
confessors or at least the role of general counselors and special gatekeepers. Still,
psychiatrists do not fully fit the image of secular confessors, for unlike priests,

whose strict duty of confidentiality is more generally respected, psychiatrists often find themselves subpoenaed to give testimony regarding their patients. Psychiatrists are often viewed as scientists able to make predictions concerning possible dangers posed by their patients, even though their ability to do so may be much greater than that of priests.

The ambiguous roles of psychiatrists also derive from the fact that psychiatrists, unlike psychologists, have an M.D. degree and usually at least three years of postgraduate medical training. Yet contemporary classifications of mental disorders have many similarities with the eighteenth-century medical classifications of complaints, despite the increasingly biological orientation of psychiatry. It is rare that one can unambiguously demonstrate the pathoanatomical or pathophysiological underpinnings of mental disorders. Instead, classifications of mental disorders represent constellations of signs, symptoms, and complaints, which are invoked as warrants for treatment and for prediction of future problems and psychopathology. Despite the ambiguity of classifications and the inability to give clear biological bases for them, the diagnosis of a mental disorder such as schizophrenia can have profound consequences for an individual in opportunities for being employed or being admitted to medical or professional school. Consider, for example, the difference between the impact that a diagnosis of diabetes or heart disease has on an electrical engineer's ability to have security clearance while working for a defense contractor, versus the impact of a diagnosis of schizophrenia or homosexuality. The somatic diagnoses are likely to have fewer adverse consequences than the psychiatric diagnoses. It is for such reasons that social and psychiatric critics such as Thomas Szasz have challenged the very notion of mental illness.

Even in the face of all these limitations and difficulties, psychiatry continues to play major gatekeeping functions. Psychiatrists are called on to testify in courts regarding insanity defenses, to determine the competency of patients, and to testify regarding the dangerousness of criminals.

Various recent legal decisions have had a significant impact on the character of psychiatric practice. In 1976 the California Supreme Court in *Tarasoff v. Regents of the University of California et al* [131 Cal Rptr 14, 551 P 2d 334 (Cal 1976)] held that a psychiatrist must take all reasonable steps required to protect those individuals, if the psychiatrist knows or should know that a patient represents a danger to those identifiable third parties. Not all state courts have followed California. There have been rejections of the Tarasoff position. Yet other courts have expanded the obligation so as to require psychiatrists to protect even those victims who might not be easily identifiable. The result has been that psychiatrists can no longer simply consider the ways in which they should treat their patients, but must be concerned with third parties, even if that concern may adversely affect the treatment of their patients. The patient must now be wary of disclosing to a psychiatrist homicidal fantasies; such disclosures may lead the psychiatrist to reporting the patient to the police or to parties threatened in the fantasies.

The law has also made it more difficult for psychiatrists to treat patients with psychopharmacological agents or electroconvulsive therapy. Courts have ruled in many jurisdictions that a patient's permission must be obtained for pharmacotherapy (for example, the use of major tranquilizers such as chlorpromazine), even if the patient has been civilly committed. One court has held that psychiatric patients could refuse treatment except in emergencies or when treatment is authorized by a guardian. Other courts have allowed a treating psychiatrist to authorize medication for a committed person if the psychiatrist certifies that the patient is functionally incompetent and therefore unable to make knowledgeable treatment decisions. This treatment choice must then be reviewed by a patient advocate and an independent psychiatrist within 15 days.

Psychiatrists find themselves torn between new obligations for the safety of non-patients and the community on the one hand, and developing rights of mental patients to refuse treatment on the other. The difficulty lies in applying the moral principles raised by *Canterbury v. Spence* regarding the patient's right to free and informed consent in circumstances where the competency of the patient to decide may be seriously in doubt. The questions raised by the readings from Gert and Culver, Abernethy, and the President's Commission indicate the problems in assessing competence in general patient populations. The problem becomes more difficult when one is forced to decide if a psychotic patient suffering from hallucinations is competent to decide whether or not to be treated with major tranquilizers that offer great promise of treating the psychosis, at the same time carrying with them risks of significant side effects. These side effects may include everything from drowsiness, depression, toxic or allergic reactions, and dry mouth to gynecomastia (men developing breast swellings), impotence, dystonia, and tardive dyskinesia (slow choreiform movements, usually of the tongue or facial muscles, but at times including pelvic thrusting, fist clenching, and wiggling of the toes and ankles). Even if these side effects may give pause to both competent individuals and judges considering the right of mental patients to refuse treatment, one must also bear in mind that these drugs have remarkably improved the capacity of psychiatrists to treat major psychiatric disorders on an outpatient basis. How ought one to apply the issues raised in the readings by Miller regarding autonomy of choices made by psychiatric patients, especially since autonomy is not an all-or-nothing, binary phenomenon, but is instead realized in degrees and in particular areas. How would you apply the considerations raised by Thomasma to the treatment of psychiatric cases? In psychiatry which is more helpful, a rights-oriented or a consequences-oriented analysis of the moral issues?

Case A

Mr. A is a 32-year-old high school physics teacher who has begun psychotherapy with Dr. Jones because of his increasing need to keep things tidy both in his laboratory and at home. There have been a number of times in which he has erupted in angry, verbal abuse of students who have failed to clean up the laboratory after an experiment. On at least three occasions he has flown into a tantrum with his wife and slapped her for not having removed her hose that were drying in the shower. Mr. A insists that his house be totally neat at all times, and re-cently he has begun spending half an hour putting the bathroom and bedroom in order as soon as he comes home. He must complete this tidying up before he can do any work or before he will speak with his wife or children. As therapy progresses, Mr. A reveals that he has repetitive feelings of anger toward both his mother and his wife. He also has uncontrollable fantasies of killing his wife. After such thoughts, which he cannot resist, he finds himself fearful of his ability to control himself and guilty for having had the thoughts. Dr. Jones concludes that Mr. A is suffering from an obsessive-compulsive disorder. He thinks it is very unlikely that Mr. A will kill Mrs. A. However, he thinks it is likely that Mr. A may slap her sufficiently to do minor but not serious injury. Dr. Jones wonders whether he should warn Mrs. A. He suspects that if he did so Mr. A would break off therapy; moreover, he is fairly certain that Mr. A would not consent to any disclosure.

Case B

Miss B, 29, has been a strict vegetarian since she entered college. She now works in a health food store and is extremely concerned about avoiding all foods with artificial additives. Her father died 15 years ago and she has been living alone with her mother since graduating from college seven years ago. Following the death of her mother, Miss B is found hallucinating by the proprietor of the health food store, apparently having visions of her dead mother. The proprietor talks Miss B into accompanying him to the emergency room of a local hospital. The psychiatric resident in charge finds Miss B to be agitated, tearful, and frankly hallucinating. When she is questioned about her feelings, she speaks incoherently and bangs her head against the wall. Still, the resident is able to get her to sign herself in voluntarily as a patient on the psychiatric service. However, when the psychiatrist suggests to Miss A that the use of a major tranquilizer would very likely help her, she refuses. She states unequivocally that she knows that such medications are poisons and cause serious side effects, including movement disorders that at times do not abate when the treatment is stopped. She insists that she wants to be treated by psychotherapy, not psychopharmacology. Though she is frankly hallucinating and psychotic, she appears to understand and appreciate the side effects that can be associated with major tranquilizers.

Case C

Mrs. C is a 53-year-old former bartender who has been suffering from end-stage renal disease for eight years. Two years ago a transplant was tried but she rejected the kidney. Since then, she has found dialysis a major psychological burden. Six months ago her husband, on whom she was extraordinarily dependent, died. It was he who cared for her and took her for dialysis. One day after completing dialysis, she announces to her physician that she does not intend to come back, that she has had enough. The physician tells her that she cannot do that; to stop dialysis would be suicide. She replies that with her husband gone and without any children, she has no one to live for and she finds her present life a burden. A psychiatrist is consulted, who finds her depressed but competent.

Case D

One Saturday at 11:30 P.M., Mr. D, a 42-year-old chronic alcoholic, appears at the emergency room of a charity hospital in a medium-sized city. He confronts one of the interns on call, Dr. Smith, and insists that she admit him. A short history reveals that Mr. D has been jobless for the last five years and living on the street. A brief physical examination shows that, aside from chronic alcoholism and an unkempt, unbathed state, Mr. D shows no signs of disease. Dr. Smith informs Mr. D he cannot be admitted because he is not sick. Mr. D responds that that is not the case. He has been reading (at the local library) the *Diagnostic and Statistical Manual of Mental Disorders* of the American Psychiatric Association, which lists alcohol dependence as a disorder. He adds that many psychiatrists hold alcoholism to be a disease for which there is medical treatment. He insists that he be treated, starting with hospitalization that evening. Dr. Smith is convinced that all that Mr. D wants is a safe place to sleep, a good bath, a shave, and some food, after which he will go back on the streets again and resume his life as an alcoholic. It is the informal policy of the hospital not to admit persons such as Mr. D, who the hospital considers to be not interested in treatment but only in shelter.

Should Dr. Jones inform Mrs. A about her husband's violent fantasies? How much of Mr. A's slapping would constitute grounds for Dr. Jones calling Mrs. A? What if, after one therapy session, he is fairly convinced that Mr. A is likely to slap his wife, although not enough to hurt her seriously? Should he call Mrs. A before Mr. A gets home so as to warn her? Would your judgment change if Mr. A had a mental disorder, such as paranoid schizophrenia, which more frequently leads to serious violent actions against others? How much of a risk to others ought there to be before a physician warns others, if that physician believes the warning will seriously compromise treatment of a patient?

At what point would the physicians be justified in giving drugs to Miss B against her wishes? In this case, the patient is well educated, well informed, and appears to understand and appreciate some of the consequences of her therapeutic choices, even though she may be incompetent in other areas of her life (for example, to decide whether or not her dead mother is talking to her). This case suggests that competence is regional and by degrees. Persons can be incompetent in only some areas and only to a certain extent. How incompetent must a patient be regarding therapeutic choices before a physician can overrule a patient's wishes? Should economic considerations play a role in such decisions, since it may be much more costly to use psychotherapy unaided with drugs in the treatment of a patient such as Miss B?

Does Mrs. C's depression override the fact that she understands and appreciates the consequences of her choices? Is the psychiatrist correct in holding her to be competent? What factual matters would change your decision in this regard? What, for example, would be your view if she refused treatment before her dialysis rather than afterwards, when one might consider that her judgment was marred by uremia. Notice, too, that the psychiatrist is playing a gatekeeping role, being called in to certify whether Mrs. C is competent to control the circumstances of her life and death. Mr. D is appealing to this same function of psychiatrists and physicians generally when he attempts to get Dr. Smith to consider him diseased and worthy of hospitalization. If you were a psychiatry resident who wandered by during the discussion between Mr. D and Dr. Smith, what would your advice be?

24. CANCER SURGERY

Many of the classical treatments for cancer developed in the latter part of the nineteenth century, when the conjunction of anesthesia and antiseptic technique made it possible to perform radical surgical interventions without high postoperative mortality. In 1889, for example, William Stewart Halsted devised the procedure of radical mastectomy for cancer of the breast, which was then developed further by J.A. Urban, who pioneered the *en bloc* extended radical mastectomy for cancer (1952). The application of radiotherapy to cancer and the development of chemotherapeutic agents made it possible to attempt less extensive surgical interventions. For example, R. McWhirter in 1955 provided the first definitive work on simple mastectomy and radiotherapy for breast cancer. In the three decades since, numerous new combinations of radiotherapy, surgery, and chemotherapy have been devised in order to achieve the same, if not better, long-range survival with less morbidity. Often, however, there has not been sufficient time to evaluate the long-range cure rates from new, less-invasive procedures, especially with cancers that grow slowly and for which an evaluation of a full cure may need to wait 15 or 20 years.

The choice of treatment must be made under conditions of uncertainty, a circumstance that highlights a general problem in medical decision making: The challenge of balancing risks of death against loss of bodily form and function. Because a number of the surgical procedures for the treatment of cancer involve major changes in the appearance and function of the person being treated, one must face the issue of what amount of intervention is worth what increase in the statistical likelihood of achieving a cure. The issue is difficult not only because one is dealing in statistical outcomes but also because it is often hard to determine the reliability of the data on which one makes predictions. Most statistical prognoses in medicine must themselves be qualified by a probability factor (for example, "There are reliable data to indicate that a surgical procedure for the cure of this cancer will offer a 75 percent chance of five-year survival, give or take 5 percent, depending on which studies one relies").

Patients and physicians must then weigh what appear not to be clearly commensurate benefits and risks. How does one compare an additional 5 percent chance of being alive in 5, 10, or 15 years with losing a breast? Deciding what the "proper" choice is depends on a judgment about the comparative worth of life extension versus preservation of body image and function. Free and informed consent in such a context is complex, for it is difficult for the physician to inform the patient straightforwardly which treatment promises the "best" outcome. This is in theory always the case. In choosing among various forms of cancer treatment, the patient as decision-maker is often forced to compare the attractiveness and costs of significantly different possible outcomes. Providing the patient adequate information will entail providing a wide range of data regarding the uncertainties involved in comparing the merits of different possible therapeutic approaches. For many patients, this will require their relinquishing a view of medicine as an unambiguous science and realizing instead that medicine usually entails the assessment of risks and the choice of options in a context of uncertainty.

What will the objective standard outlined in the *Canterbury v. Spence* decision require in circumstances such as these? Will the objective standard be sufficient, or will one instead need to rely on the subjective standard, which Capron outlines in the readings? As the range of views expands regarding what constitutes the proper therapeutic intervention, the less one will be able to appeal to the information that will be required by reasonable and prudent persons in making their therapeutic choices. The more the proper choice depends on a particular individual's understanding of his or her body image, expectations in life, and attitudes toward pain and deformity, the more the provision of information will need to be fine-tuned to the idiosyncrasies of particular patients. What do such approaches presuppose regarding patient autonomy? Consider the issues raised by Miller and Thomasma as well as by the excerpt from the President's Commission regarding "The Patient as Decision Maker."

Case A

Miss A is a 47-year-old high school chemistry teacher who has smoked three packs of cigarettes a day for the last 30 years. In addition, she consumes about four martinis a day. After being bothered by a persistent hoarseness and mild cough, she consults her physician. The family physician refers her to an otolaryngologist who makes the diagnosis of cancer of the larynx. She is found to have a 3.5-mm tumor of the middle third of the vocal chord. It is classified as Stage I and Miss A is informed that there are two possible therapeutic approaches: The first would involve an excision of the entire vocal chord. This therapeutic approach would leave her unable to speak as she had in the past and would very likely have an impact on the

ways in which she might function as a teacher. The otolaryngologist points out that with discipline, training, and corrective surgery she will very likely be able to learn to communicate in a satisfactory fashion. She can also compensate by an increased use of written handouts for her students and by writing on the blackboard, until the students accustom themselves to her new means of speaking. On the other hand, she could be treated by external radiation therapy. In the otolaryngologist's opinion, this approach might provide about the same five-year survival rate if Miss A will give up smoking completely (about 90 percent survival). Radiotherapy would not force her to learn new ways of speaking (phonation).

Case B

Ms. B is a 34-year-old attractive, unmarried television news commentator, who has never had any children. She takes pride in her appearance, which she also considers to be important for her job success. Now that she is established in her career, she has been considering marriage to a man she has been seeing for a year. When taking a shower, she notices an approximately 2-cm lump in the upper right quarter of her right breast. It appears to be freely floating in the breast and not fixed to the muscle behind the breast. On consulting her physician, she is referred to a surgeon who examines her and finds no clinical evidence of metasteses to the lymph nodes but concludes from a mammography of the lump that it is very likely a malignant tumor. The surgeon recommends that a surgical biopsy be performed and that the patient receive a modified radical mastectomy at once if the

frozen section indicates malignancy. The surgeon suggests this be done at one time with the woman under general anesthesia for both procedures. In such a procedure the total breast is removed, including the skin over the nipple. In addition, the lymph nodes from her right axilla (armpit) would be removed. Unlike the radical mastectomy, the chest muscles underneath the breast are not removed.

Ms. B asks whether the biopsy cannot be performed on an outpatient basis, giving her at least a day to decide what form of treatment she will actually accept. She indicates also that she has read that a simple excision of the area of the breast where the cancer is found, followed by radiotherapy, often produces results as good as those available through a modified radical mastectomy. Also, what she has read about the psychological impact of mastectomies on the patient, which includes depression and distaste for intercourse, concerns her very much. She notes she is not at all sure how her lover and perhaps future husband will regard her after a mastectomy.

The surgeon says that, although he favors a modified radical mastectomy, he agrees with Halsted's observation that one should take every step to avoid spread of the cancer, and he believes an immediate removal of the breast—if there is clear evidence of cancer from the frozen section—increases the odds of success. The surgeon quotes Halsted: "The division of one lymphatic vessel and the liberation of one cell may be enough to start a new cancer." Besides, he asks, "Why do you need to think things over if you know in advance what the options will be?" The surgeon adds that he believes the data are not that clear. Despite some recent studies, he judges that investigation suggesting that a modified radical mastectomy will give a better five-year survival rate for a tumor of her size than will

excision and radiotherapy should be given credence in her case. As he points out, one must remember that cancer of the breast is a very slow-growing malignancy and that metasteses may not express themselves until 15 to 20 years later. Because she is so young, he believes that the choice of excision and radiotherapy is highly imprudent. He also points out that she is on the borderline between a Stage I and a Stage II cancer of the breast with a tumor of that size (TNM classification).

The more she reads on the matter, the more apparent it becomes to her that it is unclear what "the correct treatment" is. Responsible investigators appear to disagree with the data that appear to show the equal efficacy of excision followed by radiotherapy plus chemotherapy where indicated. Moreover, the question is often rasied whether such less-invasive techniques will assure the same 15-year to 20-year survival rate as is afforded by radical mastectomy.

Case C

Mr. C, 62, was married for the second time a year ago to a 34-year-old woman. This is her third marriage. For at least six months he has noticed an irritation at the base of his penis. He has attributed it to the results of frequent intercourse and/or jock itch. However, he has noted that the irritation has now become ulcerated and therefore he consults his family physician, who then refers him to a urologist. A biopsy of the ulcer reveals that Mr. C has developed a squamous cancer of the penis. Given the size of the lesion, the urologist states that the best procedure for ensuring a cure is total removal of the penis. The glans of the penis will need to be removed in any event. Mr. C is

appalled. First, he states he is a macho individual who cannot imagine himself without his penis intact. Moreover, he is sure that his new wife will leave him if he is not able to perform in a sexually adequate fashion. He asks whether some other form of treatment is not possible. The urologist replies that given the size and location of the tumor, local excision with radiotherapy might provide only half of the five-year survival that a more radical approach could offer. As high as a 90 percent five-year survival rate is likely to be obtained through a more radical approach, especially since lymph nodes appear not to be involved.

How ought a patient to make a decision in such cases? What should Miss A's decision be if she is fairly certain that she will not be able totally to give up smoking? How should Ms. B choose, if one grants for the sake of argument that excision and radiotherapy in the presence of negative axillary nodes (no metasteses found in the nodes) will provide a 75 percent 15-year survival rate, as opposed to an 85 percent survival rate with modified radical mastectomy? Is the difference in cosmetic appearance and self-image worth an extra 10 percent chance of being dead in 15 years? How can one make such a choice? How is such a choice made in the real world where one cannot give precise percentages for future outcomes? What would be a proper choice for Mr. C? If you were the physician, how would you suggest that he decide between the two possibilities for treatment?

25. PATIENTS WITH SERIOUS BURNS

Individuals who have been seriously burned face a number of major transformations in their lives, should they be able to survive. They will often have to confront months, if not years, of painful corrective surgery and rehabilitation. The pain and travail will frequently be so severe as to make many individuals despair and to make some insist on abandoning the project of treatment. As a result, those involved in the care of burn patients must be constantly insisting, supportive, and often overbearing in their commitment to therapy. Even with successful plastic surgery, patients may have scars that leave them recognizably changed and with obvious physical signs of their burns. Such changes in self-image may be radical and deeply disturbing. In addition, the burns may have left them blind or with other disabilities due to serious injuries to extremities. Finally, some burns are so serious that there is little or no chance of survival. The issue then is whether to commit patients to the rigors of treatment when there is little likelihood of success.

The treatment of burn patients raises important questions about medical paternalism, patient autonomy, and the capacity of patients to make decisions under such severe stress. Some involved in the care of burn patients have argued that, if the patient survives, the patient will thank the physician for having been forced to agree to treatment. Nurses and others involved with burn patients have taken the view that, even if patients now despair and wish to stop treatment, such statements may not authentically reflect what will be their mature judgment once rehabilitation is completed. The treatment of burn patients presents a special context for conflict and ambivalence, where life-and-death decisions must be weighed and made by patients facing considerable pain and an uncertain future. It is difficult for patients to anticipate how they will adjust to their remaining disfigurements and disabilities. The stress of treating patients under such circumstances takes such a toll on nurses that there is considerable burnout and therefore high staff turnover.

The policy of overriding the patient's wishes at the time of the burn requires careful analysis. From a moral point of view, the argument to override patients may be based on the contention that, although the patient is not now consenting to treatment, the patient will in the future. Even though the patient at the time of the burn does not wish to live, given (1) the pains of treatment required to secure life or (2) the extent of the deformities due to the burns, most individuals, once they are rehabilitated, are pleased to be alive and appreciate the support if not force used in securing their treatment. Physicians and nurses, as suggested above, may then appeal to the future consent of the patient. Or, simply, they may argue that intervention is in a patient's best interest, no matter what the patient may wish or say. Others have also argued that such paternalistic interventions on the part of burn units are part of a social insurance policy to which we all implicitly consent so as to secure optimal treatment, should *we* be severely burned. Matters are more complicated than these portrayals would suggest. Just because a patient is willing to agree that life after rehabilitation is worth living, it does not follow that the patient, even after rehabilitation, will agree that the pain and the travail of rehabilitation were worth the quality of life secured. It may simply be that after one is forced to be rehabilitated life is better than death. One may still object to having been forced and argue that the quality of life secured was not worth the investment. In any event, one will need to address seriously the ways in which physicians and nurses acquire authority to treat patients. If that authority is gained from the actual consent of patients, then it may not be morally allowable to appeal to future consent or patients' best interests.

In considering the cases that follow, reflect on how you would apply the material in this book concerning informed consent and competency. In particular, consider the selections from the President's Commission regarding the patient as a decision-maker and the articles by Abernethy, Miller, and Thomasma. What amount of information ought to be given to patients concerning the pain, travail, and frustration they are likely to face if they decide to be treated? A full, complete, and vivid disclosure would very likely convince a great number of individuals to refuse treatment. If you would decide in favor of providing less than full disclosure, would that be on the basis of the so-called therapeutic privilege (see the case studies concerning consent to treatment)? One needs also to bear in mind the issues raised by the readings on competency. Do patients, after they are severely burned, maintain their capacities as competent decision-makers? One must remember that following extensive third-degree burns there is relatively little pain. However, the victim has experienced a major trauma. How would you use Miller's four senses of autonomy in sorting out the issues? Is it more useful to approach these questions in terms of the likely consequences of different rules or practices of respecting the wishes of patients? Or does a rights-oriented approach hold more promise?

Case A

Mr. A is an 83-year-old widower who survives a plane crash with 95 percent whole-body burns. The physicians recognize that individuals in Mr. A's condition have never survived. Given the extent of his burns, he will very likely die. At present, however, six hours after the crash, he is in no pain and is conscious and alert. He has no children or family to consult, and the physicians wonder whether they should give Mr. A the option of either trying to secure an unprecedented survival or being made comfortable until he dies.

Case B

Mr. B is a 27-year-old model and part-time nude dancer. On the way home from danc-ing in a striptease club for women, he is involved in an automobile accident in which he sustains multiple fractures and 65 percent whole-body burns. As a result of the accident, glass has penetrated both of his eyes so severely as to leave him blind. The burns are extensive, but there is a good likelihood that he can be saved. In the emergency room he is met by friends and he asks them the extent of his injury; they candidly tell him that the physicians believe he will never see, though it is likely that he can be saved. Treatment would involve months of grafting and rehabilitation, and it is unlikely that he will ever have the attractive physical

characteristics he had before the burn. Mr. B at once decides that he wants no treatment whatsoever. He would rather die than to have to readapt to a life in which few of the goals he had before could be achieved. When his physician comes into the room, Mr. B explains this to his physician in blunt terms. As Mr. B phrases it, he has enjoyed a life in which he has identified with his body, his pleasures, and his physical abilities, and he has no intellectual or other interests whatsoever. He wants to refuse all treatment and be kept comfortable until he dies.

Case C

Ms. C is a successful 33-year-old concert pianist who is severely burned (65 percent whole-body burns) while on a camping trip. She was trapped in a grass fire and after being rescued was flown to a burn center from a small local hospital to which she was originally brought by firefighters. By the time she arrives at the burn center, she is fairly heavily sedated. Three weeks into the treatment for her burns, it becomes clear that she will survive but with extensive scarring and with damage to the distal pha-

langes of the fingers of her right hand. It is clear that she will never be able to return to her career as a concert pianist. Considering how much her career has meant to her and the pain of the treatment and the months of rehabilitation ahead, she decides one day simply to refuse further treatment. The nurses and physician tell her that is nonsense and they intend to continue to treat her, no matter what she says. When her best friend visits her, she asks that he secure a lawyer to help her stop all treatment.

What would you tell Mr. A and why? How likely would survival have to be before you would actively try to dissuade him from refusing treatment—a 5 percent chance of survival, 10 percent, 15 percent? If your judgment differs with respect to Mr. B, is it because he has a good chance of survival? Or does the choice in part rest on the fact that he is young and might learn to adapt to his condition, given sufficient rehabilitation and support? How would you approach Ms. C, who is about to give up midway into the treatment? Would you respect her wishes? Or would you decide that the pain and the travail of the rehabilitation render her incompetent to choose and therefore to refuse? Try to determine what principles you would rely on in your treatment plan for each of these three patients.

26. ORGAN TRANSPLANTATION

Although organ transplantation is now widely accepted as a morally permissible undertaking, it initially raised moral concerns. The Roman Catholic theological principle of totality held that one could remove organs from an individual only if such an alteration or mutilation was undertaken to preserve the person as a whole. Thus, one could remove a cancerous uterus because the goal was to preserve the health of the woman. However, procedures such as incidental appendectomies (that is, removing the appendix not because it is inflamed but because it is easily reachable during an operation performed for another reason) raised moral qualms in the minds of some because of the principle of totality. One even finds an articulation of this view in Immanuel Kant's *The Metaphysical Principles of Virtue* (VI, 423), where he suggests that it is improper to sell or give one's hair or teeth to another. Finally, within Western society there exist concerns about the integrity of the body, concerns that have made many feel uneasy even about the transplantation of organs from cadavers.

The general public acceptance of organ transplantation changed dramatically during the 1960s when it became increasingly possible to transplant kidneys and, in 1967, hearts. This was when Dr. Christiaan Barnard performed the first human heart transplant. This successful transplantation had followed James Daniel Hardy's attempt to transplant a chimpanzee's heart into a man in 1964. The interest in the availability of organs led to a number of changes in the law. First, it became important to determine when individuals were dead. The move from a whole-body to a whole-brain definition of death, which is explored in the case studies on the definition of death, was made in part because of concerns regarding transplantation. If one waited until the heart stopped beating before declaring a donor dead to remove an organ, the organ was likely to be damaged and therefore not as useful for the recipient. Second, a move began in the late 1960s to enact legislation so that individuals could easily make their organs available for donation. These efforts resulted in passage of the Uniform Anatomical Gift Act (1968). Although the original law allows any individual of sound mind over the age of 18 to make a donation without consent of next of kin, in practice organs are usually not accepted unless the next of kin also agrees.

Currently, not only are corneas, kidneys, and hearts transplanted but also livers and lungs. With the development of recent capacities to suppress the body's rejection of foreign organs, the success rate of transplantation has increased. In addition, with the first implantation of a permanent artificial heart on December 2, 1982, a new field of transplantation was opened. The increasing capacity to transplant organs has raised the issue of the costs involved. In 1980, heart transplantation was excluded from Medicare coverage, and a number of studies have been published assessing the likely economic impact of the wide availability of various forms of organ transplantation. Often the decision to reimburse for transplantation has been couched in terms of whether or not a treatment is experimental, although such categorizations also reflect economic and other considerations. The term *experimental* is thus used as a way of declining to reimburse for treatment.

Under what circumstances may a society restrict the availability of expensive life-saving treatment such as organ transplantations? How would you apply the arguments by Gibbard to these questions? Do arguments regarding equality in health care, such as those developed by Gutmann, require either providing the care for all who need it or providing it for none? How would you apply arguments such as Daniels' regarding health care as fair opportunity, when the care involved is very expensive but will probably only extend the lives of some 50 percent of the patients treated for a period of more than five years? If heart transplantation is a part of the adequate level of health care provided to all citizens, the costs will be considerable. How would you apply the considerations raised by the President's Commission to expensive life-saving treatment, of which transplantation is an example?

In addition to economic issues, transplantation raises a number of philosophical questions. The transplantation of organs presumes a distinction between human biological and human personal life, which distinction is core to whole-brain definitions of death. One is interested in transplanting the organs of dead persons precisely because the organs are still alive. The practice of organ transplantation thus has implications for the ways in which we understand the concept of person versus the concept of being human. Transplantation, in addition, raises the question of the role of persons in determining how their bodies will be used and of who should have the authority to consent for the harvesting of organs from the bodies of dead persons.

Case A

Lobbyists for the sole medical school in a certain state approach the legislature and request funds for the establishment of a heart, lung, and liver transplant program at its medical center hospital. The hospital provides care both for indigent and paying patients. Selection for transplantation will be made without regard to one's ability to pay, but rather on the basis of need. A number of legislators criticize this plan on the grounds that the funds to support these programs would in fact benefit only a few and could be better used to improve not only education but well-baby care for the indigent. These programs, the legislators argue, would offer a greater benefit to the citizens of the state. Those who favor the creation of the transplantation program reply: How will you be able to sit back and watch individuals die who would have been saved had you developed a transplantation program?

Case B

In a university health center with an established liver-transplant program, there are two candidates for liver transplantation. Mr. Smith, 45, is suffering from cirrhosis of the liver due to years of alcoholism. Mr. Jones, 25, is a university student who received a shotgun blast to the right upper abdomen during a robbery at a fast-food outlet. The shotgun blast has irreparably destroyed the liver and right kidney. The left kidney is intact and therefore a renal transplant is not needed. Major blood vessels are sufficiently intact to permit a liver transplant. One of the robbers was shot in the head and killed by the owner of the fast-food restaurant, thus providing an intact liver for donation. A decision must be made whether to give the liver to the alcoholic or to the young student.

Case C

A number of enterprising individuals establish a corporation, located on a Caribbean island, that offers to purchase kidneys for transplantation. The corporation has built a hospital and is prepared to perform transplantations on site. It will offer $15,000 in addition to all transportation and hospitalization costs for individuals willing to fly to the island and donate a kidney. The corporation already has a long list of would-be patients throughout the world willing to purchase a kidney of guaranteed quality.

Case D

A state governor decides to remedy the shortage of organs available for transplantation by introducing a law that would make organs available for donation on death unless individuals carry with them an instrument indicating that they do not wish to participate. A number of individuals criticize the governor's proposal as tantamount to socializing bodies. The governor responds by saying that only in this fashion will there be sufficient organs to meet the needs of individuals who would otherwise die. In addition, the governor points out that a number of countries have laws similar to the one he is proposing.

How ought the legislature to decide in Case A, presuming that there are not enough funds to support not only the transplant program but also better education and a well-baby clinic? Is the consideration raised at the end on behalf of identifiable lives morally persuasive? Is it morally permissible for the legislature to choose the program that will maximize the greatest good for the greatest number, even though one will be able to identify those individuals who will die as the result of the lack of such a program? How does one assess and take account of the costs to society of having to recognize that it has decided not to save identifiable individuals?

When sufficient organs are not available for all in need, should the choice be made by lottery, by medical criteria, or by a combination of medical and social criteria? One might argue that Jones is the better candidate because he is younger than Smith and therefore would benefit more from the transplant. This argument might be bolstered if Mr. Smith had developed a disease, which might complicate the operation. Would it be proper to consider alcoholism itself as a disease, which will likely complicate the transplantation? That is, Mr. Smith may be likely to continue to drink and therefore destroy the new liver he was given. To what extent would it be appropriate to consider the cirrhosis a result of Mr. Smith's free choice, so as to judge him less deserving than Mr. Jones?

What is your view of the Caribbean organ company? Is there something immoral in offering to purchase kidneys? Individuals are often paid at higher rates for dangerous work such as the construction of skyscrapers or deep-sea diving. The risk of donating a kidney may be much less than many such risky occupations. If people truly own their own bodies, why can't they sell parts of their bodies if they so wish? One might conclude that such an arrangement would lead to the exploitation of the poor. However, the arrangement may in fact allow people to step out of poverty in a way that exposes them to minimal risk. What is your judgment of the morality of the Caribbean organ company? Is the practice of buying and selling organs contrary to the notion of the sanctity of human life? What is wrong, if anything, with making organs commodities? If you would oppose such a corporation, would your objections be objections in principle or only on the basis of likely adverse consequences? Case D raises a similar set of issues, but in a different vein. Here the question is the extent to which societies can exercise a presumptive ownership of the bodies of deceased citizens. If you were a member of that state's legislature, would you vote for or against the governor's proposal? What would be the basis for your vote?

27. SEX THERAPY AND COUNSELING

It has been difficult to make sexual behavior and sexual dysfunction objects of scientific study or medical treatment. Barriers derive from the web of cultural norms that give sexuality special significance. As was discussed in the case examples concerning decisions to reproduce, the dominant Western view during the Middle Ages was that the goals of marriage are children, fidelity, and preserving the sacrament, not the pleasures of convivial or recreational sex. Sex therapy and counseling, unlike treatment for infertility, aim at improving the sex life of individuals. Thus, they make sexual pleasure and satisfaction a central goal. This is in itself a major departure from the traditional cultural assumptions of the Christian West. These difficulties are compounded by the fact that sex therapy and counseling have often included permission to engage in non-reproductive sexual behavior, such as masturbation and oral sex. Such non-reproductive sexual behavior, as was noted in the case studies on reproduction, was strongly condemned as immoral, at least in a number of Western traditions. Finally, some therapists use surrogate sex partners, thus offending prohibitions against fornication and adultery.

The modern scientific and therapeutic approach to human sexuality has been associated with the work of individuals such as Alfred Charles Kinsey (1894–1956), William H. Masters, and Virginia E. Johnson. Kinsey, who became director of the Institute for Sexual Research at Indiana University in 1942, published *Sexual Behavior of the Human Male* (1948) and *Sexual Behavior of the Human Female* (1953). The reports revealed a wide range of sexual behaviors, from masturbation and oral sex to fornication and adultery, with a frequency that was unsuspected by many at the time. Kinsey's sociological work was followed by Masters and Johnson's study of the physiology of sexual excitement and orgasm, *Human Sexual Response* (1966), and the investigation of disordered sexual function, *Human Sexual Inadequacy* (1970), as well as the development of means for treating sexual dysfunction.

Matters are made even more complicated by the fact that many sexual disorders, which have been traditionally held to be perversions or sins, are also classified by the *Diagnostic and Statistical Manual of Mental Disorders* (DSM–III) of the American Psychiatric Association. Thus, one finds transvestism, zoophilia, pedophilia, and exhibitionism classified as mental disorders, although they have been proscribed by law in a number of jurisdictions. Sexual therapy thus offers a "medicalization" of conditions traditionally held to be sinful or criminal. In addition, the diagnosis of transsexualism, which some believe warrant surgery and hormone shots to provide individuals with the secondary sexual characteristics of the opposite sex, raises the very question of how we identify individuals as male or female.

Can the study and treatment of sexual function and dysfunction be approached as one would approach the study and treatment of cardiac function and dysfunction? Is there anything unique about sexuality? Are there values that medicine should recognize as being inherent in sexuality? Do approaches such as those of Clements and Sider suggest a way of discovering the proper goals of medical interventions? If such discoveries cannot succeed in showing medicine what ought to be done, one will need to rely on the free choices of individuals and physicians regarding what goals they wish to pursue. Are there any limits on such an autonomy-oriented approach to sex therapy and counseling? To what extent should sex therapy and counseling be a part of the "adequate level" of health care to be made available to all, as discussed in the selection from the President's Commission's report? Sex counseling also raises questions regarding the conflict of parental and child rights. Issues raised in the selection from Locke are also relevant here. What will be the likely consequences of competing views of sex counseling for our views of the family?

Case A

Miss A is the 17-year-old daughter of a very strict Roman Catholic couple who have taught their children that masturbation and pleasure in erotic fantasies are mortal sins that will lead to eternal damnation. One day Miss A is brought by her mother for a physical examination required for college admission. Miss A asks Dr. Brown whether what her mother says about masturbation is true.

Dr. Brown asks what the mother has told Miss A, and she explains that she has been informed that not only is masturbation sinful but that it will also lead to psychological and physical problems. She says that her mother has also told her that girls who masturbate tend to become promiscuous. Miss A wants to know the truth about the matter.

Case B

From childhood on, Mr. B has always felt that he was a woman trapped in a man's body. Ten years ago, in an attempt to overcome these feelings, he entered into psychoanalysis and felt that he was coming to terms with being a male. Two years into analysis he married and now is the father of two children, a son five years old, and a daughter three. The feelings of having the wrong body have persisted, and he now wishes to undergo transsexual surgery and

become a woman. His wife is aghast. She says that she loves him and cannot imagine why he wants to do this. If he wishes to make love to men, she is willing to tolerate that. He explains that he is not homosexual but wishes to make love to men as a woman. His wife becomes even more distressed and asks how will the children refer to him when he becomes a she. How can they have a father who is a woman?

Case C

Mr. C is a successful 45-year-old lawyer. He goes to a new family physician after his previous physician died of a coronary. Dr. White, wanting to have a complete history on all of his patients, carefully reviews Mr. C's life, including a detailed sexual history. Dr. White discovers that Mr. C has a shoe fetish. In fact, his only sexual release is derived from masturbating while viewing women's shoes. Dr. White suggests that Mr. C at once enter into psychiatric treatment. Mr. C protests, saying that he is perfectly

happy with his shoe fetish. He runs no risk of contracting sexually transmitted diseases or of having a divorce. He is perfectly happy with his life as it is. He asks, "Why should fetishism be a disease, if homosexuality is not?" As he points out, homosexuality is only a disease if it bothers the person who is homosexual (ego-dystonic homosexuality). Why should there not be the category ego-dystonic fetishism? His fetish, Mr. A states, is ego-syntonic.

Case D

Ms. D is a 27-year-old artist in a large California city. She consults a psychiatrist known for his ability in treating homosexuals so that they can convert to a heterosexual orientation. She explains to Dr. Black that most of her colleagues and friends are lesbians. She attempted on a number of occasions to have a homosexual relation, but each time she found it distasteful, although she liked the women as persons. She would like it very much if Dr. Black could help her change her orientation from being a heterosexual to being a homosexual. As she puts it, following DSM–III, she is suffering from ego-dystonic heterosexuality. She adds that she will be pleased if she is at least transformed into a functional bisexual.

Case E

Mr. E, 52, was until five years ago the president of a large construction firm. After his company went bankrupt, he became depressed and impotent. However, after three years he has been able to start a new business and is successful again but still impotent. He consults his internist who, after a workup, concludes that Mr. E's impotence has a psychological, not an organic, basis. In taking a sexual history the internist learns that Mrs. E is a strict, cold, unresponsive woman who has never been orgasmic. Because of her general indifference to sex, being non-orgasmic has not bothered her, although it has been a source of some distress for Mr. E. Mr. E has suggested to his wife that they seek sex therapy, but Mrs. E has refused, saying that she is pleased with the way things are. Mrs. E responded with total indifference to Mr. E's impotence. The internist refers Mr. E to a sex therapist. The sex therapist informs Mr. E that he can provide therapy that is likely to restore his potency, but he will need the cooperation of his wife because a partner is necessary. Mr. E says that his wife will not participate but that his 31-year-old secretary is willing to serve as his partner.

What information should Dr. Brown give to Miss A? Can he say that there is nothing wrong with masturbation? Or must he specify that there is nothing *medically* wrong with masturbation, so as not to challenge the views of Mr. and Mrs. A regarding the sinfulness of masturbation? Does it matter how old a child is who asks about what is proper sexual activity? How should physicians respond to such questions? Is it proper for a physician to perform transsexual surgery on a man against the wishes of his wife? Because couples can now easily divorce, can the physician simply say it is up to the patient to work out with his wife about how to come to terms with the consequences of such surgery? Do you agree with Dr. White's judgment that Mr. C is suffering from a mental disorder? If homosexuality is not a disease unless it bothers individuals, should similar conclusions be drawn with regard to pedophilia and exhibitionism? A similar question is raised by Miss D. If there is nothing normatively proper or improper about being either homosexual or heterosexual, then her request to be turned into a homosexual is as proper as a homosexual wishing to be treated so as to function as a heterosexual. Finally, how should the sex therapist treat Mr. E? Should the therapist require Mrs. E's permission? If she agrees, are there no further moral questions involved? What if Mrs. E refuses? And what if Mr. E protests that his wife has no right to condemn him to a life of sexual dysfunction?

It is difficult to answer these questions because of the wide range of views regarding proper sexual activities. In addition, many of these views depend on particular religious commitments. When they do not, they often presuppose an understanding of the discoverability of values or goals in nature, such that one can determine what is proper sexual activity and what is improper, perverse, or morally deviant. How is modern scientific medicine to come to terms with the various value viewpoints regarding sexuality?

SECTION F

Geriatric Health Care

28. ASSESSMENT OF COMPETENCY

Generally, individuals are presumed to have a right to determine the circumstances of their own lives as long as they are competent to choose, do not have a status barring them from effecting such choices (for example, minor children or prisoners), and do not have obligations to others that restrict their range of choice (for example, do not have dependent minors; are not pregnant). The presumption of competence can be defeated when individuals are shown to be unable to understand or appreciate the consequences of their choices. The difficulties lie in determining what amount of intellectual impediment to understanding the character and consequences of choices, or what degree of inability to appreciate results of actions, actually constitutes incompetence.

The problem of determining the conditions under which patients should be recognized as competent decision-makers is explored in this volume in the sections "Capacities and Competencies of Patients" and "The Role of the Patient." Abernethy's analysis in particular raises the question of what degree of incompetence should, under what circumstances, authorize paternalistic interventions. The selection from the President's Commission suggests that possessing values that diverge from conventional wisdom with regard to medical treatment should not ipso facto be taken as establishing incompetence. In addition, even if one concludes that an individual is incompetent, one may still wish to respect such a person's right to dissent from participation in procedures that are not directly related to an essential element of necessary medical care. One may wish here to examine how far Sanford Leikin's arguments with regard to assent and dissent by minors can be raised with regard to the mentally ill in general and the senile elderly in particular.

Even if one decides on criteria for competence, one will still need to face the issue of applying such criteria. The more that a false-positive determination of competence will have a significant impact on the life and health of a patient, the more one should be sure that the individual is in fact competent. If a patient is refusing life-saving treatment in circumstances where treatment will easily afford a significant period of survival, the down-side risk of a false-positive determination would be significant. On the other hand, if the individual is likely to die in any event, it may not matter much whether or not the individual refuses to accept the treatment with little promise. There one might properly have less of a concern for false-positive determinations of competence.

These issues, which are complicated enough in the general population, may be very difficult to come to terms with in geriatric medicine. One wishes to avoid stereotyping the elderly as incompetent decision-makers. Moreover, treating the elderly as incompetent involves a role-reversal that is often difficult for a family where the son/daughter must take on quasi-paternal/quasi-maternal roles. Moreover, disputes about competence may reflect ongoing conflicts between children and their parents. How ought one to balance the rights of adult children and their elderly parents? How does diminishing competence weaken the rights of the elderly to self-determination? What are the consequences of different public policies regarding presuming the elderly to be competent, even when their choices are inconvenient, costly, or vexing?

Case A

Miss A is a 78-year-old spinster who has run an 800-acre ranch for the last 50 years. She has at times hired part-time laborers but essentially she has taken care of all operations herself. Though she is no longer able to ride horseback, she gets around in a four-wheel-drive jeep. During the last five years, she has had circulatory problems in her right leg due in part to an injury she received from being thrown from a horse six years before. On a visit to her local physician it becomes clear that the circulation is seriously compromised and that an amputation will be necessary. Miss A refuses. She looks at the situation this way. She has lived her entire life on her own and she figures she can take care of her leg by herself. Anyway, if things go badly and she dies from the infection, she has lived a full life.

Her physician has always considered Miss A somewhat peculiar and has come to worry about her judgment over the last seven years, during which period she has become even more idiosyncratic, uncooperative, and hostile toward those who attempt to help her. The physician visited her house once and found it for the most part full of old boxes, newspapers, and two dozen cats. The physician believes that for her own good Miss A should be declared incompetent and forced to have her right leg amputated. He points out that she can very likely learn to use a prosthesis to get around her house and even to drive her jeep.

Case B

Mr. B is an 81-year-old retired plumber who has lived with his son and daughter-in-law since the death of his wife five years ago. In the last few years he has become increasingly anxious, irritable, irascible, and for the most part has made life miserable for his 50-year-old son and 45-year-old daughter-in-law. A physician who is consulted suggests that Mr. B take a minor tranquilizer and that this may help him to live better with his environment. For a while he does this and the medication has a marked impact on his demeanor. The younger Bs are able to have a fairly satisfactory life with the elder Mr. B. However, when the medication must be refilled, there is a delay and

Mr. B becomes agitated again and refuses to resume taking the medication. The household situation deteriorates significantly. The younger Bs ask their physician whether it would be all right to mix the medication in with Mr. B's food. That way he would never know that he is taking the drug. The young-er Mr. B adds that if they cannot do something like that, their marriage will come apart. They really do not know what other options they have, in that they do not have enough money to put Mr. B in a nursing home.

Case C

Mrs. C is an 89-year-old senile resident of a nursing home, where she has lived since the death of her daughter nine years ago. She is visited by no family members and has become progressively withdrawn and uninterested in her environment. Often over the nine years since her daughter's death, she has expressed the wish that she could die. She has found the nursing home to be an unpleasant environment and has been particularly distressed by her inability to walk around freely since her hip fracture five years before. Suddenly, she begins to refuse to eat. When asked why she does not want to eat, she simply states in a slurred voice, "No."

Under what circumstances should physicians and others override the decisions of individuals who show signs of senility? Although Miss A is idiosyncratic and uncooperative, is she really making an improper choice in deciding to try as best she can to make it on her own, as she has all her life? The disruption that a medical intervention would entail might in fact meet the criteria elaborated in the sixteenth and seventeenth centuries for extraordinary treatment. The intervention might count as an undue inconvenience, and the treatment appears to evoke a major revulsion (horror magnus) on her part. But even if the treatment is indicated and not extraordinary, does Miss A still have a right to refuse it? How senile must she be before she loses the right to refuse to have her leg amputated?

How should one resolve the issue of Mr. B? Is he so senile that he can be treated as a child and given medication without his knowledge and consent? From a very practical point of view, such deception may in fact offer the only way in which the Bs will be able to function as a family and provide Mr. B with adequate care. But at what point do they become justified in treating him no longer as an adult but as a child? In the case of the Bs, their motives appear predominantly beneficent and fairly disinterested (after all, they are shouldering the burden of taking care of an elderly father).

Finally, one must decide how to come to terms with the wishes expressed by individuals when they are senile and no longer competent. Those wishes may still reflect the settled viewpoints that those individuals had before becoming incompetent. Mrs. C had never liked the nursing home and her final decision to die may plausibly be seen as an expression of these past convictions. If one decides that she is not only incompetent but that the refusal of food should not be respected, to what extent should one force-feed her? If she tries to struggle free and pull out feeding tubes, to what extent ought one to restrain her and continue to feed her against her wishes?

Because there are no clear lines to be drawn between competence and incompetence, one must draw them, realizing that one will err in one direction or the other, either toward overdiagnosing competence or overdiagnosing incompetence. How should one establish rules for physicians, judges, and others in such areas of ambiguity?

29. THE HIGH COSTS OF GERIATRIC HEALTH CARE

Spending for health care in the United States has become a major national concern in recent years. In 1984, health-care expenditures consumed around 11 percent of the nation's gross national product (GNP), a tremendous increase from 1965 when this percentage represented about 6.5 percent of the GNP. Despite cost-containment measures in both the public and private sectors, it is likely that this upward trend will continue in the years to come.

This issue is of particular significance for the elderly because they consume such a disproportionate share of health care. It has been shown that by the late 1970s, per-capita health-care spending on people over 65 years of age was 3 1/2 times that of per-capita health-care spending on those below age 65. That percentage has undoubtedly increased since then. Although it is true that the elderly are covered by the Medicare program, as McCarthy pointed out in the reading in Section C8, Medicare does not cover all of the costs of health care for the aged. Given the deductibles, the co-payments, and the limitations on coverage, paying for the escalating cost of health care continues to be a major problem for the elderly. About a third of the health-care expenses of the aged are paid for by the elderly either directly or through their purchasing of supplementary Medigap insurance.

This issue is also of great significance to a society struggling with the problem of how to control health-care costs. We are a country whose population is getting older. In 1965, only 11 percent of the population was 65 or older; that percentage will reach 13 percent by the year 2000. Moreover, the aged are living longer and we are beginning to see a significant increase in the over-85 age group. This is a special problem for nursing home costs. Given the heavy use of health care by the elderly, we can anticipate that these demographic facts will only worsen the problem of rising health-care costs, which society pays for through such programs as Medicare.

There are many ways in which we can begin to address these questions. One relates them back to the important issues of the right to health care, which was analyzed in the readings in Section C7. We could imagine social policies that limited the growth in public expenditures on health care for the elderly either by limiting what we would provide for them or by requiring the elderly to pay a larger portion of their own health-care costs. Or we could imagine policies more generous to the elderly: providing more aid to them (say in the area of chronic nursing home care, where one currently needs to be totally indigent to receive significant public support) or by lowering the percentage that the elderly have to pay for their own health care. What does the right to health care imply for this question? What would the President's Commission have to say about it? What would Gibbard, Daniels, Gutmann, and Brody have to say about it? A second way of dealing with these issues is to relate them back to the discussion in Section C9 of the responsibilities of the individual clinician, who is often faced with the dilemma of whether or not to order expensive therapies for elderly patients. Should clinicians consider cost as a factor in deciding whether or not to order therapy? What would Fried say about that question? What would Brody say?

Case A

By the late 1960s, with the development of a new polymer plastic cement, it became possible to deal with the disability and pain of deteriorated hips by totally replacing the ball and socket and securing the prosthesis with this cement to the remaining portion of the femur and pelvis. This form of surgery is a real blessing to those elderly suffering from severely deteriorated hips, for it greatly improves the quality of their lives. It is well known that the British perform, on a population-adjusted basis, about 75 percent to 80 percent of the hip-replacement surgery done in America. As a result, there are long waiting lists, and many of the elderly suffer considerable pain and diminution of the quality of life while awaiting their turn for hip-replacement surgery. Many receiving this surgery go out of the National Health Service and secure it privately, paying for the operation out of their own pocket. The best explanation of why this occurs is that the government has limited the funds it will allocate for paying for personnel, operating rooms, and hospital beds; thus, emergency surgery takes precedence over elective surgery, and the elderly with deteriorated hips are made to wait. That is a way of controlling the costs of health care for the elderly. Is it a just way? Are the elderly in Britain being deprived of the health care to which they are entitled? What would the authors in the readings in Section C7 say about this? What do we learn from this case about the respective merits of the proposals for reforming health care advocated by Enthoven and Singer in Section C8?

Case B

Many countries have made decisions to limit by age those who may receive certain forms of health care, even if it means that those not receiving it die. The standard example of this is kidney dialysis. In chronic and severe kidney failure, fatal accumulations of toxic wastes build up in the body. Unless the body is cleansed of these waste products through the dialysis process, the patient dies. In the 1960s it became possible to keep patients alive for long periods of time without functioning kidneys. To be sure, there are significant mortality rates for dialysis-dependent patients (rates which rise as the patient grows older), but dialysis is certainly the only hope for such patients. The problem is that this form of treatment is very expensive. America spends around $1.5 billion each year on its end-stage renal disease dialysis program. Many countries have responded to this type of financial pressure by allowing dialysis centers to refuse to accept patients above age 65. These countries include Finland (89 percent of Finnish centers refuse patients above 65), Ireland (67 percent of Irish centers refuse patients over 65), and the United Kingdom (where 80 percent of centers refuse patients above 65). Some countries, such as Germany and France, have only a few dialysis centers that refuse patients over 65, whereas many other countries, such as Belgium, Denmark, Greece, Spain, and Sweden, have many centers (30 percent to 60 percent) that refuse dialysis to those over 65. Only the United States among the Western countries has no centers that refuse to dialyze patients just because they are over 65, and the cost of dialysis for all patients is covered by Medicare. Are the elderly being deprived of the health care to which they are entitled by those centers that refuse to take them, or are those centers making an appropriate selection to provide this extra health care to those who could most benefit from it? What would the President's Commission say about this question? What would Gibbard, Daniels, Gutmann, and Brody? Keep in mind that individuals who are refused dialysis die from kidney failure. Does that mean that their right to life has been violated? What would Grisez and Boyle say about that? What would believers in the sanctity of life, such as the authors of the Jewish Compendium on Medical Ethics, say about this?

Case C

The patient in this case is an elderly individual who resides in a nursing home and suffers from severe dementia and incontinence. He spends his day in bed or in his wheelchair staring at the world around him, occasionally responding in a confused way to the environment. When he develops a severe urinary tract infection—and he does so on a regular basis—he is transferred to a hospital for care until the infection is cured. Then he is transferred back to the nursing home. One might wonder, independently of any economic considerations, whether this is appropriate. Who benefits from this care? But economic considerations make this question even more pressing. It costs society a lot of money to provide all this care for this elderly, demented patient. Should physicians keep this factor in mind when deciding whether or not they should aggressively treat this patient's infection? What are the implications for this question in the views of Fried and Brody contained in Section C9? If physicians should consider cost factors, how does this affect the question of who has decisional authority in such cases? Moreover, should any decision involve the patient's family in the same way as if cost weren't a major factor? Would that depend on who is paying for the patient's nursing home and the accompanying medical care? In any case, should withholding hospital transfer and proper management of the patient's infection be ruled out as a form of killing? What would Grisez and Boyle say? What would the authors of the Jewish Compendium say?

Case D

The patient in this case is a 77-year-old gentleman who has recently been diagnosed as having oat cell carcinoma of the lung. The tumor is fairly widespread. The physicians treating the patient recommend a combination of radiation therapy and chemotherapy. They point out that this usually increases survival by many months, and also provides some palliative care. The patient refuses the care suggested, but for a very unusual reason. He is concerned that the cost of this care (including the cost of his wife staying with him near the hospital) will use up whatever money he has saved. He wants to leave as much as possible to his wife. All of the people caring for this patient are much moved by his feelings, but they are also much moved by the wife's insistence that he be pressured to accept therapy. Sadly enough, real conflict has arisen between these two loving older people, and everyone is distressed by the couple's conflict. What should be done in such a situation?

Case D raises many difficult questions. It reminds one of the social issue concerning the extent of the right to health care. Should it include helping to pay for family members being with the patient while he or she is hospitalized? Should it allow the patient to retain some funds to leave to a spouse, or should the dying patient be required to pay a share of the costs? It also forces us to think of the extent to which clinicians should take into account the economic circumstances of dying, elderly patients before they advocate life-prolonging therapy. Would it be appropriate to discuss these economic issues with the patient in all cases, or should they be discussed only in cases where someone raises the issue? How would the *Canterbury* decision apply? What would the other authors who have discussed informed consent say?

30.   INDEPENDENCE OF THE ELDERLY PATIENT

Most of us ascribe tremendous significance to our capacity to make decisions concerning ourself. We want to decide where we shall live, how we shall spend our money, with whom we will associate, and so forth. This desire is legally respected, at least in the case of most adults. In this case area, however, we will consider a group of elderly patients who may not be able to exercise this type of independent self-determination. We will look at some of the ways in which society acts to limit that independent self-determination, and we will consider the role of health-care providers in that process of limiting self-determination.

Several reasons exist why elderly citizens comprise the largest group of adults facing these limitations. Many of the elderly suffer from dementia; it is estimated that serious dementia occurs in 5 percent to 10 percent of the over-65 population and in more than 20 percent of the over-80 population. Chronic mental confusion among the elderly may also be caused by a wide variety of physical illnesses and adverse drug reactions, or may be a by-product of bereavement, isolation, and the resulting depression. Elderly patients suffering from this mental confusion are likely to be limited in their independence.

There are at least four ways by which the law allows for the limitation of the independence of these elderly citizens. They are (listed in order of extent of limitation) the following: (1) involuntary commitment to a mental health institution, (2) appointment of a legal guardian, (3) issuance of an adult protective services order, and (4) designation of a substitute payee. We shall now examine each of these ways separately.

Involuntary confinement in a mental health institution of an elderly patient suffering from confusion attributable to any of the above causes is, of course, the most extreme limitation recognized by the law on the independence of elderly patients. Such a patient is forced to live in one institution, is bound by its rules governing activities, has little if any control over financial resources, and so forth. When will society allow for this limitation? The answer to this question varies from state to state, but most states have in the last 25 years tightened up the requirements that allow a person to be involuntarily confined. This was done in response to a belief that there had been much abuse in this area. A typical situation is that found in Wisconsin, which allows involuntary confinement in a mental health institution for someone who is mentally ill, who is a proper subject for treatment, and who evidences by violent behavior a substantial probability of physical harm to self or others; or who evidences a substantial probability of physical injury to self due to impaired judgment; or who evidences an inability due to mental illness to satisfy basic needs of nourishment, shelter, health care, safety, and so forth. Are these grounds for involuntary confinement acceptable? What would John Stuart Mill say? Health-care professionals are called on to play a central role in evaluating patients to see whether they meet these criteria, and such involuntary confinements on anything more than a temporary emergency basis usually require a formal hearing at which time the health-care professional presents his or her evaluation. Many have criticized the behavior of health-care professionals in this setting, claiming (1) that they are often willing to help the family when it wishes to see the patient confined, (2) that they are insensitive to the possibility of less restrictive ways of limiting patient freedom, and (3) that they are willing to make predictions of future dangerousness despite the widely accepted professional claim that such predictions are difficult to make.

When the standards for involuntary confinement were tightened in the 1960s and 1970s, the number of petitions to the courts for involuntary confinement declined. Instead, those who were concerned about elderly patients inappropriately exercising their independence turned to petitioning the courts to appoint a guardian. Such guardians might be given plenary power over their wards' entire existence including control over their income, their health care, and where they shall live. In such cases, the involuntary appointment of a guardian may be almost as restrictive to the independence of the patient as involuntary confinement. Alternatively, the court may create a more limited guardianship, authorizing the guardian to control just the income and expenditures of the ward (be a guardian of the ward's estate) or just to make certain personal decisions which the ward has shown an incapacity to make (be a guardian of the ward's person). Appointment of a guardian requires just as formal a court hearing as do involuntary confinements; health professionals play a central role in these hearings, and many of the same issues raised in involuntary confinement hearings concerning the role of health professionals are raised in guardianship hearings. But special questions are raised during guardianship hearings because of the legal standard for appointing guardians. The standard varies from state to state, but a typical standard ("the incapacitated person standard") is that contained in the Uniform Probate Code, which defines such a person as someone

> who is impaired by reason of mental illness, mental deficiency, physical illness or disability, advanced age, chronic use of drugs, chronic intoxication, or other cause (except minority) to the extent that he lacks sufficient understanding or capacity to make or communicate responsible decisions concerning his person.

This definition of the incompetency that justifies appointing a guardian needs to be compared with the various definitions discussed by the President's Commission and with the views of Gert and Culver and of Abernethy. How would these writers evaluate this definition?

In the 1970s, as a result of its being more difficult to confine a patient involuntarily and even to appoint guardians against a patient's wishes, there emerged a significant number of elderly citizens who maintained their rights of independence but at some considerable cost to their well-being because of their limited capacities. Was this an appropriate choice? Was it a proper emphasis on rights or an improper devaluation of the appeal to the consequences for these people? These questions troubled many. Consequently, interest developed in the concept of adult protective services as a compassionate way of avoiding some of the bad consequences of accepting the right of these partially impaired individuals to remain independent. With the help of federal funding, over half of the states enacted programs of adult protective services, which can be understood as programs for assessing needs of and delivering services to the elderly so as to enable them to maintain independent living while avoiding abuse and/or neglect. Adult protection agency case workers assess the needs of these individuals and coordinate the delivery of services to meet these needs. Ideally, this should be done on a voluntary basis with the consent of the elderly individual, and, when done on that basis, there would be few who would quarrel with the concept. But what if individuals refuse this aid, perceiving it as an unwelcome intrusion on their independence? In some states, adult protective service agencies do little more than petition in the traditional manner for involuntary confinements or guardianships. Other states have experimented in the last few years with court orders authorizing entry into an uncooperative client's home and provision of services against the client's will. Such court orders raise again all of the questions about competency and about a concern for consequences versus a commitment to individual rights. We need to ask ourselves whether, in light of all these issues, there is a need and a place for these protective and compulsory services as opposed to more traditional methods such as guardianships.

These doubts and questions certainly need to be raised about one final way by which we limit the independence of the elderly, namely, the involuntary appointment of a substitute payee for a person who is receiving government benefits such as Social Security and supplemental security income. Substitute payees are appointed when the agencies judge, without any clear statutory definitions, that beneficiaries are incapable of using their funds in their own best interests. There is no formal hearing prior to the appointment of a substitute payee, and there is only minimal supervision to ensure that the substitute payees use the money in the best interests of the elderly.

Is there any way in which elderly people, concerned about their own future capacity to make decisions for themselves, can develop an alternative to these restrictive involuntary mechanisms? There has recently emerged just such an alternative, namely, the *durable power of attorney*. A power of attorney is a written authorization by which the principal gives an agent the power to make decisions on his or her behalf. Traditionally, a power of attorney ends when the principal is no longer capable of making decisions on one's own. Such a traditional power of attorney would be worthless for elderly citizens wanting to arrange their own affairs. They need to use a *durable* power of attorney, a power of attorney that becomes effective when the principal is no longer competent and which remains in effect as long as the principal is incompetent. Does this serve as a suitable way of protecting individual rights while not neglecting the consequences to the incapacitated elderly of their inability to make independent decisions? What notion of competency should be employed in deciding when such a power of attorney becomes effective? What would Abernethy say? How about Gert and Culver? The President's Commission?

Case A

This case involves a 78-year-old gentleman who had been the owner of a large furniture store, but which he sold about ten years ago, leaving him with a substantial sum of money. He and his wife planned to spend their retirement years traveling and playing golf. Unfortunately, about a year after his retirement, she suffered a stroke, lived as an invalid lovingly nursed by her husband for about two more years, and then died. The patient has never really recovered from his wife's death. For the first three years after her passing, he was very withdrawn, lethargic, and depressed. In some ways, his condition has improved in the last four years. He gets out, travels, and seems to be enjoying himself. However, there are some bizarre aspects to his activities. He often travels to distant and foreign places, then returns almost immediately, staying for just a day or two. When questioned by his children about his reasons for this, he says that he went to see or do only one thing, and he returned when he completed his goal. But his account is very inconsistent. He often buys large amounts of new clothing, most of which he doesn't wear, and then throws out the clothes and buys more. When asked why, he says that he just enjoys wearing new and fashionable things. There is no question of his not caring for himself, and he has money left for his needs for the rest of his life (including several lifelong annuities), although he has been eating into his capital. His children are concerned about his bizarre behavior. They approached his physician and asked whether he would help them in a court petition to be appointed guardian of his funds. When the physician discussed this with the patient, he was furious, saying that he was just enjoying himself as best he could, that he had made adequate provision for himself and his children, and he didn't see how his behavior was troubling anyone. What should be done in such a case?

Case B

This patient is an 82-year-old gentleman admitted to the hospital after suffering a stroke. He has undergone some rehabilitative treatment, and he can feed himself, get dressed, and wash, although he does all of this with some difficulty. He is sometimes quite confused and disoriented, although that is not usually the case, but it is happening more often. His family (a son and two daughters) report that he had been that way before the stroke, and that they had been concerned about him because he lived alone. There is no evidence, however, that they had acted on that concern. The question has arisen about where he should go when he is discharged from the hospital. The children want him to be placed in a nursing home, and he is eligible for that placement as a veteran with a service-connected disability. Alternatively, they believe that he should be confined in a state hospital. He wants to go home, insisting that he can take care of himself. One of the social workers has told him about the services of a local adult protective services agency, and he is convinced that he can manage with their help. The children believe that this plan is unrealistic, partially in light of his physical disabilities but primarily because of his increasing confusion. They want to be made guardians of his person. The social worker believes that they have ulterior motives because the father has some money and other goods that the family would like to get control of. What should be done in such a case?

Case C

The 86-year-old patient in this case has been living in a nursing home the last eight years. She was placed there by her nephew, who is her legal guardian, when she was no longer able to care for herself because of her general physical deterioration and her confused mental state. She seemed to be happy in the nursing home, was well liked, and had many friends. Recently, her mental status deteriorated further and she is no longer continent of urine. She then developed respiratory-tract infections, which got worse, and that is what led the nursing home to have her hospitalized. The guardian was out of town when she was taken to the hospital. Upon his return, he was furious about the decision to send her to the hospital. He saw no point in aggressively treating her medically in light of her deteriorating condition. He felt that she should have been left in the home and just kept comfortable. Neither the hospital nor the nursing home is sure that the guardian's authority extends that far, given that she is not in pain and is not suffering from a terminal illness. What should be done in this case?

Does the patient in Case A need to have a guardian appointed for him? If so, should it be just a guardian of his estate or also a guardian of his person? Does he meet the Uniform Probate Code's standard of lacking "sufficient understanding or capacity to make or communicate responsible decisions concerning his person"? How about the standard of responsible decisions concerning his estate? Is he a competent decision-maker? How should we assess that competency? Do we look at the decisions he makes, his reasons, his general thought processes, or what? What would Abernethy say? How would Gert and Culver respond? What would be the implications of the standards discussed by the President's Commission? Would we think about this case differently if he had less money, if we were concerned about his becoming financially dependent? Would that be enough to make his decisions non-responsible?

Can the patient in Case B care for himself? His person? His estate? Does he meet the standards for competency discussed above? Does he meet the standards for having a guardian appointed? If so, who should be appointed guardian? Should it be his family? What about the question of their motives? Would it be appropriate to appoint the adult protective services agency as his guardian? Whoever is appointed, how seriously should that person weigh his desire to go home compared to the family's concerns about his ability to care for himself?

Case C forces us to consider a very different type of question than the previous cases, which raised the question of when a guardian should be appointed. Case C raises the question of the power of a guardian. Could a patient refuse care in such a case if he or she were competent? Can a guardian refuse care on behalf of a patient in such a case? What would Grisez and Boyle say? The authors of the Jewish Compendium? The President's Commission?

SECTION G
Death and Dying

31. TRUTH-TELLING

Physicians have generally shied away from being the bearers of bad news to patients. As a first-century physicians' oath from India put it, "Even knowing that the patient's span of life has come to its close, it shall not be mentioned by thee there [in the patient's household], where if so done, it would cause shock to the patient or to others."[1] This reluctance in part stems from an all-too-human aversion to forcing others to face the reality of death. Physicians often come to regard death and disease as enemies and have a difficulty in acknowledging when those enemies are defeating their best attempts to save a patient. In addition, physicians have recognized that their confident presence itself has a beneficent influence on a patient's state. Patients not only seek hope from their physicians, but the presence of the physician can have supportive, suggestive, and placebo effects on the ways in which patients experience pain and suffering.

The issue of telling the truth to possibly terminal patients has been a recurring question in American medicine. It is raised, for example, in the first code of the American Medical Association (May 1847):

A physician should not be forward to make gloomy prognostications, because they savor of empiricism, by magnifying the importance of his services in the treatment or cure of the disease. But he should not fail, on proper occasions, to give to the friends of the patient timely notice of danger when it really occurs; and even to the patient himself, if absolutely necessary. This office, however, is so peculiarly alarming when executed by him, that it ought to be declined whenever it can be assigned to any other person of sufficient judgment and delicacy. For, the physician should be the minister of hope and comfort to the sick; that, by such cordials to the drooping spirit, he may smooth the bed of death, revive expiring life, and coun-

---

[1] "Oath of Initiation," *Encyclopedia of Bioethics*, p. 1732. (New York: Macmillan Free Press, 1978).

347

teract the depressive influence of those maladies which often disturb the tranquillity of the most resigned in their last moments. The life of a sick person can be shortened not only by the acts, but also by the words or the manner of a physician. It is, therefore, a sacred duty to guard himself carefully in this respect, and to avoid all things which have a tendency to discourage the patient and to depress his spirits.[2]

The section quoted above recognized, in its own way, that conveying the diagnosis of a terminal disease can have an adverse impact on the patient if it is not done with attention to the amount of information the patient can adequately absorb and understand. This insight argues for care and patience in conveying such information and for giving the patient an opportunity to return and ask the physician again about the meaning and significance of the diagnosis.

This important recognition that psychologically charged information must be transmitted with care has often been used as an excuse not to provide patients with all the information they might want. Surveys have shown that most patients do indeed wish to be informed of their diagnosis, whereas physicians tend radically to overestimate the extent to which patients wish to be shielded from such disclosures. One must also recognize that not informing patients about their terminal illnesses may mean they will not get their financial affairs in order, not come to terms with family and friends, not make spiritual preparations for death, and not end their days in a fully authentic fashion. By not providing the truth or distorting the truth, one may adversely affect the integrity of a patient's last months or years.

This last point should be applied with caution. Some patients do not want to know the truth. Even some of the recent court rulings regarding free and informed consent have noted that patients need not be informed if they decline information.[3] The moral duty to tell the truth and to give information for free and informed consent is thus not necessarily an obligation to force the patient to face a truth the patient wishes to avoid. There is rather a prima facie moral duty to make information available, should a patient wish to have it. If the patient requests, information can be provided instead to a family member, or the physician may treat according to what a medical professional would hold to be optimal treatment. In short, patients may choose to be treated paternalistically, if their physicians agree to shoulder such a difficult burden.

The issue of truth-telling is not confined to concerns about death. For example, physicians are often uncertain about the proper choice of treatment or the proper diagnostic procedures. To what extent should patients be informed about the full range of doubts and hesitations possessed by their treating physicians? Should patients be allowed to sit in or be invited to attend discussions among attending physicians and consultants, as they puzzle over the proper diagnosis and treatment? Physicians come to have knowledge about patients, which neither the physician nor the patient may have anticipated. If that knowledge is likely to harm the patient, the physician must then ask whether there is an obligation not to disclose. Insofar as the physician decides not to disclose the information, the four senses of autonomy, which Bruce Miller describes in the

<hr>

[2]American Medical Association Code, May 1847, Chapter I, Article I, section 4.
[3]See, for example, *Cobbs v. Grant*, 502 P.2d 1, 12, (Cal. 1972); and *Sard v. Hardy*, 397 A.2d 1014, 1022 (Md. 1977).

readings, are circumscribed. In analyzing these issues, one must ask how the President's Commission's treatment of the patient as decision-maker is to be understood in contexts where less than all the truth is disclosed. How would you apply Thomasma's views regarding autonomy and paternalism to these questions?

One is pressed to examine fundamental philosophical issues regarding the morality of truth-telling and the immorality of lying. If the duty not to lie is based on a nonconsequentialist moral grounding, one may be able to secure an exceptionless obligation not to deceive. Patients would be seen as having a right not to be told lies. But still that will not be sufficient, for patients depend not simply on physicians avoiding deception, but on physicians providing sufficient information. One will need to ask to what extent there is a positive fiduciary obligation on the part of physicians to disclose all the information a patient may want. Utilitarian or consequentialist approaches to these issues will focus more on which practices will be more or less useful in the long run. Finally, one must confront the question of the extent to which medicine may in part be a practice that depends on deception or incomplete disclosure. No one playing poker may with justification object to being deceived by poker bluffs; such are integral to the game itself. The question is whether providing less than full disclosure of information is integral, in some circumstances, to the care and comfort provided by medicine, at least as some elements of the tradition suggest. One may at the least confront a tension between the virtues of compassion and the patient's right to disclosure of information as outlined in the selection from *Canterbury v. Spence*.

Case A

Alice, aged six, has been diagnosed as suffering from acute lymphocytic leukemia. It is explained to her parents that she has at least a 90 percent chance of achieving a complete remission and that the chances of a long-term cure rate are greater than 50 percent. The parents ask the physician what they should tell Alice. Should they tell her she has leukemia? The mother wants to know how to respond if Alice asks if she is likely to die from the disease. The parents would rather not inform the child either of the diagnosis or of the prognosis. They argue that it is best to postpone such issues.

Later, one will know whether the treatment is likely to be successful or not, and Alice will have become older and more likely to understand what is at stake. Alice's parents would like to wait until then. The physician agrees. However, during the hospitalization for the first course of treatment, one of the nurses disagrees. She argues that Alice is an intelligent child and will quickly determine the nature and seriousness of the disease. Children, she argues, share a great deal of information among themselves on an oncology ward.

Case B

Mr. B is a 57-year-old electrician who has been suffering from congestive heart failure for the last five years. He has told his physician that when it gets toward the end, he does not want to be informed of the fact that he is about to die. He just wants to be kept comfortable. In fact, Mr. B would like his physician to make treatment decisions without consulting him and not to tell him about unpleasant truths. As Mr. B puts it, "It is bad enough to live with this problem without having the damn truth rubbed in my face all the time!"

Case C

For over twenty years, Dr. Frank has had Mr. and Mrs. C as his patients. He has gotten to know them very well and considers them not only patients but also close friends. Mr. C, who is a heavy smoker, comes by to have his yearly physical two days before he and his wife are scheduled to leave on a one-week vacation in London. They have looked forward very much to the trip, and it will be for them a second honeymoon. They have never been outside of the United States. As Dr. Frank examines the X ray of Mr. C's chest, he discovers findings compatible with cancer of the lung. In his judgment, it would not hurt to wait another ten days before trying to evaluate the issue further. Besides, in the meantime he can show the X ray to a radiologist for a second opinion. He decides to take two other X rays, reassure Mr. C that nothing is wrong, and contact him when he returns from the vacation.

Case D

While driving to work at the local university medical center, Dr. Smith witnesses a serious automobile accident. She stops to render aid but has no medical instruments or medication with her. One of the individuals involved is conscious and in severe pain. Dr. Smith decides to take some aspirin from her purse and give it to this individual, telling him that it will help control his pain. She suspects that if she says this in a convincing enough fashion, he will benefit from the placebo effect and will in fact experience some diminution of suffering.

Case E

Miss E, 24, has developed end-stage renal disease. Her family wants to help her acquire a transplant. Mr. and Mrs. E and their other two children, ages 23 and 21, agree to be evaluated as possible donors. Dr. Jones, while evaluating their compatibility, discovers that neither Miss E nor her brother, who is the youngest child, could have been the child of Mr. E. Should Dr. Jones reveal this information to anyone? Should he instead simply state, as he has indeed found, that no one except the mother is likely to be a good donor-candidate?

What moral rules would you appeal to in deciding what amount of information to disclose in these various cases? Would your judgment with regard to Alice change if she were 16 rather than 6? If age is an important consideration, at what age do children have a right to what amount of disclosure? Bear in mind that patients tend to find out the truth about their illnesses, as the nurse argues in Case A, even if physicians and family wish to hide it. What impact does such deception have on the patient's trust and reliance on family and physicians? How ought the conflicting views of the nurse and physician be mediated? What if the nurse insists that both her commitment to personal honesty and her professional integrity compel her to answer any questions Alice might ask? What precautions should physicians take in acting on wishes such as those of Mr. B? What if such an individual has no family to whom one can disclose information? Is the physician obliged from time to time to offer Mr. B new opportunities to learn more, in order to test whether he has changed his mind? Or should one decide that Mr. B has made a competent choice and, if the physician has agreed to honor it, the matter is settled?

What do you think of Dr. Frank's decision to inform Mr. C only after he returns from the trip? The decision presumes that the Cs will be better off not knowing the truth until after their long-sought vacation. But the time together in London may have a deeper and more profound significance for them, were they to know the truth. Perhaps if they realized this was their last trip (let us presume that they will not have money to take another), they might instead go to Rome or Jerusalem.

Is Dr. Smith in Case D actually deceiving the patient? She has good grounds for believing that if she states the aspirin will relieve pain, that it will in fact do so, at least to some degree. What is the morality of true placebos (the use of non-efficacious material under circumstances likely in part to achieve the therapeutic goal sought), given the fact that the "deceiving" statement leads to the realization of the claim made? The deception lies rather in not disclosing the mechanism by which the drug is efficacious. Finally, if you were Dr. Jones, what would you do in Case E? Is there any moral obligation to disclose such information? If you would disclose any information, to whom would you disclose it and how?

32. THE USE OF INTENSIVE CARE UNITS

Intensive care units (ICUs) were first developed in the 1950s using the recovery room as a model. At present, ICUs are a fixture of most general hospitals. They are used not only for individuals recovering from surgery, accident, or acute illness, where there is a high likelihood of recovery and return to the premorbid state, but they are also used for a great number of individuals with chronic diseases. As a result, the average age of patients in many intensive care units in the United States is frequently in the late sixties or early seventies. This circumstance suggests the diversity of purposes to which ICUs are put. They are used as vehicles (1) for short-term support and monitoring with a view to returning patients to their premorbid state; (2) in support and monitoring over indefinite periods of time in the hope that perhaps individuals involved will be able to be discharged from the ICU and from the hospital; and (3) for sustaining individuals in the last days of their lives, even though there has been a commitment not to resuscitate them, should there be cardiopulmonary arrest, or should the blood pressure begin to drop. In the last case, ICUs are employed as high-cost, high-intensity hospices. This is documented in one study that showed that about one-fifth of the individuals in an ICU were there for terminal care, and in two medical center ICUs from 40 percent to 70 percent of the deaths occurred in the ICU after "Do Not Resuscitate" orders had been written.

The amount of resources committed to ICU care is significant. In 1982 between $13 billion and $15 billion were spent for ICU and coronary care units, accounting for about 0.5% of the country's GNP. The investment of so much energy and resources raises the question of whether ICU treatment should be afforded to individuals where there is often little hope of recovery or where, if there should be hope of discharge from the ICU, there is little hope of ultimate discharge from the hospital or life beyond a number of months. There have been attempts to develop criteria for predicting whether patients who are admitted to an ICU will survive.[1] As such predictive measures become more reliable, there will undoubtedly be pressure to use them as indications for admission to an ICU.

If ICU bed capacity is not expanded, and if such predictive measures are introduced as indications for admission, the question will also arise whether patients should not be removed from an ICU when it appears that ICU treatment will no longer offer a special benefit. This would allow an ICU bed to be occupied by new arrivals instead of long-time residents for whom ICU treatment offers only a marginal benefit. This question of triage is raised by recent mechanisms for cost containment such as *prospective reimbursement.* The use of diagnostic-related groups (DRGs) to assign a fixed payment for the treatment of a disease encourages forgoing diagnostic and therapeutic interventions, which are likely to be of only marginal benefit, since hospitals are reimbursed a fixed amount per diagnostic category. The key question is how minimal does the benefit need to be before it is marginal in the sense of no longer being a necessary part of customary treatment.

To approach treatment in ICUs in this fashion will require that physicians avoid the practice of defensive medicine, that is, the ordering of all possible tests and the use of all possible resources toward the aim of prolonging life. This may require a readjustment of the legal system's attitude toward standards of care. The Office of Technology Assessment of the U.S. Congress, in a 1984 case study entitled "Intensive Care Units," noted: "The legal system, including legislators and the courts, may need to recognize the possible conflict between malpractice standards which assume quality of care that meets national expert criteria, and a decisionmaking environment in which resources may be severely limited."[2] This problem is not unique to ICUs but is integral to the DRG system and all prospective-payment systems that discourage the employment of marginally useful diagnostic and therapeutic interventions.

The very success of ICUs has thus created problems for public policy. Because ICUs can maintain individuals in states of marginal existence, this raises the issue of "do-not-resuscitate" orders, an issue explored later in this volume. Also, as the discussion regarding the case studies on the definition of death suggests, ICUs may secure survival for permanently comatose individuals, raising further the question of whether ICU resources ought to have been expended, or whether such treatment should have been discontinued before such an ambiguous therapeutic success was achieved. One needs to determine whether, when there are only marginal benefits to be derived from such care, the provision of ICU treatment is a part of the "adequate" level of health care outlined by the President's Commission. What rights, if any, do individuals have to ICU treatment? What will the likely consequences be of more stringent or lax criteria for admission to ICUs? One will also need to ponder whether it would be permissible to allow individuals to pay a surcharge and be allowed ICU care, when most consider it only of marginal benefit. Would such arrangements offend

---

[1]See, for example, W. A. Knaus, J. E. Zimmerman, and D. P. Wagner, "APACHE—Acute Physiology and Chronic Health Evaluation: A Physiologically Based Classification System," *Critical Care Medicine* 9 (1981): 591–597.

[2]Robert A. Berenson, "Intensive Care Units (ICUs)" (Washington, D.C.: Office of Technology Assessment, 1984), p. 78.

against Norman Daniels' principle of fair equality of opportunity? How would one need to make arrangements for the provision of ICU care in a health-care system committed to equality of access? On the other hand, is the provision of ICU care when there is little chance of survival or survival with sentience a form of care that should be excluded from "adequate" levels of health care to be provided to all? How would you apply Gibbard's arguments to such cases? Consult the excerpt from the President's Commission in Section 6a. Would you apply the distinction between ordinary versus extraordinary care to the choices of whether to admit a patient to the ICU?

Case A

Mrs. A, 85, suffers from organic brain syndrome secondary to diabetes. She can at times recognize her son and daughter-in-law, but she is generally confused and disoriented. Three years ago she developed cancer of the colon. The tumor is now widespread, with metastases to the liver. Even with aggressive treatment, she is unlikely to live more than a month. Her son and daughter-in-law insist that everything be done for her and that she be admitted to the intensive care unit. The attending physician suggests that the ICU does not offer her appropriate treatment. What she needs, the physician argues, is treatment aimed at keeping her comfortable and allowing her to die with as little intrusion and disturbance as possible. The son and daughter-in-law disagree; they say they love their mother and cannot see themselves giving her less than all available care. The physician would like to transfer her from the ICU, not only because the treatment is unlikely to be of benefit to Mrs. A but also because the care may entail well over $10,000 in costs that will not be reimbursed through Medicare. The ICU nurses agree with the family and argue that financial considerations should not play a role in such decisions.

Case B

For the last 25 years, Mr. B has been a chronic alcoholic. Now, at the age of 55, he is in the end stages of alcoholic cirrhosis, complicated by esophageal varices. He is hospitalized vomiting blood and is admitted to the ICU. After transfusing six units of blood, the bleeding is still not controlled and it is clear that Mr. B is in hepatic coma. At this point, the ICU is filled to capacity. Because of an automobile accident, a 25-year-old woman has been admitted to the emergency room of the hospital. She is in need of an ICU bed, would appear to be salvageable, and cannot be safely transported to another hospital. The physicians in the hospital would like to remove Mr. B from the ICU and give his bed to the accident victim. Given the fact that he is in the end stages of alcoholic cirrhosis, he will die shortly in any event.

Case C

Mrs. C, 78, has suffered a massive cerebrovascular accident. The stroke has left her completely paralyzed on the right side, aphasic, and in a deeply obtunded condition. Prior to the stroke, she had been under treatment for heart disease, hypertension, and diabetes. She appears to be developing renal failure. Her husband and her family agree to a "do-not-resuscitate" order being written on Mrs. C. The question arises of whether to admit her to the ICU; there is only one available bed left and there is concern that it may be needed by a 25-year-old woman with subacute bacterial endocarditis, who is likely to be salvageable. It is considered that both patients could be transferred to another hospital with about the same risk of health. The physicians want to know whom they should admit to the ICU. If they admit the 25-year- old woman, should they suggest that Mrs. C be transferred to another hospital's ICU or should she be managed in a general care bed, especially since the family has agreed to a do-not-resuscitate order?

How should one make choices in circumstances presented by these cases? Ought the decisions to be made on a case-by-case basis or should standard policies be developed? If you favor standard policies, should they be made on a hospital-by-hospital basis, or should the standards be statewide or nationwide? Under what circumstances would you make exceptions to such standards? Finally, how ought one to decide when the condition of two patients competing for a bed is very nearly equal? Let us imagine that they have nearly equal scores on an index of their likely survival. These sorts of questions will need to be faced the more we as a society wish to contain the cost of health care. ICUs in many other countries do not admit patients who have very little chance of survival. Do you as a citizen want to set aside funds so that you can receive ICU care, should you be 80 and have Alzheimer's disease? What conditions would you want to establish for ICU admission and treatment, recognizing that you yourself will be subject to them? Should financial considerations play a role in deciding whether to keep Mrs. A in the ICU? What role should the views of the nurses play in deciding whether to transfer Mrs. A? Are the nurses correct? Should her family have a right to demand ICU treatment? Would it be proper to remove Mr. B from the ICU? Should ICUs be used as a place to die, as is likely the case with Mrs. C? In answering such questions, determine whether it is helpful to distinguish between prolonging life and prolonging dying. How would you develop such a distinction? What should public policy be with regard to ICU admission criteria and with regard to the criteria for continued ICU treatment?

33. ADVANCE DIRECTIVES

The selections in this volume concerning informed consent support the right of individuals not only to consent to treatment but also to refuse treatment. However, they center on individuals who are competent and able to express their wishes. One of the major difficulties raised by modern technology is that individuals can now survive weeks if not months in conditions of incompetence with the support of modern medical technology. Many individuals find such a prospect abhorrent. The problem has been to find ways in which individuals while competent can establish directives for their treatment during future circumstances when they will no longer be competent and able to refuse heroic or extraordinary care.

One should note that the idea of refusing heroic or extraordinary care is not a new one. Its roots go back to discussions in the latter part of the sixteenth and early part of the seventeenth centuries regarding the extent to which individuals are obliged to accept treatment to save or prolong their lives. The distinction between ordinary and extraordinary treatment was not meant to signal a line between usual and customary treatment on the one hand, and experimental and exotic treatment on the other. Rather, the distinction was between treatment that did not constitute a serious inconvenience and treatment that constituted an undue burden on the patient or the patient's family. The burden could be either financial or psychological. The amputation of a limb could be refused because (1) the operation was painful, (2) results were uncertain, or (3) the patient had a grave horror (horror magnus) of living without the limb. This literature did not address the status of incompetent individuals, because medical technology at the time did not create a class of individuals likely to be treated for long periods of time in such a state.

With the development of intensive care units in the 1950s, along with other technological advances that allowed the process of dying to be prolonged and life often to be saved with dubious quality, questions regarding this class of individuals developed, especially in the 1970s. The goal was to provide a vehicle or method by which individuals could direct in advance how they wished to be treated, should they become incompetent. Such vehicles can in general be termed *advance directives*. They can take four forms. First, an individual may simply tell others orally how he or she wishes to be treated in the event of incapacitation. Such *oral directives* can provide the basis for physicians and courts making a substituted judgment, deciding what the patient would have wanted should the patient have been able to participate in the treatment. An illustration of this point is provided by the case of *Eichner v. Dillon* [420 N.E. 2d 64 (N.Y. Ct. App. 1981)]. Brother Fox, an 83-year-old Marianist religious, had informed Father Philip K. Eichner that, should he enter into a chronic vegetative state, he did not want his life prolonged by extraordinary means. Though New York did not have a natural death law and though Brother Fox had not written out his wishes, the court found that Father Eichner, in refusing the treatment on the basis of substituted judgment, acted legitimately.

Because of the uncertainties of oral statements, a second form preferable to the oral directive is the *living will:* a written statement in which an individual outlines under what circumstances and to what extent he or she would wish to be treated. Such living wills were met with skepticism in that they had none of the legal status of actual wills. Nor was there initially case law directly to indicate that they need be respected. Although the Hippocratic tradition did not require the treatment of hopeless patients, and although the traditional distinction between ordinary and extraordinary treatment underscored the fact that there was not a duty to save life at all costs and under all circumstances, a prevailing theme of the 1960s and 1970s indicated the contrary. There was the suggestion that life should be saved at all costs. As a result, the question arose as to whether living wills could morally and legally be respected. The interest in living wills has been widespread and widely supported. Although promoted by the Euthanasia Education Council, the use of living wills was encouraged by many groups concerned with "death with dignity." By 1974 the U.S. Catholic Hospital Association had drafted a living will. The result has been the passage in over 40 percent of the states of natural death acts that conveyed statutory recognition of written directives, creating a third form of advance directives.

However, the difficulty with this is that this legislation created instruments that were difficult to enact. Moreover, most statutes provided few sanctions other than grounds for reprimanding a physician on the basis of unprofessional conduct if the physician failed to honor a living will. A number of natural death laws require the patient to be in a terminal state for 14 days before the instrument goes into effect and allow the refusal only of artificial means of life support. It is unclear whether, by means of such instruments in states with such restrictions, one could instruct that one not be given cardiopulmonary resuscitation should one suffer a heart attack, cardiac arrest, and fail to breathe for more than three minutes. In addition, the instruments must in some states be witnessed by individuals not related to the person enacting the directive, nor by employees of the institution in which the patient is being treated. Finally, the directive to physicians provided by many of the states is a very sparse document, leaving little opportunity for patients to say in detail what they would want or would not want to have done. The major vitue of natural death laws is that they confer a special protection against liability on physicians and other health-care workers. This may not only be to the advantage of physicians but also to the patients, in that this may allay the anxiety of those who wish to respect the directive.

Even where family members are barred from being witnesses to the directive authorized under natural death legislation, it may be advisable to have a patient write a living will. Such an additional instrument can be used by the patient to express in detail what treatment is to be given and under what circumstances. The second instrument can be signed by family members. Their witness and signature would be sought not simply from a legal point of view but rather in order to enlist the family's agreement to the patient's decisions.

There is a fourth form of advance directive available through the use of *durable power of attorney* legislation. The President's Commission, in its March 1983, report, *Deciding to Forego Life-Sustaining Treatment,* indicates that most states have durable power of attorney laws, which can be used to appoint an individual to make choices about one's treatment should one become incompetent. In most cases, such legislation was not adopted with the idea of medical treatment as a central concern. Instead, the instruments provide a general appointment of power of attorney. Still, this legislation allows one to name a surrogate decision-maker. If one uses such a power of attorney, it would likely make moral, if not legal, sense to provide a living will to help the individual one appoints in making the difficult decisions that may need to be faced regarding treatment and termination of treatment.

Advance directives develop in a special way the concerns for patient autonomy and for the patient as decision-maker raised by Bruce Miller in his analyses of the refusal of life-saving treatment. A well-conceived, well-thought-out living will allows autonomy to express itself as free action, authenticity, effective deliberation, and moral reflection from a period of competence into a period of incompetence. In assessing the morality of such instruments, one will need to ask whether one can use them with a view to hastening death through the refusal of treatment, or whether that may only be a foreseen but not intended outcome. See, for example, the analysis of double effect in this volume provided in the selection from Kenny. Under what circumstances would it be proper to use an advance directive to refuse treatment? Should a condition for such an instrument being accepted be that the patient is terminal? Or may such an instrument be used to refuse treatment even when it is likely that the patient could be saved? Ought one to honor a living will that refuses treatment, should one suffer a serious burn (see the case discussion of burn patients)? What rights do patients have in these matters? What are the likely consequences of different policies with regard to the use of advance directives? Under what circumstances, if any, would the use of advance directives undermine the professional integrity of physicians? The excerpt in this volume in Section 6a from the report by the President's Commission provides analyses of the traditional distinctions between ordinary versus extraordinary care, and between intending versus foreseeing. How would you apply them to the use of advance directives?

Case A

A 45-year-old insurance salesman decides while in good health to fill out a natural death act directive in a state that requires a person to be terminal for 14 days before the directive takes effect. On the way back from having the instrument notarized, he suffers a heart attack at a bus stop. An ambulance is called. The ambulance attendants determine that very ineffective support was given to him at the scene and that Mr. A had probably stopped breathing about three minutes before they arrived and began artificial ventilation. At the hospital it becomes clear that Mr. A can very likely be saved but that he has sustained irreversible neocortical damage. The physicians treating him in the coronary care unit to which he is transferred are shown the natural death act directive but conclude that it does not apply because the patient has not been terminal for 14 days. His wife, who has arrived by that time, says the physicians' attitude is nonsensical. They are morally bound to respect her husband's wishes.

Case B

Mrs. B is a 79-year-old retired school teacher who was in excellent health prior to suffering a stroke three days previously. Her physician has on file in her medical record a living will, which she wrote out some ten years before. At that time she had indicated that, should she ever suffer a stroke of any sort, she would not want to be saved. She had watched her mother live as an invalid for about four years in a nursing home after sustaining a stroke. Mrs. B wanted to be sure she would never be exposed to such an indignity nor constitute such a burden on others. The physician is not sure whether this continued to be the view of Mrs. B. Since signing the instrument, Mrs. B never discussed the matter again. Mrs. B's home state does not have a natural death law. The stroke is a fairly massive one involving the dominant hemisphere and is likely to leave Mrs. B unable to speak and paralyzed on the right side. The physician believes that Mrs. B can probably be salvaged with the use of aggressive medical care. He also believes she is destined to spend her remaining years in a nursing home. At this point in her treatment she has developed pneumonia. If he were to fail to treat that pneumonia, she would die. He is unclear as to what he should do given the circumstances.

Case C

Mr. C is a 55-year-old former coal miner who has been retired for the last ten years because of black lung disease compounded by chronic obstructive pulmonary disease attributable to Mr. C's 40-year habit of smoking two to three packs of cigarettes a day. Over the last year and a half, he has been hospitalized three times because of his lung disease, intubated, and then slowly weaned from his ventilator and sent home. He was last discharged from the hospital six weeks before. He continues to smoke heavily and recognizes that his life expectancy is very meager. After the last hospitalization, he completed a directive to his physician in accordance with his state's natural death act. He instructed that, should he be hospitalized again, he did not want to be put on the ventilator but rather made comfortable and helped to die with as little pain as possible. He amplified this directive with a note in which he explained that he had lived a full life and could not stand being put on a ventilator again. In that note he emphasized that, should he be hospitalized and request treatment, the request should be disregarded. The last time he was hospitalized he recalls being disoriented and not being able to carry through his wish not to be intubated again. Two weeks later he is hospitalized again, gasping "Help me, help me!" Because of the directive he signed, rather than intubating the patient, the physicians sedate him so that he dies peacefully.

Case D

Mr. D is a 52-year-old stockbroker who has been living apart from his 48-year-old wife for the last year. While undergoing a coronary bypass operation, he apparently suffers from a stroke and general anoxia to the brain, leaving him with a minor paralysis on the left side and general disorientation. It is unclear as to the extent to which he will regain full function. His 35-year-old girlfriend with whom he has been living for the last year insists that everything be done. However, his wife appears, armed with a durable power of attorney, which he executed four years ago and never revoked. She insists that, should he suffer coronary arrest, he not be resuscitated. She claims that this was indeed her husband's wish, despite what the girlfriend might say.

Should the physicians honor Mr. A's request, even though the natural death act directive is not legally binding? Is it morally binding under these circumstances? What should Mrs. B's physician do? Can a living will that was written ten years before and never discussed again be considered morally and legally binding? How often should a physician discuss with a patient the patient's desires for treatment? Some states stipulate that a directive made pursuant to a natural death act will only be binding for five years. Is that a proper policy? What should the physicians do with respect to Mr. C? Is it proper simply to sedate him and allow him to die peacefully as he requested the last time he was clearly competent? Finally, should the physicians honor Mrs. D's power of attorney? Or should they instead seek a court order, arguing that his girlfriend can probably provide a better basis for substituted judgment at this juncture?

34. DNR ORDERS

The ability to resuscitate patients—the ability to rescue people from the brink of death by restoring their heartbeat and their breathing—is one of modern medicine's most dramatic achievements. In this set of cases we will be concerned with ethical issues that arise as a result of the tremendous advances in such resuscitative capacities in recent years. It is important to keep in mind throughout all of this discussion that when the heart stops beating (suffers a cardiac arrest), we have only a few minutes to restore the heartbeat before damage to the brain becomes total and irreversible and the patient dies. Therefore, the issues that arise in this area of resuscitation, particularly the question of whether or not to resuscitate, are ethical issues that need to be resolved in advance.

In the 1940s it was discovered that adrenaline could restore heartbeat and that electric defibrillation of a heart could restore a proper rhythm to the heart. If these measures were unsuccessful, the only way then available to manage a cardiac arrest was to open the chest surgically in an operation called a *thoracotomy* and directly massage the heart. In 1960 it was demonstrated that external cardiac massage could restore a heartbeat after a cardiac arrest. These types of resuscitative efforts—external massage, the delivery of oxygen under compression, the use of medications administered by direct injection or intravenously, and the application of electric shocks—soon became widespread. When it became clear that these measures could have a significant impact, most hospitals established special resuscitation teams specially trained in these techniques who could rapidly respond to notification that a cardiac arrest had occurred (in the jargon of current medicine, to the calling of a "code"). It has become customary to have a code called on all patients who have a loss of cardiac or respiratory activity unless specific instructions have been left not to resuscitate the patient.

Various studies have examined the effect of these resuscitative procedures. The initial success rate is often quite impressive (30 percent to 50 percent range), although the actual percentage of patients who recover after resuscitation so that they can be discharged from the hospital is much less, between 5 percent and 25 percent.

From the very beginning, physicians have questioned the appropriateness of cardiopulmonary resuscitative efforts in certain cases, particularly those where death is imminent no matter how successful the initial resuscitative efforts. In 1976, several hospitals, notably Beth Israel Hospital and Massachusetts General Hospital in Boston, published policies for advanced decision making not to resuscitate certain patients. Such decisions were called *Do Not Resuscitate Orders* (DNR orders) or *no-code* orders. These hospitals were following the policy statement made in 1974 in the *Journal of the American Medical Association,* which said:

> Cardiopulmonary resuscitation is not indicated in certain situations, such as in cases of terminal irreversible illness, where death is not unexpected.

Although it is not known how many hospitals nationwide have formally adopted the use of such DNR orders as a matter of policy, it is clear that a growing number of hospitals employ them. Three state medical societies (Alabama, Minnesota, and New York) have provided brief guidelines for such policies, and a number of local medical societies in association with their local bar association have collaborated to produce models for hospital no-code policies.

It is useful to have a look at one such DNR order policy, the 1981 policy of Beth Israel Hospital in Boston. The main features of the policy are as follows:

1. Orders not to resuscitate patients should be entered in the patient's record with full documentation of the patient's prognosis and of the concurrence of the patient (if he or she is competent) or of the family (if the patient is not competent).
2. The chief of service must be notified of DNR orders on competent patients and must concur on DNR orders on incompetent patients.
3. All DNR orders should be reviewed daily.
4. Competent patients must give their informed consent to a DNR order. The only

exception is when the physician believes that a discussion of such an order would be harmful to the patient. In this case, the physician and the chief of service can issue a DNR order with the consent of the patient's family.

5. DNR orders can be written for an incompetent patient provided there is proper documentation of the assessment of his or her incompetency, of the medical basis for the physician's decision, of the concurrence of the chief of service, and of the concurrence of the patient's family, if that family is available.

6. Judicial approval need not normally be obtained.

Even a brief examination of these fundamental principles of the Beth Israel DNR policy reveals many of the important questions raised by such a policy. One of them is: Who has the authority to make the decision not to initiate resuscitative efforts? The Beth Israel policy certainly creates a strong presumption that this is a decision that must involve the patient, or the patient's family if the patient is not competent. Such a presumption immediately raises the question of how we shall define competency in this particular area, keeping in mind that we are dealing with decision making by very ill people and their families, living through the crisis of a terminal illness and trying to decide what should be done for them or their family members when a cardiac arrest occurs. The reader needs to review the various accounts of competency presented in Section A1 of the readings and ask how both the President's Commission and Abernethy would understand the notion of competency in this context. The second question raised by this presumption is whether it is appropriate for this setting. The reader needs to look at the views of the President's Commission, of Miller, of Clements and Sider, and of Thomasma in Section A3 of the readings and ask how their models of decisional authority would apply to the decision made in advance not to resuscitate these terminally ill patients.

The second prominent feature of the Beth Israel DNR policy is its clear presumption that a decision not to resuscitate a patient who suffers a cardiac arrest is appropriate provided that the appropriate people have made that decision even though it means that the patient would then die, a patient who might otherwise have survived. Would this presumption be acceptable to Grisez and Boyle? Would it be acceptable to the Jewish Compendium on Medical Ethics and others who believe in the sanctity of life? Does it presuppose some stringent notion of personhood, such as advanced by Tooley and Engelhardt, or would this view be acceptable even to those who hold a wider conception of personhood? In short, the writing of a DNR order raises all the moral issues discussed in the readings in Sections B5 and B6, and the reader needs to review those ideas and to use them to evaluate the legitimacy of such policies as the Beth Israel DNR policy.

Recent studies at the Beth Israel Hospital, at Case Western Reserve in Cleveland, and at Baylor College of Medicine and its affiliated hospitals in Houston have taught us a lot about how advanced decision making regarding resuscitation is now carried on in hospitals throughout the country. One of the crucial findings of these studies is that physicians consult with patients and their family when they wish to recommend a decision not to resuscitate the patient but rarely consult with either the patient or their family when the physician's recommendation is that the patient be resuscitated. Some have criticized this practice, claiming that it shows a failure to take seriously the idea that the decision as to whether the patient should or should not be resuscitated is a decision for the patient and the family and not for the physician alone. Others have viewed this as appropriate, claiming that a physician is mandated by his moral responsibilities to resuscitate the patient in all those cases in which he or she finds resuscitative efforts medically indicated. What would the President's Commission say about this? What would Clements and Sider say? How would Miller and Thomasma respond?

Another question that emerged out of these findings is the following: Very often the physician for the patient may have views about this question different from other physicians (especially interns and residents) and nurses who are aiding the physician in the care of the patient. The Beth Israel policy, like most other policies, makes no reference to a role for these other professionals in the decision-making process. Is this appropriate? In Section A2 of the readings, what would the different models depicting the role of nurses have to say about this question?

Still another finding that has emerged from these studies is that the decision not to resuscitate a patient has varying implications for what sort of medical care the patient will or will not receive. Sometimes that decision is made even while the patient is receiving very aggressive medical care. At other times that decision is accompanied by further decisions to withhold or withdraw various medications, various procedures, and perhaps even food or water. Is that appropriate? When if ever in that spectrum of decisions do we cross the borderline between passive euthanasia (the withdrawing or withholding of care to allow the patient to die) and active euthanasia (actively killing the patient)? What would the President's Commission in the reading in Section B6 have to say about that question? What would Brody and Singer have to say about it? Grisez and Boyle? The Jewish Compendium?

Keeping in mind this background of the history of the emergence of cardiopulmonary resuscitation, of the policies that were developed to issue orders in advance to not apply these resuscitative measures in certain cases, and of the questions that arise when one examines a typical policy for DNR orders, let us now examine several cases that raise these issues.

Case A

The patient in this case is a 78-year-old male who has lived on his own for many years. He has always been a very popular man in his neighborhood, so his neighbors are always looking out for him. They report that he has a brother and a sister who moved away some time ago and who have had no significant contact with the patient in recent years, although they have an address for these family members. About two weeks ago, one of his neighbors found him on the floor unconscious. He shortly recovered, but since then he has been lethargic and uncommunicative. After two days, the neighbor who found him brought him to a hospital emergency room. A CAT scan showed a cerebral infarct. Moreover, during the medical workup, his chest X ray showed a large, dense mass in the left lobe of his lung. A biopsy has confirmed cancer. Now, by the beginning of the second week of his hospitalization, there is no evidence of any improvement in his mental status. Moreover, he has become febrile, and doctors are concerned about sepsis and possible shock. The staff is beginning to struggle with many questions about the management of this patient. One of the most crucial questions is whether, if he does go into shock and arrests, he should be resuscitated. Moreover, staff members are not entirely sure who should be making this decision.

Case B

The patient in this case is a 72-year-old woman who worked for many years as a cleaning lady in a very dusty warehouse. She has a long history of chronic bronchitis, with many incidents of bronchopneumonia. In recent years she has had more and more difficulty breathing and has been admitted to the hospital on several occasions. On some of those occasions, when her condition was very bad, she was intubated and put in the intensive care unit. She never expressed any feelings about this care. On this particular admission, she has once more been intubated, and all attempts to wean her from her respirator have failed. She has become febrile and completely disoriented. Although the health-care professionals caring for her see her case as hopeless, they are badly divided as to what to do with her. Her husband has been approached for his permission to institute a DNR order and for his agreement not to treat her current infection. He insists that she be treated for the infection and that she be resuscitated if her heart stops beating. He says that he cannot live without her because she has always taken care of him, even when she has been ill, and he wants her back.

Case C

The patient in this case is a 66-year-old widower with a history of congestive heart failure and chronic obstructive pulmonary disease. He has in the past been admitted to the hospital and put on a respirator in the medical ICU several times. On this particular occasion, his son, who lives near him, called an ambulance to take his father to the hospital because he was having difficulty breathing. On the way to the hospital, the patient arrested. He was resuscitated by the paramedics, intubated upon arrival in the emergency center, and transferred to the medical ICU. Since that time, his neurological status has fluctuated. On some occasions he seems to understand what is said to him and even attempts to respond. On other occasions he is totally nonresponsive. A CAT scan revealed an infarct in his brain. It is difficult at this point to say how likely it is that the patient can be weaned from the respirator and discharged from the hospital. It is also difficult at this point to say how severe his neurological deficits will be if that occurs. The son who lives closest to the father has asked that a DNR order be written. He says that this is what the father would have wished. He reports that the father had read in the newspaper about the natural death act, which allows patients to prepare a living will asking that aggressive health care be withheld or withdrawn when death is imminent and that they be allowed to die. The father had asked the son to make an appointment with the family attorney to fill out such a document. Unfortunately, says the son, he was unable to make the appointment before the father's latest attack. The other brothers disagree. They don't see that evidence as being persuasive because they are not sure what their father would have said, had a living will been explained to him. Moreover, the local living will, like most living wills, refers only to the withholding of care and the withdrawing of care when death is imminent, and the sons remind everyone, including their brother, that their father's death is not necessarily imminent. They feel that in light of the fact that the father has a chance to survive with some reasonable quality of life—even if there are some neurological deficits and continuing problems of congestive heart failure and chronic obstructive pulmonary disease—it would be appropriate to pull him through.

It is helpful to think of Case A and the many issues it raises by looking back at the Beth Israel DNR policy. According to that policy, these decisions, especially the ones about resuscitation, should be made by the physician in concurrence with the family because the patient is incompetent. Does that make any sense in Case A? Many members of the team treating the patient don't see why. Of what relevance are the views of the family if they have had so little to do with the patient for so many years? Would it be more appropriate to use his neighborhood friends as alternative participants in the decisional process? If so, who shall be used? What would the authors of the Beth Israel policy have to say about such a case? Looking back at the views of the President's Commission and others who have written on the decisional process, what would they say in this case?

Case B raises several crucial questions that differentiate it from Case A. The most crucial difference relates to the role of the husband. In Case B, unlike Case A, we have a family member present and he is opposed to the DNR order. The reasons that he gives are, however, self-centered and very unrealistic. What would be the appropriate way to deal with the question of decision making in such a case? Is it appropriate, contrary to the Beth Israel policy, to issue a DNR order in this case against the wishes of the husband? Could it be based on a judgment about *his* competency to make this decision? If so, what notion of competency would be involved? If not, what other basis could be used? There is another issue raised by Case B. If a decision is made to let the patient die by not resuscitating her, would it also be appropriate to extubate the patient so that she would die much more quickly? There are those who argue that the virtue of compassion calls for such a decision. This is the view of the treating physician. There are others, particularly the nurses, who believe that doing that would be morally wrong because it would be actively killing the patient. Who should make that decision? If the physician makes the decision, should the nurses who believe that it is wrong participate? In any event, is this a case where extubation would be active euthanasia? What would the President's Commission say? Does it make any difference whether it is active euthanasia? What would Grisez and Boyle say? What would Brody say? What would Singer say?

Case C raises further difficulties about the decision to write a DNR order. Part of this difficulty relates to the ambiguous evidence as to what the father would have wished. Can we take the evidence offered as sufficient proof that he would have wished the DNR order and use that as a basis for writing such an order? The Beth Israel policy talks about a competent patient consenting to a DNR order. Would the authors of this policy be willing to extend it to a patient who asks for a DNR order at an earlier stage when the patient is still competent? Would they take the evidence of this case as being sufficient to indicate that the patient would have wanted a DNR order? Secondly, there is a question of what to do about the role of the family. If this should be a decision of the family, and not of the doctor and of the patient, what are we to do given that the family is in conflict? This is not like our Case A where there was no close family member, or Case B where the family member's motives may have been inappropriate and/or based on denial. In Case C, reasonable family members are aware of the facts but are in disagreement. Should we follow the son's wishes for a DNR order, because he was closest to his father, or should we follow the wishes of the other two sons? These two decisional issues are supplemented by a third issue raised by some members of the staff. They wonder whether a DNR order is appropriate in Case

C, whatever the wishes of the patient and of the family, in light of the fact that there is no strong evidence that the patient cannot be pulled through his current crisis and returned to a quality of life reasonably approximating that quality of life with which he had lived before. What are we to make of that argument? What would the President's Commission recommend? What would Clements and Sider say about it? What would Thomasma say? How would Miller answer?

35.   THE FAMILY'S ROLE IN DECISIONS FOR TERMINAL PATIENTS

The management of terminal patients has always forced providers and recipients to raise questions about when to stop attempts to prolong the life of patients and when to start forms of care with other goals, such as keeping patients comfortable and helping them deal with the inevitability of their death. These questions have become more pressing in recent years because the ability of medicine to prolong the lives of the terminally ill has increased greatly. Because these questions have become so pressing and because the cases that raise them are so varied, we have devoted case areas 35 to 37 to these issues.

One major way of dealing with these questions is to ascertain the wishes of the patient, either at the time of decision or beforehand (with an advance directive of the type discussed in case area 33), and to follow those wishes. When we examined DNR orders in case area 34, however, we saw that there are situations in which this isn't possible because the patient is no longer competent to participate in the decisional process when the relevant decisions have to be made and has not expressed any wishes in advance. That fact led those who developed DNR policies to substitute the decision of the family for the decision of the patient. That theme has become prominent in many decision-making situations besides the decision not to resuscitate a patient who has arrested, and the following area of cases is devoted to an examination of the general theme of the role of families.

Before examining the role of the family in decision making for incompetent patients, let us first analyze the role of the family in decision making when the patient is competent. A standard analysis of that role would run like this: Strictly speaking, the only role a family has is the role that patients allow them to have. In fact, the adult patient's right to confidentiality, discussed in case area 16, would dictate that the family not even be told about what decisions are to be made unless the patient wishes them to be told. And even if, at the patient's request, they are told about the decision to be made, it is still the patient's decision, and the family can at most serve as advisors to the patient, and then only to the extent that the patient wishes them to serve in that role. Naturally, in most cases, patients will want their family to know about the decisions they have to make and will want to involve them in that decision, but that is just a fact about most patients.

An example that would help bring out the point of the standard analysis is the Florida case of *Satz v. Perlmutter*. That case involved Abe Perlmutter, who was diagnosed as having amyotrophic lateral sclerosis (ALS) in 1977. By the time the case came to court, he was virtually incapable of movement and unable to breathe without a ventilator. His death was inevitable and reasonably imminent. He was suffering immensely, and asked that he be disconnected from his respirator and allowed to die. The Florida Superior Court upheld his right to have that request honored. In that case, his family concurred in that judgment. But according to the standard analysis, that concurrence is, strictly speaking, irrelevant, and was only possible because Mr. Perlmutter involved them in the decisional process.

A number of issues might be raised about this standard analysis. Some questions relate to the question of truth-telling regarding the terminal patient discussed in case area 31. The standard analysis presupposes that terminally ill patients are fully informed of their condition by the providers and then decide what to tell their family and what role to allow their family in any decision making. But if for any of the reasons discussed in case area 31, the patient is provided with less than full information about his or her condition, then the role of the family may need to be much more prominent. Other issues relate to an appeal to such virtues as compassion and to a consideration of consequences. One might suggest that in many cases the compassionate thing is to ensure that the patient not confront life-and-death decisions without family support. Also, for the family that discovered after the patient's death that they had been left out, the consequences might be devastating. A possible compromise was proposed in one DNR policy:

> The attending physician should encourage the patient to discuss the issue with family members (if available) before deciding. If, despite such encouragement, the patient chooses not to involve or inform the family, confidentiality requires the physician to be bound by this order.

The reader must judge whether this compromise is an appropriate solution to some of the issues we have raised.

What is the role of the family in making treatment decisions for terminally ill patients when the patient is not competent to participate in the decisional process? A natural answer, one discussed above, is that the family should take the place of the patient. That answer and alternatives to it have been the subject of considerable litigation in recent years, and it is useful to review that litigation at this point.

The first of the crucial cases involved Karen Ann Quinlan, a 21-year-old woman who stopped breathing twice for at least 15 minutes each episode. The resulting damage to her brain produced a chronic vegetative state in which she was completely unaware of her environment and totally nonresponsive to it. At the time of the court case, it was also thought that she could not breathe on her own and required ventilator support. Her parents wished that support withdrawn from her so that she could die. The New Jersey Supreme Court was not willing to allow that to be done, even if the family member appointed guardian and the treating physicians concurred, without further process. The court declared:

> Upon the concurrence of the guardian and family of Karen, should the responsible attending physicians conclude that there is no reasonable possibility of Karen's ever emerging from her present comatose condition . . . and that the life-support apparatus now being administered to Karen should be discontinued, they shall consult with the hospital "Ethics Committee" or like body of the institution in which Karen

is then hospitalized. If that consultative body agrees . . . the present life-supporting system may be withdrawn. [*In re Quinlan*]

A second crucial case, reflecting a second approach, was the 1977 decision of the Supreme Judicial Council of Massachusetts in the case of *Superintendent of Belchertown v. Saikewicz.* That case involved a severely retarded 67-year-old who had been institutionalized for most of his life and who had a legal guardian rather than a family to make decisions for him. He had developed leukemia and could receive chemotherapy, which would only slightly extend his life. The guardian felt that the psychosocial trauma of the treatment for this incompetent patient made the treatment inappropriate. The court required in that case (although it later moved away from that requirement) prior judicial approval, arguing:

> We do not view the judicial resolution of this most difficult and awesome question—whether potentially life-prolonging treatment should be withheld from a person incapable of making his own decision—as constituting a "gratuitous encroachment" of medical expertise. Rather, such questions of life and death seem to us to require the process of detached but passionate investigation and decision that forms the ideal on which the judicial branch of government was created. [*Superintendent of Belchertown v. Saikewicz*]

A third approach was adopted by the Supreme Court of Florida in the 1984 case of *John F. Kennedy Memorial Hospital v. Bludworth.* This case involved a persistent vegetative patient who had insisted earlier on that he would never want to be kept alive through extraordinary life-support measures. The patient's wife requested that he be disconnected from his ventilator. The court held that her request should be honored and that more generally this right

> may be exercised either by close family members or by a guardian of the patient's person. . . . If there are close family members willing to exercise this right upon behalf of the patient, a guardian need not be judicially appointed. . . . Under this doctrine of "substituted judgment" the close family members or legal guardian substitute their judgment for what they believe the patient, if competent, would have done. [*John F. Kennedy Memorial Hospital v. Bludworth*]

As we look at this set of decisions, we can see that some allocate greater decisional authority to the family than do others. What arguments were, and can be, offered for these varying approaches? What would an appeal to consequences suggest? What would an appeal to the rights of the family suggest? What other types of arguments might be used? Also, is there any difference between these cases and the DNR orders we discussed in case area 34 where all protocols allow these decisions to be made for incompetent patients by the physicians and the family?

Case A

Mr. I, 73, has a long history of significant medical problems. He suffers both from chronic obstructive pulmonary disease (COPD) and from organic heart disease affecting his aortic and mitral valves. He has consistently refused surgery for the latter and treatment for the former, despite strong family requests. The patient says that he doesn't trust doctors and doesn't want to put himself in their hands. This, however, has not prevented his family from bringing him to the hospital emergency room several times a year for the last few years to treat acute crises, and he has in fact been treated with his grudging consent. He presented last week with a third-degree heart block. For the first time, he consented to surgery, although it was done under heavy family pressure, and it is an open question as to whether he voluntarily consented. The surgery has not been performed because it is generally believed that his pulmonary problems must be dealt with first. They, however, have worsened. The physician who treated him, and who was

doing his best despite the fact that this patient is a very difficult patient, had a long talk with Mr. I about intubation. The patient insisted that he did not wish to be intubated. At the time, his physician found him oriented, responsive to questions, but lethargic. When asked for reasons, the patient gave his familiar line on how he just didn't trust the doctors. Now he has become severely hypoxemic. The family insists that the patient is not competent, that they have to make the decisions for the patient, and that he should be intubated. The physician treating the patient does not wish to intubate him in light of his previous refusals, but he isn't sure, because he just doesn't know how to evaluate this patient's competency.

Case B

The patient in this case is a 48-year-old gentleman with a long history of diabetes and serious kidney problems. About a year ago he required a left nephrectomy. A week ago he was admitted to the hospital in a coma. His neurological status improved slightly so that he was responsive to pain and perhaps to commands, but to little else. As his treatment continued, however, his respiratory status worsened and he had to be put on a respirator. Moreover, he required medications to maintain his heartbeat. At that point, his only relative in the community, a cousin with whom he lived, was consulted, and the cousin felt that the patient's medications, which maintained his heartbeat, should be removed, saying that the man's situation was hopeless and he saw no point

to prolong the agony. The cousin contacted the patient's son, from whom the patient had been alienated for many years, and the son then spoke to the physician and demanded that everything be done to keep his father alive, including resuscitating him if he arrested. The son wanted to have a last chance to see his father and make his peace with him. The physician explained that the father's mental status made that unlikely, but the son responded that there was some chance that his father could understand, and that in any case he had expressions of regret that he had to say to his father. The cousin was furious about this, saying that the only relevant thing is that the patient should be allowed to die comfortably. What should be done in this case?

Case C

The patient in this case is an 84-year-old nursing home resident who suffers from severe and irreversible physical and mental impairment requiring that she be fed and medicated through a nasogastric tube. Her nephew, who is her legally appointed guardian, wants to remove the nasogastric

tube, even though this would certainly result in her death from dehydration in a week or less. He feels that she is not benefiting from being kept alive and is in pain and considerable indignity from her current condition. In short, he judges that she would be better off dead. The providers caring for this patient are very reluctant to follow his request, in large measure because they feel that removing the nasogas- tric tube would be equivalent to killing the patient. What should be done in a case like this?

Case A raises many important issues concerning the role of families in decision making. The first issue is the nature of competency and how it is to be assessed. One thing is clear from our earlier discussion: The role of the patient and the family changes greatly, depending on whether the patient is judged competent or incompetent. So a great deal hinges on that assessment in this case. The trouble is that this patient seems to be on the borderline. What would Gert and Culver have to say about the patient's competency? What would the various approaches discussed by the President's Commission have to say about that question? What would Abernethy have to say? If their judgment is that this patient is no longer competent to make decisions for himself, should the physician then make the decision on the basis of the family's request that the patient continue to be treated? What would the three courts whose decisions we have looked at say about that question? Keep in mind that the courts were talking about families who wished to stop treatment and that this is a case in which a family wishes to continue treatment. Does that make a difference? Finally, if we do agree that it is the family's decision to make, on what basis should family members make this decision? If we adopt the substituted-judgment rule articulated in *John F. Kennedy Memorial Hospital v. Bludworth,* is the family required, in light of the patient's long-term history of refusing medical care, to request that the patient not be intubated? And does the failure not to intubate this patient violate his right to life? What would the President's Commission say? What would Grisez and Boyle say? What would the authors of the Jewish Compendium on Medical Ethics say?

In all of the court cases we analyzed, the question was the role of the family versus the role of the court versus the role of some hospital committee. None of the decisions confront the very difficult problem about what to do about family disagreement. Case B forces us to examine that question. Whatever role we ascribe to the family, who should exercise that role when the family is in disagreement? Should it be the legally closest relative, in this case the son? Should it be the person who has been closest to the patient over the years, in this case the cousin? Of what relevance is it that the son's judgment is based on the son's own needs and the cousin's judgment is based on the patient's needs?

Case C raises still further questions about the role of the family. Just how far can the family go when it requests that care be discontinued? Should we draw a distinction between ordinary care and extraordinary medical intervention? Would withdrawing the woman's nasogastric tube really be killing the patient? Should this make a difference? The reader needs to review all of the readings in Section B6 to see what Grisez and Boyle, the President's Commission, Brody, Singer, Engelhardt, and the Jewish-Compendium on Medical Ethics all have to say about these questions.

36. HOSPICE CARE

The modern hospital stands as a tribute to the successes and hopes of contemporary medicine. The more than 7,000 registered hospitals in the United States, for example, serve more than 35 million inpatients each year. Highly specialized care is made available to these patients who usually stay in the hospital for only a brief time, and the typical hospital patient expects to get better and return to normal life. This is indeed what happens to the typical patient, and this success (together with the hope for further successes of this sort) explains the centrality of both the hospital and its health care in modern society.

Scattered throughout these hospitals, however, are some patients for whom modern medicine has much less to offer. These are the terminally ill patients whose life expectancy is measured in days, weeks, or at most months. In the past, many of them would never have been brought to hospitals. They would have stayed at home and died there. That is less of an option today. For a variety of reasons, families bring their terminally ill to die in a hospital. Unfortunately, that has given rise to many problems, for the hospital as traditionally organized often seems to be unresponsive to the needs of dying patients and their families.

What are the major problems that have been identified in this area? They include the following:

1. The primary concern of physicians and nurses seems to be with those patients who are viewed as having a good chance of surviving. Those who are dying often seem to receive less attention until they suffer an acute crisis.

2. The emphasis in hospitals seems to be on dealing with illnesses and not with painful symptoms. The dying need special attention to the management of their many painful and degrading symptoms, and this seems to be less central on the hospital agenda.

3. The hospital regulates the patient's family to a secondary place. Visiting hours and the number of visitors are often limited, and little attention is paid to family needs. The dying need their family, the family of the dying have many needs, and all of this seems less central to the agenda of the hospital.

4. Hospitals seem to be organized to fight death until there is nothing left to do. This is, after all, an appropriate attitude for its normal patients. But the terminally ill do not necessarily benefit from such an attitude, so the hospital as normally organized may be inappropriate for them.

In short, it is often claimed that the terminally ill need institutions and programs that place primary emphasis on their true needs (symptom relief, close contact with family, attention to personal and spiritual concerns) and not on attempting to prolong life and cure diseases. It is also often claimed that the contemporary hospital, as normally (and perhaps appropriately) organized, is not necessarily the best place to meet these needs. Out of these claims has grown the modern hospice movement.

The term *hospice* derives from a medieval French designation for places of rest constructed in out-of-the-way sites to house wandering pilgrims. The term was resurrected in the mid-nineteenth century by the Irish Sisters of Charity who created facilities for the special care of the dying, based on the notion of an earthly pilgrimage to an ultimate Holy Land. But the modern hospice movement's real development began with the founding in 1967 by Dr. Cicely Saunders of St. Christopher's Hospice in Sydenham, England (St. Christopher, it should be noted, is the patron saint of travelers).

St. Christopher's Hospice serves a 1.5-million patient population drawn from a six-mile radius. It has both an inpatient and an outpatient program, both of which emphasize symptom relief and personal caring rather than high-technology attempts to prolong life. This is particularly evident in the 70-bed inpatient unit. Visiting hours are long, and children and even family pets are allowed in. Patients are encouraged to talk about their feelings when they want to, and they are expected to continue activities (such as having a cocktail before dinner) that give them pleasure. Painful and distressing symptoms are anticipated, rather than responded to, and the highest priority is on relief of these symptoms. When the patient finally dies, family and staff members are encouraged to stay with the body as long as they wish. The home-care program provides a similar emphasis, and this enables St. Christopher's to serve a larger population.

St. Christopher's Hospice has set an example that has been followed in many places. In North America, the pioneer hospices were the Connecticut Hospice in New Haven, which began in the mid 1970s as a home-care program and then expanded to become an inpatient program as well, and the Palliative Care Service of the Royal Victoria Hospital in Montreal, which pioneered in the creation of a hospice unit within a large general hospital. Further growth of the hospice movement in North America was hampered by the difficulty in getting hospice care paid for by third-party insurers. That has changed in recent years when hospice care became eligible for funding under Medicare. Moreover, many Blue Cross and Blue Shield plans are paying for such services as long as various standards are met. It is clear that these developments in reimbursement represent at least in part a hope that hospice care may be less expensive than regular hospital care, because of its emphasis on outpatient care and because hospices are not committed to extending life as long as possible.

Hospice can be defined as a commitment to provide on an outpatient basis, in a special inpatient unit, or in a regular inpatient institution, care based on the following principles:

1. The main emphasis in hospice care must always be on the needs of the patient as a person and not just on the needs of a body suffering from a disease.

2. When the patient chooses hospice care, he or she is choosing care that emphasizes control of symptoms rather than prolongation of life. This is not a decision for some medical technology and against others. Rather, it is a decision for the goals that will be used to determine which care ought to be provided and which ought not to be provided.

3. Patients are entitled to aggressive pain relief that anticipates needs rather than merely responds to these needs and which is not concerned about addiction.

4. In addition to aggressive symptom relief, hospice care attends to the related social, psychological, and spiritual needs of patients and their family by encouraging active patient–family interaction, by re-creating a home milieu even in the hospice, and by using an interdisciplinary team that includes such professionals as social workers, counselors, and clergy, as well as physicians, nurses, and allied health professionals.

5. Hospice care attempts to ensure that outpatient care and inpatient care are coordinated, jointly meet these goals, and are available on a 24-hour, seven-days-a week basis.

6. Hospice care provides bereavement support for the family after the patient dies as part of its commitment to meeting all of the related needs of both the family and the patient.

Many important questions are raised by the emergence of the hospice movement. To begin with, the hospice movement has always stressed the involved informed choice of the patient to seek hospice care rather than more traditional care. In doing so, it has acted in keeping with the emphasis in the President's Commission on patient-centered decision making. Should we always accept that patient-centered orientation? Are there situations when hospice care would be too premature and pessimistic and should be rejected? What would Clements and Sider say? Thomasma? Miller? Should hospice care be something that relatives can choose for patients who are no longer competent? Should parents be able to choose it for children? Should adolescents be able to make that choice for themselves? Then there are questions related to the withholding of life-prolonging care in the hospice situation. What would Grisez and Boyle say about such a decision? What would the authors of the Jewish Compendium say? What would the President's Commission say? Finally, questions arise about the relation between hospice care and cost containment. Is hospice care something that ought to be part of Singer's national health plan? Should it be part of Enthoven's consumer choice program?

Case A

The patient in this case has recently been diagnosed as having a stage C2 colorectal cancer (disease extending beyond the muscularis mucosa with positive draining lymph nodes). Such patients have a median survival rate of 10 to 12 months; about 15 percent of such patients survive for five years. A common form of treatment would be surgical resection of the tumor and radiation therapy. In part, this would give the patient the best chance, but in part it would also provide symptom relief. The patient in question does not really wish any of these more aggressive forms of care, nor does he wish any chemotherapy. He says that he wishes to enter into a hospice program and merely be kept comfortable, without using any aggressive techniques, until he dies. His family and health-care providers are having a lot of difficulty with this decision, in part because there is a modest but real five-year survival rate for patients in this condition, in part because they think that surgical resection and radiation therapy would give him a longer median survival rate, and in part because they believe that he is underestimating the significance of the surgery and the radiation therapy for relief of symptoms.

Case B

The patient in this case is a 72-year-old gentleman who presents with significant weight loss, gastrointestinal bleeding, and pain in his abdomen at night. An abdominal ultrasound reveals a tumor of the pancreas. This particular tumor has a very high mortality rate, and there is a general feeling among the team managing the patient that this patient would benefit most from a hospice-type approach. Unfortunately, the patient is sufficiently demented so that it is impossible to discuss this choice with him. There is, moreover, no family available. The physicians recognize that there is at least one aggressive option open, a total pancreatectomy, a procedure that has a significant mortality rate, and only a modest success rate. Some of the physicians are concerned, however, about denying this man the best chance for survival and simply turning to a hospice-type approach, without the informed consent of either the patient or the family. They are particularly concerned because the tumor is confined to the head of

the pancreas and there are no lymph node metastases, so this is the type of patient who might benefit from surgery. Others don't see it that way. They see, on the contrary, any decision to proceed with a surgical procedure that has great risk and only a modest benefit as requiring the informed consent of the patient and his family. They also feel that the palliative approach of a hospice program is the more reasonable approach to adopt in a setting in which there is no possibility of patient and/or family involvement.

Cases A and B force us to think very carefully about the criteria for enrolling a patient in hospice care. The ideal candidate, in light of the philosophy of hospice care that has been outlined above, is the patient suffering from a terminal illness and a short life expectancy who can get significant symptom relief without aggressive medical care; who would benefit very little from aggressive medical care; and who in light of that chooses a program that attends to the patient's personal needs and the need for symptom relief rather than aggressively attempting to prolong life. Cases A and B involve some but not all of these factors. In Case A, there is a patient who can be cured or whose life can be significantly prolonged, but the patient chooses a palliative hospice approach. Moreover, the patient refuses certain aggressive measures that can be quite palliative and symptom relieving. Is this an appropriate patient to admit to a hospice? Is the choice of hospice care, and for certain forms of hospice care, primarily a matter of patient autonomy? Does it also need to involve a clear-cut medical judgment that supports it? What would the President's Commission have to say about this question? What would Clements and Sider, Thomasma, and Miller have to say about this question? Would the patient's choice in Case A be acceptable to the authors of the Jewish Compendium on Medical Ethics? Case B raises a different set of questions. Here there is a strong argument, in light of the patient's condition, for the appropriateness of hospice care and for the inappropriateness of extensive surgery. But we do not have the concurrence of the patient or the family who might speak for the patient. Absent such a concurrence, which approach should be adopted? How do we make the choice between hospice care and attempts at curative care when the patient and/or the family cannot participate? What would the authors just cited say about that question? Would their view be different if we had a patient who had a tumor like the patient in Case A, but whose mental status and family condition were like the patient in Case B?

Case C

The patient in this case is a 68-year-old gentleman with a 60-pack–year history of smoking who presents with a 4-cm tumor in his left lung diagnosed as squamous cell carcinoma, with evidence of only modest lymph node involvement, and with evidence of metastatic disease in his other lung. After a full explanation of his prognosis, he indicates that he wishes to avoid any aggressive therapy and simply receive palliative care, and that in order to achieve this, he wishes to be enrolled in the local hospice program. He cannot pay very much, because he has limited means, but he knows that hospice care is covered by Social Security. His physician in-

forms him that such coverage is covered by Social Security only if the patient has less than six months to live, and his prognosis is not that dim. The patient insists that hospice care is what he needs, that he certainly might die within the next six months, and that the physician should not be so overzealous in enforcing unfortunate rules.

This case raises many additional issues. Should reimbursement for hospice care be limited in this way? Should this patient's wishes for enrollment be respected? Is the physician the agent of the patient or of society? How far can a physician go in stretching the truth to help a patient?

37. SUICIDE AND EUTHANASIA

Both Plato and the Judeo-Christian tradition have interpreted individuals as custodians of their lives on behalf of God. As a result, suicide has been regarded as a moral evil, a point that is illustrated by the selections from the Canadian Law Reform Commission and the Jewish Compendium on Medical Ethics. In contrast, philosophers such as Seneca and David Hume have defended its moral propriety. Whereas in ancient times many agreed with Seneca, such has not been the case recently. With few exceptions, the general approach of Anglo-American law has been to condemn both suicide and killing at the behest of the victim. The arguments against allowing competent choice to authorize suicide and euthanasia have been varied. Those involved in public policy often reflect the view that the state should enforce moral law and that the citizen has obligations to the state, which preclude either euthanasia or suicide. As Blackstone put it in his *Commentaries on the Laws of England* (1765–1769), "[T]he suicide is guilty of a double offence; one spiritual, in invading the prerogative of the Almighty, and rushing into his immediate presence uncalled for; the other temporal, against the king, who hath an interest in the preservation of all his subjects . . ."[1] In addition, there have been concerns that such liberties would lead to abuse and that individuals might fail to discharge their duties—a person committing suicide might fail to pay outstanding debts. However, in the case of terminal patients, and in the presence of liberal bankruptcy laws, many of these concerns are blunted.

One singular exception in the Anglo-American legal tradition must be noted: The history of Texas law, which had never prohibited suicide and, until 1973, had no law against aiding and abetting suicide (aiding and abetting suicide is now a felony in Texas). In fact, during the first few months of the Texan Republic, there was no law against dueling; thus, one could interpret murder not as the taking of someone's life but as the taking of life without permission. Although dueling was outlawed in Texas in December 1836, the Texas courts

[1] William Blackstone, *Commentaries on the Laws of England*, Vol. IV, p. 189.

took the position that aiding and abetting suicide was not a crime, because suicide was not a crime. Regardless of what "may have been the law in England, or whatever that law may be now with reference to suicides, and the punishment of persons connected with suicide, by furnishing the means or other agencies, it does not obtain in Texas." [*Grace v. State*, 44 Tex. Crim. 195, 69 S.W. 530 (1902).] The court can be interpreted as taking the position that even if one held that suicide was wrong, free individuals have a right, if competent, to be aided in it by willing others. As a result, until 1973, when aiding and abetting suicide were criminalized, Texas offered individuals an opportunity to commit suicide—as the Roman philosopher Seneca had suggested—should the pains and frustrations of this life outweigh its pleasures and rewards. Seneca had noted that no one could complain of existence here; if it were not rewarding, one could end it.

One of the distinctions of Texas law was that it did not discourage people from willing their death or the death of others, as long as those involved were freely consenting. Traditionally, as the selection from Kenny indicates, one could take both active and passive steps that would likely expedite death, as long as one simply foresaw that death might come more quickly but did not intend it, all within the constraints of the doctrine of double effect. As the selection from the President's Commission in Section 6a shows, this distinction has remained an important one. The distinction between foresight and intention may in fact be more significant than the distinction often drawn between active and passive euthanasia, that is, between expediting death by omission or commission. The second distinction obscures the morally significant role of intentions. Consider, for example, whether wilfully omitting the act of stopping a person in a wheelchair about to fall over a cliff is any less heinous than shoving the person over. Where there are differences they will in part depend on fiduciary obligations established by context, status, and contract. Finally, if one agrees with the Texans, then what is most important is the consent of those involved. This approach is a liberty-oriented one in which injuries do not occur if those involved agree. It is an approach that accents the rights of persons to choose the circumstances of their own deaths.

One needs to recognize that the cases to which rational suicide and active euthanasia could apply are infrequent. Most individuals contemplating suicide do so not on the basis of clear and rational reflection and choice, as did Seneca, but rather under the compulsions of mental pressure and disorder. In most cases physicians are able to control pain and discomfort so that the choice of an active and deliberate intervention to expedite death is not a serious option. On the other hand, choices are frequently made to discontinue treatment or to use pain-killing medication, foreseeing that such choices will bring death sooner. Undoubtedly, many of the individuals involved in such choices will not make them within the constraints of the doctrine of double effect, as outlined by Kenny in this volume. They rather intend death, not simply foresee death. They may thus be considered as engaging in euthanasia in the strict sense that they are making choices aimed at expediting an individual's death, so as to make the dying less painful, clearly and forthrightly willing that death take place more quickly. However, because what they do is indistinguishable in external form from the actions undertaken by those acting within the constraints of double effect, few new public policy questions are raised.

The matter is different when an action would forthrightly expedite death. One might think here of cases in which all artificial feeding and fluids have been discontinued so that a permanently comatose individual will die. One might ask what the moral difference is between the decision to omit such treatment and the decision to end that life quickly, except that the second choice is cheaper. Or one might think of the case of an individual who is conscious and dying in agony of a disease where one decides to withdraw all medications that prolong life. One might reasonably ask why not, in such a circumstance, simply expedite the individual's death if the person so requests. Are the barriers against such policies simply utilitarian? Are they based on the supposition that such forthright acts would have an adverse impact on our social constraints against murder in general or against the abuse of the defenseless in particular? Or are Grisez and Boyle correct in holding that every act in the strict sense of killing a person is immoral?

One must note that in a number of countries, unlike the United States, aiding and abetting suicide does not appear to be a crime. It is possible for a physician or another person to provide a patient with the means to expedite death and not face criminal charges. In fact, the Netherlands now allows active euthanasia in certain circumstances. For those who would fear that such policies will lead to the horrors of Nazi extermination camps for the unfit, perhaps the example of Texas is instructive. Texas required the deliberate and free choice of competent individuals and excluded involuntary euthanasia or interventions by the state. It would appear that the individual and liberty-oriented policy did not lead to abuse and was secure against the dangers of exploitation. Do you believe adopting such a policy would have positive or negative consequences? Would a permissive policy of this sort be morally allowable, even if it did not lead to abuse? Is there something intrinsically immoral in such a policy?

Case A

Mr. A is a 52-year-old diabetic who has been blind for five years and impotent for seven years because of his disease. He now appears to be developing renal failure, and he has difficulty in walking because of poor circulation to his legs. He has been living alone since his divorce three years ago. He concludes that it is not worth continuing life as it is and decides one day not to take his insulin. He is fairly sure that he will be dead before anyone discovers him. He has few friends or others who are likely to visit his apartment.

Case B

Following an industrial accident ten years ago, Mr. B was left wheelchair-bound and with intractable chronic pain of his back and lower extremities. There have been repeated surgical attempts to alleviate the pain, but they have failed. For the last three years he has attended a chronic-pain clinic, but little progress has been made in blunting the daily suffering he experiences. He is 64 and had been extremely dependent on his wife. She died a year ago from a coronary. He has spent a great deal of time discussing his plight with one of the physicians at the pain clinic. As Mr. B sees it, he has nothing and no one to live for. He is consumed by his pain and restricted by his physical disabilities. He asks the physician to give him a prescription for enough pain medication so that, should he take it all, it would bring about his death. Mr. B argues that he and not the physician will be responsible for his own death, for the physician could always argue that he had simply given Mr. B suffi- cient pain medication to tide him over to the next visit.

Case C

Five years ago, Mrs. C watched her older brother slowly die of Alzheimer's disease. She found it to be a terrible experience for the whole family and vowed that she would never be the occasion of such suffering for others. She has now been diagnosed as suf- fering from the disease. She has resolved that she will put her financial and personal affairs in order and then kill herself. As she reasons, this will be an act of love and benef- icence to her family and is therefore not immoral.

Case D

Miss D is a 37-year-old former singer. Her career was brought to an end when she de- veloped amyotrophic lateral sclerosis (Lou Gehrig's disease). The demands of the dis- ease and her unfulfilled life have left her recurringly depressed and disconsolate. She is finally admitted to a nursing home. She is not yet on a ventilator, but her capacity to breathe unassisted is now severely limited. She realizes that she will either have to choose to be put on a ventilator or face a death that is likely to be marked by a dis- tressing struggle to breathe. She finally asks her physician to give her an overdose of morphine or an injection of some drug so as to allow her to die quickly and painlessly.

How would you compare these four cases? The first individual is omitting treatment with the intention of expediting his death. Is he guilty of committing suicide? If his plans came to the attention of the police, should they intervene to stop him? Does his plight reflect a lack of caring on the part of others? If so, how should that influence your judgment? Is he right that death is a reasonable choice under the circumstances? What do you make of Mr. B? It would have been allowable under previous Texas law for his physician to have provided him with medication he could have then used to commit suicide. Would such an action be morally justified? Would it in fact be a beneficent action? Is Mrs. C's choice a beneficent one? Is it immoral? What about Miss D? Is it immoral to deny her the means for a quick and painless death? If you answer yes, who should kill her? A physician? A nurse? A member of a special profession of euthanizers? Or should it be done by a friend?

These cases suggest conflicting moral intentions and obligations. They are particularly vexing because in our culture we have not seen individuals as having a right or a responsibility either to end their lives or to aid others in ending theirs. As we are able increasingly to save or prolong the lives of individuals so as to place them in circumstances they may find worse than death, these questions will become more pressing. Does our ability deliberately to prolong life lead us to a position where, under certain circumstances, we may be allowed (or obliged) deliberately to end life? Would we be well-advised to return to the legal position of Texas before 1973 or to adopt the current position of the Netherlands? What restrictions would you place and in what circumstances and for what reasons?

38.   DEFINITION OF DEATH

The definition of death draws the line between human biological life and human personal life. In this respect, as Engelhardt suggests in this volume, the definition of death raises questions similar to those raised by abortion. Depending on when one holds that the fetus becomes a person, one is likely to see special moral issues surface regarding the rights of women to terminate the pregnancy. So, too, the definition of death marks the line between stealing organs from a person and harvesting them from a corpse. It indicates when murder is no longer possible and that, instead, affronts against the body must constitute desecration of a corpse rather than assault, battery, and manslaughter.

The traditional approaches to the definition of death in the West have been whole-body oriented. In the Jewish tradition, death took place when an individual breathed his or her last breath (although some recent arguments have attempted to rely on a precedent that death occurs with decapitation). So, too, St. Thomas argued that all of the soul is in all of the body (*tota in toto, tota in qualibet parte*). In contrast, many modern understandings of the definition of death presuppose the localization of mental functions in the brain. They depend as well on drawing the line between the principle of life and the principle of personhood. That is, one is forced to draw a distinction between those processes that maintain biological functions and those that make sentience and consciousness possible.

The prevailing common-law understanding of the definition of death until recently recognized the whole-body definition of death. Death was defined as "the cessation of life; the ceasing to exist; defined by physicians as a total stoppage of the circulation of the blood, and a cessation of the animal and vital functions consequent thereon, such as respiration, pulsation, etc."[1] In the spirit of this traditional definition, cases were decided that appear to us now as incongruous. One court addressed the question as to which of two individuals survived the other, if only by a few seconds. This case involved two people killed in an accident; one of them was decapitated and the carotid arteries were squirting blood after the trauma; the other died from internal injuries. The decapitated individual was held to have outlived the nondecapitated individual, even though both sustained injuries at the same time and the decapitated person's head was a number of yards distant from the body. [*Gray et al. v. Sawyer et al., Gray et al. v. Clay et al.*, 247 S. W. 2d 496, 497 (Ky. App. 1952).]

The 1950s and 1960s raised practical issues that required a theoretical reconsideration of the definition of death. The development of intensive care units made it possible to sustain, if only for a brief period of time, brain-dead but otherwise alive individuals. Their status raised both financial and psychosocial questions regarding their care. In addition, as has been noted in the discussion of cases on organ transplantation, the capacity to transplant organs raised the issue of when bodies were dead and therefore their organs available for harvesting. As a result, the Ad Hoc Committee of the Harvard Medical School to Examine the Definition of Brain Death was organized to study the practicality of

---

[1]*Black's Law Dictionary*, 4th ed rev., 1968.

a whole-brain definition of death. It published a positive report in 1968.[2] This was followed by the 1969 report of the Ad Hoc Committee of the American Electroencephalographic Society on EEG Criteria for Determination of Cerebral Death, which offered precise criteria for applying a whole-brain–oriented definition of death.[3]

Beginning with Kansas in 1970 and Maryland in 1972, some 20 states moved to adopt by statute the whole-brain definition of death. Many of the statutes provided that death could be determined on the basis of either cardiorespiratory or brain-oriented criteria. The provision of two sets of criteria underscored the fact that what was at stake was both the *conceptual* definition of death and the *operational* definition of death. The conceptual definition of death can be seen as focused on what it means to be here in the world. A definition of death that is brain-oriented on a conceptual basis presupposes that an intact brain is a necessary condition for the life of a person. An operational definition of death can be seen as focusing on particular criteria useful in determining whether someone is dead according to the accepted conceptual definition. Thus, even if one holds that an intact brain is the necessary condition for being a person alive in this world, one may still use cardiorespiratory-oriented criteria to determine death when these are convincing indices of the brain's destruction.

In 1975, the American Bar Association proposed a definition of death that accented the brain alone as the central focus of concern. "For all legal purposes, a human body with irreversible cessation of total brain function, according to usual and customary standards of medical practice, shall be considered dead." States such as Montana and Tennessee adopted statutes influenced by this recommendation. However, in July 1981, the President's Commission for the Study of Ethical Problems in Medicine and Biomedical and Behavioral Research offered a Uniform Determination of Death Act, which underscored both cardiorespiratory and brain-oriented criteria. "An individual who has sustained either (1) irreversible cessation of circulatory and respiratory functions, or (2) irreversible cessation of all functions of the entire brain, including the brain stem, is dead. A determination of death must be made in accordance with accepted medical standards."[4] In its discussion on the proposal, the President's Commission underscored its view that the whole-brain–oriented definition of death did not focus on the brain because of its being the sponsor of consciousness. Instead, it argued that definitions of death properly focused on the brain because either (1) the brain was the primary organ without which life could not continue, or (2) the integrated functions of the body as a whole would collapse with the loss of brain or cardiopulmonary function.

By this interpretation and by stressing the inclusion of brainstem death in whole-brain death, the President's Commission precluded a neocortically oriented or higher-brain-center–oriented approach. The result has been to put individuals who have permanently lost consciousness but still have brainstem

---

[2]*Journal of the American Medical Association* 205 (1968): 337–340.
[3]*Journal of the American Medical Association* 209 (1969): 1505.
[4]President's Commission for the Study of Ethical Problems in Medicine and Biomedical and Behavioral Research, *Defining Death* (Washington, D.C.: U.S. Government Printing Office, 1981), p. 2.

function in a limbo where they cannot be declared dead, but where, according to a later President's Commision report, it appears that they may be starved to death. "Other than requiring appropriate decisionmaking procedures for these patients, the law does not and should not require any particular therapies to be applied or continued, with the exception of basic nursing care that is needed to ensure dignified and respectful treatment of the patient."[5] Subsequently, two court decisions have supported the probity of stopping all treatment, including the provision of food and water to such individuals with the consent of relatives and in the absence of any indication of a previous contrary wish on the part of the patient [see *Barber v. L.A. Co. Sup. Ct.,* No. 69350 (Cal. Ct. App. Oct. 12, 1983) and *In re Conroy,* N. J. Sup. Ct., A-108 (Jan. 17, 1985)].

In assessing the issues raised by the definition of death, you will need to decide the role that the concept of person should play. Does one need to have an awareness of self to be a person, and therefore to be alive, as Tooley contends? Or does the definition of death involve more than the life of persons as moral agents and include a general concern for the sanctity of the life of humans? Examine how, for example, you would apply the arguments of Devine and Sumner to the issue of the definition of death. Does the President's Commission's recommendation side more with views of Devine and Sumner rather than with the views of Tooley and Engelhardt?

Case A

Mr. and Mrs. A, when shown their 17-year-old daughter, who has suffered severe brain damage due to an automobile accident, refuse to accept the fact that it is highly unlikely that she will survive. On the third hospital day it is clear to the physicians that Miss A is brain-dead. They inform the parents that their daughter has died. The parents become enraged and assert that the hospital is simply trying to kill their daughter. They can tell their daughter is alive, for she is warm to the touch and breathing with the aid of the respirator. Moreover, the mother points out that she can feel her daughter's pulse. The mother shouts, "If you turn off the respirator and kill my daughter, I will have murder charges brought against you!"

Case B

Mr. B, while drinking in a bar in a state that does not have a statutory definition of death, gets into an altercation with one of his fellow-imbibers. They step outside to settle matters and Mr. B is shot in the head. He is rushed by an ambulance to the local medical center, where he is found to meet all of the criteria for whole-brain death. Moreover, he is found to be carrying a driver's license on the back of which he has signed an instrument for the donation of his organs. He is pronounced dead, and his heart, kidneys, and corneas are removed for transplantation. When charged with murder for having shot Mr. B, Mr. S responds, "I may have assaulted and attempted to kill him, but he was alive until the physicians took out his heart. If you are going to find a murderer anywhere, he is in the medical center, not in this cell."

---

[5]*Deciding to Forego Life-Sustaining Treatment,* March 21, 1983, p. 6.

Case C

Mrs. C, a 31-year-old woman in the 20th week of her pregnancy, is shot in the head during a hunting accident. She is rushed to the local hospital where it is determined that she is brain-dead. Her husband asks that they attempt to keep her body alive as long as possible so as to prevent the child from being born so prematurely. He wants the child to have a good chance for survival. The physicians agree and have her transferred to a university medical center, where a team is ready to keep her body alive until the baby can be delivered.

Case D

After a routine appendectomy and while in the recovery room, the daughter of Mr. and Mrs. D begins to have difficulty breathing. Before this is discovered, the 12-year-old Miss D has sustained irreversible neocortical damage. Neurological assessment reveals that her cortex appears to be totally destroyed, although the medulla is still intact. She is at best destined to a life of profound unconsciousness. The physician suggests that all further support be withdrawn. The parents, however, have consulted a lawyer and intend to sue for $5 million, funds sufficient to keep Miss D alive for the rest of her expected life. The physicians are very upset; they point out that were there not the issue of a malpractice suit, they believe that the parents, and any sensible person, would simply allow Miss D to die. In fact, they contend that because the neocortex is dead, Miss D is indeed dead.

How would you as a physician attempt to come to terms with the demands of the As? Would it make any difference to your answer whether or not they were paying for the costs involved in the care of their daughter? What if the person involved was not a child but a father whose pension rights, which the family would inherit, would not vest unless the father "lived" another three days? Would it be proper to defer declaring death for three days? In your consideration of this matter, bear in mind two different but equally important issues. First, the definition of death is a fact. Individuals generally are not asked to consent to the death of their closest kin. On the other hand, sudden death is difficult to come to terms with. The difficulty is compounded when the death is declared on a brain-oriented basis. Recall, for example, how hard it was for our culture to move from a whole-body to a whole-brain definition of death. The As are being asked to make this transition at a time of great stress and over a period of a few hours.

Do you agree with Mr. S's contention that he did not kill Mr. B? Do you have any difficulty in talking about the status of Mrs. C? One has to come to terms with the fact that she is dead, while her body is alive, sustaining the life of her fetus. Finally, what do you make of the issue raised in Case D? If you believe that the whole-brain definition of death makes sense not simply because you cannot be hurt if your brain is dead but because *you* are not there, is it plausible that you are there if the only difference is that your brainstem has been spared? In short, how much brain function is required for a person to be considered still alive? If you were on the jury in the malpractice suit, would you award funds to keep Miss D alive?

39. AUTOPSIES AND ORGAN DONATIONS

Throughout human history, societies have placed great significance upon the proper disposal of human cadavers after death. What constitutes proper disposal of the cadaver has, however, varied greatly from one society to another. In ancient China and Egypt, for example, mummification and embalming were used to preserve as much as possible the tissues of the body so that they could be reused by the spirit following a period of purification. Traditional Christian and Jewish societies, on the other hand, felt strongly that the only appropriate method for final disposal of the cadaver was burial in the ground. Zoroastrians thought that such burial was impious, and left bodies to be eaten by birds. In other Eastern societies, and more recently in the West, cremation was viewed as the proper method of disposing of a cadaver.

Although societies have disagreed about what they viewed to be the most appropriate way of disposing of the dead, they have agreed in raising strong moral objections to non-approved means of disposing of the cadaver. It is this opposition that has, on many occasions, brought organized societies into conflict with medical science, which has wanted to study some of the cadavers (in dissections and autopsies) and, in recent years, to use some of the parts of the cadaver for other human beings (organ donations). Historically, the lack of availability of human bodies had an adverse impact on medical knowledge in both the ancient world and on medieval physicians who relied upon ancient authorities such as Galen, who was forced to dissect only nonhuman mammals.

What we are looking at is a conflict between the needs of medicine on the one hand and the rights of the family of the deceased on the other. Members of the family will often be opposed on an individual level to an autopsy or an organ donation, in part because of a subconscious feeling that "the body deserves to be allowed to rest in peace" and in part out of a feeling that such postmortem activities represent a desecration of the body. Family members are reinforced in these feelings by socially and religiously based perceptions that this is not the proper way to treat the dead. Finally, family members may be reinforced in these feelings by concerns about whether or not the use of the cadaver in this way will make it impossible to have an open-casket viewing of the deceased. These individual and social feelings are reinforced by legal restrictions, to be discussed below, on postmortem uses of bodies. There is, of course, another side to the story, and this is the medical need for autopsies, dissections, and organ donations. The medical need for autopsies and dissections begins, naturally, with a recognition of the importance of the dissection of the human cadaver for the study of anatomy in general and for the study of the causes of the death of the particular patient on whom an autopsy is being performed. In the past, medicine has had to resort to such criminal means as grave robbing and fighting over the remains of executed felons in order to obtain bodies for study. Moreover, there is often the need to perform an autopsy when there are suspicious deaths, and necessity for these medico-legal autopsies has been recognized for a long time. Finally, in recent years, there is the need to obtain organs so that they can be transplanted in other human beings.

Each state in the union has enacted its own laws, which are attempts to deal with these issues by compromising between the interests of the various parties.

Let us begin by looking at typical statutes governing autopsies and at some tricky cases that have arisen in connection with them. In general, it is possible to distinguish two types of accepted autopsies: medico-legal autopsies and non-medico-legal autopsies. Medico-legal autopsies are autopsies that coroners and medical examiners are empowered in certain cases to conduct independently of the wishes of the family of the deceased. The most common of these are cases of death due to violence or to suspicious or unexplained causes. Other such cases might include those in which death was sudden and unexpected, or in which an individual died in an institution other than a hospital or nursing home, or in which no physician is prepared to certify the cause. Obviously, these latter cases are elaborations of the idea of an individual dying under suspicious circumstances. It is important to keep in mind that the fact that the coroner and medical examiner are entitled to perform the autopsy without the family's permission does not mean that they will always perform an autopsy in each of these cases. All that it does mean is that consent from the relatives of the deceased is not required.

This is what distinguishes medico-legal autopsies from non-medico-legal autopsies. Statutes authorizing these types of autopsies usually specify quite clearly who it is that may give consent for such autopsies. The usual list makes reference to a surviving spouse, an adult child, a parent, other next of kin, and those assuming responsibility for burying the deceased. Some, but by no means all, of the statutes spell out what to do when there is disagreement among family members or, alternatively, when no family members are present at all.

It is interesting to see the compromise that has been struck by these typical state statutes between the interests of society on the one hand and the interests of the family of the deceased on the other. In the cases of the non-medico-legal autopsies, it is quite clear that priority has been given to the interests of the family of the deceased. In these statutes, at least as long as there is a family member present, their consent is an absolute requirement for allowing an autopsy. The interests of society in advancing medical knowledge have been treated as secondary, even in those case where the patient's hospital course has been very perplexing and where it is felt by the physicians that there will be a great deal to be learned from performing the autopsy. The situation is very different in the case of the medico-legal autopsies. Here the law has decided that the interests of society in ascertaining whether there was foul play in the death of the patient must take precedence over the wishes of the family. It is easy to understand why this would be so in cases in which the family itself is suspected of the foul play. We would hardly want to give any preference to their wishes. It is more controversial as to why this should be so in those cases in which there is no reason to suspect the family. The reader might ponder this question in the following way: There is clearly some appeal to consequences, which argues for the social benefit of allowing medico-legal autopsies even without the consent of the deceased's family. There is also an appeal to the consequences, which talks about the social benefits of allowing such autopsies in non-medico-legal cases where the physicians are strongly convinced that there is a great deal to be learned from this particular autopsy. What arguments can be offered to allow the appeal to consequences in one case to outweigh the rights of the family but not in the other case? Does it have to do with a mistrust of physicians and a trust in coroners and medical examiners? Does it have to do with a fear that any other results would lead to physicians always overriding the wishes of the family?

With this background in mind, let us look at a number of cases that raise interesting ethical issues concerning autopsies.

Case A

Late one afternoon, a father heard a thump in his 18-year-old son's room. He went up to investigate. When the son did not respond, the father called an ambulance, which took the son to the hospital. The son was declared dead upon arrival. There was no history of illness and no immediate explanation of the sudden death. Although there was no particular reason to suspect that this was a case of foul play, the medical examiner ordered a complete post-mortem examination. The father, who was an Orthodox Jew (as was his son), strongly objected. He argued that his religious faith and the religious faith of his son prohibited autopsies after death, and he believed that his religious rights and the rights of his deceased son should take precedence.

Case B

This case involves a sad conflict between the parents of a young child who died shortly after birth, having suffered from a wide variety of problems since birth. The physicians in question asked permission for an autopsy, in part so that they could understand better the causes of this child's death and in part so that they could see if there was anything that the parents would need to know about potential problems affecting future children. The mother was very concerned to know the exact cause of her child's death, in part because she was concerned about the question of future children but primarily because she simply wanted to know why her child suffered and died. The father couldn't see the point in any of that. He was very distraught at the thought that his young child's body would have an autopsy performed on it. He just wanted the child to be left alone and buried.

Case A raises in a very dramatic fashion many of the questions that we have just been examining. The standard statutes governing autopsies would allow the medical examiner to conduct an autopsy in this case without the permission of the family. Is that morally correct? Given the absence of any suspicion of foul play, why should that autopsy be allowed? On the other hand, can we really rule out the possibility of foul play? And might there be other reasons why we would want to insist on an autopsy against the wishes of the father? There are, however, still further issues raised by the case. It is important to keep in mind that the medical examiner is not required by law to perform the autopsy, but merely allowed to do so without this family's consent. How should the medical examiner take into account the extent of his or her own suspicions about the case and the extent of the family's opposition based on their religious beliefs before deciding whether or not to perform an autopsy?

Case B calls our attention to a real problem that often arises under the statutory provisions mentioned above. In truth, as one of the health providers put it, if he had known in advance that there was going to be this type of conflict in the family, he probably would never have asked for permission for the autopsy. But now, it is too late for that. The mother really wants the autopsy and the father really doesn't. Is there some appropriate rule as to whose wishes should prevail? Should it be that all of the equally close relatives must agree before an autopsy can be performed? Is it enough that one person agrees? Shall we take the case in which the two parents are in strong disagreement as special? What moral appeals might be used to deal with this ambiguity, which is often found in autopsy statutes?

There are somewhat different laws governing organ donations and the donation of entire cadavers for use by medical schools. The reason for this is that in 1968 the National Commission on Uniform State Laws along with the American Bar Association proposed the Uniform Anatomical Gift Act, which was then adopted by the state legislatures. The main provisions of the act are as follows:

1. Gifts of organs or the entire cadaver can be made prior to death by any person of sound mind at least 18 years of age and by family members either before or after death. The consent of family members is voided if there is knowledge that the deceased or any member of higher rank opposed the donation.

2. A variety of documents for making organ donations were authorized. Among these documents are, at least in some states, donor cards on driver's licenses.

3. In most states, the time of death at which the gift goes into effect is to be determined by the donor's attending physician, or by the physician certifying the death. Also in many states, the physician who determines death is banned from participating in transplantation of organs from the donor.

Case C

It is clear that the enactment of the Uniform Anatomical Gift Act represents a major social decision to put high priority on obtaining organs for transplantation and, to a lesser degree, cadavers for study. Nevertheless, despite this high priority, there continues to remain a shortage of appropriate organs, particularly kidneys, for transplantation. This is due in part to a failure to get an adequate number of advanced donations from those in the 18- to 25-year-old age group. These are the prime donors, for if they do suffer death in an accident (the largest cause of death in this age group), their organs are very suitable. A second problem is the unwillingness of organ transplant centers to accept organs donated in advance by the deceased if the family is in disagreement with the gift. Their feeling in part reflects legal concerns but it also reflects an intuitive belief that it would be wrong to add to the burden of the family suffering the traumatic death of a family member by taking the organs against the family's wishes. All of this has led to an extensive public debate. There are those who would argue that we need to move forward much more aggressively to obtain donations of organs, either by accepting organs donated in advance—even if the family disagrees at the time of death—as the law allows, or by changing the law to presume that organs may be taken at the time of death unless the deceased indicated otherwise during his or her lifetime or unless the family objects at the time of death. Such methods are called *presumed consent* schemes and are already in place in many countries. The essential feature of such a scheme is that there is a presumption in favor of permission for organ donations. In about half of the countries with such presumed consent schemes, physicians still consult the families of the deceased to make sure that they have no objection to the organ donation. In the remaining countries that have a presumed consent scheme, physicians proceed without asking unless a prior objection has been raised by the family or by the deceased.

What moral appeals could be used to justify such schemes in either of the variations discussed above? What moral appeals could be used in opposition to them and on behalf of the scheme developed in the Uniform Anatomical Gift Act? What would the appeal to consequences say about these issues? What would the appeal to compassion say? If we went to one of the presumed consent schemes, which of the above two would be more appropriate? Would any such scheme be compatible with the values inherent in the standard autopsy laws, which provide great deference to the wishes of the family? If not, do we have strong reasons for distinguishing autopsies from organ donations?

APPENDIX

Codes of Ethics

Hippocratic Oath

I swear by Apollo Physician, by Asclepius, by Health, by Panacea and by all the gods and goddesses, making them my witnesses, that I will carry out, according to my ability and judgment, this oath and this indenture. To hold my teacher in this art equal to my own parents; to make him partner in my livelihood; when he is in need of money to share mine with him; to consider his family as my own brothers, and to teach them this art, if they want to learn it, without fee or indenture; to impart precept, oral instruction, and all other instruction to my own sons, the sons of my teacher, and to indentured pupils who have taken the physician's oath, but to nobody else. I will use treatment to help the sick according to my ability and judgment, but never with a view to injury and wrong-doing. Neither will I administer a poison to anybody when asked to do so, nor will I suggest such a course. Similarly I will not give to a woman a pessary to cause abortion. But I will keep pure and holy both my life and my art. I will not use the knife, not even, verily, on sufferers from stone, but I will give place to such as are craftsmen therein. Into whatsoever houses I enter, I will enter to help the sick, and I will abstain from all intentional wrong-doing and harm, especially from abusing the bodies of man or woman, bond or free. And whatsoever I shall see or hear in the course of my profession, as well as outside my profession in my intercourse with men, if it be what should not be published abroad, I will never divulge, holding such things to be holy secrets. Now if I carry out this oath, and break it not, may I gain for ever reputation among all men for my life and for my art; but if I transgress it and forswear myself, may the opposite befall me.

A Patient's Bill of Rights

American Hospital Association 1973

On 6 February 1973 the American Hospital Association's House of Delegates approved A Patient's Bill of Rights. Other historically significant documents in the United States, which predated this Bill of Rights, were a document drafted by the National Welfare Rights Organization (1970) and the preamble to the Standards of the Joint Commission on Accreditation of Hospitals. The AHA Patient's Bill of Rights, printed in full below, has been influential in the development of similar documents in other parts of the world.

The American Hospital Association presents a Patient's Bill of Rights with the expectation that observance of these rights will contribute to more effective patient care and greater satisfaction for the patient, his physician and the hospital organization. Further, the Association presents these rights in the expectation that they will be supported by the hospital on behalf of its patients, as an integral part of the healing process. It is recognized that a personal relationship between the physician and the patient is essential for the provision of proper medical care. The traditional physician-patient relationship takes on a new dimension when care is rendered within an organizational structure. Legal precedent has established that the institution itself also has a responsibility to the patient. It is in recognition of these factors that these rights are affirmed.

1. The patient has the right to considerate and respectful care.

2. The patient has the right to obtain from his physician complete current information concerning his diagnosis, treatment, and prognosis in terms the patient can be reasonably expected to understand. When it is not medically advisable to give such information to the patient, the information should be made available to an appropriate person in his behalf. He has the right to know by name, the physician responsible for coordinating his care.

3. The patient has the right to receive from his physician information necessary to give informed consent prior to the start of any procedure and/or treatment. Except in emergencies, such information for informed consent should include but not necessarily be limited to the specific procedure and/or treatment, the medically significant risks involved, and the probable duration of incapacitation. Where medically significant alternatives for care or treatment exist, or when the patient requests information concerning medical alternatives, the patient has the right to such information. The patient also has the right to know the name of the person responsible for the procedures and/or treatment.

4. The patient has the right to refuse treatment to the extent permitted by law, and to be informed of the medical consequences of his action.

5. The patient has the right to every consideration of his privacy concerning his own medical care program. Case discussion, consultation, examination, and treatment are confidential and should be conducted discreetly. Those not directly involved in his care must have the permission of the patient to be present.

6. The patient has the right to expect that all communications and records pertaining to his care should be treated as confidential.

7. The patient has the right to expect that within its capacity a hospital must make reasonable response to the request of a patient for services. The hospital must provide evaluation, service, and/or referral as indicated by the urgency of the case. When medically permissible a patient may be transferred to another facility only after he has received complete information and explanation concerning the needs for and alternatives to such a transfer. The institution to which the patient is to be transferred must first have accepted the patient for transfer.

8. The patient has the right to obtain information as to any relationship of his hospital to other health care and educational institutions insofar as his care is concerned. The patient has the right to obtain information as to the existence of any professional relationships among individuals, by name, who are treating him.

9. The patient has the right to be advised if the hospital proposes to engage in or perform human experimentation affecting his care or treatment. The patient has the right to refuse to participate in such research projects.

10. The patient has the right to expect reasonable continuity of care. He has the right to know in advance what appointment times and physicians are available and where. The patient has the right to expect that the hospital will provide a mechanism whereby he is informed by his physician or a delegate of the physician of the patient's continuing health care requirements following discharge.

11. The patient has the right to examine and receive an explanation of his bill regardless of source of payment.

12. The patient has the right to know what hospital rules and regulations apply to his conduct as a patient.

No catalogue of rights can guarantee for the patient the kind of treatment he has a right to expect. A hospital has many functions to perform, including the prevention and treatment of disease, the education of both health professionals and patients, and the conduct of clinical research. All these activities must be conducted with an overriding concern for the patient, and, above all, the recognition of his dignity as a human being. Success in achieving this recognition assures success in the defense of the rights of the patient.

Principles of Medical Ethics

American Medical Association

PREAMBLE:

The medical profession has long subscribed to a body of ethical statements developed primarily for the benefit of the patient. As a member of this profession, a physician must recognize responsibility not only to patients, but also to society, to other health professionals, and to self. The following Principles adopted by the American Medical Association are not laws, but standards of conduct which define the essentials of honorable behavior for the physician.

I. A physician shall be dedicated to providing competent medical service with compassion and respect for human dignity.

II. A physician shall deal honestly with patients and colleagues, and strive to expose those physicians deficient in character or competence, or who engage in fraud or deception.

III. A physician shall respect the law and also recognize a responsibility to seek changes in those requirements which are contrary to the best interests of the patient.

IV. A physician shall respect the rights of patients, of colleagues, and of other health professionals, and shall safeguard patient confidences within the constraints of the law.

V. A physician shall continue to study, apply and advance scientific knowledge, make relevant information available to patients, colleagues, and the public, obtain consultation, and use the talents of other health professionals when indicated.

VI. A physician shall, in the provision of appropriate patient care, except in emergencies, be free to choose whom to serve, with whom to associate, and the environment in which to provide medical services.

VII. A physician shall recognize a responsibility to participate in activities contributing to an improved community.

Current Opinions of the Judicial Council of the American Medical Association—1984

2.01 Abortion. The Principles of Medical Ethics of the AMA do not prohibit a physician from performing an abortion in accordance with good medical practice and under circumstances that do not violate the law. (IV)

2.03 Allocation of health resources. A physician has a duty to do all that he can for the benefit of his individual patients without assuming total responsibility for equitable disbursement of society's limited health resources. To expect a physician in the context of his medical practice to administer governmental priorities in the allocation of scarce health resources is to create a conflict with the physician's primary responsibility to his patients that would be socially undesirable.

Limited health care resources should be allocated efficiently and on the basis of fair, acceptable and humanitarian criteria. Priority should be given to persons who are most likely to be treated successfully or have long term benefit. Social worth is not an appropriate criterion.

Utility or relative worth to society should not determine whether an individual is accepted as a donor or recipient of tissue for transplantation, selected for human experimentation, or denied or given preference in receiving scarce health care treatment or resources. (I)

2.04 Artificial insemination. The informed consent of the woman seeking artificial insemination and her husband is necessary. The prospective parents should be informed that any child conceived by artificial insemination is possessed of and entitled to all the rights of a child conceived naturally. (I, V)

2.05 Artificial insemination by donor. Physicians have an ethical responsibility to use the utmost caution and scientifically available screening techniques in the selection of donors for use in artificial insemination. Relying only upon the verbal representations of donors as to their health, without any medical screening, is precarious. The donor should be screened for genetic defects, inheritable and infectious disease, RH factor incompatibility and other disorders that may affect the fetus. When the physician is not equipped to fulfill these responsibilities, the services of a skilled medical geneticist or other appropriate specialist should be sought.

Since the identity of donors usually should not be available to recipients or the offspring that may result, the risk of inadvertent inbred and serious undesirable genetic and biological consequences should not be ignored. Physicians have an ethical and social responsibility to avoid the frequent use of semen from the same sources. (I, V)

2.08 Costs. While physicians should be conscious of costs and not provide or prescribe unnecessary services or ancillary facilities, social policy expects that concern for the care the patient receives will be the physician's first consideration. This does not preclude the physician, individually, or through medical organizations, from participating in policy-making with respect to social issues affecting health care. (I, VII)

2.09 Fetal research guidelines. The following guidelines are offered as aids to physicians when they are engaged in fetal research:

(1) Physicians may participate in fetal research when their activities are part of a competently designed program, under accepted standards of scientific research, to produce data which are scientifically valid and significant.

(2) If appropriate, properly performed clinical studies on animals and nongravid humans should precede any particular fetal research project.

(3) In fetal research projects, the investigator should demonstrate the same care and concern for the fetus as a physician providing fetal care or treatment in a non-research setting.

(4) All valid federal or state legal requirements should be followed.

(5) There should be no monetary payment to obtain any fetal material for fetal research projects.

(6) Competent peer review committees, review boards, or advisory boards should be available, when appropriate, to protect against the possible abuses that could arise in such research.

(7) Research on the so called "dead fetus," mascerated fetal material, fetal cells, fetal tissue, fetal organs, or the placenta should be in accord with state laws on autopsy and state laws on organ transplantation or anatomical gifts. Informed and voluntary consent, in writing, should be obtained from a legally authorized representative of the fetus.

(8) In fetal research primarily for treatment of the fetus:

A. Voluntary and informed consent, in writing, should be given by the gravid woman, acting in the best interest of the fetus.

B. Alternative treatment or methods of care, if any, should be carefully evaluated and fully explained. If simpler and safer treatment is available, it should be pursued.

(9) In research primarily for treatment of the gravid female:

A. Voluntary and informed consent, in writing, should be given by the patient.

B. Alternative treatment or methods of care should be carefully evaluated and fully explained to the patient. If simpler and safer treatment is available, it should be pursued.

C. If possible, the risk to the fetus should be the least possible, consistent with the gravid female's need for treatment.

(10) In fetal research involving a viable fetus, primarily for the accumulation of scientific knowledge:

A. Voluntary and informed consent, in writing, should be given by the gravid woman under circumstances in which a prudent and informed adult would reasonably be expected to give such consent.

B. The risk to the fetus imposed by the research should be the least possible.

C. The purpose of research is the production of data and knowledge which are scientifically significant and which cannot otherwise be obtained.

D. In this area of research, it is especially important to emphasize that care and concern for the fetus should be demonstrated. There should be no physical abuse of the fetus. (I, III, V)

2.10 Genetic Counseling. Two primary areas of genetic diagnosis are: (1) screening or evaluating prospective parents before conception for genetic disease to predict the likelihood of conceiving an affected child; and (2) in utero testing after conception, such as ultrasonography, amniocentesis, and fetoscopy, to determine the condition of the fetus. Physicians engaged in genetic counseling are ethically obligated to provide prospective parents with the basis for an informed decision for childbearing. In providing information to couples who choose to reproduce, physicians should adhere to the Principles of Medical Ethics and standards of medical practice.

Technological developments in the accuracy of predicting and detecting genetic disorders have created a dilemma for the physician who for personal reasons opposes contraception, sterilization or abortion. The physician should be aware that where a genetic defect is found in the fetus, prospective parents may request or refuse an abortion. A dilemma may also exist for physicians who do not oppose the provision of these services (contraception, sterilization or abortion).

Physicians who consider the legal and ethical requirements applicable to genetic counseling to be in conflict with their moral values and conscience may choose to limit such services to preconception diagnosis and advice or not provide any genetic services. However, there are circumstances in which the physician who is so disposed is nevertheless obligated to alert prospective parents that a potential genetic problem does exist, that the physician does not offer genetic services, and that the patient should seek medical genetic counseling from another qualified specialist.

Physicians, whether they oppose or do not oppose contraception, sterilization or abortion, may decide that they can engage in genetic counseling and screening but should avoid the imposition of their personal moral values and the substitution of their own moral judgment for that of the prospective parents. (II, IV, V, VI)

2.12 In vitro fertilization. The technique of in vitro fertilization and embryo transplantation enables certain couples previously incapable of conception to bear a child. It is also useful in the field of research directed toward an understanding of how genetic defects arise and are transmitted and how they might be prevented or treated. Because of serious ethical and moral concerns, however, any fertilized egg that has the potential for human life and that will be implanted in the uterus of a woman should not be subjected to laboratory research.

All fertilized ova not utilized for implantation and that are maintained for research purposes shall be handled with the strictest adherence to the Principles of Medical Ethics, to the guidelines for research and medical practice expressed in the Judicial Council's opinion on fetal research (2.09), and to the highest standards of medical practice. (I, IV, V)

2.13 Organ transplantation guidelines. The following statement is offered for guidance of physicians as they seek to maintain the highest level of ethical conduct in the transplanting of human organs.

(1) In all professional relationships between a physician and his patient, the physician's primary concern must be the health of his patient. He owes the patient his primary allegiance. This concern and allegiance must be preserved in all medical procedures, including those which involve the transplantation of an organ from one person to another where both donor and recipient are patients. Care must, therefore, be taken to protect the rights of both the donor and the recipient, and no physician may assume a responsibility in organ transplantation unless the rights of both donor and recipient are equally protected.

(2) A prospective organ transplant offers no justification for a relaxation of the usual standard of medical care. The physician should provide his patient, who may be a prospective organ donor, with that care usually given others being treated for a similar injury or disease.

(3) When a vital, single organ is to be transplanted, the death of the donor shall have been determined by at least one physician other than the recipient's physician. Death shall be determined by the clinical judgment of the physician. In making this determination, the ethical physician will use currently accepted and available scientific tests.

(4) Full discussion of the proposed procedure with the donor and the recipient or their responsible relatives or representatives is mandatory. The physician should be objective in discussing the procedure, in disclosing known risks and possible hazards, and in advising of the alternative procedures available. The physician should not encourage expectations beyond those which the circumstances justify. The physician's interest in advancing scientific knowledge must always be secondary to his primary concern for the patient.

(5) Transplant procedures of body organs should be undertaken (a) only by physicians who possess special medical knowledge and technical competence developed through special training, study, and laboratory experi-

ence and practice, and (b) in medical institutions with facilities adequate to protect the health and well-being of the parties to the procedure.

(6) Transplantation of body organs should be undertaken only after careful evaluation of the availability and effectiveness of other possible therapy. (I, III, V)

2.14 Quality of life. In the making of decisions for the treatment of seriously deformed newborns or persons who are severely deteriorated victims of injury, illness or advanced age, the primary consideration should be what is best for the individual patient and not the avoidance of a burden to the family or to society. Quality of life is a factor to be considered in determining what is best for the individual. Life should be cherished despite disabilities and handicaps, except when the prolongation would be inhumane and unconscionable. Under these circumstances, withholding or removing life supporting means is ethical provided that the normal care given an individual who is ill is not discontinued.

In desperate situations involving newborns, the advice and judgment of the physician should be readily available, but the decision whether to exert maximal efforts to sustain life should be the choice of the parents. The parents should be told the options, expected benefits, risks and limits of any proposed care; how the potential for human relationships is affected by the infant's condition; and relevant information and answers to their questions. The presumption is that the love which parents usu-

ally have for their children will be dominant in the decisions which they make in determining what is in the best interest of their children. It is to be expected that parents will act unselfishly, particularly where life itself is at stake. Unless there is convincing evidence to the contrary, parental authority should be respected. (I, III, IV, V)

2.15 Terminal illness. The social commitment of the physician is to prolong life and relieve suffering. Where the observance of one conflicts with the other, the physician, patient, and/or family of the patient have discretion to resolve the conflict.

For humane reasons, with informed consent a physician may do what is medically necessary to alleviate severe pain, or cease or omit treatment to let a terminally ill patient die, but he should not intentionally cause death. In determining whether the administration of potentially life-prolonging medical treatment is in the best interest of the patient, the physician should consider what the possibility is for extending life under humane and comfortable conditions and what are the wishes and attitudes of the family or those who have responsibility for the custody of the patient.

Where a terminally ill patient's coma is beyond doubt irreversible and there are adequate safeguards to confirm the accuracy of the diagnosis, all means of life support may be discontinued. If death does not occur when life support systems are discontinued, the comfort and dignity of the patient should be maintained. (I, III, IV, V)

Code for Nurses: Ethical Concepts Applied to Nursing (1973)

International Council of Nurses

The fundamental responsibility of the nurse is fourfold: to promote health, to prevent illness, to restore health and alleviate suffering.

The need for nursing is universal. Inherent in nursing is respect for life, dignity and the rights of man. It is unrestricted by considerations of nationality, race, creed, color, age, sex, politics or social status.

Nurses render health services to the individual, the family and the community and coordinate their services with those of related groups.

NURSES AND PEOPLE

The nurse's primary responsibility is to those people who require nursing care.

The nurse, in providing care, promotes an environment in which the values, customs and spiritual beliefs of the individual are respected.

The nurse holds in confidence personal information and uses judgment in sharing this information.

NURSES AND PRACTICE

The nurse carries personal responsibility for nursing practice and for maintaining competence by continual learning.

The nurse maintains the highest standards of nursing care possible within the reality of a specific situation.

The nurse uses judgment in relation to individual competence when accepting and delegating responsibilities.

The nurse when acting in a professional capacity should at all times maintain standards of personal conduct which reflect credit upon the profession.

NURSES AND SOCIETY

The nurse shares with other citizens the responsibility for initiating and supporting action to meet the health and social needs of the public.

NURSES AND CO-WORKERS

The nurse sustains a cooperative relationship with co-workers in nursing and other fields.

The nurse takes appropriate action to safeguard the individual when his care is endangered by a co-worker or any other person.

NURSES AND THE PROFESSION

The nurse plays the major role in determining and implementing desirable standards of nursing practice and nursing education.

The nurse is active in developing a core of professional knowledge.

The nurse, acting through the professional organization, participates in establishing and maintaining equitable social and economic working conditions in nursing.

Code for Nurses (1976, 1985)

American Nurses' Association

PREAMBLE

A code of ethics makes explicit the primary goals and values of the profession. When individuals become nurses, they make a moral commitment to uphold the values and special moral obligations expressed in their code. The Code for Nurses is based on a belief about the nature of individuals, nursing, health, and society. Nursing encompasses the protection, promotion, and restoration of health; the prevention of illness; and the alleviation of suffering in the care of clients, including individuals, families, groups, and communities. In the context of these functions, nursing is defined as the diagnosis and treatment of human responses to actual or potential health problems.

Since clients themselves are the primary decision makers in matters concerning their own health, treatment, and well-being, the goal of nursing actions is to support and enhance the client's responsibility and self-determination to the greatest extent possible. In this context, health is not necessarily an end in itself, but rather a means to a life that is meaningful from the client's perspective.

When making clinical judgments, nurses base their decisions on consideration of consequences and of universal moral principles, both of which prescribe and justify nursing actions. The most fundamental of these principles is respect for persons. Other principles stemming from this basic principle are autonomy (self-determination), beneficence (doing good), nonmaleficence (avoiding harm), veracity (truth-telling), confidentiality (respecting privileged information), fidelity (keeping promises), and justice (treating people fairly).

In brief, then, the statements of the code and their interpretation provide guidance for conduct and relationships in carrying out nursing responsibilities consistent with the ethical obligations of the profession and with high quality in nursing care.

INTRODUCTION

A code of ethics indicates a profession's acceptance of the responsibility and trust with which it has been invested by society. Under the terms of the implicit contract between society and the nursing profession, society grants the profession considerable autonomy and authority to function in the conduct of its affairs. The development of a code of ethics is an essential activity of a profession and provides one means for the exercise of professional self-regulation.

Upon entering the profession, each nurse inherits a measure of both the responsibility and the trust that have accrued to nursing over the years, as well as the corresponding obligation to adhere to the profession's code of conduct and relationships for ethical practice. The *Code for Nurses with Interpretive Statements* is thus more a collective expression of nursing conscience and philosophy than a set of external rules imposed upon an individual practitioner of nursing. Personal and professional integrity can be assured only if an individual is committed to the profession's code of conduct.

A code of ethical conduct offers general principles to guide and evaluate nursing actions. It does not assure the virtues required for professional practice within the character of each nurse. In particular situations, the justification of behavior as ethical must satisfy not only the individual nurse acting as a moral agent but also the standards for professional peer review.

The Code for Nurses was adopted by the American Nurses' Association in 1950 and has been revised periodically. It serves to inform both the nurse and society of the profession's expectations and requirements in ethical matters. The code and the interpretive statements together provide a framework within which nurses can make ethical decisions and discharge their responsibilities to the public, to other members of the health team, and to the profession.

Although a particular situation by its nature may determine the use of specific moral principles, the basic philosophical values, directives, and suggestions provided here are widely applicable to situations encountered in clinical practice. The Code for Nurses is not open to negotiation in employment settings, nor is it permissible for individuals or groups of nurses to adapt or change the language of this code.

The requirements of the code may often exceed those of the law. Violations of the law may subject the nurse to civil or criminal liability. The state nurses' associations, in fulfilling the profession's duty to society, may discipline their members for violations of the code. Loss of the respect and confidence of society and of one's colleagues is a serious sanction resulting from violation of the code. In addition, every nurse has a personal obligation to uphold and adhere to the code and to ensure that nursing colleagues do likewise.

Guidance and assistance in applying the code to local situations may be obtained from the American Nurses' Association and the constituent state nurses' associations.

CODE FOR NURSES

1. The nurse provides services with respect for human dignity and the uniqueness of the client, unrestricted by considerations of social or economic status, personal attributes, or the nature of health problems.

2. The nurse safeguards the client's right to privacy by judiciously protecting information of a confidential nature.

3. The nurse acts to safeguard the client and the public when health care and safety are affected by the incompetent, unethical, or illegal practice of any person.

4. The nurse assumes responsibility and ac-countability for individual nursing judgments and actions.

5. The nurse maintains competence in nursing.

6. The nurse exercises informed judgment and uses individual competence and qualifications as criteria in seeking consultation, accepting responsibilities, and delegating nursing activities to others.

7. The nurse participates in activities that contribute to the ongoing development of the profession's body of knowledge.

8. The nurse participates in the profession's efforts to implement and improve standards of nursing.

9. The nurse participates in the profession's efforts to establish and maintain conditions of employment conducive to high quality nursing care.

10. The nurse participates in the profession's effort to protect the public from misinformation and misrepresentation and to maintain the integrity of nursing.

11. The nurse collaborates with members of the health professions and other citizens in promoting community and national efforts to meet the health needs of the public.

Code of Federal Regulations

SUBPART A—BASIC HHS POLICY FOR PROTECTION OF HUMAN RESEARCH SUBJECTS

§46.101 To What Do These Regulations Apply?

(a) Except as provided in paragraph (b) of this section, this subpart applies to all research involving human subjects conducted by the Department of Health and Human Services or funded in whole or in part by a Department grant, contract, cooperative agreement or fellowship.

(b) Research activities in which the only involvement of human subjects will be in one or more of the following categories are exempt from these regulations unless the research is covered by other subparts of this part:

(1) Research conducted in established or commonly accepted educational settings, involving normal educational practices, such as (i) research on regular and special education instructional strategies, or (ii) research on the effectiveness of or the comparison among instructional techniques, curricula, or classroom management methods.

(2) Research involving the use of educational tests (cognitive, diagnostic, aptitude, achievement), if information taken from these sources is recorded in such a manner that subjects cannot be identified, directly or through identifiers linked to the subjects.

Source: 46 FR 8386, January 26, 1981

(3) Research involving survey or interview procedures, except where all of the following conditions exist: (i) responses are recorded in such a manner that the human subjects can be identified, directly or through identifiers linked to the subjects, (ii) the subject's responses, if they became known outside the research, could reasonably place the subject at risk of criminal or civil liability or be damaging to the subject's financial standing or employability, and (iii) the research deals with sensitive aspects of the subject's own behavior, such as illegal conduct, drug use, sexual behavior, or use of alcohol. All research involving survey or interview procedures is exempt, without exception, when the respondents are elected or appointed public officials or candidates for public office.

(4) Research involving the observation (including observation by participants) of public behavior, except where all of the following conditions exist: (i) observations are recorded in such a manner that the human subjects can be identified, directly or through identifiers linked to the subjects, (ii) the observations recorded about the individual, if they became known outside the research, could reasonably place the subject at risk of criminal or civil liability or be damaging to the subject's financial standing or employability, and (iii) the research deals with sensitive aspects of the subject's own behavior such as illegal conduct, drug use, sexual behavior, or use of alcohol.

(5) Research involving the collection or study of existing data, documents, records, pathological specimens, or diagnostic specimens, if these sources are publicly available or if the information is recorded by the investigator in such a manner that subjects cannot be identified, directly or through identifiers linked to the subjects.

§46.109 IRB Review of Research.

(a) An IRB shall review and have authority to approve, require modifications in (to secure approval), or disapprove all research activities covered by these regulations.

(b) An IRB shall require that information given to subjects as part of informed consent is in accordance with §46.116. The IRB may require that information, in addition to that specifically mentioned in §46.116, be given to the subjects when in the IRB's judgment the information would meaningfully add to the protection of the rights and welfare of subjects.

(c) An IRB shall require documentation of informed consent or may waive documentation in accordance with §46.117.

(d) An IRB shall notify investigators and the institution in writing of its decision to approve or disapprove the proposed research activity, or of modifications required to secure IRB approval of the research activity. If the IRB decides to disapprove a research activity, it shall include in its written notification a statement of the reasons for its decision and give the investigator an opportunity to respond in person or in writing.

(e) An IRB shall conduct continuing review of research covered by these regulations at intervals appropriate to the degree of risk, but not less than once per year, and shall have authority to observe or have a third party observe the consent process and the research.

§46.111 Criteria for IRB Approval of Research.

(a) In order to approve research covered by these regulations the IRB shall determine that all of the following requirements are satisfied:

(1) Risks to subjects are minimized: (i) By using procedures which are consistent with sound research design and which do not unnecessarily expose subjects to risk, and (ii) whenever appropriate, by using procedures already being performed on the subjects for diagnostic or treatment purposes.

(2) Risks to subjects are reasonable in relation to anticipated benefits, if any, to subjects, and the importance of the knowledge that may reasonably be expected to result. In evaluat-

ing risks and benefits, the IRB should consider only those risks and benefits that may result from the research (as distinguished from risks and benefits of therapies subjects would receive even if not participating in the research). The IRB should not consider possible long-range effects of applying knowledge gained in the research (for example, the possible effects of the research on public policy) as among those research risks that fall within the purview of its responsibility.

(3) Selection of subjects is equitable. In making this assessment the IRB should take into account the purposes of the research and the setting in which the research will be conducted.

(4) Informed consent will be sought from each prospective subject or the subject's legally authorized representative, in accordance with, and to the extent required by §46.116.

(5) Informed consent will be appropriately documented, in accordance with, and to the extent required by §46.117.

(6) Where appropriate, the research plan makes adequate provision for monitoring the data collected to insure the safety of subjects.

(7) Where appropriate, there are adequate provisions to protect the privacy of subjects and to maintain the confidentiality of data.

(b) Where some or all of the subjects are likely to be vulnerable to coercion or undue influence, such as persons with acute or severe physical or mental illness, or persons who are economically or educationally disadvantaged, appropriate additional safeguards have been included in the study to protect the rights and welfare of these subjects.

§46.116 General Requirements for Informed Consent.

Except as provided elsewhere in this or other subparts, no investigator may involve a human being as a subject in research covered by these regulations unless the investigator has obtained the legally effective informed consent of the subject or the subject's legally authorized representative.

An investigator shall seek such consent only under circumstances that provide the prospective subject or the representative sufficient opportunity to consider whether or not to participate and that minimize the possibility of coercion or undue influence. The information that is given to the subject or the representative shall be in language understandable to the subject or the representative. No informed consent, whether oral or written, may include any exculpatory language through which the subject or the representative is made to waive or appear to waive any of the subject's legal rights, or releases or appears to release the investigator, the sponsor, the institution or its agents from liability for negligence.

(a) Basic elements of informed consent. Except as provided in paragraph (c) or (d) of this section, in seeking informed consent the following information shall be provided to each subject:

(1) A statement that the study involves research, an explanation of the purposes of the research and the expected duration of the subject's participation, a description of the procedures to be followed, and identification of any procedures which are experimental;

(2) A description of any reasonably foreseeable risks or discomforts to the subject;

(3) A description of any benefits to the subject or to others which may reasonably be expected from the research;

(4) A disclosure of appropriate alternative procedures or courses of treatment, if any, that might be advantageous to the subject;

(5) A statement describing the extent, if any, to which confidentiality of records identifying the subject will be maintained;

(6) For research involving more than minimal risk, an explanation as to whether any compensation and an explanation as to whether any medical treatments are available if injury occurs and, if so, what they consist of, or where further information may be obtained;

(7) An explanation of whom to contact for answers to pertinent questions about the research and research subjects' rights, and whom to contact in the event of a research-related injury to the subject; and

(8) A statement that participation is voluntary, refusal to participate will involve no penalty or loss of benefits to which the subject is otherwise entitled, and the subject may discontinue participation at any time without penalty or loss of benefits to which the subject is otherwise entitled.

(b) Additional elements of informed consent. When appropriate, one or more of the following elements of information shall also be provided to each subject:

(1) A statement that the particular treatment or procedure may involve risks to the subject (or to the embryo or fetus, if the subject is or may become pregnant) which are currently unforeseeable;

(2) Anticipated circumstances under which the subject's participation may be terminated by the investigator without regard to the subject's consent;

(3) Any additional costs to the subject that may result from participation in the research;

(4) The consequences of a subject's decision to withdraw from the research and procedures for orderly termination of participation by the subject;

(5) A statement that significant new findings developed during the course of the research which may relate to the subject's willingness to continue participation will be provided to the subject; and

(6) The approximate number of subjects involved in the study.

(c) An IRB may approve a consent procedure which does not include, or which alters, some or all of the elements of informed consent set forth above, or waive the requirement to obtain informed consent provided the IRB finds and documents that:

(1) The research is to be conducted for the purpose of demonstrating or evaluating: (i) Federal, state, or local benefit or service programs which are not themselves

research programs, (ii) procedures for obtaining benefits or services under these programs, or (iii) possible changes in or alternatives to these programs or procedures; and

(2) The research could not practicably be carried out without the waiver or alteration.

(d) An IRB may approve a consent procedure which does not include, or which alters, some or all of the elements of informed consent set forth above, or waive the requirements to obtain informed consent provided the IRB finds and documents that:

(1) The research involves no more than minimal risk to the subjects:

(2) The waiver or alteration will not adversely affect the rights and welfare of the subjects;

(3) The research could not practicably be carried out without the waiver or alteration; and

(4) Whenever appropriate, the subjects will be provided with additional pertinent information after participation.

(e) The informed consent requirements in these regulations are not intended to preempt any applicable federal, state, or local laws which require additional information to be disclosed in order for informed consent to be legally effective.

(f) Nothing in these regulations is intended to limit the authority of a physician to provide emergency medical care, to the extent the physician is permitted to do so under applicable federal, state, or local law.

SUBPART C—ADDITIONAL PROTECTIONS PERTAINING TO BIOMEDICAL AND BEHAVIORAL RESEARCH INVOLVING PRISONERS AS SUBJECTS

§46.301 Applicability.

(a) The regulations in this subpart are applicable to all biomedical and behavioral research

Source: 43 FR 53655, Nov 16, 1978

conducted or supported by the Department of Health, Education, and Welfare involving prisoners as subjects.

§46.302 Purpose.

Inasmuch as prisoners may be under constraints because of their incarceration which could affect their ability to make a truly voluntary and uncoerced decision whether or not to participate as subjects in research, it is the purpose of this subpart to provide additional safeguards for the protection of prisoners involved in activities to which this subpart is applicable.

§46.306 Permitted Research Involving Prisoners

(a) Biomedical or behavioral research conducted or supported by DHEW may involve prisoners as subjects only if:

(1) The institution responsible for the conduct of the research has certified to the Secretary that the Institutional Review Board has approved the research under §46.305 of this subpart; and

(2) In the judgment of the Secretary the proposed research involves solely the following:

(A) Study of the possible causes, effects, and processes of incarceration, and of criminal behavior, provided that the study presents no more than minimal risk and no more than inconvenience to the subjects;

(B) Study of prisons as institutional structures or of prisoners as incarcerated persons, provided that the study presents no more than minimal risk and no more than inconvenience to the subjects;

(C) Research on conditions particularly affecting prisoners as a class (for example, vaccine trials and other research on hepatitis which is much more prevalent in prisons than elsewhere; and research on social and psychological problems such as alcoholism, drug addiction and sexual assaults), provided that the study may proceed only after the Secretary has consulted with appropriate experts includ-

ing experts in penology medicine and ethics, and published notice, in the Federal Register, of his intent to approve such research; or

(D) Research on practices, both innovative and accepted, which have the intent and reasonable probability of improving the health or well-being of the subject. In cases in which those studies require the assignment of prisoners in a manner consistent with protocols approved by the IRB to control groups which may not benefit from the research, the study may proceed only after the Secretary has consulted with appropriate experts, including experts in penology medicine and ethics, and published notice, in the *Federal Register,* of his intent to approve such research.

SUBPART D—ADDITIONAL PROTECTIONS FOR CHILDREN INVOLVED AS SUBJECTS IN RESEARCH

§46.401 To What Do These Regulations Apply?

This subpart applies to all research involving children as subjects, conducted or supported by the Department of Health and Human Services.

§46.402 Definitions

The definitions in §46.102 of Subpart A shall be applicable to this subpart as well. In addition, as used in this subpart:

(a) "Children" are persons who have not attained the legal age for consent to treatments or procedures involved in the research, under the applicable law of the jurisdiction in which the research will be conducted.

(b) "Assent" means a child's affirmative agreement to participate in research. Mere failure to object should not, absent affirmative agreement, be construed as assent.

(c) "Permission" means the agreement of parent(s) or guardian to the participation of their child or ward in research.

(d) "Parent" means a child's biological or adoptive parent.

(e) "Guardian" means an individual who is authorized under applicable State or local law to consent on behalf of a child to general medical care.

§46.403 IRB Duties.

In addition to other responsibilities assigned to IRBs under this part, each IRB shall review research covered by this subpart and approve only research which satisfies the conditions of all applicable sections of this subpart.

§46.404 Research Not Involving Greater Than Minimal Risk.

HHS will conduct or fund research in which the IRB finds that no greater than minimal risk to children is presented, only if the IRB finds that adequate provisions are made for soliciting the assent of the children and the permission of their parents or guardians, as set forth in §46.408.

§46.405 Research Involving Greater Than Minimal Risk but Presenting the Prospect of Direct Benefit to the Individual Subjects.

HHS will conduct or fund research in which the IRB finds that more than minimal risk to children is presented by an intervention or procedure that holds out the prospect of direct benefit for the individual subject, or by a monitoring procedure that is likely to contribute to the subject's well-being, only if the IRB finds that:

(a) The risk is justified by the anticipated benefit to the subjects;

(b) The relation of the anticipated benefit to the risk is at least as favorable to the subjects as that presented by available alternative approaches; and

(c) Adequate provisions are made for soliciting the assent of the children and permission of their parents or guardians, as set forth in §46.408.

§46.406 Research Involving Greater Than Minimal Risk and No Prospect of Direct Benefit to Individual Subjects, but Likely to Yield Generalizable Knowledge About the Subject's Disorder or Condition.

HHS will conduct or fund research in which the IRB finds that more than minimal risk to children is presented by an intervention or procedure that does not hold out the prospect of direct benefit for the individual subject, or by a monitoring procedure which is not likely to contribute to the well-being of the subject, only if the IRB finds that:

(a) The risk represents a minor increase over minimal risk;

(b) The intervention or procedure presents experiences to subjects that are reasonably commensurate with those inherent in their actual or expected medical, dental, psychological, social, or educational situations;

(c) The intervention or procedure is likely to yield generalizable knowledge about the subjects' disorder or condition which is of vital importance for the understanding or amelioration of the subjects' disorder or condition; and

(d) Adequate provisions are made for soliciting assent of the children and permission of their parents or guardians, as set forth in §46.408.

§46.407 Research Not Otherwise Approvable Which Presents an Opportunity to Understand, Prevent, or Alleviate a Serious Problem Affecting the Health or Welfare of Children.

HHS will conduct or fund research that the IRB does not believe meets the requirements of §§46.404, 46.405, or 46.406 only if:

(a) The IRB finds that the research presents a reasonable opportunity to further the understanding, prevention, or alleviation of a serious problem affecting the health or welfare of children; and

(b) The Secretary, after consultation with a panel of experts in pertinent disciplines (for example: science, medicine, education, ethics, law) and following opportunity for public review and comment, has determined either: (1) That the research in fact satisfies the conditions of §§46.404, 46.405, or 46.406, as applicable, or (2) the following:

(i) The research presents a reasonable opportunity to further the understanding, prevention, or alleviation of a serious problem affecting the health or welfare of children:

(ii) The research will be conducted in accordance with sound ethical principles:

(iii) Adequate provisions are made for soliciting the assent of children and the permission of their parents or guardians, as set forth in §46.408.

§46.408 Requirements for Permission by Parents or Guardians and for Assent by Children.

(a) In addition to the determinations required under other applicable sections of this subpart, the IRB shall determine that adequate provisions are made for soliciting the assent of the children, when in the judgment of the IRB the children are capable of providing assent. In determining whether children are capable of assenting, the IRB shall take into account the ages, maturity, and psychological state of the children involved. This judgment may be made for all children to be involved in research under a particular protocol, or for each child, as the IRB deems appropriate. If the IRB determines that the capability of some or all of the children is so limited that they cannot reasonably be consulted or that the intervention or procedure involved in the research holds out a prospect of direct benefit that is important to the health or well-being of the children and is available only in the context of the research, the assent of the

children is not a necessary condition for proceeding with the research. Even where the IRB determines that the subjects are capable of assenting, the IRB may still waive the assent requirement under circumstances in which consent may be waived in accord with §46.116 of Subpart A.

(b) In addition to the determinations required under other applicable sections of this subpart, the IRB shall determine, in accordance with and to the extent that consent is required by §46.116 of Subpart A, that adequate provisions are made for soliciting the permission of each child's parents or guardian. Where parental permission is to be obtained, the IRB may find that the permission of one parent is sufficient for research to be conducted under §46.404 or §46.405. Where research is covered by §§46.406 and 46.407 and permission is to be obtained from parents, both parents must give their permission unless one parent is deceased, unknown, incompetent, or not reasonably available, or when only one parent has legal responsibility for the care and custody of the child.

(c) In addition to the provisions for waiver contained in §46.116 of subpart A, if the IRB determines that a research protocol is designed for conditions or for a subject population for which parental or guardian permission is not a reasonable requirement to protect the subjects (for example, neglected or abused children), it may waive the consent requirements in Subpart A of this part and paragraph (b) of this section, provided an appropriate mechanism for protecting the children who will participate as subjects in the research is substituted, and provided further that the waiver is not inconsistent with federal, state or local law. The choice of an appropriate mechanism would depend upon the nature and purpose of the activities described in the protocol, the risk and anticipated benefit to the research subjects, and their age, maturity, status, and condition.

(d) Permission by parents or guardians

shall be documented in accordance with and to the extent required by §46.117 of Subpart A.

(e) When the IRB determines that assent is required, it shall also determined whether and how assent must be documented.